I0820122

SITTING BULL'S WAR

Sitting Bull, in the all-too-common dress of a humble spiritual man, photographed by David F. Barry in 1883.

SITTING BULL'S WAR

THE BATTLE OF LITTLE BIG HORN AND THE FIGHT FOR BUFFALO AND FREEDOM ON THE PLAINS

PAUL L. HEDREN

PEGASUS BOOKS
NEW YORK LONDON

SITTING BULL'S WAR

Pegasus Books, Ltd.
148 West 37th Street, 13th Floor
New York, NY 10018

First Pegasus Books cloth edition November 2025

Interior design by Maria Fernandez

Library of Congress Cataloging-in-Publication Data is available.

ISBN: 978-1-63936-983-6

10 9 8 7 6 5 4 3 2

Printed in the United States of America
Distributed by Simon & Schuster
www.pegasusbooks.com

For Marvin Kaiser,

a spirited friend

ABOUT THE AUTHOR

Paul L. Hedren is a retired National Park Service historian and superintendent whose thirty-seven-year career led him from Minnesota to Wyoming, Montana, Utah, North Dakota, and Nebraska. His many books have received numerous honors, including a Spur Award from the Western Writers of America, a Western Heritage Wrangler Award from the National Cowboy & Western Heritage Museum, and multiple Best Book awards from the Little Big Horn Associates. He is a lifelong student of the Great Sioux War, and he is often found exploring the trails, battlefields, back corners, and sacred sites of that intriguing 1870s Indian war. When not in the field, Paul resides in Omaha, Nebraska.

ALSO BY PAUL L. HEDREN

John Finerty Reports the Sioux War

Rosebud, June 17, 1876: Prelude to the Little Big Horn

Powder River: Disastrous Opening of the Great Sioux War

Ho! For the Black Hills: Captain Jack Crawford Reports the Black Hills Gold Rush and Great Sioux War

After Custer: Loss and Transformation in Sioux Country

Great Sioux War Orders of Battle: How the United States Army Waged War on the Northern Plains

We Trailed the Sioux: Enlisted Men Speak on Custer, Crook, and the Great Sioux War

Traveler's Guide to the Great Sioux War: The Battlefields, Forts, and Related Sites of America's Greatest Indian War

The Great Sioux War, 1876–77: The Best from Montana The Magazine of Western History

Campaigning With King: Charles King, Chronicler of the Old Army (with Don Russell)

Fort Laramie in 1876: Chronicle of a Frontier Post at War

With Crook in the Black Hills: Stanley J. Morrow's 1876 Photographic Legacy

First Scalp for Custer: The Skirmish at Warbonnet Creek, Nebraska, July 17, 1876

CONTENTS

	War Country, 1872–1877 map	viii
	Medicine Line Country, 1877–1881 map	x
	Sitting Bull's War Timeline	xi
	Preface	xix
1.	A Time in the West	1
2.	Railroaders on the Yellowstone	28
3.	Buffalo and Borders	56
4.	Black Hills Mayhem	71
5.	War Comes to the Cheyennes First	100
6.	The Great Ascendancy	120
7.	Stopping the Gray Fox	142
8.	We Wish to Live!	169
9.	One Day in June	186
10.	A Dangerous Time	225
11.	The Hunted	251
12.	Red Fork and Belly Butte	278
13.	Cruel Fate of the Cheyennes	305
14.	Shock and Despair in the Pine Ridge	318
15.	Defiance	350
16.	The Starving Years	374
	Epilogue	409
	Acknowledgments	424
	Bibliography	427
	Notes	452
	Index	538

Fort Peck Agency
Missouri River
MONTANA
TERRITORY
Ash Creek
Cedar Creek
Cedar Creek
Spring Creek
Powder River Depot
Yellowstone River
Tongue River Cantonment (1877)
Fort Pease
Big Horn (1873)
Arrow Creek (1872)
Big Horn Post (1877)
Crow Agency
Little Big Horn
Crow's Nest
Rosebud Creek
Tongue River
Powder River
Little Powder R.
Lame Deer
Belly Butte
Fort C. F. Smith (ruin)
Wolf Mts.
Little Big Horn River
Rosebud Creek
Powder River
Tongue River Heights
Sibley Scout
Goose Creek Camp
Bear Lodge Butte
ROCKY MOUNTAINS
Big Horn River
Big Horn Mountains
Fort Phil Kearny (ruin)
Cloud Pk.
Fort Reno (ruin)
Cantonment Reno
WYOMING
TERRITORY
Red Fk.
Belle Fourche River
Red Fork Powder River
Middle Fk.
BOZEMAN TRAIL
War Country
1872-1877
0 20 40 60 80 100
MILES
Fort Fetterman
North Platte River
Laramie Mts.
Laramie Pk.
Laramie River
TOM JONAS 2025

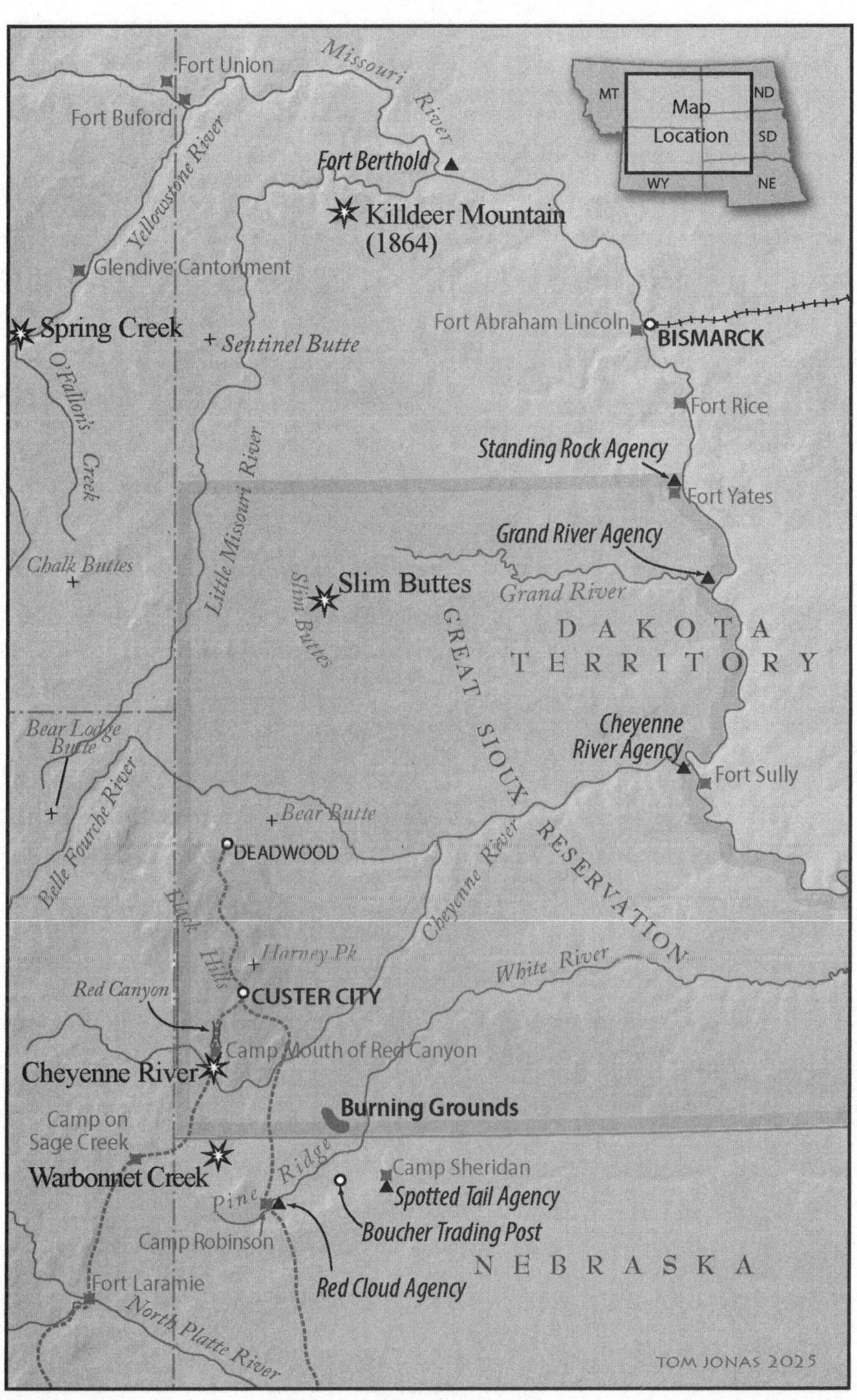

Fort Union
Missouri River
Fort Buford
Yellowstone River
Fort Berthold
Killdeer Mountain
(1864)
MT
ND
SD
WY
NE
Map
Location
Glendive Cantonment
Spring Creek
Sentinel Butte
Fort Abraham Lincoln
BISMARCK
O'Fallon's Creek
Fort Rice
Standing Rock Agency
Fort Yates
Little Missouri River
Grand River Agency
Chalk Buttes
Slim Buttes
Slim Buttes
Grand River
DAKOTA
TERRITORY
GREAT SIOUX RESERVATION
Cheyenne River Agency
Fort Sully
Bear Lodge Butte
Belle Fourche River
Bear Butte
DEADWOOD
Black Hills
Cheyenne River
Harney Pk
White River
Red Canyon
CUSTER CITY
Camp Mouth of Red Canyon
Cheyenne River
Burning Grounds
Camp on Sage Creek
Warbonnet Creek
Camp Sheridan
Pine Ridge
Spotted Tail Agency
Camp Robinson
Boucher Trading Post
NEBRASKA
Fort Laramie
Red Cloud Agency
North Platte River
TOM JONAS 2025

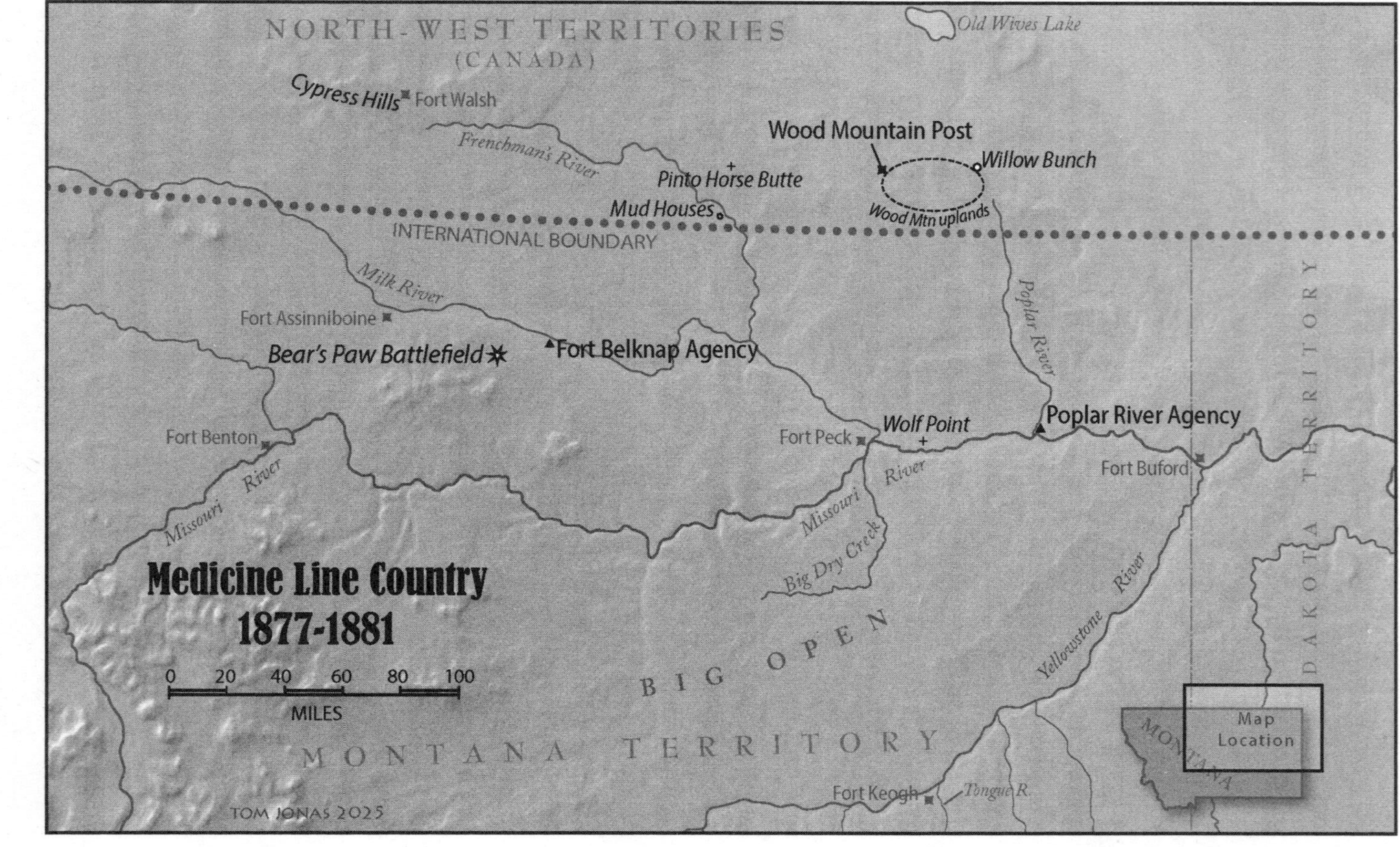
NORTH-WEST TERRITORIES
(CANADA)
Old Wives Lake
Cypress Hills
Fort Walsh
Frenchman's River
Wood Mountain Post
Willow Bunch
Pinto Horse Butte
Mud Houses
Wood Mtn uplands
INTERNATIONAL BOUNDARY
Milk River
Fort Assinniboine
Bear's Paw Battlefield
Fort Belknap Agency
Poplar River
Wolf Point
Poplar River Agency
Fort Benton
Fort Peck
Missouri River
Fort Buford
Big Dry Creek
Yellowstone River
Medicine Line Country
1877-1881
0 20 40 60 80 100
MILES
BIG OPEN
MONTANA TERRITORY
DAKOTA TERRITORY
Map Location
MONTANA
Fort Keogh
Tongue R.
TOM JONAS 2025

SITTING BULL'S WAR TIMELINE

1866

Late December: Sitting Bull, wearing a red shirt obtained at Fort Union to better distinguish himself, dares soldiers he's warring with at nearby Fort Buford to kill him.

1871

Fall: Northern Pacific railroad surveyors in the east probe the Dakota Badlands and reach the Yellowstone Valley, while surveyors in the west reach Pompeys Pillar.

1872

August 14: Arrow Creek fight with railroaders. Openly exposed to the enemy, Sitting Bull brazenly smokes his pipe and taunts death.

August 18: Gall engages soldiers and their commander, David Stanley, at the mouth of the Powder River.

1873

August 4: In a third year of railroad surveying work, Miniconjou warriors ambush soldiers on the Yellowstone above the mouth of the Tongue River.

August 11: Miniconjou and Cheyenne warriors again strike soldiers on the Yellowstone, near the mouth of the Big Horn River.

Summer: Northern Boundary surveyors plot the international border across Dakota.

1874

February 9: Lieutenant Levi Robinson is killed by Oglala raiders near Laramie Peak, and that same day agency clerk Frank Appleton is killed at Red Cloud Agency.

April 4: On Rosebud Creek Miniconjou warriors engage the Yellowstone Wagon Road and Prospecting Expedition of Bozeman.

Summer: Northern Boundary surveyors plot the international border across Montana and lay the stone heaps.

July and August: An expedition led by George Custer explores the Black Hills and on August 2 discovers paying gold.

August 8: A courier from Custer's camp reaches Fort Laramie with reports of Black Hills gold. The news is telegraphed to the nation. Custer triggers a gold rush.

1875

Early June: Fellowes Pease and others from Bozeman establish Fort Pease on the Yellowstone below the mouth of the Big Horn River, attempting to open trade with Crows and Sioux.

Mid-June: Lakotas and Cheyennes Sun Dance on Rosebud Creek, embracing the spirit of unity and determined to protect a homeland.

Summer: A second government expedition explores the Black Hills, determined to establish its mineral worth.

Early August: Spotted Tail visits with miners in the Black Hills and scoffs at their presence and paltry gold recoveries.

September 23: On the White River midst thousands of onlooking Sioux, Little Big Man disrupts the proceedings of a government commission attempting to purchase the Black Hills.

November 3: President Grant convenes a council of war in the White House and determines to clear the northern plains of disruptive Lakotas and Northern Cheyennes.

December 3: An edict is served to the Lakotas and Cheyennes ordering them to relocate to the Great Sioux Reservation before January 31, 1876, or be considered hostile and passed to the military.

1876

March 3: The besieged surviving Fort Pease complement is relieved by soldiers from Fort Ellis.

March 17: Soldiers strike and destroy Old Bear's Northern Cheyenne village on the Powder River, drawing first blood in an erupting Indian war.

Early May: Desiring strength through unity, Sitting Bull's summons all traditional Lakotas and Northern Cheyennes to join him on Rosebud Creek.

Mid-May: Sitting Bull experiences the first of two powerful dreams, one of great clouds colliding, but the storm subsiding and the white cloud drifting serenely away.

June 6: In the midst of the great ascendancy, Hunkpapas conduct a Sun Dance on Rosebud Creek. In another dream Sitting Bull sees soldiers coming, heads down, hats falling off. They are to die as they "have no ears."

June 9: Little Hawk and fellow Cheyenne warriors taunt a soldier camp at the mouth of Prairie Dog Creek, serving notice that the lands beyond belong to the Northern Indians.

June 17: Some 750 Sioux and Cheyenne warriors engage 1,250 soldiers and scouts on Upper Rosebud Creek. After a day-long fight the blue coats hold the field, but then turn away.

June 24: Sitting Bull's village, now nearly 5,000 strong, pauses on the Little Big Horn River. That evening he again prays, this time for the well-being and survival of his people.

June 25: Sitting Bull's great camp on the Little Big Horn is attacked by blue coats. By day's end, George Custer and five companies of cavalry lay dead.

June 28: On the Upper Little Big Horn at the mouth of Lodge Grass Creek, the great Lakota and Cheyenne alliance of traditionals begins to disperse. Never again would it be so mighty.

July 17: Northern Cheyenne traditionals led by Morning Star fleeing the White River Agency are confronted at Warbonnet Creek. Buffalo Bill Cody takes a much-celebrated "First Scalp for Custer."

Late August: In the shadows of Sentinel Butte the surviving Lakota alliance disperses into four major bodies.

September 9: Blue coats attack and destroy a Miniconjou camp in the Slim Buttes. The camp's primary chief, Iron Plume, is killed.

September 20: At the agencies government commissioners commence collecting signatures on a forced agreement that surrenders the Black Hills. One individual signs with a blanket covering his eyes. The Black Hills are lost.

October 20: Sitting Bull and Nelson Miles meet face-to-face on Cedar Creek, each stridently serving notice that they wanted the other out of the buffalo country.

October 21: Miles strikes and destroys Sitting Bull's camp on Cedar Creek. Another village and its contents are lost and the surviving alliance is further shattered.

Mid-October: Soldiers punitively confiscate all ponies and firearms at the Sioux agencies along the Missouri River and in the Pine Ridge.

November 25: Soldiers attack and destroy a massive encampment of Northern Cheyennes on the Red Fork of the Powder River in the southern Big Horn Mountains.

December 16: Sitting Bull, the Oglala, is murdered near the Tongue River Post, dashing any hope of Crazy Horse surrendering there to Miles.

December 18: Soldiers strike and destroy Sitting Bull's camp on Ash Creek, further shattering the coalition holding with the great chief.

1877

January 8: Crazy Horse and Miles fight inconclusively at Belly Butte on the Tongue River, each having imagined destroying the other.

February 28: Little Wolf's Northern Cheyenne followers surrender at the White River Agency.

April 14: Touch the Clouds' and Roman Nose's Miniconjous surrender at Spotted Tail Agency.

April 21: Morning Star's Cheyennes surrender at the White River Agency.

April 23: Old Wolf, Two Moon, and their Cheyenne followers surrender at Tongue River Post, all but ending Cheyenne participation in Sitting Bull's War.

April 30: Sitting Bull leads some 860 followers cross the Medicine Line into Canada, believing that his people's future now lay in the north.

May 6: Crazy Horse and 898 Oglala followers surrender at Red Cloud Agency.

May 7: Miles strikes and destroys Lame Deer's village on Muddy Creek, an engagement remembered as the last armed clash of Sitting Bull's War.

May 27: Crook punitively orders the relocation of the Northern Cheyennes in the Pine Ridge to the Indian Territory.

Late July: Crook withdraws his consent for a buffalo hunt, betraying a promise made to Crazy Horse that, in part, induced his surrender.

September 3: Crook orders Crazy Horse's arrest and deportment to Fort Marion, Florida.

September 5: Crazy Horse is slain at Camp Robinson while resisting arrest.

October 17: Sitting Bull meets with General Terry at Fort Walsh, in Canada's Cypress Hills. Terry had ventured north to lure the chief back to the States, but Sitting Bull all but tells him to go to the devil.

1878

Summer: Sitting Bull's alliance in Canada continues to grow, now tallying some two thousand people representing each of the Lakota *Oyates* and even refugee Nez Perces. But a seeming life of serenity and plenty disappears when the buffalo in Canada all but vanish.

1880

January 29: White Gut and some 300 Hunkpapas surrender at Poplar River.

June 14: Little Hawk and 585 Oglalas surrender at Fort Keogh. Soon Iron Thunder and 132 other Oglalas also surrender there.

September 8: Big Road, He Dog, and 200 Oglalas surrender at Fort Keogh.

October 30: Spotted Eagle and Rain in the Face surrender 494 Sans Arcs, Miniconjous, and Hunkpapas at Fort Keogh.

1881

January 2: Gall and some 300 Hunkpapas surrender at Poplar River.

February 10: Crow King and 350 Hunkpapas surrender at Fort Buford.

April 11: Low Dog and 135 Oglalas surrender at Fort Buford.

July 19: Sitting Bull and 187 followers surrender at Fort Buford. When meeting with the post commander the next day, he expresses the simple wish to be remembered as the last of his tribe to surrender his weapon.

AN END, BUT NOT THE END

1878

September 9: Three hundred Northern Cheyennes under Morning Star and Little Wolf flee Indian Territory bound for their Montana homeland. Bitter travails lay ahead, including brutal killings at Fort Robinson in January 1879.

1881

Mid-September: Sitting Bull and 172 others are punitively exiled down-river from Standing Rock Agency to Fort Randall in the farthest corner of the Dakota Territory.

1883

By winter's end, 1882–83, the last of the once mighty Buffalo North is all but wiped out by hide hunters.

April 28: Sitting Bull and the exiled Hunkpapas at Fort Randall are permitted to return to Standing Rock.

1890

December 15: In the early days of the Ghost Dance crisis in Dakota, on the Grand River not far from his birthplace, Sitting Bull is killed by an Indian policeman while resisting arrest.

PREFACE

Many years ago my family and I attended an evening campfire program at Theodore Roosevelt National Park in North Dakota's rugged Little Missouri badlands. I'm not clear any longer whether the program's theme that evening was the buffalo of the park, or the Indian heritage of that remarkable place. Both are powerful subjects there and in the whole of western North Dakota. But I've evermore been haunted by a short Carl Sandburg poem, "Buffalo Dusk," recited by that ranger during her program. It played straight into several lifelong themes central to my own studies of the American West, the buffalo of the Great Plains, the Indian people who built lives around those majestic creatures, and, further, that time when, for buffalo and Indians, their world turned upside down. The Sandburg poem:

> *The buffaloes are gone.*
> *And those who saw the buffaloes are gone.*
> *Those who saw the buffaloes by thousands and how*
> *they pawed the prairie sod into dust with their*
> *hoofs, their great heads down pawing on in a*
> *great pageant of dusk,*
> *Those who saw the buffaloes are gone.*
> *And the buffaloes are gone.* [1]

I've spent most of my adult life writing about one of the great sagas occurring on the plains, the Great Sioux War, or, as some call it, the Custer

War, and others the Black Hills War. By whatever name, this calamitous war swept the northern plains clean of its free-roaming Indian people. I've guided readers to the many sites of that war. I've told stories large and small of its battles and skirmishes. I've analyzed military methodologies employed in that war. I've explored uniquely the consequences of that war: Once Indian people no longer roamed the northern plains, a second transcontinental railroad pushed to completion, the great northern buffalo herd was decimated in direct consequence, and an enduring cattle empire blossomed. But wafting through my studies always were the simple disturbing essences of that Sandburg meditation. The buffaloes are gone. And those who saw the buffaloes are gone. And where was that story?

The Great Sioux War is traditionally told a single way, through the perspectives of Ulysses S. Grant, his government, and the American Westering movement. Pinned to such justifications as obstructing the construction of another transcontinental rail line, an unwillingness to sell the revered Black Hills—alluring gold country to the Whites—and the refusals of many Indians to conform to a famous treaty that ended a previous northern plains Indian war, the president opted for a coercive end, finally, to this Indian obstruction on the northern plains. Washington sicced an Old School senior general on those Indians, and in the mid-1870s he delivered a succession of military campaigns into the Powder and Yellowstone River country with the sole intent of achieving the president's and country's aim of sweeping aside that obstruction.

But the war immediately turned into a quagmire, complicated by a vigorous foe equally determined to retain a traditional lifeway on the buffalo prairie and by the ever formidable northern plains weather. One campaign succeeded another, and then another. We know the names of the officers who commanded those respective movements and the nature and number of their troops. We know the days they marched, and numbers of miles they traversed. We know their battles and the names of their casualties.

That version of the story is enticing and easy to pursue and complicated only by the depth of the tale being told, an inevitable pursuit of varied and new source material, and the variety of voices brought to bear. History shows that there are still fresh ways to tell "this" story. Most writers, of course, particularly of late, and even when telling a traditional military story, have also paid heed to the Indian people targeted in the war's many campaigns and battles. And still, through it all, this version of the war story has consistently been a Washington-centric, top-down narrative of treaties, commissioners, obstruction, campaigns, and battles. I've told this version myself many times.

I consciously intend that the work in hand defy the standard tradition. This is a unique history of the Great Sioux War, carefully and deliberately told through the eyes of its victims, the Lakotas and Northern Cheyennes of the northern plains, the tradition-embracing people of the buffalo prairie. They witnessed this war from the inside. They endured it and suffered it. Their voices are heard on almost every page. This is not an involved military history, or a history of two cultures in conflict. This is Sitting Bull's War, an Indian history of a cataclysmic, decade-long struggle on the northern plains to preserve and sustain a traditional way of life, a story that ended tragically as a people's world indeed was turned upside down. This is an epitaph for a lifeway.

Sources allow for this. Although tradition long held that Indian accounts of the Great Sioux War were irreconcilable, or, as one esteemed scholar described them, personal and maddeningly detached, such dismissals are plainly wrong, and regrettable. Even while Hunkpapas, Miniconjous, and Oglalas were still being chased across the plains, individuals appeared at Sioux agencies from time to time, usually inquiring about surrender terms, and were carefully interviewed by agents and military overseers. Their reports, in turn, were circulated widely through government channels and simultaneously fed to newspapers where they comprised literal "hot news" from the warfront. Later, particularly in the early twentieth century, curiosity led inquisitors to seek out and interview survivors of the war, most especially the revered native traditionals with their long hair, who quietly practiced the old ways, lived to an old age in the shadow of the buffalo, and were willing to tell their stories. The internet makes virtually all of this readily accessible today, but its unique richness has been barely exposed.

The killing of Custer usually drove this curiosity, but to get to the events of that horrific day, June 25, 1876, interviewers and interviewees necessarily reflected on the rest of those days. I endeavored to examine and utilize virtually every accessible Indian account of this war, whether in private collections, publications, or archives far and wide. Ultimately, I collected much more than I could use, and I am sure that I missed things, but I believe that my endnotes and bibliography are robust and nearly exhaustive. I was aided as well by the informative labors of genealogists, collectors, and narrowly focused scholars whose own work fills countless published monographs and internet website pages. I also unhesitatingly embraced the work of biographers, vintage and current, who, often mining the same source material as well as finding much that was new, rounded out completely the lives of critical individuals who played central roles in or gave voice to this remarkable story. Such biographies, too, are acknowledged in my bibliography.

My choices of language are deliberate. The native peoples of this story refer to themselves as Indians, or Lakotas, and Northern Cheyennes, and even Sioux, the botched French translation of a Chippewa word, and they do so to this day. But native peoples then and more so now use some words cautiously. Native American and Amerindian, for instance, do not appear in this book aside from here, once. That I was born in New Ulm, Minnesota, of stout Swedish-German stock, and am Native American too, further drives the point. For the Teton bands I embraced the terminology in James R. Walker's *Lakota Society*. I occasionally utilize Lakota and Cheyenne words, but cautiously, readability being a guide point, and commonly use English names, Crazy Horse, for instance, rather than *Tasunka Witko*, or Good White Buffalo Cow Woman, instead of *Pte San Waste Win*. English names were commonly used in their own day too. I use plural forms of native groups, conforming to the rules of Standard English. I prefer the word buffalo, not bison, the scientist's term. I am at heart and by training a geographer. These are the northern plains, not Northern Plains, or northern Plains, though indeed a subset of the Great Plains, and an individual might be a Plainsman, not a plainsman. I commonly but not consistently use modern names for streams and landmarks but usually also acknowledge alternatives. And I am an ardent field man. One reads landscapes like books, and this is a story in which landcover, streams, hillocks, buttes, and divides are timeless and critical, and such detail overflows here. My endnotes are conventional and exhaustive, touching all sources critical to the narrative at hand and often amplifying or rounding out particular points.

This then is the unique story of an Indian war, America's greatest Indian war. This was indeed a conflict between cultures and mindsets, with distinct winners and losers. It ultimately closed the American frontier. But at what cost? This is *Sitting Bull's War: The Battle of Little Big Horn and the Fight for Buffalo and Freedom on the Plains.*

1
A TIME IN THE WEST

"As I now think back upon those days, it seems that no people in the world were ever any richer than we were."
—Wooden Leg, Northern Cheyenne

The day was months in the making. On the morrow, July 19, 1881, after more than five years of bloody war and anxious political wrangling, Sitting Bull was surrendering himself and his followers at Fort Buford, Dakota Territory. A newsman from the Saint Paul and Minneapolis *Pioneer Press* had arrived and was providing his readers—and ultimately the nation—with captivating details. The reporter had scampered north and joined Jean Louis Legaré's lumbering Buford-bound wagon train midway on its journey from Willow Bunch, Canada, a crossroads in the Wood Mountain uplands just north of the international line. He was struck first by the overwhelming impoverishment he encountered, people in rags, some nearly naked, all with the stark look, he thought, of not having eaten properly in days, perhaps meaningfully in months. That captured but half of a lamentable scene.

Captain Walter Clifford of the Fort Buford garrison had also separately joined the caravan on its southward trek. He had been dispatched by Major

David Brotherton, Buford's commanding officer, escorting wagonloads of foodstuffs intended for the famished people. Clifford knew Sitting Bull before the war when he served as an agent at Fort Berthold and Brotherton had assumed that his appearance now would not be misconstrued. The captain's wagons reached the plodding string of Sitting Bull's mostly screechy Red River oxcarts and a few saddle ponies north of the Sand Buttes, a landmark in far northeastern Montana midway on the trail between Wood Mountain and the sprawling army post. The provisions were a godsend. Already the people in the convoy, more than two hundred Indians and Canadian mixed-blood drivers, had nearly consumed what limited foodstuffs they started with.[1]

The anxious chief recognized Clifford quickly and even forced a slight smile when learning that the chief's daughter, who had fled the doting father with a suitor a while earlier, had now moved downriver to the Standing Rock Agency at Fort Yates and was safe, and fed, and in fact happy. In the days before this final journey Sitting Bull had heard otherwise, that she was in shackles, telling Clifford: "If they punish my daughter, who has done nothing, what will they not do to me." He had long ago acknowledged that most Americans held him accountable for the death of Custer, and he was sure that punishment awaited him now. Clifford calmed his fears but the apprehension lingered.[2]

That evening an old Indian woman drew the camp's attention when she cried out a clear, repetitive refrain. The buzz of the camp quieted and her voice carried across the campfires. Clifford found the scene and her words almost mesmerizing and had an interpreter listen carefully and tell him what it was she was saying, in "her exact words."

> Be brave, my friends, be brave.
> The White men have brought us food;
> they will not hurt us;
> their hearts are full of pity for us.
> My father and my mother, be not afraid,
> your hunger once more is stayed,

and there is still food in abundance.
My brother and my sister, comb your hair,
and paint your faces with vermilion,
for the Great Spirit has softened the hearts of our enemies,
and they feed us with food.[3]

—~—

For nearly two years the US Army had chased Sitting Bull and his followers across the buffalo prairie of Dakota, Wyoming, and Montana, driven to end that unfettered lifeway and secure all the Sioux people at agencies on the Great Sioux Reservation in the Dakota Territory. Sitting Bull escaped the cordon and crossed the mysterious Medicine Line into British America in midsummer 1877, intent plainly on distancing himself from that tireless, deadly army, and subsisting as long as possible on buffalo. But in the end it was the matter of subsistence that overwhelmed him. The buffalo in Canada had disappeared, hunted to virtual extinction but for the few escaping into the Big Open country of Montana, a land that no longer welcomed the stalwart chief. His Canadian hosts had, at best, tolerated his presence, even while repeatedly declaring that he and his people were American Indians, not Canadian, and their own larder was always closed. These years later, Sitting Bull's people were indeed starving. Ultimately, the day coming was all about food, just as the old woman had chanted. In the end, it was always about food.

The caravan camped on the open prairie seventeen miles north of Fort Buford on the evening of July 18. Brotherton was well alerted to their pending arrival and had been encouraged to sequester his garrison so as not to alarm them when the procession made its way through. Buford's soldiers recognized the importance of this day, too. Most had gone to war against Sitting Bull. The lone Seventh Cavalry company in the garrison had been almost wholly reconstructed after Little Big Horn—the heart of this particular company had perished with Custer. The three Seventh Infantry companies present had helped bury the Little Big Horn dead.[4]

The Sitting Bull caravan reached Fort Buford at noon on July 19. Dispersed and barracked soldiers notwithstanding, the arrival attracted considerable attention, much as it would have, the *Pioneer Press* reporter thought, had it passed through the streets of Saint Paul—Sitting Bull and fellow headmen riding ponies in the van, six army wagons carrying women and children following behind, and twenty-five or thirty Red River baggage carts trailing all.[5]

Brotherton directed the chief and drivers to a broad sward between the southernmost army buildings and the Missouri riverfront near the boat landing. There, after lodges were erected, he entered the camp and shook the chief's hand. Both agreed that any public statements would be made the next day, after everyone had been well fed. First, however, Brotherton, his adjutant, and several members of the post guard undertook the surrender of Indian weapons and ponies. Warriors detested the move but that simple measure had long ago become the standard, inflexible imposition on all returning Lakotas, an act some called the Rule of 1876, reflecting the time when it was first imposed.[6]

Sitting Bull surrendered two weapons. On July 19 when all arms were collected, he gave to Brotherton a smoothbore Northwest trade gun, an antique weapon in 1881 even in Indian circles. But he acknowledged also that he had another firearm. He and Brotherton agreed that that gun might be surrendered the next day. Meanwhile, he gave his horse to Harriet Clifford, wife of Captain Clifford, telling her as he did so: "eleven years ago I shook hands with you . . . now I shake hands with you again and make a present of my horse." He then rather abruptly spun away and entered his lodge. One Bull, Sitting Bull's nephew raised as a son, remembered that only after the weapons and ponies were taken away were rations distributed.[7]

The night passed quietly. At 11:00 A.M. on July 20, Sitting Bull led a small delegation of headmen, including Four Horns and One Bull, to Brotherton's quarters, where surrender formalities occurred. Uniquely in the mix was the chief's six-year-old son, Crow Foot, carrying his father's relatively new, brass tacked, Winchester carbine. An aura of pomp and dress pervaded the room, onlookers including a red-coated North-West Mounted Policeman, the brass buttoned and proper Major Brotherton and a contingent of blue-coated officers from his garrison, and several guests, including the *Pioneer Press* reporter. But Sitting Bull's appearance mirrored the weariness of his own lot. According to the reporter, the lone newsman among them, the heralded chief's dress amounted to a worn and dirty calico shirt, a pair of black leggings, a shabby, threadbare blanket wrapped about his waist, and a calico kerchief tied turban-like around his head and partly concealing his eyes.[8]

The sullen Sitting Bull seated himself at the major's left side. Brotherton opened the council, outlining the government's intent for Sitting Bull. He and his people would be sent to Fort Yates, where the larger portion of the Hunkpapa Sioux already resided. They had nothing to fear, he assured them, so long as they remained peaceable. The major then turned to the chief, indicating that he could now proceed. The reporter remembered that Sitting Bull sat perfectly silent for nearly five minutes, as if making a review of his past life. "So long as he maintained his silence there was nothing about the man to indicate the strength of will which has made his name so famous." He then spoke, first talking calmly to the other Indians present. Those remarks were not interpreted.[9]

After that brief utterance Sitting Bull turned to his young son, directing him to take up the Winchester and present it to Major Brotherton. This done, the chief followed with a remark that fitted not only the moment, but the ages:

> I surrender this rifle to you through my young son, whom I now desire to teach in this manner that he has become a friend of the Americans. I wish him to learn the habits of the Whites and to be educated as their sons are educated. I wish it to be remembered that I was the last man of my tribe to surrender my rifle.

Sitting Bull's comments then trailed into a review of other surrenders and his apprehension over being here today. "I have never received good news from here," he declared. He wished to continue the old life and trade on either side of the line. He wished for the freedom to visit his old friends north of the line, including Major Walsh and Inspector Alexander Macdonell of the Mounted Police—Macdonell the Red Coat in the audience now. He acknowledged leaving some Lakota families in Canada, but hoped that they might join him and other Hunkpapas variously now at Poplar River and at Standing Rock on a different reservation of their own choosing on the Little Missouri River.[10]

When the chief finished, several other Indians present offered remarks, mere echoes said the reporter of what Sitting Bull had said. Brotherton, in turn, was in no position to challenge or promise anything Sitting Bull had said or sought but merely to assure everyone that the government was dealing with them in the best manner possible. And on that note he dismissed the gathering and consigned the Indians to the care of Captain Clifford, who escorted them to their camp and tended a distribution of new blankets for all.[11]

The next days were filled with calm and an abundance of foodstuffs while the army wrangled with arrangements necessary to transport these 188 Lakotas to Fort Yates, the military post aside the Standing Rock Agency, the downriver home of most Hunkpapas. The first reports of the surrender reached Bismarck and Saint Paul by telegraph on June 19, the day of Sitting Bull's arrival at Fort Buford, and they and others filled columns in those city newspapers and nationwide for days to come. The *Pioneer Press* reporter's filings were soon augmented by correspondence and official reports from others in attendance. Never lost in the shower of words were those of the great chief: "I wish it to be remembered that I was the last man of my tribe to surrender my rifle."[12]

And thus ended Sitting Bull's War. This conflict, spanning nearly two years on the battlefield and three more in a wearying political imbroglio, plus years before that of maddening intrusions into the buffalo country—and a lifeway—cost the American government millions of dollars, atop a casualty tally numbering in the many hundreds of Indians and Whites, whose blood fell on some two dozen fields of honor across the northern plains. Most significantly, and a point not lost on many then or today, it ended a unique lifeway for all time, a lifeway once marked with untold richness and freedom on the buffalo prairie of old.

Sitting Bull's life changed forevermore at Fort Buford. The central figure in this story of a long and difficult war was fifty years old when the conflict ended. He was born in 1831, likely on the Grand River in Dakota, near an obscure location known as Many Caches and ironically close to where his life ended in 1890. He earned his name, Buffalo Bull Sits Down, as a teenager after counting his first coup. The name easily translated as Sitting Buffalo Bull or simply Sitting Bull. He counted many other coups in young adulthood, mostly fighting with the Crows, and was wounded three times, including in the foot. He ever after walked with a noticeable limp. Throughout life he exhibited the four Lakota cardinal virtues of bravery, fortitude, generosity, and wisdom, all behaviors of one possessing great personal and social discipline and consciousness.

Sitting Bull was no man of pretention at Fort Buford in 1881, and was never such a man. He dressed plainly and typically wore but a single eagle feather recognizing his first coup. The *Pioneer Press* reporter at Fort Buford called it shabby attire, doubtless a reflection of a terrible time but also missing the point. The chief's simple dress exemplified a lifeway. While respected as a brave and accomplished warrior and a Hunkpapa war chief by the time he was twenty-six, Sitting Bull was foremost a humble man. Moreover, in adulthood he developed an admired reputation as a holy man, possessing gifts of prophesy obtained from dreams, visions, and direct communications with *Wakan Tanka*, the Great Mystery. In the greatest of all Lakota self-sacrifices and dream inducers, Sitting Bull Sun Danced many times, and the visions derived were sometimes astounding. His nephew, White Bull, a Miniconjou, vividly remembered his heavily scarred arms, back, and breast. And his followers likewise never forgot the remarkable vision that came to him on Rosebud Creek in June 1876.[13]

Surrounding Sitting Bull throughout the war and in those final days was foremost his extended family. While his marital status throughout life was complicated, in these critical years his family included two wives, Four Robes and her older sister, the widowed Seen by Her Nation. Three children by previous marriages, two daughters and a son, also lodged with them, and Seen by Her Nation brought two children to the family which he adopted. Of his earlier children, he was particularly fond of the eldest girl, Many Horses, who had run away just before Sitting Bull returned to America. That loss tormented him greatly, especially when learning, incorrectly as it turned out, that she was then being held in irons. With Seen by Her Nation, the son, Crow Foot, was born in 1873, and with Four Robes twin sons were born just days before the Little Big Horn battle. Two other children were born in Canada. One of the twin sons died later in 1876 and the son from a first marriage died in 1877 but the others, aside from that daughter, were with him now.[14]

This complex man, once a great warrior and now a devout holy man, and ever a dedicated father, was remembered in those days of turmoil for his willingness to advise, encourage, sympathize, explain, and simply converse. Those observing him from afar, particularly Whites, saw a stoic man, but around family and friends he was ever capable of a gentle smile and a hearty laugh. Mostly his friends remembered a good man who always put the well-being of others before his own. His people's welfare was his foremost obsession.

Americans have long struggled to grasp the worth of the Great Plains, their chief breadbasket and protein source since the late nineteenth century, and much later a blind-eye source of coal and natural gas. The lands west of the Missouri River reaching to the Rocky Mountains were never subtle. In their vast openness the Plains could be perplexing, often overwhelming, and sometimes deadly, and all the while vibrant and beautiful. Geographers in the twentieth century were quick to dissect the Great Plains, enumerating and characterizing its whole and its many subsections—southern, central, and northern plains—high plain—a mosaic of grasses that were tall, mid-sized, and short, and vibrant with wildflowers and other broad-leaved plants—lands bisected by intermittent and continuously flowing waters, with major and lesser water courses, some navigable—land that was humid in places, or subhumid, or arid—land mostly treeless and once filled with prairie dogs, antelope, wolves, and buffalo. What to make of it, then or now? Mostly, Americans recognize the Great Plains today as an essential sector of the endlessly fascinating American West, or Wild West.[15]

For early Americans, the feature characterizing the Great Plains foremost was not its seemingly endless flatness or dryness but its buffalo, by far the region's dominant species. While American buffalo were once found from the Rocky Mountains eastward to the Atlantic Seaboard, their true home was on the Great Plains. And while continually nibbled at on the eastern margins to the point of elimination, through most of the eighteenth and nineteenth centuries the plains population remained robust and seemingly limitless. Early observers were spellbound by what they confronted. A traveler in western Kansas in 1871 encountered a great herd of buffalo, recording countless smaller herds of some fifty to two hundred animals that were utterly inseparable from other similar smaller herds, the sum comprising one mass of animals that encumbered his way for twenty five miles. A Santa Fe–bound traveler several decades earlier reported seeing buffalo covering the entire landscape for three days.[16]

Calculating buffalo numbers has never been easy. Estimates based on subsistence requirements and range carrying capacities suggest a one-time Plains buffalo population of twenty-two to twenty-five million animals. But human predation and environmental conditions took an enormous toll. By the time of Sitting Bull's War scholars have estimated that some four million animals still comprised a so-called southern herd, all south of the nation's first transcontinental railroad, and that another two million buffalo sprawled the hills and valleys of the northern range. The Sioux people distinguished those masses, calling one simply the "Buffalo South" and other "Buffalo North," referring to ranges as well as animals. For generations they revered all manner of the animal and made it a cornerstone of their lives, but by war's end it was all but a mere memory. "I wish I had some of that meat now," recalled the Oglala warrior Eagle Elk decades later. "It had strength in it."[17]

The Sioux people thrived in this vastness of land and animals, evolving a culture perfectly suited to the Plains and the varied bounty they beheld. By Lewis and Clark's time, the Sioux people sprawled the Upper Missouri Country in what became the Dakota Territory, east and west of the Missouri but mostly west where they were continually drawn by the richness of resources and opportunity. In that west lay the lands of the Kiowas, Cheyennes, Crows, and others. The Sioux, a numerous people, easily wrested and occupied what they wanted—conquest demanded both—sometimes driving enemies away and sometimes, as with the Cheyennes, forging bonds of alliance that endured through innumerable wars with the Whites, including Sitting Bull's War. By the 1860s, Sitting Bull's people had wrested most of eastern Montana from the Crows, too. The great chief never found accord with those people and warred incessantly with them to the very end of their collective days on the prairie.[18]

By the mid-nineteenth century the domain of the seven divisions or *oyates* of the Teton Sioux sprawled westward from the Missouri to the Big Horn Mountains, and from the Canadian prairies southward to the Republican River Basin in present-day Kansas. Each of the seven divisions favored sectors of this distinctive and resource-rich homeland, and within each major division were bands and aligned bands—*tiyospayes*—who parsed it all the more. All lived day-to-day lives rather independent of one other. The Brulés or Sicangus, always the largest of the divisions, dominated lands from the southern Black Hills, White River, and Pine Ridge southward through the Niobrara and North Platte Rivers to the Republican itself. Their focus was buffalo hunting on the central plains, particularly in the Republican River country, while also availing themselves of the natural riches of the Black Hills and Pine Ridge. The Oglalas, second largest of the *oyates*, scattered over lands west of the Brulés, roughly stretching from the North Platte River in Nebraska and Wyoming northward into the Powder River Basin, with the Big Horn Mountains a natural western boundary. Both groups were typically considered Southern Lakotas, a distinction that played large in their history, especially in the days of America's overland migrations and the wars and treaties long preceding Sitting Bull's War. Both bands at midcentury favored trading opportunities at Fort Laramie on the North Platte. Trading intercourse there and on the Missouri River factored large in this approaching apogee of the Lakota horse and buffalo culture.[19]

The Miniconjou Sioux favored lands stretching westward from the Missouri along the Cheyenne, Belle Fourche, and Moreau Rivers to the northern Black Hills and beyond, a territory teeming with buffalo and the natural resources of the Hills themselves. Sitting Bull's people, the Hunkpapa Sioux, the third largest of the Lakota *oyates*, regarded the lands of the Moreau, Grand, Cannonball, and Little Missouri Rivers as their natural early and mid-nineteenth century Plains homeland, but also often hunted west of the Little Missouri in the Lower Yellowstone Basin and adjacent wilds farther west yet, sandwiched between the Yellowstone and Missouri. At midcentury the Lower Yellowstone remained Crow Country until the Hunkpapas pushed those people toward the mountains and came to fully dominate almost all of today's eastern Montana. The Hunkpapa attachment to and familiarity with the northernmost of Sioux Country helps explain why the closing days of Sitting Bull's War and its entire long aftermath took place in that land between the Yellowstone and Missouri Rivers, and eventually straight north into Canada. For the Hunkpapas, this was an evolved natural homeland from well before the 1870s war.[20]

The smallest of the Teton divisions, the Blackfeet, Two Kettles, and Sans Arcs occupied much of the same ground as the Miniconjous and Hunkpapas and those people interspersed themselves band by band and individually among them, often by marriage. Collectively, these five Teton groups, last to abandon their forest homeland in Minnesota, were once known as the Saones (from *chan* [trees, forest] + *oni* [to live among]), but that distinction had all but disappeared by the mid-nineteenth century. These five bands were drawn to trade at Fort Pierre on the Missouri, in the center of the Dakota Territory, although Miniconjous were also known to trade at Fort Laramie, and from time to time the Hunkpapas carried on a testy trade at Fort Union, located at the confluence of the Yellowstone and Missouri Rivers. For decades, Fort Union had been the trading haven of the Crows.[21]

The seven Lakota *oyates* each had their own governing councils and religious leaders prescribing norms that regulated daily, seasonal, and religious lives. Sun Dances, the most important of Lakota religious ceremonies, were held each summer, often in the foothills of the Black Hills, sometimes occurring band by band but as often in great communal gatherings where the Lakota people affirmed their oneness. The Sioux enjoyed a fluid society where, born into one *oyate* or *tiyospaye* an individual might by marriage or choice move to another whenever suitable or desirable. For the Lakotas, fusion and fission of bands was a recurrent feature of life, in which Miniconjou one year, an individual might become an Oglala the next. Entire bands might realign, as occurred with the *Wajajes* in the 1860s when choosing to identify as Oglala rather than Brulé. Similarly, in the days of treaties, agencies, and attempted government order, bands might align in ways serving their own interests. A Miniconjou band, retaining its identity, might settle among the Brulés, for instance, at the Brulé agency on the White River and not their own on the Missouri, invariably to the consternation of local government officials.[22]

While the Sioux are ever remembered as buffalo people, it was in fact horses that enabled their distinctive lifeway. At their disposal was an animal that could do the work of dogs but much more efficiently, and carry people, and facilitate hunting and war. The Sioux had acquired horses by 1680 through Indian trading networks, and once mounted this already populous people easily followed the buffalo onto the open prairie. While the Sioux were skilled herdsmen, they were not noted as breeders to the extent needed to sustain their own individual and tribal demands. Instead, stealing horses from others, chiefly from the Crows, became the norm. Stealing horses was always the better bargain, with glory added to the allure.[23]

The Sioux are sometimes characterized as a nomadic people but that misses a subtle truth. While movement was a constant in their lives, smaller family bands, or two or three aligned bands, followed regular seasonal courses. Indians camped on the same streams and hunted the same regions in the same seasons, always within the same home ground, so long as essential needs were met—suitable water, fuel, grazing, shelter in winter, and access to buffalo. A remarkable Hunkpapa woman turned twentieth century Lakota historian, Josephine Waggoner, recalled that all the camping places had names and were used year after year. Moreover, she said, Indians had a map of the country—a figurative map—layered with year-round water courses, mountains, and roadways. "Directly east of the camp about a hundred miles," Waggoner remembered so poignantly, "was the headwaters of the Little Missouri, whose rough banks and badlands were impassable except for travois traveling. Directly west was Goose Creek, which could be followed to the Laramie country in Wyoming. The headwaters of the Cheyenne River was not very far away, which could be followed into the Black Hills."[24]

Waggoner's roadways were mere travois trails that sometimes visibly scored the ground. Implicit in her recollection was a dependence on watercourses. The Sioux were in fact a river people. While they largely disdained the Missouri because of its proximity to Whites and their riverboats and military posts, almost every other flowing watercourse in their northern plains universe served them perfectly, from the North Platte and Niobrara in the south, to the White, Cheyenne, Moreau, and Grand in the east, to the Little Missouri, Powder, Tongue, Rosebud, and Red Water in the west and north. Those streams and their endless smaller tributaries featured magnificent stands of cottonwoods and cedars, providing necessary fuel, with cottonwood bark even providing winter forage for horses, and with nutritious grasses covering adjacent hillsides. Virtually every one of the devastating clashes of Sitting Bull's War occurred on the waterways, great and small, of the northern plains.

Within this Lakota universe, the most important physical feature at its very core was the Black Hills, a sacred place that was home to powerful spirits, and no mere landmark but always a destination. This well-watered, piney, elliptical shaped upland in western Dakota with its jutting rocky interior—featuring Black Elk Peak (formerly Harney Peak) reaching an elevation of 7,244 feet and noted as the highest summit between the Rocky Mountains and French Alps—spans some one hundred twenty miles north-south by fifty miles east-west. Seen from afar the Black Hills indeed loomed dark, luring, and mystical on the horizon. Indians traveled long distances each year to cut lodge poles there, avail themselves of diverse flora and fauna different from the plains, and fulfill religious obligations. By the time of Sitting Bull's War, most Lakotas embraced an additional value, a reverential one, borne out of a multigenerational familiarity with that landscape and tempered now by the action of Whites, who had poked about its interior since the 1830s and ultimately snatched it away after gold was confirmed there by Custer in 1874. He Dog, a nephew of Red Cloud and long-time close personal ally of Crazy Horse, spoke for most Oglalas and Lakotas when he remarked that the Black Hills were "the Heart of the Earth."[25]

Sioux Country was dotted with other striking physical landmarks recognized by the people of the seven Lakota *oyates* and their allies. On the near northern margins of the Black Hills are several striking uplifts possessing considerable reverential value to Lakotas and Cheyennes, including Bear Butte in Dakota and Inyan Kara and Bear Lodge Butte (Devils Tower to the Whites), in Wyoming. The Cheyennes, long present in the Black Hills before the Sioux, particularly cherished Bear Butte then as now as their sacred mountain, home of their Four Sacred Arrows. For the Sioux, these striking prominences were places to fast, pray, and worship. Farther north in Dakota were the Slim Buttes, Short Pine Hills, and Sentinel Butte, prominent way stops figuring directly in varied Indian and soldier movements during the course of life and the coming war. To the west on Montana's Rosebud Creek was Deer Medicine Rocks, a small but noticeable stony protuberance layered with rock art documenting and foretelling all manner of Indian tradition and history. Scattered elsewhere was the Pine Ridge in Nebraska and Rawhide Butte and Hat Creek Breaks in Wyoming. These were among the obvious, oversized places in Sioux Country, but in truth every corner had a protruding glacial boulder, unique bend in a stream, a stony cairn, a specific location where someone fought or died in an intertribal clash, and all were memorable and meaningful.[26]

The Sioux Country on the northern plains, a land so long dismissed and confusing to Whites, was to Indians a place of remarkable diversity, overflowing with abundant physical and natural resources that, in all, were perfectly suited to peoples who embraced the buffalo and sought only to live in the manner of their ancestors. And it had now become a land and lifeway worth fighting and dying for.

One other dimension of Indian land plays continually through this story. While Whites described and understood lands having discernable legal bounds and entitlements, such notions were all but meaningless to Lakotas and Cheyennes who lived and thought in terms of place, not physical possession, and whether waterways, highlands, sacred ground, hunting land, Crow land, buffalo trails, a Buffalo South and Buffalo North. When treaty commissioners at Fort Laramie in 1851 described Sioux, Cheyenne, or Crow country, Indian people standing before them understood their words abstractly. Fixed boundaries on maps were meaningless. When treaty commissioners in 1868 prescribed a Great Sioux Reservation and unceded hunting lands, again Indian people understood what they were being told, at least conceptually. River bounds and agencies might be static, but until the time of the stone heaps placed along the international border in the early 1870s no lines or concepts of lines existed on the ground. Such disparate views of land and land ownership perplexed Indians and Whites throughout this coming time of travail.

Sitting Bull and other fervent traditionals were renowned for their disdain of Whites, avoiding the inducements of presents, overtures, treaties, and agencies, and regarding with contempt those kin who did. And yet ironically the horse and buffalo culture that comprised the central focus of their lives made them strikingly dependent upon Whites, or at least the material trappings uniquely provided by White traders. Saint Louis–based company men operating from stationary posts like Forts Union, Pierre, and Laramie—rogue traders operating on the margins—and itinerant trading caravans coming from British America all provided an array of knives, awls, metal arrowheads, cooking kettles, blankets in an array of colors, yard goods, decorative materials, and, most importantly, firearms, lead, and powder—materials that easily became essential elements of Lakota life. Traders were accepted as necessary evils, men who felled timbers in the river bottoms for their stockades and to fuel their cooking and heating stoves and the voracious fireboxes of their steamboats, but whose industrial goods were fair compensation. Traders in turn sought furs, especially by midcentury Plains buffalo. Indian tanned buffalo robes quickly became a prime commodity.[27]

While company traders and their posts dominated the business, independent traders often operated in their proximities, sometimes relatively nearby and openly, but as often deliberately in the shadows, where small unscrupulous outfits intentionally unseen brokered merchandise that was usually carefully governed and often prohibited. Whiskey was long a scourge in the Indian trade, a potent and damning commodity that was never eliminated and invariably available from these clandestine traders. But in the time of Sitting Bull's War, the greater scourge was access to new model firearms and fixed ammunition (cartridges). Regulated or not, and always outrageously expensive, Lakota warriors readily obtained all the firearms they could afford, usually new model Henry and Winchester repeating rifles, plus sufficient fixed ammunition to sustain themselves on the hunt and in battle. As war approached, this so-called night trading with rogue outfits was not merely occurring at isolated locales in the Pine Ridge and along the Missouri River but with outfits taking their business straight to the Indian camps themselves.[28]

The greatest of the clandestine traders operating on the northern plains in the 1860s and 1870s were the Plains Métis, a mixed-blood people of part-Canadian French and part-Plains Cree heritage and who themselves had been pushed onto the Plains from their long-held homeland in the Red River country of British America. The Plains Métis were formidable buffalo hunters who ranged on both sides of the border and brokered their furs and meats to their advantage, sometimes in Canada and as often in Saint Cloud and Saint Paul, Minnesota. As the buffalo range contracted westward the Métis followed and by the middle 1860s had established themselves on the Frenchman's River in Rupert's Land (soon to become a segment of the North-West Territories when that vast Hudson's Bay Company holding was acquired by Canada), and also in the Milk River country of Montana, where they brokered furs and meats at Fort Benton. What made the Métis problematical for American authorities was their mobility, which enabled them to circumvent restrictions, and their willingness to trade with the Sioux, providing whiskey, arms, and ammunition in exchange for buffalo robes. For the Métis, the border was their shield. That this business enabled Lakota resistance to American expansion seemed only to tempt and delight the Métis.[29]

The Eastern Sioux resented these mixed-blood incursions onto their hunting ground. The two groups fought incessantly, and the clashes were invariably unfavorable to the Sioux. A fight between Yanktonai Sioux and Métis near Fort Union in 1856 was particularly costly for the Sioux, who lost as many as eighty warriors, while the Métis lost perhaps eight of their own. Reflecting on those troubles, a Fort Union bourgeois noted: "It appears that the Half Breeds get the better of the Sioux. At least they are not afraid to continue their annual excursions into their country, and are known to be as good if not better warriors than the Indians." This persistent ill will followed the Métis into Montana. As Sitting Bull's people ventured into the Yellowstone River country in the mid-1860s they too at first were alarmed by this competition for the same land and buffalo. The Lakotas called these mixed-bloods the *Slotas*, or Grease People, and often fought openly with them and rarely found common accord until changing fates in the coming years altered circumstances in compelling ways.[30]

The notion of Northern Sioux and Southern Sioux gained new meaning in the early 1860s when the Hunkpapas and Blackfeet, and Oglalas and Brulés all found themselves enmeshed in two different streams of war spilling across the margins of Lakota Sioux Country. Many Dakota Sioux Indians fleeing the terrible shambles in Minnesota in 1862 took refuge in Northern Lakota Sioux camps that winter and fell prey next year to a vigorous onslaught of troops from the East. Sitting Bull was not present in those fights though doubtless was horrified by the continual news, including of the fight at Whitestone Hill in September 1863, occurring well east of the Missouri River, where upward of three hundred Dakota Indians were killed, another 150 captured, and winter provisions destroyed. But indeed Sitting Bull and his followers were present at an equally disastrous affair at Killdeer Mountain the next year. In the shadows of that imposing butte located in the eastern breaks of the Little Missouri badlands, troops assaulted a broad mix of Eastern and Western Sioux in July 1864. Indian casualties may have numbered 150, and again a village and its wherewithal were destroyed. Sitting Bull's foremost counterpart there was the dynamic Dakota Sioux leader Inkpaduta, a central figure in the Minnesota War and its aftermath and a lingering, almost tragic figure in the Sitting Bull War yet to come.[31]

The Oglalas and Brulés, meanwhile, had no role in the warfare in Dakota but were caught in troubles on the Platte River at the same time. Access to the Colorado gold fields drew blood across the central plains in the early 1860s, mostly involving Arapaho and Southern Cheyenne Indians, and soon reached a fever pitch. That warfare spilled northward after Colorado militiamen ruthlessly slaughtered a peaceful village of Cheyennes belonging to Black Kettle at Sand Creek, Colorado, in November 1864. Word of that atrocity spread throughout Indian Country and in the north drew Oglalas and Brulés, long-time allies of those Cheyennes, into a retaliatory war that enflamed the Platte River Valley in 1864 and then spread into Wyoming the next year. Repeated clashes along the South and North Platte Rivers and soldier forays into northern Wyoming were dramatic, and while not on the scale of the bloodletting at Whitestone Hill, Killdeer Mountain, or Sand Creek, they rendered the Colorado and Overland Trails virtually impassable without stiff military intervention. Those events also brought into focus an emerging Oglala Lakota warrior, Crazy Horse, then twenty-five years old, whose heroics and charisma were noticed by both sides.[32]

This allied Indian resistance on the Platte and in Wyoming served Whites another lesson, too. Gold had also been discovered in western Montana at this time. A new trail blazed to those far reaches that coursed across the eastern foothills of the Big Horn Mountains required heavy fortification because it passed through the very heart of the Lakota's buffalo country. A residual supply base from the Wyoming war, Fort Connor on the Powder River, was seen as but one of several posts serving this new purpose.

Recognizing this as yet another potential crisis, the government attempted a peace accord with the Lakotas at Fort Laramie in 1866. While negotiations were underway, the untimely arrival of soldiers bound for a trail through the buffalo country that had not yet been accorded by treaty shattered the proceedings and triggered two full years of all-out war. The army stayed its course, occupying Fort Reno—the old Fort Connor—and established Fort Phil Kearny on Big Piney Creek east of the Big Horns, and Fort C. F. Smith on the Big Horn River north of the Big Horns in Montana. Lakotas and Cheyennes besieged all three posts almost immediately. Tremendous battles fought nearly within their sight claimed astounding numbers of casualties on both sides, especially in a fight known to the Sioux and Cheyenne as the "hundred in the hand" battle, remembering the number of people killed. Whites remembered it as the Fetterman Massacre.[33]

This war in the late-1860s is sometimes remembered as the Bozeman Trail War but better remembered as Red Cloud's War, because that patriarchal Oglala had masterminded Indian resistance throughout its course. The war brought notoriety to a number of other Lakotas and Cheyennes more than Red Cloud—Little Wolf of the Northern Cheyennes, White Bull and High Back Bone of the Miniconjou Lakotas, Man Afraid of His Horse, American Horse, and Crazy Horse of the Oglalas, names that would surface again in affairs to come.[34]

Red Cloud's War had ramifications of an even greater sort in the manner in which it was brought to a close. On the bloody trail itself across Wyoming and Montana, the Sioux and their allies had stymied virtually all movements on the road short of those covered by heavily armed military escorts. By now, the army was principally caring for its own and rarely others. And soon enough, the trail's obsolescence seemed at hand. With the looming completion of the nation's first transcontinental railroad, anticipated in early 1869, Montana-bound citizens could more easily and safely travel by rail to a junction in Utah, and continue northward from there on a near trouble-free Montana Road to Virginia City, Helena, and the other vibrant gold camps dotting the western mountains. The Sioux meanwhile demanded the complete abandonment of the Bozeman road and its protectorate forts, a matter the government conceded easily enough.

Again commissioners met Indian representatives at Fort Laramie, this time in 1868, and dished up a prewritten accord largely crafted in Washington. In its seventeen articles, the government prescribed establishing a defined home for the Lakotas, not one much mirroring the Sioux Country then occupied by the seven *oyates* that stretched from the Platte to the Yellowstone and the Missouri to the Big Horns, but instead land in southwestern Dakota Territory. That this new reservation included the Black Hills was a true oversight—Whites still knew virtually nothing at all of the Hills. The White treaty-makers imagined all Lakotas living on this reservation and no longer anywhere else in the Sioux Country of old. Their treaty also prescribed a single agency for the Sioux, on the Missouri, where farming and schooling would be introduced, and patented land, clothing, and annuities distributed. As a practical measure, the government allowed an unceded territory west of this new reservation to the summits of the Big Horns, where no Whites could settle or even traverse and where Indians might continue to roam and hunt, and also buffalo hunting in the Republican River Basin, that a particular cause célèbre of Spotted Tail and his Brulés. And the government agreed to the abandonment of the hated military posts on the Bozeman Trail and the full closure of that road itself.[35]

Indian representatives at the proceedings saw what they wanted in the document, the abandonment of the forts and road foremost, and believed that they would never become farmers or send their children to schools or ever be obliged to do so. Some were open to living near an agency but that was an abstraction for most, and for some even abhorrent. Little could any of the signers imagine that this document would guide virtually all future relations with the government. A case was made by some later that they did not know what they were signing, which may partly be true, but signing began no less on April 29, with the Brulés first, followed by the Oglalas on May 25, and Miniconjous and Yanktonais on May 25 and 26. The proceedings then shifted to Fort Rice on the Missouri River where representatives of the Hunkpapas, Blackfeet, Two Kettles, Sans Arcs, and Santees signed on July 2. Red Cloud was the longest holdout, signing a copy of the document retained for him at Fort Laramie on November 6. He waited to first personally witness troops abandon the Bozeman road. In all more than 184 Lakota, Yanktonai, Arapaho, and Santee headmen marked the document, their names duly recorded for all time. Sitting Bull's name was not among them. He agreed to nothing. His land, the northern buffalo prairie, served him well. That was his home and he intended to stay.[36]

By the mid-1860s during Red Cloud's War, Sitting Bull's people had indeed spread fully into the Lower Yellowstone country, drawn as always by the bountiful buffalo herds. This had largely been the home of River and Mountain Crows before this. Those people, now pushed farther west, continued hunting the same northern buffalo range as did the Métis, Gros Ventre, Assiniboine, Yanktonai Sioux, and other northern plains Indians. This expanding Northern Lakota universe now spanned the drainages of the Little Missouri in the east, the lower Powder and Tongue Rivers and Rosebud Creek farther west, and all of eastern Montana north of the Yellowstone to the Missouri, a land itself that came to be known as the Big Open.[37]

With few exceptions, Sitting Bull's people took no part in Red Cloud's War, focusing at the same time considerable parallel enmity on a different military post emerging at the confluence of the Yellowstone and Missouri Rivers, Fort Buford, established in June 1866. After the Killdeer Mountain episode Sitting Bull watched soldiers occupy the aged Fort Union trading post, and then witnessed this new construction two miles east. As Sitting Bull viewed it, those Whites—soldiers no less—represented a new and direct threat to the buffalo prairie, his home. He openly preyed on the new fort for nearly two years. While never mustering the same strength and warrior mass as did Red Cloud against the forts in the Big Horn country, his annoying presence at Buford was continually obstructive, whether threatening and occasionally killing herders and woodcutters, running off stock, firing hay stacks, volleying into the fort, or, on one occasion, seizing the post's sawmill and beating the circular blade with a maddening glee. The garrison saw itself continually besieged.[38]

All the while, Sitting Bull's people did occasional business at the nearby and still functioning Fort Union and although the chief was rarely present there or at any of the other independent houses the local traders maintained nearby, the Upper Missouri veteran Charles Larpenteur remembered confronting him outside his shop one day. Sitting Bull had come to talk with Whirl Wind, an Assiniboine chief whose people were trading with Larpenteur. Larpenteur warned Sitting Bull about the depredations being committed at Buford and that those soldiers would one day be strong enough to chastise him. Sitting Bull scoffed at the notion. "I have killed, robbed, and injured too many White men to believe in a good peace," he proclaimed. "I'd rather have my skin pierced with bullet holes." And to the Assiniboines who listened intently, he warned them not to stick so close to the Whites. Do as he did, he declared. "Go into the buffalo country, eat plenty of meat, and when they wanted a good horse, go to some fort and steal one." "Look at me," he continued, "see if I am poor, or my people either. The Whites may get me at last, as you say, but I will have good times till then. You are fools to make yourselves slaves to a piece of fat bacon, some hard-tack, and a little sugar and coffee."[39]

On another occasion, in December 1866, Sitting Bull actually taunted death at the confluence. While again visiting Fort Union he waved a white cloth and parlayed with the agent in charge, Fellowes Pease. In a long talk Sitting Bull declared his intent to kill every soldier at the army fort. He wanted Pease to give him a red shirt so that the Buford defenders could more easily recognize him, and said that he would throw off his robe when next he was there. Pease obliged and then hurriedly sent word to Fort Buford, where soldiers were ordered to concentrate their fire on the Indian wearing the red shirt. Sitting Bull may or may not have exposed himself in a red shirt at Fort Buford. No one there afterward mentioned any more of the episode, but this pretense, if not an actual show of hubris, was dramatic, and attention getting, and a plain sign of bursting contempt for White people. Sitting Bull relished the theatrics. An act of actual hubris a few years hence was all the more dramatic and potentially self-sacrificing.[40]

In the coming years agencies evolved on the Great Sioux Reservation, not the lone station imagined by the treaty makers but respective stations for each of the principal Lakota *oyates*, with three located on the Missouri and another on the North Platte. Those locations changed from time to time but each, wherever initially or permanently situated, became centers for the relentless acculturation labors envisioned by the government. Some Lakotas of each *oyate* took easily to agency life, many having resided around trading posts for years, and some even serving as intermediaries in the business. Others married traders and were now raising mixed-blood children who, as they themselves grew older, continued the tradition of employment, particularly in the roles of language translation. Many of these agency people were pragmatists who increasingly saw the futility of the old life, despite never ceasing to consider themselves Lakotas.[41]

Sitting Bull represented the old life. Increasingly in the days following the consummation of the Fort Laramie Treaty of 1868 he emerged as the pillar of Indian independence on the northern plains, steadfastly dedicated to living on his own terms, on his own ground, and making his way hunting buffalo in the long tradition of the Hunkpapa Lakotas. He drew to his camp a fluctuating lot of similarly minded independent people and bands from all the Lakota *oyates*. They saw themselves living a superior life dedicated to the hunt, and where they were not dictated to by a government or anyone. By now this had become an almost inflexible tradition. Wooden Leg, a Northern Cheyenne whose people came and went among the Sitting Bull people, expressed the simplicity of it all, telling his biographer that "we had but to kill and eat. As I now think back upon those days, it seems that no people in the world ever were any richer than we were. That is all anybody needs—a good shelter, plenty of food, plenty of fuel, plenty of good water."[42]

By the mid-nineteenth century the Northern Cheyennes had followed a course much like that of their steadfast Lakotas allies, the Oglalas, with whom they developed many common bonds through marriage and kinship, shared common words, and even dressing alike. They occupied much of the same ground as the Oglalas, from the Black Hills and North Platte River to the Yellowstone, but preferred the seclusion of the unique valleys of the lower Powder, Tongue, and Rosebud in Montana. The Northern Cheyennes split from southern kin early in the nineteenth century, the two peoples drawn in different orbits by the quest for horses and trading opportunities. The last common gathering of all Cheyenne bands was thought to have occurred in 1838. Mostly the Southern Cheyennes now resided in the Indian Territory (today's Oklahoma) but familial ties between the southerners and northerners remained strong and movement between the two groups was constant. Many southern people took active roles in Sitting Bull's War. The Northern Cheyennes had also signed a treaty at Fort Laramie that contained the same government assimilation intents and prescribed for them a reservation apart from but aligned with their southern kin in the Indian Territory. The treaty also allowed a reservation prospect with the Brulés or any other Lakota *oyate*, or, oddly, even with the Crows, who were mortal enemies. The Northern Cheyennes were given a year to decide the matter. In the meantime they drew rations with the Oglalas at Red Cloud Agency. The Northern Cheyenne population in the mid-1870s was some 1,700 people, or roughly half that of their Oglala friends.[43]

What was slowly emerging in those years was a distinction between traditionals and agency people, or "non-treaty" and "treaty" Indians. Often the groups held each other in contempt, as only family could, traditionals labeled as "wild" or "hostile" or "northern," and agency people derisively dismissed as "loafers" or "stay around the fort people" or "friendlies," all names that quickly gained currency in White contexts as well. In 1876 the Commissioner of Indian Affairs, John Quincy Smith, summarized it conveniently: "For several years past a camp of Sioux on the Yellowstone River have been known as the northern, or hostile, or non-treaty Sioux, or more commonly as Sitting Bull's band. They are in no sense a recognized band or branch of the great Sioux Nation, but consist of representatives from all the bands, who have rallied around one as their leader who claims never to have been party to any treaty with the United States, and who styles himself chief of the followers whom his personal power and avowed hostility to civilization and the United States Government have attracted around him." Smith's view was politically charged. With but the rarest exceptions contemporary Whites in America never did grasp what this coming war was all about, and certainly not as the tradition-minded Lakotas viewed it.[44]

Whether northerner or southerner, or treaty or non-treaty adherent, there existed across Lakota society and among allies a distinct, visible fluidity of movement between the northern camps and emerging agencies, especially in the summertime when the outward draw was buffalo hunting, communal councils, and Sun Dances, and often enough in the winter when government rations neatly supplemented the hunt. This movement drew the increasing ire of agency officials responsible for clothing and feeding their charges and enforcing edicts on matters like censuses and arms sales. This simple reality persisted until Sitting Bull's War delivered a fatal end.

At one such summer gathering, likely in 1869 and as likely on Montana's Rosebud Creek, a remarkable event occurred. All the Lakota bands were present in greater and lesser numbers, plus many Cheyennes. And all were aware of the forces aligning against them, evidenced in the emerging realities of a reservation in Dakota, and agencies, and notions of themselves described as wild, non-treaty Indians. These were two different Lakota worlds, a transformative one, as already embraced by Red Cloud and Spotted Tail and many of their Oglala and Brulé adherents, or one preserving a life on the buffalo prairie, living in the manner of the ancestors.

Voices in the councils that summer spoke to the desire of embracing one leading man to represent them all, a person of experience, one with demonstrated and respected leadership qualities, and especially an individual exhibiting great wisdom. The council leaders chose Sitting Bull as their consummate chief. Sitting Bull's uncle, Four Horns, also a deeply respected Hunkpapa chief, led the movement, with Black Moon and other Hunkpapa headmen at his side, and Makes Room and Lame Deer rendering Miniconjou support, and Spotted Eagle offering the endorsement of the Sans Arcs. With sweeping approval, Four Horns spoke for all when saying, "we have elected you as our war chief, leader of the entire Sioux nation. When you tell us to fight, we shall fight, when you tell us to make peace, we shall make peace." This was perhaps a tenuous assumptive role at first, calling for a diplomat not an authoritarian, and something more akin to a temporal focal leader of the last free traditionals than a supreme chief in any Whiteman sense, but Sitting Bull accepted the burden. His place was on the buffalo prairie.[45]

As the decade of the 1860s drew to a close Sitting Bull and his adherents had firmly established themselves in eastern Montana's Lower Yellowstone country. The landscape possessed all the essential qualities critical to a good life, with permanently flowing waters in the river's main stem and tributaries, luxuriously wooded valleys, inviting grazing in grassy bottoms and adjacent hillsides, and the northern buffalo herd ever in reach. They had wrested this land from the Crows, with whom they still fought and not merely because both vied for the same ground and same buffalo, but also because the Sioux relished stealing Crow horses. The Crows were adept breeders, and thieving from such an enemy usually meant that the animals were already broken for use. Successful horse stealing, too, brought social and political prestige. In truth, both tribes pleasured in stealing the other's stock, despite the fatalities that inevitably occurred. Lakotas and Crows killed one another not because they were so different but because they were so much alike.[46]

With Sitting Bull as the obvious beacon, fervent traditionals made a new home in the north—Four Horns's, Black Moon's, Gall's, and Long Dog's Hunkpapas; Lame Deer's and White Bull's Miniconjous; Spotted Eagle's Sans Arcs; He Dog's, Black Twin's, and Crazy Horse's Oglalas; Two Moon's, White Bull's, Little Wolf's, and Old Bear's Northern Cheyennes. All would play critical roles in the coming days of war. The bands moved their camps as nature prescribed, always to good grass and bountiful hunting, and invariably staying within a same three hundred mile radius. (Picture today's Miles City, Montana. With that community as the hub, a radius of 150 miles captures this universe.) They fought with the Crows and Métis and avoided the Whites. They welcomed agency kin in summer, friends and extended family who brought coffee, sugar, flour, and other agency bounty. And they enjoyed the last unfettered days on the buffalo prairie, ever.

2
RAILROADERS ON THE YELLOWSTONE

"We pulled up all [the stakes] we saw and threw them away."
—Eagle Elk, Oglala Lakota

At the dawning of the 1870s, Sitting Bull's people confronted an array of new challenges and opportunities across the northern plains. While having largely displaced the Crows and now fully commanding virtually the entire Lower Yellowstone Basin, seasonal migrations also took Lakotas northward, drawn as always by buffalo. This brought them into the lands of the Assiniboine, Yanktonai Sioux, and Santee Sioux, with whom they were at peace. This was also the land of the Métis, who themselves were well established in the Milk River country north of the Missouri but who also commonly hunted and traded south of the river.

The Lakota-Métis relationship was problematical from the start. The Canadians were skilled market hunters, their wanton consumption of flesh and bone quite different from that of the northern plains Indians. All vied for the same buffalo resource but the Métis hunted year-round, taking away valuable hides in the fall and winter seasons, and meats and fats year-round. The meats were dried, pulverized, and mashed with fats into pemmican, and packed into eighty- and one-hundred-pound bags called *taureaux*. The product was a hunter's and trader's staple. The Métis traded with everyone, including Lakotas and Lakota enemies alike. Always a formidable people, those mixed-bloods were well-armed and capable defenders of their camps and property, as experienced by Yanktonai and Santee Sioux in previous years. Sitting Bull viewed the Métis pragmatically. Remembered the Hudson's Bay trader Isaac Cowie, Sitting Bull "did not care to arouse the Métis against him" but let them live.[1]

The Métis interlopers worried American officials, too, especially when the Lakotas embraced them. In the winter of 1869–70 a Métis sleigh caravan traveled as far south as the mouth of the Powder River and traded in Sitting Bull's camp. White Bull, Sitting Bull's nephew, remembered the occasion. The Slotas brought tobacco, knives, files, guns, powder and ball, and red and blue blankets. Good guns were especially prized but expensive, White Bull recalled, costing as many as five dressed buffalo robes. A single robe bought two pounds of gunpowder. It was the guns and powder that were central to the Lakota-Métis courtship, despite repeated government attempts to curb it.[2]

Those northernmost Montana lands in the Upper Missouri drainage were already a hotbed of intrigue and turmoil. As Sitting Bull and his followers had earlier preyed on Fort Buford at the confluence of the Yellowstone and Missouri, an odd mix of Santees and Yanktonai Sioux mostly from the east, plus a few Tetons, were now fostering the same mayhem in the wilds above Buford as far as the mouth of the Musselshell River, and up the Milk River to the shadows of Fort Browning, an Assiniboine–Gros Ventre agency post. They were particularly troublesome at Fort Peck, a trading post established on the Missouri in 1867 by the Durfee & Peck Company, a Leavenworth, Kansas, based trading outfit that operated widely in the Upper Missouri country. At Peck they killed woodhawks—men who supplied steamboats with fuel—and herders, and ran off stock. Government agents were outraged, labeling those Indians "wild" and "hostile" and laying especial blame on the mixed-blood traders of the British possessions who enabled their actions. It was into this brew that the Hunkpapas had come.[3]

Sitting Bull's people readily connected with the Milk River Métis, obtaining desired stocks of weaponry and munitions, and also strident encouragement that was disconcerting to American agents. The Métis openly promoted Lakota war-making against the Americans, and opposed the construction of the Northern Pacific Railroad. So contentious had this Métis influence become, with whiskey, munitions, and such ill-boding advice, that the superintendent of Montana's Indian affairs in Helena sought direct military intervention to suppress this "gang of illicit traders and outlaws." The Helena official learned from the Milk River agent at Fort Browning that between seventy-five and one hundred British mixed-bloods had established winter quarters south of the border on Frenchman's Creek, a tributary of the Milk about midway between Browning and Fort Peck and were regularly importing illegal merchandise expressly for the Indian trade. This illegality was not merely occurring south of the border, but also within the bounds of lands set aside as a reservation for the Assiniboines and Yanktonai Sioux.[4]

American officials reacted quickly. The Milk River agent had no suitable force for intervention, but Colonel John Gibbon, commanding troops at Fort Shaw in the District of Montana, did, and promptly dispatched two companies of infantry to strike and destroy the Métis settlement. After awaiting the late arrival of a guide from Fort Peck, Gibbon's force swept north along Frenchman's Creek in the predawn hours of November 2, 1871. No resistance was encountered, although the Métis claimed that their village sat on British soil, not American. Such pleadings were to no avail. Gibbon's soldiers burned two trading houses and their associated outbuildings, nine structures in all, along with their entire contents of liquor, ammunition, Indian trade goods, and general merchandise. One trader was absent, apparently hunting, and another arrested and escorted to Helena. The mixed-bloods in the community, some sixty families, plus a handful of aligned Santees, and even a Catholic priest, were allowed to remain on Frenchman's Creek, a simple momentary gesture of goodwill acknowledging the foreigners' own destitute plight, but only upon assurances that they would refrain from future illegalities. The destruction of the trading enterprise was immediately lauded as a complete success, but the property loss soon became a political issue, and as a long-term solution to a troublesome situation the action only proved illusory.[5]

The Milk River agent also sought an opportunity to confer with Sitting Bull directly, especially considering intelligence received suggesting that his followers intended to obstruct the Northern Pacific Railroad surveys. Sitting Bull's people generally refused all open intercourse with the Whites although they often quietly traded at Fort Peck, and on one occasion even expressed a desire to meet with a government agent to discuss making peace. The agent sent presents of tobacco and invited Sitting Bull and his chiefs to come to the fort. Sitting Bull remained aloof, but sent Black Moon, Long Dog, and other head men to speak on his behalf, and what the agent heard at several meetings was disconcerting. Black Moon professed peaceful intents but also laid out a number of strident demands. He wanted the railroad stopped as this advance was occurring without Indian consent and would destroy the game in their country. To that point, Black Moon was especially emphatic: "How could they live when the game was gone? They would die and would rather choose to die like brave men fighting." White soldiers and citizens must also be kept out of the Indian country, he continued. And Fort Buford and the Musselshell trading post must be abandoned. If the Great White Father would do these things, Black Moon said that they would have peace. In reply, the agent tried patronizing, offering food and the generous intents of the government, and rationalized the merits of the railroad and settlement. He also threatened military intervention if needed. In truth he was baffled. His report to his superior in Helena was fraught with frustration.[6]

The most confounding news circulating in the traditional camps in 1871 was indeed that of survey work both projected and partly already underway for a new railroad, the Northern Pacific. Some of those same Northern Indians had very recently witnessed the advance of two other railroads, the

Union Pacific through Nebraska and Wyoming, and the Kansas Pacific through Kansas to Denver, and some had even fought against those railroad men. Arriving with both lines were towns and cities and new White enterprise across the central Plains. Often it was said that the Overland Trails of an earlier era divided the buffalo herds. While that may have been so, it was those railroads that sealed the herds' fate. Such ill-boding outcomes—settlements, the destruction of natural resources, the loss of homelands—were not lost in the Northern Indian camps. This prospective new railroad, intended to connect Saint Paul, Minnesota, with Seattle, Washington, posed complications of an equally horrific sort. Its projected route across Dakota and through the Yellowstone Valley aimed at the very heart of the traditionals' universe and threatened the ultimate destruction of their buffalo prairie.

As yet, however, there was little tangible evidence of this new road. Likely the Northern Indians knew nothing of work already underway in Minnesota, where in 1870 and 1871 iron rails advanced westward from the hamlet of Duluth, at the head of Lake Superior, or of a connecting line advancing northward from Saint Paul. But when those rails crossed the Red River of the North into Dakota Territory in 1872 and survey work and track laying proceeded westward from there toward the Missouri, a new reality hit home.[7]

Foremost heralds of this news among the Lakotas were the agency people at Grand River and Cheyenne River, nominal homes of the Hunkpapas and Miniconjous and where some of Sitting Bull's closest allies visited from time to time. A report from the Cheyenne River agent to his superiors foretold of the fierce resistance anticipated when the railroaders reached the Yellowstone Valley. Similarly, the Grand River agent had no concern over agency people interfering with the line, but he feared that those living in the Yellowstone country would wage open war on the Whites. Many times, the agent reported having discussed "this railroad business" with his charges. News of the railroad was arriving in northern Lakota camps from other directions also, including by way of Yanktonais and Santees at Fort Peck, who were similarly learning of it from downriver kin.[8]

Other government officials were equally alarmed. Colonel David Stanley, commanding the army's Middle District of Dakota at Fort Sully on the Missouri, was sure that the Hunkpapas would fight vigorously once the line crossed the river, and even before then would harass and annoy "as they always have." Ultimately he projected that this entire Sioux question "will only be solved by an Indian war of some magnitude." Soon enough Stanley would live his own prophesy.[9]

Likewise, Jasper Viall, the Indian Bureau's superintendent in Helena, understood that the proposed Northern Pacific route would cross a several-hundred-mile-section of territory in the Yellowstone and Powder River country occupied by a thousand lodges of Teton Sioux. Sitting Bull controlled those lodges, and from what Viall was learning it was the chief's intention to resist the survey and the road itself. Viall characterized those Sioux as numerous, powerful, and hostile. "Should these Teton Sioux offer any obstruction to the Northern Pacific Rail Road, a sanguinary war may soon be inaugurated."[10]

A similarly ominous report originated at Fort Buford in mid-June 1871. "It is rumored," penned a correspondent for the *Army and Navy Journal* who signed his letter simply "Tepee," "that the principal chiefs of the hostiles on the Yellowstone have held a great council of war, and their object was to stand by each other and attempt with all their might to defeat the plans of the Northern Pacific Railroad Company in running a railroad through their country."[11]

Despite the bluster, in 1871 the eastern and western surveys of the railroad experienced no obstruction or harassment whatsoever. Still, though they were well escorted by troops should difficulties arise, the surveyors reported sensing Indians watching their every move. Both movements occurring that fall were brief. Amounting to simple alignment searches, one headed west from Fort Rice on the Missouri in September, crossing Dakota and the Dakota badlands, and then turning around upon reaching the Yellowstone. The other worked east from Fort Ellis, near Bozeman, in November, aiming down the Yellowstone, through Crow land, and nearly reaching Pompeys Pillar, upstream of the mouth of the Big Horn River.

The Crows were quite indifferent to the notion of a railroad, preferring that fight to fall to the Sioux. Weather brought closure to both surveys, and the parties did not intersect. If anything, the Northern Indians pleasured in uprooting survey stakes planted by the railroad parties, seemingly erasing their presence.[12]

Buried in one of the exchanges between Milk River and Montana Indian Bureau officials in the summer of 1871 was a brief mention, easily unnoticed, that Sitting Bull has as his "chief soldier," an unnamed "Sandwich Islander." The writer was plainly referring to Frank Grouard, estranged offspring of a White Mormon missionary and a Polynesian woman and lately a Fort Peck mail rider who somehow, somewhere, fell in with the Sioux. He claimed that he had been captured by Sitting Bull's people near Fort Peck when he was nineteen. He was now twenty-one. Grouard's features were dark and his hair long and black, and in most circles he readily passed as an Indian, or some thought a Black man. Details on those early doings and especially his crossing over to the Northern Indians are murky. Principal accounts of his life, first recorded in 1876 by a fellow Plainsman and separately later by a biographer, often conflict.[13]

This first mention of Grouard as a "chief soldier" appears in a letter dated May 19, 1871, and plainly places him in an Indian context. But oddly, Grouard is apparently also the unnamed scout from Fort Peck who guided troops to the Métis camp on Frenchman's Creek in November of that year, or so he tells us. How it was that Grouard could cross from a Lakota camp and be acknowledged as a Fort Peck guide expressly serving military interests, and then apparently return and be readily accepted in Lakota tipis, no less than Sitting Bull's and Crazy Horse's, and earn the name Standing Bear, or more commonly Grabber, is perplexing but verifiably true. What is equally true is that in the coming Indian war Grouard became a key voice and often a central figure in the action, including the war's opening salvo, and particularly in a tragic episode occurring near its end.[14]

White Bull, a leading Indian informant on the events of the early 1870s and of the coming war, was present with Sitting Bull's people. In later years, he provided an interviewer with a direct sense of the perpetual movement of the camp and the critical events occurring at the time. Although venturing northward from time to time, almost to the Missouri River, or east to the Little Missouri badlands, Sitting Bull's people more commonly roved the Lower Yellowstone country, availing themselves of the lands north and south of the river and ever driven by the daily and seasonal needs of the camp. Summer pauses were of two and three night's duration, with the people intently hunting, drying meat for winter, and preparing robes and clothing. White Bull remembered Sitting Bull's people joining a large camp of Oglalas, Miniconjous, and Sans Arcs in 1871. He said those people journeyed southward together that summer to the White Mountains—the Big Horns—and back again along the Little Big Horn River, with the collective camp holding a traditional Sun Dance at the Big Bend of the Yellowstone. Other tradition-minded people enjoyed this same simple routine, a life following the buffalo in the lands of the Lower Yellowstone.[15]

While life in the Yellowstone country could seemingly be measured by its simplicity, an unease shadowed the Lakota camps that fall of 1871. Josephine Waggoner recollected learning that the people were aware of the soldiers they sometimes observed in their country. That the soldiers were not on any friendly mission became a continuing topic of conversation in the council lodges. The foretold matter of a railroad had validity it seemed, and these tradition-bound people only saw such intrusions into their buffalo country as outright invasions. These Northern people were not signatories to any treaty that might have established bounds or entitlements, and although the soldiers of 1871 had departed with the advent of cold weather, the elders agonized over what might be coming when the land warmed again.[16]

Routine exchanges between the traditional camps and agencies heightened the sense of worry. As happened in Indian Country in the early days of the Great Sioux Reservation, devout traditionals occasionally ventured to the agencies. An instance of the sort occurring at Cheyenne River Agency in March 1872 had immediate and widespread repercussions. One hundred and fifty Sans Arcs led by Spotted Eagle came in, partly to trade but apparently mostly to consult with the local agent about the Northern Pacific Railroad. Spotted Eagle was a close ally of Sitting Bull and may, in fact, have gone to Cheyenne River on his encouragement. The agent arranged a council with the chief and his headmen. Present on the occasion was Colonel Stanley from nearby Fort Sully and officers from the small Cheyenne River military post. Of several subsequent reports, Stanley's was the most revealing. In Spotted Eagle the officer encountered a man about thirty years old, tall, active, very intelligent, and surprisingly well informed, not only about the prospective railroad but also about persistent rumors of White interest in the Black Hills, and even the recently arrived telegraph line at Fort Sully. Spotted Eagle objected to everything, and his tone, Stanley recollected, was sometimes sharp and bitter.[17]

Spotted Eagle had come from Rosebud Creek in Montana and while at Cheyenne River refused all rations and presents. He was obviously agitated and when given an opportunity to speak, did so plainly and forcefully. "He knew," Stanley reported, "of the intention to run the [rail] road through his country. He stated that neither himself, or any Sioux properly authorized to speak for his people, had ever given their consent to this, and that they never would give their consent, or listen to any proposition to that effect. He said that he would fight the rail road people as long as he lived, and would tear up the road, and kill its builders."[18]

Stanley attempted to mollify Spotted Eagle, but the effort seemed only to harden him. "I tried to show him that the road would be built however bitterly he might fight it, and that his course would probably bring ruin upon his people. He admitted that perhaps this was true, but said that driving off of the buffalo was death to his race, and he would fight knowing he would be beaten in the end." The Cheyenne River agent departed the exchange exceedingly distressed. All the Sans Arcs present opposed the railroad, and any agent's effort would not be sufficient, he was sure, to prevent the coming difficulties. This railroad, he wrote later, is perfectly "obnoxious to them."[19]

Sitting Bull's resolve to resist the Northern Pacific stiffened that spring as rumors and forecasts of all sorts reached him. Government agents, in turn, were well aware of the looming troubles. The commanding officer at Fort Stevenson, Dakota, located near the Fort Berthold Arikara agency upriver of Grand River, warned his superiors in Saint Paul in April that when the railroad dared to cross the Missouri two thousand Northern Indians were prepared to oppose it, *en masse*. The officer provided names: Sitting Bull, Black Moon, Iron Dog, Iron Horn, Four Horns, Long Dog.[20]

Oddly, Sitting Bull also received counsel from another more distant quarter. His counterpart from an earlier day, Red Cloud, acknowledged leader of the Oglala Lakotas now residing at the Sioux agency on the North Platte River east of Fort Laramie, had been invited to join a delegation of Sioux leaders and agency men bound that summer for Fort Peck, to meet with government commissioners intent on stemming this hostility toward the railroad. Red Cloud declined the invitation but wished that a message be carried along and passed to Sitting Bull. Red Cloud had visited Washington on several occasions since ending his own war with the Whites and the weight of those visits brought to him a different understanding of the government and its irrepressible forces. "Tell Sitting Bull," he said, that "I shall do as my Great Father says and make my people listen. Make no trouble for our Great Father. His heart is good. Be friends to him and he will provide for you." In course Red Cloud's message was delivered. Sitting Bull openly scoffed at what he heard. Four years earlier Red Cloud had touched the pen at Fort Laramie and since that time he had become exactly what Sitting Bull despised. Sitting Bull ignored the gathering at Fort Peck as well.[21]

But in 1872 the traditional people did not ignore the army columns pressing eastward from Fort Ellis and westward from the Missouri River later that summer, each aiming it seemed at the very heart of the buffalo prairie. By midseason Sitting Bull's camp had grown significantly as like-minded bands gathered for the Sun Dance, held again on the Yellowstone at the Big Bend. With him were Black Moon's Hunkpapas, Crazy Horse's Oglalas, Steam Boat's Miniconjous, Circling Bear's and Spotted Eagle's Sans Arcs, and a number of Brulés and Cheyennes. Late in the four-day dance, scouts came with a frantic warning that soldiers were approaching fast from the west. The chiefs counseled and directed that the camp be broken, the women and children sent eastward toward Rosebud Creek and then to the Tongue to await the warriors' return, while a strong war party of some five hundred men rode west to confront the soldiers head-on.[22]

The warriors readily found the army camp on the north side of the Yellowstone, opposite the mouth of Arrow Creek (today's Pryor Creek, just east of modern-day Billings). Large numbers of horses, mules, and cattle in the soldier camp proved irresistible lures to many of the younger men, who became impossible to restrain and whose movements in the early dawn hours of August 14 triggered a frenzied exchange of gunfire that continued past daylight. One warrior, the Hunkpapa Plenty Lice, was killed early in the clash and fell into soldier hands, and fifteen cows and four mules were driven off by the attackers. The fighting soon tapered into exchanges of long-range shooting between warriors positioned on the higher ground north of the river, and soldiers obscured in a sprawl of timber and an adjacent slough stretching across the riverfront. The desultory exchange was broken only by warriors who would occasionally ride forth in demonstrations of daring, intentionally drawing fire and earning honors. Crazy Horse was among them, charging the soldier line and attracting fire but escaping unharmed, with onlookers whooping boisterous approval. Spotted Eagle did so, too, though he was slightly wounded and his horse killed. Afterward, Spotted Eagle intently passed word back to Cheyenne River that he had fought these soldiers, and would do so again.[23]

But no greater honor was earned at Arrow Creek than by Sitting Bull himself. In an episode so utterly imaginative that it surpassed all others, it even now remains foremost in the annals of the American West as an act of audacity and fearlessness in the face of an enemy. White Bull witnessed it all. After watching the fighting intently that morning, the chief always encouraging his followers by his presence and timely words, Sitting Bull, at an opportune moment, laid down his own gun, picked up his long slender pipe bag, and walked deliberately beyond the Indian lines onto the open prairie, as if, White Bull thought, "taking a stroll through the camp at evening." When a hundred yards out, and in clear sight of the warriors behind him and the soldiers plainly in his fore, Sitting Bull sat down, drew the stem and bowl from his pipe bag and fixed them, filled the bowl with tobacco, struck a spark with a flint and steel, and began puffing away "in his usual leisurely fashion." Those behind him were astounded, and even more so when he turned his head and urged followers to join him.[24]

"It was amazing," White Bull remembered. Not one to ignore the dare, he and another Sioux warrior, Gets the Best of Them, and two Cheyennes went forward and when reaching Sitting Bull sat down beside him. Sitting Bull passed the pipe and they all smoked. Meanwhile bullets kicked dirt around them and whizzed overhead. "Our hearts beat rapidly," White Bull remembered, "and we smoked as fast as we could. But Sitting Bull was not afraid. He just sat there quietly, looking around as if he were at home in his tent, and smoked peacefully."[25]

When the pipe was smoked out, Sitting Bull pulled out his tamper, cleared the bowl, and returned everything to the bag. He then rather nonchalantly rose and walked back to the safety of the Indian line. White Bull and the others again watched in astonishment, and got up themselves and ran back. Gets the Best of Them was so excited that he forgot his arrows and White Bull went out again and collected them.[26]

"It was the bravest thing Sitting Bull had ever done," White Bull concluded. But at this place, in this first demonstration against the Northern Pacific Railroad, in plain sight of hundreds of tradition-bound warriors like himself, he may simply have been driven to show his own complete contempt for those Whites who dared to enter his world. The episode was forceful, dramatic, and never forgotten.[27]

When Sitting Bull returned to his tethered pony on the ridge he took up his weapons, mounted, and called out, "That's enough! We must stop! That's enough!" It was about noon, White Bull recalled. But Crazy Horse was unwilling to stop so abruptly. He turned to White Bull, a close friend, and urged him to join in making one more circle toward the soldier line. They dared each other to go first, but it was Crazy Horse who rode off, with White Bull on his tail. As they made their sweep, Crazy Horse's pony was shot dead beneath him. He tumbled unhurt and ran back afoot. White Bull and his horse returned untouched.[28]

Such was the Battle of Arrow Creek. The soldiers later reported one of their own killed, three wounded, and a civilian mortally wounded. Sitting Bull's people lost two of their own killed outright, Plenty Lice and a Miniconjou warrior who was the nephew of chief Lame Deer, plus one other, the Brulé Hawk Dog, brother of chief Spotted Tail, who died later of wounds, and additionally perhaps a half dozen wounded. The warriors left fourteen dead ponies on the field. After the soldiers moved on, Plenty Lice's family returned and found his remains. His body had been tossed into a fire and only scorched bones remained. Other warriors also returned and unearthed the soldier remains and stripped them of their clothing.[29]

Neither side claimed victory but the results were telling. So terrified by the experience were the railroad surveyors that they adjusted their line of scrutiny and headed for the Musselshell Valley, forty miles to the north, instead of continuing down the Yellowstone to a presumed rendezvous with a second column. The warriors abandoned the field that afternoon, returning to their families downriver. By then they were hearing other foreboding news.[30]

In western Dakota an entirely different gambit of observation, harassment, and direct challenge was playing out. A column of soldiers marching west from Fort Rice on the Missouri on July 26 ambled the Heart River westward, reaching the Dakota badlands a week later. Their trail soon took them down O'Fallon Creek in eastern Montana to the Yellowstone. The column's sense of ease while crossing Dakota soon gave way on O'Fallon to continuous trouble, beginning when Sioux warriors fired into their camp at daybreak on August 16, killing a mule, wounding five more, and drawing fire from the camp's sentinels. A day later after the soldiers reached the Yellowstone and turned upriver bound for the mouth of the Powder, warriors struck again, particularly chasing a surveyor who had strayed beyond the safety of the column. The attackers were Gall's band of warriors, Hunkpapas mostly, who had begun shadowing the soldiers when they reached Montana.[31]

At thirty-four years old, Gall was one of Sitting Bull's foremost lieutenants and a lifelong friend. He was a stocky man, with intense eyes and a strikingly handsome face. He was also among those traditionals uniquely unafraid to visit an agency or trading house from time to time, whether visiting kin or seeking some necessary accoutrement. Gall was among Hunkpapas who fought in Red Cloud's War, and stood with the war chiefs who met with Father De Smet at Fort Rice in 1868 when the Black Robe strove to obtain signatures on the Fort Laramie Treaty. Gall was the first to sign on July 2, doing so as Man that Goes in the Middle, a favorite name from childhood. Whether he fathomed the nature of the document has forever remained in question. Gall would be at Sitting Bull's side throughout the coming war.[32]

Gall knew well why these *wasicus*—big talkers, the Sioux epithet for White people—were there but still possessed the audacity to pause his attacks and talk. At the mouth of the Powder on August 18 in plain sight of the soldiers, he rode forward to the western riverbank, laid down his weapon, and sought to speak with the leader of the trespassers advancing from the east. Stanley, near the fore of the column, came forward, also laid down his pistol, and walked to the opposite bank. At bankside, they were separated by perhaps thirty or forty yards of shallow, chalky colored water. Stanley asked to meet Gall on a sandbar in the middle of the stream but the wary war chief refused, and from the bank partly questioned and partly taunted the soldier chief. Why was he on Sioux land? "Go home and make no marks upon the ground." Stanley offered to buy the land and give the Indians presents, but Gall cut him short, screaming back: "You lie." Finally, Stanley noted, Gall threatened to "bring all the bands and give us a big fight." Stanley watched other warriors thread their way through the generally obscuring brush at bankside and backed away, sensing his own vulnerability, and almost immediately shots rang out, aimed mostly at the soldier chief, his interpreter, and those around him. Soldiers retaliated and for the next half hour both sides poured an inconsequential fire on each other, the warriors and soldiers mostly obscured by the bushy undercover along the riverbanks.[33]

What Stanley did not know until much later was that Gall had sent a courier upriver to find Sitting Bull, who, when learning of this threat in the east, even then was leading two hundred warriors down the Yellowstone, having started when the gunsmoke had barely cleared at Arrow Creek. Opportunely, upon reaching the Powder, Stanley's surveyors had more or less completed their summer task and two days later the soldiers turned on their heels and followed the trail home, with Gall shadowing them all the way. When crossing the Little Missouri badlands, Stanley dispatched segments of his supply train, partly to procure additional stores and partly simply to return empty wagons. After completing survey work in the Little Missouri Valley, he also dispatched elements of his soldier complement.[34]

These scattered movements provided the trailing warriors unique opportunities to cause additional trouble. On one occasion near Heart Butte on October 2 warriors engaged five of Stanley's well-armed Santee Sioux scouts in a running fight that lasted the better part of the day. The Santees lost two horses and some equipment but no lives. East of there again on the Heart River on October 3 the soldier column suffered its first military casualty, an infantry officer named Eben Crosby, who was ambushed and killed while hunting antelope barely a mile from camp. Gall was directly implicated in the killing and some allegedly reported seeing him waving Crosby's fresh scalp near the camp.[35]

By then the returning column was well scattered along the Heart, and Gall's warriors remained alert and opportunistic. On October 4, Stanley's own cook, a Black man named Stephen Harris, was killed when venturing too far from the wagons. That same day, also on the Heart, Lieutenant Lewis Adair was ambushed and mortally wounded while scouting ahead of his command. A rescuer killed Adair's assailant, a Hunkpapa warrior from Gall's band, Little Red Horn, but barely escaped with his own life. Adair died the next day.[36]

This pursuit brought Gall's warriors to the proximity of a new post, Fort McKeen, emerging at the confluence of the Heart and Missouri near the projected Northern Pacific Railroad crossing of the Missouri. The post was still under construction that fall and in repeated and sometimes bloody episodes, eerily similar to Sitting Bull's siege of Fort Buford five years earlier, Lakota warriors, allegedly from Cheyenne River and Grand River, and now with Gall's band among them, attacked and killed mail carriers on the trail between Forts McKeen and Rice, assailed Arikara scouts employed at the post, and in mid-October ambushed wood cutters. In that episode soldiers used an artillery piece to rout the assailants. A more brazen attack occurred on November 3, when warriors struck the post's saw mill and trader's store. The garrison defended itself adequately, driving the warriors up the Heart, but not before eliciting an outburst from one of the attackers to the effect that if the soldiers killed even one warrior, they would stay around and kill ten blue coats in retaliation.[37]

Gall's name surfaced one other time late in this fractious year. On November 7 Stanley reported to a superior that he had just learned that Gall was seen at one of the Grand River trading houses bartering twenty-three buffalo robes for Henry cartridges and three kegs of gunpowder. Stanley ended his note with a sarcastic quip: "Let the proper officer of the government take the responsibility of bartering the blood of citizens and soldiers of our country for buffalo robes."[38]

Sitting Bull did not go into Dakota Territory with Gall after watching Stanley's soldiers depart the Yellowstone. Instead, he returned to Rosebud Creek, where an Oglala Indian, Wolf Ears, found him in early October. Wolf Ears had attended the summer gathering at Fort Peck where government commissioners met with Indian and White representatives from each of the Sioux agencies, intent on explaining, justifying, and pressing consent for the construction of the new railroad. Wolf Ears was swayed by the government's case and obtained permission from his agent to visit the northern camps and carry a conciliatory message to friends. In due course he found No Neck's and Sitting Bull's camp on the Rosebud and was afforded a council with those two and other headmen and was asked many questions. Sitting Bull set the opening tone, telling Wolf Ears: "You are one of our soldiers and left us but yesterday, and I think you will tell the truth for you have been with the Whites but a little while."[39]

Wolf Ears explained where he had been and what he had heard, and how the Great Father wished that they should all be on the "good road" and not make any trouble. The Great Father wished, he continued, to build a railroad through their country, but he would take care of them if they would listen. Sitting Bull's reply was short and oddly, probably intentionally, vague, at least in Wolf Ears's retelling. "They had but little country left," Sitting Bull said, "and the game was growing less every year. Soon they must go to the Whites but they wish[ed] to keep what country they had." No Neck, the other principal chief present, was much more strident, speaking "against eating the White man's food or letting them build the road." He said "the White man will feed us a few years and then let our children starve. The Great Spirit gave us the game to live on and I am not going to the Whites until it is gone."[40]

Wolf Ears had five such councils that fall with Hunkpapas and Miniconjous. His message was the same and so mostly were the responses, although Lone Antelope, a Miniconjou chief, thought that the course Wolf Ears encouraged was good, and that "we should be friends to all." In the same accounting of his travels, Wolf Ears provided a sense of the size and nature of the Northern Indian camps that season. The village of Sitting Bull, No Neck, and Four Horns on Rosebud Creek numbered some 130 lodges, with another 105 lodges of Grand River Hunkpapas camped separately but nearby. During Wolf Ears's visit twenty-five other lodges of Hunkpapas departed for Fort Peck. On the Yellowstone not far from the mouth of the Powder, Wolf Ears noted a camp of 250 Miniconjou lodges, with Lone Antelope among their chiefs. And in the Powder River headwaters were forty lodges of Oglalas, mostly relatives of Red Cloud. Lone Antelope told Wolf Ears of other smaller camps of Indians scattered about. Wolf Ears also reported that buffalo were plentiful north of the Yellowstone but not so much on the south side. Wolf Ears's report was compelling, less for his effort at urging the Sioux to accept a railroad and White man's food than for insights into the nature and fervor of the Northern Indian camps at the close of a challenging year. [41]

Shortly after the observant Wolf Ears departed the Indian camps on the Yellowstone, some two hundred lodges of Black Moon's and Long Dog's Hunkpapas went north to Fort Peck, where in December they drew rations. There were no buffalo in that vicinity or on the Yellowstone, the local agent observed, and the people were hungry. The agent also acknowledged that Sitting Bull and fourteen other lodges were camped at the head of the Red Water River, some fifty miles away. Some of those Hunkpapas may have been among those noted by Wolf Ears as trailing north at the time of his visit. The agent observed that these people preferred peace and provisions over further warfare and starvation, and in addition to rations he was liberally distributing clothing and blankets. [42]

On one occasion in December, Black Moon and the Fort Peck agent conversed about the Baker fight, as the Arrow Creek episode of August 14 was coming to be known among the Whites. Black Moon told him that some 1,400 warriors had participated in the clash, and that they had actually started out intending to fight Crows but learned of those soldiers and charged them instead. Black Moon's number does not comport with other accounts, but that his people still fixated on the Crows resonates. In some Lakota circles, enmity with that old enemy remained more important than stopping a railroad, although the agent closed his letter predicting that opposition to the Northern Pacific Railroad should be expected next year, particularly from the south, meaning from tradition-minded Indians other than the Hunkpapas. [43]

Other government officials were seeing matters much the same way. A particularly telling insight penned by an officer with Stanley that summer said all. In a letter to his wife written while still in the field, Clarence

Bennett of the Seventeenth Infantry predicted that "We are going to have a big Sioux War. Next year will be the death struggle of the Sioux. We will have to put in this country a great many hundred troops by the thousands to whip them effectually for all time." Bennett was correct in part. There would be a big Sioux war. But he underestimated the number of troops required for it by a few thousand.[44]

As tumultuous as events had proved to be for the Northern Indians in the Yellowstone country, chaos of another sort dominated the lives of the Southern Lakotas at much the same time. Since the signing of the Fort Laramie Treaty, the Oglalas and Brulés willing to attach themselves to an agency, even if only seasonally or when not hunting buffalo in the Republican River Basin or the Powder River country as permitted by the treaty, squabbled over agency locations as variously proposed. The government preferred the Missouri, where the Brulés were now congregating because annuities could be delivered there more easily by steamboat, or at Fort Laramie, long the preferred trading home of the Oglalas. While Sitting Bull's followers eyed Métis traders and railroaders, Red Cloud's Oglalas were relocated down the North Platte River to a location in Nebraska thirty miles east of Fort Laramie, and then moved again northward in the Pine Ridge country. Spotted Tail, meanwhile, finessed the relocation of his people westward from the Missouri, which he disliked for numerous reasons, to more welcome locations along the White River and in the Pine Ridge.

This wrangling over agency locations for the Oglalas and Brulés vexed the government until 1873, when all parties agreed to respective agencies along the White River in Nebraska's Pine Ridge. That they were located in Nebraska and not on the Great Sioux Reservation in Dakota perplexed many people, especially land-hungry Nebraskans, but momentary contentment justified the decision for the time being. The locations came to be known as Red Cloud Agency and Spotted Tail Agency, or collectively often simply as the White River or Pine Ridge agencies. Red Cloud Agency was located eighty-two miles northeast of Fort Laramie, and roughly 125 miles north of the Union Pacific Railroad line at Sidney, Nebraska. Spotted Tail Agency was more distant, 125 miles from Fort Laramie and 170 miles from Sidney. In a parallel interim measure, the Northern Cheyennes and Northern Arapahos also received rations and annuities at the Oglala agency, which they too called the White River Agency. Both agencies were endlessly chaotic and figured deeply in coming events, as did a well-scored trail westward from both places heading into the buffalo country of the Powder, a pathway soon to be known variously as the Red Cloud or Powder River Trail.[45]

In the Yellowstone country, Lakota problems with the Métis surfaced again. In April 1873 Métis men fired on several young Lakotas, wounding one and capturing his horse. Sitting Bull sent ten scouts to locate the interlopers who were discovered corralled at the mouth of the Rosebud on the south bank of the Yellowstone. He followed his scouts with one hundred warriors to the Métis corral. They rather immediately found it impenetrable. Its defenders were well-armed, including with a small cannon. The fight that ensued was an unequal confrontation. The Sioux were mostly armed with bows and arrows and a few old trade guns. The Slotas were armed with long-range guns and plenty of powder. At best a few Slota horses were killed, but the Sioux suffered greatly, with nine named warriors killed among others whose names are forgotten. Many more were wounded. Finally, as White Bull recalled, Sitting Bull cried out an order: "We have fought enough. We can do no more. Let's go home." This time the young men obeyed him.[46]

Peaceful trading with the Métis was a paradoxical thing. Not all Métis had befriended the Sioux and not all Sioux were as acquainted with them and their ways as were the Hunkpapas. What the Sioux feared most was the Métis' capacity to kill buffalo. They made regular hunting forays throughout the year and killed animals by the thousands, serving market needs almost exclusively and taking meats and fats, and retaining the skins in season.

Summer skins were valueless and the wastage was astounding. No one was more destructive, thought White Bull. This alone may have been an overriding consideration prompting the Rosebud confrontation. As White Bull told of it, Métis caravans were not known to venture this far south into Sioux Country, and their doing so now was costly—to the Sioux.[47]

The Métis episode also revealed a critical dimension of Lakota life that vexed them now and throughout the coming war: They lacked dependable access to modern weaponry, fixed ammunition, and loose powder and lead. By whatever source, serving that need was complicated, and timing was always an issue especially in the coming years when the government carefully regulated agency arms trading or banned it outright. That, in turn, led to a near total dependence on the illegal marketplace inevitably existing in the back country. Access concerns merely laid atop the parallel issue of the enormous costs associated with acquiring weapons and munitions. Addressing this with a people the Lakotas befriended one day and warred against the next only complicated matters.

Gall was among those who frequented the agencies. In April 1873 he visited Fort Peck and openly traded furs for arms and ammunition. Reportedly, he had access to all he was able to pay for. The medium of exchange was, as always, tanned buffalo robes. The business peeved military authorities. Colonel Stanley, who learned of Gall's presence at Fort Peck and had fought him the previous fall, labeled it an issue of gravity. The notion, he suggested, of the Indian department prohibiting arms sales was a "dead letter" because traders at those places would never refuse arms and ammunition to Indians. An army surgeon familiar with the matter was similarly outraged, writing several years later specifically of the illegal trading occurring at Fort Peck. "Since 1872," he wrote, "some parties have stationed themselves at that place for the purpose of obtaining a monopoly in bartering with the Sioux, and the only inducement to bring their customers forward was the offer of arms—Winchester rifles."[48]

In defending himself later that fall, Fort Peck agent A. J. Simmons revealed some of the complexities inherent in regulating such trade on the Milk River Reservation. This was foremost the designated home of Gros

Ventre and Assiniboine Indians. Many Mountain and River Crows who had yet to be congregated on the Crow Reservation south of the Yellowstone were also there, as were even some scattered Yanktonai and Santee Sioux from the Missouri River in Dakota. These people were not hostile, Simmons declared, but extremely friendly and well-disposed to the Whites. Hunting, for them, was an essential element of agency life and self-support. The agent noted the existing multiple outlets for the legal trade of firearms by firms properly permitted to do so and who were duly submitting monthly reports on their sales. The agent was discreetly silent on the well-known Métis trade occurring simultaneously on the margins of the reservation and sometimes even within its bounds. How Gall got his guns and ammunition can only be surmised.[49]

Among the Northern Indians, this matter of arms trading was not confined to Fort Peck. In mid-July the Grand River agent similarly reported a pleading coming from his charges that they be furnished with quantities of powder and ball for hunting purposes. "They are much in need of many articles they manufacture from the skins obtained by hunting." This agent was relatively new and at a loss what to do.[50]

The Grand River agent's puzzling query came on the heels of an outburst of hostilities occurring that May and June at Fort Abraham Lincoln, the renamed and expanded Fort McKeen. The post had been directly fired upon on two separate occasions, and those episodes were followed by another incident on June 17 when a surveying party working along the Heart River was attacked and forced to retire to the safety of the post. The garrison was duly mustered on each occasion, and army accounts said five warriors were killed and eleven others wounded altogether. The army reported losing only one of its own killed, an Arikara scout. A party of Sioux Indians numbering nearly one hundred was implicated in the episodes. Gall's name was linked to the Heart River encounter.[51]

As Gall had dogged the army column in 1872 on its return from the Yellowstone, so did he and a band of warriors again shadow a new column a year later as it ambled westward, apparently again bound for the buffalo country. This time warriors at first were rarely seen aside from pony tracks. Lakota camps farther west were well alerted to this sequential invasion, which had been foreshadowed, too, by the incessant, annoying movement of steamboats on the Yellowstone beginning in early June, depositing supplies and forage at an army camp established first at the mouth of Glendive Creek and then moved to the south bank of the Yellowstone eight miles upriver. One boat ventured farther upstream to the Wolf Rapids, just downstream of the mouth of the Powder. The Lakotas knew of such boats on the Missouri, but they were rarely seen on this long reach of the Lower Yellowstone.[52]

The soldiers from the east made their way to the Yellowstone and the mouth of the Powder without interruption. Their particular interests were west of there, in a reach of the Yellowstone Valley not yet explored by railroad surveyors, and they especially focused their attention on the north bank of the river. Most of the traditionals were then camped in the Rosebud drainage farther along. All were aware of these soldiers, even while the Hunkpapas remained transfixed by the lingering Métis, who had not yet departed the Yellowstone country.[53]

Soon, however, all bands turned their attention to this looming soldier threat. From camps along the Yellowstone, warriors tracked the soldier advance, and on August 4 just upstream of the mouth of the Tongue a small band confronted a party of blue coats who had advanced well ahead of their wagons. As those soldiers lazed in the hot midday sun several warriors attempted to run off their horses and they taunted the Whites to fight. The soldiers charged the attackers but the warriors stood their ground, even though well exposed, and then withdrew to a dense copse behind them. As the Whites advanced they quickly confronted 250 warriors, mostly Miniconjous with a few Hunkpapas and Brulés, who emerged from the cottonwoods. Both sides backed off and the exchange of fire degenerated into a fight not unlike the Arrow Creek encounter, sparked by long-range shooting, taunts, and individual dashes into the open to demonstrate daring. Neither side gained an advantage.[54]

When the fighting opened not all the soldiers and wagons of the strung-out column had come up, and Rain in the Face, a thirty-eight-year-old Hunkpapa warrior, seized an opportunity to harass other blue coats still coming on. With five or six others they circled downstream and confronted two men riding alone far ahead of the others. The warriors killed them both, one with arrows in the back and the other with a death blow to the head. Those were the only two Whites killed this day, and although neither man was mutilated or scalped their pockets were rifled and their horses and equipment taken. Rain in the Face was ever after linked to the killing of one of them, a civilian named John Honsinger, an army veterinary surgeon. The Hunkpapa never shied from this claim and later brandished a watch and saddle recognized as belonging to the veterinarian. In Indian Country that claim was disputed, however, with some holding that a warrior named Prairie Chicken killed the man.[55]

The assembling mass of soldiers this day was daunting and after three or four hours warrior gunfire diminished and then ceased altogether. Warriors fired the grass behind them and disappeared, the rising curtain of blue smoke from the dense green grass quickly shrouding the scene. No known Indian account of the day mentions their own casualties, but soldiers claimed that two warriors were killed and perhaps a half dozen wounded.[56]

Sitting Bull was not in the fight, and neither was White Bull. The two and most of their people apparently remained in camp that day. But those soldiers were close enough and the camps were vulnerable. While the record is unclear it seems that Sitting Bull principally oversaw the safe flight of his followers. The soldiers, meanwhile, camped on the field that evening and in the morning continued their deliberate advance upstream. Two days later they encountered the tell-tale remains of a recently abandoned village, presumed to be Sitting Bull's, with tipi poles, camp kettles, clothing, saddles, playthings, and foodstuffs scattered about, and the grass nibbled short. The next day the soldiers encountered yet another abandoned camp that seemed to have been this time hastily vacated. The Indian trail from both sites tracked westward and then crossed the Yellowstone several miles short of the mouth of the Big Horn River. The soldiers themselves found the river an impossible obstacle and continued their own march westward, hugging the north side.[57]

What the soldiers missed were five different traditional camps scattered up the lower Big Horn: Hunkpapas, Sans Arcs, Miniconjous, Oglalas, and Cheyennes. But warriors in those camps did not miss these hated *wasicus*, and just below the mouth of the Big Horn River in the breaking light of August 11 they struck again. A small number crept through the brush at riverside and fired across and into the army camp. Soon a few shots became many, mostly aimed at the soldier's horses. One soldier was killed, as were four horses, with many other horses wounded before being led away. Meanwhile other warriors crossed the Yellowstone both above and below the soldier camp and engaged soldier pickets. The soldier camp divided. Some met the attackers coming from downstream, dispersing them, and others advanced on the apparent greater threat coming from upstream. A bounding chase ensued covering several miles before the warriors scattered.[58]

Only one Indian name emerges in the various contemporary accounts of the day, that of Gall. A newspaperman noted simply: "One conspicuous Indian in a red blanket, supposed to be Gall, an important chief, had his pony shot dead from under him. He leaped on a fresh horse and got away." An unnamed Indian informant said much the same thing at the Grand River Agency several months later: "We were under several leaders, among them Gall. Sitting Bull [was] not in the fight." Several accounts of the day also mention Indian women, old men, and children gathered on a distant hillside south of the river watching the spectacle and themselves drawing long-range artillery fire from the soldier camp, which readily dispersed them.[59]

By midmorning the so-called Big Horn River fight was over. A Miniconjou informant at the Cheyenne River Agency mentioned later that four warriors were killed and twelve others wounded in the two engagements on the Yellowstone, plus twenty-six ponies killed.[60]

The soldiers continued their westward trek, reaching Pompeys Pillar on August 15 where they encountered surveyor's stakes marking field work accomplished the year before. At this point the surveyor's duties were complete and the return journey to Dakota began, with the soldiers mostly following the Musselshell Valley eastward toward the supply camp on the Yellowstone, and from there overland across western Dakota to the Missouri. Indian harassment at this stage of the work was slight, and the men in the column turned their attention instead to hunting buffalo.[61]

—

On reflection, although one of the officers returning from the eastern 1872 railroad survey predicted that "we are going to have a big Sioux war," what occurred a year later was considerably less obstructive and hardly matched the rhetoric. The government understood that it faced an obstacle on the Yellowstone River and to protect the survey work intended in 1873 assembled a military escort substantially stronger than had been deployed in the two previous years. But Lakota resistance, while annoying, was never particularly insurmountable. The two notable clashes occurring in August did not stop the surveyors, and this a reflection as much on the Lakota's own inability to coalesce against this threat, or a simpler statement yet that the soldier presence was no threat at all, annoying though it may have been, with some northern bands fighting, others hunting as usual, and still others stalking traditional enemies. But warriors did love pulling survey stakes. Eagle Elk, an Oglala hunting in the Yellowstone country that fall, recalled encountering surveyor stakes, and learned that the *wasicus* intended to make another iron road. "We pulled up all we saw and threw them away." In a similar vein, Rain in the Face remembered with obvious delight that he and fellow Hunkpapas "made some trouble for the men who were building the great iron track north of us."[62]

But in reality it was the nation's crippling financial woes, the soon famous Panic of 1873, that halted the Northern Pacific's construction at Bismarck, the railroad town that emerged on the Missouri. Tracks reached there that summer and the company commenced regular service thereafter, even as the line suffered insolvency and faced both a formidable bridging challenge on the Missouri and the Indian frontier in the west. Many laid the blame for the nation's crisis on the Northern Pacific alone, and indeed its financial woes helped bring on the bankruptcy of Jay Cooke & Company, its principal underwriter and the one-time renowned financier of the Union Cause during the Civil War. But there was no one cause of this national crisis that also witnessed European financial markets failing, the closure of the New York Stock Exchange, the Gold Exchange shutting its doors, other banks crumbling, manufacturers ceasing operations, rampant unemployment, and dozens of other railroads failing too. And worse yet, there was no easy or quick recovery.[63]

The warriors on the Yellowstone paid no heed to who it was leading the soldiers they fought twice this year, eying them merely as despicable *wasicus*. Some may have recognized Stanley in one of the support columns, the man they confronted at the mouth of the Powder the year before, but he did not lead in the two engagements. Yet history tells us that the soldier directing the blue coats in those fights was no less than George Armstrong Custer, an individual highly regarded among the Whites and one of the Great Father's most renowned Indian fighters. Custer was not known to the Northern people, and in fact was himself new to the northern plains, but from those days on the Yellowstone onward the lives and legacies of two critical people—Sitting Bull and Custer—would repeatedly intersect, each a symbolic figurehead of causes that were worlds apart and yet inexorably linked.

In Sioux Country, Indian winter counts—pictorial calendars—in the south remembered the year as the last time the Southern Lakotas hunted buffalo in the Republican River country, a right that had been guaranteed them by the Fort Laramie Treaty. Stripping that entitlement was a crippling blow, particularly for Spotted Tail's Brulés.[64]

Many Southern Lakota winter counts also remembered the year as when the Oglalas and Brulés inflicted a horrific bloodletting on the Pawnees. In a distinctly one-sided affair between traditional enemies, on August 5, in a secluded, watered canyon of the Republican—a place ever after remembered as Massacre Canyon—some seventy-five Pawnee men, women, and children were slain.[65]

A mix of Oglalas and Brulés perpetrated the Pawnee killings and some say that Crazy Horse played a role there, too. Indian accounts are uncommonly silent about Crazy Horse on the northern plains that year, and White Bull plainly asserted that his friend was not in the Yellowstone country that season. Still, modern scholars place him there, confronting soldiers in the north. No evidence supports this, and a better case is made for his involvement in the events in the south, bolstered when his name was brandished by the Red Cloud agent in the same foul vein as Little Big Man and Little Hawk, outlaws all, he declared, responsible for committing the "depredations on this frontier the past year."[66]

Meanwhile, for Sitting Bull and the Northern Indians, that fall a welcome calm again settled on the rivers and land. The Northern people had endured three consecutive years of *wasicu* incursion into their homeland, each mightier than the one before. But always the Whites disappeared. For the time being, the buffalo prairie seemed safe. And yet even the dreamers among them had to have imagined that this condition was fleeting.

3
BUFFALO AND BORDERS

"The Whitemen were excellent shots."
—Wears Horns, Hunkpapa Lakota

The momentary respite enjoyed in the Northern Indian camps during the winter of 1873–74 was not experienced in the south where the White River agencies were the epicenter of mayhem unlike anything witnessed since the creation of the Great Sioux Reservation. The inability to hunt buffalo in the Republican River country enraged the southerners and made them completely reliant on government issues of beef, bacon, and flour, and shortages were rampant. Critical to the acquisition of stores were accurate counts of the people being subsisted, and agency Indians fiercely resisted the process. In turn, without sound numbers agent requisitions were based on estimates that varied widely and inevitably never met the moment. Complicating matters, too, this season's winter was a difficult one and the Northern Indians, Sioux and Cheyenne alike, appeared at the agencies in unprecedented numbers, sometimes doubling the known tallies of people to be fed. The dilemma was not quickly or easily resolved, and in the face of hunger other troubles arose.[1]

Given the scarcity of foodstuffs at the Red Cloud and Spotted Tail agencies, many residents, both long-time and new arrivals, lashed out irrespective of consequence. The Red Cloud agent tallied the deaths of Whites and Indians killed—the bloodshed cut both ways—from January 1873 through July 1874 and his list was alarming. Herders and teamsters were particularly vulnerable, with ranchers and freighters killed in the Niobrara Valley and as far south as the North Platte River near Scott's Bluff, where Indians "are daily killing cattle in that vicinity." At Spotted Tail Agency, warriors drove off agency herders and issued their own beef. No single individual or band was immediately identified with these troubles, but Little Big Man seems to have again been at the center of trouble, having already been specifically noted by the Red Cloud agent in a similar regard some months earlier.[2]

The bloodshed spread, particularly southwestward toward and beyond Fort Laramie, the initial agency for the Oglalas and Brulés and a fixture on the principal road northward from the Union Pacific Railroad and Cheyenne, Wyoming. In the years since the great treaty of 1868, the river corridors in the region had filled with ranches. All were easy targets now for raiders who swept through that country in January and February, attacking hunting parties and preying on ranches in the North Platte and Laramie River valleys, thieving horses, mules, and cattle, and challenging stockmen, some of whom were their own mixed-blood kin.[3]

One of the more alarming and attention-getting episodes occurred on February 9, likely involving the same raiders then sweeping through the Fort Laramie countryside. That day Lieutenant Levi Robinson and a corporal riding with him were ambushed and killed by raiders on Cottonwood Creek, forty miles west of Fort Laramie. The two had separated from an army wood cutting detail, apparently intent on hunting but falling prey themselves. A cavalry contingent from the fort recovered their bodies the next day. Both were riddled with gunshots and arrows and had been scalped. The raiding party was next seen above Horse Shoe Creek southeast of Fort Fetterman, seemingly east bound to the White River agencies. The identities of the warriors were never known.[4]

An equally disturbing event occurred on the same day, February 9, at Red Cloud Agency, fully one hundred miles east of the Levi Robinson episode. At Red Cloud, agent John J. Saville had been warned that Indians intended to kill him in retaliation for the slaying of an Indian in the Platte country a short while before. Saville ignored the threat and traveled to the Spotted Tail Agency to confer with the agent there about jointly calling for troops to protect their interests. The nearest military support was at Fort Laramie, eighty-five miles distant. Saville left his chief clerk, Frank Appleton, in charge. That night a warrior named Kicking Bear of Crazy Horse's Hunkpatila Oglala band stealthily entered the agency compound. Bypassing a sleeping watchman, Kicking Bear made his way to Saville's quarters where he confronted Appleton at the front door, uttered something unintelligible, and shot him with his Winchester. The clerk died several hours later. Kicking Bear successfully fled the scene.[5]

Within months these two episodes and other recent bloodshed triggered deployment of troops to the agencies, bringing about the establishment of Camp Robinson near Red Cloud—aptly named for the recently killed Levi Robinson—and Camp Sheridan near the Spotted Tail Agency. The deployments had been eagerly anticipated by civilians and the military alike. From the start, both little posts, each picturesquely situated but noticeably almost always undermanned, found themselves enmeshed in all manner of Indian restiveness. Not limited to the Pine Ridge and White River countryside, the unease spread north soon enough to the Black Hills as well. Militarization of the agencies also triggered the flight of most of the lingering Northern Indians from these southern agencies, but not before resupplying themselves with arms and munitions to the fullest extent possible. Whites were alarmed. "Crazy Horse has declared for war," exclaimed the highly agitated Agent Saville in a telegram to superiors in late February.[6]

Sitting Bull had made a memorably contemptuous statement to White invaders when he so brazenly smoked his pipe near Arrow Creek, Montana, on August 14, 1872, bullets buzzing about him like bees and onlookers on both sides equally agape. Now, two years later, Crazy Horse and his close friend Little Big Man, made contemptuous statements of their own amid the wave of raiding in the Pine Ridge and North Platte country. This was a volatile time at the southern agencies, and it steeled Crazy Horse and

Little Big Man in their resolve to resist reservation life. It also induced other like-minded contemporaries to join them. As those fervent warriors saw it, it was plainly disheartening to see the transformations underway since the days of the Fort Laramie Treaty. Ranches and cattle now dotted the lands north of the Union Pacific Railroad and along the great avenue between the booming rail line, the cattle town of Cheyenne, and the aging military post farther north on the Laramie River. They were hearing, too, of the buffalo slaughter underway on the central plains south of the railroad.[7] A railroad—the wanton killing of buffalo—cattlemen. This land had become inhospitable, dangerous, and disgusting. If there was solitude and sanctity in their world, it only existed now on the buffalo prairie in the north among like-minded, tradition-embracing people.

Food shortages plagued another reservation in the far north country too, and one agent's interim solution was as ironic as it was resourceful. At Milk River Agency at Fort Peck on the Upper Missouri, a newly arrived agent discovered that, but for the scantiest number of live cattle in his corrals, the supply of fresh beef was all but exhausted, and sufficient replacement stocks impossible to obtain in midwinter. Moreover, his stores of dried buffalo and pemmican were also fully exhausted. Fortunately, the agent reported, considerable quantities of dried meat and pemmican were available for purchase "in his vicinity," at "12 cts per lb. for Dried Buffalo meat and 14 cts per lb. for Pemmican." The source was the Durfee & Peck Company, licensed traders on the reservation, who were selling meats packed by the Métis people who also lived within the bounds of the reservation. These were the same people who were market hunting the northern buffalo herd to the great consternation of the Lakota people, even as they quietly purveyed arms, whiskey, and defiant advice to those same Indians. The agent bought the meats. The Métis quandary, meanwhile, only became more complicated in the coming months.[8]

In the Northern Indian camps in the Yellowstone country that late winter, however, the issue was not railroad surveyors or Métis buffalo hunters. Rather, it was a wagon caravan ambling east across the divide from the mountain settlement of Bozeman and threading its way down the Yellowstone River to points unknown. The train—twenty-two wagons, some 150 well-armed miners and Plainsmen, plus several hundred horses and mules, twenty-eight yoke of oxen, two pieces of artillery, and a motley array of dogs—was barely distinguishable from the other columns in previous years, although this one included no men wearing blue.[9]

The citizens of Bozeman knew the outfit as the Yellowstone Wagon Road and Prospecting Expedition. The expedition was intent on exploring the head of navigation on the Yellowstone River, where perhaps one day a wagon road might connect river traffic with their town. Its members also intended to prospect for gold in the Wolf Mountains, the rugged uplands of the upper Rosebud and Tongue River region. Montana had a fiery territorial governor named Benjamin Potts who was as intent on developing settlement as he was on removing the Indian impediment. He may have foreseen this expedition as a means to so stir the wild Sioux and Cheyenne that the army would be forced into action against them. The hoped-for outcome in eastern Montana would be to clear the land of those people. Washington rejected Potts's political scheme outright, but the expedition proceeded. However motivated, the expedition opted for travel in the late winter since many knew that the Indians in the Lower Yellowstone country tended to congregate along the Powder River well east of where they planned to go. For most of the expedition's participants, gold was the driving force.[10]

The caravan made its way eastward in the late winter drear following the north bank of the Yellowstone. A Chinook wind had recently cleared the snow but the nights and northerly winds remained bitterly cold. The prospectors slowly pressed on until the end of March 1874 when they crossed the still mostly frozen Yellowstone River downstream of the mouth of the Big Horn. Once across, they angled southeastward toward Rosebud Creek. Several of the wintering camps of Northern Indians were located up Rosebud Creek, including Red End of Horns's band of Two Kettles

Sioux and Hump's band of Miniconjous. Those Indians were keenly aware of these unwelcome *wasicus*, especially when the expedition ascended the countryside south of the Yellowstone. In turn, the Whites had also seen Indians, including one occasion in the uplands between the Big Horn and Rosebud where they confronted twenty-five warriors. Every night the Whites circled their wagons, secured their stock inside, and dug and nestled in long trenches capable of securing six or eight men. "We called them dug-out dwellers," remembered Wears Horns, a Hunkpapa warrior in the Two Kettles camp.[11]

While the broader Tongue and Powder River drainages harbored many wintering Northern Indian camps, later secondary accounts identify Sitting Bull and Crazy Horse among them, but neither of those Lakota leaders was involved in this episode. At that very time, Sitting Bull and his followers were known to be hunting buffalo on Big Dry Creek, near Fort Peck, while other Sioux were hunting buffalo near the Bear's Paw Mountains. Assertions, meanwhile, that Crazy Horse was in the north in these months are unsubstantiated and conflict with contemporary accounts placing him in the Pine Ridge and Fort Laramie countryside at the same time. The resistance confronting these unwelcome *wasicus* appears chiefly to have come from Red End of Horns's and Hump's camps, and they alone proved formidable, even while costly to themselves.[12]

The caravan's cross country trail to the Rosebud was a slog over mostly dry and waterless ground, and always under the watchful eye of Indians. The wagons reached the Rosebud on April 3 and circled at the mouth of Greenwood Creek. In the morning darkness of April 4 a jittery picket shot at distant shadows and three of the party's dogs rushed forward, barking and disappearing in a distant coulee. Only one returned, with an arrow deep in its body. Then shots rang out from that same coulee and other points around the camp. A few rounds from the caravan's artillery pieces stilled that opening fire.[13]

The shooting and booming cannon fire drew other warriors from the upriver camps and in the morning light a general fight ensued. Warriors occasionally rode close enough to the expedition's dug-outs that dogs would emerge from beneath the wagons and chase after them. Warriors shot several with arrows, but also suffered from heavy fire themselves and retreated to distant hills. "The Whitemen were excellent shots," remembered Wears Horns. One warrior tied a red eagle feather to his coup stick and held it aloft as a target and bullets hit the feather. "The warriors knew that they were not fighting soldiers, because soldiers were poor shots." It was an unfair advantage since the warriors were mostly armed with bows, arrows, lances, and war clubs. The clash ended when the Whites fired one of their cannons one more time, as if signaling, and then charged, surprising their assailants who fled up Rosebud Creek, pushed by other salvos from the big guns.[14]

The prospectors remained in camp that day. In the prominent coulee in their fore they found the heads and paws of their two missing dogs, the Indians having roasted and eaten them in the darkness. Wears Horns claimed that two warriors were killed and others wounded. The Whites later claimed they collected seven scalps, killed ten ponies, and captured thirty more that were tied together in a deep draw. They said they suffered only one of their own wounded but also had twenty-one horses and two oxen killed, requiring them to burn three of their wagons for lack of animals to put in harness. Before departing camp the Whites scattered about pieces of pemmican and biscuits infused with strychnine, as if baiting and poisoning wolves. The Brulé warrior No Flesh remembered that the Indians were suspicious of the food and did not touch it.[15]

The clash on the Rosebud caused many in the train to wonder just what it was they were doing in that country and some argued for returning to Bozeman. Their cries grew ever more insistent in the days ahead, but others, drawn by notions of gold in the Wolf Mountains, urged crossing over to the Tongue. After the fight on the lower Rosebud, however, the party remained together and continued up that stream. Oddly, their own stocks of ammunition were running short, despite the comfort of a seeming overabundance at the beginning of the outing. The Indian trail served as a "wide road," remembered one of the members, and there remained a lingering sense of an Indian presence. Evening camps were always well fortified. The trail up the Rosebud turned onto Davis Creek and then onto Ash Creek in the Little

Big Horn drainage. The prospectors were following a timeworn Indian pathway from drainage to drainage that, coincidentally, was the same one Sitting Bull's massive village would travel two years later.[16]

On Ash Creek on April 12 warriors struck again. As herders pushed their animals to water that morning watchful warriors sensed an opportunity to run off the stock. Several cannon salvos scattered the attackers but also startled the expedition's animals and pushed them toward the waiting Indians. Only a heroic charge of one of the herders rushing to the fore and turning the herd stemmed a near catastrophic loss, while gunfire from the camp further frustrated the attackers who fled to the surrounding hills. As happened downstream, the clash quickly devolved into another fruitless and mostly one-sided affair. Losses that morning included the deaths of one member of the party and one warrior.[17]

The prospectors pushed on, half retreating and half attempting to make something of their folly, crossing overland from Ash Creek to the Little Big Horn River a few miles below the mouth of Lodge Grass Creek, and then up Lodge Grass. The weather meantime turned foul. On April 16 Indians again harassed the train and engaged in a running fight, but as before effective long-range small arms fire and occasional volleys from the artillery pieces stemmed the assaults. Farther up Lodge Grass the expedition encountered the Old Bozeman Road and turned westward onto it. One member of the party quipped that no wagon had been over that trail since it was abandoned six years earlier. But ruts were plainly visible and it "seemed good to have a road to follow once more." In due course the prospectors reached the ruins of the old Bozeman Trail post on the Big Horn River, Fort C. F. Smith, and camped within the shadows of its weathered adobe walls. By then, any trailing warriors had disappeared.[18]

The expedition disbanded in Bozeman several weeks later, a dismal and public failure and an abject lesson once again of the impenetrability of the Lower Yellowstone, a conceded Indian country. They had suffered one man killed and two wounded, plus the loss of an untold number of horses, mules, and oxen. Worse yet, aside from a few "colors" panned in the Big Horn drainage, the men found no worthwhile gold.[19]

As with the railroad surveys in 1872 and 1873, the interlopers in 1874 had not contended with the entire might of the Northern Indians but only two disparate bands whose warriors may or may not have been involved in the resistance of earlier years. Wears Horns reflected years later on this particular invasion of the buffalo country. The pride in having turned away those *wasicus* was plainly apparent in the interview, as was the awe of well-stocked wagons, superior weaponry, and astonishing sharpshooters. If anything, the disparity of weaponry was Wears Horns's lasting memory. "The warriors did not have good guns," he plainly confessed to his interviewer. "Bows and arrows against rifles is *sica* (no good)."[20]

One member of the Yellowstone Expedition paid particular heed to the warrior firearms used against them in April 1874, evident when he and others combed about Indian positions after their clashes. He specifically mentioned .50 caliber needle guns, referencing government Springfield breech-loading rifles that were often modified from their original condition. He also noted a Sharps cavalry carbine taken from a fallen warrior, plus Spencers and Winchesters, weapons readily identified by the expended metallic cartridge cases left behind. But far more common, he said, were old muzzle-loading rifles and revolvers, and bows and arrows. Indian access to modern weaponry was proving its worth, but Wears Horns's quip spoke to the Northerners' continuing challenges of obtaining weapons of quality and in quantity in the face of relentless White invasions.[21]

The firearms trade was a dilemma throughout Sioux Country. Outright bans at the agencies were coming but had not yet been imposed, even while agents dutifully reported monthly sales and often actually justified Indian acquisitions. John Saville at Red Cloud Agency said, "I found it necessary to open an ammunition trade for the Indians to purchase enough to kill their cattle." At the agencies firearms were always difficult to obtain, and exceedingly expensive, but the trade for metallic cartridges, bar lead by the pound, kegs of powder, and caps was commonplace and endlessly referenced in monthly reports.[22]

At the Cheyenne River Agency on the Missouri River, agent H. W. Bingham was less circumspect about selling weapons to those in his charge, repeatedly endorsing arms sales generally, but only, he said, to the "friendly or civilized Indians at this agency." The licensed Durfee & Peck trader at Cheyenne River acknowledged that sales averaged about ten guns per annum, along with requisite quantities of powder, balls, and caps. But such loose munitions were appropriate only for single-shot muzzle loading rifles, not the newer repeating cartridge guns. The Cheyenne River agent also acknowledged the challenge of regulating trade with outside Indians, reporting in one instance in March 1874 that runners had recently come from a large camp of Miniconjous and Sans Arcs located north of the Black Hills seeking to trade buffalo robes for ammunition. The agent labeled the runners and distant camp "hostile" and forbade any such trading.[23]

Farther north at Fort Peck, local agent William Alderson also solicited and forwarded monthly reports on weapons transactions occurring among the several licensed traders on the Milk River, one of whom defensively called arms dealing the very "foundation of the Indian trade." But Alderson also acknowledged his inability to control all such business, particularly referencing nefarious trading occurring on the Musselshell River southwest of him. On the Musselshell, he claimed, was an individual not taking "special pains" to ascertain whether he was doing business with hostile Indians. (By now agents generally labeled virtually all non-agency Indians—implying Sitting Bull Indians—as "hostile.") The local agent knew those traders by name and in one communication labeled them "unsuitable" people.[24]

The Musselshell matter exploded when the Fort Peck agent reported to the Commissioner of Indian Affairs that a lawless trader was attempting to lure heretofore peaceful Yanktonai Sioux from Milk River to that place for "trafficking purposes," promising unlimited quantities of loose ammunition and breech-loading guns if they would join him. With no deputy marshal or detective anywhere near the agency, Alderson decried his powerlessness to enforce the "regulations of the Department relative to the ammunition question." The matter begged a response, and finally a US Indian Service detective from Helena investigated the various trading houses in the Milk River country, including those on the Missouri and Milk Rivers and on Frenchman's Creek. The detective initially found nothing especially awry at any of those places, aside from bookkeeping references to whiskey trading on Frenchman's Creek, but his final report addressed several critical matters. For one, the scale of ammunition pouring through those places to the Milk River and Teton Sioux people was daunting. It included cartridges for all manner of pistols and modern rifles, among them Sharps, Spencers, and needle guns, plus sizeable quantities of conventional loose powder, lead, and caps.[25]

The detective's final report also revealed several other complexities of the arms trade in that critical borderland region. He learned from the local priest at the Métis community on Frenchman's Creek, for example, that traders from Wood Mountain, Canada, appeared from time to time expressly to trade ammunition with local Indians. None of those suspect Métis were present when the detective was there. The investigator also learned, or more likely reaffirmed, the well-understood truth that local Indians, friendly and peaceable and permitted to trade without restriction, in turn freely traded with unfriendly or hostile neighboring Indians. The detective's report included a statement from a Yanktonai Indian, Good Dog, who told how he traded two horses to Gros Ventres at Fort Buford for two Henry rifles and ammunition, and how from those same Gros Ventres and wood hawks at Buford he and his people could always get all the weaponry they wanted. Good Dog knew, too, that such trading was occurring with the Hunkpapas.[26]

While nearly all of the agents in Sioux Country grappled with the conundrum of legal and illegal arms trading, one further alarming report nearly eclipsed all others. Colonel John Smith, newly arrived peace enforcer at Red Cloud Agency and founder of nearby Camp Robinson, reported in early May 1874 distressing news regarding mixed-bloods. A camp of some seven hundred Red River mixed-bloods were now on a tributary of the Big Horn River and trading arms and munitions to the Northern Indians. Furthermore, they were attempting to persuade the Northerners to withdraw from the agencies. There was plainly no simple solution to this mix of peaceable and hostile crosscurrents.[27]

Meanwhile, barely had the Northern Indians deflected one late-winter invasion of the northern prairie country—the Yellowstone expedition—when other intrusions loomed. The first occurred in the borderlands north of the Missouri River in an episode that seemed of little consequence, although it became more than yet another annoyance in buffalo country. The other was a deliberate invasion of the Black Hills in Dakota that was not only greatly disturbing from its start but also portended a continuing, even explosive nightmare.

In the more minor affair, borderlands surveyors of the US Northern Boundary Commission and their Canadian counterpart were actively planting permanent markers on the landscape, Sometimes the markers were tall black cast metal posts, placed at one-mile intervals. Other times, they were eight-foot-tall glacial stone or heaped earth pyramids spaced three miles apart. Their line was plainly visible and ultimately stretched from Lake of the Woods in northern Minnesota westward to the Rocky Mountains. For the first time, the heretofore nebulous boundary separating the lands of the Great Mother in the north from those of the Great Father in the south were being delineated.[28]

During the three-year-long boundary survey crews and escorts from both governments labored on respective sections of the line. By year's end 1872 the demarcated boundary reached from its eastern start in the lake country of northern Minnesota to the Red River of the North. A year later all of northern Dakota Territory was marked, that season's work terminating in the Wood Mountain country northwest of Fort Buford. While Colonel David S. Stanley and his troops clashed with Lakota warriors on the Yellowstone that year, the surveying work in Dakota in 1873 was peaceful throughout. Taking no chances, however, the American and Canadian crews were well protected, the Americans by a complement of soldiers and the Canadians by a force of specially recruited and armed Métis guides and scouts. The Indians of the region mostly came to understand that the new "stone heaps" defined a political landmark of potentially useful purpose.[29]

When work resumed in 1874 difficulties with the Hunkpapa Sioux and others at Fort Peck were anticipated as the line advanced westward across northern Montana to the mountains. Once again both governments assembled sizeable complements of surveyors and support staff. This year's American soldier escort assembled at Fort Buford, while its Canadian counterpart of Métis scouts was joined in the field by elements of the newly created North-West Mounted Police, a 275-man complement of scarlet-coated constables. As respective crews advanced into the buffalo country west of Wood Mountain, they occasionally encountered Sioux, Assiniboine, and Plains Cree people but no resistance. If anything the labors of 1874 were memorable for the challenges of surviving an oft-waterless, alkaline prairie, and hunting buffalo, which the American surveyors first encountered in July and thereafter killed rapaciously. By mid-September the Americans had completed their labors and the crews withdrew from the line and largely dispersed at Fort Benton on the Upper Missouri.[30]

During the 1874 fieldwork, American and Canadian surveyors did have several noteworthy encounters, not with Indians or buffalo directly but with the detritus of Métis market hunters. Such systematic hunting was common on the northern plains broadly, and especially locally in the Frenchman's River locale (the stream was known as Frenchman's River north of the border), where surveyors came across the putrid wreckage of recent killing and pemmican production, evident always, as one Canadian noted, by the sheer numbers of buffalo recently killed that "strew the country & in some places still pollute the air." Nearby were the camping places of the mixed-bloods, discerned by their lodge circles and barren ground, the heaps of ashes marking cooking pits, and especially by the mountainous piles of broken buffalo bones that had been boiled to extract fats for pemmican production.[31]

In early July two of the American surveyors, Captain James Gregory and Lieutenant Francis Greene, explored ahead of their party for a passable wagon crossing of Frenchman's River. The valley before them was some eight miles wide, with only two suitable wagon crossings within sixty miles and neither of those close at hand. On their way, they encountered a small, unpretentious hovel called Fort N. J. Turney, just north of the international line. The fort was "imposing only in name," quipped Greene, amounting to a simple log stockade of about eighty feet on a side enclosing a storehouse and dwelling occupied by two independent traders and a handful of mixed-blood employees. All were highly agitated, having been riled the day before by Sioux Indians from Fort Peck who had been feasted but then ran off with nine of the complement's eleven horses. The traders were so disillusioned, Gregory observed, that they were prepared to burn their compound and abandon the country.[32]

In a letter to his parents written a few days later, Greene added several interesting details. Fort Turney survived, he wrote, on the barter of "red flannel, ammunition, guns, bridles, and saddles to the Indians for robes, [and] from such places as this come the improved breech loaders and fixed ammunition found on the Indians in every fight." Greene was unknowingly echoing the observations of the US Indian Service detective who had investigated the many trading houses on the Milk River Reservation just months before, and perhaps even this one. Such trading camps on Frenchman's River had long vexed American authorities, but to the Métis, the unheralded and despised lot of hunters and entrepreneurs, those same posts were profitable and irrepressible. Moreover the Métis had come to appreciate the usefulness of the soon heralded "Medicine Line."[33]

The supposed Sioux Indians from Fort Peck harassing the traders at Fort Turney were in fact unnamed Yanktonai Sioux, not Sitting Bull's people. That same spring and summer the core of the Northern Indian camps, particularly Sitting Bull's Hunkpapas, were traveling customary paths along the Lower Yellowstone, ranging from the forks of the Powder to the Rosebud, variously hunting and engaging an old enemy, the Crows.

Strangely, Frank Grouard, the odd mixed-blood still among them, remembered how the warriors in Sitting Bull's camp at the time were strikingly short of fixed ammunition and eagerly awaiting an unnamed overdue party from an agency bringing cartridges and other supplies.[34]

Standing Bear, an Oglala who often lived among the tradition-bound Miniconjous, meanwhile, recalled his people slowly traveling the Cheyenne River valley in Dakota that spring and summer, and that Crazy Horse's Oglalas were camped and hunting farther west yet. This placed those Miniconjous in an unenviable position to witness the most egregious invasion of Sioux Country yet, the army's 1874 foray into the Black Hills, the land He Dog had called the "Heart of the Earth."[35]

4

BLACK HILLS MAYHEM

"I am here to kill the White men who are trying to take [my] land."
—Little Big Man, Oglala Lakota

Rumors of gold in the Black Hills had tantalized Americans for decades, but into the 1870s the legacy of discovery was spotty. Tales from previous decades offered no shortage of murky details, undetermined values, and tragic endings, invariably death at the hands of Indians. The Black Hills lay squarely in the heart of Sioux Country. The first scientific explorations of the region, Gouverneur Warren's survey in 1857 and William Raynolds's in 1859, delivered only the vaguest of specifics. Indians themselves sometimes contributed to the allure. Northern plains traders recalled tales of natives showing specimens of yellow metal from time to time—whether pyrites or actual gold was never specified—and reports of Black Hills placer gold being exchanged at Fort Laramie and at Missouri River trading posts. Father Pierre De Smet supposedly saw Black Hills gold himself, but hushed the account to protect his "children." However fanciful the enticements, as late as 1862 the realities of gold in California, Colorado, and Montana drew the nation's exploring fervor elsewhere and not to this corner of Indian Country, where Whites were simply not welcome. Moreover, in 1868 the Fort Laramie Treaty with the Sioux locked this prospective El Dorado tightly within the bounds of the new Great Sioux Reservation. But it was the very creation of that reservation that changed the story forevermore.[1]

With the establishment of Lakota agencies on the Missouri and White Rivers came the inevitable cocreation of military posts at or near each, their respective garrisons ostensibly serving as guardians of government administrators, employees, and property. The new agency posts complemented an existing string of older forts, including Randall, Sully, Rice, Buford, Laramie, Fetterman, and Ellis, created in an earlier era and scattered across a broader span of the northern plains. The army quickly came to grasp a void in its garrisoning efforts, however. It lacked a post in the very heart of Indian country, somewhere north perhaps of the Black Hills. The difficulties railroad surveyors experienced in Dakota and Montana played heavily in this thinking, as did the existence of recognized Indian pathways between the various Sioux agencies and the Yellowstone country.[2]

On the simple premise of reconnoitering a site for such a military post, a sizeable column of cavalry and infantry numbering nearly a thousand men embarked from Fort Abraham Lincoln on July 2, 1874. Within the column's ranks were Arikara and Santee Indian scouts, an army band, trained engineers, university geologists and naturalists, a photographer, three newspapermen, a mix of artillery pieces, and more than one hundred wagons. Tellingly tucked within the expedition, as well, were two experienced miners. The column traveled under a simple proviso in the Fort Laramie Treaty that permitted government officers, agents, and employees to enter the reservation in the discharge of duties. Finding a suitable location for a military post was one such justifiable duty. This formidable column was led by George Custer, still a relative unknown in northern Indian Country.[3]

Grand River and Cheyenne River Lakotas were the first to notice the column's movement, and one so obviously bound for the Black Hills. But it was Lakotas from the south who encountered it first. A small band of Oglalas from Red Cloud Agency, five lodges of Stabber's people, were camped on Castle Creek cutting lodge poles and hunting when they were discovered by the column's Arikara scouts, who advanced under a flag of truce. At perhaps seventy years of age, Stabber, or One Stab, was long prominently connected with affairs in the Platte and Pine Ridge country and had even visited Washington as recently as two years earlier. Within the month, July 1874, he and his people had been with the Northern Indians on the Powder, where they learned of the fights with the Bozeman exploring party. Stabber was contemptuous of Whites but unafraid now to confront these scouts and their interpreter, and he and two others, Slow Bull and Long Bear, talked at length with them. Their interpreter explained that the column sought someone familiar with the interior of the Hills who might willingly guide it. Slow Bull found the encounter intimidating. These were traditional enemies after all. Yet they all shook hands and agreed to meet the soldier chief. As they rode off, the camp behind them packed and fled.[4]

Slow Bull was struck by the soldier chief's visage. He had "yellow hair, long yellow mustache and chin whiskers." They shook hands and talked about General John Smith, the commanding officer at the new Camp Robinson, whom the yellow-haired one called a "strong friend." The soldier chief explained that he sought someone who would stay with him and guide them deeper into the Hills. Stabber alone agreed and went along, forcibly perhaps. The three were given coffee and bacon and Slow Bull and Long Bear mounted and rode away, fearful of being chased and killed by the Arikaras. They quickly rejoined their camp in its flight from the Hills and headed for Red Cloud Agency, where they promptly reported the encounter to their agent, J. J. Saville. Saville told them that the yellow-haired chief was Custer, a man not then known to them. Slow Bull and Long Bear were positive that the old man, Stabber, would be killed by the soldiers. Stabber, in fact, was closely held all the while as though a prisoner, but after guiding the *wasicus* for several weeks was released by the yellow-haired one and returned to the agency unharmed.[5]

Stabber's band was not the only one aware of these soldiers in the Hills. Farther north in Miniconjou country, Standing Bear, an Oglala who often aligned with the Miniconjous and who was already a voice in reporting the movements of the Northern people that spring, recalled traveling that summer upstream of the Forks of the Cheyenne, likely on today's Belle

Fourche River, and learning of White men exploring the interior. Those Miniconjous hunted a while, counseled, and then headed for Sitting Bull country, plainly intent on avoiding the invaders.[6]

A similar circumstance occurred in the southern Black Hills among other Oglalas who were hunting and gathering tipi poles. In May a band of about thirty lodges of Big Road's people had leisurely skirted the southeastern Black Hills, entering by way of Spring Creek. On Rapid Creek in the thick forest, women and children labored cutting and stripping lodge poles while men hunted bear. There one of their own warned them of soldiers heading their way. The band quickly departed for the Oglala agency where in evening councils they learned that the "soldiers were up there to get the white and yellow metals in the hills." Word was disseminating quickly. Almost certainly this was news from Stabber's people spreading throughout the Oglala camp circles. "Everyone thought that something should be done about it," the Oglala informant Black Elk told an inquirer many years later.[7]

But no effort was made to impede the soldier invaders who continued their way into the interior. Their travels were largely effortless, everyone extolling the splendor of the grass, the floral-laced valleys, and the profusion of wild berries and rippling cool streams. The ease of day-to-day travel may have been a simple reflection of the deeply worn Indians trails that the column often followed, and perhaps also recognition of Stabber's counsel, although never once was the old Oglala acknowledged in any soldier report or newspaper account. "In no portion of the United States, not excepting the famous blue-grass region of Kentucky, have I ever seen grazing superior to that found growing wild in this hitherto unknown region," extolled the yellow-haired soldier chief.[8]

All along, the column's scientists paid continuing attention to the mineralizations encountered but what they saw was deemed of little value. That is, until the labor of the column's two practical miners turned the tale. On July 30 the troops reached the French Creek valley in the central Hills and while some in the party climbed prominent mountains the two prospectors reported finding gold colors in the stream. What they found were visible specs of gold though apparently nothing of measurable value. The next day, however, the prospectors worked a gravel bar farther downstream where their recovery turned promising. And on August 2 about two miles below today's Custer City the prospectors found excellent colors in the streambanks. They sank a hole in one of the sidebars and in bedrock sands recovered pinhead size flakes of placer gold, enough to yield, they thought, ten cents to the pan. After three pans the pair had enough free gold to take to Custer's tent. The miners did the conventional goldfield math. At ten cents a pan and working with sluice boxes, a day's labor might yield $50 or $75. Someone even thought $150. Prospective gold country needed paying yields—enough gold to return more than a typical day's wages of $3.50 to $5—and some of the observers believed they had found it.[9]

The news captivated the camp, and Custer himself wasted no time in announcing it. On August 3 he led five companies of his cavalry and a handful of staff on a reconnaissance aimed in a southwesterly direction toward the Cheyenne River. Beyond lay Fort Laramie and the nearest telegraph station. Custer carried hastily drawn reports, including from the newsmen, and a satchel of mail. Again he followed obvious Indian trails, and that evening at the mouth of Red Canyon—a locale soon renowned during the heady days of the gold rush—he bade adieu to a lone rider who commenced a nighttime journey over uncharted ground to Fort Laramie, ninety miles distant. The courier's horse's hooves were wrapped in leather boots to obscure its iron shoes. Summer nights were short, and the rider needed four days to pass through treacherous Indian country. Eventually reaching Rawhide Creek, southeast of the Rawhide Buttes, he followed it southward until it intersected with the well-scored Fort Laramie–Camp Robinson military road. Soon after reaching the old post on the morning of August 8, he spread news of gold in the Black Hills nationally by telegraph. Custer had unleashed a gold rush.[10]

On August 6 Custer's Black Hills Expedition charted a course for home, exiting the Hills in a northeasterly direction toward Bear Butte and then a northerly course into the Little Missouri drainage before turning east to Fort Lincoln. Shortly beyond the Belle Fourche River the soldiers encountered four Cheyenne Indians en route to their White River agency in Nebraska. From the Cheyennes, they learned that Sitting Bull, camped then on the Tongue, was aware of the column and preparing to intercept it in the tangle of the Short Pine Hills in the Little Missouri drainage. The column passed that way in due course, but no such confrontation occurred, although the soldiers repeatedly encountered fresh pony trails and vast burned-over tracts that destroyed the grazing and scattered the game—Indian statements that they were well aware of the column's movement.[11]

For their parts, Sitting Bull and Crazy Horse were indeed conscious of this incursion into Lakota sacred ground, but offered no resistance. Doubtless it was Miniconjous annoyingly burning the prairie. The Miniconjous, in fact, were greatly alarmed, confronting their agent in August and demanding to know why it was that a soldier column "had passed over the Sioux Reservation and penetrated the sacred soil of the Indians, the Black Hills." The alarmed agent reported to the Commissioner of Indian Affairs that he has "been obliged to use every means to prevent the Indians at this agency from going against Genl Custer in force."[12]

While Custer explored the Black Hills, Crazy Horse's followers and other Oglala traditionals hunted buffalo in the Powder River country. Sitting Bull's people remained likewise occupied farther north in the Lower Yellowstone and Big Open country, where, when not hunting, they preferred horse raiding in Crow Country. Sitting Bull had oddly, if rightly, called the Black Hills a "food pack," a strange notion for a Northerner who was always somewhat detached from affairs in the south, but one deftly explained by Standing Bear, an Oglala, some years later. Standing Bear remembered hearing Sitting Bull use that expression and inherently knew of the natural riches of the Hills, as any Southern Lakota would. As Standing Bear explained, he felt that "we Indians should stick to it. Indians would rove all around, but when they were in need of something, they could just go in there and get it." For some, it was as simple as that. To outsiders, the concerns of the Southern and Northern Lakota people could seem quite different, but to all, it was proving obvious that the *wasicus'* covetous interest in exploring and invading Indian country was endless.[13]

The nation's citizenry, meanwhile, saw the Black Hills in a different light. Custer's announcement of gold, cautious as he and his scientists played their assessments and pronouncements, captivated America. The nation was subsumed by hard times. The Panic of 1873 brought on severe hardships and in its chaos and pain nothing stirred a population more than notions of gold for the taking "from the grass roots down." Within months jumping off places like Fort Pierre, Yankton, and Sioux City on the Missouri, and Sidney and Cheyenne on the Union Pacific in Nebraska and Wyoming boomed with prospectors, speculators, dreamers, and the down and out. The Grant Administration confronted a crisis. How would it mollify a depressed electorate and reconcile a new gold rush in country lying squarely within an Indian reservation? Stemming this tide would soon prove a near impossibility, although at first the government and its army uncharacteristically held for the Indians and the Fort Laramie Treaty.[14]

An odd attempt at countering the gold news played out barely weeks after Custer completed his exploration. Members of a Sioux Commission investigating affairs at the Spotted Tail Agency turned their attention to the Black Hills, as if seemingly puzzled if not thoroughly annoyed by the breaking news of a gold discovery. The impromptu survey was led by Samuel Hinman, an edgy Episcopal missionary active in Indian affairs in eastern Nebraska. Hinman led a small delegation into the Hills in August, accompanied by the Spotted Tail agent and others from that agency, an escort of cavalry from Camp Sheridan, and several miners. Within days his entourage crossed Custer's trail and thereafter mostly followed its same interior course. While Hinman's party often viewed the same sights, climbed the same peaks, and panned the same placer sands, his assessments were unenthusiastic. Where the yellow-haired one found rich soils,

Hinman thought them poor and the grasses thin. While fragments of white quartz were everywhere, Hinman found no evidence of mineral wealth. And his practical miners, supposedly men experienced in the California and Colorado gold country, found no traces of gold or other precious metal whatsoever. The priest's search for a permanent agency location along the White River was similarly unproductive. Hinman's assessments attracted no national attention and his report was buried.[15]

In the face of Black Hills gold fever surging irrepressibly, particularly in gateway communities, Lieutenant General Philip Sheridan, the army's commander in the Trans-Mississippi West, took an approach reminiscent of his Civil War tactics. In September, Sheridan, headquartered in Chicago, ordered post commanders in Dakota and Nebraska to seek out prospecting parties organizing for the Hills and "burn the wagon trains, destroy the outfits, and arrest the leaders." Local organizers, residents, and political operatives were outraged and challenged Sheridan's authority. But the matter had been directed by the president himself and was separately affirmed by the Interior Department and sustained by a federal district court. That fall and winter 1874–75 soldiers aggressively pursued trespassers, indeed occasionally destroying their trains and more frequently locating and evicting working parties. Ironically, Sheridan, here upholding the sanctity of the Black Hills as treaty-bound Indian country, was the one who had unleashed Custer to begin with.[16]

The growing Black Hills fever also drew the ire of many Sioux agents and their residents. Henry Bingham, agent at the Cheyenne River Agency, was particularly perplexed, writing the Commissioner of Indian Affairs in late October that Cheyenne River Indians knew of White men in the Black Hills "working the ground." While they did not wish to make war on those invaders they were prepared to do so if the government did not "drive the miners out of their country." A month later Bingham again reported that prospectors were seen near the agency, obviously Black Hills bound. This time he could add that troops from the adjacent Cheyenne River Post and Fort Sully were in pursuit. Such chases mostly proved fruitless, however, and resolute prospectors continually evaded the army cordon.[17]

—~~—

The handwringing in Indian Country and Washington over the Black Hills dilemma continued through the winter. Despite striving to uphold the intents of the Sioux treaty and the integrity of the reservation, pressure to do otherwise mounted steadily, and Washington scrambled for an alternative course. Conventional thinking in such crises was inevitably to organize and dispatch a commission to the affected Indians to explain, cajole, and inevitably push an Anglo-desired outcome. That strategy often included inviting Indian delegations to Washington where such discussions occurred at higher levels, not least in the deliberately intimidating environment of the White House.

An inkling of this old ploy revealed itself in late March 1875 when John Collins showed up at Red Cloud Agency. A well-known Omaha and Cheyenne businessman and current post trader at Fort Laramie, Collins was also a close friend of President Grant's. Collins sought an audience with Red Cloud and other Oglala headmen. Red Cloud Agent James Saville was flabbergasted by the trader's appearance and openly questioned Collins's authority for undertaking such a mission. Nonetheless, in short order the famed Oglala and several others appeared. Collins explained that he had come on behalf of the Great Father, not to make promises but simply to hear what they had to say about White men going to the Black Hills to hunt for gold. Collins assured Red Cloud and the others that the president was telling citizens not to go there, and when that occurred soldiers were continually seeking them out and bringing them back. But there were too many roads to the Hills, he lamented, and not enough soldiers to keep White intruders out of Indian country. Getting to his overarching point in short order, Collins asked: "Do you want to make a treaty with the Great Father for the Black Hills? Is it not better to sell the country between the two Cheyenne Rivers?"[18]

Red Cloud had seen this gambit before. In plain terms he told Collins that he did not believe that the Great Father "has not soldiers enough to keep the Whites out of our country." He wanted no commissioners coming to talk with the Sioux. "They pray to God to help them," Red Cloud said, "but they all lie to me and want to steal everything I have." Soundly rebuffed, Collins continued to the Spotted Tail Agency where he met with several Brulé headmen, and on returning to Fort Laramie a week later telegraphed Grant. Of three things he was sure, he told the president: the Indians were willing to sell the Black Hills, but if commissioners were sent to treat with them nothing would come of it. To that end, they desired to go to Washington themselves. Collins had, at best, a simple sense of the White River people, the Southerners with whom he was treating, but he knew nothing at all of the Northerners. Plainly, however, a stratagem for opening the Black Hills had begun.[19]

The cold season passed quietly in the Northern camps. The devout traditionals, with Sitting Bull's seventy lodges visibly at the core of a diverse amalgam of like-minded people from the other Lakota *oyates* and the Northern Cheyennes, increasingly isolated themselves from the agencies, whose residents they viewed as surrendering to the ways and wiles of the Whites. Twice recently the buffalo country was invaded, variously by prospectors roaming the Rosebud and Big Horn countryside and by surveyors placing stone heaps north of the Missouri. But like the railroad surveyors before them, they all went away. The soldier invasion of the Black Hills was different. While those blue coats also went away, on their heels came trespassers who were now digging the ground. Lakota winter counts remembered other episodes not to Indian liking, too. On his winter calendar American Horse sketched a flagpole with a tomahawk buried in its side, recalling the chaos erupting at Red Cloud Agency when the Oglalas cut up a flagpole because the agent had tried to hoist an American flag. Blue Thunder, a Yanktonai at Grand River, chose to remember Rain in the Face being imprisoned at Fort Lincoln for the presumed killing of an army veterinarian. Army expeditions, gold-seeking intruders, tensions at the agencies, arrests—there was indeed much to talk about in the lodges and around the council fires that winter.[20]

Spring comes slowly on the northern plains, its arrival measured by some as the time of "ice-out" on major rivers like the Yellowstone and Missouri when their waters again flowed freely. Among the northern people this was also the time of emerging new grasses, the budding and leafing of trees, and the movements of the herds, all causes for rejoicing and thanks. Interlopers embraced springtime, too, this season including boatmen.

Steamboats had ventured into Sitting Bull's world in 1873, when soldiers and surveyors explored the Yellowstone Valley, but they never advanced beyond Wolf Rapids, a dangerous, turbulent constriction just below the mouth of the Powder. Now, in late May 1875, a steamboat appeared again, its military passengers intent on examining the mouths of the Tongue and Big Horn Rivers, anticipating a presumptive day when troops might permanently occupy the Yellowstone country. On that journey the boat threaded its way through Wolf Rapids safely, its captain taking advantage of the seasonal high waters. It continued upriver, pausing to allow surveys of the confluences of the Tongue and Big Horn. The boat continued on, determined also to find the head of navigation on the Yellowstone. It bypassed Pompeys Pillar and threaded an upriver narrows known as Hell Roaring Rapids before turning around just above that stricture at a point more or less straight south of today's Billings. At that turnaround, the boat had traveled some 250 river miles above the mouth of the Powder.[21]

Near the Arrow Creek or Baker's battleground of 1872 the boatmen encountered a large camp of Mountain Crows headed for the buffalo country. The passengers told of seeing massive herds crossing the Yellowstone between the Tongue and Big Horn, migrating north into the rugged prairie of the Big Open. Inevitably, Sitting Bull's presence entered the conversation, and the Crows spoke disparagingly of him and his people, emphatically asserting that the Big Horn country belonged to them and that they would fight the Sioux to keep it. One of the boatmen observed that the Crows were well armed with Sharp's carbines, lately a military weapon. No Sioux were seen at any time on the journey, although the boat's captain recalled having passed a hastily abandoned Indian camp among the trees at the mouth of the Tongue, tipi fires still smoldering. No Lakota or Cheyenne informant speaks of this steamboat incursion, perhaps simply because the interlopers came and went by water, and rather hurriedly.[22]

What came in the boat's wake, however, was an invasion of yet another sort. Fellowes Pease of Bozeman was the government agent to the Crows from 1870 into 1873 and an ardent advocate for the opening of commercial prospects in the Lower Yellowstone Valley. In early June 1875 Pease led a party of like-minded promoters downriver aboard three mackinaws, hoping to connect with the steamboat then known to be plying the river toward them. They missed the steamer by days and misfortune befell two of their mackinaws when they snagged and sank, but they salvaged most of their property and continued to the mouth of the Big Horn. On the Yellowstone's north bank just below the Big Horn confluence in a lengthy plain known ever after as the Pease Bottom, the party erected a log stockade some two-hundred-feet square with two corner bastions. They christened the outpost Fort Pease. Pease's avowed intents were lofty, imagining at his little post a transfer trade with steamboats at this near head of navigation on the river. It would be an equivalent of Fort Benton on the Missouri, and also the opening of an amicable trade with the Crows and Sioux.[23]

But Fort Pease was doomed from the start, as if foreshadowed by the sinking of two of its boats so early on their outbound journey. The little fort and its imposing flagpole proved an enormous exasperation to Sitting Bull and his people, who resented this intrusion into the heart of the buffalo country just as they had every other incursion. As Pease erected his fort Sitting Bull's people were fighting Crows nine miles downstream, likely the same Crows encountered by the steamboat a short while earlier and drawn here by their former agent. Sitting Bull may actually have visited the fort, too, if only to vent his wrath and demand that it be torn down. The chief and Pease had actually met face to face some years earlier at Fort Union during the infamous red shirt episode at Fort Buford. But Fort Pease endured a while longer, suffering what one newsman characterized as a perpetual state of war with the Sioux. Six of its forty original inhabitants were killed that season and another nine wounded. Pease, the dreamer, captured no Indian or transfer trade and brokered only occasional wolf skins. For the time being, however, he refused to abandon this dreamy if irritating thorn in the buffalo country.[24]

That spring 1875 word spread through the Northern Indian camps of a proposed Sun Dance on Rosebud Creek. In mid-June a phenomenal assembly of traditionals gathered at the mouth of Lame Deer Creek, a few miles above the revered Rosebud landmark Deer Medicine Rocks. They included Sitting Bull's Hunkpapas, Spotted Eagle's Sans Arcs, Crazy Horse's and Black Twin's Oglalas, and Lame Deer's and Spotted Elk's Miniconjous. Notably present too were Little Wolf and his Northern Cheyenne followers, and the Cheyenne holy man, Ice, or White Bull, who later provided a detailed accounting of the gathering. The ceaseless intrusion of White people into the buffalo country was the common talk of the circles, evidenced yet again by the emergence of a trader's fort at the mouth of the Big Horn. And those episodes atop the repeated movements of soldiers, surveyors, and miners on the Yellowstone in seasons past, and surveyors of another sort in the far north leaving behind the stone heaps, and last year's soldier invasion of the Black Hills, with a tide of prospectors poking about those waters now. It was a time for unity, a survival instinct not yet demonstrated by the traditionals in their previous efforts at repelling the intruders and protecting a homeland.[25]

With the usual deliberation, a circular Sun Dance arbor was erected, with a great cottonwood pole at its center strewn with various religious offerings. On the appointed day and time people from the camps gathered to witness a special dance by Sitting Bull, one consciously resonating with the theme of unity. The great Hunkpapa's entry was stirring. He dressed plainly that day in a breechcloth and moccasins but was painted strikingly, his body smeared over with yellow clay, his face painted black, with two black bands painted around each of his wrists and ankles, a black disc representing the sun ornamenting his chest, and a black crescent representing the moon covering his right shoulder. He approached the scene astride a black horse, a gift from Ice.[26]

After entering the arena Sitting Bull dismounted and danced around the center pole, pressing forward and back several times. After dancing a full circle he turned to the people and called out, "I wish my friends to fill one pipe and I wish my people to fill one pipe," respectively inviting Cheyennes and Sioux to each fill pipes in an act of intertribal unity. From Black Crane, a Cheyenne, he took a pipe in his right hand, and from a Hunkpapa he took a Sioux pipe in the left, and invited the two to join him at the center pole. With the people around all singing, Sitting Bull held both pipes in front of him, the bowls directed toward the pole, and he again danced forward and back, as though, White Bull retold, he were approaching an enemy.[27]

Three times Sitting Bull advanced on the pole, one time declaring, "I have nearly got them." After a fourth approach, he spread his arms and swept them through the air and closed them over his chest. He then lifted his hands to the sky and offered the pipes to the Great Spirit, proclaiming, "We have them. The Great Spirit has given our enemy into our power."[28]

When Sitting Bull finished the dance, he sang out the full meaning of his vision, exclaiming: "The Great Spirit has given our enemies to us. We are to destroy them. We do not know who they are. They may be soldiers." The thronging Lakotas and Cheyennes were mesmerized. Hundreds of onlookers joined Sitting Bull in his song of triumph and thanksgiving, a massed crescendo rising above the camp and filling the people with a new hope that they could endure in the buffalo country.[29]

In the Black Hills, mining parties continued to evade the army's porous cordon and were scouring nearly every rivulet in the central Hills, and they had Sioux agencies and agents on edge. If an answer existed to this growing crisis, it apparently only existed in Washington. Already a delegation was forming at the White River agencies to visit the Great Father and discuss these concerns. Whites conveniently believed such a visit might soften the Indians on the question of relinquishing the gold country, a point alluded to by John Collins barely a month earlier. In preliminary talks with Saville at Red Cloud Agency, Red Cloud himself insisted that Crazy Horse be included in the delegation. Acknowledging Crazy Horse's outsized influence in Oglala affairs, the agent sent messengers to the Northern Oglala camp, as if believing that the chief and an ally, Black Twin, might somehow be induced to participate. Crazy Horse's reply was curt, urging only that the delegation be heavily weighted with traditionals. Ultimately thirteen Oglalas and six Brulés traveled to Washington in May 1875, where they joined representatives from Cheyenne River and Grand River. All were agency people but not necessarily accommodationists, and none were amenable to opening the Black Hills. The effort was a resounding failure.[30]

In a twist of fate, as the Sioux delegation passed Cheyenne headed east it encountered government surveyors assembling for a second exploration of the gold country. This one was to assess the merits of the Black Hills mineralization more carefully and perhaps even determine a fair value. The effort seemed of little relevance to the Indian delegates, however. Red Cloud and Spotted Tail told the scientists they only wanted the miners removed.[31]

The ensuing exploration was commonly known as the Newton-Jenney Expedition, after its principal geologists Henry Newton and Walter P. Jenney, both late of the Columbia School of Mines. Supporting the pair was a sizeable corps of scientists and engineers, plus customary newsmen and yet another photographer. An infantry and cavalry escort assembled at Fort Laramie, this one much smaller than the one accompanying Custer in 1874. Custer's was foremost a military expedition. Doubtless, the simple fact that Custer had traveled so largely unthreatened also was a factor in this planning. Departing Fort Laramie in late May the Newton-Jenney Expedition threaded its way northward to a point near present-day Newcastle, Wyoming, where it turned into the Hills and eventually reached the same streambeds that Custer's prospectors had worked the year before.[32]

Jenney's assessments of gold were disheartening. French Creek was at best an intermittent stream with little grade and inconsequential water.

Mining prospects did improve somewhat as the scientists ventured northward onto Spring, Castle, and Rapid Creeks. Jenney thought those placers would pay but probably not sufficiently to cover the costs of hydraulic mining. While Jenney found gold enough to prompt the settlement of the Black Hills, he believed that after the placers were exhausted stock raising would become the principal livelihood of the inhabitants. But the newsmen threw Jenney's cautions aside, trumpeting GOLD FOUND IN ABUNDANCE, one account declaring that prospectors were taking "gold at the rate of from $5 to $25 a pan."[33]

While Custer had encountered Stabber's small band of Oglalas in the Hills in 1874, a year later the Newton-Jenney Expedition chanced onto no Indians at all, just occasional abandoned hunting camps. Instead, Spotted Tail found them. Sitting Bull and the Northern Indians had long been contemptuous of Spotted Tail, who so pragmatically embraced Whites and the cultural transformations inherent in the Fort Laramie Treaty, but the wily fifty-two-year-old Brulé had never forsaken the interests of his people. That summer after returning from Washington he persuaded his agent, Edwin Howard, to join him and other Brulé chiefs on their own exploration of the gold country. Their purpose was not to pocket riches but to satisfy their own curiosity about the richness of the country and the extent to which the government was fulfilling its promise of keeping the Hills clear of miners.[34]

In early August Spotted Tail's small entourage, including Agent Howard, several interpreters, and twelve Brulé chiefs and headmen, plainly traveling under a fluttering American flag, reached French Creek, which they found alive with miners. They passed the reoccupied stockade erected the previous winter by the first invaders to enter the Hills (and who were summarily evicted). Now, they found endless miners' shelters scattered along the creek bottom. The scene was disturbing and clearly showed the hollowness of the government's claim of removing trespassers. Spotted Tail met with some of the miners one evening and scolded them roundly for invading the Hills. He also watched men working the sluices and panning dirt. The gold recovery he viewed was miniscule, but for a few small particles in a pan. The chief was sure that the miners were deceiving him and letting much of the gold wash over with the sand. He and his entourage then posed for two stereographic images taken by the exploring expedition's photographer.[35]

Before departing French Creek, one of the Newton-Jenney newsmen sought an interview with the chief. The two had encountered each other before, apparently in Cheyenne, and the exchange was cordial but to the point. "I have come to see the White man dig gold," Spotted Tail declared. "I want to see so as to know for myself. There is much talk about this country. The Whites want it. I want to see it before I let them have it." Spotted Tail acknowledged that he previously had known of gold in the Black Hills and was afraid of Whites going there and finding it. The reporter pressed the matter of the Indians selling the Hills, and Spotted Tail's reply first touched the duplicity evident everywhere. "I would like for the Great Paper Man to give one of his papers to the Great Father. Tell him to come here so that he can see for himself that there are miners here; that his government, in letting them come and stay here, is violating the treaty, and failing to keep the promises made to the Sioux."[36]

The reporter pressed the sale issue again. "Are you willing now to sell the country to the Great Father for a just price?" "Of course, the Sioux are going to sell the Black Hills," Spotted Tail replied, but "if the Great Father wants it, he must pay a big price."[37]

An army officer witnessing the interview added a compelling detail in an account he provided a different newspaper. Asked whether there will be a war with the Northern Indians, Spotted Tail spoke realistically and from the heart. "I don't want to go to war on either side. I want to be at peace. [But] the Indians are all angry because the miners are in this country."[38]

By now the government had evolved its own preferred if predictable solution. Instead of futilely attempting to exclude Whites from the Black Hills it would aggressively pursue negotiating a new agreement with the

Lakotas for the purchase of the gold country. In southern Sioux Country the notion was timeworn, having been broached repeatedly, as with Collins in March, in the meetings with Red Cloud, Spotted Tail, and the others in Washington in May, and by the newsman in the face-to-face encounter with Spotted Tail most recently. In the wake of the failed negotiations in Washington, President Grant authorized the appointment of a commission to treat with the Sioux for the relinquishment of the Black Hills as well as other lands and entitlements farther west. By late August seven commissioners led by Senator William Allison of Iowa passed through Fort Laramie, where they were joined by John Collins as the commission's secretary, all bound for the White River agencies.[39]

As the Black Hills tempest erupted in the south, the Northern Indians enjoyed a certain normalcy in the Yellowstone country. When not tormenting the Crows or the little Fort Pease traders hovel, they performed the Sun Dance and went hunting. But such reverie was interrupted when some seventy-five Oglalas and Brulés from the White River agencies found their way to the summer camps then sprawled along the Tongue River. The entourage was led by Young Man Afraid of His Horses, a distinguished warrior in the days of the Bozeman Trail War and an individual much like Red Cloud with great influence in Oglala affairs. Within the delegation were two agency interpreters, one of them Louis Richard (known as Reshaw in Indian Country), plus Frank Grouard, the puzzling Sandwich Islander who had recently surfaced at Red Cloud Agency after living several years in the Northern camps. Bearing gifts of tobacco, Young Man Afraid had come to encourage the Northern people's participation in a council convening soon at Red Cloud Agency. The council's purpose was to discuss ceding the Black Hills to the government.[40]

The wheedling took place both individually and in a massive council, with Young Man Afraid and his cohorts extending and explaining the government's invitation. Everything about the intent seemed abhorrent to the Northern people. Grouard, the lone observer offering an account of the episode, remembered that Crazy Horse told him face to face that he had no intention of going but would not oppose any of his people doing so. Ultimately, as many as a thousand people attended the internal council and no one favored making a treaty. Big Breast, a Brulé in the Oglala camp, was among the first to speak, telling everyone that he did not want to part with the land, but if anyone present was "in favor of selling their land from their children, let them go." Sitting Bull's was the most strident voice of all. In a long harangue directed principally at Louis Richard, he said that he was not going in. He was no agency Indian. He told Richard to "tell the Great Father that I do not want to sell or lease any land to the government." Reaching down for a pinch of dirt, he said with a dramatic flourish, "not even as much as this." Over the next few hours nearly one hundred more Indians expressed similar resolve.[41]

The great summer camp dispersed soon after Young Man Afraid's delegation departed. For the most part the Miniconjous, Sans Arcs, and Hunkpapas preferred remaining aloof in the Yellowstone Country, as did some Oglalas and Cheyennes. But two sizeable bands of Cheyennes and Oglalas separated from the northern fold. After Young Man Afraid's departure the Cheyennes counseled separately and many embraced visiting the White River Agency, drawn less by the Black Hills matter as the prospects of being fed. Hunting had been difficult for the Cheyennes that season and government food was always a lure. While Little Wolf and Morning Star led their followers to the Pine Ridge, other Cheyenne notables, including Old Man Chief Old Bear and council chiefs Box Elder and Black Eagle, opted to lead their people to familiar northern haunts, a decision with devastating consequences a few months hence.[42]

The Northern Oglalas had a different strategy. Young Man Afraid and interpreter Louis Richard reported to Agent Saville that attitudes about the Hills were divided in the Oglala camp and that some were coming in, notably among them the avowed traditional, Little Big Man, and perhaps Crazy Horse and Black Twin, too. Those Oglalas "will agree to any treaty . . . made by the Indians at this agency," Saville ecstatically reported to the

Commissioner of Indian Affairs. Saville was delusional. He and the messengers had entirely misunderstood the Oglala's intent. Those people ventured southward from Tongue River toward Bear Lodge Butte—Devil's Tower—to hunt in the midst of favored ground, and to monitor the coming summit at Red Cloud Agency. From there Little Big Man would lead followers to the agency, but not to embrace any treaty action ceding the Black Hills. Rather, his intent was to obstruct the proceedings in any way possible.[43]

A successful Black Hills council might well have been a crowning achievement for the Grant Administration. It would climax peaceably an unforeseen and painful economic and political nightmare, and in consequence also forestall or even avert an expensive Indian war. Instead, Commissioner Allison was charged with achieving an outcome unattainable in Sioux Country, and the affair proved a blistering sore from the start. The gold country brimmed with miners, and the Sioux, agency dwellers and Northerners alike, were largely unwilling to yield any more of their current homeland. That homeland had already suffered a diminishing blow when the Republican River buffalo country was stripped from the Sioux. Impediments of other sorts also arose. After squabbling for days over where to conduct the commission's business, whether at one or another of the White River agencies or somewhere between, the southern chiefs consented finally to meet on a plain above the White River nearer Red Cloud Agency, just north of Crow Buttes, a revered landmark from another day. Crowning the location was a singularly tall cottonwood tree, ever after heralded as the Council or Lone Tree.[44]

The gathering quickly proved to be no mere enclave of White River people. Allison estimated an attendance of 4,500. John Collins thought it was many thousands more, including agents and sizeable contingents from the distant Standing Rock, Cheyenne River, and Lower Brulé Agencies, plus scattered Yanktonais and Santees, and Cheyennes and Arapahos, atop thousands from the local agencies. In this midst, as well, were as many as four hundred Northern Indians, mostly Oglala adherents of Little Big Man, and all stalwart opponents of any sale. After his arrival Little Big Man alone sowed discord in all the camps and soon enough threatened the proceeding itself.[45]

The Lakotas counseled among themselves continuously. They knew what they faced and understood the fundamental questions: would they sell the Black Hills, and for how much? Spotted Tail's views were commonly quoted. Yes they would sell, he often declared beforehand, for $6 million. Newspaper accounts and Allison's report noted that figure, but other figures as well: $7 million, $30 million, $50 million. Plainly, some Lakotas were open to such a sale at the start, and others to long-term leasing arrangements, but those were views of agency people who understood accommodation as an accepted way of life. Little Big Man, present at many of the internal councils, continually threatened the chiefs, telling them that he would kill them if they signed any treaty. Plainly, his obstructive view was taking hold.[46]

The proceedings opened on September 20, the commissioners seated beneath a grand canvas awning facing northward, the council tree behind them. Opposite were representatives from the gathered agencies seated in a crescent. In Allison's preliminary remarks he addressed both the mining ground in the Black Hills and the government's oddly-timed desire for reclaiming the hunting lands west of there to the summits of the Big Horn Mountains in Wyoming—the unceded lands of the Fort Laramie Treaty. One chronicler later rightly labeled the Big Horn rhetoric as a "supremely stupid move," particularly in light of the already nearly insurmountable obstacle at hand. Allison realized quickly that he faced two disparate audiences, one seemingly willing to sell the Hills if a large price could be obtained, and a smaller but resolute lot who opposed parting with the Hills whatever the consideration.[47]

Attitudes steeled on September 23 when Little Big Man, whom Agent Saville had earlier called the "most irreconcilable of the 'Hostiles,'" led some fifty painted, armed, and mounted warriors into a gap in the council arena.

Small, muscular and nearly naked, his scarred breast freshly painted, and with eyes that gleamed wickedly, Little Big Man lofted a Winchester in one hand and a belt of cartridges in the other and bellowed that he would kill any commissioner who would steal his land. Warriors behind him dashed right and left as if anticipating or even willingly provoking a fight, and some of them singing, "The Black Hills is my land and I love it, and whoever interferes will hear this gun."[48]

One of the interpreters looked at Allison and blurted, it "looks like hell to pay here in a few minutes." The small complement of troops guarding the commissioners deployed and faced down the challengers. Amazingly, no shots were fired, largely through the speedy intercession of Young Man Afraid of His Horses and an Oglala who also bore the name Sitting Bull. The two had ridden forward to challenge the Northerners, Sitting Bull gripping an engraved Henry rifle given him by President Grant just that spring for interceding in the so-called flag pole affair at the agency. He would kill "the first Indian who fired a shot," he proclaimed. When Young Man Afraid and Sitting Bull positioned their own followers between the commissioners and their angry kinsmen, Little Big Man and the Northerners gave way, riding to a hill nearby. But the strident Northerner had succeeded in delivering a powerful message of opposition.[49]

The Little Big Man episode colored the proceedings from then on. In the days after, the commissioners heard from the leading chiefs of the various bands, and their responses were clearly shaped by Little Big Man's rhetoric. Spotted Bear, a Miniconjou from Cheyenne River, called the Black Hills a "big safe. Our Great Father has one, and so have we. That is the reason we can't come to a conclusion very quickly." Red Dog, an Oglala, was slightly conciliatory, declaring that "we want to be taken care of for seven generations ahead," and might give up the Black Hills, "where there is gold, in the center, [but] not to include the pine." Stabber, the aged Oglala who had confronted Custer the year before, told Allison: "Give us as many millions as we have asked, [because] we know that those hills will support us for seven generation to come." Even Red Cloud and Spotted Tail, plainly amenable to a sale before the council began, moderated their tone. Red Cloud demanded compensations of many confusing sorts—money, cattle, horses, wagons, clothing, arms, ammunition, mowers, scythes, furniture—and for generations. The demands baffled the commissioners. Plainly, enthusiasm for the sale was waning.[50]

The question of price, whether monetary or material support for generations, was never resolved. For their part, the commissioners played an illogically poor hand, variously offering $400,000 annually for the mining rights in an agreement running until the gold ran out, when the land would revert to the Sioux. Or perhaps they might receive $6 million, payable in fifteen equal annual installments. Amid sharpening frustration, the discussions drew to a close. Little Big Man and the hardliners had prevailed. Allison returned to Washington frustrated and bitter. In his report on the failed Black Hills purchase attempt, he angrily blamed the Northern Indians for the standoff and declared that the spirit and temper of the Sioux would never change until those people had felt the power of the government. Northern traditionals and agency residents alike only saw themselves as being robbed.[51]

After his standoff with the Black Hills commissioners at the Lone Tree, Little Big Man and the other Northerners fled the Pine Ridge Country for Crazy Horse's camp. It had moved northwestward in the intervening weeks, crossing the shallow divide from the hunting grounds in the Bear Lodge Butte country to the Powder River valley and then continuing farther west onto Otter Creek, a lush tributary of the Tongue. Along the way, Lone Horn or One Horn, a venerable old Miniconjou in the Northerners' mix, separated and continued to Sitting Bull's camp, then at the mouth of the Powder. During the proceedings in the south, Lone Horn had scolded Red Cloud, Spotted Tail, and the others who seemed so willing to sell the Hills, calling them selfish and cheap. "We are not the only ones in the Sioux nation," he implored. "Raise up your heads and look to the north and the west. There are Sioux still out." Sitting Bull was pleased when he heard this and praised his friend. "Brother, it is well that you have said that; these hills are a treasure to us Indians."[52]

Lone Horn died that winter. Some said it was on account of watching the Black Hills fall to the Whites. The purchase attempt had failed, but the Whites were not deterred. As Black Elk, the elder, told his young son, "the Black Hills would be just like melting snow held in our hands, because the *wasicus* would take that country anyway." White possession did not occur quickly, but that fall and winter prospectors continually strengthened their presence in the gold country. Red Cloud and the others complained of this continually, and the Great Father and his soldiers did nothing about it.[53]

Little Big Man's followers were not the only Pine Ridge people to depart the White River country that fall. Big Road, an Oglala traditional who often frequented Red Cloud Agency but preferred the Powder River buffalo country, led his followers to Crazy Horse's camp. Primarily, he wished to hunt, but he also wanted to escape the frantic chaos in the Pine Ridge. Young Black Elk, an alert twelve-year-old Oglala in the band and much later an important informant of events associated with Sitting Bull's War, provided his biographer with a careful description of the journey, measured as always by landmarks encountered along the way—Warbonnet Creek, Sage Creek, the Plains of the Pine Trees, Powder River, and the Tongue. He was describing a common pathway from the Pine Ridge to the buffalo country that others had labeled the Powder River Trail. Big Road's people encountered buffalo when reaching the Powder and slowed their pace to lay in meat and robes, but in due course they continued to the Tongue and the Northern Oglala camp.[54]

Others headed north that fall as well. Agent Saville reported to the Commissioner of Indian Affairs in mid-October that many Indians were leaving his agency for the Tongue and Yellowstone, supposedly to hunt. Most were leaving their families behind, he noted. "There appears to be no hostile feeling," he thought. Cheyennes and Arapahos were among those fleeing, including Little Wolf's people. Little Wolf had come from the north when summoned in August and attended the great council, telling Commissioner Allison that the Cheyennes also had an interest in the Black

Hills. He wanted guns, ammunition, and money. The White man would become rich. "We want him to make us rich also." He was ignored.[55]

The Black Hills matter reverberated throughout the Northern Indian camps that winter but for the most part the people seem to have taken the intrusion in stride. By now Lakota and Cheyenne traditionals had experienced White duplicity for generations, and the cycle of events in the 1870s were merely its present form. Sitting Bull and his followers wished only to be left alone, to live an independent existence mirroring a time when the Lakotas maintained firm control of their homeland, when their buffalo culture flourished, and when traders and trading posts in Sioux Country were just enough to satisfy their wants. But some among them could also be prophetic. Late in life, Eagle Elk, an Oglala traditional customarily in one of the northern camps, likened his world to a big island, with the *wasicus* like great waters washing all around it, nibbling off the edges, and the island getting smaller, smaller, smaller. This notion may have been his own, or perhaps it was the metaphorical contrivance of the old man's biographer, but it was apt. Sitting Bull, Crazy Horse, and the Lakotas and Cheyennes huddled through another bitter northern plains winter likely with no sense of the enormous political storm then gathering against them. The reservation and its agencies, the new military posts, the succession of railway surveys, the persistent invasion of Sioux Country by explorers and traders and most recently by miners, and now the theft of their "Heart of the Earth," all this was surely foreboding.[56]

In Washington on November 3, a gathering at the White House sealed the Northerners fate. Present that day was President Grant, who called the meeting, his Secretary of War, William Belknap, Secretary of the Interior, Zachariah Chandler, one of Chandler's assistants, Commissioner of

Indian Affairs, Edward P. Smith, and two army generals, Sheridan from Chicago, and George Crook, newly arrived in Omaha and commanding the sprawling Department of the Platte encompassing the entire southern half of Sioux Country. The Black Hills gold rush weighed heavily on Grant, as did treaty obligations with the Sioux. The nation's interests, still embroiled in the devastating Panic of 1873, welcomed the complete opening of the Black Hills. Until now, Grant had stood with the Indians and was the one who imposed the army's interdiction efforts. While that was proving a near impossibility, the removal orders remained in place.[57]

If official minutes or notes of the meeting were taken, none are known to survive. But chatter afterward from several of the attendees and orders rippling through War Department channels in subsequent weeks make abundantly clear what was discussed that day.

Certainly, the president and his attendees addressed the Black Hills situation head-on. The country needed this economic boost, both to its financial markets and the relief a gold rush afforded an underemployed population. Crook brought the most current news, having visited the gold country in August where he met with miners, saw actual placer gold, and orchestrated his own removal effort. Even now troops remained in the midst of the French Creek diggings ensuring that miners were not working that ground. Grant acknowledged that he could not openly ignore the guarantees and prohibitions in the Fort Laramie Treaty and would not rescind previous orders forbidding this occupation by miners. But he finessed the matter by ordering the withdrawal of troops from their policing and interdiction duties, thus quietly permitting the rush to ensue. The thinking may simply have been that in light of the failed Black Hills purchase attempt at Red Cloud Agency, perhaps a flood of prospectors would induce the Sioux to negotiate a sale after all. Within days interdiction activities in both the Departments of Dakota and Platte ceased, evidenced most directly when the complement of troops on French Creek withdrew and returned to Fort Laramie. The army would not impede the Black Hills gold rush any longer.[58]

The White House conferees certainly also discussed the Northern Indians. Little Big Man's disruptive behavior at the Allison Commission proceedings was chilling and begged a reflection on the similar repeated obstructions exhibited by the non-treaty people since the time of the Fort Laramie Treaty. As the Washington conferees saw it, they were one Lakota people. No one distinguished traditionals from non-traditionals or Northerners from agency people, although figureheads like Crazy Horse, Sitting Bull, and now Little Big Man stood out. Furthermore there existed an established reservation for the Sioux people, with individual agencies for each of the subtribes. The questions now were simply how and when to make the non-treaty people embrace the reservation. A precedent already existed. Sheridan's army had just waged a successful war on the southern plains against the Southern Cheyennes, Comanches, and Kiowas, forcing them onto reservations in the Indian Territory. The conferees easily agreed that the time had come to force the non-treaty people living in the Yellowstone Country to submit. Crook later quoted Grant as saying that the Sioux must go to the reservation "or be whipped." On this point there was no disagreement in the White House.[59]

Figuring in this growing call for war was a report received by Commissioner Smith on November 9, submitted by Erwin C. Watkins, an Indian Service inspector working directly for the Commissioner. Watkins was a long-time roving agent for the Indian Service. In this instance, he was charged with investigating "the attitude and condition of certain wild and hostile bands of Sioux Indians in Dakota and Montana." Almost certainly before embarking on his tour into Sioux Country Watkins was briefed on or more likely read a communication from the commanding officer at Fort Ellis, near Bozeman. Dated March 8, 1875, it had subsequently circulated widely in the War and Interior Departments. The Fort Ellis commander's letter was a scathing indictment of Sitting Bull and his followers, noting the country the chief and traditionals occupied, the identities of the various bands and band leaders who rallied with him, their collective open hostility toward Whites, their ease of trade for arms and ammunition, their ability to lure agency warriors to their fold, always fully armed and mounted, and in all a people proving a perfect obstacle to peace from north of the Platte to the British line. The letter seethed with invective in an oddly similar manner to Watkins's report eight months later. Watkins, it seems, knew how to frame his questions, and already knew the answers.[60]

While Jenney was surveying the Black Hills gold country and Allison attempted to buy that land, Watkins traveled the Upper Missouri country interviewing agents and agency residents. His report of November 9 was explosive, especially when coming on the heels of the disastrous purchase effort in September and the consequential White House meeting that had just occurred. Watkins pointed fingers, calling Sitting Bull and the other chiefs and head men following him as "untamable and hostile." They roamed freely over Western Dakota and Eastern Montana, he noted, including the rich valleys of the Yellowstone and Powder Rivers in what was "probably the best hunting ground in the United States, [and] a Paradise for Indians."[61]

Those Sitting Bull Indians "have never accepted aid or been brought under control," Watkins lamented, and they boast that "United States authorities are not strong enough to conquer them." And they claimed, moreover, to be the "Sovereign Rulers of the land," and to "own the wood, the water, the ground, and the air." Watkins plainly gathered his information from agency Indians living along the Missouri in Dakota and Montana, people largely at odds with their tradition-minded kin in the buffalo country, and whose anxiety was palpable. Sitting Bull's people were rich in horses and robes, Watkins observed, and thoroughly armed with breech-loading guns, pistols, and bows and arrows. "Fortunate indeed is the man who meets them [and] escapes with his scalp."[62]

At one point Watkins branded the Sitting Bull Indians "as uncivilized and savage as when Lewis and Clark first passed through their country." But it was plainly apparent, even then, that Watkins never understood the venerable forty-five-year-old Hunkpapa, his followers, or their world, at one critical point assuring Commissioner Smith that those "Indians number, all told, but a few hundred warriors, and these are never all together, or under the control of one chief." "One thousand men under the command of an experienced officer, sent into their country in the winter," he wrote, "would be amply sufficient for their capture or punishment." Agents at

Cheyenne River, Fort Yates, and Fort Peck certainly knew better, and so would have Saville at Red Cloud Agency, whom Watkins never spoke with. A knowledgeable contemporary later called the inspector's work simple "fiction." But in the end it was Watkins's vitriol and numbers . . . a few hundred warriors . . . one thousand men under the command of an experienced officer . . . and notions of finally ending Lakota nomadism that captivated the Washington elites. His admonition to "send troops against them in the winter, the sooner the better, and whip them into subjection," circulated widely and quickly, including to Sheridan and Crook, with whom Watkins apparently met personally.[63]

At the White House meeting Grant sanctioned war. So too did Interior Secretary Chandler and Commissioner of Indian Affairs Smith. Watkins bolstered their case with his incendiary report. They agreed to lead this campaign with a summons. On December 3 Secretary Chandler instructed Commissioner Smith to order the Sioux Indians living beyond the bounds of the Great Sioux Reservation to remove themselves to their respective agencies before January 31, 1876, and remain there or be "regarded as hostile and turned over to the military." Chandler's instruction and Smith's letters to the agents formed the official edict upon which Sitting Bull's War, or what others soon called the Great Sioux War, was grounded.[64]

For Sitting Bull, Crazy Horse, and the Lakota and Cheyenne traditionals clinging fervently to a life in the buffalo country, a cannon fuse was lit.

5
WAR COMES TO THE CHEYENNES FIRST

"At Powder River the soldiers attacked our camp and destroyed everything, and that made us mad."

—Two Moon, Northern Cheyenne

December was a difficult time to declare an Indian war, at least as President Grant had unleashed it. The firebrand US Indian Inspector Erwin Watkins, who had so recently surveyed the Lakota agencies in the Upper Missouri Country, favored sending troops against Sitting Bull's people immediately, in the winter, "when the Indians are nearly always in camp, and at which season of year they are the most helpless." That, of course, was already a well understood maxim in military circles. Winter campaigning was most promising when weather conditions were brutal, the grazing thin, the ponies were stressed, and the simple thoughts in Indian camps focused on mere survival until the renewal of spring. Watkins's counsel notwithstanding, Interior Secretary Zachariah Chandler first framed Grant's consent to this war in an edict, an odd, perhaps even well intended ultimatum to the Northern people to submit at one or another of the Sioux agencies before January 31, 1876, or face an unleashed army. It proved a fool's gambit, and was troubled from the start.[1]

The charge of distributing Chandler's ultimatum passed first to the Commissioner of Indian Affairs, Edward Smith, who transmitted the directive by mail to the various agents administering the agencies serving the Great Sioux Reservation, and also to Fort Peck, haven of Sitting Bull's Hunkpapas. Because none of the agencies were connected by telegraph, the letters took two to three weeks to reach the Nebraska and Dakota agents. In one instance, it took nearly four weeks, and to snowbound Fort Peck fully seven weeks, within days of the letter's ultimatum.[2]

In due course the respective operatives acknowledged receiving the communication and commenced a response. In several instances, the directive was passed on rather passively to local agency Indians with an added charge that *they* carry the order to "Sitting Bull and the other wild bands." The agents at Lower Brule and Crow Creek on the very margins of this developing tumult acknowledged Smith's letter but rather dismissively reported that Sitting Bull and the other wild and lawless Indians did not visit their agencies. The last operative to receive the communique, William Alderson, agent at Fort Peck, endeavored first to send a reliable White courier to the Northern camp, but when that failed sought to induce friendly Indians to carry the message.[3]

White Bull, Sitting Bull's Miniconjou nephew, remembered the season as a bad one, a harsh winter with much snow. He later recollected that no runners came telling them to come to the agency. Travelers, yes, he said, but no runners. Ironically, in too many instances conveying the summons became the burden imposed on agency people, mostly kin, charged with the onerous task of warning family and friends of a government demand to forego a lifeway on the buffalo prairie or face a war.[4]

James Hastings, successor to Saville at Red Cloud Agency, dispatched a bevy of couriers to the Northern Oglala and Northern Cheyenne camps in January. As with other agents, Hastings's effort was confounded by deep snows but also at Red Cloud by prospective couriers demanding an onerous reward for their services. They wanted presents worth at least one hundred fifty dollars. Hastings's gifts in the end amounted to tobacco and cloth. Short Bull, youngest brother of He Dog, remembered that as many as one hundred people went out from the agency to coax the Northern Oglalas in. The bands of Crazy Horse, He Dog, Holy Bald Eagle (Black Twin), and Big Road questioned the couriers and chose to deliberate the matter in a grand council convened on the Upper Tongue. Some agreed to comply, but mostly they were hunting then, Short Bull recalled. "They had to shoot for tipis," but they would come to the agency in the spring, he remembered. Young Black Elk, in Crazy Horse's camp, was perplexed by the runners from the Soldier Town. That was a foolish thing to say, he told his biographer. "It was very cold and many of our people and ponies would have died in the snow. Also, we were in our own country and were doing no harm." Hastings, when eventually reporting on the Oglala response, allowed that he had not received any word as yet from couriers sent to the Cheyenne camp, located on the Tongue one hundred miles beyond the Oglala camp.[5]

Black Elk's reflection that the Northerners were in their own country and doing no harm nicely captured a general sentiment in the camps. So did Short Bull's, allowing that some, maybe many people would return in the spring when it was possible to travel easily again. Until then the people were contentedly hunting buffalo and surviving the winter. The Cheyenne River agent, Horace Bingham, reported a similar response when his couriers returned. The "hostiles," in Bingham's language, received the invitation and warning in good spirit, he wrote, and without ill feeling. They were hunting buffalo presently but come early spring "they will visit this agency to dispose of their robes and skins, when the question as to their future movements can be thoroughly discussed."[6]

Cheyenne reaction was divided, much as in the other Northern camps. Like so many of their allies among the Northern Oglalas, the Cheyennes had kinship ties to the White River and even among Southern Cheyennes in the Indian Territory. No one wanted a war. In the face of the hard winter, the Northern Cheyenne bands mostly resolved to endure the season but then come in. Such was the determination particularly of Old Bear, Box Elder,

Black Eagle, Two Moon, and their followers. They would come in, but only when the weather moderated.[7]

John Burke at Standing Rock actually engaged a messenger to carry Smith's edict to Sitting Bull's camp, but that runner was intercepted en route and his horse taken from him. Thwarted, Burke requested an extension of time to fulfill his obligation and give Sitting Bull more time to comply. He then engaged Johnny Bruguier in a second attempt to relay the critical edict. Bruguier was a well-known local mixed-blood of Yankontai-French Canadian heritage. Educated in Saint Louis, he was fluent in the Sioux language, his mother's tongue. The Sioux called him "Big Leggins" for the heavy leather chaps he favored.[8]

Of these concerted efforts to contact the Northern people, Burke's resonated more than any other because Bruguier and the thwarted courier before him were purposefully directed to Sitting Bull's camp. Sitting Bull had long ago emerged as the dominant Lakota figurehead on the northern plains. While Crazy Horse had gained notoriety in various confrontations in the Pine Ridge Country, and Little Big Man was remembered as the foremost instigator of the recent Black Hills purchase foment, Sitting Bull was recognized all along by Indians and Whites as the one individual whose demeanor and aura rallied like-minded traditionals to an original way of life. It was Sitting Bull who led the fierce resistance in the recent cycle of intrusions, whether by action or word. His resolve, characterized as obstructive by so many, had captured the nation's attention as he rebuffed surveyors and exploiters probing the interior of Sioux Country, as well as White House conferees, investigator Watkins, newspapermen, and now Chandler and Smith. Smith's edict to the Sioux agents in this surge to war was not simply a challenge to lure the last of the traditionals to the reservation, but to compel Sitting Bull's submission.

Bruguier was nearly a month in locating Sitting Bull's camp, then on the Lower Tongue. And once he arrived, he was slow to gain credibility. Some thought him a spy sent by the army, but Sitting Bull took a liking to him and admired his bravery for delivering a message despite the danger of winter travel. Remarkably, the two struck up a friendship and by one account the chief adopted him as a brother, much as had occurred with Frank Grouard several years earlier. The chief plied Bruguier with questions every evening as they sat by the open fire in his lodge. In Josephine Waggoner's version, the more the chief learned, the sadder he became. Bruguier warned that armies were ready to march against him as soon as weather permitted. In Waggoner's telling, the old chief knew that this lifeway was coming to an end.[9]

Early in 1876 it was plain to the agents across the Great Sioux Reservation that the Northerners belonging to their respective agencies were not returning in any appreciable numbers. Each agent had done his part to convey the notice, whether placing the burden on the shoulders of local residents or by specifically engaging messengers. Hazy reports that Northerners would return in the spring were meaningless. To the agents in the field and to Smith and Chandler above them, January 31 was an inflexible deadline. On February 3 Sitting Bull's people—the hostile Sioux—having refused to comply with the summons, were turned over to the War Department "for such action on the part of the Army as [they] may deem proper." Grant, Sherman, and Sheridan now had their war.[10]

The prospect of an all-out war on the northern plains was difficult to imagine in the Indian camps that winter, but not so at the Sioux agencies, where on January 17 operatives were instructed by Washington to cease selling arms and ammunition to all residents. Already agents had been carefully monitoring this traffic, with licensed traders in their realms duly filing regular reports on all such transactions. Never once did their business appear irregular. The new order, however, restrained the agents all the more and they in turn asked, if rhetorically, how residents would then kill their beef cattle or hunt the small game in the vicinity? Agents likewise defended their residents, characterizing them as disciplined and evincing no hostile dispositions. But then agents imposed the restriction on weapons sales—and watched young men leave the agencies and not return. Hearing this, new Indian Commissioner John Q. Smith was unmoved.[11]

At the same time agents, licensed traders, and Indian inspectors pointed to related problems. A licensed trader at Cheyenne River admonished his agent, asserting, for example, that denying regulated trade would only drive the business to "unscrupulous Whites and half breeds." Another trader pointed to the recognized, sometimes vigorous gun sales occurring beyond local jurisdictions, whether by so-called nighttime trading known to be occurring in the outback or in open trading with Indians and intermediaries occurring in places like Bismarck, terminus of the Northern Pacific Railroad, where Indians could "purchase all the guns and ammunition that they could find the means to pay for." Or, they could trade with the Métis, the ever annoying Red River mixed-bloods from Canada. Reports of gun trading with the Canadian Métis indeed remained common in the Fort Peck region on the Upper Missouri, but more recently the commanding officer at the Cheyenne River Agency post noted illicit trading between Métis and Indians as far south as Bear Butte, just north of the Black Hills.[12]

One independent trader operating in Brule City, across the Missouri from the Lower Brule Agency, openly challenged his local agent, insisting that such sales were entirely legal and that he would make a "test case" of it if a ban was imposed. The arms and ammunition dilemma perplexed government agents throughout the coming war, and similarly challenged Sitting Bull's people as they sought to replenish stocks of materials consumed in their own defense.[13]

The people in the Northern camps, meanwhile, mostly settled in for winter. As always, the bands were scattered along the Little Missouri or the lower reaches of the Powder and Tongue. Indian accounts make abundantly clear that four major concentrations of Lakotas and Cheyennes kept to the buffalo country that season. That land had been home for this generation of traditionals since the days of Red Cloud's War, which itself was already a decade in the past.

Short Bull, He Dog's brother, remembered encountering assembled Northern Oglalas on the Upper Tongue River when he and others delivered the government's ultimatum. Shave Elk (Thomas Disputed), an Oglala ordinarily aligned with Big Road's people, confirms this, as does He Dog himself. The Oglalas drifted down the Tongue later that winter and in the proximity of the mouth of Otter Creek, some sixty miles above the Tongue's mouth, they encountered another sizeable Indian group, the Cheyennes. Otter Creek, a secluded forty-mile-long Tongue River tributary, was a favorite Cheyenne wintering haven. A short while before, the Cheyennes had been visited by Last Bull, who brought his family to Old Bear's camp from the White River Agency. Last Bull carried dire news: "Soldiers are coming to fight you," he said. Soldiers intended to fight all the Cheyennes and Sioux who were living off the reservation. He did not know what forts they would come from or who would lead them, but the news, in the words of the great Cheyenne informant Wooden Leg, "disturb[ed] our peace of mind."[14]

In early March, a column of soldiers traveled down the Yellowstone from the mountainous west, reaching Fort Pease on March 4. They had come to relieve the beleaguered and besieged civilian complement at that place and escort it to Bozeman, its point of origin nine months earlier. The fort's inhabitants had given up all hope of successfully trading with the Crows and Sioux and gladly left behind an empty outpost. Still, they left an American flag fluttering overhead in perfect defiance. Only nineteen of its original forty-six men remained, the others having fled earlier or had been killed by the Sioux. The soldiers conducting the relief excursion encountered no resistance coming or going.[15]

The Oglala and Cheyenne camps combined and crossed over to the Powder River but then almost immediately began splintering. Old Bear's Cheyennes were the first to part, his people intent on heeding the government's summons. Their decision was doubtless guided by Old Bear himself, a fifty-four-year-old Cheyenne Old Man Chief, and perhaps hastened by soldier movement on the Yellowstone just days before and coming so closely on the heels of Last Bull's warning. Old Bear's course took his people up the Powder. The fervent but cautious traditional was embittered over the invasion of the Black Hills, but he was unwilling now to go to war with the Whites. He Dog and his followers, a small lot of eight or ten lodges, joined Old Bear's Cheyennes. The words of warning from his brother, Short Bull, may have driven his decision. The remaining Cheyennes parted as well. They headed down the Powder intent on joining Sitting Bull's camp or perhaps simply to hunt buffalo in that direction.[16]

Crazy Horse's and Big Road's people, meanwhile, continued eastward, traveling up the Little Powder River, perhaps bound as some thought for the Bear Lodge Butte and Belle Fourche countryside, normally a rich haven for buffalo. On that trail a short while later, the Oglala body divided again. Big Road and some thirty-five families made for the Pine Ridge. For those Cheyenne and Oglala bands departing for the south, the matter was simple. No one wanted war. Crazy Horse and Black Twin, meanwhile, elected to remain on the Little Powder. It was early March, the season of welcome warm winds and thawing on the northern plains.[17]

The Cheyennes remaining in the buffalo country continued down the Powder but instead of encountering Sitting Bull's camp came instead to the combined camps of Lame Deer's and Spotted Elk's Miniconjous. Those bands spent much of the winter on the lower Tongue, dividing their time between harassing Fort Pease, raiding the Crows, and hunting. The aligned Cheyenne-Miniconjou camps closed the late winter on the Yellowstone, camped near the mouth of the Powder.[18]

Sitting Bull spent the latter part of the winter on the Lower Tongue, where Bruguier had brought him word of the government summons. More recently he led his Hunkpapa followers down the Yellowstone to the mouth of the Powder. From there, although it was still late winter, he continued eastward cross-country to the Little Missouri Valley. Some of his people, including Gall and his followers, were frequent traders at Fort Berthold on the Missouri, below the mouth of the Little Missouri. There, working through intermediaries, their quest for munitions was foremost. But by early March Sitting Bull's people moved again, westward from the Little Missouri following Little Beaver Creek into the Blue Mountains in southeastern Montana.[19]

This continual drift of Sioux and Cheyenne bands along the major watercourses and drainages of the northern buffalo country belies the notion, at least as the Sioux agents and many later chroniclers assessed it, that these Northerners were mostly a snowbound people unable to return to the agencies as summoned. That particular winter was indeed a difficult one, and the snows impeded movement, but the Northern people were not immobile. Normal camp needs—fuel, fodder, sanitation—and routines necessitated moving from time to time, even in winter. Wooden Leg, the Cheyenne, plainly explained to his biographer that bands moved to and from the hunting grounds all the time. The messengers that January were honest about this. But the Northerners seemed defiant also or plainly oblivious to the forces gathering against them. Dire warnings like that delivered by Last Bull to Old Bear's Cheyennes were an exception.[20]

Old Bear's Cheyennes and a small scattering from the other bands and He Dog's cluster of Oglalas tallied together perhaps seventy-five occupied lodges (an official army count on March 17 of 105 lodges included an untold number of wickiups and shelters). They were perhaps 475 people in all as they made their way up the Powder. They had nearly reached the mouth of Thompson Creek, almost to the Wyoming line, when the entourage was broadsided by a springtime blizzard. Such storms are commonplace on the plains in the spring when warm temperatures plummet suddenly, fierce winds howl, and heavy, wet snow buries the budding grasses. The people made no pretense about continuing southward but chose to wait out the storm and resume travel when the land had dried again sufficiently. As always, "wolves"—Indian scouts—covered their advance, and hunters, too, maintained a careful vigil. There was no indication of soldiers anywhere.

Last Bull's warning of soldiers coming for them had the camp's attention, but on that evening of March 16, in the chill of another wintery night, there seemed no cause for alarm. Besides, the people were heeding the government's directive.[21]

Before the snows flew that day or maybe the day before, the camp welcomed to its midst Little Wolf, another of the four Cheyenne Old Man Chiefs and also the Cheyenne Sweet Medicine Chief, meaning that he presided at major councils. Traveling alone likely from the downriver camp, Little Wolf had apparently come to visit his relative, Box Elder (also known as Maple Tree), a nearly blind, eighty-one-year-old holy man. Box Elder was the keeper of *Ox'zem*, a Cheyenne Sacred Wheel Lance possessing great spiritual power, including the ability to conceal the presence of Cheyennes from their enemies. Little Wolf was opposed to this seemingly inevitable war, but he was a brave military tactician and many in the camp were comforted knowing that he would help protect them if soldiers struck. Still, no one anticipated trouble.[22]

Old Bear's camp was nestled in a stand of dormant cottonwoods that ran along the west bank of the Powder. It was wedged protectively between a mostly frozen river on one side and a sharp twenty-foot-tall break, edging a higher open bench on the west side. Beyond the higher bench, hills rose dramatically, blocking any conventional passageway from that side. Intermittent cross-cutting drainages like Thompson Creek that sliced through every few miles provided some access, however. The camp's ponies, as many as eight or nine hundred, grazed the snow-covered bottomland surrounding the lodges and on the upper bench. No herders guarded the animals that frigid night.

Little did the camp know that soldiers were creeping upon them from another direction entirely that night, having threaded their own way through the lofty mountainscape in the west and now massing up Thompson Creek. They were guided to the village by none other than Frank Grouard, the mixed-blood who had resided in Sitting Bull's camp a few years earlier but more recently had gone over to the Whites at Red Cloud Agency. Army officers respected Grouard, who boasted that he "carried a map of the country" in his mind. "From the Platte river to the British possessions, and from the Black Hills to the Big Wind range of mountains," he claimed, "the country was an open book to me." Grouard believed that he had led the soldiers to Crazy Horse's camp because in the breaking morning light he saw lodges and ponies he had seen in the Oglala camp. In truth, he saw lodges and animals belonging to He Dog's people, and particularly a buffalo pony, a spotted one, very fast, that may actually have belonged to Crazy Horse but had been borrowed now by his friend. "I knew this village by the horses. Knew every horse there," Grouard later crowed.[23]

The soldiers, emerging from the recesses and crags of Thompson Creek, struck shortly after daybreak, coming from several directions, with some sweeping the ponies in their fore and others attacking the camp straight on from the south. An old man in the village who had risen early that morning and walked to the top of a nearby hill to pray saw the soldiers advancing and started screaming toward the camp: "The soldiers are right here! The soldiers are right here!" But it was too late. Black Eagle, whose tipi was on the south side of the camp, remembered bullets striking around him "like the patter of raindrops in a hard storm."[24]

The attack was a complete surprise. Women shrieked as bullets tore through the lodges. Children cried for their mothers. Old people scrambled to get out of the way. People rushed frantically from their homes in every direction, some carrying packs of precious belongings and others dragging children. The attack came from the south, so the people mostly fled northward through the cottonwoods, and kept that bearing until reaching the mouth of Flood Creek, the next drainage beyond, where they turned west and scrambled into its deep recesses.[25]

Warriors rallied, some assisting the vulnerable ones in their flight and others scrambling for weapons and ponies as they attempted to meet the initial assault. The only horses accessible were those few to the north and a few others scattered through the camp. Wooden Leg roped one. It belonged to Old Bear, the chief of the band, and it became Wooden Leg's war pony. He first assisted in carrying children to safety. Antelope Woman, better known later as Kate Big Head, remembered ruefully that the soldiers "got between our camp and our horse herd, so all of us had to run away afoot." That was a telling statement, adding burden in the painful days ahead. Old people needing help the most were assisted by warriors and able women. Elbow Woman, Box Elder's daughter, coaxed her father onto a pony and led him to safety, he all the while cradling the Sacred Wheel Lance in his arms.[26]

After assisting with the evacuation, warriors both mounted and afoot turned southward toward the village. Some took positions in a cluster of rocks that formed a perfect breastwork—the best on the field—on the high bench just northwest of the tipis. Others hid behind rocks on the rising ground fronting the towering hills in the west. Still others skittered to the trees in the bottomland and advanced toward their homes. All faced soldiers who had established lines across the northern and western periphery of the camp. Some warriors remembered Little Wolf's voice above the din, urging warriors to be strong and fight like men. An officer in the engagement recalled hearing of "an Indian chief in full war costume, riding and running up and down among his men on the cliffs, haranguing them and animating their valor." He had to be describing Little Wolf, though he labeled him Crazy Horse, every soldier's bogeyman.[27]

Several other episodes stand out. Powder Face, a Cheyenne warrior firing at the soldiers from behind trees, took aim at one and shot him through the head. A short while later after the soldier line was abandoned, he and two friends rushed the dead man and ceremonially touched him, an act of counting coup. Elsewhere Wooden Leg, Two Moon, and Bear Walks on a Ridge, skirting the icy river, encountered a wounded soldier struggling in the snow. Two Moon had a repeating rifle and fired at the soldier but missed. Bear Walks on a Ridge fired his muzzle-loading rifle and hit the man in the head. Another Cheyenne warrior joined them and they rushed the soldier and beat and stabbed him to death. The unnamed Cheyenne took the soldier's carbine. Wooden Leg took the man's coat.[28]

As the morning progressed the warriors watched in horror as soldiers began looting the tipis and then collapsing and firing them, destroying their contents—robes, munitions, fresh and dried buffalo meat and other foodstuffs, horse gear, clothing, personal possessions. The destruction began at the northern end of the camp and visibly progressed southward, lodge by lodge, until all the lodges were in smoky flames and ultimately reduced to ashes. "From a distance we saw the destruction of our village," Wooden Leg remembered. "The Cheyennes were rendered very poor. I had nothing left but the clothing I had on, with the soldier coat added. My eagle bone flute, my medicine pipe, my rifle, everything else of mine, w[as] gone." Two Moon likewise later reflected on the destruction. "At Powder River the soldiers attacked our camp and destroyed everything, and that made us mad."[29]

When the soldiers finished their fiery work and abandoned the camp one lodge remained standing. Inside was an old woman stretched out on a couch, sick. Grouard was summoned and interviewed her. She told him that Sitting Bull was down river some sixty miles and that this village belonged to Crazy Horse. She apparently was an Oglala and those details were truthful, if misleading without context. Indeed, Sitting Bull then was thought to be down river. And if an Oglala, she belonged to He Dog's band, which normally aligned with Crazy Horse. That little detail, added to Grouard having already seen Oglala ponies that morning, colored the identity of this village for decades to come. The old woman was left alone, Grouard dismissively noting, "as nobody in the command wanted her, she was left there."[30]

The soldiers departed in the early afternoon, riding southward. Warriors watched from a jutting bluff south of Thompson Creek. The last movement of the departure was the push of the corralled pony herd, driven by the army's handful of White and mixed-blood scouts. Warriors fired down on the herders. The last shots of the Powder River fight belonged to them.

That afternoon the Cheyennes assessed the destruction. Black Eagle remembered that after the soldiers went away the young men started back into the village. The stench of burned buffalo skin lodges, leather clothing, robes, meats, and furs overwhelmed the senses. Everything was reduced to piles of black smoldering rubble. Men and woman picked over the remains but found little to salvage. The clothing the people wore that morning when they fled their lodges was all they possessed. The people, too, saw the one standing lodge. "We went to it," remembered Wooden Leg. "There was the missing old blind woman. Her tepee and herself had been left entirely unharmed. We talked about this matter, all agreeing that the act showed the soldiers had good hearts." In light of it all, Wooden Leg's consideration seems striking.[31]

The people also tended their casualties. Antelope Woman remembered that "not many of our people were killed, but our tepees and everything that was in them were burned." Accounts tell of several warriors wounded and two Cheyennes killed, a young boy who was herding or gathering ponies that morning, and Chief Eagle, brother of White Hawk, shot in the abdomen early in the fight while also chasing horses. Chief Eagle's remains were elaborately wrapped by family members who swaddled him in a red blanket, a soldier overcoat, and a buffalo robe. They placed him in a stony niche north of the camp, the preferred Cheyenne way of burial. Cheyennes later observed four dead soldiers on the field, two in the camp and two others upriver where the Indian ponies were gathered before being driven away. The army noted six others wounded.[32]

The people did not move far that day. Most camped in the trees just north of their destroyed village and in the remaining daylight poked about the smoldering debris, searching especially for food. Small morsels were pulled from some of the lodges, but hardly enough to sustain the camp's nearly five hundred people. Half-clothed women and children suffered immensely. "Our hearts were bad when our babies and children cried from the cold," remembered Two Moon. Later that day the chiefs gathered and agreed to send wolves on the soldier trail. Perhaps they might reclaim some of the ponies. Ten warriors having ponies were chosen, including Wooden Leg and three Sioux. Black Eagle counseled them. "Follow them up," he said. "They cannot sleep with our horses to watch them." That evening too, Box Elder, the eighty-one-year-old holy man, spent time in prayer. Embracing *Ox'zem*, the Sacred Wheel Lance, he invoked the Lance's concealing power to cover the movements of the wolves as they trailed the soldiers, hopeful of recapturing the stolen ponies.[33]

Prayer and an entirely unsuspecting, unprepared army led to unexpected success. The wolves shadowed the soldier column as it made its way south and halted at the mouth of Lodge Pole Creek, today's Clear Creek, twenty-one miles from the battlefield. The herd was driven beyond the army camp. Oddly, the animals were left unguarded that night, the prevailing thinking perhaps simply being that an army camp nestled between the destroyed village and the Indian herd was security enough. From high ground west of the Powder opposite the camp, Wooden Leg and the wolves sized up the matter instantly. "One Cheyenne would whisper, 'I see my horse.' Another would say, 'There is mine.'"[34]

The wolves waited until late in the night and slipped down among the animals and slowly pushed them up Lodge Pole Creek. After the movement was well underway there came the slightest reaction from the soldier camp. A few shots were exchanged but to no consequence. Wooden Leg and the wolves drove the ponies harder several miles up Lodge Pole Creek and then veered onto a succession of northerly branches and around another unanticipated soldier contingent heading south, until eventually circling back to the Powder. The audacious act netted the return of nearly two thirds of the original herd. Later, several other wolves returned to the high ground above the next day's army camp hopeful again of capturing more ponies, but instead watched the soldiers kill the rest.[35]

Taking back the ponies was an extraordinarily heroic and memorable achievement, the first of several occurring in the coming months, in what was otherwise soon a protracted, bleak war.

On the morning of March 18, Old Bear's bedraggled Cheyennes began their own trail away from the Powder River carnage. The Cheyennes followed He Dog's lead. He knew the way to Crazy Horse's camp, forty-five or fifty miles distant. Most everyone walked. The few ponies remaining in the camp were scattered among the old people and vulnerable ones, or given to warriors who remained far behind to cover the flight. The people were cold and hungry and another day of melting snow muddied the ground and made the trail difficult. Their path took them across the Powder and north and east, across the Little Powder River, and eventually onto the secluded East Fork of the Little Powder. Always they looked to the rear. The people had learned that the wolves sent after the ponies met with success but as yet, after the first day on the trail, the animals had not yet been returned.[36]

The recovered ponies reached the people near the end of the second day's travel. Black Eagle remembered that a rider from the south arrived earlier in the day announcing that the horses were near. Then a cry arose through the bands when heralds proclaimed: "All get up and be happy. We have recovered all our horses." In truth, not every horse was returned, but enough familiar stock to allow warriors to again be mounted and most women, children, and old people to ride. Upon returning to the camp, Wooden Leg sought out Chief Old Bear and returned the horse he had taken when the camp was first attacked. Old Bear thanked him and gave the pony to his woman while he remained afoot.[37]

On the fourth day the beleaguered, starving lot reached Crazy Horse's camp. After Big Road's people departed, the remaining Oglala camp was small, maybe thirty or forty lodges in all. Crazy Horse came out and learned from He Dog the essences of the Powder River attack. His people came out as well and received the Cheyennes hospitably, welcoming them and calling out: "Cheyennes, come and eat here." Wooden Leg recalled with evident joy and respect that there were only a few Oglalas and many Cheyennes, yet "they fed us to fullness and gave us temporary shelter and robes."[38]

Crazy Horse was then thirty-five years old. His reputation as a fierce warrior and complex, fervent traditional was plainly understood among both his Northern Oglala followers and these Cheyennes, who themselves had so long cultivated bonds of friendship between the peoples. But the attack upon the Cheyennes at Powder River and their arrival in Crazy Horse's camp now thrust upon him a different role. Here, people looked to him for wise counsel. He Dog remembered that Crazy Horse ordinarily attended very few councils and never spoke when he did. "There was no special reason for this," He Dog said. "It was just his nature." Short Bull remembered that Crazy Horse "had black eyes that hardly ever looked straight at a man, but they didn't miss much that was going on all the same."[39]

That evening Crazy Horse hosted a council of chiefs and elders and listened intently to Cheyenne accounts of distress and need. With Old Bear, Little Wolf, and Box Elder looking on, Two Moon spoke for the Cheyennes, reminding everyone of the ruthlessness of the attack, of pony soldiers driving women and children to the hills, of burning their homes, and stealing their horses. We "now have hatred" toward the Whites, he declared. And they are coming here to fight you, too, he warned. Give us arms and horses and we will fight them "until we are all killed or they are driven back." The words were stirring. "*Hau! Hau!*" reverberated through the council. Others rose one by one and agreed to stay together and fight. And the reticent one, Crazy Horse, capped it, concluding, "I am glad you are come. We are going to fight the White man again." The chiefs agreed to break camp in the morning and find Sitting Bull's people, a large and well provisioned alliance that would certainly share this fervor for resistance.[40]

In the forenoon of March 28 the Old Bear–Crazy Horse–He Dog coalition headed north, skirting the highlands of the eastern Powder River valley. In previous weeks, Sitting Bull had returned from the Little Missouri, reaching those same highlands by way Little Beaver Creek. Many knew the locale as the Blue Mountains, south of today's Ekalaka, Montana, a dramatic timbered landscape between the Little Missouri and Powder River drainages. It was another of the favorite haunts of the Northern Indians because it offered abundant clean water, wood, hunting, and seclusion. Hampered midway by another springtime snow, the Cheyennes and Oglalas were three days on their short but difficult journey before finding Sitting Bull's camp at the head of Little Beaver Creek in the lee of the Chalk Buttes. The Cheyennes knew the place as Charcoal Butte.[41]

Sitting Bull's Hunkpapas greeted the refugees graciously, welcoming them and immediately feeding them. His camp was a large one, more than the Cheyennes and Oglalas combined. At his direction two double lodges were set up in the middle of the camp, one for men and the other women.

He told his own people to make room for them, and give them tipis if they could. They came with more than mere lodges, also offering robes, blankets, clothing, powder and ball, and horses. "Oh, what good hearts they had!" Wooden Leg told his biographer many years later. "I never can forget the generosity of Sitting Bull's Uncpapa Sioux on that day."[42]

Lame Deer's band of Miniconjous also joined Sitting Bull's camp during its time in the Chalk Buttes. Wooden Leg remembered their arrival, coming about the same time the Cheyennes appeared, he said. The Cheyennes and Miniconjous were friendly, with occasional intermarriages and people from each band living at their whim with the other. The two peoples had allied most recently in the persistent harassment of Fort Pease at the mouth of the Big Horn.[43]

The feasting and recovery lasted a week, but the daily joy was tempered in the evening councils where headmen from the four bands discussed the probabilities of war. The government's ultimatum in midwinter spoke of a consequence of war, and at Powder River a brutal, unforeseen attack had just been served on the Cheyennes, people actually heeding the government's call. When interviewed several years later after surrendering at Fort Yates in 1881, Low Dog, an Oglala, reflected on the anguish expressed in the councils. Our people were talking about the chief of the White men who wanted the Indians to live where he ordered, he remembered, and do as he said, and he would feed and clothe them. "Little I thought then that I would have to fight the White man, or do as he should tell me," he explained. "Why should I be kept as a humble man, when I am a brave warrior on my own lands," Low Dog implored. "The game is mine, and the hills, and the valleys, and the White man has no right to say where I shall go or what I shall do. If any White man tries to destroy my property, or take my lands, I will take my gun, get on my horse, and go and punish him." In spring 1876, such thoughts were virtually universal among the Northern people.[44]

Low Dog's blistering sentiments were echoed often in the councils. Two Moon reminded the elders of the sufferings of the Cheyennes at Powder River. Sitting Bull repeated his own life-long refrain. He would not go to the reservation nor would he accept any rations or other gifts coming from the White man government. And while he did not seek a war with the Whites, he would fight if attacked. All the more, the wisdom of Sitting Bull's counsel was plain to see. He and his followers "were wealthy in food and clothing and lodges, in everything needful to an Indian," Wooden Leg remembered, and he was admired by all "as a man whose medicine was good—that is, as a man having a kind heart and good judgment as to the best course."[45]

There was not much debate about a course of action, Two Moon recalled. "All agreed to stay together and fight." That conclusion was becoming ever more apparent among these resilient traditionals and had been ordained at the Sun Dance the previous summer when these same people assembled and embraced a spirit of unity, and seeming inevitability. There, Sitting Bull had foreseen enemies coming to them and that they would be destroyed. Only then, he proclaimed, would the people endure in the buffalo country.[46]

The four bands could not stay in the Chalk Buttes area much longer, however, before consuming its available resources, particularly grass and wood. But the grasses across the plains were greening and the days growing longer, gradually erasing the harshness of winter. The chiefs agreed to move north to the next stream flowing into the Powder. As they commenced the trail the bands took up what became a familiar order, one they embraced in all of their movements that spring and summer, and one also reflective of long-standing traditions in Lakota society that prescribed a particular order of travel from camp to camp. Councilors from the respective bands took the lead, selecting places for smoking, rests, and overnights. Camp police, *akicitas*, rode the flanks, maintaining order and providing security, while wolves ranged the distant margins, now doubly watchful for soldiers. The Cheyennes, the put upon people, led the procession. Their Oglala friends followed, the Miniconjous trailing next, and the Hunkpapas closing the body. The horse herds followed the people, usually driven by young boys coming of age. And trailing all were other warriors, ensuring the safety of the procession.[47]

—m—

Many years after the Powder River fight Short Bull, He Dog's brother and one of the wolves who recaptured the Cheyenne ponies, offered an interesting perspective on the March 17 episode. It was a "turning point," he told an interviewer in 1930. "If it had it not been for that attack by Crook on Powder River, we would have come in to the agency that spring, and there would have been no Sioux war."[48]

Short Bull's belief had some validity, at least as he grasped the matter in another day and time. Indeed Old Bear's and He Dog's people were headed for the White River Agency that early spring, not dutifully ahead of the January 31 deadline so arbitrarily imposed by the government but complying no less. Had not troops so coincidentally found them as they did, the two bands may have escaped this early wrath, just as Big Road's people avoided it. But there was another truth in play that spring, one that was perhaps beyond Short Bull's comprehension. Sitting Bull and Crazy Horse had no intention of complying with an arbitrary government demand to fatefully cede a lifeway, and in the end, Sitting Bull's War was purely a conflict meant to impose the government's will and sweep the buffalo country clean of the last of its free-roaming Indians. When war came to the Northern Cheyennes on March 17, it came to all the Northern People.

He Dog remembered the event in an honoring song fashioned for him that venerated the Cheyenne and Sioux people caught in the Powder River fight.

> The soldiers charged our village, my friend cried,
> soldiers and Sioux charge, and my friend cried.[49]

6

THE GREAT ASCENDANCY

"Our council men told us that we would have to fight for our country, and that would be the only way we could retain it."

—Red Horse, Miniconjou Lakota

An Indian war was breaking on the northern plains. The Cheyennes assaulted on the Powder River on March 17 immediately sought out their friends, the Northern Oglalas, who were camped several days north and east of Old Bear's ruined village. The Cheyennes' impoverishment overwhelmed the Oglalas and in course the aligned camps turned to Sitting Bull's people in the Chalk Buttes, where a recovery commenced. There in nightly councils the chiefs and elders of the assembled bands debated these events—an ultimatum, a devastating attack, the invasion of the Black Hills, the continuous prowling along the Yellowstone. If this was indeed a time of war, what might their best course be? Mostly the counsellors embraced notions of shielding the people and their daily wherewithal. At Powder River the Cheyennes lost foodstuffs, personal possessions, lodges, and many of their ponies. At Whitestone Hill, and Killdeer Mountain, and Sand Creek, in times gone by aligned bands like these lost possessions, *and* people too.

Pressing Sitting Bull's growing camp were simple conventional needs, and the Chalk Buttes were quickly stripped bare. Late in this second week of April the aligned people made their way northward from Little Beaver Creek. Their route took them across the headlands of O'Fallon Creek and onto Sheep Creek, a small tributary of the Powder. Along the way, likely on Sheep Creek, Wooden Leg recalled that Spotted Eagle's Sans Arcs joined the camp, adding some fifty-five additional lodges of stalwart traditionals to the fold. The Sans Arcs, long-time Sitting Bull allies, were angered by the news of the unforeseen cavalry assault on the Cheyennes on Powder River. Their arrival swelled the consortium to some 380 lodges, and more than 2,400 people.[1]

Also about then on Sheep Creek or perhaps from the Chalk Buttes camp, Crazy Horse broke from the bands and struck for the Black Hills country, alone. The evidence is thin, but he apparently sought time for self-reflection, a thread common in his life. The separation would have been of no consequence had a resident at the Spotted Tail Agency not linked Crazy Horse's name to a murderous episode occurring in the southwestern Black Hills. On April 16 four Custer City residents were surprised and killed in Red Canyon, southwest of Custer City. The incident was ever after remembered as the Metz Massacre. Those brutal killings were rather immediately pinned on a White outlaw known as "Persimmon Bill" Chambers and his gang of cutthroats, including some Pine Ridge malcontents. Much later, He Dog hinted at Crazy Horse's involvement in the episode, but Crazy Horse may simply have served once again as a convenient Plains bogeyman.[2]

Sitting Bull's coalition of Northern Indians, meanwhile, continued their slow drift westward, recuperating horses, hunting buffalo, and eventually reaching the Powder, where a small band of Blackfeet Sioux joined them, adding a sixth camp circle to the new alliance. This band was particularly heralded for bringing with them many extra ponies that were distributed as gifts. And more kept coming. A short while later, Lame White Man and his band of Cheyenne followers joined. Lame White Man, known especially for his courage in battle, was a respected Southern Cheyenne Council Chief who had lived among the northern people for a long while. With him were eight Southern Cheyenne families. The band had departed the White River Agency weeks earlier and spent the intervening days searching for the Cheyennes in the north. Unaware of the attack on the Powder River, they had crossed the heads of the Powder, Tongue, and Rosebud before doubling back and encountering Old Bear's trail east of the Powder. Lame White Man's band tallied some ten lodges, and folded in with the Cheyennes.[3]

As the days passed in mid-April the bands lingered in the greening bottomland of the Powder above the mouth of Sheep Creek. Across the river was the mouth of Mizpah Creek. This expansive campsite was broad and lush and possessed all the critical elements a sprawling village needed. At hand were superb grazing, rushing springtime water, and abundant shade and wood in the riverside cottonwoods. Soon, other scattered small bands and individuals joined, a few Brulés aligning with the Oglalas, and a straggle of Santee Sioux, or "No Clothing People" as Wooden Leg referred to them. That destitute lot of some fifteen small lodges followed the charismatic sixty-one-year-old chieftain Inkpaduta, perpetrator of the bloody Spirit Lake Massacre in Iowa in 1857 and at one time one of the most feared Indians on the northern plains. Lately, Inkpaduta and his people mostly lived in the Wood Mountain country of Canada, but they crossed into Montana from time to time to hunt buffalo. They were without horses and relied on dog travois to haul their lodges and bundles, a reflection of an earlier day and time. Although friendly with Sitting Bull, whether they intended to participate in his war is debated, but there was safety here, and these fervent traditionals welcomed them. They folded in with the Hunkpapas. These odd-lot smaller parties of Blackfeet Sioux, Southern Cheyennes, and Santees helped grow the Sitting Bull coalition to some 415 lodges.[4]

In evening councils, usually held in Sitting Bull's camp, One Bull, the chief's adopted son, recalled how his adoptive father emerged as a strategist. Sitting Bull was quick to send runners for horses. "Don't spare anyone," he proclaimed. "If you meet anyone, kill him and take his horses. Spare nothing." Sitting Bull's challenge led his nephew, White Bull, to join a party of Miniconjous and Sans Arcs bound for the Black Hills country to prey on the marginal mining settlements. The raid was successful. White Bull alone returned with six horses, one he presented to Sitting Bull and another to his father.[5]

In council, the elders concluded to cross from the Powder River to the Tongue. Their trail led them a short distance up Mizpah Creek and then straight west over hill country to the head of today's Johnson Creek, and then westward again and down Pumpkin Creek to its confluence with the Tongue. "We camped in two or three places between the [Powder] and Tongue river, one sleep at each place," remembered Wooden Leg. "The grass was coming up everywhere, and our horses were growing stronger." It was about the first of May in the season of the Lakota's Green Leaves Moon.[6]

War fervor intensified in evening councils on the Tongue. Rain in the Face remembered the resolve, a willingness to "fight the White soldiers until no warrior should be left." But if a war with the Whites was truly upon them, Sitting Bull had two overarching concerns, both of comparable magnitude. First, a camp of 415 lodges could not sustain a prolonged and costly war. The attack on Old Bear's camp of seventy-five allied Cheyenne and Oglala lodges had been devastating. That camp had counted some 475 people, with perhaps 110 men of fighting age. The present village on the Tongue tallied upward of 610 men capable of fighting but also another 2,000 vulnerable women, children, and old people. In a time of war, Sitting Bull needed help. Early in their pause on the Tongue, the Hunkpapa chief dispatched runners to scattered camps in the buffalo country and to the distant agencies calling on traditionals to join him on the Rosebud. He likely had Big Road's sizeable body of Oglalas and Gall's Hunkpapa followers foremost in mind. Those people normally aligned with him, but they also returned to their agencies periodically. Agency Indians, he knew, also went west to hunt when winter subsided, but how much he could depend on this now was an open question.[7]

Sitting Bull had a second concern. He needed an adequate supply of arms and munitions sufficient to sustain a war. Already his Hunkpapas had resupplied themselves when in the Little Missouri country late that winter. Where the Little Missouri crosses today's Montana–North Dakota border, they had met a Métis trading caravan operating there in March and early April, much to the consternation of agents at Cheyenne River who reported the matter to superiors in Washington. Similarly, White Bull remembered Miniconjous from the Northern camps obtaining guns at Cheyenne River from traders "inside and out," meaning from legal but probably mostly illegal operators. Earlier that winter, Gros Ventres from Fort Belknap had visited Sitting Bull's camp while hunting buffalo and traded powder and arms. They then coyly complained of that intercourse when returning to their agency, telling their agent that the Lakotas had robbed them, and knowing full well their losses would be replaced. Such supplies were precious but limited, even in the best of times, and the Hunkpapas had already shared some of their excess with Old Bear's strife-torn Cheyennes.[8]

People with ties in the south relied on one particularly notorious trader operating in the Pine Ridge country, an individual as devious as any Métis trader. The well-connected Frenchman, stocky, bearded, twenty-nine-year-old Francois or Francis Boucher (pronounced Booshay in Indian country), was an occasional employee of the Spotted Tail Agency and a trusted relative of Spotted Tail. By day, beginning in 1872, Boucher operated a small independent trading house on Bordeaux Creek in the Pine Ridge roughly midway between the Red Cloud and Spotted Tail agencies. He also served as Spotted Tail's personal interpreter from time to time. More importantly for Sitting Bull, Boucher was known as a "night trader," one who trafficked in illegal merchandise in the remote "Burning Grounds," a labyrinthian black-clay badlands north of the White River just across the Nebraska-Dakota border. Boucher drew the ire of the licensed trader at Spotted Tail Agency in February 1875 when that trader reported these alleged illegal activities. But Boucher's conventional operation lay beyond the ordinary bounds the White River agencies and their adjacent army garrisons. Doubtless, too, on account of his close ties to Spotted Tail, the accusation of illegal activity was conveniently ignored. Boucher's illicit labors turned ever more brazen and visible—and no doubt more profitable—as the war advanced. Inevitably, the military took notice and intervened, but not yet.[9]

Before long, Sitting Bull's call to action reached the agencies. A trader operating on the Milk River remembered a runner visiting with the Santees, noting the chief's call to gather on Rosebud Creek and imploring their help. While the Santees seemed outwardly sympathetic, none of them journeyed to the Northern camps. That same runner, however, "had better success with the renegades, as we realized that their camp was growing less near the approach of spring." Agent Burke at Standing Rock likewise reported the departure to the "hostile camp" of 100 Indians aligned there, mostly in March, and a few more thereafter. In the south, Little Big Man himself carried Sitting Bull's message to the Pine Ridge people, particularly to Big Road's traditionals. The Black Elk family belonged to that band and Young Black Elk remembered the occasion: "My father told me we were going back to Crazy Horse and that we were going to have to fight from then on, because there was no other way to keep our country."[10]

The first and most perplexing agency arrival in Sitting Bull's camp appeared in early May on the Tongue when twelve lodges of Kill Eagle's Blackfeet Sioux and another fourteen lodges of Hunkpapas trailing west with them from Standing Rock reached the camp. These likely were the same Indians that Agent Burke reported as leaving in March. The oddity here was that Kill Eagle's people were not drawn to the war at all but simply to the Yellowstone Country to hunt buffalo. "I was in want of lodges, robes, and skins," Kill Eagle told an interviewer some months later. The band hunted successfully en route, killing twenty and thirty buffalo on some days, and was warmly welcomed in Sitting Bull's camp. But when the Blackfeet people learned of the maelstrom they had stepped into, they wanted to get away immediately but were not permitted to leave. Some tried doing so and had their horses confiscated or shot outright. Insults thereafter were showered on those newcomers continually. Sitting Bull's camp population grew measurably but Kill Eagle's people were a ceaseless burden until they finally escaped in midsummer. Until then his lodges folded in with the small Blackfeet circle, which itself was close to and now under the watchful eye of the Hunkpapas. Importantly, however, Kill Eagle proved a keen witness to most of the summer's events, and when finally returning to his agency became one of the first to report on the great chief and his war.[11]

By now the camp's wolves were aware of another troop movement, this one north and west of them. A column of soldiers was slowly making its way down the north side of the Yellowstone and had reached the proximity of Pompeys Pillar above the mouth of the Big Horn River. The presence of cumbersome wagons and a swollen Yellowstone lessened the immediacy of any threat to the village, and no Indian chronicler at this stage mentions these troops, though soldier accounts remembered the loss of some of their own animals on the night of May 2, and their Crow scouts lost all their animals—thirty-two in all, "gobbled by the Sioux." "The Crows had a good cry over their loss," said one of them.[12]

Conventional camp needs, particularly of forage, obliged a move from the mouth of Pumpkin Creek up the Tongue to the mouth of Ash Creek, where the people spent nearly a week, and then farther south to the mouth of Foster Creek, where they spent four more days. Both were lesser affluents entering the Tongue from the east. At the Foster Creek camp the largest band yet of newly arriving Northern Indians aligned with Sitting Bull's village. These were Black Moccasins' people. Also known as Dirty Moccasins, the chief brought some thirty lodges of Northern Cheyennes to the fold. Black Moccasins was an Old Man Chief, another of the revered Northern Cheyenne counsellors like Old Bear and Little Wolf, who came now from the Pine Ridge country. They followed the plainly scored Powder River trail straight to the Powder, journeyed down that river through Old Bear's ruined camp, crossed over to Otter Creek, and continued down Otter and the Tongue until meeting their fellow Cheyennes and Sitting Bull. Wooden Leg was elated. "These Cheyennes brought extra ammunition, sugar, coffee, and tobacco."[13]

The arrival of Kill Eagle's Blackfeet Sioux, the fourteen other Hunkpapa lodges traveling with him, and now Black Moccasins' Cheyennes grew

Sitting Bull's camp to some 470 lodges, with upward of 3,000 people. It was the middle of May. That soldiers were again in the Yellowstone Country, however, was a dark foreshadowing of the government's wintertime resolve. As the young Oglala Black Elk had expressed it, this fight was inevitable or they'd lose their country. For the Oglalas in the south as with Sitting Bull's people in the north, their country, their homeland was this very buffalo prairie.

After some ten days on the Tongue, the village moved west, across broken high ground—the headlands of today's Sweeney Creek—and then on to Rosebud Creek, taking almost a week and mostly hunting buffalo all the while. This year buffalo were plentiful across that divide and the Cheyennes were still replacing lodges and robes lost on the Powder two months before. In nightly councils during the crossover chiefs and elders gathered to discuss their next movements, plus the constant dribble of news from scouts shadowing the soldiers on the Yellowstone. Some of the Crow scouts in that enemy force had, in fact, lost ponies. Young warriors were eager to fight those hated intruders, but the elders urged them to stay away from the Whites. Sitting Bull did not want a fight either. He and the others urged a defensive war, unless the enemy threatened women and children. Then they would fight to the death. Anyway, fighting wasted energy, they insisted, and young men should instead be concerned with providing food and clothing for their families. Restraining young warriors became a constant challenge.[14]

When Little Big Man reached the Pine Ridge Country in early May carrying Sitting Bull's call to the traditionals to join the chief on Rosebud Creek, he encountered a people enraged. The Black Hills gold rush was in full flower and the best roads there, those from Sidney, Nebraska, and Cheyenne, Wyoming, were crowded with prospectors and freighters. Both avenues crossed the Pine Ridge and Powder River Trail; the Sidney road bypassing Red Cloud Agency directly. Death on the roads had become a common epitaph, and newspapers far and wide paraded lurid reports of Indian scares, chases, face-to-face encounters, named and unnamed fatalities, some with arrows sticking from them, others having been scalped. Raiders ran off cattle and horses from the agencies and local ranches, and even lingered about the Black Hills settlements, opportunistically running off horses there, too. Despite the mayhem, the rush proved unstoppable, and for many Oglalas the Black Hills invasion merely lay atop the unfathomable demand that Lakotas cede the buffalo country west of it.[15]

George Crook went to Camp Robinson and Red Cloud Agency in mid-May partly to investigate the turmoil, but also to enlist Oglalas and mixed bloods for his coming campaign. He had commanded the expedition in March that struck Old Bear's village, although he was not on the battlefield that day. His recruiting effort now was a dismal failure, openly opposed both by the local agent and Red Cloud himself, largely because it would have drawn otherwise peaceable Lakotas into a war. This strategy of pitting kin against kin had served Crook well among southwestern tribes in Arizona, but it proved a failure here. The ever pragmatic Red Cloud attempted to explain those matters to Crook, lecturing him bluntly. "The Gray Fox must understand that the Dakotas, and especially the Oglalas, have many warriors, many guns and ponies. They are brave and ready to fight for their country. They are not afraid of the soldiers or their chief. Many braves are ready to meet them. Every lodge will send its young men, and they all will say of the Great Father's dogs, 'Let them come!'"[16]

The Gray Fox had his own brush with death on that same trip. As he departed Camp Robinson for Fort Laramie on the morning of May 16, he and his party rode through scattered Sioux camps for three or four miles. Beyond the camps as his party continued up the White River valley they repeatedly noticed Indians posted on prominent points along the way, as if somehow anticipating something. They also noticed smoke curls rising behind them but did not comprehend their meaning. At noon the entourage paused for a meal at the head of the valley and a mail carrier from Fort Laramie passed by. After exchanging compliments the rider continued toward Camp Robinson. He never made it. A few miles beyond warriors ambushed and killed him. Crook learned of this after reaching Fort Laramie and realized that the ambush was meant for him, and that the billowing smoke behind his party was a signal to conspirators that he had departed the White River post. The details were confirmed later; only the size of Crook's escort had prevented an attack. Years later word circulated that the assassination plot had been Red Cloud's doing.[17]

Little Big Man's prime objective in coming to the Pine Ridge was to lure north Big Road's band of traditional Oglalas. Those people had separated from Crazy Horse's camp on the Little Powder River some two months earlier, partly drawn south by the government's summons but also spurred by conventional habits. The Black Hills and Pine Ridge were familiar ground to Big Road's people, and kinship ties in the south were strong. The band readily connected with the Northern traditionals, too, in that time when many Oglalas conveniently divided their time between north and south, much as Gall and his followers divided their time between the Missouri River agencies and the Lower Yellowstone country. Crazy Horse's and Sitting Bull's strident Northerners relied on these frequent go-betweens because they always returned with trade essentials.

The departure of so many Indians at one time from camps in and around Red Cloud Agency was noticed but never exactly measured (and has often been over, or under, estimated). The agency's locale was densely populated with scattered camps of Oglalas, Cheyennes, and Arapahos, much as Crook had noted. Among so many camps, some people easily slipped away. Big Road's departure occurred under cover of darkness, and his people, as Young Black Elk recalled, "traveled fast." When the local agent awakened to the situation, he underplayed it. Reporting in early June, he said simply that by his best estimates some 400 Sioux, including women and children, had gone north—as they did every summer, he emphasized—and so did 400 Cheyennes. Another report provided by an army officer who actually encountered the procession west of the agency, put the estimate at 100 lodges, including, he said, 600 fighting men. If indeed 100 lodges was an accurate tally, which comports reasonably with other known figures, the warrior count was more nearly 150, with a total camp population of perhaps 650.[18]

Young Black Elk provided additional details. He remembered his group being joined near Warbonnet Creek by some Cheyennes and other Sioux, including a small band of Short Bull's Oglalas. On May 17 at Sage Creek, the next principal drainage west, his party overtook an oxen train of freighters bound for the Black Hills. The Oglalas briefly harassed the train but did not dally long. Mostly that was a young man's escapade. Young Black Elk, age thirteen at the time, recalled Little Big Man coming up and telling the young men to ride out and attack the Whites. Black Elk did so with a few others and remembered bullets whizzing about but no one getting hurt, not even horses. The chance confrontation ended abruptly when a column of soldiers appeared on a distant crest behind the train. The attackers hastened away, but the soldiers did not pursue them. Why the troopers did not give chase seems puzzling. Perhaps they saw themselves as greatly outnumbered, or maybe the Indians in flight did not seem a serious threat and certainly not elements of what would become an all-powerful enemy capable of destroying elite army regiments. Meanwhile, other small bands joined Big Road's people as they traveled the Powder River Trail by way of Bear Lodge Butte.[19]

The ascendant camp reached Rosebud Creek at a point seven or eight miles above its mouth in mid-May, about the time in the Lakota calendar of good berries. Like many of the water courses in this remote landscape, the Rosebud flowed north. Tracing it backward, this well-watered stream ran nearly one hundred miles from its confluence with the Yellowstone southward into headlands deep in the Wolf Mountains. Throughout its course the secluded valley featured luxurious grasses in its bottoms, diverse hunting of buffalo, deer, and elk, and extraordinary topographic anomalies. The Rosebud was known for its rugged side hills and named buttes in its lower reach and striking sandstone walls and monoliths at midstream. Amid the latter were the revered stand-alone Deer Medicine Rocks that were heavily strewn with ancient and recent petroglyphs. The valley made a dramatic narrowing in the stream's upper reach where its meandering waters emerge from the Wolf Mountains, having originated in springs and rivulets scattered across a broad highland where, straight south, lay the Tongue River and the Big Horn Mountains. Sioux and Cheyenne people had hunted and camped in the Rosebud Valley yearly since arriving a generation earlier, and the Rosebud was a favorite locale now for annual Sun Dances, as occurred there just a year before when the Sioux and Cheyenne embraced bonds of unity. Two years earlier the valley had witnessed another of the lead-ups to this war, when Sioux warriors fiercely resisted a party of Bozeman prospectors passing through its lower reaches.[20]

On the day of Sitting Bull's arrival on Rosebud Creek, another band joined the six circles. These were Charcoal Bear's Northern Cheyennes, some ten lodges that folded in neatly with the Cheyenne circle. Charcoal Bear was a Cheyenne medicine man—a healer, not a prophet—and the keeper of *Esevone*, the Sacred Medicine Hat, and Sacred Hat Lodge. The arrival of this important individual and these sacred objects brought great joy to the Cheyenne people, and their lodge was raised immediately in the center of the Cheyenne camp.[21]

The ascendant village remained in place for a week as the people hunted the plentiful buffalo encountered in the crossing from the Tongue and that were now also found on the hillsides west of the Rosebud. Late in the week occurred one of the singular episodes that marked these months of May and June. Its focus was Sitting Bull, the one who always worried about and prayed for the well-being of his people. He was the people's lodestone and prophet, now almost singularly rallying them to a defense of the buffalo country and a lifeway.[22]

One Bull, Sitting Bull's beloved twenty-three-year-old nephew and adopted son, recalled years later that "something or somebody" prompted the mystic to climb a nearby butte and commune with the great mystery, *Wakan Tanka*. There he sat on a lichen-covered rock, praying and meditating and then falling asleep. In a dream, Sitting Bull looked to the east and saw a high wind raising considerable dust. It was coming straight toward him. At the same moment a white cloud, an Indian village at the foot of snowcapped mountains, was sailing smoothly against the gale. Behind the storm Sitting Bull could see soldiers, their weapons and accoutrements glistening in the sun, charging straight into the cloud. Thunder pealed, lightening crackled, and torrential rains fell, but then as quickly the storm subsided and the white cloud drifted serenely eastward before passing out of sight.[23]

As One Bull recounted it, when Sitting Bull awakened he returned to the village and summoned the chiefs and headmen of the bands and told them of his "terrible dream." It was a bold vision, reflecting the peril his people faced in the wake of an ultimatum, the attack on Cheyenne friends at Powder River, and now soldiers prowling the Yellowstone, coming, he saw, to wipe them out. But Sitting Bull also saw a glorious victory for the Northern people. The storm subsided. The soldiers disappeared. The white cloud drifted calmly away. The vision was captivating but ominous. Elders that day instructed the wolves to watch intently and to look eastward for an approaching enemy.[24]

Watching for an enemy did not mean engaging that enemy, however. Rain in the Face remembered the exuberance that summer of the young warriors, who always "delighted with the prospect of a great fight." The elders repeatedly tempered the young men's ardor, but some stole away anyway, seeking opportunity. On one daring encounter, warriors found two soldiers and a teamster from the Yellowstone army camp out hunting several miles upriver of their camp. They were ambushed and killed. The teamster's body was riddled with bullets, and one soldier was scalped and the other found with two butcher knives buried in his skull. Soldiers from the camp pursued the attackers, but the Indian trail vanished. On other occasions warriors visibly taunted the camp from jutting hilltops south of the river, and tried running off army horses. But just as suddenly the threat disappeared.[25]

The needs of the camp and the desire to distance it from the Yellowstone soldiers prompted a move. For three consecutive days the six sprawling circles trailed slowly southward until reaching another open bottomland with inviting grazing at the mouth of Greenleaf Creek, thirty-two miles upstream of the Rosebud's mouth.[26]

The great news on reaching Greenleaf was the arrival of Big Road's Oglalas, a few aligned Cheyennes, and some Brulés, all from the White River and adding some 100 lodges to the sprawl. A noteworthy lot of individuals arrived in this mix, too, not the least Little Big Man, the prominent disrupter of the Black Hills purchase affair eight months earlier who had served as Sitting Bull's messenger to these Oglalas. Arriving as well was Short Bull, He Dog's brother, and his small band of Oglalas, and Jack Red Cloud (Above Man), the eighteen-year-old son of the great chief. Young Red Cloud had departed the agency without his father's consent and quietly carried along the chief's engraved Winchester rifle received in Washington the year before. Also in the mix was the impressionable Young Black Elk. As with Wooden Leg, Black Elk later shared extraordinary memories of these days with Sitting Bull. Here at the mouth of Greenleaf, Black Elk stared in amazement when first seeing a valley full of tipis and more ponies than could be counted. The newcomers readily folded in with the already sizeable Oglala and Cheyenne circles. Tempering the day's joy, however, Wooden Leg remembered a cautionary note shared by the newly arrived Cheyennes, warning kinsmen that "lots of soldiers are being sent to fight the Indians."[27]

The newcomers also brought news of the continuing invasion of the Black Hills and such details were shared in nightly councils. There, according to Red Horse, a Miniconjou who often attended the assemblies, the leaders agonized over the Whites trespassing in the Black Hills. They also worried about government demands that the Indians cede the Big Horn country, and about the ever-wearisome notion of a railroad building through the Yellowstone Valley. All these concerns simmered contentiously. "Our council men told us that we would have to fight for our country, and that that would be the only way we could retain it," Red Horse explained.[28]

Big Road's coming signaled the bold success of Sitting Bull's call to the traditionals to join him, but the arrival of others, only sometimes named, continued as well, and reflected another reality in the Lakota world that the great chief understood well. Charcoal Bear's Cheyennes and Big Road's bands of Oglalas and Cheyennes added some 110 lodges to a camp that now swelled to more than 580 lodges and nearly 3,700 people. But agents across the Great Sioux Reservation saw another exodus. A quip echoing from Standing Rock and Cheyenne River alone was telling. An unnamed informant noted that "there remain only old men, women, and children, the warriors being on the hunt; but all the tracks from these agencies led toward the location of Sitting Bull." A short while earlier the commanding officer at Fort Abraham Lincoln had said much the same. The young men are leaving with their best ponies, the officer quipped. "They say they are going to fight the Crows, but . . . they are going to join Sitting Bull." Whether these young men accompanied named bands or traveled alone, the trickle continued in the days to come.[29]

Late in the pause at the mouth of Greenleaf Creek, Sitting Bull was again drawn to prayer. He called his nephew, White Bull, his adopted brother Jumping Bull (Little Assiniboine), and the son of a friend to join him as witnesses, and at midday the four made their way to a hilltop overlooking the camp. Sitting Bull dressed plainly. His hair was unbound and he was without feathers or paint and carried only his pipe, its stem wrapped with silver sage. On the hilltop, he stood facing the sun and lit the pipe. After pausing in contemplation, he raised the pipe, its stem upward, and prayed. White Bull remembered his words:

> *Wakan Tanka*, save me and give me all my wild game animals and have them close enough so my people will have enough food this winter, and also the good men on earth will have more power so their tribes get along better and be of good nature so all the Sioux nations get along well. If you do this for me I will Sun Dance two days and two nights and will give you a whole buffalo.[30]

The four smoked the pipe in communion, and when they finished Sitting Bull wiped his face with the sage and they set off for camp. Yet again the great chief invoked themes close to his heart: peace and plenty for his people, sacrifice for *Wakan Tanka*. That evening in a grand council, it was announced that the Hunkpapas would hold a Sun Dance.[31]

In early June the great village moved south, the Cheyennes again leading and the Hunkpapas trailing. They filled a campsite below the Deer Medicine Rocks, some forty-five miles above the Yellowstone. The six camp circles sprawled on both sides of the creek for nearly a mile. Early in the move, the chief and his nephew White Bull rode off and hunted for buffalo. The pair soon killed three. Sitting Bull selected the fattest cow and asked White Bull to help him turn her onto her stomach with her bushy chin on the ground and her legs propping just so. He then filled his pipe, observed the sacred ritual of lifting it to the sky, the four quarters of the world, and then to the earth, and prayed to *Wakan Tanka*. "Here is the whole buffalo I promised. In three days I will perform the Sun Dance and you will have the red blanket." By red blanket, he meant his own blood.[32]

As promised, a unique Sun Dance was organized. It was distinctly a Hunkpapa Sun Dance, one remembered ever after as Sitting Bull's Sun Dance. Hunkpapas largely undertook the ritualistic preparation of the site, first selecting a dance arena on the valley floor just downstream of their own camp. Then the Hunkpapas cut, delivered, and raised a cottonwood tree in the center of the grounds, a tree some thirty-five feet tall by one observation. To that sacred tree, with branches and heart-shaped leaves still fluttering in the crown, preparers and attendants affixed rawhide cutouts of a man and a buffalo. Surrounding the pole at its base were buffalo skulls, and around those centerpieces the Hunkpapas erected a circular arbor large enough for participants and their attendants, drummers, and onlookers. The entryway faced east. Although this was a Hunkpapa Sun Dance, participants were invited from the entire camp, and throngs of observers came, pressing the arbor all around.[33]

On June 6 Sitting Bull purified himself in a sweat lodge ceremony and entered the arena. He was plainly dressed. He performed the ritualistic pipe ceremony and then sat down, his back against the pole, his legs outstretched and his arms resting against his thighs. As friends and family members sat nearby, Jumping Bull stepped forward and commenced a piercing operation, beginning at the wrist of the chief's left arm. Jumping Bull pricked skin with a trade awl, raised the flesh, and sliced off a bit the size of a match head. Working upward, he repeated the cuttings forty-nine more times. Jumping Bull then grasped Sitting Bull's right arm and repeated the ritualistic cuttings fifty more times. Bleeding profusely and with tears streaming down his face, Sitting Bull cried out, not in pain but in sacrifice and supplication to *Wakan Tanka*. After about thirty minutes, Sitting Bull's offering of a "red blanket" was complete.[34]

The revered traditional raised himself, his hands dripping with blood, turned to his right, and commenced a slow, methodical dance around the pole. It rained hard later that day, but still the great chief danced through the day and into the night. As the sun rose the next morning, Sitting Bull maintained his pace, slower now, trance-like. He had not eaten or taken water for more than a day. In his stupor came a great dream. Soldiers coming, upside down, falling from the sky like so many grasshoppers. And a voice spoke to him: "I give you these, because they have no ears." The soldiers would suffer a great loss. "They are to die." But the voice also delivered a stark warning. His people must not touch the spoils of their victory. If they violated that command they would forever be at the mercy of the White man.[35]

At about midday the chief faltered as if about to faint. Several rushed forward and eased him to the ground. Someone sprinkled him with water. When he awakened he spoke in a low voice to Black Moon, his cousin and fellow Hunkpapa band leader, telling of his vision and asking that he share it with the pressing onlookers. Black Moon stepped forward and in a loud voice repeated Sitting Bull's words of soldiers coming down like grasshoppers, their heads down and hats falling off. They would die as they "have no ears." Each of Sitting Bull's words and phrases were heavy with thought, but the people knew exactly what he meant. The *wasicus* would not listen; they never listened, as demonstrated again and again in decades of one-sided treaty councils and commissions. Wrote a later chronicler, a "murmur of wonder built to exultant cries." A great victory was coming. Sitting Bull had seen the finale. *Wakan Tanka* would care for its own.[36]

On the morning of June 8 the great village packed and moved upstream a few miles to the mouth of Muddy Creek (today's Lame Deer Creek), a small affluent draining the pine-covered highlands south of Rosebud Creek. The Hunkpapa Sun Dance arbor and centerpiece cottonwood pole remained, with a "Whiteman's scalp not quite dry" fluttering from the pole. A later observer was sure that it belonged to one of the soldiers in the Yellowstone River army camp killed several weeks earlier. Scattered elsewhere was a litter of signs. In the bare earth, a drawing of hoof prints and figures of soldiers and Indians, and between them dead men facing the Indians. Stones painted red. A buffalo calfskin stretched over four sticks and tied with cloth and tobacco offerings. These were intentional signs that the Sioux medicine was strong, or so many thought later, including the Arikara scouts accompanying a soldier column following the same course.[37]

Hunting again largely occupied the men of the six circles. Buffalo remained abundant in the countryside west of the Rosebud, and the large camp needed to eat. Wooden Leg remembered hunting, but he also remembered that he and ten others struck off on a unique quest of their own, seemingly as much interested in finding soldiers as buffalo. Since some of them had been in Old Bear's camp, the warning from the Cheyennes arriving with Big Road that soldiers in the south were coming to fight them resonated powerfully. The eleven, with pack horses in tow, departed the Greenleaf Creek camp just ahead of the Sun Dance. They trailed east, up Greenleaf, over the low divide to the Tongue, and up the Tongue to Hanging Woman Creek, opposite today's Birney, Montana. Hunting was meager, merely four buffaloes at the start, so the party determined to cross to the Powder and follow it upstream. They passed the charred ruin of Old Bear's camp along the way and for a while followed the same course in reverse that Big Road's people took in coming from Red Cloud Agency. This was familiar ground to Wooden Leg. After their attack on Old Bear's camp, the soldiers had driven the Cheyenne pony herd up this same stretch of the Powder to

Lodge Pole Creek, where on March 18 trailing Cheyenne wolves, Wooden Leg among them, stole most of them back.[38]

Wooden Leg and the Cheyennes now reached the mouth of Lodge Pole Creek and turned west, again apparently much more intent on discovering soldiers. One of them, Lame Sioux, ranging the hills far northwest of the others, indeed found the enemy. He beckoned for the others to hurry along. In the headlands of Prairie Dog Creek in the foothills of the Big Horn Mountains was a soldier camp. It was nearing dark, and the hunters turned wolves hid until well into the night. Then they dressed, painted themselves, and ventured onward. In the distance they saw soldier campfires burning brightly, but it was a big sprawl and they dared not get too close.[39]

Late in the night the party edged closer. Fires still smoldered but when the wolves could see the entire scene, the soldiers were gone. The soldier trail led down Prairie Dog Creek. The abandoned camp was rich with booty, including a beef carcass with many fragments of meat remaining on the bones, and close by a box of army hard crackers. It had been raining, but Wooden Leg said that this made the crackers all the better. He and his party ate what they wanted and cooked beef shreds on the fire coals. "We enjoyed a fine breakfast," he boasted, and they then set off on the soldier trail.[40]

The shod horse prints and wagon ruts led to another camp, this located where Prairie Dog Creek empties into the Tongue. The wolves did not venture close but skirted widely to the west. The Tongue was a raging river but they rode their ponies and led their pack animals through the swift current and hid overnight among the cottonwoods on the stream's north bank. In the breaking morning light they climbed the high sharp cliffs on the Tongue's left and approached the massive encampment. The activities below were puzzling. People were riding this way and that, and soldier horses seemed within grasp. Wooden Leg and his friends momentarily contemplated crossing the river again and stealing some of those horses but in the end agreed that such a move was too risky. Anyway, conveying this news of soldiers advancing northward had to be carried to the great camp on Rosebud Creek.[41]

The hunter-wolves momentarily divided. Wooden Leg and five others commenced a hurried overland ride to Sitting Bull's camp while the remaining five agreed to shadow the soldiers, but in short order they, too, rejoined the party. Their trail took them northward from the Tongue onto the headlands of Rosebud Creek. There, late in the day, they killed a buffalo and after sharing the raw liver, built a small fire and roasted pieces of meat. They then moved on until late in the night when they stopped to eat again and rest their ponies. No soldiers or soldier scouts trailed them. In the breaking day of June 8, they continued down Rosebud Creek until reaching the great camp of their people nestled at the mouth of Muddy Creek.[42]

"We wolf-howled," Wooden Leg recalled, and Cheyennes from the upstream camp flocked to them "to learn why we had given the alarm." The wolves advanced into the Cheyenne circle and told their story to the elders. Some Sioux were at hand, and they in turn hurriedly rushed the news to their own circles. Soon the entire massive village was in a frenzy, with heralds riding about shouting: "Soldiers have been seen. They are coming in our direction."[43]

Councils were called. Young men wished to go out and meet the threat, but the chiefs would not allow it. The notion of soldiers in the south was an ominous one, but so too was the lingering presence of soldiers on the Yellowstone. At the moment neither force appeared imminently threatening. Still, these new soldiers needed watching, and the Cheyennes appointed twenty-eight-year-old Little Hawk and his friend Crooked Nose to lead a party in that direction. Several Sioux warriors joined the band, which may ultimately have numbered around ten.[44]

Wooden Leg's return was not the only excitement this day. From the east came another band of allies, some 130 Two Kettles in perhaps 20 lodges from Cheyenne River Agency, all under Runs the Enemy. The newly arrived Two Kettles folded in with the Miniconjous. As the Miniconjou circle was near the Cheyennes, Runs the Enemy recalled being drawn to the commotion there as the Cheyennes selected warriors to shadow this new enemy in the south.[45]

Little Hawk's party traveled south through the night and most of the next day, following the same course along the Rosebud just taken by Wooden Leg's hunter-wolves. On approaching the mouth of Prairie Dog Creek across the Tongue, they found that the soldier camp had not moved. As dusk settled across the scene the warriors advanced to the brink of the towering bluffs lining the river's north side and commenced shooting into the camp, particularly aiming at the wagons and profusion of canvas tents below. The wolves' gunfire was startling but managed only to riddle canvas and splinter ridge poles and wagon boxes. We "thought [the] soldiers were sleeping," Little Hawk recalled, but they "must have been sitting up with guns in their hands for a rain of bullets met [us]." [46]

The momentary clash was spontaneous and inconsequential. When it subsided, the tally was but two soldiers and some horses wounded. Yet it served as an eye-opening notice to the *ve'ho'es*—the Cheyenne name for White people—that the lands beyond the Tongue belonged to the Northern People. The soldiers rallied and drove the attackers off, but not beyond their ability to continually watch the camp. Doubtless they were startled when, the next morning, the soldier camp broke and commenced moving to the south, as if intent on distancing itself from the great enclave on Rosebud Creek. That Indian target was imagined but not yet precisely understood by those soldiers, or those invaders on the Yellowstone.

Word of the soldier withdrawal reached Sitting Bull's camp quickly as it continued up the Rosebud from Muddy Creek to just short of the mouth of Davis Creek, an otherwise inconsequential drainage coming from the west. But that same mostly dry wash was the timeless pathway west to the Little Big Horn Valley. Reports of good hunting had come from the west. [47]

In evening councils, the elders renewed their debate over fighting the soldiers, whether those in the south or the north. Foolish Elk, a twenty-two-year-old Oglala among Crazy Horse's people, wondered whether the soldiers had come to fight or perhaps make a treaty, a notion not particularly farfetched for one who had already seen much from the *wasicus* in his years.

As before, a consensus was embraced to defer any aggressive movement against these known enemies, particularly an action that might jeopardize the cohesiveness of the allied camps or endanger its numerous dependents and worldly possessions. But perhaps the soldiers were scared. As Wooden Leg expressed it: "We supposed that the combined camps would frighten off the soldiers." Besides, word had come of still other soldiers sighted in the east.[48]

Whether precisely sensed or not by those in the great enclave, soldiers were invading buffalo country from all directions. The people in Sitting Bull's camp, meanwhile, had drawn tightly together and, in fact, were growing stronger, as dribbles of warriors from the agencies continued to find their way to the Northerners. But the villagers also seemed to have missed much. Already weeks ago a column of soldiers diverting from the Yellowstone had ventured up the Big Horn River and down the Little Big Horn and Tullock Creek. Those soldiers acknowledged seeing abandoned Indian campsites but no Sioux or Cheyenne Indians. From that same Yellowstone River camp Crow army scouts had ventured across the river and ascended high ground between the Rosebud and Tongue and reported observing telltale evidence—agitated buffaloes, campfire smoke—of Sitting Bull's people in motion. But nothing came of it. The villagers seemed wholly oblivious to those incursions. Even now as the six circles continued southward from Muddy Creek up the Rosebud other soldiers were on a new trail, exploring the Lower Powder and Tongue River valleys and in due course would discover the wide imprint of the great Indian trail itself. In later life, Wooden Leg mused at that notion, quipping, "Our trail . . . that summer could have been followed by a blind man." And farther north and east a steamboat was plying the Lower Yellowstone, having advanced beyond Wolf Rapids to the mouth of the Powder. Soldiers in the west and south and now east were pressing the core of Sioux Country. Fully comprehended or not, a lifeway hung in the balance.[49]

7
STOPPING THE GRAY FOX

"Remember the helpless ones at home! This is a good day to die!"
—Crazy Horse, Oglala Lakota

It was now the middle of June. Sitting Bull's camp of Lakota and Northern Cheyenne traditionals had grown to more than 600 lodges and 3,800 people, men, women, and children committed to sustaining a way of life in the buffalo country. The odds against them were growing. Most had ignored the Great Father's unfathomable summons to the reservation in Dakota, invariably proclaiming that they were non-treaty people intending to live a free life wherever they wished, as generations before them had. But the brutal strike on Old Bear's Cheyennes on the Powder River three months earlier, and the repeated ominous warnings from agency kin that more and more soldiers were headed for the Yellowstone country, foreshadowed a different tale. All the while, Sitting Bull repeatedly proclaimed that he wanted no war, but would fight to protect families, homes, and this lifeway. His own visions lately suggested a great battle ahead, but also an astonishing Indian victory, and he was ever more intent on staying this course.

Little Hawk's news of the soldiers in the south turning and apparently marching away from the Tongue was a momentary relief in the great camp as it continued its deliberate ascent of the Rosebud Valley. By June 12 the Cheyenne circle, leading a well strung-out procession, reached the mouth of Davis Creek, some eighteen miles above their previous camp at Muddy Creek. Young Two Moon remembered those movements and how the Cheyennes and Oglalas, leading the spectacle, often had their lodges set up at the day's destination well before the final bands arrived. Scouts continually protected the margins of the body, a duty that rotated daily among all the bands.[1]

This was familiar ground, especially to the Cheyennes, who considered the Wolf Mountains of the upper Tongue and upper Rosebud as their own unique domain. It was a land rich with roots, berries, and game that they knew well. It was also a land reluctantly ceded by the Crows as the more populous Cheyennes and Sioux pushed them farther west in recent decades, though the Crows, merely now living beyond the Big Horn River, were near enough, and ceaselessly annoying.[2]

Joining the expansive camp about now was Medicine Cloud, an Assiniboine from Fort Peck, and seven other Assiniboines and Hunkpapas. Dispatching them on May 21, their agent had sent them on a quizzical, if not well-intended, mission to lure Sitting Bull away from this explosive predicament. The messengers reached the village in the middle of June and offered Sitting Bull the agent's assurances that he and the Hunkpapas would be treated well at Fort Peck. The appeal was predictably rebuffed, and Sitting Bull's *akicitas* restrained the couriers in camp. The Assiniboines may have had no desire to become entangled in a war, but in coming days, they would witness much.[3]

Sitting Bull's *akicitas* restrained other reluctant visitors, too. In late May a small band of Brulés from Spotted Tail Agency made their way to the ascendant village solely for the purpose of bringing home relatives and children belonging to the wife of a band leader, Bear Stands Up. Like Medicine Cloud's small party, Bear Stands Up was keenly aware that Sitting Bull's soldiers watched the camps closely and kept the people together, but he had no intention of joining the war and unhesitatingly told Sitting Bull so. Sitting Bull, puzzlingly asked how the Brulés were being treated at their agency and inquired about two notorious traders there, Bissonette and Boucher, meaning the old-time trader Joseph Bissonette, and the lately better known Francis Boucher. "If the troops come out to him he must fight them," the chief admitted, "but if they do not come out, he intends to visit this agency [meaning, evidently, the Spotted Tail Agency], and he will counsel his people for peace." In this instance Sitting Bull did allow Bear Stand Up and his small band to depart, but they did so by dark of night and shrewdly took a roundabout way home, traveling well east of the Black Hills to avoid making contact with anyone, Indian or White.[4]

On June 15, after three days at the mouth of Davis Creek, the great camp turned to the west and ascended the shallow divide, bound now for the Little Big Horn Valley. The grazing and game resources on the Rosebud were all but exhausted and word had come of buffalo in the west. After a movement of nearly twelve miles, the village spread out that afternoon near the crest. It was a dry camp with no water, Wooden Leg recalled, but the coulees were full of plum thickets. We spent "one sleep here."[5]

That morning before the camp moved, Little Hawk, bearer of the striking news that soldiers had been spotted on the Tongue but then had turned away, departed again. Leading three other warriors into the upper Rosebud Valley, they were intent partly on hunting buffalo but were also desirous of stealing horses from the *ve'ho'es*. As they rode up Rosebud Creek they encountered another small camp of Cheyennes, Magpie Eagle's people, descending the stream intent on joining the coalition. Two warriors from that camp joined Little Hawk's party. At about noon the next day beyond the Big Bend of the Rosebud they encountered a herd of buffalo bulls. Little Hawk shot one, breaking its back. It dragged itself to the creek where the hunters killed and skinned it, planning to roast some meat. As they went about the task a larger herd of cows came into view farther up the valley. Leaving one of their own behind to tend the cooking fire, Little Hawk and the others went forward seeking a fatter animal. Before making a kill Little Hawk happened to look back at the man at the cooking fire and saw him frantically motioning for them to return. They did so, and when they reached their friend he told of seeing two men, leading horses, peering into the valley from a distant ridge.[6]

Little Hawk and the others assumed that the friend had seen some Sioux and thought to "have some fun with them." As they rode forward, carefully obscuring themselves in the pines, and peering ahead over a ridge, they saw before them a horrific sight. "It seemed as if the whole earth were black with soldiers," Little Hawk remembered. It had to be the movement again of those soldiers in the south. The Cheyenne wolves were so close they feared being seen. One of them urged that they go back to where they were roasting the meat, but Little Hawk instead turned and started riding pell-mell overland, northward through a tangle of rough ground, in the direction of the great camp. The others followed without hesitation. The first section was rough. Little Hawk recalled that he "left a good many locks of his hair in the brush." On high ground before the riders dropped again into the Rosebud Valley they looked back. They could still see the soldiers, slowly making their way into the Rosebud headlands on a course that would take them straight toward the buffalo cooking fire. Little Hawk's reflection of the moment spoke devotedly of a buffalo-centric people. "If they had not killed the buffalo," he told an interviewer in 1908, "they would have kept on and ridden right into the soldiers. The buffalo bull saved their lives."[7]

Little Hawk's party split when crossing the Rosebud, with Magpie Eagle's people cutting for that camp. Little Hawk and his followers, meanwhile, raced their ponies as fast as they could, not down the Rosebud Valley but on a northwesterly course, over the undulating Wolf Mountains and eventually onto the South Fork of Ash Creek. Ahead, somewhere on Ash Creek, they knew they would find the great village.[8]

On June 16 the six great Indian circles continued their course across the shallow divide between Davis Creek and Ash Creek, the latter an eleven-mile-long, well-watered tributary known by many names—Sundance, Ash, and more recently, Reno. It led directly to the Little Big Horn River. A Crow

Indian familiar with the Davis-Ash course referred to it as the Lodge Pole Trail, a reflection that it and the Little Big Horn led straight to lodge pole harvesting ground in the Big Horn Mountains, not far to the south. The Cheyennes leading the procession stopped for the day a mile beyond the mouth of the South Fork of Ash Creek. The camp that rose was a linear one, a simple reflection of the pinched nature of the valley in that locale, with the Hunkpapa circle nearly a mile above the South Fork confluence. The place was idyllic, covered with luxuriant bottomland and hillside grasses, scattered ash and cottonwood trees along the watercourse, clean water in the mainstem and south fork, and a strikingly tall ridgeline to the north. Some warriors had advanced ahead that day, intent on stealing horses from the Crows, while others hunted the abundant buffalo in the Little Big Horn Valley.[9]

To this well-scattered camp, Cheyennes below, Hunkpapas above, Sans Arcs in the middle where the South Fork met the mainstem, Little Hawk vividly recalled his return in the predawn hours of June 17. He and his companions had ridden hard since discovering soldiers advancing their way. We "howled like wolves" to announce ourselves, he remembered. Some early rising Sioux greeted them and asked who they were, Sioux or Cheyenne? The Sioux in turn sent a runner to the west to notify the Cheyennes that several of their own had come in, and furthermore with dire news. Soon the whole camp east to west was thoroughly astir, heralds announcing that scouts had returned. Soldiers were coming, and warriors needed to "get ready and go meet them."[10]

Young Two Moon and several companions in the Cheyenne camp heard the howling and ran forth. Little Hawk's news was startling. Those soldiers in the south had not ridden away after all, but were returning, and had already crossed the Tongue and were now advancing straight down Rosebud Creek. "I think there are Indians with them, too," Little Hawk blurted. Young Two Moon and his friends were agitated and agreed with Little Hawk that they must get ready and set out. Young men across the camps caught the fervor, brought in their ponies, assembled personal war kits, and commenced spiritual preparations for battle. Some were ready to ride out almost in an instant, fully prepared for a hard fight.[11]

In the rush of the moment, chiefs and elders met in a grand council and objected as before to any notion of sending warriors from the camp toward these soldiers, telling heralds to call out: "Young men, leave the soldiers alone unless they attack us," and "We must not divide our great power." If war came, it should be defensive. But others argued differently. Rain in the Face recalled the desire to meet those soldiers "at a safe distance from our camp." This time, no one listened to the chiefs. What loomed was an imminent threat to women, children, the elderly, and the collective well-being of a great camp, the strongest motivators any warrior could have. In the view of most, the only logical response was a calculated attack on those soldiers to drive them away.[12]

Preparations for battle varied. Each warrior had a particular way of dressing, painting, and ornamenting himself and his pony to ensure a protective power in the coming fight. For some it was intentionally elaborate dress, for others plain clothing or little clothing at all. Rubs of spiritual clays and herbs were common, as were body paintings of symbols or sometimes full shadings in blues, reds, and blacks. Arm bands, breast plates, and whistles were sometimes added, plus ornamentation with endowed *wotawe*—medicine charms—and horned or feathered headdresses, or merely one or two feathers. Some sang sacred songs. Arrangements often occurred under the guidance of a father or spiritual advisor. No one neglected these sacred rituals, though some undertook them when nearly upon the enemy and not now. Wooden Leg noted almost casually that he had his weapons, war clothing, paints, and medicines, and simply "slipped away" that evening.[13]

For some the preparations were exceedingly intricate. The Miniconjou White Bull, Sitting Bull's nephew, donned a red flannel breech cloth that draped to his ankles, dark blue woolen leggings decorated with broad strips of blue and white pound beads, and matching beaded moccasins. Over a simple shirt he suspended a thong across his right shoulder, draping war medicines beneath his left arm. Around his waist he wrapped a cartridge belt, and crowning all was a feather bonnet with a long single tail of red and white feathers, commemorating battle wounds and honors. Should he be killed in the looming fight, he wished to die in fine clothing. "Besides," White Bull recollected, "such fine war-clothes make a man more courageous."[14]

Crazy Horse's preparations were perhaps the most elaborate of all and were commented upon by many. His friend He Dog remembered that Crazy Horse never donned a warbonnet. "A medicine man named Chips had given him power if he would wear in battle an eagle-bone whistle and one feather and a certain round stone with a hole in it. He wore the stone under his left arm, suspended by a leather thong that went over his shoulder. The one central feather . . . in the middle of the war-eagle's tail, that was the feather he wore in his hair." Another friend, Eagle Elk, an Oglala in Big Road's band, remembered the same details but noted too that Crazy Horse also conventionally wore an ear stone, a small endowed stone suspended with buckskin ties woven through his hair. Eagle Elk and White Bull both recalled the war chief's plain dress: hair hanging loose, moccasins, a simple calico shirt. Crazy Horse's long-time friend and spiritual advisor, Chips, or Horn Chips, an Oglala holy man, was not with him now, but a stand-in carefully supervised these preparations. Do this before going into action, his mentor proclaimed, and "no bullet would touch him."[15]

Young Two Moon remembered warriors streaming out of the Ash Creek camp singly and in pairs in the dim breaking light. The most logical route took them in a southeasterly direction across the divide and onto Thompson Creek, the next Rosebud drainage above Davis Creek. Little Hawk had reported enemy soldiers on Rosebud Creek and warriors needed to be ahead of them. Soon the loners and small parties were corralled by a line of Cheyenne soldiers, who stopped their advance. Only when a solid band was assembled did this first party, now some two hundred strong with nearly sixty Cheyennes among them, continue. They moved cautiously, with Sioux and Cheyenne scouts well in the lead and warrior societies policing the immediate fore and margins.[16]

An even larger band followed, a mix from all of the assembled circles on Ash Creek, with Crazy Horse in the fore and Sitting Bull in the group's midst. Sitting Bull, armed now with a Winchester and wearing two feathers, was still seriously weakened from the Sun Dance ordeal just eleven days before but his presence was heartening to those at his side. "Sitting Bull came along to encourage the warriors," Eagle Elk remembered. The great spiritualist was closely tended by his nephews, One Bull and White Bull, and a friend, Old Bull, who traveled at his side throughout the day.[17]

Yet a third group of warriors also departed the Ash Creek camp in the breaking light, this one guided by Little Hawk. Barely hours before, Little Hawk had delivered the alarming news of this soldier advance on the great camp. He rode now at the head of some seventy Cheyenne and Lakota warriors on the same direct course he had just taken, following Ash Creek's South Fork and through the Wolf Mountains, bound directly for that same upper reach of Rosebud Creek where he had seen the enemy.

Runs the Enemy, the Two Kettles chief who led twenty lodges of followers to the coalition a week earlier, recalled that by daybreak almost everybody able to ride a horse or hold a gun had mounted and ridden out to meet the soldiers. But another recollection suggests a more thoughtful offensive *and* defensive strategy. Shave Elk, an Oglala in the Big Road band plainly remembered that only "part of our men went out to fight [the soldiers]. The remainder was left to guard the villages in the direction of the Yellowstone," meaning certainly any threat from the north. Sitting Bull would not have allowed the village to remain defenseless. The Ash Creek camp contained nearly 2,900 women, children, and old people. With them, too, was Kill Eagle's small pocket of Blackfeet Sioux, some seventy-five people, who had come west only to hunt and were still restrained from leaving by camp *akicitas*. Others bristled at being left behind. The eager thirteen-year-old Black Elk of Big Road's band was instructed by his uncle to remain behind and tend the helpless ones. He had proven himself, he thought, in the encounter with Black Hills freighters in May and was ready for war now, but he obligingly stayed behind, even while others his age went forward.[18]

Allowing that perhaps one hundred men of fighting-age remained in the camp as its shield, upward of 750 warriors rode south, in three distinct groups, all bent on intercepting soldiers daring to invade the buffalo country and imperil the people. But this was not Powder River. These soldiers had been spotted coming on and would be stopped. As one chronicler noted much later, not since the days of the Bozeman Trail War had Sioux and Cheyenne warriors gone out in such numbers to attack soldiers. And they went prepared, dressed in war clothing, wearing protective *wotawe*, singing sacred songs, and many carrying the latest modern guns.[19]

The warriors riding the Rosebud Valley had barely turned south when they encountered the fifteen or twenty Cheyenne and Sioux lodges of Magpie Eagle's camp. Magpie Eagle was a Southern Cheyenne, a survivor of Custer's attack on the Cheyennes at the Washita in the Indian Territory in 1868, and lately a resident at the White River Agency. Little Hawk had encountered these same people at the start of his hunting foray two days earlier and several of them had joined his party. They were aware of the soldiers upstream, having been alerted to that danger by those with Little Hawk the day before. Many of the camp's warriors joined those riding south now.[20]

The two bands riding on Rosebud Creek had closed on one another by now. Just beyond Magpie Eagle's camp they paused long enough to consult, water and briefly rest their ponies, and make final personal preparations for a fight. Some warriors brought along war clothing and spiritual medicines when they hurriedly streamed out of the Ash Creek camp and these essential needs were tended now. To the chagrin of those around him, Young Red Cloud pulled from a container his father's long-tailed feather bonnet and put it on. He also carried his father's Winchester. Young Red Cloud's friends shrugged and only saw an impetuous agency boy.[21]

As individual preparations continued, four warriors from the bands, Young Two Moon and White Bull of the Cheyennes, and two Sioux men, were sent ahead to scout for the enemy. The day before Little Hawk had seen Indians with the soldiers doing the same and this was no time to be caught unaware. The pause near the mouth of Trail Creek was short and soon most of the warriors continued their ascent of Rosebud Creek. *Akicitas* maintained order and restrained anyone inclined to dash ahead, and even made individuals stop talking. They had not yet come to the Rosebud Narrows, a distinctive four-mile restriction where the valley tightened. It was a perfect place for an ambush, or to be ambushed. Immediately beyond lay the Rosebud's Big Bend, where the stream turned abruptly to the west. Around several other bends and slightly to the south was where Little Hawk had spied the soldiers. The distance was closing.[22]

The four scouts hugged the western timbered edge of the valley and approached a distinctive imposing hill blocking any view beyond. As they ascended the rise but not quite having reached its top, the wolves were startled to be fired upon by soldier scouts—Crow Indians—who were already scattered across that crest. Those soldier scouts had watched the wolves approach and also saw in the distance the greater mass of Sioux and Cheyenne warriors coming their way. Two Moon and the others fired back. The exchange was brief. Somewhere behind those soldier scouts, unseen, was that mass of troops that Little Hawk discovered—a whole earth "black with soldiers."[23]

The warriors behind rushed to the sound of the firing. Dog and Weasel Bear, both Cheyennes, remembered the moment: "They shoot. We shoot. They run." The soldier scouts indeed turned and dashed away, soon disappearing into a deep dry hollow a mile and a half short of the Big Bend. The hollow angled upward in a southwesterly direction and was a natural channel ascending onto ground behind the long ridge fronting the west side of the Narrows. The wolves and oncoming Sioux and Cheyenne warriors trailed the soldier scouts up that same dark draw. This was familiar ground to some. Ahead in another stricture at the top, in a place ever after remembered as the Gap, was a distinctive buffalo jump, a timeless stony ledge long known to many Indian people who lived and hunted in the area.[24]

As warriors streamed up the draw and reached the upper end of the Gap they paused long enough to survey new ground. Through the Gap straight south some grasped the presence of blue coats milling along Rosebud Creek, a mile or so distant. After having turned at the Big Bend, the stream now oriented in an east-west direction. West of the Gap, warriors also plainly saw high ground blocking any other views of the creekside—a long ridge stretching to the west that others would soon call the Camel-Back Ridge. As warriors crowded at the head of the Gap some continued chasing the soldier scouts southward, toward the soldiers, until veering out of sight to the right. Many other warriors ascended the high ground on either side of the Gap and continued their own press southward. Shots pattered in the distance as the soldier scouts rode nearer to the creek, with some warriors still on their heels. More and more Sioux and Cheyenne fighters crowded the high ground east and west of the Gap and milled southward, puzzled by the extent of what might be a whole earth "black with soldiers." What they saw below them was shocking.

Lining both sides of the creek bottom for more than a mile were soldiers lazing in the morning sun. No one was mounted. Some horses were at creekside drinking and others grazed in the bottomland and adjacent benches. Horses always drew Indian attention. And everywhere were soldiers, in long random lines stretching from the mouth of the Gap westward to where Rosebud Creek bends again to the south. Farther to the west yet, warriors glimpsed a mass of horses, a herd plainly belonging to these soldier invaders. For a moment most of the newly arrived warriors paused in surprise at the sprawl—east and west—hundreds of soldiers, maybe thousands. The patter of gunfire diminished, but then picked up again as warriors here and there advanced to rocky outcroppings on the lower east shoulder of the Gap and to knobs and ridges below the Camel-Back Ridge and commenced opportunistic shooting into the soldier mass, just as had occurred when Cheyennes fired down on these same soldiers at the mouth of Prairie Dog Creek eight days earlier.

Shooting was crackling in the west, too. Little Hawk's Cheyennes had also reached the field, retracing tracks up Ash Creek's South Fork and through the Wolf Mountains, and were now sparring with soldier scouts nearer to the army's horse herd. Iron Hawk, a fourteen-year-old Oglala known to his family then as Runs in Circle and riding among those Cheyennes, remembered how they reached the field a bit later than those who rode up Rosebud Creek. The initial fighting in the west turned momentarily tense, with Crow and Shoshone army scouts charging and pushing back the mixed lot of warriors. Occasionally, the combat was hand-to-hand. "It was all mixed up fighting," Iron Hawk recalled. "We charged the Crows back, we were going south," he remembered.[25]

As the fighting intensified, several realities played out at once. The still oncoming Sioux and Cheyenne warriors confronted a soldier force on Rosebud Creek that was vastly superior to their collective mass of barely more than 750 fighters. The invaders tallied no less than 1,250 men, fully armed and capable, and among them 250 Crow and Shoshone allies, all vigorous hereditary enemies of the Sioux. Facing them also was a vast, sprawling landscape. Scattered prominences and rocky outcroppings lay east and west, a vast high ridge south of the creek loomed behind the soldiers, and a substantial if dry drainage crosscut the field from the distant west. Countless smaller draws that cut-up the Rosebud's foreground made hurried direct movements difficult if almost impossible. Before day's end, nearly every square yard of this landscape, almost thirteen square miles in all, had pony, shod horse, and foot tracks across it, and oftentimes blood trails. Such was some of the evidence of what became known as the Battle of Rosebud Creek.[26]

Sioux and Cheyenne warriors fought aggressively, often heroically but exceedingly individualistically, motivated by proving one's self-worth and counting coup. Years later the great Cheyenne informant Wooden Leg explained this unique circumstance to his biographer. "If some aggressive war was contemplated," he said, their war chiefs "agreed upon the plans. But when any battle actually began it was a case of every man for himself. There were then no ordered groupings, no systematic movements in concert, no compulsory goings and comings. Warriors of all societies mingled indiscriminately, every individual went where and when he chose, every one looked out for himself." The Hunkpapa warrior Bear Soldier put it even more bluntly: "Chiefs have little influence after battles start," he said. It was as though 750 individual battles were fought against an enemy operating with a rigid command structure and having an aggressive central authority, an individual who commanded his battle from the onset.[27]

By now Sitting Bull and Crazy Horse had arrived, the chiefs having threaded their way up the same draw from Rosebud Creek as the others. Pausing momentarily at the head of the draw, Sitting Bull scanned about, and then moved to a higher conical knob on his right. His vista afforded him a long view south through the Gap and the high ground on either flank. The ride from the Ash Creek camp, some thirty-two miles, was exhausting, but the chief's encouraging words echoed widely: "Steady men! Remember how to hold a gun! Brace up, now! Brace up!" While doubtless watching the action unfolding on that side of the field, no account suggests any other movement on the battlefield before the chief simply inauspiciously returned to camp, apparently accompanied by Old Bull. His nephews White Bull and One Bull by now had each plunged into the fight.[28]

Crazy Horse's presence on the field was appreciated by many as well. Early in the headlands of the Gap, after surveying the action and doubtless stimulated by the reactions and boldness of others, he pulled up, waved his Winchester aloft, and shouted to those around him: "Hold on, my friends! Be Strong! Remember the helpless ones at home! This is a good day to die!" The memorable cry was electrifying. And then, with the shrill notes of his eagle bone whistle penetrating the air, he rode into the Gap, his many friends at his side each too screaming loudly, "this is a good day to die!"[29]

By now the gunfire in the west had slackened but then erupted almost immediately along the entire rise north of the creek; that is, along the full extent of the army's position. Dismounted blue coats advanced on those warriors still annoyingly plinking at the camp from the rises and hillocks south of the Camel-Back Ridge. No warrior position was yielded quickly, and two blue coats were wounded in this initial soldier charge, the first army casualties of the engagement. But the soldier advance faltered. Higher yet, along the broad crest of the dominating Camel-Back Ridge, the shooting intensified as increasing numbers of warriors surged over that towering ground, scanned southward and often taunted the soldiers below. They found safety for themselves behind the shelves of rock and timber scattered along the crest. In the soldier lines below, one man thought the crest a frightening "mass of humanity." A civilian in the soldier midst said the Indians seemed "as thick as blackbirds."[30]

Almost simultaneously, action on the east side of the field drew attention to that quarter. Mounted soldiers had gathered at the mouth of the Gap and with their own trumpets blaring charged northward into the swirling fray. They took the fight especially to the high ground on their right about midway into the Gap, near the aged buffalo jump. Knowing they should dodge such open confrontations, the warriors withdrew, some onto the next of the succession of ridges behind them, some into the rocky ground to the west, at the eastern foot of the Camel-Back Ridge, but more into the rock-strewn highlands above the buffalo jump. The soldiers swerved in that direction, dismounted, withdrew their horses to several rocky prominences just below the buffalo jump, and climbed afoot into the high ground themselves. The shooting was intense but largely ineffectual, a screen of billowy white gunsmoke clouding everything, but warriors there were slowly driven to rocks and hillocks farther north.

Early in the fighting, one of Camp Robinson's intermarried Frenchmen, Baptiste "Big Bat" Pourier, an individual well known in the Northern Indian camps but now scouting for the army, spotted Crazy Horse and directed those around him to focus their shooting on him. But "they couldn't even hit his horse," Big Bat lamented. "I myself fired at him four times but missed him and I was a good shot them days too. The Indians say this was because of his great medicine."[31]

What Crazy Horse likely had spotted were the cavalry horses withdrawn in the care of a few holders to the rocks below the buffalo jump. Others did, too. Young Two Moon recalled eyeing four horses—cavalry horses were typically linked and withdrawn by fours—and he and a friend, Black Coyote, plus two other Cheyennes and two Sioux behind them, set out to capture those mounts. They raced forward but were driven back by sharp carbine fire. As the would-be raiders fled, "the soldiers came near overtaking them and were shooting at them fast," Young Two Moon remembered.[32]

A Southern Cheyenne chief, Comes in Sight, saw those horses, too, or perhaps he was tempted simply to expose himself in an act of daring, courageously letting soldiers shoot at him as he and two others made a showy run. Accounts vary, but however motivated, in one such run across the western length of the Gap above the buffalo jump Comes in Sight's pony was shot from beneath him. He tumbled to the ground, gathered his bridle, and started running afoot, zigzagging to his friends well north of him. Bullets kicked dust all around. Warriors on the margins watched in dread, but suddenly from their midst sprang a young rider on a gray pony galloping straight toward the fleeing Cheyenne. The rider rode slightly past, wheeled about, and snugged up tightly beside him. Comes in Sight jumped on and the two rode to safety. The heroine that morning was Comes in Sight's sister, Buffalo Calf Road. This mother of two in her mid-twenties, an excellent horsewoman and fearless warrior in her own right, had ridden south from Ash Creek that morning with one of the Cheyenne bands. Her act of selflessness was never forgotten, and to this day the Northern Cheyennes refer to the Rosebud battle as the "fight where the girl saved her brother."[33]

The soldiers charged a second time in the Gap, joined side-by-side by the army's Shoshone and Crow allies who had rallied to the gunfire. The combined enemy line pushed the warriors to the next highlands behind, which by now were veering away in a natural northwesterly curve. Some warriors at that point abandoned this fight in the east altogether and rode farther west to a rallying point at a prominence ever after remembered as Conical Hill, at the westernmost extent of the Camel-Back Ridge. The knob that Sitting Bull occupied at the battle's start was abandoned by now, and the great egress to and from Rosebud Creek also lay behind soldier lines.

Again the fighting devolved into a continuous exchange of long-range shooting, broken by a number of memorable episodes and with neither side yielding ground. White Bull tells of facing a charging Shoshone warrior riding a fast sorrel with white stockings. He came straight for White Bull and when close fired twice, but missed. White Bull fired back, twice striking the sorrel in the fore-shoulder. The horse fell and the Shoshone leapt and ran. White Bull chased him for a moment and shot again, laming him in the right leg. He wheeled about and joined his comrades as they rode to the west. In later years White Bull was often heralded as "the man who lamed the Shoshone." He remembered those Shoshone warriors as the bravest and best he had ever fought.[34]

A civilian in the midst of the soldiers clinging then to the toe of the Camel-Back Ridge remembered one peculiar instance involving Yellow Ear Rings, a warrior he had known at the Grand River Agency in Dakota. In the fighting with the Crows, Yellow Ear Rings's gun jammed. Figuring this was his death knell as Crows raced toward him, he climbed atop a boulder before him and began chanting:

> *I, Yellow Ear Rings, love these hills and valleys,*
> *My friends are in number as the grass.*
> *But now I am nothing.*
> *My friends, I am leaving you.*
> *You may even now count me dead.*

Yellow Ear Rings repeated himself, but his act of extraordinary bravery inspired his followers, one of them screaming out: "Yellow Ear Rings, you are too brave to die. We will not let you die. If you are to die, we shall also die with you." And his followers rose as one man and flew at the Crows and put them to flight. As he later retold it, "his death chant saved his life."[35]

Wooden Leg sensed the sometimes simple essences of the fight, telling his chronicler: "Our Indians fought and ran away, fought and ran away. The soldiers and their Indian scouts did the same. Sometimes we chased them, sometimes they chased us." Iron Hawk, an Oglala in He Dog's band, said much the same thing. "It was all mixed-up fighting. There was a brave Cheyenne with me and a man by the name of Sitting Eagle. I was about fourteen years old at the time. This was a pitiful long stretched-out battle."[36]

An even more peculiar episode involved Above Man, later in the reservation period called Jack Red Cloud. The heralded chief's eighteen-year-old motivated son had donned his father's feather bonnet that morning, much to the dismay of Lakota warriors around him, especially the older chiefs. After witnessing attempts at running off cavalry horses, and the heroic episode of the sister saving her brother, he may have been spurred to also make a successful daring run, just as others were doing. So, he galloped alone into the fray.[37]

Midway into his ride Young Red Cloud's horse was shot from beneath him. He tumbled unhurt, but what then followed was a sequence of humiliations witnessed by many that haunted him the rest of his life. One observer, Wooden Leg, was especially critical. "According to the Indian way," he told his biographer, when unhorsed like this, a "warrior was supposed to stop and take off the bridle from the killed horse, to show how cool he could conduct himself. But young Red Cloud forgot to do this. He went running as soon as his horse fell." That action alone defied a simple imperative that a warrior should either escape with his bridle, or die trying, a matter of death before dishonor.[38]

Crow scouts, likely the same ones who shot young Red Cloud's horse, watched the unfolding action closely. Bull Doesn't Fall Down and two others chased Young Red Cloud. Instead of resisting his assailants, the feckless boy whimpered and begged for mercy. The Crows summarily seized Young Red Cloud's feather bonnet and his rifle—the ornate Winchester given to his father in Washington. They taunted and laughed at him, and then whipped him with their riding quirts, berating him as a mere boy with no right to possess such honors. Then, in an "eloquent expression of contempt," they let him go instead of killing him. It was an act of humiliation worse than death.[39]

Crazy Horse and two others witnessed the spectacle and charged the Crows, saving the young man, a critical attribute among Oglalas, but they refused to look at him afterward, shaming him for his behavior in running so quickly without facing his enemy. But this was no time for a lengthy scorning. To the south the warriors could see soldiers ascending and advancing westward along the crown of the Camel-Back Ridge, pushing the warriors in front of them farther west toward Conical Hill. Soldiers now more or less occupied all of the advantageous ground in the area of the Gap. But no warrior dallied. Most simply joined others and rode westward themselves, safely beyond the range of any gunfire from the crown of the ridge and anxious to join those gathering on Conical Hill.[40]

Unlike those warriors on Conical Hill who had long views of the Rosebud Valley south of the Camel-Back Ridge, the warriors fighting in the Gap were unaware of soldier movements—and opportunities—elsewhere on the field. For one, the army's sizeable horse herd remained circled at the west end of the stream's east-west reach, and those extra horses and ponies tended by young herders were a perfect target for a raid. The Cheyenne and Sioux warriors on Conical Hill had mostly ridden cross-country from Ash Creek, and when the battle opened they initially sparred with Crows and Shoshones. But that encounter slackened when intense gunfire in the east drew most of the army's auxiliaries into the Gap, leaving the horse herd an irresistible target.[41]

Seizing the moment, a band of Cheyennes rode the back side of Kollmar Creek, the pronounced dry drainage that cut across the field from the west. They rode directly toward the horses and made a surprising swoop that captured a small bunch. One luckless Shoshone boy was killed outright in the attack, the boy's slayer pausing long enough to dismount and take the youth's scalp, a gruesome slice from "the nape of the neck to the forehead, leaving his entire skull ghastly and white." The boy's name was not memorialized but he was the first fatality on the army side in the Battle of the Rosebud. Sharp soldier fire from the hill south of the creek and overlooking the scene drove the raiders away.[42]

Elsewhere on that front the Indians in the west, particularly those hovering around Conical Hill, became a deliberate target of two different soldier advances. The enemy was sizeable enough to be scattered widely yet be effective. One element was engaged in the Gap, another ascended the crown of the Camel-Back Ridge, while a smaller complement rode to the crest of the prominent ridge south of the creek, and yet another mounted unit—the largest intact command on the field—advanced westward along the southern fore of the Camel-Back Ridge. For those several soldier units operating on or near the Camel-Back Ridge, their plan seemed simply to push and ideally disperse the warriors in their front, as if to sweep the field.

But no ground on the Rosebud battlefield was yielded without a contest. Warriors across the Kollmar drainage and Camel-Back continually found advantageous ground upon which to dismount and fire on the soldiers, and when pushed would simply mount and retreat to the next hillock or draw behind them. Some have insisted that this was Crazy Horse's design, the notion of drawing soldiers farther and farther to the west, up the Kollmar drainage and ultimately beyond conventional support, as if being lured into a well-intended trap. More likely what occurred was the simple run of events, warriors following independent inclinations alone or among scattered friends, but with no one dominant man orchestrating some overarching design. It was likely the same among the soldiers who followed their own carefully prescribed directives that sent them against their enemy. The warrior Eagle Elk, riding among the Oglalas, said as much. Crazy Horse "was not trying to guide the warriors, he was just fighting like the rest of us." The Cheyenne warrior Limpy expressed it in the plainest terms: "We fight hard. By and by [those] soldiers chase us." Limpy made a sign indicating a running right. "Soldiers stop and we chase them."[43]

Exploding gunfire in the west drew warriors to the scene, most of them necessarily riding widely around soldier positions along the crowns of the Camel-Back and Conical Hill after soldiers successfully occupied those positions. The lures were the cavalrymen who had reached the rocky headlands of Kollmar Creek, where they dismounted and seemed intent on holding that position. The shooting intensified as more and more warriors streamed onto the scene, and then turned furious when those soldiers unexpectedly began to withdraw. Puzzling things were occurring elsewhere on the battlefield, too. Word was spreading among the warriors that the soldiers fighting in the Gap had also withdrawn from their farthest position and were now consolidating at the mouth of that distinctive feature. To the warriors, such turnings could well mean that they were succeeding in this fight. These invaders from the south had not yet abandoned the field, but the battle imposed on them stalled their advance northward toward a vulnerable village on Ash Creek. This was no time to slacken and here was an opportunity to cut some of those soldiers off entirely.

Everything up Kollmar became a target. When the soldiers in this farthest reach of the drainage dismounted, holders withdrew their horses to the depths of the broad dry wash behind them. Some warriors perhaps thought the successful horse raid in the soldier camp a while earlier could be duplicated now. "We made a dash" at those horses, Runs the Enemy remembered. "The charge we made was enough to scare anybody." The soldiers, however, held their ground as they continued to back away, but at an ever visible cost. We "shot down a good many of their horses, for there were lots of them lying on the ground, wounded and dead."[44]

As the soldiers backed away, they yielded valuable defensive ground, too. The head of the Kollmar drainage was a natural overviewing bulwark, a ground strewn with sizeable rocks and broad views in every direction. As the soldiers stepped backward, some protecting the horses in the swale and others straddling the southern shoulder of the drainage, warriors quickly occupied that same rocky ground and poured a ruinous fire on the enemy. The soldiers called their conscious withdrawal a retrograde movement. Warriors, in turn, saw themselves aggressively pushing those soldiers eastward, down Kollmar to Rosebud Creek, two miles distant.[45]

As in the Gap, opportunities for heroics along Kollmar presented themselves. Easily the most distinctive episode early in this stage of the fighting involved an eighteen-year-old Cheyenne warrior named Limpy. The young man had experienced a crippling leg injury years earlier—hence his name—but had survived, walking with difficulty because of leg bones that had mended improperly. This was Limpy's first experience in battle and he watched other Cheyenne and Sioux warriors fighting fearlessly. He did so as well.[46]

In the swirl in the upper Kollmar, as the soldiers were pushed backward, step by step, Limpy rode with Yellow Black Bird, Comes in Sight, Young Two Moon, White Bird, and Dog, some of them already prominent in other episodes this day. In stalking the soldiers, they came to a cluster of sand rocks, common features in the upper end of the swale and some of them large enough to hide humans and horses, and tall and flat enough to stand atop. They stopped and fired into the soldiers pushing the horses. But they pushed too hard and in turn were attacked by soldiers from the left in retaliation, some of them the horse guard. For a moment the warriors seemed almost trapped. As they huddled behind the sand rocks Young Two Moon argued that they should flee to the distant high ground two hundred yards behind, but do so one by one so that the others could defend the rider in flight. And in that manner one by one they made their escape, except for Limpy.[47]

Limpy was the youngest in the group and obligingly agreed to head out last. He had barely begun his ride when his pony went wild, kicking and jumping and bucking him off, and then dropping dead from a bullet. Young Two Moon shouted out to Limpy to be ready to jump on his horse, and he rode out, bullets whizzing about. Young Two Moon closed on Limpy but he was too crippled to simply jump on the pony's back, and the attempt failed. Soldiers watched the action intently, too, and served up hot fire from the left. Limpy hobbled to one of the sand rocks in his fore and waited for Young Two Moon's return. When he headed out Limpy climbed to the top of the rock. When Young Two Moon approached a second time, Limpy jumped from his perch onto the pony's back and the two Cheyennes escaped together, Limpy clutching his revolver and prized silver mounted bridle tightly. Young Two Moon had honorably rescued a fellow warrior.[48]

Reflecting on his narrow escape many years later, Limpy blurted: "When you are in a tight pinch like that it seems like you don't have no feelings. It seems like your feet don't even touch the ground." Before the fighting ended Limpy was given a new horse, not a led animal but one captured in the battle, and he and his five companions joined another body of warriors and charged again into the fight.[49]

On their withdrawal, the dismounted blue coats continued to hug the southern shoulder of the Kollmar drainage, some pushing the horses in the depths of the swale and others back-stepping slowly along the rise and crown of the grassy top. The soldiers faced west and sometimes returned Indian fire. Warriors hounded the line, using to their advantage small hillocks on both sides of the shoulder, its periodic creases, and the scattered sand rocks throughout its upper course. These were the same advantages reluctantly surrendered moments before by the *wasicus* as they inched eastward. And all along warrior numbers increased, especially as others arrived from the now fully faded clash in the Gap. Soldiers there had withdrawn completely and, curiously, were riding away, down Rosebud Creek. Just now, in the early afternoon, the Rosebud battle focused on the Kollmar drainage.

For a while the fighting seemed at a stalemate. Warriors doggedly pressed the soldiers as they backstepped, but never succeeded in cracking their cohesiveness and order. Still, many on both sides doubtless could sense—or fear—that a cataclysmic moment loomed. Somewhere ahead those soldiers would necessarily turn their backs on their attackers, dash for their horses, and attempt a run to soldiers in the east. That would be the moment to bring them down.

The Kollmar drainage broadens visibly at a point about half a mile above its mouth, where its otherwise narrow tight bottom affords an easy crossing from the south to the north. The few soldiers who had remained mounted all along saw it first and halted the movement at that point. Straight north on the crown of the Camel-Back Ridge, other soldiers witnessed this spectacle, too. The hounding Sioux and Cheyenne warriors easily imagined the soldiers on Kollmar turning away, dashing for their horses, and attempting to cross the dry bottom to escape to safety with the troops on the ridge top. Already, when the soldier line paused their mounted soldiers paused, too, making themselves especially inviting targets. And just behind the blue line were those attractive horses, jittery, and now tightly confined in a pocket in a deep crease of the drainage.

The orderly soldier line that had characterized nearly the entire withdrawal along Kollmar Creek collapsed on two near simultaneous triggers.

On the ridgeline one of the mounted soldiers who had paused was shot from his horse. The bullet sliced across the man's face from his left temple to just beneath his right eye, blinding him instantly. A witness remembered that as he fell, blood spurted from the penetrating wounds and he spat more from a full mouth. Sioux warriors charged right over the soldier's prostrate body. One chronicler noted that the soldier was lucky not to have been struck by the hooves of galloping ponies. Several Shoshone scouts quickly rushed to his side.[50]

That startling event seemed to prompt the anticipated dash. The *wasicus* indeed turned their backs on their enemy and made for their horses, some still conscious of the ever-present danger in their rear, some simply on the run. Witnessing that, mounted warriors attacked, delivering a "savage fire" as they dashed forward from nearby ravines and into the fleeing troopers. Other warriors emerged from the narrow winding creek bottom above the horse herd, and still more raced across the ridgeline from the west and southwest. "We did not circle the soldiers," remembered the Oglala, Eagle Elk, "we just rode in among them all mixed up, and killing the nearest ones with knives and war clubs. Sometimes we would knock them off their horses, then jump down and beat them to death."[51]

The fighting turned hand-to-hand. Near the horses, White Shield, a Cheyenne, watched a soldier attempt to mount. White Shield rode between the trooper and his horse and killed him, counted coup, and took his bugle. Another Cheyenne, Scabby, watched a soldier nearby struggling with his horse and rode over and tried to strike him with his quirt. The soldier caught the whip and pulled Scabby from his pony and shot him. The soldier escaped. Scabby managed to crawl a short distance out of the fray and was discovered and carried away when the shooting ended. He survived the battle.[52]

Red Hawk, an Oglala, remembered a tall soldier on foot shooting at a charging Indian but managing only to hit the warrior's horse. Red Hawk turned on the soldier as he attempted to reload and shot him in the breast. Soldiers later told of watching comrades who had run out of ammunition clubbing their attackers, and one, a recruit it was later told, apparently preferring a fatal bullet from his own gun to the torture of being pierced by spears and arrows, surrendering his carbine to the nearest warrior, only to have his skull crushed by the blow of a war club. Yet another soldier, also a young man, was shot at point blank and fell to the ground, gravely wounded. The fighting swept over him. A while later other warriors appeared. The soldier thought they were friendly Crows and hailed them. But they were Sioux warriors, who struck him repeatedly with tomahawks, disemboweled him, and cut off his hands and feet.[53]

Weasel Bear was drawn to the horses and thought he could capture three or four with saddles on. As he tried leading them away he saw where they were shot through their bodies. He left them to die. Young Two Moon saw the same horses and noted that the saddlebags were empty, quipping that "some Sioux had already been there." But the young Cheyenne continued his own quest and captured a soldier gun and "heap soldier cartridges off all soldier saddles." He proudly told of using that carbine in other battles that summer. Soldier saddlebags were as much a lure as the horses themselves because they invariably held foodstuffs and boxes of pistol and carbine ammunition.[54]

The tenor of the fight at the Kollmar Crossing changed when Shoshone and Crow army scouts charged into the fray, coming from the northeast and likely drawn by the crescendo of gunfire. They threaded their way across the dry creek bottom, through the milling soldiers, and straight into surging Sioux and Cheyenne warriors. A few peeled to the left and fought off those warriors in the proximity of the soldier shot from his horse—warriors only learned much later that this was an esteemed officer. Those Shoshones helped move the wounded man to medical care. Other army scouts pushed the warriors out of the crossing and west to the sand rocks. The Two Kettles chief, Runs the Enemy, grimly remembered the arrival of those army scouts, observing: "Had it not been for the Crow scouts we would have charged right through to the soldiers. The Crow scouts were between us, and received fire from both sides." But it was close to the end. The Crow and Shoshone push of Sioux and Cheyenne warriors on Kollmar Creek was the final gasp of the great battle on Rosebud Creek. It had been nearly a day-long fight. As he rode away, Eagle Elk thought simply that this enemy was as tired of fighting as he and his companions were.[55]

The warriors withdrew slowly that afternoon, those on Kollmar necessarily circling widely between that drainage and the soldiers occupying Conical Hill, the imposing redoubt that had changed hands during the course of the battle. The route to their Ash Creek camp followed Little Hawk's overland trail. By then, warriors and ponies had been in constant motion for twelve hours or longer, with no letup for eating, resting, or watering the animals. Tall Bull, a Cheyenne, remembered simply that we "thought we had done enough for one day." Iron Hawk recalled that word had spread that they should quit and go back and take care of their women, adding pointedly that "there was no finish fight here," and that these soldiers would come after them. Iron Hawk's sense that these soldiers posed a continuing threat prevailed among most of the warriors as they departed the battlefield. Some considered staying and chasing a while longer but no one did. The ponies were exhausted, and, besides, there were many wounded to care for.[56]

For the most part, wounded warriors were carried away by friends and family. The soldiers that evening counted thirteen dead Indians scattered across the vast field. One other badly wounded warrior, evidently a Cheyenne involved in the horse raid at the western bend of the stream earlier in the day, was killed the next morning.

Warriors in turn had killed nine soldiers and wounded another thirty or forty. Whatever the casualty number, the lingering presence of such an imposing body of troops posed a considerable threat to the massive Sitting Bull camp. Four men, including the Cheyennes Lost Leg and Howling Wolf, stayed behind to watch the soldier force, much as Little Hawk had done the day before. If it moved northward at all, whether that afternoon, in the coming darkness, or in the morning light, they would warn the village. But what they witnessed at first was only confusing. The mule soldiers vacated Conical Hill and took up a new camp on the crown of the Camel-Back Ridge, midway along its course, and most of the other soldiers for a while milled about the Big Bend but then turned back and encamped midway along the east-west reach, about where they were when the battle opened that morning. Soon the mule soldiers abandoned the ridge altogether and joined the massive camp. Throughout the night countless campfires flickered across the Rosebud bottom. This plainly remained a threatening enemy.[57]

Many weeks later the warriors in Sitting Bull's camp learned that the man commanding the soldiers at Rosebud Creek was Brigadier General George Crook, the Gray Fox as Red Cloud called him. This was the same man who had traveled to Red Cloud Agency several times that spring attempting, unsuccessfully, to recruit Oglala Sioux to guide his campaigns into the buffalo country. The Oglalas refused to join Crook, insulted to be asked to pit kin against kin, and some even trying to kill him on his second visit. At Rosebud Creek Crook fought well, with a superior force, and he inflicted costly numbers. By one count as many as thirty-six Indians were killed in the fight, including fourteen outright on the field, eight dying of wounds that night, and four dying the next morning. Additionally, Indian counts variously noted another sixty-three (or perhaps eighty-six) warriors wounded. The wounded were carefully returned to Ash Creek, some on horseback and others on hastily fabricated travois. Mostly the victim's names are lost to history. Kill Eagle, the Hunkpapa chief who had remained at Ash Creek, noted additionally that 180 Indian ponies were lost in the Rosebud fight.[58]

Despite the human toll, it was a great battle. Some in the Ash Creek camp could remember others—on the Dakota prairie in the early 1860s, in this same Powder and Tongue River country in the days of the Bozeman Trail, and on the Powder River most recently. But often villages were involved, where the devastation and human tolls were always shocking. Rosebud was different. There 750 warriors rode out to directly challenge an army daring to invade the homeland of these Northern Indians, soldiers intent on severing their right to live where they chose, forcing them to subsist on agency beef and flour instead of buffalo, and otherwise deny them the timeless lifeway of their forebearers.

Weeks earlier Sitting Bull had had a great vision of soldiers falling upside down, hats falling off, into an Indian camp, and that the Indians would defeat those soldiers. Was this great battle on Rosebud Creek a fulfillment of that vision? In succeeding nights, the chiefs and elders in the great camp debated the matter carefully and concluded that the Rosebud fight, massive and heroic as it was, was not what Sitting Bull had seen in his vision. Soldiers had not struck their village. Another great battle loomed somewhere in the future.[59]

SITTING BULL AND THE RED SHIRT.

ABOVE: Sitting Bull's red shirt episode at Fort Buford in 1866, illustrated in Nelson Miles's *Personal Recollections* (1897), was the first of many notable expressions of sheer contempt shown by the chief in his long struggle with the white invaders of the revered buffalo country. *Author's Collection.* BELOW: Métis Red River cart convoys of this sort were commonly seen on the prairies of Dakota and Montana in the 1860s and '70s, whether hunting buffalo or trading contraband wares, including firearms, to the Northern Indians. *Montana Historical Society.*

Spotted Eagle, a Sans Arc Lakota, was a fervent Sitting Bull ally who figured prominently in nearly every episode of the 1870s war, from fights with railroaders to the Little Big Horn to the showdown with General Terry in Canada. *Montana Historical Society.*

White Bull, a Miniconjou Lakota, was Sitting Bull's nephew and at his side throughout the long course of the 1870s war. He was also one of the war's longest living survivors, reaching the year 1947. *The Dickinson Press.*

Gall, a Hunkpapa Lakota war chief, was a steadfast Sitting Bull lieutenant throughout the war. He suffered tremendously at the Little Big Horn where he lost two wives and three children in an opening fusillade of the battle. *State Historical Society of North Dakota, 00022-H-11190.*

ABOVE: Massive heaps of glacial till or prairie sod, seen being piled here in 1873, marked the US-Canada border, the sacred Medicine Line of Sitting Bull's day. *University of Calgary Collections.* BELOW: Spotted Tail (second left) and other Brulé chiefs investigated the Black Hills gold diggings on French Creek in August 1875. Among Spotted Tail's party was the interpreter, Francis Boucher (right), the otherwise notorious night-trader who provided arms and munitions to the Northern Indians during the war. *Dakota Wesleyan University.*

Little Big Man, an Oglala Lakota, was an enigmatic figure in the 1870s war. A fervent Crazy Horse ally, he nearly singularly disrupted the Black Hills proceedings in 1875. He fought valiantly alongside Crazy Horse in many of the war's great battles but then switched allegiances in 1877 during war chief's final days at Camp Robinson. *Denver Public Library, Western History Collection, X-31790.*

He Dog, a lifelong friend of Crazy Horse, remained at the war chief's side through nearly every episode of the 1870s war, including his fateful surrender and horrendous death in 1877. *Nebraska State Historical Society, RG2955.PH00007.*

Big Road, a fervent Oglala Lakota traditional, figured in nearly every episode of Sitting Bull's War, including the Canadian exile, and afterward remained a staunch nonprogressive in the earliest days of the reservation. *Wikimedia Commons.*

Black Elk, an Oglala Lakota, (left)—seen here with a friend, Elk, during Buffalo Bill Cody's Wild West tour of England in 1887-88—befriended John Neihardt in the 1930s and provided a distinctive accounting of Lakota life during those final memorable years on the buffalo prairie. *Anthropological Archives, Smithsonian Institution.*

Wooden Leg, a Northern Cheyenne, provided Thomas Marquis with his own compelling narrative of life and war on the buffalo prairie in the 1870s. Their book, *Warpath* (1924), is a timeless classic and remains a vital resource today. *Mark Gardner Collection.*

One Bull, a Miniconjou Lakota, was Sitting Bull's nephew, adopted son, and constant companion through every phase of the war and its aftermath. Memorably, One Bull was Sitting Bull's lone companion on the evening of June 24, 1876, when the two crossed the Little Big Horn to pray, the great chief pleading for his people, "We wish to live!" *Mark Gardner Collection.*

Two Moon, a Northern Cheyenne, fought valiantly in the Powder River, Rosebud, and Little Big Horn battles, but later scouted for the army in the final days of this long war for the buffalo prairie. *James Brust Collection.*

Red Horn Bull, an Oglala Lakota warrior, was shockingly wounded in the face in the Little Big Horn fight but recovered and died on the Pine Ridge Reservation years later. *Library of Congress, LC-K2-53.*

Little Wolf and Morning Star, Northern Cheyenne Old Man Chiefs, figured in many distinctive episodes of Sitting Bull's War, but are remembered foremost for leading their people in 1878 from an anguishing exile in the Indian Territory to their northern plains homeland. *Anthropological Archives, Smithsonian Institution.*

Susan Iron Teeth, a Northern Cheyenne, suffered the loss of her husband and two sons in the Red Fork battle and endured the painful Cheyenne exile in the Indian Territory, but later provided Thomas Marquis with an extraordinary account of perseverance during those trouble-filled years. *Buffalo Bill Center of the West, PN.165.1.92.*

Sitting Bull (front left), an Oglala Lakota pragmatist murdered by Crows at the Tongue River Cantonment in December 1876, poses here a year earlier with Swift Bear (front center), Spotted Tail (front right), Omaha businessman Julius Meyer (back left), and Red Cloud (back right), en route to Washington to meet with the President. *Nebraska State Historical Society, RG2246.PH000008a.*

ABOVE: This dramatic and near contemporary depiction of the slaying of Crazy Horse in September 1877 was drawn by Amos Bad Heart Bull, a Lakota historian and graphic artist. *University of Cincinnati.* BELOW: The Sitting Bull Council at Fort Walsh, Canada, in October 1877, proved an embarrassment to the American government in its attempt to induce the surrender of the exiled Sioux and return them to Dakota. *New York Graphic, December 1, 1877, Author's Collection.*

Newsman Jerome Stillson sketched this somber image of Sitting Bull on the occasion of an interview at Fort Walsh in the late evening of October 17, 1877. The interview, one of the first ever with the proud Lakota leader, captivated American readers with its endearing glimpses of a dedicated family man and fervent traditionalist. *Harper's Weekly, December 8, 1877, Author's Collection.*

This striking photograph of Spotted Eagle's camp along the Yellowstone River at Fort Keogh in November 1879 offers a blunt look at a war-weary Northern Indian village near the end of Sitting Bull's War. *Archives & Special Collections, Mansfield Library, University of Montana, 81.0492.*

Cleansing the northern prairie of natives in the 1870s and '80s had two cruel manifestations, the removal of its free-roaming Indian peoples and the complete destruction of the buffalo herds, the signature ungulate of the grasslands. This enormous pile of buffalo skulls, a monument to that latter pathetic legacy, awaits transformation into bone meal fertilizer in Detroit in 1892. *Burton Historical Collection, Detroit Public Library, DPA4901.*

8

WE WISH TO LIVE!

"Father, save the tribe, I beg you. Pity me, we wish to live!"
—Sitting Bull, Hunkpapa Lakota

Rosebud was a long hard fight in a day punctuated beginning and end by difficult, wearying rides from a distant Ash Creek camp. Warriors and ponies were physically consumed. Some 750 Sioux and Cheyenne fighting men rode south that morning, June 17, and confronted a substantially larger enemy. Chroniclers among the soldiers were at once astounded by those uncanny attackers and their seeming incalculable numbers and boldness, convincing themselves that evening that they had been assaulted not by hundreds but by thousands of "hostile" warriors. No one in that evening camp could grasp the Plains Indian style of warfare confronted that day, or the sheer determination the fighters exhibited, especially on such a sprawling battlefield.

During the Rosebud fight, a surprising lot of self-assured warriors challenged soldiers in one sector of the field, then dashed off to confront other soldiers over the next hill, and then circled around to engage them again in some other quarter. Often, as the Cheyenne warrior Dog remembered, it was as if there were "three fights going on" almost simultaneously. Such was the fluidity of Indian movements. But it was also a costly fight. Perhaps twenty warriors, maybe more, were killed on the field, with others dying later, and many more wounded and their pony stock severely used up.[1]

Most of the exhausted Rosebud warriors returning to Ash Creek were jubilant over their accomplishments. Two Moon remembered a "great fight, [with] much smoke and dust." White Bull effused over a "hard fight, a really big battle. I lived up to my good name and counted five coups." Eagle Elk boasted that "nothing touched me all day. I think it was the quirt that protected me," referring to a treasured, charmed buffalo-hide riding whip he carried in battle. But some had restrained views. The Oglala Iron Hawk merely remembered a "pitiful long stretched-out battle."[2]

Assuaging everything at the moment was the simple fact that this enemy from the south had been stopped, if perhaps only momentarily. Indian wolves remained on the field that afternoon and evening ready to report any soldier movement. Meanwhile, the warriors returning to camp as darkness came on were greeted by cooking fires and women going about feeding hungry fighting men. Young boys rushed to tend the ponies, watering them and ushering them to hillsides to graze. Wounded men were delivered to the care of families, and the deceased were borne home too, and the grieving began.[3]

A few warriors lingered on the distant margins of the Rosebud battlefield through the night and at the earliest crack of light the next morning, watched and listened as bugles broke the calm. Soldier horses and mules were drawn in and the blue coats prepared for some manner of movement. The commotion was confusing at first, and the wolves could only imagine a resumption of the troop movement northward, down Rosebud Creek, where they'd quickly encounter the obvious pony trail from the day before, a trail that would lead this enemy straight to the great Ash Creek camp. But to their utter astonishment, the wolves watched instead as the blue coats commenced a departure from the field heading south, straight for the Tongue and Big Horns. The soldiers were abandoning the Rosebud.

The wolves fixed their stare, and as that dust trail grew fainter in the distant hills they turned north and raced pell-mell to Ash Creek. The soldiers were retreating.

Heralds spread the news throughout the stretched-out camp and the reactions were rapturous. Any lingering doubts of victory were cast aside. As one chronicler observed, "even the mourning people stopped to make a little sound of joy." Weasel Bear concluded that "the Great Spirit was with us. We whipped the White soldiers and drove them back south." As Runs the Enemy expressed it, "the general sentiment was that we were victorious in that battle, for the soldiers did not come upon us, but retreated back into Wyoming." Turning back was the key. The soldiers in the south no longer posed an imminent threat to this camp and its vulnerable ones.[4]

Some on Ash Creek momentarily contemplated assembling and challenging the soldiers again, but that ardor was dashed quickly. Shave Elk captured the sentiment. "We did not pursue [them] because we were not particularly anxious to fight if the soldiers would leave us alone." Besides, as He Dog observed, those soldiers had Crow and Shoshone allies, who were dangerous enemies who might somehow find the sprawling village while the warriors were away.[5]

But a small lot of Sioux and Cheyenne, some twenty men in all, did return to the battlefield, not necessarily intent on engaging soldiers again but to scour the place for plunder. Dead horses littered the field, Standing Bear recalled. Ammunition was the biggest lure and the scavengers picked it up everywhere, sometimes even in scattered piles, a point speaking to frenzied life and death struggles occurring across the field during the course of the fight. Standing Bear also remembered the discovery in the soldier camp of disturbed soil with the remains of a fire built atop it. Assuming immediately that this was a grave, he and several others dug and indeed discovered at least a corner the battlefield's mass soldier burial. Some retrieved blankets used to wrap the dead, and one warrior cut a diamond ring from a man's finger, while another collected a watch, and yet another scalped one of the bodies and carried that piece of flesh home on a stick. Others in the party also found the grave of the Shoshone boy killed by

Cheyennes in the horse raiding episode. Though no informant mentioned doing so, the scavengers likely also gathered the remains of the fallen Indians abandoned on the field. As they departed, Standing Bear recalled looking south and seeing the dust of the soldier column on the far horizon between the Rosebud and Tongue, but "we went home."[6]

On Ash Creek, June 18 was a chaotic day. For some, it was a day almost entirely devoted to caring for the wounded, the dying, and the dead. As many as thirty warriors returned with battle wounds. Mostly they were recoverable, although some men clung precariously to life and several died that day in camp. In the lodges devoted to the fatalities, the deceased were tended by family members, who dressed their fathers or sons in fine clothing, wrapped them in blankets and skins, and buried them according to custom. The Sioux preferred scaffold or tree burials while the Cheyennes when possible commonly placed their dead in caves or crevices on nearby rocky hillsides. In this locale a precipitous rocky ridgeline defined the northern margins of the slender valley. Black Sun, a Cheyenne victim who died in the camp, was buried in a hillside cave. Time was of the essence as it was customary to relocate camps, especially after so many deaths.[7]

Intentionally, several of Rosebud's dead were left in the camp in tipis standing in respective tribal circles. No less than three such lodges dotted the site when the camp moved on. The uppermost lodge was in the Sans Arc circle located on the north bank of Ash Creek opposite its confluence with the South Fork. That band's circle was positioned centermost in the strung-out village. Inside lay the body of Old She Bear, a Sans Arc shot through the hips in the battle and carried home by his brother. Old She Bear suffered a lingering death. When others in the great village departed for the Little Big Horn, the warrior's wife and a few kinsmen remained behind until he expired some days later. His preparation for burial was remembered by a family member, with Old She Bear's face painted red, his body dressed in ceremonial buckskins and then swaddled in a buffalo robe, and the remains placed atop a squat legged scaffold. Cooked soup and meat were laid aside the bier, and a brightly decorated tipi was raised over him. Only then did those family members depart, barely ahead of the site being overrun by others, who on their own arrival curiously noted the warm fire pits. On June 25 this lodge drew considerable attention when soldiers encountered it and when they and their Arikara allies plundered, shredded, and burned everything completely.[8]

The Northern Cheyenne warrior American Horse told of two other Indians wounded in the Rosebud fight who died in the camp and were "left there in lodges." Wooden Leg, the reliable Cheyenne informant added details, noting that a Burned Thigh Sioux (Brulé) and a Miniconjou died after arriving in the camps. The few Brulés in the massive village were aligned with the Oglalas, whose camp circle was located alongside the Cheyennes, while the Miniconjou circle stood between the Oglalas and Sans Arcs. Those funerary lodges were downstream of Old She Bear's tipi.[9]

Wooden Leg also noted that the Hunkpapas lost the greatest number of warriors at Rosebud, but the handling of their dead was unlike the others. Moving Robe Woman, a Hunkpapa informant twenty-three years old then, remembered that seven dead warriors were carried by travois to the Little Big Horn River when the camp moved the next day, and there they were placed in a funerary lodge adjacent to the Hunkpapa circle. This, too, was a conventional occurrence until all funerary rites could be honored.[10]

After devoting nearly all of June 18 to Rosebud casualties, the great village took up the trail again on June 19. As always, the Cheyennes led, traveling down Ash Creek to just short of its confluence with the Little Big Horn River, and crossing southwesterly to a new site in the broad bottomland along the east side of the river. The day's journey was a short one, barely seven miles. Again, the Cheyenne camp, located the farthest upstream on the gushing Little Big Horn, defined one extent of the great encampment while the Hunkpapa circle, farthest downstream, defined its other end.

Unlike the Ash Creek encampment that was distinctively linear in that narrow valley, the sprawl now filled the entire width of the bottom land. As Wooden Leg suggested, "the only strict rule of camp circle location was that none should be up ahead of the Cheyennes nor behind the Unkpapas."[11]

Conditions along the Little Big Horn were perfect, perhaps the finest yet on this two-and-a-half-month odyssey from the Powder to the Tongue and up the Rosebud. The Little Big Horn Valley was familiar ground to these Cheyennes, who summered there almost annually and hunted the great buffalo herds that invariably ranged the uplands farther west. They were guides and cordial hosts in country that was new for many of the Sioux. This again became a time for hunting, berry picking, and root digging. The water was particularly sublime, the stream wide, cold, clear, and flowing abundantly from the Big Horn Mountains, thirty-five miles straight south. The Hunkpapa Good White Buffalo Woman (Mrs. Spotted Horn Bull in another day) marveled at what she saw. "The country was good; there was rich grass for the ponies, and sweet water; the fields glowed with prairie flowers of yellow and red and blue; there were buffaloes in the valleys and Indian turnips on the hills for digging. We were rich in provisions."[12]

The great village spent five days in this camp. The people relished a seeming break from the ever-present pressures of this absurd war, so plainly meant to end their life on the buffalo prairie. They were relieved most immediately from the pressures of soldiers in the south. We "did not suppose that the White men would care to follow us further into the rough country," remembered Rain in the Face. Moreover, here the general demeanor of the camp changed from one of recovery and mourning after the grueling and costly Rosebud fight to one of jubilation after learning that they had defeated that enemy. The Rosebud triumph may not have been the great victory Sitting Bull had foreseen in his Sun Dance vision, but a sizeable army column had indeed been turned away.[13]

Soon after settling in, the camp was roused upon the arrival of Gall, Crow King, and their sizeable bands of Hunkpapa followers. When Sitting Bull dispatched couriers to the agencies in early May requesting traditionals join him in this war, he foremost had in mind Big Road's considerable band of Oglalas and these equally devoted bands of Hunkpapas. Those chiefs and their people were not averse to visiting their agencies from time to time, where among their many ordinary routines they also commonly availed themselves of opportunities to connect with outlying traders. At war's end, Gall explained himself, telling a newspaperman that he had gone to Standing Rock that spring to visit relatives, and he furthermore detailed his return, making no mention of the Sun Dance or Rosebud Creek fight. These Hunkpapas, Gall's sixty lodges, and Crow King's fifty-four lodges, added upward of 165 warriors to the fold.[14]

Another band also joined the great camp early in this pause. Where Gall's people traveled west from Standing Rock ahead of or at least oblivious to a soldier movement also coming from that direction, Hollow Horn Bear, a Brulé traveling west with some twenty Two Kettles warriors, consciously trailed those soldiers for two days in the Heart River valley in Dakota. When learning that those soldiers were led by George Custer, a figure increasingly well-known on the Middle Missouri, the band diverted from their original intent of chasing horses to a pell-mell ride to Sitting Bull. There, at least some pinned a figurehead name to what was still an elusive notion of soldiers coming to the buffalo country from the east. As yet no such headlining names were attached to the *wasicus* already on the Yellowstone or those defeated on Rosebud Creek. The Two Kettles people apparently folded in with the Sans Arcs, bringing that collective number of lodges, in Hollow Horn Bear's estimation, to sixty-five.[15]

Some time each day was spent in common council, where the chiefs and elders from the many circles met in one camp and then the next in another day. The chiefs of the different circles were considered equals, but among them they also acknowledged one honorific Old Man Chief, Sitting Bull, who though his counsel, inspiration, and foresight was a lodestone in this time of war. News now that Custer was coming and seeking a fight was disturbing and much discussed. Some Cheyennes remembered his bloodthirstiness on the southern plains. Lakotas more recently recalled his exploration of the Black Hills and the tempest he had unleashed. Some also remembered fighting him on the Yellowstone, although they had learned his identity much later. At best the chiefs agreed to not seek out the soldiers as they had at Rosebud, but, as Two Moon put it, "let them come to us." Lone Man, a well-scarred Oglala Sun Dancer, remembered Sitting Bull adding his own words of encouragement: "We shall remain together as a Sioux nation and we must never retreat in the face of danger, no matter what the odds. We must defend our rights, our families, and our hunting lands."[16]

Evenings were times for celebration and dancing, particularly victory dancing after the Rosebud clash. Never before had the Lakotas taken the battle so consciously to the *wasicus*. Even the great fight on the Piney ten years before did not compare. The soldier chief that day was not nearly as capable as this soldier chief, and nor were the numbers alike. In each circle, warriors regaled others about their great war deeds. Best of all occurred among the Cheyennes, where the story of Buffalo Calf Road Woman, the sister who saved her brother, was told and retold.[17]

In the days after the Rosebud fight, scattered individuals and small clusters of friends joined the camp. They traveled without families, were not aligned en route or presently with any known band leader, and some, though not all, were heeding Sitting Bull's call to the defense of the buffalo prairie. They sheltered in wickiups that customarily dotted the margins of camps like this, sometimes close to their own tribal circles but just as commonly scattered haphazardly among the willows and underbrush at riverside. The most puzzling of these newcomers were five Arapahos from the White River Agency. They had started out in search of Shoshones but ran instead into a Sioux party who brought them to camp. At first the Arapahos were greeted skeptically. Most of the Sioux believed they were spies for the army and detained them, confiscating their arms and ponies. But some among the Cheyennes recognized the men and ultimately Old Two Moon interceded, declaring that "these Sage People are all right. They have come here to help us fight the soldiers. Do not harm them, but give them back their property." The five were released and in the days ahead fought steadfastly alongside their Cheyenne friends.[18]

Another band appeared, as well. Late in the respite, ten lodges of Oglalas under Foolish Elk joined the camp. He told inquisitors years later that he fought in the Rosebud battle and was wounded slightly, explaining how he and his followers arrived on that field from an entirely different direction and pitched in, and then from its proximity exited straight west to the Little Big Horn Valley. He remembered the engagement as a great victory, but he also understood that other troops were in the Indian country and that the villagers could ill afford any further loss of men and ammunition. Ironically, after Rosebud, Crow army scouts who had separated from the southern army column the day after the fight, observed Foolish Elk's people. The Crows, who were themselves headed to their agency beyond the Big Horn River, chose not to engage. Foolish Elk's meander took his band down the Little Big Horn to this communion with Sitting Bull's camp.[19]

After five days at this place the chiefs chose to move downstream, perhaps as far as the mouth of the Little Big Horn. Before this, the elders had planned simply to continue buffalo hunting and gradually move upstream toward the mountains, but hunting scouts reported great herds of antelope grazing the tablelands west of the Big Horn River and north and west of their present camp. That was desirable meat and skin, too, and on that account the camp headed north, deeper into precarious Crow Country. On June 24 the Cheyennes took down their tipis, packed belongings, and commenced the trail, passing each of the other circles as they made their way down the valley. The Oglalas and the others followed in natural order, the Hunkpapas trailing all.[20]

The presence of soldiers in the south remained foremost in the consciousness of the people. Wooden Leg passed it off. "We had driven [them] away . . . and it seemed likely it would be a long time before they would trouble us again." Nowhere in his narrative or in any other is there an overt concern shown for the soldiers operating on the Yellowstone, a similar distance away. Then, too, Hollow Horn Bear had warned of soldiers coming from the east. Soldier movements on the Yellowstone River had been the object of considerable attention a month and a half earlier, but not now. In fact, troops there were concentrating and probing the very back country that these people had traversed just weeks before. In spite of it all, in Sitting Bull's camp, this past week had been one of hunting, berry picking, and victory dancing, and the greater focus now it seemed turned simply to antelope.[21]

The journey on June 24 was a short one, perhaps eight miles, and most of the people established camps before noon at yet another inviting expanse of Little Big Horn bottomland, this one on the west side of the river several miles below the mouth of Ash Creek. The valley here was nearly a mile wide, with a lush grassy floodplain that rose gently to the west, providing ideal camping grounds and attractive grazing for the camp's substantial herd of more than ten thousand ponies. Dense stands of cottonwoods fringed the riverbanks here and there, and a massive slough south of the Hunkpapa circle showed where the river had once followed a different course. Beard, the Northern Cheyenne, distinctly remembered that this was the season when the cottonwoods shed their seeds, often creating a summer snow of glistening white. The river was thirty, sometimes fifty feet across and occasionally five and six feet deep, and still running bank-full with mountain snowmelt. Abutting the river's east side was a long expanse of rugged cliffs. Some were nearly three hundred feet high, forming a nearly impassable ridgeline broken only infrequently by coulees and drainages, the most prominent being Ash Creek itself, several miles upstream. A large dry wash four miles to its north opened about opposite the lower end of the new sprawling camp, about where the Cheyennes established their circle. Some in the village knew this wash as Water Rat Creek while others called it simply Dry Creek. Most, however, knew it as Medicine Tail Coulee.[22]

The village sprawled for about a mile, the camping order partly reflecting the simple travel scheme adopted that spring, with the Cheyennes always in the fore, the Hunkpapas trailing all, and in-between the four other major bands and lesser groups. When reaching the new site the bands randomly scattered along the river and into the width of the floodplain, with their exact positions evermore etched into the lore of what was to come.

Marking the massive village's farthest northerly extent was the Cheyenne circle, tallying now some 125 lodges and comprising the third largest band in the encampment. Notions of a general village-inclusive "circle" were misleading. Sprawl was a better description of what unfolded. Behind the Cheyennes and snugging the sinuous river were the seventy-five lodges of Miniconjous, while farther south and west the Sans Arcs raised their near sixty-five lodges. Aside and partly behind them stood the Blackfeet Sioux circle of twenty-two tipis, with Kill Eagle's twelve lodges of hunters and war resisters in their midst. The Sans Arcs and Blackfeet formed the camp's smallest independent circles. Farthest from the river and shouldering the Cheyennes camped to their north were the Oglalas, the second largest circle in the encampment numbering upward of 155 lodges. Randomly spaced in their midst were an untold but smaller number of Brulé lodges, people camping neighborly with the Oglalas just as they had all spring and as they did in the Pine Ridge country. Defining the southern extent of the great camp was the Hunkpapa circle, the largest in the village at nearly 300 lodges. Among the Hunkpapas were the Santees—the fifteen humble tipis of No Clothing People led by the seemingly ageless Inkpaduta. The massive Hunkpapa circle touched the river on its east side, had an all but impassable slough to the south that stretched westward partway across the valley floor, and the open prairie in the west where some of the Hunkpapa lodges neighbored with the Oglalas.[23]

Sitting Bull's own crowded skin lodge stood on the southernmost margin of the Hunkpapa camp. Twelve people resided with him, including his two wives, his mother, two adolescent daughters, a young son, two stepsons, his sister, and twin sons born in the previous camp just days before. Gray Eagle, the brother of his wives, also resided in the lodge. One Bull, Sitting Bull's newly married nephew, occupied an adjacent lodge, and he and Gray Eagle chiefly tended the family's pony stock, some twenty animals. They picketed them close by night and tended to their watering and grazing needs by day.[24]

Simple, peaceful routines immediately engaged the villagers. Herders drove the camp's ponies variously to water and then to graze, with individual and tribal herds scattered across the prairie north, west, and south of the camp. Usually such duties befell younger boys, but just as often older men also tended this important task, as in the instance of Sitting Bull's family. Elsewhere children bathed and frolicked in the river, men fished, women went to the hillsides to dig turnips, meals were prepared, and many anticipated an evening of social dancing. Good White Buffalo Woman remembered this as a comfortable camp.[25]

But the painful legacy of the Rosebud battle lingered. The Hunkpapas carried to this place the seven bodies of their deceased men, a movement that began on Ash Creek. A funerary lodge was again erected, this time on the southern margin of the Hunkpapa circle. Elsewhere, Julia Face, an Oglala, remembered several seriously wounded men being tended in their circle. One, a warrior named Plenty Lice, died a day later. Another, Julia Face's husband, Rattling Hawk (also known as Thunder Hawk), who had been seriously wounded in the hip, recovered in due course.[26]

In the midst of this ordinary hubbub Magpie Eagle's small band of mostly Cheyennes joined the camp, adding some fifteen or twenty lodges. Their trail began weeks ago at the White River Agency in Nebraska. The Rosebud fighters from Ash Creek encountered the band on Upper Rosebud Creek the day of the fight and many from the camp participated in the battle. Since then the band had continued its own deliberate, almost nonchalant meander down the Rosebud, hunting and steering clear of others, until angling west on Davis Creek and following the well-scored trail to the Little Big Horn. The band mostly folded in with the Cheyennes, enlarging that circle now to some 145 lodges.[27]

The week's arrivals, Gall's and Crow King's 114 lodges of Hunkpapas, the approximately ten lodges or wickiups belonging to Hollow Horn Bear and his Sans Arc friends, the ten lodges of Foolish Elk's Oglalas, and now the twenty lodges of Magpie Eagle's Cheyennes grew the great camp to some 765 lodges, with a population of nearly 4,900 people, with perhaps 1,100 men of fighting age scattered throughout. Among the Cheyennes, they looked still for the arrival of the valorous Old Man Chief Little Wolf and his followers, who were thought then to be in the buffalo country somewhere to the east.[28]

Sitting Bull's call to the defense of the buffalo prairie had indeed proved enormously effective. The camp had more than doubled in size since dispatching couriers to the agencies five weeks earlier calling on the traditionals to join him. In size, the camp had no relative comparison. The Black Hills purchase fracas near Red Cloud Agency a year and a half earlier had drawn thousands of Lakotas and Cheyennes too, but they were largely agency people. The great treaty enclave at Fort Laramie in 1851 had drawn twice as many people, but they represented all of the Plains tribes. This Little Big Horn camp was filled with Lakota and Northern Cheyenne traditionals and was almost certainly the largest of its sort ever seen on the northern plains. Such a sizeable gathering would never occur again.

Numbers do not lie, nor do Indian accounts of this emotional time. Often it is asserted that the camp during this interim between June 17 and June 25 also welcomed a deluge of agency people, the often so-called "summer roamers." But that claim is not supported in the historical record, aside from vague statements like that of Wooden Leg's, who noted when commenting on the arrival of the Arapahos that "some more of our own people from the reservation joined us here." He was perhaps referring simply to Magpie Eagle's band. He noted too that "likely some Sioux also arrived, but I am not sure about that." Perhaps in that instance he was simply reflecting on the arrival of Foolish Elk's Oglalas and Gall's mix of Hunkpapas.

Sitting Bull had consciously summoned the traditionals to the fold. They responded and are acknowledged specifically in Indian accounts, by name and sometimes repeatedly. Doubtless scattered unattached individuals like

Hollow Horn Bear and his Sans Arc friends also arrived, but that hardly constituted a deluge of agency people. Otherwise someone, somewhere would have noted it, particularly if those surging new arrivals were led by a recognized band leader. Any contrasting notion plays against another reality inherent that summer of 1876. While agency people ordinarily came to the northern buffalo country to hunt, many plainly stayed away in this time of calamitous war. Safety dictated their course. A network of military posts aside the agencies surrounded them, and they could observe the wartime orchestrations occurring against their Northern kin first hand. What they saw was distressing. Many Lakota people consciously stayed home this year. The silence in the historical record tells us so.[29]

In the center of the great camp near the river's edge a large yellow council tipi was raised and that evening the chiefs and elders from the various circles gathered to discuss the day's events and the camp's prospects and business. They quickly agreed to remain at this place one more day to allow the people to fully avail themselves of the resources and attributes at hand, and heralds were instructed to convey that word. The counselors also acknowledged the largely unsubstantiated but nagging threat posed by soldier invaders lurking in the north along the Yellowstone River. There were also the routed soldiers on Goose Creek in the south. The chiefs agreed to dispatch wolves in the morning in those directions to shadow them. Meanwhile, to protect the camp itself, the assembled elders instructed representatives from the many warrior societies present to serve as guards now, shielding the camp and particularly restraining zealous young men who might wish to sneak away and somehow engage or incite conflict unnecessarily. But no overt action was directed at the known enemies north or south, and the elders sensed no eminent threat. We "did not think the soldiers would come that far to fight us," recalled the Oglala Shave Elk.[30]

The assembled head men again also affirmed Sitting Bull as the Old Man Chief of the aligned bands. Wooden Leg explained this many years later, reflecting on the matter in personal terms. "I am not ashamed to tell that I was a follower of Sitting Bull. He had a big brain and a good one, a strong heart and a generous one. In the old times I never heard of any Indian having spoken otherwise of him." Iron Hail (Dewey Beard in another day) expressed it more plainly. "As long as we were all camped together, we looked on him as head chief. We all rallied around him because he stood for our old way of life and the freedom we had always known."[31]

This, indeed, was Sitting Bull's camp.

The evening gave way to social dancing in nearly all of the circles, large and small, the people moving from camp to camp, singing, gathering around drums and great fires, older women providing plenty of food, younger women flirting with younger warriors who were heroic in the Rosebud fight. The young men were always "after the girls," Wooden Leg admitted. "My mind was occupied mostly by such thoughts as regularly are uppermost in the minds of young men. I was eighteen years old, and I liked girls." The scene in one of the Sioux camps was momentarily more somber when a handful of young men, some twenty Sioux and Cheyenne who had lost relatives in the Rosebud fight, pledged to throw away their own lives in the next battle. The Suicide Boys danced, too, theirs a "Dying Dance." The dancing and drumming were kept up all night by all the people, remembered the Cheyenne warrior Brave Bear.[32]

Despite the precautions, some young warriors were intent on evading the *akicita* cordon thrown up around the camp. Spotting soldiers in the north, perhaps even fighting them, was a beckoning opportunity for glory, just as the Rosebud warriors basked now in what they had accomplished. Earlier in the day, two Cheyennes, Wolf Tooth and his cousin Big Foot, hobbled their ponies north of the village. After dark they inched around the guards, feigning the need to check on their hobbled animals, and once away struck eastward, keeping at first to brushy draws as they threaded their way into the Little Big Horn highlands. At first they thought they were the only two that had somehow escaped with this intent, but they soon ran into others, eventually as many as fifty. Alas, "the nights were short," Wolf Tooth lamented, and the cross-country distances were daunting. But the thought of somehow warning the camp of approaching soldiers, just as Little Hawk had done on the eve of the Rosebud fight, was a luring opportunity.[33]

Even in the general frivolity of the evening, some could not shake the precariousness and vulnerability of a camp filled with so many devout traditionals. The people there knew that soldiers lurked near enough, and that unease atop last winter's government ultimatum, the vicious attack on the Powder River, and a victorious if costly battle eight days ago on Rosebud Creek were thunderclaps of warning. The night before, Box Elder, the eighty-one-year-old Cheyenne holy man, dreamed of soldiers coming, and urged elders and warriors to tie their best ponies close to their lodges. This was the same spiritualist who prophesied that the Cheyennes would recover their ponies after the Powder River fight. Some did not believe the old man, but those close to him "recalled that, in the past, Box Elder's prophesies had always come true." In fact, while the young people danced on the evening of June 24, and cautious elders like Box Elder fretted, a soldier column was force-marching its way up Rosebud Creek, hounding Wooden Leg's well-beaten Indian pathway so wide that a blind man could follow it.[34]

At the far southern end of the camp, Sitting Bull fretted, too, and as he was so often wont to do, went off and prayed. What occurred that night, especially in hindsight, was another of the extraordinary moments in the wartime life of this great leader, akin perhaps to his audacious prayer in the midst of the Arrow Creek fight in 1872 and his episodes of prayer on Rosebud Creek barely a moon earlier. Prayer was often a relatively solitary matter, and it invariably occurred on some accessible though remote vista at the time of the setting sun. Here, from the southern extremity of the Hunkpapa circle, as Sitting Bull scanned east and west, such a luring vista beckoned. It was due east, across the Little Big Horn, not on the obvious pinnacles on the high foreground jutting the river, but on a shadowy ridge behind, nearly a mile distant, a perch ever after known by others as Sharpshooter Ridge.[35]

Sitting Bull and one other, One Bull, walked there, and we principally know this story by way of that young nephew. After wading the river and climbing a steep dry coulee on the front ridge, the two crossed eastward through another deep coulee. They ascended the northern end of the long, slender ridge east of the coulee, one that offered on its southern tip a distant view of the Ash Creek drainage. From its northern end they had a broad view northward of the tangled Medicine Tail Coulee, and from that point westward a sweeping view of virtually the entire Indian village across the river, a camp now speckled with evening dance fires. There Sitting Bull fashioned an altar. He carried with him four slender offering sticks fashioned from chokecherry boughs. To their tops he had affixed tiny prayer ties, simple buckskin bags filled with a mix of trade tobacco and willow bark. He planted the sticks firmly in the ground on the cardinal directions, about three feet apart. Within that sacred space he laid a folded buffalo robe, prepared his pipe, and, standing first, offered it as always to the six powers: the four quarters of the earth, the Great Mysterious One above, and Mother Earth. He sang a thunder song, and to the God who had promised him a great victory he prayed for knowledge of things to come, intoning softly:[36]

> Great Spirit, pity me. In the name of the tribe I offer you this sacred pipe. Wherever the sun, the moon, the earth, the four points of the winds, there you are always. Father, save the tribe, I beg you. Pity me, we wish to live! Guard us against all misfortunes or calamities. Pity me.[37]

He then sat and smoked his pipe and when he was finished, he and One Bull returned home. His small altar remained on the hill, marking yet another personal and very private episode in an explosive story, one capped with the simple humble pleading:

"We wish to live!"

9

ONE DAY IN JUNE

"It was a glorious battle. I enjoyed it. I was picking up head-feathers left and right that day."

—White Bull, Miniconjou Lakota

Sunday, June 25, 1876, in the time of the red berries, dawned cloudless. It looked to be another hot day, much like the others Sitting Bull's camp had experienced since arriving on the Little Big Horn River almost a week earlier. White Bull remembered a hot, windless, lazy morning. Many young people had only barely found their way home after a long night of social dancing and reverie enjoyed throughout the scattered camps. But daily duties beckoned. Horses needed watering. Young Black Elk estimated a collective camp herd numbering perhaps ten thousand ponies. Others thought it even larger, perhaps nearly twenty thousand head. Witnesses a day later concluded a sum greater than that. Gradually horse tenders drove family and tribal stock to open river stretches north and south of the massive village, and when the animals would drink no more pushed them back onto the open prairie to graze. Close-in forage was nibbled off. Good grass was farther out now, north, west, and south. Only when the ponies had settled down again did most of the herdsmen return home for a morning meal, leaving but a few tenders behind to watch the animals.[1]

In the quiet of the morning attention turned to simple routines. Individuals and families went to the river to bathe, swim, and fish. Emily Standing Bear, an eight-year-old Oglala girl, remembered she and other children taking baths and being taught to swim, "although the water was chilly because the sun was barely up." White Shield, a Cheyenne, took his nephew fishing and delighted in watching the boy dutifully catch grasshoppers for him. Wooden Leg, a carouser the night before, ate a late morning meal and then went to the river with his brother, where they bathed in the cool water, talked a while about the good times enjoyed the prior night, and fell sound asleep under the cottonwoods.[2]

Hunters scattered widely in all directions that morning, some northeast into the Tullock Creek drainage, some up Ash Creek into the rugged Wolf Mountain highlands, and others ranging westward. An Oglala, Eagle Elk, remembered joining those roaming west. Prospects quickly proved meager so they cut their hunt short and returned to camp. Women, too, quickly commenced their daily ways, variously tending family burdens in and around the lodges. Some took up the endless tanning of animal skins. Others ventured through the river bottom and onto the hillsides in search of berries and prairie turnips. Tipsinna or tipsin—a root staple among the plains people—was in full bloom now and prime for harvesting.[3]

At about midmorning on a hill by the Oglala circle, the twenty Sioux and Cheyenne boys who had taken the suicide vow the night before gathered and were paraded through the Oglala camp and then led to the Cheyenne circle. The boys rode together, flanked by old men who shouted their names and announced to onlookers: "look at these boys well; they would never come back after the next battle." The parade grew longer as it circled about, chiefs and elders falling in behind the boys as they wove through the northern end of the village. Ultimately, they returned to the hill where they had started. The boys then scattered to their home lodges.[4]

From the Crazy Horse and Big Road circle, a small group Oglalas, six men and a woman led by Black Bear, departed for Red Cloud Agency.

Black Bear and his friends had ventured out several weeks earlier to retrieve horses that were variously lost or absconded with when Indians, likely among Big Road's people, departed Red Cloud for Sitting Bull's camp. Having recovered their animals, Black Bear's group simply wished now to return to the Pine Ridge. Although the evidence is thin, it seems highly probable that Young Red Cloud, shamed in the Rosebud fight and still brooding, joined Black Bear's party on this return. The eighteen-year-old was unable to dodge the onus of cowardice and had been shunned since the battle eight days before. Black Bear's pathway led his small band and their horses east, up Ash Creek.[5]

Behind the Black Bear party three Hunkpapas, Brown Back and his sons, Hona, or Little Voice, and Deeds, also rode eastward, up Ash Creek, Unlike Black Bear, they were searching for lost horses. Separately, two others, Two Bear and Lone Dog, both Sans Arcs, also rode up Ash Creek to fetch a horse wounded in the Rosebud fight and abandoned in the old camp. No one anticipated trouble. Plainly, the countryside near and far from the Little Big Horn village was alive with Indians this morning, whether they were opportunistic glory seekers like Wolf Tooth and Big Foot who snuck out of camp the night before and with others were now ranging the highlands in the Little Big Horn–Rosebud divide, or were among the morning's wave of horse tenders, travelers, hunters, and turnip diggers.[6]

In the massive yellow council lodge in the heart of the village, many of the chiefs and older men assembled and agreed easily to remain in the camp another day. But a more compelling conversation quickly centered on Sitting Bull, his prayer, and the contemplations the night before. The chief was not present now, but earlier in the day he had spoken to a select group of leaders, including Crazy Horse, where he reflected on his sequence of dreams. In one telling, Sitting Bull fervently believed that soldiers were headed for this village and the people would be forced to engage them. But "the day would belong to the Lakotas for the signs have further revealed that every soldier will die by his own sword." Looking directly at Crazy Horse, Sitting Bull allegedly remarked: "You will emerge from this conflict with added laurels," and "in the coming battle prove your worth as a daring leader." The seated council members were at once mesmerized and terrified by what they heard.[7]

Unknown to the elders or anyone else in the Little Big Horn village, a column of soldiers idled not more than fifteen miles away, near the eastern crest of the Davis Creek–Ash Creek divide. By midday from scattered perches in the high country around those soldiers, wolves and buffalo hunters watched intently, and some Indian people behind those White men had already been shot at.

The Cheyennes at Little Big Horn eagerly awaited the arrival of Little Wolf, another of their revered Old Man Chiefs. The fifty-six-year-old was a devout traditional and fearless warrior. He was also something of a pragmatist, itself a reflection of too many years' experience fighting White men. Like Big Road and Gall, he traveled widely this spring, and lately was visiting kin at White River Agency. Resolved again to join the Cheyenne traditionals in the north, he was sensitized to the robust militarization occurring across the Pine Ridge country and the word of fresh cavalry having arrived to patrol the highly trafficked and vital Powder River Trail. This time, Little Wolf intended to go north to encourage his Cheyenne friends and kin to get out of this war. He had departed the White River country on June 15, hastening up the Powder River Trail. He then routed westward cross-country through Montana to Rosebud Creek. His band reached the Rosebud about when Sitting Bull's village was relocating on the Little Big Horn, and there they immediately encountered the alliance's distinctive pony and travois trail scoring the valley. They also found the distinguishing fresh prints of shod horses. Little Wolf's small band of seven lodges—perhaps forty-five people—had fallen in behind soldiers. His own wolves advanced and carefully shadowed those *ve'ho'es* as they rode late in the day and into the night, and now idled at the head of Davis Creek.[8]

As Little Wolf's warriors roamed on lower Davis Creek the next morning, several chanced onto a crate of army hardcrackers and other matter apparently dropped from a soldier pack mule. The warriors eagerly pried at the box, oblivious to a small lot of soldiers closing on them fast. Several shots from the blue coats rang-out and scattered the Cheyennes. From points of safety they turned and watched again, and then began stalking those Whites as they picked-up the dropped possessions and returned to their column.

What happened in consequence folds neatly into another of the many perplexities of the day. For his part, Little Wolf chose to trail the soldier column cautiously. He might well have directed one or more of his band to elude the soldiers and ride pell-mell to a camp located, at best, somewhere up the trail. The village's pony and travois tracks would lead one there. Little Wolf was almost certainly unaware of the parallel instances of troop sightings and warnings preceding the Rosebud fight, details that may have impelled a different course now. Perhaps, as well, Little Wolf may simply have thought it better to shadow the soldiers a while longer until the village location became obvious. Conversely, the cracker box episode triggered an entirely different reaction unknown to Little Wolf. When the soldier chief ahead learned that shots had been fired at Indians on his back trail, and with that news coming atop other reports from his scouts telling of various Indian sightings in front of him, he determined to hasten forward. From that point on, Little Wolf's Cheyennes were chasing the dust.[9]

Elsewhere across the Little Big Horn–Davis Creek highlands, Black Bear's small party of Oglalas, pushing horses recovered from the Oglala herd, also encountered fresh shod horse tracks in the divide. Their pathway eastward was veering out of the Ash Creek drainage toward Thompson Creek on the same route taken eight days earlier by warriors riding out to intercept the soldiers advancing from the south. Some in this small band may in fact have been among them. Black Bear's band slowed long enough to investigate the tracks and then noticed White men in the distance with a dust trail behind them. Believing they had again spotted those soldiers from the south, they momentarily contemplated retracing their trail to the village, but as that column was moving fast, they doubted whether they would reach the camp first. Instead, they continued toward the divide. Black Bear's band also encountered three Cheyennes who told of trailing those soldiers and of the encounter over the cracker box. Those Cheyennes resumed trailing the soldiers, but, "as we were not hostile," Black Bear's Oglalas pressed on toward Red Cloud Agency.[10]

Wolf Tooth and his cousin Big Foot, young Cheyennes determined to find soldiers and earn honors this day, had joined a small band of similar-minded warriors who evaded yesterday's *akicita* guard at the village and made their way eastward. Eventually, they turned onto the north fork of Ash Creek. About "halfway to the head of the creek" they observed a rider on the ridge south of them who was frantically summoning them to the crest. When they reached the top the lone rider started hollering in Sioux. Big Foot, who spoke some Sioux, learned that soldiers had passed south of there and were headed for the village. Some among the soldiers saw this band of Indians, "forty or fifty" by one measure, "sixty or seventy" by another, on a hill watching the advance. Wolf Tooth, Big Foot, and the band turned, intent on warning the camp. But by the time they neared the north end, chaos had erupted in the south. It was now approaching midafternoon.[11]

Yet other warriors were even closer to the unfolding action. Two Bear and Lone Dog, Sans Arcs who set out that morning for the Ash Creek camp to retrieve the horse wounded in the Rosebud fight, encountered soldier scouts just west of that former village site. The Sans Arcs turned abruptly and attempted to evade the enemy, but one of the army scouts shot and killed Two Bear. In his own hurried escape, Lone Dog encountered other Sioux, passed the alarm, and continued a feverish ride, northward now on a diagonal from Ash Creek. By the time he reached the Little Big Horn's east side about opposite the Sans Arc circle, shots were resonating at the south end of the village.[12]

Brown Back and his sons, Little Voice and Deeds, were in the mix of horsemen riding frantically ahead of the advancing soldiers and their allied Indians. On their flight they followed the creek's course straight to the river, intent on alerting the camp but hounded closely by army scouts, just as Two Bear and Lone Dog had been. Again shots were fired, wounding Brown Back in the leg. As the father and his sons neared the river, Deeds's horse was spent, and as he mounted behind his brother he was shot and killed and fell into the brush. Brown Back and Little Voice raced on and reached the Hunkpapa circle just ahead of shots from soldiers who were also then peppering the southern end of the huge camp. Ever after Deeds was remembered as the first traditional killed in this fight, although that distinction might as easily belong to the Sans Arc Two Bear.[13]

Not everyone along Ash Creek was trapped in the frenzy. Near the lower end of the drainage two hunters, Brave Bear and Long Sioux, Southern Cheyennes, who this morning had been roaming the highlands southeast of there, saw a long line of blue coats riding swiftly toward the camp. Taking a parallel course, they attempted to keep pace, but their horses were exhausted. From the highlands upstream and south of the creek's confluence they watched the action unfolding down the valley, "where smoke and dust was rising," and then heard the pop-pop of gunfire. Long Sioux thought it sounded like a "good many . . . Indians chasing buffalo."[14]

As reports of these early afternoon sightings and encounters with oncoming soldiers began reaching the camp, initial reactions were confused. Runs the Enemy, a Two Kettle Sioux, recalled warriors and women alike arriving with warnings that soldiers were near, but many in the village, he said, simply did not believe it. It made no sense, he thought. The soldiers that had threatened them before had gone back toward the Big Horn Mountains and were not possibly near enough to attack again. Anyway, soldiers never attacked Indians in the daytime. And so "we sat there smoking." But very quickly other screams ran through the camp. "The soldiers are here! The soldiers are here!" and bullets whizzed through the southern lodges. On that horrific note, Runs the Enemy dropped his pipe and ran frantically to his lodge.[15]

Indeed, it was the stirring dust from dry ground, the crackle of bullets reverberating in the south, and clouds of rising white smoke that shocked the great camp. Soldiers had threaded their way across the river and down the valley from the mouth of Ash Creek, fanned into a frontal line, and charged the village, halting and dismounting just short of the southernmost string of lodges. The Hunkpapa Little Soldier faced the brunt of the initial attack. The "bullets sounded like hail on tepees and tree tops. [I] could see bullets hit dirt. I was armed with my bow and arrows."[16]

The Hunkpapa Good White Buffalo Woman, wife of Spotted Horn Bull, remembered this opening moment vividly. In relating her story of the war a few years later she halted her narrative at this point, thought for moment, and then struck her hands sharply together to imitate the rattling of carbine fire, and continued: "Like that the soldiers were upon us. Through the tepee poles their bullets rattled. The women and children cried, fearing they would be killed, but the men, the Hunkpapa and Blackfeet, the Oglalas and Miniconjous, mounted their horses and raced to the Blackfeet tepees." Moving Robe Woman, another Hunkpapa, was no less distraught. "Women and children were running away from the gunfire. In the tumult I heard old men and women singing death songs for their warriors. I saw a warrior adjusting his quiver and grasping his tomahawk. He started running toward his horse when he suddenly recoiled and dropped dead. He was killed near his tipi." But Moving Robe Woman was unafraid. She ran to a nearby thicket, got her black horse, painted her face crimson, and circled into the chaos.[17]

Like an explosive wave rocking the entire village, shrieks of terror rippled from south to north, circle by circle in a matter of moments. In the annals of Western American history, nothing was as terrifying as an Indian village under attack by soldiers. Sadly, it was such a common occurrence that almost every Plains Indian man, woman, and child was haunted by such recollections. In army circles this was plainly understood doctrine, a steadfast belief that the surprise attack of a camp and the destruction of foodstuffs, shelters, possessions, and ponies hastened the desired outcome of defeat. It drove these soldiers now and throughout this war.

Sitting Bull was idling in his lodge when the soldiers attacked. Beside him were Black Moon and Crow King, two steadfast Hunkpapa allies, and Kill Eagle, the Blackfeet band leader and war resister. The three were once again engaged in dissuading Kill Eagle from departing the camp. It was a nagging matter and had been so since the time of that band's arrival in early May. They represented a puzzling inconsistency in this camp. Other groups had freely departed all along, like Black Bear and his small circle of Oglalas who had struck out for Red Cloud Agency that morning. The reasoning behind Sitting Bull's continuing restraint of the Blackfeet chief and his people is unclear. One chronicler presumed that while Kill Eagle was reluctant to fight, he was also embittered by the White man's continuing treachery. That alone, plus some inducements, had proved restraint enough. Perhaps. Elsewhere in and around the lodge were Sitting Bull's wives, seven children, including newborn twin sons, and his mother. And into that robust chatter, Fat Bear, a Hunkpapa, burst, screaming the alarm.[18]

Sitting Bull, a stout middle-aged counselor, was no warrior but he was instantly animated. He helped a wife and several children onto a pony staked at his lodge and urged her to run with the rest of the women. When his family was out of harm's way, he mounted another pony brought up by one of his sons and galloped off, first ensuring that his mother reached safety. As quickly, he was back among followers, conspicuously rallying those around him. White Bull, in his own lodge in the Sans Arc circle, reacted quickly when the shooting began. Riding south to the Hunkpapas, he saw his uncle in the moment: Winchester in hand, no special dress, no feathers, riding a black horse, yelling continually, "Brave up, boys, it will be a hard time—brave up." Those around him were the first to rally in defense of the camp.[19]

Throughout the sprawling village, Hunkpapa criers mounted swift ponies and spread the alarm, screaming, "Chargers are coming! Chargers are coming!" meaning, of course, enemy cavalry. People almost universally remembered the opening chaos: mothers screaming for children; tearful, frightened youngsters; young and old scrambling to the north and west, away from the attack in the south; old men and women singing death songs; old men calling young warriors to battle; warriors rallying, shielding families, and scrambling for ponies and arms. Some horses had been staked near lodges, but most of them, as in Sitting Bull's instance, were given to the vulnerable ones so they could flee.[20]

Already people were dying. Moving Robe Woman remembered a warrior near her, perhaps Bear With Horns, a Hunkpapa, who was killed in an opening salvo. White Bull may have witnessed this death too, recalling an old Lakota man, wounded before any resistance was organized, who died several days later. White Bull remembered him as the very first casualty of the fight. Unfathomably, two of Gall's wives and three of his children were also killed in the opening salvos. His lodge, like Sitting Bull's, was located on the exposed southern periphery of the Hunkpapa circle. When the shooting began Gall was elsewhere in the camp, but he had imagined his family fleeing northward with the others. Catching a horse, he quickly rode northward himself but was unable to find them. Turning toward the riverbank he followed it to the south, encountering other villagers who had taken haven there, but again, he found no family. Returning to the Hunkpapa circle, in the shallow bend of the former river channel just beyond his lodge, he found them. They each had been shot by soldiers. Gall was enraged. "It made my heart bad," he later remarked, and "after that I killed all my enemies with the hatchet."[21]

The initial attack shocked the great village, but the people reacted instinctively, securing vulnerable ones, with boys and others bringing in horses from distant grazing in the west and north. They brought some from the south, too, though the army's Indian allies had run off many of those animals. In quick time, warriors commenced necessary, often obligatory, religious rites and ablutions as they prepared to join the fight. For some, individual preparations, as with Crazy Horse, were exceedingly elaborate and time-consuming, while others finished theirs in but a moment. The Oglala warrior Foolish Elk, wounded but not incapacitated in the Rosebud fight, remembered the ease of his own preparation, as well as a general haste as he and others hurriedly mounted horses at hand, grabbed guns, and bounded upriver to join the fight.[22]

—

The focus of all attention remained in the south where some ninety-five soldiers had dismounted and held a line more or less fronting the southernmost string of Hunkpapa lodges, seventy-five or a hundred yards beyond. Through enveloping clouds of white gun smoke, soldiers scattered indiscriminate carbine fire, targeting lodges, animals, and people. The soldiers' horses at the onset of this dismounted fight were withdrawn into the cottonwoods at riverside and put in the care of horse-holders—the cavalry's habitual "every fourth man." Warriors remembered one or more of the lodges on the periphery of the Hunkpapa circle being set afire. One was likely the funerary lodge containing the Rosebud fatalities.[23]

Hunkpapa warriors were the first to rally in the camp's defense. Their return fire was scattered but effective, stemming any additional soldier advance northward toward or into their circle. They were resolute fighters, and this was the most populous group in the village. Veterans of the battle later thought that "it was sure hard luck for [those soldiers to strike] the Hunkpapa camp first." Charging Bear, a young Oglala, remembered those hard-pressed Hunkpapas, too, but also how it "was a grand thing to watch" as warriors from the other camps raced to help them.[24]

Warriors knew better than to openly challenge a deadly soldier line, but the blue coats' unprotected margins east and west offered ideal opportunities to hurt them on vulnerable sides. Some warriors rode widely to the west, circling the soldier line altogether and placing themselves behind the enemy. There they confronted soldier scouts who were mostly intent on gathering Hunkpapa ponies. The army scouts offered little resistance, although as Gall later recollected, "it made us mad to see Indians fighting us." Already the nature of the fighting in the south was shifting. What began as an unforeseen attack on the upriver end of the great encampment was met by a piecemeal defense at first, as vulnerable ones were sent away and ponies drawn up. But that condition rapidly evolved into an offensive fight for the defenders. The ninety-five soldiers in the line were no match for the Indians pouring from the sizeable camp, one now thoroughly aroused and rallying. For some warriors, if not most, they were driven also by Sitting Bull's prophesy of a great victory, as foretold in his Sun Dance vision several weeks before.[25]

The soldier line wavered under the intense pressure. Brave Bear, among Cheyennes riding fast for the south, remembered joining Sioux warriors and that they were all "coming thick." Just then the soldiers broke for their horses at the river. The traditionals by now were incurring other casualties, including one, maybe two warriors killed outright, several more wounded, and no less than ten noncombatants killed, including Gall's family; but the soldiers were losing lives also, and now they sought a better defensive position east of their initial line. Barely half an hour had elapsed since the shooting began.[26]

The soldier position in the timber proved untenable almost immediately as the 130 men in the attacking force—the surviving skirmishers having rejoined the horse-holders—contended with jittery animals and increasing numbers of warriors pressing from all sides. Adding to the chaos, the Indians set fire to the tall, dry grass running throughout the entire cottonwood grove. Acrid smoke now merged with obscuring clouds of dust and gun smoke. Some warriors later thought the soldier position a good one. With water and trees for protection, the blue coats might not have been driven out. But the pressure intensified. Iron Hawk, a Hunkpapa, recollected that the Indians by now "were so thick that [the *wasicus*] would have been run over and could not have lasted but a short time if they had stood their ground in the woods." And so, indeed, the soldiers ran.[27]

The soldiers' retreat from the riverside timber southward proved a sheer hell. As the blue coats raced their horses into open ground, warriors at first cleared the way, fearing that they were being charged. But when they realized that the soldier were not attacking but instead attempting a frantic escape, they wheeled their ponies and closed on them right and left, swarming "like a cloud of mosquitos." Crazy Horse was on the scene by now, animating all, and leading his own followers directly into the soldiers' flight, with warriors striking with war clubs and knocking troopers from their horses, others using bows and arrows, some firing revolvers and Winchesters virtually point-blank. The consequences were devastating. One Bull killed two soldiers with his tomahawk. Charging Bear, an Oglala riding with Crazy Horse, remembered maneuvering his pony aside "a big soldier with red hair" and shooting him in the throat with an arrow, and when he fell he "took the big soldier's gun and ammunition belt and rode after [his] chief into the smoke and roar of the battle." Wooden Leg watched soldiers fall, and horses limp and stagger, with sounds of Indian tremolos and eagle bone whistles shrilling the air, amidst "yells of the kindred and the shouts of the Whites." One also heard, Wooden Leg remembered, contemptuous jeering, with someone blurting: "You are only boys. You ought not to be fighting. We whipped you on the Rosebud. You should have brought more Crows and Shoshones with you to do your fighting."[28]

The soldier retreat hugged the west bank of the river. The Ash Creek confluence used on their approach was on a different bearing and would have obliged a longer ride across ground even more exposed than this. The soldier destination was not apparent at first, but many warriors remembered the flight. White Bull recalled that from the moment the soldiers turned tail, swarming Sioux were on their heels, riding them down. "It was like a buffalo hunt," he said. These expressions, running buffalo . . . a buffalo drive . . . a grand chase, would be common descriptors this day. Among Lakotas and Cheyennes, and by whatever metaphor, it was apt. It translated into pure mayhem and death.[29]

After nearly a mile, those soldiers in the lead reached a point where the eastern bluffs aligned with the river. They turned toward the water and commenced crossing, plainly angling for the high ground on the opposite side. But even that effort, like nearly everything else for the blue coats, was nightmarish. This was no natural river crossing, and riders and horses slipped, slid, and plunged over steep cutbanks into a river still surging in its June rise. As the soldiers slowed and bunched, Flying Hawk, an Oglala, remembered that "we got right among [them] and killed a lot with our bows and arrows and tomahawks." Wooden Leg, likewise, was directly among them. With a carbine just taken from a fallen soldier, "I knocked two of them from their horses into the flood waters." Red Feather, an Oglala, saw a soldier fall from his horse, his foot caught in his stirrup, and get dragged through the water. From the other bank, warriors shot soldiers as they floundered. "I could see lots of blood in the water," recalled the young Cheyenne Brave Bear.[30]

And still the soldier anguish continued. The east bank of the Little Big Horn was as steep and treacherous as its west side and horses slipped and slid in ground wetted by the first to cross. Some tumbled backward. Those who reached the eastern bank faced other warriors who had crossed below and scattered death anew here and in the long steep draws that led survivors to the bluff top. Only on the top could adrenaline-pulsing soldiers savor their first small respite since the fight began. Behind them, warriors lurked in the carnage, killing wounded blue coats, stripping the dead, gathering weapons and cartridges, and catching runaway horses. Upward of thirty-one soldiers and allied scouts were killed in what came to be remembered as the Little Big Horn Valley Fight, this against Indian casualties numbering perhaps eight warriors killed in the buffalo chase alone, atop another twenty defenders and noncombatants killed elsewhere. But while this contingent of soldiers was repulsed, they were not the only ones on the field in this early phase of the great Battle of the Little Big Horn, and attention was quickly drawn elsewhere.[31]

As the fight opened at the south end of the village, a second column of cavalry, larger than the first, had followed the same course down Ash Creek that the attacking force had, but turned short of the creek's confluence and was making its way northward, threading draws and ridges east of the Little Big Horn River and roughly parallel to it. This second column was mostly unnoticed by a camp already in the turmoil of a surprise attack. Most noncombatants fled north and west to the high bench beyond the village, a position affording a broad look at everything occurring in the camp below, plus logical routes of escape behind them if they too were threatened. But some noncombatants fled eastward, crossing the river at the Medicine Tail Coulee ford, and making their way into that dissected dry watercourse. Some took higher ground to the south, intent on watching the fighting in the valley. It was those villagers, women mostly, who first spotted this second column of soldiers. Some momentarily watched as those blue coats maneuvered high in the Medicine Tail drainage, while others scattered through the camp with warnings that another column of soldiers threatened.[32]

Tall Bull had returned to the Cheyenne circle when the soldiers in the south began their retreat, partly to offer assurances to the vulnerable ones that the blue coats were running away and partly to encourage the women to secure their lodges and meats, when he heard the cries that more soldiers were coming their way. He had a pair of field glasses and scanned eastward and watched those *ve'ho'es* moving along the high ridges east of the river. White Shield, who earlier had been fishing with his nephew, remembered looking into the distance and seeing soldiers on white horses. They "could be seen a long way off," he recalled. Those soldiers were advancing now toward the river. Some Cheyennes rushed to the river's edge and from scattered brush and tree cover fired across the stream and into the leading soldiers. White Shield and others, meanwhile, crossed the stream south of the coulee and also immediately closed on the enemy, which, under fire, had drawn up and dismounted on the bench above the coulee's mouth. Among the warriors gathered at the river was one named Mad Wolf, who counseled: "No one should charge yet—the soldiers are too many. Just keep shooting at them." [33]

At the crossing in the south, bloody now with soldier and Indian casualties, White Bull remembered the moment when he heard the alarming news. He was fighting those retreating soldiers when someone from behind started yelling that troops were coming from the east toward the north end of the camp, three miles downriver. He and most of those around him spun their horses and galloped northward. Some riders returned by way of the village, usually assisting the return of a wounded friend or to change horses. White Bull and others crossed the river almost at once and rode the narrow toe-line at water's edge until it opened into Medicine Tail Coulee.[34]

Charging Bear, fighting alongside Crazy Horse, was sure that they would have killed all those soldiers at the riverside if not interrupted by a messenger. Racing a lathered horse, the man cried out: "Brothers! Come quickly! More soldiers are attacking the camps!" Knowing that meant an attack on women and children, Crazy Horse's bone whistle shrilled out, calling warriors back. He pointed with his rifle to the other side of the river, opposite the lower camps, and screamed: "They are near the helpless ones! Let's go!" Eagle Elk, an Oglala caught in the mix, remembered being in "a river of warriors" streaming northward. As he passed the smoky copse where the first soldiers had fought in the timber, he saw an unhorsed one who had lost his gun and was being chased by Lakota boys who were shooting at him with bows and arrows. The soldier did not escape.[35]

Eagle Elk's "river of warriors" streaming northward to the new threat were astounded by what they soon encountered. Whether riding through the camp, funneling through the brush and timber at riverside, or crossing the river and variously riding low ground northward to the mouth of Medicine Tail Coulee or climbing to the heights of the adjacent fronting ridge, warriors saw before them a mass of soldiers, some threading down the coulee and others maneuvering in the higher ground behind them. "They seemed to fill the whole hill," remembered Runs the Enemy, the Two Kettles chief. "It looked as if there were thousands of them, and I thought we would surely be beaten."[36]

Gall, seething over the loss of his wives and children, watched as Lakota warriors raced northward when one of his own followers, Iron Cedar, caught his eye, hailing him from high ground across the river. Gall rallied those immediately around him and bounded toward Iron Cedar. When they reached that higher ground, they too saw the soldiers maneuvering near the mouth of the coulee. Most of them were dismounted now, with horses having been withdrawn behind them by horse-holders. Those cavalry mounts particularly drew Gall's attention. Sensing their vulnerability, he and his followers began firing into the soldier flank, keying on the horse-holders, and yelling, waving blankets, and scattering many of the mounts into the hands of watchful women.[37]

The response to this second attack on the great village was almost instantaneous and furious, as enraged Cheyennes, by simple proximity to their own circle, confronted the approaching enemy first and stalled their attack near Medicine Tail Coulee's mouth. As they did, other warriors, Lakotas mostly, arrived from the south and simultaneously besieged the southern flank and rear of those advancing blue coats. The Indians' combined frontal and flanking fire was devastating. A Cheyenne, Soldier Wolf, remembered, that they fought in the bottom for "quite a time," and that two soldiers were killed and left there. "But soon," he said, "the Indians overpowered the soldiers and they began to give way, retreating slowly, facing the front." Horned Horse, an Oglala, also remembered the soldiers wavering and then how the "command reeled back toward the bluffs."[38]

For his part, Sitting Bull had ranged widely. In this opening hour of what many came to know as the Battle of the Little Big Horn, he was never caught in the midst of the most dangerous fighting but yet always seemed close enough to observe and assess virtually everything occurring in both brutal attacks. Riding the black pony brought in by One Bull, he, like so many others, first tended to the safety of his family, ensuring their flight to the bench north and west of the camp to join many other noncombatants. When returning to the Hunkpapa circle, he continually encouraged the warriors as they rallied to deflect the initial assault. At a distance, he trailed the action as it flowed from the first line of fighting to the timber at riverside and on to the bloody river crossing. Some women and young boys who had not fled milled through the battle scene, killing wounded soldiers and poking and stripping the dead, despite Sitting Bull's admonishments against doing so. Several accounts tell of Sitting Bull's presence for one such fatal moment—the death of a Black man named Isaiah Dorman, a civilian interpreter for the army on this campaign.[39]

—~~—

Dorman, a freeborn forty-four-year-old Pennsylvanian, had a long history on the Minnesota and Dakota frontier. He had arrived there in 1853 and secured employment as an officer's striker, including with young Alfred Sully, at Fort Ridgely on the Minnesota River. His employment with Sully continued into the Civil War and brought him to Dakota in 1863, where he remained variously engaged as a mail carrier, wood hawk, and interpreter in and around Fort Rice. He had also accompanied the Dakota segment of the 1871 Northern Pacific Railroad Survey. Dorman married a Lower Yanktonai woman and was fluent in the Lakota language.[40]

Early in the flight from the timber, Dorman's horse was killed and tumbled atop him, pinning him beneath it. Other soldiers rode by and acknowledged him, but inexplicably ignored him, perhaps simply because he appeared hopelessly wounded. Runs the Enemy remembered seeing the Black man in this fix but also merely rode on. The Hunkpapa Bear's Ghost remembered seeing Dorman and that he was wounded in the breast but still able to talk. When Hunkpapa women scoured the field a while later several recognized the interpreter, who remained alive and stranded. They knew him as Black Hawk or, jocularly, Teat, and berated him for siding with the Whites in this war.[41]

As one woman raised a gun and prepared to shoot Dorman, Sitting Bull, watching nearby, blurted out: "Don't kill that man, he is a friend of mine." Sitting Bull then stopped and provided Dorman with water. The reaction may seem odd, but it is in keeping with the chief's befriending such middlemen, and likely remembering meeting Dorman and sharing food and tobacco some years before, as he had more recently with Frank Grouard. But the women paid Sitting Bull no heed, and when he mounted and continued to the north, Moving Robe Woman shot Dorman dead. She had learned earlier that her brother, Deeds, was killed on Ash Creek and in anger she and others slashed the Black man, mashed his body with stone mauls, and cut off his head. A soldier who viewed the remains two days later said that Dorman's body looked "as though it went through a hash machine."[42]

For a moment, the soldier force operating in the Medicine Tail Coulee had divided itself. One component was operating near the mouth, seemingly originally intent on striking the camp at its midsection. The other, larger than the first, was making its way northward out of the drainage, ascending the long ridge in front of it, and heading, some thought, for the village's lower end. But increasing numbers of warriors were engaging those troops too, at first warriors from the east, including some who had been hunting that morning, and others, like the Cheyenne friends Wolf Tooth and Big Foot, still opportunistically seeking glory. The very movement of these soldiers from Ash Creek northward had blocked any simple return to the camp, but all were perfectly positioned now to harass these blue coats. They seized the moment, dismounting, creeping close, and loosing arrows and gunfire from the many gullies bisecting the upper drainage. Those warriors from the east were soon joined by a mix of other oncoming fighters. "Although it was natural that tribal members should keep together," Wooden Leg later recalled, "there was everywhere a mingling of fighters from all of the tribes." Gall likewise remembered that "all the Indians were mixed up then," and so it remained for the remainder of the day.[43]

The cresting of that long ridgetop posed an immediate dilemma for this lot of blue coats. When surmounting the ridge they lost any manner of cover, and once exposed they and their horses began taking devastating Indian fire. As they pressed northward onto a prominence known later as Battle Ridge, the soldiers in the rear dismounted and attempted to provide covering fire. Low Dog remembered how the soldier shooting was extremely inaccurate as they dually struggled to load and fire while still holding the reins of skittish horses. For the Rosebud veterans, the action playing out resembled the soldier retreat along the southern shoulder of Kollmar Creek, although here the fighting was all the more intimate and intense. Determined warriors inflicted casualties and increasingly spooked army horses that reared and escaped their holders, further exacerbating the plight of those men.[44]

At the same time, the soldiers that had advanced down Medicine Tail Coulee nearly to the river's edge were slowly withdrawing northeastward following the shoulder of an angular draw subsequently known as Deep Coulee. They plainly hoped to rejoin the blue coats on the higher ground, but they were hunted at every step. An unnamed Cheyenne visiting the ground a few years later told a soldier with him that it was like "herding" those soldiers up the hill. The blue coats fought well and successfully joined the others, but they had suffered scattered casualties along the way. Once joined again, the combined soldier force doggedly pursued its northward course, but they were stringing out noticeably and suffering harassment from ever increasing numbers of warriors filling the adjacent draws east and west. Rain in the Face reflected imaginatively on their predicament: "Those soldiers were followed by our warriors, like hundreds of blackbirds after a hawk."[45]

The Oglala Shave Elk acknowledged the steadiness with which the soldiers pushed up the hill, and also how only then did the "battle begin in good earnest."[46]

The focus of this great fight was narrowing to a sequence of straight-line ridges, draws, and hilltops north of Medicine Tail Coulee on an otherwise geographically opaque and nameless landscape. The reunited troops continued their advance northward but were precariously stretched-out. Some warriors thought they were pushing the Whites. More likely, the northward movement was a self-directed attempt to reach the high ground on the soldier's horizon, a half mile distant, or to apparent open ground beyond, suggesting another drainage leading to a probable river crossing.

Evidence of any greater intent—striking the north end of the village as some chroniclers have supposed—is thin, but three matters were clear: that the blue coat force was making a deliberate move north; that it was disjointed and exposed to an ever-surging body of incensed warriors; and that a catastrophic outcome was ever more probable, with the crucial tipping toward that end beginning simply enough in the column's rear.[47]

Most warriors remembered their own advance on these soldiers. Flying Hawk, riding with Crazy Horse, recalled he and other mounted warriors turning from the fighting in the south to the extreme north end of the camp, crossing the river, and ascending a deep ravine that brought them "very close to the soldiers on their north side." Flying Hawk could only be referring to Deep Ravine, the next bisecting draw north of Deep Coulee. Meanwhile other influential leaders, Two Moon, Crow King, Gall, and Rain in the Face among them, led followers up Deep Coulee and challenged the soldier's left flank. One early chronicler aptly noted that Indians commanded virtually every little gully and ravine running from the sides of the ridge, and every little bunch of sage. He remembered a stinging, persistent harassment.[48]

Midway to the distant horizon the troops paused on a feature ever after remembered as Calhoun Hill. There a portion of the force dismounted and challenged warriors pressing their flanks and rear. The Oglala Red Hawk remembered how the soldiers fought bravely but their horses, whether held by every fourth man or individually, were unmanageable. Some got away. Others would rear up and fall backward. Protecting those animals was critical and when any were lost, dismounted troopers were doubly disadvantaged. Cast afoot in a dire fight, they had also lost the reserve ammunition carried in their saddlebags. In the moment, each side was still delivering a galling fire. The Oglala Red Feather recalled that if either side showed a head, an adversary would shoot at it. And still, Red Hawk declared, "the Indians kept coming."[49]

Fallen soldiers and lost horses were simple gifts. Sioux and Cheyenne fighters at the Rosebud had captured a number of soldier carbines and revolvers, plus ammunition scrounged from saddlebags or loosely collected from the field later on, but now they were doing so on a much greater scale, and the consequences were immediately telling. White Bull remembered that "if it had not been for this they could not have killed them [all] so quickly."[50]

But overcoming the soldier line did not come without cost. The soldier defense on Calhoun Hill was gallant. Indians remembered a difficult fight and that many of the Lakota and Cheyenne casualties in this segment of the battle occurred in the face of these skirmishers scattered along this ridge. Gall, standing on the site ten years later, offered details without hesitation, telling an interviewer that eleven warriors were killed here.[51]

Two Moon saw an opportunity to weaken the soldier flank and he challenged his warriors to follow him in a charge. When they were assembled he led them up the sloping ground and into withering enemy fire. The Cheyenne attack faltered and the warriors fell back, regrouped, and charged a second time. The result was the same. Yet a third charge was made, and this time the Cheyennes drove the soldiers back in panic. For Two Moon, after this, "the fight . . . was merely a slaughter."[52]

The confusion the Cheyenne attack caused in the rear presented other opportunities. White Bull saw a man waver in his saddle, and he raced forward on his pony to count first coup. The dying man fell from his horse. White Bull jumped from his pony, struck the man with his quirt, and took his revolver and cartridge belt. Almost in the same moment he saw another soldier with yellow hair aim his carbine at him. "I dodged it," he said, and grabbed and wrestled with the man. "The soldier was strong and brave," White Bull admitted, but "I lashed him across the face with my quirt," and struck him again. "He drew his pistol. I wrenched it out of his hand and struck him with it three or four times on the head, knocked him over, shot him in the head, and fired at his heart." It was a hard fight, he allowed, "but it was a glorious battle. I enjoyed it. I was picking up head-feathers right and left that day."[53]

The soldier line faltered. "The Indians were overwhelming," remembered Red Hawk, watching as those men fell back steadily, though in an orderly fashion behind the forward mounted troops who were still inching northward toward the horizon. By this time, too, as he explained in a 1906 interview, "Indians were taking the guns and cartridges of the dead soldiers and putting them to use." Gall also recalled this withdrawal, telling a Chicago newspaperman in 1886 that those soldiers afoot "never broke, but retired step by step." Yellow Nose, a twenty-two-year-old Ute raised by Southern Cheyennes, sensed an enveloping despair in that withdrawal. He labeled it a retreat shrouded with a mantle of dread if not panic. In their first position, the soldiers knelt and took deliberate aim, he remembered, with every fourth man holding the horses. In subsequent movement, every soldier again took possession of his own horse. But the mounts had grown wild with fright, and their rearing and plunging made it impossible for the soldiers to shoot with steadiness and accuracy, and riderless horses were soon stampeding in every direction.[54]

The soldier movement in its entirety seemed to lack central control, and their disorder was proving increasingly fatal. Warriors infiltrated every crevice the landscape offered and seized every opportunity to pour on a withering fire. Another critical factor was that the soldiers were getting more distant from possible help. Instead of withdrawing to the south where other soldiers were still presumably maneuvering, these besieged blue coats continued their northward push, away from any possible relief, apparently aiming still for the highest point on their horizon. But they were no longer an organized force. Instead, they were a flailing, tactically impotent body of men, obviously led by the mounted soldiers ahead of them, but trailed by a dishevelment of mounted, dismounted, and wounded men, with the entire force painfully nipped at front to back by their enemy. The column, as one later scholar described it, had lost its tactical cohesion and was disintegrating. One senses that even the soldiers at this point realized that this battle was no longer being fought for victory, but for their own survival.[55]

The strung-out line presented repeated opportunities for open assaults and demonstrations of great courage. Lame White Man, the respected Southern Cheyenne leader whose small band of followers had lived among the Northerners for years, watched this scattered enemy line stagger northward and rallied those around him, crying out: "Young men, come now with me and show yourselves to be brave." Indians leapt up, including some already prominent in this war—Comes in Sight of the Rosebud eight days earlier and Waterman, the determined Arapaho interloper—and rallied to the chief, who screamed again: "Come. We can kill all of them." The rush was bold and deadly, as mounted Cheyennes and Sioux charged into horsed and unhorsed soldiers, driving away animals, clubbing panicked blue coats, counting coup even on living enemies. An observer watched some soldiers put pistols into their mouths and end their own lives. But the soldiers sustained a deadly return fire, one bullet striking Lame White Man in the breast and killing him instantly. White Bull watched this spectacle and was moved by the apparent recklessness of such an inspirational leader. He had never seen a man so willingly "throw his life away," he said later.[56]

Perhaps inspired by Lame White Man's challenge, Yellow Nose, another Southern Cheyenne, rode into the fray. Spotting a soldier carefully guarding a stars and bars flag—a company guidon—he shot the man, snatched the staff and its flag, and used it to count coup on the fallen trooper. As he held the flag high for others to see, soldiers rushed to the man's aid and fired at the Cheyenne at close range. A bullet gashed Yellow Nose's forehead, blinding him with his own blood and fatally wounding his pony. He was in a dire fix, but he escaped, cleansed the blood from his face, and within moments rejoined the fight. Yellow Nose's flag episode was brazen. The Cheyennes forever remembered it, much as they did the girl saving her brother at the Rosebud.[57]

By now the trailing companies of the advance to the north, the segment held in the recesses of Medicine Tail Coulee when the attack began, faced annihilation. Their rearmost defense had collapsed, and warriors wreaked havoc on the thinning flanks, wounding and killing soldiers, scattering horses, and segmenting ever smaller groups of survivors who persistently rallied for one another until they too were overrun. Meanwhile, the leading segments of this frail line had passed that high point on the horizon that seemed to have beckoned them from the start and began following another ridgeline dipping to the northwest. But they had all but reached the limits of their advance and when looking back, they could plainly see that no effective force was following them.

Sioux and Cheyenne warriors ever after remembered personal episodes of bravado. Some were widely witnessed, and, often carefully documented, and they have become features of the general lore. Doubtless many more became personal family tales, reserved for retelling in lodges, cabins, and reservation homes, where, generations later, the heroics remain vibrant, even today. Perhaps the most consequential, an episode that was indeed widely witnessed and documented, focused on the charismatic warrior-chieftain Crazy Horse, who at the perfect moment made a charge that hastened the end for these despicable blue coats.

Crazy Horse arrived at the ridge fight by way of Deep Ravine, and in its head he and his followers had added their own fire to the soldier flank, loosing arrows and gunshots at any exposed *wasicu*. "He fired as fast as he could load his gun," Flying Hawk recalled. Clouds of smoke and dust billowed across the scene and yet through those obscuring shrouds opportunities for heroics presented themselves. Warriors to the left had stalled the advance of the soldier line as it ambled the broad shoulder of a nameless ridge leading to the river. Warriors eastward of them on the opposite side of the crest had run off horses being held in a dimple of that crown. The soldier line farther to the right was thinning to near total annihilation. Those men had been engaged in the ridgetop clash the longest, with most of their horses having been run off or released. They were strung-out survivors now being cut apart piecemeal as they feebly attempted to keep pace with the northward movement of the surviving effective force. In that sector Flying Hawk remembered "there was only a few of them left."[58]

White Bull, who had engaged bravely in the fighting near Calhoun Hill, had worked his way farther north and joined the party of warriors assembled with Crazy Horse. Here their competitive nature again served them well, and much as they did in the fight with railroad surveyors on Arrow Creek in 1872, they goaded each other into striking the soldiers before them. As at Arrow Creek, Crazy Horse saw the perfect moment and struck first. Mounting his pony, with the scree of his eagle bone whistle rising above the din, he charged straight into the soldier line. "The soldiers all fired at once," Red Feather remembered, "but didn't hit him." And the soldiers panicked and scampered right and left, splitting, as He Dog said, into two bunches and leaving each alone to face oncoming warriors. Crazy Horse rode straight through. His charge had divided the soldier line.[59]

Waterman, the Arapaho, watching the episode from afar, remembered Crazy Horse as "the bravest man I ever saw." White Bull, He Dog, Red Feather, and others followed and peeled right and left into the enemy, clubbing and stabbing soldiers to death. "This charge seemed to break the morale of the survivors," White Bull believed. "They all ran, every man for himself, afoot and on horseback." One small concentration formed on Calhoun Hill on the right, another group clustered in the center, and still another gathered on the high ground on the left, a landmark ever after legendarily remembered as Last Stand Hill. As one chronicler aptly put it, the killing now was quick and one-sided.[60]

Great charges by Crazy Horse and others that afternoon electrified those around them, but already across this battle ridge from south to north a determination and certainty were playing out. This fight had but one inevitable outcome, the complete destruction of this soldier command. Gall, the broad-shouldered Hunkpapa, was interviewed carefully on the field in 1886 at a tenth anniversary gathering of battle survivors. He gave voice to the hard fighting on another sector of this ridge, around Calhoun Hill, where he figured prominently. Those soldiers "never broke," he told transfixed newspapermen and officers, but, leading a sizeable band of Hunkpapas, Miniconjous, and Sans Arcs, "we charged through them." And we brought "special fire against the troopers who held the horses while the others fought. As soon as a holder was killed, by waving blankets and great shouting the horses were stampeded. The soldiers fought desperately and hard and never surrendered." Some warrior chieftains achieved ends with bold, dazzling charisma. Measured against the likes of Sitting Bull, Crazy

Horse, and White Bull, Gall seems to have achieved his desired ends by exercising simple if repetitive quiet resolve.[61]

Red Hawk, an Oglala active throughout the fighting around Calhoun Hill, also recalled the soldier gallantry exhibited there, costly though it was to warriors around him. Already Lame White Man was killed leading fearless charges on that front. Eagle Elk remembered another warrior, an Oglala Sioux named Red Horn Bull, shot through the jaw and horribly bloodied. Wooden Leg saw the same individual. "He wobbled dizzily as he moved along. He fell down, got up, fell down again, got up again. As he passed near to where I was I saw that his whole lower jaw was shot away. The sight of him made me sick. I had to vomit." Others saw him, too, remembering how his jaw was hanging on his breast, his teeth showing like a necklace. Friends tore up a cloth and tied his jaw back onto his head. Somehow, the horribly maimed Red Horn Bull survived the battle and died on the Pine Ridge Reservation years later.[62]

The fall of Calhoun Hill and the entire ridgeline under such pressure was all but inevitable. Scattered survivors attempted to make their way northward, but few succeeded. The movement was frantic. The ingenious phrase "buffalo chase" appears often in many warrior accounts and aptly reflects those final anxious movements. And as the Calhoun sector and ridge quieted, warriors themselves surged northward to the battle's last scenes.

The soldiers at the head of this northernmost column, strung-out, vulnerable, and continually diminishing now, were confronting their own difficulties. Mostly the mounted remnants of the smaller force that originally advanced down Medicine Tail Coulee, these blue coats were the least diminished of the troops advancing along the extended ridge leading to an ever-beckoning high point on the horizon. But upon reaching that high point the column's direction changed in a pronounced way as they descended on a northwesterly course along a broad grassy shoulder that at its farthest western extent dropped to the river. Ahead presumably were several crossings, not yet actually seen. Advancing perhaps a quarter of a mile along the slope, the column inexplicably halted, as though pondering a course ahead or perhaps waiting for those behind to close-up.[63]

But the pause proved catastrophic. It allowed warriors to strike with fury and they did. Wolf Tooth, the adventuresome Cheyenne who snuck out of camp early that morning, was among friends, Cheyennes mostly, attacking on the column's right. Those warriors had shadowed these soldiers for miles. Other attackers funneled to the front of the soldier column from the crossings straight ahead, while more, Two Moon and White Bull among them, struck at the column's left. The near encirclement was complete and reckoning. "This made the soldiers turn," Wolf Tooth recalled, and they "went back in the direction they had come." The soldiers' mystifying pause proved providential for the Indians, and fatal for the blue coats. As Shot in the Eye, an Oglala arriving on the field by way of one of those crossings ahead, put it, "this gave the Indians plenty of time for their warriors to scatter and secure the best positions around [this] little command." The soldiers advanced no farther, and having turned and stopped, they surrendered the offensive, however feeble their offensive momentum was at that point.[64]

The Indian onslaught was furious. White Bull and others watched some of the soldiers dismount and return a steady defensive fire, momentarily stalemating an assault. Nonetheless, as warriors watched in amazement, a daring Cheyenne, wearing a feather bonnet and an animal skin, made several mounted passes in front of the soldiers—an honor-earning bravery run—drawing fire but escaping harm each time. Iron Hawk heard a Cheyenne say the bold warrior was "bulletproof." All along, more warriors kept streaming to the scene, and the clouds of smoke and dust grew darker. Iron Hawk heard another voice blurt out: "Now they are going, they are going." The gray horses held by the dismounted soldiers were bolting and stampeding toward the draw to the south, Deep Ravine. For some warriors, chasing loose horses became an irrepressible lure. For the soldiers, the loss was disastrous.[65]

Into this chaos rode an unexpected lot of warriors, a mix of nearly twenty young Cheyenne and Sioux men, the Suicide Boys. These were individuals who had lost a relative in the Rosebud fight and the night before had pledged to throw away their own lives in the next battle. They charged as a group, some helping to scatter the gray horses and others jumping from their ponies and engaging soldiers in hand-to-hand fighting. They paid a heavy toll, and most were maimed or killed, but so were soldiers. Others joined the surge. Wolf Tooth, a primary informant, saw panic everywhere. "There was no time for the soldiers to take aim or anything," he recalled. Some started to run, but they were killed before they got far.[66]

Others joined the killing spree. The fearless young Cheyenne, Buffalo Calf Trail Woman, riding alongside her husband, Black Coyote, was one of few women to ride into the fray. Armed with a six-shooter pistol, she fired many shots into the soldiers. Late in the fight she saw a young Cheyenne who had lost his pony, and took him up on her own and rode toward the river where the freed soldier horses were gathering. Fearlessness and warrior-like gallantry had marked her at Rosebud, too, where she was remembered as the Girl Who Saved Her Brother. Here she was known among the Cheyennes as Brave Woman.[67]

By now the soldiers had nowhere to go but to the hill behind them, a refuge already drawing frantic survivors from the ridgeline fighting south of there. "Last Stand Hill," so warmly revered in the present day, is not the same prominence it was on June 25, 1876. Its original small, pronounced crown has been shaved-off repeatedly over the years to accommodate the trappings of a popular national park. But the destination was not its top anyway. Physical geographers refer to such rises and knolls as hogbacks, landforms having gentle faces with sharply dropping backslopes. This prominence on the Little Big Horn hillside was easily accessible from its west and south, but not so its north or east. And it was manifestly exposed. It was a poor position to stage a defense, although it was the best within reach.

Thus the remnants of the battered column rallied on the west face of the hill. Two Moon thought they may have numbered perhaps 105 at this point, judging from the complement of 212 that had maneuvered at the start in Medicine Tail Coulee. Beleaguered they were now but that did not mean defenseless. Many warriors remembered the moment of a fierce, even deliberate concentrated volley of fire rising from the soldier cluster. Warriors scrambled for cover and then watched a group of soldiers run a short distance southwestward from the hill toward the head of Deep Ravine, an obvious point of steady Indian emergence. The soldiers "scattered some in going down," Two Eagles recalled, but in those headlands they took cover in the sage and tall grasses and formed what many have assumed, then and now, was a defensive position—a skirmish line. If relief for this command was somehow en route it would only come from the south. Instead, those soldiers met not assistance but the same biting resistance that by now was being meted out across every inch of this field. Iron Hawk remembered watching those soldiers run downhill, but he also saw Hunkpapas that "ran right up . . . and encircled them from all sides."[68]

Almost simultaneously, a rider on a sorrel horse emerged from the knot of soldiers, the concentrated gunfire perhaps intended as his shield. Stunned warriors were surprised as the soldier galloped past. Many fired in vain and others quickly commenced a chase, including for a while Crazy Horse, but this soldier's horse was fast and long-winded. Turtle Rib, a Miniconjou among the pursuers, thought "the soldier rode like the wind." It appeared that the trooper might outpace his trailers as he bypassed Calhoun Hill and disappeared into Deep Coulee. As he gained that ravine's southern shoulder and descended into Medicine Tail Coulee the rider may even have seen soldiers in the south, barely a mile away. They told later of seeing him. But just then an Indian bullet struck him in the back and killed him. Cheyennes believed that it was fired by one of their own, Old Bear, a young warrior by that name and not the famous Old Man Chief and prophet.[69]

Behind the valiant rider, in the circle on Last Stand Hill, what few horses remained were either killed outright to become breastworks or were released. The soldiers had nowhere to run and readied for a final desperate fight. Yellow Nose, the young Southern Cheyenne who earlier had captured the soldier flag, remembered the unique chaos of running horses that filled the air with blinding dust, atop clouds of smoke from constant gunfire, and mixed with the din of yelling Indians and rattling musketry. Some warriors attempted to capture animals on the spot. When White Bull's own pony was hit, he caught one from this group as some rushed his way. Oddly, most of the surviving horses made for the river, and, as Runs the Enemy recalled, when they reached the water they were so thirsty they stopped and drank and drank. We captured the horses with their saddle bags, he said, "That gave us a chance to load up with shells and blankets and everything that the soldiers carried with them."[70]

The running of the horses signaled the end, and the great confusion was over quickly. Standing Bear expressed it well. "I could see Indians charging all around me. Then I could see the soldiers and Indians all mixed up and there were so many guns going off that I couldn't hear them. The voices seemed to be on top of the cloud." Rain in the Face remembered plainly that "the soldiers fought desperately and hard and never surrendered." Hollow Horn Bear, the Brulé living among the Sans Arcs, thought the soldiers fought as hard here as at any other place on the field.[71]

Many others remembered the final fury. Eagle Bear, an Oglala, noted that "we could not ride in a circle around [them] because they were on one edge of the hill. There were great numbers of us, some on horseback, others on foot. Back and forth in front of [them] we passed, firing all the time. Then suddenly we rode right into [them] and killed all who were still alive." White Shield, a Cheyenne, was among those who joined the swarm. "The Indians made a charge," he told an interviewer in 1908, "and killed all the wounded with hatchets, arrows, [and] knives." This last surge was largely inspired by the chiefs. Low Dog screamed to his followers: "This is a good day to die: follow me." Crow King told an army officer several years later that "every chief rushed his horse on the White soldiers and all our warriors did the same, every one whipping another's horse." Gall, virtually everywhere it seemed, told the anniversary crowd in 1886 that "the dust and smoke was black as evening. Once in a while we could see the soldiers through the dust, and finally we charged through them with our ponies."[72]

Among those soldiers at the last were several who had drawn attention almost all along. During the course of the soldier advance from Medicine Tail Coulee four distinctively attired soldiers wearing buckskins rode at the head of the column. They could be seen continually consulting with one another, and endlessly peering about and seemingly plotting a course. They were plainly in charge. As soldiers always rallied to their flags, all along this bunch had in its midst a different one, larger than the others, swallow-tailed with a red top and blue bottom and large white crossed soldier knives on either side. When the advance collapsed beyond Last Stand Hill, the man with the flag was killed. A Cheyenne warrior whose name is lost to history wanted that flag, but as he rushed to pick it off the ground another blue coat leapt out and fought him hand to hand. The warrior beat the soldier to death with his war club, but another *ve'ho'e* shot him in the groin. The Cheyenne warrior grew dizzy and fell. When he regained consciousness, the flag was gone, and those buckskin soldiers who rallied to it were corralled on Last Stand Hill with the others. There the death of the last one was ever after a vivid memory belonging to another Cheyenne warrior.[73]

Yellow Nose, heroic in the capture of a soldier stars-and-bars flag earlier on Battle Ridge and, like Crazy Horse and Gall, among the everywhere warriors on the battlefield, remembered a lone man at the end wearing buckskins and shouting loudly to the soldiers around him. "The appearance of this man was so striking and gallant that [he] decided that to kill him would be a feat of more than ordinary prowess." Yellow Nose rode into the fray. The buckskin soldier was bareheaded and armed only with a pistol, he recalled. As he neared the soldier he was fired upon, and his pony bolted to the side and ran beyond the man. Yellow Nose turned and charged the soldier again, jumping to the ground just as the buckskin man fired his last shot. The soldier drew a knife but Yellow Nose struck him in the back of the head with his club and he sank to the ground in a heap. He grabbed the knife and slashed him across the throat. "He quieted down." Yellow Nose laughed and said: "Big man. Big man." Yellow Nose later came to believe that he had killed the soldier chief who led these blue coats. Others remembered that buckskin-clad soldier, too. He had "blue marks pricked into the skin above the wrist."[74]

Soldier resistance wholly collapsed. In their terror some men threw away their guns and when confronted by a warrior begged for mercy.

Others used their pistols at close range, but when their guns were emptied, there was no time to reload. Several used their carbines as clubs. A few feigned death. And a handful ran. Carbine fire still reverberated southwest of the hill across the head of Deep Ravine where skirmishers were sent earlier in this closing episode. A small number of soldiers from Last Stand Hill—estimates vary, seven, ten, maybe fifteen—rose from their breastworks and ran toward them. Those that made it joined a few other survivors from that position and continued running into Deep Ravine, where warriors hunted and killed them all. Big Beaver recalled how none of those soldiers shot back. "My idea is that they used all their ammunition and were making this last effort to get away." The last desperate stand of what was a substantial second attacking force occurred in the recesses of Deep Ravine. Red Horse noted the inevitable: "The Sioux did not take a single soldier prisoner, but killed all of them; none were left alive for even a few minutes."[75]

Wooden Leg recalled the moment when the guns went silent. "Warriors who had crept close began to call out that all of the White men were dead. All of the Indians then jumped up and rushed forward. All the boys and old men on their horses came tearing into the crowd amid an atmosphere full of dust and smoke. Everybody was greatly excited. It looked like thousands of dogs might look if all of them were mixed together in a fight."[76]

The silence drew women and children to the field. During much of the fighting many of the camp's noncombatants had massed on the bench west of the village, able to flee farther west if circumstances required but also able to watch the progression of the fight as it crept along the ravines and ridges east of the river. The ever churning clouds of dust and gun smoke were telltale indicators of the action. But even as they struggled on the eastern hillsides, many noncombatants returned to their circles and assisted the coming and going of warriors and the care of wounded men streaming back. And as the firing ebbed many were lured across the river and onto the field itself, drawn by the inevitable bounty of dead soldiers and horses. Some were involved, too, in the final killings.

The Miniconjou Iron Hail (Dewey Beard of another day) remembered chancing on a dying soldier laying on the ground, surrounded by a cluster of taunting Indians. They made gestures to strike him, and he was almost crazy waiting for the death blow. Women in the crowd were laughing. Then an Indian rode up with his son draped over his horse. He was singing a death song in his honor. When he saw the soldier he pulled up sharply, threw his leg over his pony, and jumped to the ground with a pistol in hand. He walked up to the blue coat and shot him dead without a word.[77]

Elsewhere Two Eagles watched a Cheyenne woman rummaging the field. Her hair was cut short in mourning for a son killed in the Rosebud fight. She carried an ax. When a soldier got up in front of her, two warriors near her grabbed and pinned the man to the ground while the woman killed him with the ax. Antelope Woman (Kate Big Head) was drawn to the field even while the last of the fighting raged and watched a similar killing. A living soldier sat on the ground, bewildered and rubbing his head. Three Sioux men surged on him and pinned him flat on his back. While two held the soldier down the third sawed off his head with a sheath knife.[78]

Impressionable boys watched these final killings. Thirteen-year-old Black Elk knew he should be happy about this. "These *wasicus* had come to kill our mothers and fathers and us, and it was our country." As he told an interviewer years later, they were very foolish to do this and this is what they deserved. But as he walked about he tired of looking at the chaos. "I could smell nothing but blood and gunpowder." Smoke and dust still blotted the sun. His stomach clenched and he felt sick.[79]

Charging Bear, another young Lakota, remembering the final moments, recalled years later a blood-smeared friend dying in agony as well as a young soldier "with hair like the morning sun and both eyes shot out. [He] had blown off the back of his own head." And he thought of the soldier he had killed "and the way he had clawed at my arrow in his throat before he died, his blue eyes wide open. I got off my pony, vomited, walked dizzily a few steps and fell. Lying there on the ground, I cried. In half an hour I had got my fill of war."[80]

Black Elk's and Charging Bear's reactions were uncommon. Hundreds of people scrounged the half-mile-long ridge from Calhoun Hill to Last Stand Hill seeking plunder, much as had the women who scoured the sprawl of the valley fight after those soldiers were repulsed. Women searched-out the dead, stripped soldiers of usable clothing, luring jewelry, and utilitarian leather wear, and rummaged laden saddlebags astride dead horses. Men likewise combed the grounds and searched the dead for weapons, ammunition, and other trophies. Flags and bugles were special treasures. No less than six flags were taken from this field. Scalping, too, was widespread.

Sitting Bull was not among those who inspected the field. After departing the bloody scene of the valley fight, he made his way through the village and joined noncombatants gathered on the hillside west of the camp. As the fighting progressed northward toward Last Stand Hill, he returned to the camp, to look after women and older men who had returned, and to tend wounded men returning or being delivered to home lodges. He contemplated telling the women to strike the lodges, but was overtaken by young warriors who had just come down from the fight and who called out: "No use to leave camp; every White man is killed." Some on the battlefield recalled his stern warning from the time of the Sun Dance about not touching the spoils of their victory, but only Sitting Bull and those of his own band heeded the warning. In truth, there was no controlling the victorious Lakotas and Cheyennes as they went about doing to an enemy what they always had done. But this failure to heed Sitting Bull's warning grieved the chief. He was sure it would be a curse on the people. "For failure on your part to obey," he openly lamented, "henceforth you shall always covet White people's belongings." As one chronicler added, "the specter of dependence on the Whites would haunt him to his dying day."[81]

~

Even during the heaviest of fighting in the north some warriors remained conscious of the original force—the first soldiers—who had attacked the village earlier that afternoon. The surviving White men remained a distinctive threat to the camp now. When the Medicine Tail Coulee danger captured the camp's attention, those blue coats had been largely abandoned by the warriors and for a while the soldiers held a nearly quiet bluff-top position above their river crossing. The soldier force there was also strengthened as other soldier segments scattered before, now joined them. But late in the fighting in the north, they could be seen advancing again and had come to within plain sight of Medicine Tail Coulee, where some had spotted the lone rider scrambling southward toward them until he was killed in the depths of that draw. At first, these advancing soldiers seemed oblivious to warriors bounding toward them. Red Horse recalled how chiefs had directed Sioux men to watch those soldiers on the hill and prevent the two forces from uniting. Facing an onslaught of warriors, however, those soldiers quickly recoiled and returned to their hilltop position, where Indians soon corralled them and shot at them from the ridge tops surrounding the position.[82]

The fighting on the southern field was costly but quickly stalemated. The soldiers drew their mounts and newly arrived pack mules into the center of a broad if irregular encirclement and quickly entrenched. From time to time, warriors made bold dashes against the soldier lines, but their impenetrability quickly stung. A fifteen-year-old Sioux boy, Breech Cloth, made one such dash against the east line at dusk, but his horse threw him, and he was shot and killed attempting to run away. His brother had been killed in the Rosebud fight, and he told his relatives that he would die in the same way if there was any chance to fight soldiers again. Standing Bear remembered joining other warriors at sunset to discuss what they might do. "We couldn't get at the soldiers so we decided we would starve or dry them out," he told an interviewer many years later. Some warriors stayed through the night, but most returned to the camp. White Bull, the Cheyenne sometimes referred to as Ice, added philosophically: Why "lose men recklessly?"[83]

The village, meanwhile, remained a hive of activity. Late in the day, Little Wolf and his small band of Cheyennes reached the camp. Since chancing on the soldier column the day before and where this morning some of his warriors had been shot at by those men on Davis Creek, Little Wolf's people had shadowed the blue coats as they crossed the divide and descended Upper Ash Creek. They watched the column divide several times and continued trailing its rearmost element, especially its ever-desirable pack train. They watched too when later one of the segments that had ridden far to the southwest joined the soldiers on the hilltop overlooking the Ash Creek-Little Big Horn confluence. Then, they had watched the mule train join that command. By the gunfire reverberating and then subsiding to the north, they had a sense of a major fight occurring elsewhere and then dying out. Only then did they depart the Ash Creek drainage and ride widely northward to the great camp. But even that approach proved challenging. When descending Medicine Tail Coulee the band first encountered Sans Arc warriors, a people not familiar with these Cheyennes. They surrounded Little Wolf's people, some shouting "Kill them! Kill them!" Wooden Leg and a Southern Cheyenne elder, Yellow Horse, reacting to the commotion, recognized kin and intervened. Only then was the band taken to the Cheyenne circle where they learned fully of all that had transpired across the valley and upon the west-facing ridges east of the river.[84]

Elsewhere in the camp chiefs and elders agreed to consolidate the sprawling village into a smaller, concentrated mass. Heralds proclaimed the directive, and in a fluid motion the near eight hundred lodges scattered across the six great circles were disassembled and the people and their property relocated to the floodplain and hillside below the Cheyenne circle. The new camp was a helter-skelter sprawl of willow shelters, tent-flies, and sometimes mere buffalo robe bedding thrown on the ground. Standing Bear remembered the pandemonium. He also remembered that he could not sleep because he "kept recalling the horrible things he had seen. It seemed that everyone was excited and moving around and the whole village did not sleep a wink." The ceremonial lodges in the former camp were packed, as were the lodge poles and covers belonging to nearly every family. We "were packed for moving away quickly if necessary," remembered Kate Big Head. Behind them some lodges remained standing in the old camp, now covering dead warriors from the day's battle. That area had become a literal dead camp.[85]

While notions of a great victory filled the hearts of many of the people that evening, heralds proclaimed it should be a night without celebration. Instead, it should be a quiet time for families to care for the wounded, and to mourn. Such compassion was widespread in the circles but may have originated with Sitting Bull. Moving Robe Woman recalled him saying: "We shall not celebrate tonight. There are too many of our warriors killed." Another Hunkpapa, Good White Buffalo Woman, remembered that "while our hearts were singing for the victory [we] had won, there were wailing women in the village, for they had their dead." Indeed, the fight had been a great victory, the complete realization of Sitting Bull's stunning Sun Dance vision, but the grief was overwhelming. Victory dances could wait.[86]

Informed tallies of Indian fatalities suggest that as many as forty-five or fifty Lakota warriors were killed, plus another ten women and youths. A common Cheyenne count is six or seven men killed. Actual numbers and many identities are lost to history. Whatever the great toll, the anguish was widespread and palpable. Burial details varied. Already some of the deceased were interred in rocky crevices west of the village while a few others were lofted to scaffolds in the riverside tree cover. Still others were placed in funerary lodges scattered through the old camp, and some were carried along with the families when the camp dispersed to be buried elsewhere. Soldiers in the distant army circle saw burial pyres and heard the rhythmic drumming and singing of mourning songs. They interpreted it as a night of revelry.[87]

A curious thing happened late in the day. Several Cheyenne women combing the battlefield made their way to Last Stand Hill. In the midst of dead horses and severely mutilated soldiers they came across one individual who was stripped naked, visibly shot several times, but not mutilated in any manner. They were sure the man was named George Custer, an individual they had encountered on the southern plains many years before. One of the women stuck the point of a trade awl into each of his ears, "to improve his hearing," it was said, as he had not listened to the peace talk in the south and, not listening, had brought about his own death. But the Custer name was not spoken in the camp that evening nor in the days that followed, and the northern traditionals did not know this identity for many weeks.[88]

Aside from the Cheyenne women, the Lakotas and Northern Cheyennes at the Little Big Horn had no sense of who they had defeated. At best, some speculated that it was again the soldiers from the south, those troops, too, led by an individual still unknown to them. Some Hunkpapa women, as with those Cheyennes, may have recognized one individual, Isaiah Dorman, the Black man killed in the valley fight, but no one knew that a soldier named Marcus Reno led that attack. In truth, as Wooden Leg later quipped: "It made no difference to us." At its simplest, the villagers had defended a camp of steadfast traditionals, men, women, and children, from a daring attack, and they had destroyed a despicable enemy. It came on a day that at its start had dawned so placid and ordinary for people dedicated to life on the buffalo prairie.[89]

10
A DANGEROUS TIME

"We can go nowhere without seeing the head of an American."
—Sitting Bull, Hunkpapa Lakota

On June 25, 1876, this Indian war came home to Sitting Bull and his loyal coalition of traditionals. The near five thousand Lakotas and Northern Cheyennes camping with him along the Little Big Horn River were committed to a simple life on the buffalo prairie, as in the days of their forebearers. But on that day, they were attacked by a Whiteman army, and they destroyed it. Many events stretching through the years had foreshadowed this almost inevitable climactic and transformative moment. The Indians had suffered relentless hounding in the buffalo country by railroaders, prospectors, and surveyors; the invasion of the Black Hills, their "Heart of the Earth"; and the March attack on peaceful Northern Cheyennes on the Powder River, people agreeably heeding the government's summons. There was also the recent receipt of an incomprehensible mandate from the Great Father demanding the midwinter surrender of their lifeway, and repeated warnings from agency kin and officials that soldiers were massing against them. But in the midst of this chaos there were favorable signs: a dramatic Sun Dance vision portending a great victory, the turning back of the soldiers on Rosebud Creek, and now this triumph at the Little Big Horn.

Many in the Little Big Horn encampment that evening savored the day's victory, but sages and elders among them saw dire consequences. The camp had lost some sixty killed and countless others severely wounded, many of whom would die in the days ahead. By contrast, the people had killed 263 soldiers, Indian scouts, and civilians in the valley and hillside fights. It was the height of their ascendency. From that day forward, the story of Sitting Bull's War turned dramatically against the traditionals. The consequences came slowly at first, but nothing would ever be the same again. It was indeed a day, as history is wont to echo from time to time, that lives in infamy. The Whites would never forgive it. The traditionals would always remember it with pride but regret terribly what came after.

In the dawning of June 26, the huddled villagers were ever mindful that elements of the blue coat army, crippled but still menacing, remained bunched on a ridgetop six miles south of their drawn-up camp. In the early morning hours, warriors streamed in that direction to continue the fight. A few Sioux warriors, "the watching party" as Standing Bear called them, had kept an eye on the soldiers through the night, plinking at them occasionally to declare their continuing presence and ensure that no one escaped. When other warriors came on, most of the overnighters went home, and the new arrivals gradually renewed the fight. The soldiers were in a tight fix, but the action around the hilltop, dramatic in moments, quickly proved pointless. As the Brulé warrior Hollow Horn Bear later explained, through the night the soldiers had burrowed deeply into the ground like prairie dogs, where Indian guns and arrows could not reach them. This was not a position that could be rushed. This could never be another Last Stand Hill.[1]

Warriors persisted no less in challenging the prairie dog circle, rising and shooting from time to time, and sometimes charging the entrenchments outright. In one instance, sensing soldier vulnerability on the south side, warriors rushed the line and nearly succeeded in breeching it. Long Road, a Sans Arc, got close enough to strike a soldier with his coup stick but as he turned to run, he was shot dead. The Whites mustered a counter charge and scattered the attackers. Doing so, they overran Long Road's body. One of the blue coats later crowed that he "was the only dead Indian left in our possession."[2]

On a ridge northeast of the soldiers a Miniconjou, Dog's Backbone, huddling among White Bull's followers, watched bullets kick dust around him and cautioned those within earshot: "Be careful. It is a long way from here but their bullets are coming in fierce." Barely had he blurted his warning when he was shot in the head and tumbled to the ground. Standing Bear and others crawled over to the man and saw how the bullet had entered above an eyebrow. He was killed instantly.[3]

As absorbing as the hilltop fighting had become, alarming news began to run the camp around midday. Men ranging down the Little Big Horn Valley searching for ponies had encountered other blue coats advancing their way. Among those soldiers, they could plainly see long guns—some manner of artillery and in this instance, Gatling guns—and walking soldiers, men they particularly despised because they were armed with deadly long-range rifles. While some continued to shadow those soldiers, others raced to the camp to spread the frightening news.[4]

Wooden Leg remembered the chiefs counseling. Many wondered whether this sighting represented the return of the Rosebud soldiers? But Little Wolf, the Cheyenne Old Man Chief who had arrived late the day before, noted that the soldiers who struck from the east yesterday and likely these approaching from the north now had Corn Indians with them, meaning Arikaras, not Crows or Shoshones. They could not be the soldiers from the south. Some wished to rise up and attack those blue coats immediately, just as had occurred on the Rosebud. The chiefs and counselors thought they had fought enough, however, and that the village should, as Wooden Leg remembered, "continue in our same course—not fight any soldiers if we could get away without doing so." This cautious refrain had successfully guided the camp since the sighting of soldiers on the Yellowstone in the spring. But the elders also agreed to break camp and move up the Little Big Horn toward the mountains away from all blue coats.[5]

The chiefs' reluctance to engage formally did not deter some warriors from riding in that direction anyway, whether to eye this threat themselves or perhaps even intervene. White Bull had been among those watching the soldiers in the south through the night, but after sunup he had returned home to eat and sleep. Around midday he remembered his father awakening him with news of trouble in the north. White Bull, the Sans Arc Many Lice, and one other rode downriver together and quickly encountered others doing the same. When nearing the soldiers, they exchanged a few shots with the blue coats in the lead and successfully ran off some of their horses. But they never fully engaged, acknowledging that the blue coat force outnumbered them greatly. In due course the warriors returned to camp, some arriving before everyone broke for the south, others following later in the camp's traces.[6]

The oncoming threat in the north and the camp's departing preparations brought about a deliberate if slow closure to the fighting with the entrenched soldiers on the hilltop. Sitting Bull was particularly outspoken on the matter, proclaiming that morning: "Let them live. They are trying to live. They came against us and we have killed a few." Reflecting on that same point several years later, Low Dog suggested that it was a chiefs' decision to break off the fight, a consensus prevailing by then that those men had been punished enough, and that "we ought to be merciful and let them go." Red Horse, a Miniconjou chief in the camp, was considerably more dogmatic, telling an interviewer a short while later that it was the coming of the walking soldiers that saved the others. "Indians can't fight walking soldiers; they are afraid of them, and so we moved away."[7]

Some less sympathetic warriors regretted the disengagement. Two Moon was sure the soldiers could have been starved out. Flying Hawk assured an interviewer many years later that given time, "we could have killed all the men that got into the holes on the hill." He Dog was similarly positive, saying, "we would have worn them out in a few days." Red Hawk was likewise insistent that if it had not been for more soldiers coming from the north, they could have wiped out the hilltop command "in another day or two." Each spoke in hindsight, imagining a luxury of time they did not have. The great village by now was threatened again, and once more it needed to be in motion.[8]

The movement southward began in the late afternoon. Again, the Cheyennes led. The withdrawal was deliberate, and somber, a movement plainly dictated by the threat posed from the oncoming soldiers. Some families carefully transported wounded fathers and sons on travois. Pony herds were pushed in unison on the hillsides west of the long caravan, and watchful warriors skirted the procession and trailed all. Behind them the grasses were fired, and soon a cloak of white smoke and dust obscured the parade from the puzzled onlookers burrowed into the hillside across the river.[9]

Abandoned behind the people was another camp of the dead. Scattered about were funerary lodges, new burials along Shoulder Blade Creek (the drainage from the west that bisected the heart of the initial camp), standing lodge poles, a litter of meats and other foodstuffs, buffalo robes, undressed skins, blankets, cooking pots, and personal possessions, most of it abandoned by the mourning families. Also scattered across the dead camp were fifty or sixty ponies and American horses, almost all of them wounded, plus many Indian dogs. Most disturbing to the soldiers coming onto the smoldering field the next morning was the profusion of bloody army uniform and body parts, gauntlets, cavalry saddles, and severed human heads. Such things portended other grisly discoveries strewn across the hills to the left, where one oncoming officer thought he had sighted "buffalo lying down."[10]

For the people in the great village, the late afternoon travel stretched into late evening. It was a determined, nonstop movement of some fourteen miles up the Little Big Horn to the mouth of what some then knew as Box Elder Creek, likely today's Sand Creek. Along the way, they passed their grazed-over post-Rosebud victory camp. There in the darkness the caravan stopped and rested until daybreak. They slept in the open much as they had done the night before. Next morning, June 27, they continued their ascent of the Little Big Horn Valley and by midday reached the mouth of Lodge Grass or Wood Lice Creek. In a broad flat just below the creek's mouth, they established a formal camp in the customary fashion, with Cheyennes at the upstream end and Hunkpapas at the tail end downstream.[11]

That evening the chiefs and elders assembled in a grand council held openly in the Oglala circle. The chiefs announced tallies of their dead in the Little Big Horn fight. The numbers varied and did not include noncombatant casualties or deaths occurring along the departure trail. Wooden Leg, an observer of the gathering, reported that an Oglala chief announced to the assembly that the Big Chief of the soldiers two days ago was a man called Long Hair—Custer. "I know it was him," the Oglala asserted. Some Oglalas, in fact, had had close contacts with this man, both on the Yellowstone in 1873 and again in the Black Hills in 1874. No one discounted the Oglala's assertion, but no one else made such a claim just then either. The combined counsellors also reckoned with the inevitable breakup of the massive village, commencing almost certainly on the morrow. This camp was simply too big and its needs for grass, wood, water, and food too vast to hold together much longer, particularly under the duress of the blue coat threat.[12]

That evening while the great camp of traditionals held together one final time, dancing occurred in most of the camp circles, with warriors telling of their experiences in the fight and their glorious coups. The dancing did not carry on very long into the night, however. Some people in fact were still in mourning and took no part in it at all. One chronicler later lamented that there would be no such celebration of massed traditionals again for many years to come.[13]

The next morning, June 28, the spinoff of bands began. Already in the darkness the day before, the five Arapahos who had appeared in the camp in the eight-day respite between the Rosebud and Little Big Horn quietly slipped out of camp. They disappeared into the Wolf Mountains, headed, two of them later reported, for Red Cloud Agency. Aside from their Cheyenne hosts, no one else noticed their departure. Also barely noticed was the departure that morning of Magpie Eagle's twenty lodges of Cheyennes. This independent-minded band joined the great village the day before the Little Big Horn fight after slowly descending and hunting the Rosebud Valley during the time of the Rosebud fight. They were headed now for the Black Hills country and eventually to the White River Agency. They trailed directly east out of the camp. In due course, several from that band, all Southern Cheyennes, continued through the Pine Ridge Country bound farther south still for the Southern Cheyenne agency in Indian Territory. In early August J. D. Miles, the agent there, reported their arrival and noted details elicited from their descriptions of the Rosebud and Little Big Horn fights. He also noted their possessing now sugar, coffee, arms, horses, and scalps taken in the latter battle.[14]

Nearly all the remaining Cheyennes separated and continued up the Little Big Horn, overnighting near the mouth of Pass Creek, in the shadows of the Big Horn Mountains. From there the next day they ventured even closer to the mountains, intending to lay over and replenish food stocks and lodge poles. The various departures stripped most, though not all, of the Northern Cheyenne circle from Sitting Bull's mix of devout traditionals. At Little Big Horn, the apex of this movement, the Cheyennes comprised one of the largest circles in the great camp, some 145 lodges (152 with Little Wolf's late arrival), adding more than two hundred fighting men to the coalition.[15]

Meanwhile, the surviving camp turned to the southwest that morning of June 28 and ascended Lodge Grass Creek, advancing to a camp some thirteen miles upstream. The pause was memorable on two counts. That evening the villagers were startled by a bugle call. It blared in the distance, and upon reconnaissance, warriors saw a line of ten or fifteen soldiers riding abreast, all dressed in blue uniforms, astride army horses, and displaying a fluttering stars-and-bars soldier flag. Dogs barked in alarm. Women shrieked: "The soldiers are coming!" Word had passed the camp not long before that soldiers were, in fact, not following this exodus but had stopped on the Little Big Horn battlefield and were burying their dead. But now this. The alarm was but short lived. The people in the village soon recognized the chargers as Indians dressed in soldier clothing and riding army horses captured three days ago. They were doing this "just to fool us," Young Black Elk remembered.[16]

From that camp another splintering occurred. The next morning the remaining Cheyennes, most under Two Moon, ascended the narrow neck of land to the west that separated Lodge Grass Creek from Rotten Grass Creek. The Rotten Grass drainage, a picturesque tributary of the Big Horn River, was another buffalo-hunting range the Cheyennes favored. Like those Cheyennes who chose to remain in the Little Big Horn Valley and were now in its Big Horn Mountain headlands, Two Moon's people were seemingly intent on continuing southward to the foothills to hunt. But after three days on Rotten Grass Creek, they turned about and retraced their trail to the east, evidently resolved to realign with kin. Sitting Bull was the ever stalwart traditional Two Moon had rallied with in the immediate wake of the Powder River fight. His lone regret in parting from the revered chief, Two Moon said, was that "I did not see him again."[17]

That the soldiers in the Little Big Horn Valley appeared to have stopped there to bury their dead was not entirely true. A small column of cavalry had in fact advanced from that force and had just reached the mouth of Lodge Grass Creek on the Little Big Horn, a mere thirteen miles behind Sitting Bull's surviving coalition. The soldiers reported encountering scaffolded Indian dead on the trail and an endless scattering of discarded property. They saw also that the Indian enclave had divided and was now trailing in three different directions. But at that point the soldiers followed no trail and merely turned about. Surprisingly, this nearness was not reported in any of the dispersed Indian camps.[18]

The Lakotas, absent now all their Cheyenne allies, continued their own ascent of Lodge Grass Creek, reaching its headlands in the Big Horn foothills. There they intended to hunt, gather poles, and, most of all, stay beyond the reach of hounding soldiers. As with the Cheyennes who were principally gathered in the headlands of the Little Big Horn River, the immediate draw for the Sioux was the glimmering, snow-covered, White Mountains, the Big Horns. Splashed across their fore was a luxurious spread of grassy vales and trickling springs draining toward Lodge Grass Creek. Running bank full, that stream coursed through an equally stunning small valley speckled with brush and intermittent stands of cottonwoods. Again, life went on as in the days of old, and only in hindsight does one realize that for these tradition-minded people, these were their final days of unfettered freedom on the buffalo prairie. They restocked food packs, feasted, victory danced, sang endless kill songs, and dispatched word to the agencies of their great success over the *wasicus*, even inviting kin to join them. One Bull remembered the reverie lasting some ten days.[19]

During this unique, midsummer pause, the Cheyennes camping in the Little Big Horn headlands often ranged southeastward, partly drawn by abundant buffalo in the Tongue River country and partly attentive to the soldier camp that seemed permanently parked in the foothills along Goose Creek, a tributary of the Tongue. The soldier camp was barely forty miles distant. The Cheyennes had discovered the *ve'ho'es* a month ago, just ahead of the Rosebud fight, and they were continually conscious of their presence now. On a hunt in early July in the foothills southeast of the Little Big Horn, Cheyenne hunters had spotted a contingent of soldiers by mere chance. The blue coats, numbering perhaps thirty in all, were four or five miles from the Indian village and riding that way. The hunters hurriedly reported the alarm, and the Little Big Horn camp began to scatter, band by band, in several directions. To initially protect the scrambling exodus some fifteen or twenty warriors rode forth and secreted themselves along the soldiers' line of approach.[20]

The soldiers had witnessed some of this movement, too, and from high ground in the distance could see commotion in the village. They continued their own cautious approach northwestward, following the evident traces of the old Bozeman Road. When the soldiers reached the broad glide descending into the Little Big Horn drainage, the secreted warriors, well bolstered now by others, confronted them, screaming and firing shots that pushed the blue coats into a dense stand of upland timber.[21]

The parties exchanged gunfire, and the warriors rushed the position, riding right and left of the soldier's tree cover. They were threatening enough to push the unmounted blue coats higher into the rugged mountainside. In one exchange, the Cheyenne warrior High Bear was killed. With no strong inclination to follow the soldiers into the mountainscape, the warriors broke off the confrontation. Turning, they carried High Bear's body back to camp and brought along the horses the soldiers had inexplicably abandoned, each mount with its saddlebags fully packed.[22]

The warriors saw no more of those men, but they recognized one of them as Frank Grouard, whom they had come to despise and who lately had frequented Red Cloud Agency, administrative home for some of these Cheyennes. Grouard had consistently guided the troops coming from the south and had had visible roles in both the Powder River and Rosebud episodes. In a lull here, one warrior derogatorily screamed out to him in Sioux: "Standing Bear, [Grabber to the Sioux] do you think that there are no men but yours in this country?"[23]

Conventional camp needs brought an end to the Lakotas' near idyllic if short-lived odyssey in the Big Horn Mountains. Rather than any immediate threat from soldiers, it was the need for grazing and hunting that kept them moving. During the second week of July, shortly after the Cheyennes clashed with the small soldier contingent, Sitting Bull's followers crossed from the Lodge Grass Creek headlands into the Little Big Horn drainage and overnighted northward near the mouth of Pass Creek. Their trail continued down the Little Big Horn to Ash Creek, turned east, and then looped up and over the well-worn Ash Creek–Davis Creek divide to Rosebud Creek. When near the Little Big Horn battlefield, a handful of curious warriors from the bands seized the opportunity to look it over. The soldiers were gone and the burials of their dead were shockingly wanting, the Oglala warrior Red Hawk recalled. The stench from decaying human and animal flesh was so overwhelming that the exploration was cut short.[24]

On Rosebud Creek the Lakotas momentarily realigned with some of the Cheyennes whose own trail had brought them from their diffusion in the Little Big Horn headlands directly east onto the Rosebud drainage and then down that creek. Referring to the Rosebud fight, Wooden Leg recalled passing "the ground where we had fought the soldiers" and camping a few miles below that place. They overnighted around or perhaps slightly downstream from the Rosebud Narrows, and then camped again below the mouth of Davis Creek. A day later, they were near the mouth of Muddy Creek, where they reunited with the Lakotas. At the Muddy Creek camp the Cheyennes danced and talked of their great battles, but Wooden Leg recalled no dancing in the other tribal circles.[25]

Uniquely, and by apparent simple chance, three soldier couriers traveling Tullock Creek and Rosebud Creek at nearly that same time somehow missed these Lakota and Cheyenne bands. At one point on July 10, the soldiers miraculously avoided sixty Indian herders pushing ponies down the Rosebud. Their own trail took them up the Rosebud Valley, through the heart of the Rosebud battlefield, across the divide to the Tongue, and to the army camp in the south, where they arrived unscathed on July 12. It was a big country, and many things could go unnoticed.[26]

The combined Lakotas and Cheyennes continued down Rosebud Creek, camping near the sacred Writing Rock, just above the Sun Dance camp of early June. Exploring both places during a hurried overnight stop, Young Black Elk lamented that soldier horses had thoroughly defiled the Sun Dance circle. Game was scarce and as Young Black Elk observed, the land was heavily grazed and trampled from what had been a continuous parade of Indians and soldiers passing this drainage throughout May and June. In turn and in a conscious act of defiance, the valley behind the Indian parade was set ablaze after the people passed. As a White chronicler traveling that same ground several weeks later grimly lamented: "The Indians have burned off every blade of grass their ponies left undevoured, and for miles below us the scouts report it even worse." But the Lakotas and Cheyennes relished such thoughts. Let those "soldier horses starve," Young Black Elk scowled.[27]

The Indian caravan continued to the mouth of Greenleaf Creek, and from there in mid-July ascended that creek and crossed the narrow divide to the Tongue River. The crossover was familiar to many of the people, for this was the same trail traveled by Big Road's and Little Big Man's Oglala traditionals from Red Cloud Agency in late May. It was also the same route the small Cheyenne hunting party that included Wooden Leg had taken when they discovered troops maneuvering in the south. The combined circles camped one day when reaching the Tongue. Their location was the mouth of Beaver Creek, a small tributary entering from the east. The isolated site proved noteworthy on several counts.[28]

Since early May a small band of Blackfeet Sioux led by Kill Eagle had trailed with Sitting Bull's Lakota coalition. Long counted among the Missouri River Progressives, or Friendlies, Kill Eagle led twelve lodges of followers west that spring—to hunt, but not to engage in Sitting Bull's War. And yet on the Tongue River just below this place he aligned with the great chief and trailed with him through the time of the ascendency. He and his people were in the camp at the time of the Rosebud and Little Big Horn fights, but they did not participate in either action. Kill Eagle was scorned often and severely for this reluctance, or at least so he told an interviewer at the Standing Rock Agency in September. He had attempted as recently as the morning of June 25 to lead his people away from the great camp but was again forced or induced to stay. Here now at Beaver Creek was one more chance to flee.[29]

The sprawl of the Tongue River camp apparently placed the Blackfeet circle aside or very near the Cheyenne circle, and that evening Kill Eagle courted the Cheyennes with a feast of wild turnips. Among those Cheyenne chiefs, Kill Eagle explained his predicament, and they pitied him, one saying: "These Sioux who are kindred to you have abused you, [but] now this day you have honored us with your attention." The Cheyenne chiefs agreed that he should be allowed to go his own way and offered to stand between him and Sitting Bull's *akicitas*. So, under cover of darkness, Kill Eagle and his people took flight. At daybreak Sitting Bull's police gave chase, but by then the Blackfeet were well on their way eastward to Standing Rock Agency. Several weeks later, after arriving at the agency, the Standing Rock military agent interviewed Kill Eagle. In the aftermath of the Rosebud and Little Big Horn battles, military authorities had taken over the Sioux agencies, and the officer who quizzed Kill Eagle provided a forty-seven-page report that overflowed with details on the affairs in Indian Country through the summer. Kill Eagle had been an eyewitness through it all, and his interview drew national attention.[30]

At the Beaver Creek camp, meanwhile, most although not all the Cheyennes departed as well, breaking again from the still relatively whole coalition. They trailed up the Tongue to begin for them a succession of travels that led through their own favorite hunting country in the valleys of Otter Creek, Pumpkin Creek, and the Powder River. They remained aligned in principle with Sitting Bull's avowed dedication to a traditional life on the buffalo prairie, but the season also demanded robust hunting. Behind them the massive village was straining all grazing and hunting resources.[31]

The Lakotas, meanwhile, trailed down the Tongue and camped next at the mouth of Pumpkin Creek. Then they continued a relatively reverse course following the same trail they blazed in April in the earliest days of the ascendancy. Their route followed Pumpkin Creek, Johnson Creek, and Lower Mizpah Creek eastward until reaching the Powder River, some thirty-six miles above its mouth. Sitting Bull's simple intent was to hunt and carefully avoid the surging military traffic crowding the Yellowstone Valley. Already some among his circles had been to the Yellowstone and witnessed "fire boats" plying the river in numbers too many to count.[32]

While on this travel other small groups and bands also peeled away. Medicine Cloud, an Assiniboine dispatched by the Fort Peck agent in late May specifically to find Sitting Bull and extend an appeal to quit this disastrous war, was allowed to depart the camp and return to his agency, where he arrived on July 25. Medicine Cloud disavowed participating in the fights in June, but he did acknowledge that one member of his original party, a Hunkpapa Sioux, was killed at the Little Big Horn. Another individual returning with him now had in his possession a gray horse branded US and C7. When the agent pressed the man on how it was he possessed this animal, he told him only that it was acquired in trade from a Standing Rock Indian. "I am of the opinion," the agent wrote, "that he participated in the fight and obtained the horse in that way." As he closed his report, the agent asked for guidance on what to do with government property found in Indian possession, and what to do with Indians who possessed such property. In this instance the agent, not wishing to jeopardize any future contacts, allowed the individual to keep the horse.[33]

Separately, Rain in the Face, the resolute Hunkpapa and vigorous defender of the buffalo country, also departed. He and six others made their way to the Standing Rock Agency, where they claimed to be peaceable and willing to give up their arms. Upon learning through intermediaries that they would also lose their ponies, however, and that their surrender must be unconditional, they immediately turned away and fled westward.[34]

The dramatic battlefield successes in the north and continuous peevish affairs in the Pine Ridge Country during the early days of Sitting Bull's War variously inspired and riled the Oglala Sioux and their agency neighbors, the Brulés, Northern Cheyennes, and Arapahos. Pine Ridge residents east and west were thoroughly enmeshed in the full-blown Black Hills gold rush, where a boundless tide of prospectors and nonstop stage and freight traffic from Sidney, Nebraska, and Cheyenne, Wyoming, turned once crude roads through and near the agencies into dust-clouded thoroughfares. There seemed to be no let-up in sight. Compelling, too, was news from the north delivered by Black Bear's horse recovery party and more recently the five Arapahos and Magpie Eagle's band of Cheyennes. They all told of astonishing Indian victories and delivered Sitting Bull's fresh invitation to join him. Such news resonated widely at the Red Cloud and Spotted Tail agencies and elsewhere.

Among the Northern Cheyennes still in the Pine Ridge Country, Morning Star, or Dull Knife as the Sioux commonly referred to him, held his people out of the war. A wise and seasoned pragmatist, he was the fourth of that tribe's Old Man Chiefs, a sixty-six-year-old veteran who a contemporary characterized as a chief of the "old school," measured by inspiring courage, selflessness, and intelligence. He was a devout traditional. Like Little Wolf, he had endured the sting and perfidy of the Whites. Lately around Camp Robinson, he also witnessed the sweeping martialing activities plainly rising against the Northern people. One might imagine him thinking the Northerners had no chance in this war.[35]

Morning Star and other Cheyenne leaders at the agency also contended with the government's continued insistence that they join the Southern Cheyennes in the Indian Territory. For a while this spring the Old Man Chief contemplated leading his people there to live among those kin. But the freedom and hunting prospects of the Buffalo North beckoned, and some among his people eagerly wished to join their kin there.[36]

By now, the Pine Ridge and Missouri River agents knew well of Custer's death, and that word spread widely among the locals. In the Yellowstone country Custer's name had already drawn connections here and there, but his death hardly portended any immediate sense of consequence or urgency. Throughout America, however, Custer's death on June 25 changed everything, including the trajectory of this Indian war. The death of such a Civil War hero spawned complexities impossible yet to fathom in buffalo country. The Red Cloud agent asserted that the news and the attendant martialing widely underway were inspiring young Sioux and Cheyenne men to flee the agency for the northern camps. Those Oglalas and Cheyennes themselves might simply have thought the season's victories, coupled with Sitting

Bull's repeated calls to join him, were inspiration enough. Whatever the case, that alone seems to have inspired Morning Star. In mid-July he opted to lead his people north. Doing so, he almost immediately thrust himself into a confrontation of more consequence than he could possibly imagine.[37]

Several warriors among Morning Star's people later provided details that round-out the tale of a small but crucial episode that unfolded in the breaking light of July 17 on the banks of Warbonnet Creek, Nebraska. The day before some six or seven hundred Cheyennes and a few Sioux led by Morning Star, Turkey Leg, and Standing Bear departed the proximity of the White River Agency and by evening were paused a mile or two short of Warbonnet, a small, languid tributary of the Cheyenne River. They had only begun a journey on the well-scored Powder River Trail and were no more than fifteen miles from their agency.[38]

Word of Morning Star's flight had been anticipated, already passing through military channels from Camp Robinson to Fort Laramie and on to a column of cavalry then policing the Powder River Trail ahead of the Cheyennes. On the morning of the seventeenth a handful of Cheyenne wolves, including Beaver Heart, Buffalo Road, Yellow Hair, and four or five others, were scouting ahead of the camp. They ran head-long into the blue coat cavalrymen, who themselves had bounded eastward the day before and were now secreted along the cut banks of Warbonnet Creek. Both sides exchanged a few scattered shots, unhorsing Beaver Heart and Yellow Hair. Yellow Hair was killed. His companions dashed back to the camp. The people from a distance witnessed the clash, and with blue coats blocking their westbound trail they hurriedly reversed course and scurried back to the agency, soldiers hounding them all the way.[39]

The army ever after remembered the encounter as the Skirmish at Warbonnet Creek, an eloquent name for an otherwise hasty little affair. The clash achieved the return of Morning Star's Cheyennes to presumed agency control, if only momentarily. Within a day or two and apparently unknown to the blue coats, most of those same Indians merely divided into smaller bands and again struck the trail, angling west on a slightly divergent path and with one and all vowing "to keep away from all White people."[40]

Trifling as it was, to the outside world the Warbonnet Creek episode resonated from coast to coast, newspapers heralding the fight as a victory of sorts in an otherwise embarrassing Indian war. There, the well-known stage actor and Plainsman, William F. "Buffalo Bill" Cody, scouting for the cavalry that day, killed and scalped the lone Indian casualty, Yellow Hair, and proudly lofted the knot of hair amid the cheer, "First Scalp for Custer." Within weeks Cody showcased the scalp, Yellow Hair's knife, and other Indian trophies gathered from the scene in playhouse windows nationwide, and reenacted the fight in theater limelights. In the moment, the Warbonnet Creek fight was instantly gratifying for Cody and the many soldier witnesses, but the stage performances were even more electrifying and generated welcome support for Sheridan's Indian war, particularly in a tragic season when, for the Whites, it was needed most.[41]

Warbonnet Creek was but one encounter with Indians in the Pine Ridge Country that summer, though no other had such resonance. Two weeks later agency warriors harassed the Cheyenne River stage station, a critical stop on the Cheyenne–Custer City road. Infantrymen from nearby Camp Mouth of Red Canyon rallied and drove the attackers off. The next day those same raiders struck the south-bound stagecoach as it made its way from Custer City to the Hat Creek station, adjacent to the army's Sage Creek camp. They all but wrecked the coach and wounded one of the four passengers before the harried travelers reached Hat Creek. That same day, farther west on Elkhorn Creek another band of like-minded raiders harassed an army freight train bound for Fort Fetterman. In that instance the wagon boss was killed, a teamster wounded, and three wagons burned before frantic survivors reached the post. These and other assaults in that locale paled in comparison with the great battles bloodying the north, but collectively they sustained a view widely held by the public that general mayhem now gripped the southern span of Sioux Country. The army responded by transferring additional troops to this margin of the war zone from as far away as Texas and San Francisco.[42]

Similar mayhem tormented a swath of countryside north of the Black Hills. In days past the north country was a common traverse for Miniconjous and others journeying from the Missouri River to the buffalo country and to the Hills themselves. It was a land spotted with revered landmarks such as Bear Butte and Bear Lodge Butte. Now it sprawled with hay cutters, stockmen, and prospectors serving the interests of the northern mining communities. For a while, Centennial Valley, north of Deadwood, became a figurative No Man's Land where Indian confrontations were commonplace. The most notorious killing by Indians in that locale was of Reverend Henry W. Smith, "Preacher Smith of the Black Hills," a founder of Deadwood. Smith was shot five miles north of the mining camp on August 20 while making his way to nearby Crook City to preach.[43]

Other confrontations were occurring in the Yellowstone country. The core of the great village had made its way toward the Powder River in late July and had slowly descended to within eighteen miles of its confluence with the Yellowstone. Persistent stories of steamboats plying the river, and reports of stockpiled and abandoned army stores at the mouth of the Powder lured sizeable parties from the camp northward to investigate, and that in turn brought on two back-to-back clashes with soldiers.[44]

A boat landing on the south bank of the Yellowstone barely downstream of the mouth of the Powder had been the focus of considerable soldier activity in June and July. It was serving as an army supply depot for necessary stores of food and grain delivered there by river steamer. As troops continued to maneuver on the Yellowstone, particularly upstream, the depot's soldier complement relocated, momentarily leaving behind caches of bacon, beans, coffee, and apples, and sacks of oats and yellow corn. Ascending the river on August 1 was a boat delivering yet another complement of troops for the coming campaign. When that steamer passed Wolf Rapids just downstream of the Powder River landing and came within its sight, passengers observed Indians scurrying about, salvaging such foodstuffs and grain as they wanted. The boat discharged several companies of foot soldiers who skirmished with and scattered the scavengers. But the Lakotas merely retreated to the distant bluffs beyond reach of the soldier rifles. For their part, the foot soldiers returned to the boat and continued upstream, and delivered a lively report.[45]

A second boat, also troop-escorted, reached the landing on August 2, its soldiers determined to remove the remaining stores. Perhaps as many as two hundred warriors openly challenged them. Anticipating trouble, those soldiers brought along a Gatling gun and a twelve-pounder Napoleon field piece. The latter was put into service and effectively scattered the attackers into the bluffs at the farthest extent of the gun's range, and thus shielded the soldiers landed and commenced reclaiming the stores. The warriors continued their challenge, but such fearlessness proved costly, with one White and one warrior—Runs Fearless, a friend of Crazy Horse—killed. Of the affair, Young Black Elk remembered his relatives bringing home generous quantities of corn, "which we parched and feasted on. It was very good."[46]

All along the leading chiefs and elders routinely counseled, such assemblies having started in the earliest days of the ascendency. A Métis trader a few weeks later met with one who was there and remembered hearing of the unique conversations occurring among the elders. Sitting Bull challenged the traditionals to think of other options for sustaining their buffalo life. In a speech to the council, Sitting Bull reportedly said: "We can go nowhere without seeing the head of an American. Our land is small, it is like an island in the middle of the sea. We have two ways to go—to the land of the Great Mother, or to the land of the Spaniards." The metaphoric cliché—a small island in the middle of the sea—may belong to the Métis informant, but the prospect of fleeing the Yellowstone Country and even America itself seems to have entered open Lakota deliberation for the first time. One reason was that soldier traffic on the Yellowstone had become ominous. The river was flooded with troops and boats, and Sitting Bull in early August was already pondering a way to escape.[47]

Even though so close to the Yellowstone, Sitting Bull and most of his followers went nowhere near that menacing water. Instead, they continued a slow deliberate trek, trailing from the Powder eastward, across the O'Fallon Creek drainage, and on to Beaver Creek. Aside from a few Cheyennes with kinship ties among the Oglalas, no others of that tribe remained in the enclave, the last having departed for the south and west. All along, too, small family bands scattered, some intent on hunting, others bound for an agency, whether there to unite with kin or avail themselves of wintertime bounty. On this trail Inkpaduta, the impoverished Santee band leader, departed the core, along with Long Dog, a bullet-scarred Hunkpapa band chief who would have a prominent role in events soon to come. Having had enough of this war, their combined thirty lodges struck off northward, bound for the Missouri River. Rivermen noted them crossing the Yellowstone near today's Glendive on August 22.[48]

Beaver Creek, a well-watered north-flowing stream, originated in the Blue Mountain headlands, where this coalition had first assembled after the assault on Old Bear's Cheyennes in mid-March. Now, the remaining aligned people followed that stream northward and then pivoted to the east, crossing rolling ground toward Sentinel Butte, a prominence in the broken western badlands of the Little Missouri River. Most of Sitting Bull's followers were bound for the Little Missouri, familiar ground to the Hunkpapas, Miniconjous, and Sans Arcs, but not the Oglalas. In calmer times Eagle Elk, an Oglala among Crazy Horse's people, remembered how in this Moon of the Black Cherries the people always scattered after having come together for the Sun Dance. "But this time it was different," he said. In these days of war this once mighty coalition had proven itself immensely capable, defeating Crook's soldiers coming at them from the south, and destroying Custer's command on the Little Big Horn. At the time they had numbered nearly five thousand people in six major camp circles. They were a quarter fewer now and still a formidable body, but here in the shadows of Sentinel Butte, the coalition dispersed.[49]

Four major groups emerged from the split. Sitting Bull rallied most of the Hunkpapas, all along the largest of the circles. He led them on a northeasterly course for the Killdeer Mountains, a secluded upland in the eastern breaks of the Little Missouri badlands. His people were drawn by reports of buffalo near the confluence of the Little Missouri and Missouri Rivers, due north of the Killdeer uplands. With him were the No Neck, Black Moon, and Four Horns bands. Despite a tortured history, including the devastating Sitting Bull–Sully clash in 1864, the Killdeer Mountain locale was renowned for its consistently good hunting and seclusion, qualities long favored by the great chief and the Hunkpapas.[50]

A second sizeable body of aligned Miniconjous and Sans Arcs, mostly under Eagle Shield and Spotted Eagle, separated from the mass and headed in a southeasterly direction, reportedly bound for the Cheyenne River Agency. A third group, mostly Miniconjous and Oglalas, headed southward, too, but soon split, with some forty lodges of Miniconjous under Red Horse and Iron Plume (commonly called by some American Horse, the elder) angling in a southeasterly direction toward the Slim Buttes, while a larger body of mostly Oglalas led by Crazy Horse, Little Big Man, and Big Road continued directly southward. The Red Horse and Iron Plume bands were purportedly bound for the Pine Ridge agencies while Crazy Horse's and Big Road's people eyed hunting and raiding prospects in the northern Black Hills. During these days of breakup, a sense of intentional evasion was in play, or at least it was according to Eagle Shield, who testified to it during an interrogation at the Cheyenne River Agency several months later. "The Indians," he confided, "when the trail became too large, would scatter to hide it, and come together again at some previously appointed place." Perhaps so.[51]

The free-roaming traditionals faced many obstacles in this changing season. They were particularly aware of fresh troop movements north of them. Soldiers there seemed to multiply almost daily and were now intentionally blocking Yellowstone River crossings. Long Dog and Inkpaduta would soon encounter such an obstacle as they trailed to Fort Peck. Moreover, the soldiers from the south were known to have taken the trail again and were advancing northward to join the blue coats on the Yellowstone River. Despite the constant and intentional Indian back-firing of their trail, that ploy was proving no deterrence to these soldiers. Then too, couriers and kin from the agencies brought word of conditions there and were advising the bands to submit soon, perhaps under some manner of armistice. Agency people said the army was suggesting ever more stridently that incoming Indians lay down arms, submit to arrest, and be held accountable for the blood spilled in the summer. Conveniently ignored was just who started this war. Civilian agents were aghast, as were agency chiefs. What few Northern Indians who did visit an agency from time to time invariably departed hastily when learning of the army's demands.[52]

In this waning summer season, the persistent problem of ammunition became acute. In the Rosebud and Little Big Horn battles warriors had fired thousands of rounds in weapons of all makes and manufactures. At the Little Big Horn, they, in turn, collected hundreds of army carbines and revolvers, plus thousands of rounds of ammunition from soldier cartridge belts and saddlebags. But army weapons fired distinctive .45 caliber cartridges that were unusable in the odd medley of Indian guns in hand, particularly the popular and common Winchester and Henry .44 caliber rifles and carbines. What was especially needed now was a supply of bar lead and loose gunpowder. Agency traders were prohibited from trafficking in such munitions and weapons, but in that void shrewd kin and traders were still prospering, including one nefarious trader in the south.[53]

In other days, the Northerners routinely carried on a robust trade with Métis traders from British America. Soldiers operating on the Yellowstone through the summer had largely precluded that source, however, which made agency trade on the Missouri and in the Pine Ridge even more critical. Black Bear, a Brulé from the Spotted Tail Agency who surrendered at Standing Rock that fall, told of his own entrepreneurial trafficking in munitions. Ponies and buffalo robes were his prime medium of exchange, he said, commodities that could be readily exchanged with licensed traders. Other instances were hinted at by the *New York Herald* when it reported that fall of the coming and going of the steamboat *Carroll* at Cheyenne River Agency. The boat carried 26,000 rounds of ammunition that were unloaded and quickly disappeared into the western hinterlands on the backs of pack mules. The same story related instances of nearly 100,000 rounds similarly trafficked through Standing Rock Agency, and 138,000 rounds passing into Indian Country through Fort Benton. The report was alarming. Whether any of this reached the warring camps will never be known, and there shortages persisted.[54]

Easily the most infamous and still unchecked illegal trading operation in Sioux Country was that orchestrated by Francis Boucher, the daytime operator of an independent trading house on Bordeaux Creek in the Pine Ridge. Boucher was also the widely scorned night trader operating in the isolated "Burning Grounds," the black-earth feature on the White River just across the Nebraska-Dakota Territorial line straight north of his trading post. Most Whites knew that he benefitted by his close relationship with Spotted Tail, his marital relative. and that he served as the chief's personal interpreter. In the 1870s the stout Frenchman was at Spotted Tail's side during most of the Brulé chief's delicate dealings with Whites. Capturing widespread notice in this time of war was the duo's trip in June 1876 to Fort Laramie and Cheyenne. While Spotted Tail made social rounds in Cheyenne, including a visit to the theater, Boucher purchased a sizeable load of fixed ammunition that the two subsequently transported to the Pine Ridge on their return. Among the agency Indians, Spotted Tail was perhaps on the best terms possible with the military and other Whites. He always claimed that his people needed the ammunition for hunting, but from Pine Ridge, Boucher's trail northward suggests otherwise.[55]

Boucher's reputation as a shadowy trader followed him. An officer at Fort Laramie who joined Crook in the field that summer penned a letter that circulated in eastern newspapers lamenting Boucher's ammunition purchase in Cheyenne. "A fresh party of Indians starts out fully equipped," the officer bemoaned. A resident on the Cheyenne–Fort Laramie road likewise complained to the Wyoming Territorial congressional delegate that when Boucher and Spotted Tail passed his place they had with them forty thousand rounds of ammunition. Surely such ammunition should be seized by military authorities, the delegate asserted, before it "finds its way into the hands of the hostile Sioux." The Spotted Tail agent also noted Boucher's load of cartridges, but puzzlingly sidestepped the matter with a closed-eye quip: "I have every reason to believe he sold [the lot] in direct violation of the law." What everyone feared, in fact, was indeed *fait accompli*. Boucher's load disappeared shortly after reaching the Pine Ridge. Deadwood's newspaper, the *Black Hills Weekly Pioneer*, finished the story, noting in its July 29 issue how Boucher's four-mule team was "traced to a point between Rapid City and Crook City, where the trace was lost until he was next seen with an empty wagon." Boucher vigorously denied the allegation of chicanery in his own letter to an Omaha newspaper, but circumstantial evidence was damning.[56]

The *Pioneer*'s story pointed if but vaguely to the wilds beyond the Black Hills as Boucher's trading locale but Indians themselves when returning to agencies that summer and fall helped affirm a unique place, the Burning Grounds, a sprawling remote locale along the White River that perplexed agents, army generals, and the nation's newspapers alike. When returning to Fort Peck in early August, Medicine Cloud specifically told his agent that ammunition supplies came from "the 'Burning Grounds,' beyond the Black Hills on White River." That small detail—on the White River—is critical and pinpointing. Little Buck Elk told the same Fort Peck agent in September that their ammunition source was "traders from the Burning Grounds." Boucher's operation would soon enough be investigated and curtailed, but not yet.[57]

Francis Boucher was not the only source of ammunition for the Northerners during this critical period. When, late in summer, Sitting Bull's followers trailed to the Killdeer Mountain country, they were drawn chiefly by its prospective solitude and by word of a sizeable buffalo herd nearby. At hand, too, slightly downstream of the Little Missouri–Missouri confluence was the Fort Berthold Arikara Agency, the welcome setting of Hunkpapa intermarriage and trade in previous years and where Hunkpapas might still visit relatives when opportunity arose. But newer tribal alliances between the Arikaras, Hidatsas, and Mandans strained Hunkpapa ties of old, as did the reality of Arikaras now scouting for the army. On August 21 ten or twelve Hunkpapas appeared on the Missouri's west bank in the proximity of the agency. They made known their wish to cross and trade. On other days such trade was desirable, but plainly now these Hunkpapas were unwelcome, so much so the Arikaras fired on them. The Lakota warriors departed in haste, dropping three Seventh Cavalry canteens as they fled. Our Indians, said the local agent, could see where those Hunkpapas had been.[58]

In the days and weeks following the death of Custer, the Lakotas and Northern Cheyennes basked in the glories of that remarkable day in June, even as they strove to lay in a larder of berries, roots, and meats to sustain the camps in the coming winter months. All the while, they evaded troops who were traversing the revered buffalo country. But a play on Eagle Elk's refrain that "this time it was different" proved increasingly telling. Soldiers had trailed the great camp. Crisscrossing the range, they were swarming the Yellowstone Valley and its vital river crossings. Soldier numbers on the Yellowstone were climbing beyond anything previously known, in fact, with each successive steamboat arrival. This time indeed was different.

The Little Big Horn battle was also an awakening for Sheridan's Army. His plan for a conclusive wintertime strike on the Northern Indians, the Sitting Bull traditionals who had not heeded the government's call to the agencies, had been thoroughly stymied. The Powder River fight in March had only succeeded in inspiring the Northerners. Sheridan's summer campaign had likewise proven an unimaginable failure. But the general who would not take defeat as an answer in the Civil War had the capacity to reinvent his campaign. The arrival of additional infantry, cavalry, and even artillery from throughout the land this late summer and fall was already telling. What came next not only doomed the people attempting to live a free life as in the days of old, but also the very consummate resource that held them there. As well, Sheridan already harbored plans to permanently garrison the Yellowstone Country, a move virtually guaranteeing the permanence of his campaign to sweep the northern plains clean of those buffalo people and open it to railroaders and cattlemen. The painful evidence of Sheridan's resolve and capacity awaited the Northern people this fall.

11
THE HUNTED

"It seemed to us that everything was upside down."
—Charger, Miniconjou Lakota

Long Dog, a Sitting Bull ally and fervent traditional, departed the great camp while it made its way from Powder River to Beaver Creek. With him were Inkpaduta and his small band of Santees. Both bands may simply have been seeking hunting opportunities beyond the Yellowstone but just as likely they sought to escape the war entirely. In recent tribal councils Sitting Bull had spoken of fleeing to Canada, a land yet untrammeled by annoying railroaders and prospectors. Inkpaduta knew that land and its people well. Whether he and Long Dog discussed such freedom is unclear, but these Hunkpapas and Santees were the first of the wartime people to head in that direction deliberately. Others followed in course.

As the combined thirty lodges of Hunkpapas and Santees ambled north, they headed first for the Big Open country between the Yellowstone and Missouri Rivers in far eastern Montana. Flee as they might, war was still almost impossible to escape. Plying the Yellowstone ahead of them was a steady parade of steamboats, including just then a pair traveling in relative unison. On August 23 slightly below Glendive Creek, Long Dog's warriors chanced onto and fired into the first of those boats as it paused to take on wood. The shooting caused great alarm among the passengers, and a soldier among them was killed. When they could, both boats continued upstream. Behind them Long Dog's and Inkpaduta's people crossed the river and continued northward.[1]

Long Dog's trail soon crossed the Yellowstone-Missouri divide and followed a course in the valley of Red Water River, a Missouri tributary. This land was a tangle of rugged grasslands challengingly bisected by dry and flowing watercourses. In the Red Water Valley they encountered an immense buffalo herd and slowed to hunt. But soldiers from the Yellowstone, learning of the assault on the boats and the death of a soldier, trailed them northward. The soldiers encountered the same buffalo herd, but not Long Dog's people. From afar the Hunkpapas and Santees saw the blue coats and fled in panic, abandoning their lodges, and hastening to the Missouri. On September 6, they crossed below Wolf Point, a river landmark on the Fort Peck Reservation, nominal home of Assiniboines and Upper Yanktonais.[2]

Long Dog's appearance caused an immediate stir, and on September 11 the local agent, Thomas Mitchell, found them on Porcupine Creek, a Milk River tributary north of the Fort Peck trading post. They traveled openly, and the agent said they talked freely of going to the Wood Mountain country in the British Possessions after pressing their immediate need to make new lodges and lay in meats before winter set in. Four days later other troops arrived by Missouri River steamer, but the Hunkpapas and Santees had long departed. A tenuous alliance with the Métis and buffalo and freedom from the Americans beckoned.[3]

In the great break-up near Sentinel Butte, a band of Miniconjous and Sans Arcs aligned with Eagle Shield and Spotted Eagle had cut from the body and was bound for the Cheyenne River Agency. One of them, Swelled Face, later admitted that "they had concluded to quit the war." When the Miniconjous and Sans Arcs neared the Missouri River, twelve men from the band approached officials at the agency, saying the main camp was behind them, near the forks of the Grand River. They said they were out of rations, short of ammunition, and questioned the government's terms for coming in. The government's response was distressing. Without pause, the commanding officer of the Cheyenne River army garrison said any surrender must be unconditional. Warriors would be dismounted and their firearms confiscated. They would be held as prisoners and subjected to such punishments and other treatments as higher authorities might dictate. Almost simultaneously the officer and those around him proceeded to disarm and arrest the men. The civilian agent present protested vigorously but was ignored. Agency Indians were likewise astonished and some, perhaps many, feared the day when this, too, would be forced on them. Separately, the commanding officer sent couriers to the camp forewarning of the terms they faced if they came in. No one else appeared. From afar, the Cheyenne River Miniconjou Charger (Martin Charger of another day) reflected plaintively: "It seemed to [us] that everything was up-side down."[4]

The lands far to the west of Cheyenne River Agency, in fact, were dotted with Indian camps that fall, mostly a disassembling of the various bands that had turned south from Sentinel Butte. Some soon became aware of what happened to the twelve men who presented themselves at Cheyenne River. Others were chiefly occupied with hunting, and still others were intent on continuing the trail to the Pine Ridge agencies. The largest intact body was that of aligned Oglalas and a few remaining Cheyennes, who, one and all, were content to continue resistance, especially when learning of the stern measures they faced if they chose to come in. Crazy Horse, for one, was incensed by the news from Cheyenne River. Most were aware, too, that a sizeable body of soldiers was on their backtrail, but they believed the scattering of the bands and the dreary fall weather would obscure their movements. Still, they were cautious. Those soldiers, the Miniconjou Swelled Face remembered, "passed within nine miles of us and did not attack us, but went on and attacked a small party farther south."[5]

Another mixed band of some thirty-seven lodges, mostly Miniconjous with a few Sans Arcs, Oglalas, and Brulés, largely belonging to the

Miniconjous Iron Plume and Roman Nose, were camped in the lee of the Slim Buttes in western Dakota. In the morning drear of September 9, the trailing blue coats attacked them. No episode in Indian warfare was more frightful than an assault on an unsuspecting Indian encampment. "We were coming in, to give ourselves up," the Miniconjou Red Horse later exclaimed. "It was early in the morning, still dark and misting. We were all asleep." In the shriek of gunfire and bullets ripping dewy skin lodges, warriors gathered what arms they could in the dark, slashed their way out of tipis, hid their women and children among the upslope rocks, and attempted to resist.[6]

Defense of the camp was initially weak. They were a small concentration of merely 235 people, with perhaps fifty warriors, facing an initial attacking force of 150 chargers, supported later that morning by nearly eighteen hundred other soldiers and civilians arriving from the north. Dependents fled westward and southward. Some followed the brush line along the small creek flowing through the camp and succeeded in reaching higher ground to the west. They then escaped the field altogether through the crags of the pine-topped Slim Buttes. Warriors, meanwhile, did what they could, seizing advantageous perches in the west and commencing a steady if largely ineffectual long-range exchange of gunfire with the soldiers. Most of the fight's few casualties occurred in the opening moments of the rainy, pitch-black morning.[7]

Only with dawn light did the attackers fully comprehend that the small camp held bounteous quantities of buffalo robes, dried meats, and other foodstuffs, plus saddles, tin ware, and the general wherewithal of Indian lives. Having seized the camp, the blue coats devoured most of the dried meats and berries, but the greater share of property was simply piled high and set ablaze. Soldiers lorded over souvenirs from the Little Big Horn fight—a swallow-tailed cavalry stars-and-bars flag, soldier clothing, saddles, a glove marked with the name of a fallen Seventh Cavalry officer, and horses branded US and 7C. Two good conduct passes—notes helping "good" Indians pass safely through the countryside—were also found in the lodges, one of them signed by F. C. Boucher, the scorned Pine Ridge trader.

The soldiers also gathered and distributed two hundred Indian ponies. One Indian eyewitness later told an interviewer that this story might have been different, but ironically, "most of the men were out trading for ammunition." The Whites, meanwhile, heralded the encounter as "a bright page in the history of this expedition." For the most part these were the same soldiers humiliated at the Rosebud in June. For them, any conquest in Indian Country was a substantial victory in this otherwise dismal year of war.[8]

As soldiers prowled the field they encountered a deep ravine in the west filled with Indians. One of the attackers, a White man among the column's many scouts, brazenly stood fully exposed on the rim and was shot dead. That brought on more soldiers who poured "a rain of hell," as one newspaperman called it, into the ravine's brush and obscuring recesses. In due course, a mixed-blood interpreter from Red Cloud Agency negotiated a surrender, and slowly twenty-eight people were coaxed into the open, many of them frightened women and children. With them was Iron Plume, the camp's primary leader, and his brother Charging Bear, the same young Miniconjou who had been repulsed by the blood and gore he witnessed at Little Big Horn. Iron Plume was grievously wounded, a bullet having slashed across his abdomen. He emerged from the ravine pressing a bloody rag against his belly, his hands barely containing entrails protruding right and left.[9]

The soldier in charge, Gray Fox George Crook, and doctors were summoned and the medical attendants attempted to bind Iron Plume's wound. One officer remembered how he never once groaned. Iron Plume refused a hypodermic of morphine, and the doctors declared his wound fatal. With Crook's trusted mixed-blood, Frank Grouard, and the Red Cloud mixed-blood both interpreting, the soldiers interviewed some of those who surrendered, including Iron Plume. The chief spoke freely, saying this was a village of mixed Lakotas, mostly belonging to the Cheyenne River Agency. He also warned that Crazy Horse's camp, perhaps numbering as many as three hundred lodges, was close at hand, somewhere nearer the Little Missouri River. With a certain palpable defiance, he seemed to dare Crook to pursue any other Indians in the region, suggesting that the result would be the same as Custer's fate. But he also allowed that the Sioux were pretty well tired of the war.[10]

Red Horse and Burnt Thigh were among those who fled westward that morning in the attack's opening salvos and located Crazy Horse's camp, eight or nine miles distant. The chief and his lieutenants, He Dog and Kicking Bear among them, gathered warriors and rode to Iron Plume's village, reaching the heights in the Slim Buttes late that afternoon. What they observed through the rain and murk below was not the mere 150 chargers that struck the camp in the morning but an extraordinary array of horse and foot soldiers that vastly outnumbered their own riders. Still, they carefully descended to the same perches occupied by the camp's initial defenders and added to the desultory fire. Some attempted to run off the captured ponies but were turned away by the soldier horse guard and pickets. Several times the general shooting became so intense that the soldiers organized sorties to drive the harassers back. As at the Rosebud, the long-range of infantry rifles proved consequential. Only when darkness descended did the gunfire subside.[11]

By now pangs of hunger and the prospect of resupply in Deadwood motivated this undersupplied and exhausted soldier command, not the chance to strike another Indian camp. When the column continued south in the morning, two of the surrendered men and nine women and children, some of them wounded, were released, but others were taken along. Among those led away were Charging Bear, Iron Plume's brother, and his wife. The surrendered people with the troops were neither hostages nor prisoners nor guides, it seemed, but were photographed as curiosities as they later passed through the Black Hills. They were released when they reached Camp Robinson some weeks later. In turn, Spotted Tail later orchestrated their return to the Cheyenne River Agency.[12]

Conditions on the ravaged battlefield at Slim Buttes were grim. More than the burned lodges, some fourteen fatalities, mostly battered women and children, lay scattered across the field and in the ravine that for a while had sheltered refugees when the attack began. Dispersed as well were the captives that Crook had released, including Iron Plume's wife. Iron Plume had died in the night. Crook obliged the released people to tell their kin that the army would hunt them all until everyone had surrendered. That notion, well known and executed by generals like Crook during the Civil War, meant complete abdication and was, of course, abhorrent to the traditionals.[13]

Short Bull, a young warrior in the fight alongside Crazy Horse, remembered that Indians ever after called the Slim Buttes encounter "The fight where we lost the Black Hills." It was a puzzling notion because it seemed to place an undue importance on such a small and seemingly inconclusive engagement. Yet those Miniconjous, Sans Arcs, Brulés, and Oglalas watched as two thousand soldiers continued southward a day later and then days after entered the Black Hills. While soldiers had accompanied exploring parties combing the gold country in 1874 and 1875, those episodes were brief and transient. These troops on the other hand seemed more like occupiers, joining thousands of miners churning the streams and constructing towns. The legality of this invasion of the western quarter of the Great Sioux Reservation remained in question, but even then another government commission was forming to address that political nightmare. Indeed, the Black Hills, the "Heart of the Earth" as He Dog once so eloquently called them, were all but lost to the Sioux. And while those troops from Slim Buttes departed the Black Hills in mid-October, a permanent military presence in that coveted land had only begun.[14]

When the government last dispatched a commission to Sioux Country to purchase the Black Hills, in September 1875, a Sioux war nearly erupted in the Pine Ridge. Agency chiefs wavered, never exactly embracing the notion of signing away that coveted land, but also ever conscious of their people's subsistence needs. Hunger was a prevailing consideration, and subsequent commissioners used it advantageously. Moreover, in 1875 Northerners tried in one instance to disrupt the proceedings forcibly when Little Big Man led fifty armed warriors into one council session and threatened to kill any commissioner who would steal his land. In the end, the purchase effort was sidelined, the commissioners went home, and the White invasion of the Black Hills merely continued apace.

At Congress's direction, a new commission was authorized in the annual Indian appropriations bill in August 1876. Again, it would address Indian surrender of the Black Hills. This time commissioners dispensed with any notion of negotiating with the Sioux, predicating any continued subsistence of agency people, who would starve otherwise, on the relinquishment of all rights and claims to the lands west of the 103rd meridian and inside the forks of the Cheyenne River. The commission also promised construction of three wagon roads across the reservation to facilitate Black Hills development. Red Cloud later complained that that boundary was never fully explained and that "Indians did not understand the White man's way of bounding tracts." "They cannot understand," he said, "except by landmarks like hills and streams." Such a complaint had no currency in Washington.[15]

To further buttress their demands, the commissioners carried with them a fully prepared document requiring only signatures. And that document added one more twist. Commissioners also sought complete relinquishment of the unceded hunting lands west of the Great Sioux Reservation. For the Pine Ridge people and all Lakotas, the choice was starve or cede not just the gold-rich Black Hills country but also the hunting lands of the Powder and Yellowstone River Basins—the Northerner's revered Buffalo North. Because Congress had abolished the treaty system in 1871, the commissioners called their paper Articles of Agreement, coyly avoiding, they believed, the stipulation in the 1868 Fort Laramie Treaty that required land cessions of any sort to be consented to by three-fourths of all adult male Lakotas. It was cede or starve.[16]

The nearby Camp Robinson garrison was bolstered substantially through the summer and the added troops ensured calm. But no Northerners were on hand to disrupt the proceedings anyway. Where in 1875 government commissioners assembled representatives of all the Sioux people in one grand council, this time each of the Lakota *oyates* would be consulted separately. In long episodes of speech-making at both Pine Ridge agencies, local chiefs and elders almost universally placed matters of subsistence in the fore, especially if buffalo hunting was in peril. The commissioners, in turn, merely pointed to the paper and assured the signers that what they sought—continued annuities and protection—was provided for there. Again, a heap of promises! The Oglala Little Wound scoffed and asked where the $25,000 was that had been promised when the hunting rights in the Buffalo South were forfeited. A commissioner acknowledged that the sum had not yet been paid but said that the president had not forgotten the obligation and was still trying to secure the funding from Congress.[17]

At the agencies the give-and-take stretched over several days. Finally, the commissioners abruptly pointed to the document and said that it was time to sign. Marking the paper took several more days, commencing at Red Cloud Agency on September 20, and then at Spotted Tail Agency three days later. At each, an agent or secretary would write a name and individuals scrawled an X to affirm consent. They were somber affairs. Most chiefs and head men touching the pen were conscious of what they were doing, even if with great reluctance. Some did so bitterly. Fire Thunder, an Oglala, found the document so shameful that when he stepped to the table he covered his eyes with his blanket and touched the paper blind. Sitting Bull, not the resistant Northerner but the agency Oglala, spoke aggressively against the document and threatened those who seemed willing to sign. He was ushered from the proceedings in disgust. Two Strike, a Brulé, said only, "The reason we are afraid to touch the pen and are silent before you is because we have been deceived so many times before."[18]

From the Pine Ridge the commissioners traveled a circuitous route by rail to Bismarck and then descended the Missouri River, procedurally explaining, cajoling, and securing signatures at Standing Rock Agency on October 11, Cheyenne River on October 16, Crow Creek on October 21, Lower Brule on October 24, and the Santee Agency in eastern Nebraska on October 27. The meetings were often contentious. Headmen voiced concern for subsistence and welfare, or they challenged the paper's simple vagaries. Would the payments last as long as there was a hill standing, Flying Bird, a Miniconjou, posed? Was this merely a loan of the Black Hills to the Whites, Long Rock, another Miniconjou, wondered? Commissioners deftly offered nearly any assurance necessary to obtain marks on the paper. Their mission ultimately a success, the signed agreement passed through Interior Department channels to President Grant, who commended it to Congress on December 22 and asked for its special consideration. The Senate ratified the agreement on February 28, 1877. At last, the government had eliminated the Black Hills from Sioux Country.[19]

In the days and weeks following the fight in the Slim Buttes the focus of the northern camps turned solely to survival, driven by ceaseless quests for buffalo. Aside from the many soldiers and steamboats crowding the Yellowstone and its traditional river crossings into the Big Open country, blue coats were notably absent from other waterways and hunting grounds beyond that valley. The summer soldiers seemed to have gone home. The people in the camps had no way of understanding the government's strategic shift in waging this war, nor could they possibly comprehend that those river soldiers, mostly hated infantry now largely encamped at the mouth of the Tongue, constituted the greatest threat yet to their freedom. Those soldiers operated under a new mandate to create not one but soon two massive forts on the Yellowstone, plus a third on the Middle Powder, further allowing the army to continue this war and ensure an inevitable new order on the buffalo prairie. The people in the camps simply turned their attention to buffalo. Time was of the essence. Normal hunting and gathering cycles had been disrupted throughout the summer, and the long seasons of cold and snow were coming soon.[20]

Sitting Bull learned of the Slim Buttes fight within days of its occurrence when refugees found their way to his camp. After a pause in the Killdeer Mountain country, he began making his way westward again, toward the Big Open, variously intent on hunting, securing munitions if possible at

Fort Peck, and apparently nearing himself to Canada, should he opt for that greatest of escapes. It was well remembered among his people that the Santees had fled to Canada after their war in Minnesota in 1862, and the Canadians had welcomed them. Sitting Bull's own followers had traded with the Métis in Canada's Wood Mountains almost continuously since the winter of 1870–71, and in the years since he had maintained a casual but often productive relationship with those mixed-bloods. Sitting Bull presumed that Long Dog's band of traditionals, having split from his camp in August, were already there.[21]

Word of the Great Chief's movement was well known in the Upper Missouri Country in late September when Little Buck Elk, a Hunkpapa, and three others appeared at Fort Peck on September 23, having come directly from the chief's camp. In conversation with the local agent, Little Buck Elk told among other things of ammunition being supplied by the southern trader Francis Boucher in the Burning Grounds in the southeastern Black Hills country. But the Hunkpapa had come foremost with a query from Sitting Bull, who wondered whether ammunition might be available at Fort Peck? The agent was aghast, reporting to his superiors that he immediately dispatched a runner to Sitting Bull informing him that no munitions were available at that place or anywhere on the reservation. He did allow that if the chief wished to come in and surrender arms and government property he would be treated kindly. Little Buck Elk told, too, of the Custer fight, admitting to being present but adeptly avoided confessing that he had any role in the affair. "Indians were as thick as bees at that fight," he allowed, and "there were so many of them they could not all take part in it."[22]

Of equal interest, Little Buck Elk also provided particulars on Sitting Bull's movements in mid-September. Barely a few days earlier when the Hunkpapa departed the camp, the chief was on Beaver Creek, southeast of the mouth of the Powder. Another camp of Hunkpapas was nearby in the Blue Earth Hills, the vast forested tract in the southeastern corner of Montana. That band may in fact have been united Miniconjou and Sans Arc refugees, loosely aligning with other Hunkpapas. By now those scattered places were familiar landmarks in the saga of this war, the creek a standard pathway between the Little Missouri drainage and the Yellowstone, and the Blue Earth Hills a favorite sanctuary for these traditionals. Word of this movement spread widely. In army spheres, it triggered an alert that the great chief was again approaching the Yellowstone and searching for ammunition, a report that quickly reached the soldiers hutted at the mouth of the Tongue.[23]

Somewhere along Sitting Bull's trail from the Killdeer Mountains, likely in the Little Missouri country, he was joined by twenty-seven-year-old Johnnie Bruguier, an unlikely but not unknown Missouri River mixed-blood. Bruguier was among the messengers dispatched by the Standing Rock agent the previous January to deliver a final warning to the Northerners to submit or face a war. The year before he had interpreted for that same agent during the first of the Black Hills negotiations. Bruguier was fluent in the Lakota language, his mother's tongue, and routinely interpreted at Grand River and Standing Rock. He was also well educated. His father, a successful French-Canadian trader on the Middle Missouri, had providing each of his male children with an education at the Christian Brothers College in Saint Louis. But Johnnie was complicit in a recent killing at Standing Rock, and rather than defend himself and clear his name, he had fled. Lawmen believed he intended to disappear in the flotsam of the Black Hills mining camps. Others thought he was headed to Minnesota to be among Red River mixed-bloods. Instead, he sought obscurity in a not-so-distant Northern Indian camp, and apparently chanced onto the very camp belonging to Sitting Bull. It was a bold move, but Bruguier's familiarity with the Hunkpapas and their language saved him.[24]

While most Hunkpapas knew Bruguier a few were suspicious. They questioned why a man in White man's clothing might ride into an Indian camp so brazenly. Some even threatened to kill him, but Sitting Bull intervened and welcomed him to his lodge. The venerable chief again showered favor on such a self-assured and gregarious middleman. Bruguier talked frankly about the war, of forces circling and in the field presently, all aiming to defeat the Northern Indians. And he talked of the fates of those surrendering at an agency. It was Bruguier who allegedly told Sitting Bull and these Hunkpapas that it was Custer leading the soldiers they killed at the Little Big Horn. Spotted Bear, a Hunkpapa in the camp, claimed it was the first they had heard of this. Perhaps so, even if Cheyenne women had identified Custer late in the day of the battle. The Oglala He Dog remembered learning the soldier's identity some two weeks after the fight "when a Missouri River Sioux brought out the news." Whatever the case, Bruguier was welcomed and befriended. As a fugitive, the safety and isolation of the Hunkpapa camp served him well. His presence would also soon serve Indian interests.[25]

As Sitting Bull's people crossed the Yellowstone on October 10, having descended Cabin Creek, a small tributary downstream of the mouth of the Powder opposite Bad Route Creek, his wolves reported the movement of army wagons east of them. The Indian camp was headed northward for the Big Dry, following Bad Route Creek. Big Dry Creek, across the northern divide, was a broad watercourse leading to the Missouri River and Fort Peck. It was a landscape almost always heavy with buffalo. But the wagon soldiers were in the way. Sitting Bull's wolves wanted to fight, but the chief, innately cautious, counseled against interfering. Still, young men, emboldened by the successes of the summer and incensed by the army's attack at Slim Buttes, rushed off.[26]

Late that evening warriors struck the soldiers at their overnight camp at the Spring Creek crossing (today's Sand Creek), some fourteen miles west of their Glendive supply camp, capturing forty-seven government mules from the westbound train. The raiders lingered and the next morning again harassed the train as it pressed on for the fledgling Tongue River post. At the Clear Creek crossing seven miles further along, Indian gunfire grew so persistent and sometimes vigorous, the government train and its mix of civilians and foot soldiers turned back. One recalled having to "fight our way through to Glendive." Several days later, refitted and accompanied by a measurably strengthened escort, the wagons again took the trail. As before, warriors harassed the train. In this exchange, Sitting Bull's nephew, White Bull, so brave and heroic at the Little Big Horn, was wounded in the left arm, a bullet breaking the bone. "It was a hot fight," White Bull recalled. "Four soldiers were wounded that day." White Bull was helped back to camp where his wounds were tended. "They gave me medicine for four days, and made me well again," he remembered. "I was almost dead."[27]

Sitting Bull had no role in those clashes. If anything, he consistently pressed his people to disengage and continue to the Big Dry. But he also acknowledged there was a point to be made, and perhaps even something to be gained. On the morning of October 16 as the troops and wagons continued westward, they encountered a note scrawled on a piece of white cloth tied to a stick, the handiwork of the chief's newfound literate middleman friend, Johnnie Bruguier. As Johnnie explained later, what occurred was unique and distinctly of the chief's inspiration.

> Yellowstone
>
> I want to know what you are doing traveling on this road. You scare all the buffalo away. I want to hunt on the place. I want you to turn back from here. If you don't, I will fight you again. I want you to leave what you have got here, and turn back from here.
>
> I am your friend,
>
> Sitting Bull
>
> I mean all the rations you have got and some powder. Wish you would write as soon as you can.[28]

Shortly thereafter, two riders from the Indian camp, Bear Face and Long Feather, appeared. Both were Standing Rock Lakotas who the agent recently sent to encourage Sitting Bull to end the war. They approached the column under a white flag and were led to the commander. Their pleading on the chief's behalf was no different than the essence of the note. The trains were scaring the buffalo, but Sitting Bull was tired of fighting and his people were hungry. He was willing to make peace but wanted now only to hunt, and for that he needed ammunition. The army commander told the couriers that he was in no position to negotiate and certainly would not provide ammunition. The couriers asserted that Sitting Bull then would merely continue to Fort Peck to trade. The exchange was brief and seemingly innocuous, although when the soldiers continued on, they left beside their trail two sides of bacon and 150 pounds of hard bread, small tokens of a continuing hope to end the conflict, if only on the government's terms. The Indians harassing the train to this point disappeared altogether, even as Sitting Bull led his people northward up Bad Route Creek and into the forked headlands of Cedar Creek where buffalo had been spotted.[29]

Meanwhile, a column of soldiers led by Colonel Nelson A. Miles of the Fifth Infantry joined the wagon train. Alarmed when the Glendive train had not appeared as anticipated, they had come hastily from the Tongue River camp. At thirty-seven years of age, Miles was a complex man. An aggressive, seasoned Indian campaigner, he had brought his regiment to Montana from Kansas in the wake of the Little Big Horn disaster, arriving on one of the many steamboats plying the river that season. He was dually charged now to establish the Tongue River post, one of the new army garrisons intended to be permanent in the heart of the buffalo country, and to take the war to Sitting Bull. Apprised of the apparent nearness of the chief's camp, he immediately determined to intercept him and either oblige his surrender or destroy his camp. Few of the people comprehended just then that a new reality had set in. In Miles, they now faced a determined, unbending agent of the government, an officer as resolute in effecting a new order in the buffalo country as Sitting Bull was in clinging steadfastly to the vestiges of yesterday. Miles would dog the great chief to the end.[30]

As the wagon train continued to the Tongue River camp, Miles's column of foot soldiers and a lumbering artillery piece pivoted to the north and ascended Cedar Creek, a shallow, nearly treeless drainage reaching to the far horizon. Some eight or ten miles up the stretch they were again confronted by the two Standing Rock Indians, Bear Face and Long Feather, who once again advanced under a white flag. Behind them in the distance, a crowd of onlookers, perhaps as many as 150 warriors, were visible on the skyline. Taken to Miles, the two couriers told him that Sitting Bull was willing to have a meeting and discuss surrendering his people. This suited the colonel immensely, and the two riders returned to the watchful audience on the horizon, this time accompanied by one of Miles's officers. There, with Bruguier interpreting, arrangements were made for a council of a few necessary participants drawn from each side. They would meet between the lines. [31]

The stage was set. What occurred on the afternoon of October 20, 1876, was an episode distinct in an already distinctive, convulsive saga, a moment when the Great Chief looked face-to-face at his enemy and made his case for a life in the buffalo country.

The day was sunny but bitterly cold. Onto the broad, treeless stage Sitting Bull and Miles each rode forward accompanied by small retinues of counselors and interpreters. They pulled up on the prairie thirty yards apart, dismounted, and stepped forward. The leading figures were each suitably attired for the season but made no grand spectacle. The chief, swaddled in a thick buffalo robe, was in plain dress. Miles wore a unique fur cap and a long, caped, dark blue overcoat trimmed with bear fur. Indians ever after referred to him as "Man with the Bear Coat," or simply "Bear Coat" Miles. Sitting Bull wore no feathers or ornamentation but, as always, clutched his pipe bag. No one was armed, at least visibly. Among those at Sitting Bull's side was Big Leggins Bruguier, his trusted new interpreter. [32]

Sitting Bull spread a buffalo robe between them and urged that they sit. Miles consented to kneel but refused to sit. Bruguier sat between them. Sitting Bull first conducted a pipe ceremony, ritualistically invoking the supreme powers in the prospect of peace. Miles opened the exchange, circling his driving point with small matters, particularly the return of the mules taken a week earlier. Then he reached the issue of consequence, telling the chief bluntly that he meant to deliver the Sioux to the reservation, peacefully he hoped, but forcibly if necessary. Sitting Bull bristled. "Give us back the buffalo your soldiers scared away from us," he retorted. If Whites had not come into his country there would be no war. He wanted peace, he conceded, but on the old terms, with arms, the ability to trade, and the liberty to hunt and roam at will on the Plains. Miles later characterized

Sitting Bull's demands as an "old fashioned peace." Bear Coat was inflexible, and their differences irreconcilable. Miles broke off the council near sunset and the parties returned to respective onlookers far behind. Sitting Bull and his warriors quickly disappeared, returning to their camp in the headlands. Before parting, however, he and Miles agreed to talk again in the morning.[33]

In the Indian camp that evening, the contentiousness of the day boiled over, and a number of chiefs and head men confronted Sitting Bull. Some wished to attack the soldiers outright, but that ardor was calmed. Others wished to accede to Bear Coat's demands, Bear Face and Long Feather particularly espousing such a view. Conditions were dire, the wavering ones noted, and they were ready to yield, even if it meant surrendering firearms and ponies. But mostly the people needed to eat. Sitting Bull struggled to retain his resolve but managed to calm the dissenters.[34]

Next morning the people were alarmed to see the soldiers advancing up the east fork of Cedar Creek toward them as if ready to strike the camp, and when the chiefs and warriors departed for the talk the women and children struck the lodges and prepared to flee. The meeting with Bear Coat Miles that morning was even more tumultuous than the one the day before. Sitting Bull surrounded himself with a greater delegation of counselors, eight or ten now, including Gall, Black Eagle, Bull Eagle, and Red Skirt. The chief dominated the exchange, repeating his demands for unfettered freedom in the buffalo country. Miles zealously repeated his demands from the day before. Fearing the soldiers might be wiped out right then, Bruguier sometimes delicately avoided translating some of the officer's intemperate remarks. In utter frustration, Sitting Bull told Bear Coat that there could never be a peace between the peoples. "God Almighty made him an Indian and did not make him an agency Indian either, and he did not intend to be one." As the council dispersed, Miles warned Sitting Bull that to reject the government's terms would be considered a hostile act, and he would attack immediately.[35]

Bear Coat Miles's attack on Sitting Bull's Cedar Creek village on the late morning of October 21 only served to harden the chief's view of a duplicitous government, and of Whites, daring to speak of peace, but only on government terms. Barely had he and his entourage returned to the camp when shrill cannon fire announced the commencement of Miles's assault. Bullets from infantry rifles soon pelted what remained of this buffalo hunting enclave, the fragile remnant of a once-mighty alliance of Hunkpapas, Miniconjous, and Sans Arcs. Miles never tallied the size of the camp aside from declaring, speculatively, that it held "about a thousand warriors." Bear Coat's attack achieved the scattering of the inhabitants and the complete destruction of hastily abandoned property, the all too frequent consequence of yet another hurried flight. One White scout among the attackers was struck by the richness of the Indian property—lodge covers often taken but not always the poles, tons of carefully dried buffalo meat and backfat, hundreds of parfleches stuffed with dried berries, plus cooking utensils, furs, and skins of all sorts. This was the fourth such brazen attack on traditionals this year, and the first directed consciously and specifically at Sitting Bull. He and those same kin allies were in the immediate cross fire at Little Big Horn, too, but the nature of that fight saved the village. Not here.[36]

For a short while, warriors put up a gallant defense. They burned the grass between the soldiers and the camp, even as some seized the advantageous ridge defining the scene's northern horizon and shooting from there, all to cover fleeing dependents. At one point White Bull, his shattered arm in a sling, attempted to rally followers, yelling out, "Come on, let's go and rub them out." But Sitting Bull restrained him and urged that he shield the vulnerable ones instead. Casualty tallies varied—one, maybe five Indians killed, and an untold number of ponies, American horses, and mules lost. Two soldiers were wounded. Most of the people fled in a southeasterly direction, opposite the blue coat's charge. They crossed the shallow divide onto the headlands of Bad Route Creek in the direction of the Yellowstone, with slow-paced foot soldiers on their heels after first ensuring the complete destruction of the camp.[37]

For many in the village, this attack was a final straw. They had grown weary of this war and were increasingly willing to submit. Emissaries from the agencies made clear the government's terms for surrender. Ever more attractive were the simple laying down of arms, loss of ponies, and a release from this terror, all in exchange for food. On Bad Route Creek yet another seemingly inevitable separation occurred, with the aligned Miniconjous and Sans Arcs continuing a direct course toward the Yellowstone, headed, most thought, for the Blue Earth Hills to hunt and replace lodge poles as they continued to the Cheyenne River Agency. The Hunkpapas, however, had no interest in the Blue Earth Hills and cut for the north, but then almost immediately split again. Sitting Bull, Gall, Black Moon, Four Horns, and Iron Dog—some one hundred lodges of people holding steady to the mystique of the buffalo country, continued northward, still drawn by Fort Peck and even British America. Others, with Bear Face and Long Feather among them, fled eastward in the direction of the Standing Rock Agency. They were finished with this war.[38]

Conspicuously riding with Sitting Bull was Big Leggins Bruguier. When eluding the US Marshal in Dakota and heading west to the Indian Country, he scarcely imagined aligning with the most notorious of Northern Indians and joining this all-out war against the Whites. Already he was conspicuously visible, whether writing letters or serving as interpreter. At Cedar Creek, he rode bravely into the fight, much to White Bull's and Sitting Bull's surprise and approval. Such entanglements complicated his fix as a fugitive, but this was not the time or place to find a way out. Sitting Bull's plain course was north toward Fort Peck. Perhaps an opportunity would present itself there.[39]

The Miniconjous and Sans Arcs who safely reached and crossed the Yellowstone pulled-up. Instead of continuing toward the isolated Blue Mountain sanctuary immediately, they milled conspicuously in the river valley, curious about Bear Coat Miles's movements and hardly less certain of their own. Miles's overtures on Cedar Creek had swayed many of these Lakotas, and now, two days after the confrontation there, Bull Eagle, a Miniconjou, and several other chiefs crossed the river again and approached the soldiers. They suggested another council. Miles remembered Bull Eagle from the second Cedar Creek meeting. In meeting with them now, the colonel learned that Sitting Bull and his Hunkpapa followers had separated and were bound for the Missouri while other Hunkpapas from that circle had fled toward the Standing Rock Agency. The chiefs sought mixed options. Some told Miles they had no willingness to yield directly, but Bull Eagle and others were much more amenable and expressed a desire to do so now. Nothing resolved, they agreed to continue their exchange the next day.[40]

Their meeting the next day, October 27, took place over a meal. Again, others, all Miniconjous, joined Bull Eagle. Yesterday's willingness by some to submit at an agency was tempered by a desire to hunt first. The people lacked clothing, they declared, their ponies were worn, and no one had meat. Miles had no patience for delays, however, and repeated the strident tone he used with Sitting Bull, telling the chiefs again that he was prepared to advance his foot soldiers against them forthwith if they dallied. This time his coercion worked. The people agreed to submit immediately. Miles knew that he was in no position to subsist so many people—he unrealistically estimated two thousand Indians in three or four hundred lodges—and neither did he have a sufficient force to escort them to Cheyenne River.[41]

Instead, Bear Coat offered a unique proposal. The people should turn themselves in at Cheyenne River within thirty-five days. Five chiefs or headmen among them would have to surrender now, accept being held hostage, and assent to being delivered to Saint Paul, Minnesota, as guarantors of their followers' surrender. The headmen consented to the terms, and after a brief dally among themselves five stepped forward. Surrendering as hostages were Red Skirt and White Bull, the elder, both Miniconjous, Black Eagle and Red Sun (Sun Rise), both Sans Arc chiefs, and Foolish Thunder, a Sans Arc warrior. Two days later the five headmen and a small soldier escort, plus an interpreter, commenced an overland and steamboat journey, not to Saint Paul but to Cheyenne River Agency, where they were released to the local agent. Bear Coat was ecstatic, telling his superior, General Terry in Saint Paul, that he considered this "the beginning of the end."[42]

The reality was less convincing. In due course some thirty-five or forty lodges of Miniconjous and Sans Arcs appeared at Cheyenne River. Most belonged to the hostages. The rest of the people continued into the Powder River Country and eventually joined the large encampment of Oglalas aligned with Crazy Horse. Bull Eagle, seemingly one of the more compliant ones during the councils, did not go in immediately. Neither did Spotted Elk, who later confessed that the promises and agreement were mere ruses that bought time and relief from the dogged soldier pursuit. As for Miles, he returned with his soldiers to Tongue River thinking he had achieved a complicated surrender.[43]

Sitting Bull had no way of knowing of the drama playing out on the Yellowstone. From the time of his separation on Bad Route Creek, he led his Hunkpapas north to the Big Dry country nearer Fort Peck. He needed to hunt and hoped to trade with the Yanktonais. He was in want of ammunition, and if none could be secured at Fort Peck, he was prepared to continue north to Wood Mountain to trade with the Métis. Many of his people also needed lodge poles, which might also be acquired through trade. As the Hunkpapas neared the Missouri, Iron Dog and 119 lodges of followers, seeking refuge among the Yanktonai camps, continued to the river and camped in the bottoms midway between Wolf Point and the trading post. There he deliberately sought out the Fort Peck agent and surrendered four government horses and one mule captured during the most recent engagements with American troops. Iron Dog inquired especially about food and ammunition but wished also to discuss surrender terms. Johnnie Bruguier went along. Separately, Bruguier gave the agent a government check in the amount of $182, payable to Captain George W. Yates, a recognized Seventh Cavalry fatality at the Little Big Horn. Doubtless the note had been taken from the man's body.[44]

Isolated in northeastern Montana, Fort Peck Agency was long a hotbed of intrigue and intercourse between various Indian and mixed-blood peoples, and it was particularly inviting now because no soldiers were stationed there. Many Hunkpapas, having drawn rations at the post over the years, were familiar with its operations and people. Many had intermarried with the Yanktonais, which itself opened trading opportunities of both regular and irregular sorts. Coming to discuss the prospects of surrendering was a logical move. Conversely, the government's terms of surrender were well known by now among the Sioux agents, and military authorities, whether at hand or nearby, carefully monitored them. In this case, that scrutiny came from the post commander at Fort Buford, 115 miles downriver. The agent laid out simple, inflexible terms—unconditional surrender, and the delivery of all arms and ponies. Iron Dog and the agent haggled, but the chief dejectedly agreed. In return, he and his people were rationed for the day. A formal surrender was put off to the next day, but before it occurred the Hunkpapas learned of the advance of soldiers aboard an approaching steamboat. Distraught, they fled. Most went south and reunited with Sitting Bull, although some went north and crossed the border into Canada. The Fort Peck agent had seen plenty, however, telling the commanding officer of the boat escort that those Northerners were impoverished. They had no lodges and their horses were as "thin as shadows." "I don't think they can stand the winter if kept stirred up." [45]

The troops aboard the boat had not come to occupy the trading post or commence a campaign against the Northerners. Instead, they came merely to deliver supplies for Miles, who had already orchestrated a renewed campaign, this one focusing on Sitting Bull directly. Miles boasted of a network of spies at the different agencies who regularly obtained information from locals and from runners who were continually coming and going between the agencies and Northern camps. Apprised of Sitting Bull's nearness to Fort Peck now, Bear Coat chortled to his superior in Saint Paul at the opportunity presenting itself. "I will endeavor to keep them divided and take them in detail," he declared, which was military jargon for defeating an enemy piecemeal. [46]

When Miles reached the trading post several weeks later, Sitting Bull and the Hunkpapas were gone. He did consult with Johnnie Bruguier, however, who had lingered among the mixed-bloods and flotsam there. Miles also combed the countryside south of the river for several weeks more. Snow had obliterated all traces of the great chief, who by now was the government's and army's foremost nemesis. Bear Coat returned to Tongue River to refit and rest but left behind a small complement of foot soldiers to continue observing and reconnoitering. When Sitting Bull again appeared in Fort Peck's proximity in yet another attempt to secure munitions, the local officer was alerted. This time he successfully trailed the band south up Red Water Creek and a fork, Ash Creek, into its headlands. At midday on December 18 he struck the camp, which largely belonged to the followers of Sitting Bull and Iron Dog. The location in the high divide between the Missouri and Yellowstone drainages was barely north of the Cedar Creek affair of two months earlier.[47]

Weather conditions were dire. Those trailing the Indians and those being trailed were buffeted by cycles of Northers—vicious polar winds capable of dropping temperatures to -50°F—and had to tromp through snow sometimes two feet deep. Sitting Bull's camp, well sheltered along the timber-lined creek, was caught entirely unaware. Some inhabitants were away, hunting, but those warriors remaining put up a stiff resistance that allowed the women and children to flee to the south just before the soldiers stormed the lodges. Neither side reported casualties, but the blue coats destroyed some 122 tipis and sixty ponies and mules, and gathered nearly three hundred buffalo robes and caches of dried meats and other comestibles. Retaining the camp's foodstuffs, blankets, and buffalo robes, the soldiers distributed them among themselves, while the harried inhabitants fled into the winter snow and cold, protected by barely more than what they possessed on their persons.[48]

Those were the last of the once mighty and irrepressible Northerners still aligned with Sitting Bull. They were now a bedraggled coalition, and they splintered yet again. The indomitable chief and his small retinue, refusing the abhorrent prospect of submitting, fled south in search of Crazy Horse. "I still remember the bitterness of the suffering of the Sioux that winter," the Hunkpapa Good White Buffalo Woman remembered, "before we went north into the land of the Red Coats." The soldiers meanwhile returned to the newly christened Tongue River Cantonment, where they too were soon in search of the great Oglala, Crazy Horse. Bear Coat Miles was indeed determined to defeat the Northern Indians in detail.[49]

The government, meanwhile, and its outspoken and steadfast War Horse, General Phil Sheridan, was even then implementing another deliberate retaliatory policy at the Sioux agencies: the mass confiscation of all ponies and firearms. Such confiscations were already compulsory with the Northern Indians as they surrendered, but the policy was now imposed on agency people too, a tactic virtually ensuring the complete subordination of all Lakota peoples on the Great Sioux Reservation. Sheridan, commander of the vast Military Division of the Missouri headquartered in Chicago, had implemented a similar policy on the southern plains following the Red River War of 1874–75. Indian peoples there had endured the widespread confiscation of ponies and firearms. Then as now, the animals went to public sale in White marketplaces, with the proceeds used to purchase cattle intended to feed the thoroughly subsumed people. Government authorities imagined the policy would speed the ultimate transformation of Indians from buffalo hunters into self-supporting, independent agriculturalists. But in Sioux Country, Lakotas never imagined themselves as Minnesota or Iowa farmers, and how much of this beef stock was simply consumed rather than bred has never been examined. Remaking Indian people into farmers was no more than a perverse dream.[50]

The Pony Campaign was consciously delayed at the Sioux agencies until October, when the nearness of winter naturally discouraged outward migrations into the buffalo country. It was also a time when many traditionals normally returned to the agencies, whether to visit kin or avail themselves of wintertime rationing. Sheridan, moreover, had imagined that by then his organized campaigns of the summer and fall also would induce greater movement out of the buffalo country and toward the agencies. Indeed, the collective successes at Slim Buttes, Cedar Creek, and Ash Creek, combined with Bear Coat's ceaseless hounding were plainly bringing about such surrenders. As Sheridan saw it, ceding the buffalo country was precisely what this war was about.

A column of cavalry and infantry implemented Sheridan's plan at Standing Rock and Cheyenne River agencies. Mostly the troops came from Fort Abraham Lincoln and were supported by local garrisons as the column swept down the Missouri at mid-month. The focus was Hunkpapa and Yanktonai residents at Fort Yates, and Miniconjous and Sans Arcs at Cheyenne River. In the Pine Ridge, a separate column of cavalry dismounted Red Cloud's Oglalas and Red Leaf's Brulés, both sizeable bands aligned with Red Cloud Agency. To Sheridan's dismay, confiscations did not occur among Spotted Tail's Brulés. Commanders there and Crook himself did not wish to disrupt the general rapport they enjoyed with that chief.[51]

The widespread unhorsing and disarming actions dismayed and shocked the agency Indians. Many believed Lakota society could not function without its mounts or firearms, whether it was agency residents employing ponies to draw wagons or using firearms for local hunting and even the routine slaughter of agency beeves. The Hunkpapa woman turned Lakota historian, Josephine Waggoner, writing years later, personalized the trauma: "No one in this machine age could ever understand the love between master and horse. The love of a man toward a spirited, courageous horse was wonderful. It was like the love of a beloved child, only a man is dependent on a horse." Charger, a Cheyenne River Miniconjou, described the burden imposed on the agency people. "It was a pitiful sight to the Indians to see their ponies driven away to be seen no more. That night all over the camp Indians were weeping over the loss of their property. Rations were issued to them every week. The Indians went after their rations on foot and came back, often packing heavy loads on their backs." Little No Heart, another Miniconjou, put the confiscations in practical terms, complaining that "those arms were not presents to us; we traded horses for most of them. By taking those arms from us, we have lost the opportunity of collecting many furs and robes, which we could have sold for much money." Officers reported that the number of arms confiscated proved negligible as was the ammunition seized. Yet Sheridan and his commanders were convinced that agency ponies and munitions routinely benefited the Northerners.[52]

Accountability for the unhorsings was shockingly lax. Subsequent tallies suggested that as many as two thousand Indian ponies, American horses, and mules were seized from Standing Rock Hunkpapas on the Missouri's west bank and from Yanktonais on the east bank. Rations would be withheld if the Indians resisted. Twenty-two hundred animals were seized at Cheyenne River, and nearly three thousand at Red Cloud. The ponies from the Missouri River agencies were variously driven to auction houses in Saint Paul and Yankton. Of some four thousand animals gathered at the river agencies, the majority died of various causes or were siphoned off or stolen outright while en route to the sale yards. The proceeds purchased 315 cows and eight bulls for Standing Rock, and 650 cows and nine bulls for Cheyenne River. At Red Cloud Agency some of the confiscated ponies were retained and given to Indian allies when wintertime campaigns were organized, and army officers readily hand-picked mounts for their personal use. The rest were variously driven to sale at Sidney, Fort Laramie, and Cheyenne. Receipts from the Red Cloud sales were never used to purchase cattle for agency residents, and the funds were never accounted for. The hypocrisy and sheer vindictiveness of Sheridan's unhorsing campaign was embarrassing even at the time, and the action remains controversial in Indian Country these many years later.[53]

Bear Coat Miles's campaigns north of the Yellowstone and its two convincing clashes on Cedar Creek and Ash Creek largely cleared the vast Big Open country between the Yellowstone and Missouri of free-roaming Northern Indians, even though that land remained the most alluring buffalo country on the northern plains. But the countryside south of the Yellowstone still teemed with tradition-minded people. Remnants of the Miniconjou and Sans Arc bands scattered at Cedar Creek still tarried after their surrender conference with Miles on October 28. Cheyennes who split band-by-band from the great Rosebud–Little Big Horn coalition in July and August stayed out as well. Most notable of all was the sizeable alliance of Oglalas led by Crazy Horse and Big Road. Those chiefs and followers resolved to sustain a traditional life on the buffalo prairie, and furthermore, if necessary, to persist in this war. But those Cheyennes and Lakotas had not yet confronted Bear Coat's foot soldiers, or the new body of troops once again advancing out of the south. Although disparate, these forces would make for these people a long and calamitous winter.[54]

12
RED FORK AND BELLY BUTTE

"I run for my life. Soldiers everywhere. There is no time to snatch up even a robe."

—Beaver Heart, Northern Cheyenne

The nature of Sitting Bull's War changed dramatically in the fall of 1876. An army bulldog, Bear Coat Miles, had been unleashed in Montana and was now operating from an increasingly imposing outpost on the Yellowstone in the midst of the revered buffalo country. Already Miles and his infantry had twice confronted Sitting Bull's people and cleanly swept them from the Big Open Country north of the Yellowstone. Near year's end, and with no letup, he was turning his focus to the traditionals roaming south of the river. Miles and his government knew some of them as the followers of Crazy Horse, a fervent ideologue of Sitting Bull's and the second great bogyman of the war. But Miles was not the only army commander to put Crazy Horse and his people in his crosshairs.

At that same time in the Nebraska Pine Ridge, Gray Fox Crook had organized yet a third campaign against the traditionals. His targets were mostly Oglalas and Cheyennes who refused to return to their agency. While he did not coordinate with Miles, like his counterpart Crook focused specifically on Crazy Horse and his scattered alliance in the Powder River

Country. The Gray Fox had commanded the two previous army campaigns originating in the south, and while neither effort succeeded in driving many traditionals into an agency, both had wreaked havoc enough among peoples where attacks on villages and ceaseless hounding disrupted the ordinary movements and needs that defined their lives. Still, the lesson was not yet wholly served.

The Gray Fox's third orchestration again involved a substantial corps of fresh troops, well equipped and outfitted this time for long wintertime service, and he again headed into the Powder River Basin. As on his second campaign, he was supported by a sizeable contingent of Indian allies. On his summer movement Crook had with him some 250 Crows and Shoshones. He marched this time with nearly four hundred Indian allies, including Oglalas, Cheyennes, and Arapahos recruited at Red Cloud Agency, a contingent of Pawnee Scouts, hereditary enemies of the Sioux brought up from the Indian Territory, and Shoshones and Bannocks recruited at their agency in western Wyoming. Many of the Sioux and Cheyenne volunteers had kin in the northern camps and were conscious of the cultural and familial compromises posed by their joining the army, but Crook's assurances and inducements resonated. Here was the chance to be mounted and armed again, he offered, and he assured them that food for their families would be plentiful while they were away. But Crook also obfuscated, telling his native allies that this was a campaign directed at others and not their own people. That that somehow resonated at all seems puzzling, but it worked. Most of Crook's Indian scouts wore army uniforms, but not the Sioux and Cheyennes, whom the general insisted "dress as the Indians always do."[1]

Uniquely, too, Crook supported this campaign from a forward supply cantonment established in mid-October on the Middle Powder River, near old Fort Reno, a relic of the old Bozeman Trail days. Dubbed Cantonment Reno, this fully garrisoned infantry outpost operated much like Miles's cantonment on the Yellowstone, though on a less robust scale. Sheridan fully endorsed bastions of the sort located in the heart of the northern buffalo country. He believed such fixtures ensured making permanent the transformation underway and that once these contested northern plains were cleared of their roaming natives, those peoples could never return.[2]

When the followers of Two Moon, Old Bear, and Little Wolf broke from the great Rosebud–Little Big Horn coalition in July, those Cheyennes ascended the Tongue, simply intent on avoiding soldiers and hunting a favorite game-rich swath of country ranging from the Middle Powder west to the Big Horn River. There, in this time of the summer moon, the Cheyennes were joined by Morning Star and his people. After confronting the soldier obstacle on Warbonnet Creek in the Pine Ridge, their subsequent pathway north was unobstructed. With Morning Star's arrival, three of the four Cheyenne Old Man Chiefs were together and they remained so through the winter, a matter of endless comfort to the Cheyenne people. Other small bands from the White River Agency also joined, bringing with them the dire news of the taking of the Black Hills and the unhorsings and disarmings occurring at Red Cloud and the other Lakota agencies. All agreed that they were safer in their own country, merely, as the Cheyenne woman Iron Teeth recalled, killing buffalo, tanning skins, and storing berries for the wintertime.[3]

That fall, the continual movement of the Northern Cheyennes again brought some near the Little Big Horn battlefield, and Wooden Leg and a small party of hunters combed that evocative ground. They recalled their own good deeds there during the fight and places where Cheyenne kinsmen fell. They were particularly drawn to a hunt for cartridges that Wooden Leg noted were profusely scattered about, in singles and even in full boxes. Wooden Leg's friends planned to give their finds to others, but he was glad to keep what he found for himself. "I was the only one of this party having a soldier rifle," he boasted. The Cheyenne trail eventually took them to a remote haven in a southern extremity of the Big Horn Mountains, where they planned to spend some of the winter. The place, as one chronicler aptly noted, was a natural fortress, with limited access, immense, sharply rising walls protecting three sides, and the steady flow of the Red Fork of the Powder River running through the heart of the place. Most Northern Cheyennes were present, tallying perhaps twelve hundred people occupying some two hundred lodges and shelters. Nearly three hundred were warriors. "[We] wanted to keep entirely away from all White people, wanted to be left alone," Iron Teeth remembered. "They said that nobody would trouble us in this place so far away from other people."[4]

And yet, an enemy lurked. Approaching from the south behind those unsuspecting Cheyennes was Gray Fox Crook, not seeking Cheyennes particularly but determined at the onset of his third movement to locate and engage Crazy Horse, the general's principal war-time nemesis. But two chance encounters with Indians in late-November north of the Powder River Cantonment changed Crook's trajectory. On November 20 his Arapaho and Oglala scouts encountered a lone young Cheyenne warrior, Many Beaver Dams, in the eastern foothills of the Big Horns. Many Beaver Dams was traveling with a small party making its way to the Cheyenne camp in the southern Big Horns. The scouts passed themselves off as members of his tribe, and before he discovered the ruse they seized him and brought him to Crook. The young warrior revealed the location of Crazy Horse's camp, then on Rosebud Creek near where the fight of June 17 had occurred, and that the Cheyennes had crossed over to the other side of the Big Horns, meaning in this instance the west side of the mountains.[5]

Crook resolved to force-march his soldiers to the Rosebud, but even before commencing the movement his scouts encountered another young warrior, Sitting Bear, a friendly Oglala from Red Cloud Agency, who approached under a large white flag. Sitting Bear had been sent by the Red Cloud agent some while earlier to encourage Crazy Horse to submit. He departed the war chief's camp several days earlier and was headed now for the Pine Ridge. He told Crook that the chief had been forewarned of this soldier advance by the friends of Many Beaver Dams, who, when their compatriot had not returned, fled in that direction. The war chief had learned as well that a sizeable portion of Sitting Bull's people, doubtless the same Miniconjous and Sans Arcs that had conferred with Bear Coat Miles some weeks earlier, were south of the Yellowstone and moving toward the Tongue, seeking to align with the powerful Oglalas. Crazy Horse intended to move his camp to the Tongue River to meet them.[6]

Sitting Bear's news was at first disappointing. Crook had fixated on finding and destroying Crazy Horse, but the Oglala had other news that proved just as animating. Many of Beaver Dams's people, the Cheyennes, were not obscurely on the other side of the Big Horns as he had described, but in fact hidden now in a canyon on the very stream that Crook's soldiers were then passing. Because those people were plainly the closest of any potential enemy, Crook changed course on the spot and dispatched his mounted troops and Indian auxiliaries into the mountains to locate and destroy that Cheyenne camp.[7]

By now the Cheyenne camp on the Red Fork was alerted to Crook's soldier presence, and the council chiefs dispatched four wolves—Hail, Crow Necklace, Young Two Moon, and High Wolf—to locate and follow the blue coats' trail, a challenge eased greatly by the season's continuing and ever deepening snows. The wolves found the trail easily enough, and then the soldier camp. Well after dark on the evening of November 23, two of the Cheyennes, Crow Necklace and Young Two Moon, stealthily infiltrated the auxiliary's camp, intent simply on purloining food and running off some ponies. As they lingered on the margins they recognized two Cheyennes, plainly if perversely now scouting for the enemy, and heard the babble of four different native languages, Pawnee, Shoshone, Arapaho, and Cheyenne. The wolves did not dawdle and fled into the night with several Arapaho ponies and rode hard for their own camp.[8]

The council chiefs gathered the next morning to receive the scouts' report and the ensuing debate was stirring. The wolves told of spotting and even infiltrating a great soldier camp, a camp itself frighteningly close to their own, and that among the aligned Indians were Cheyennes. The wolves implored the chiefs to scatter the village, Young Two Moon forewarning that "if they [the soldiers] reach this camp I think it will be a big fight." Black Hairy Dog, a venerated holy man and keeper of the Cheyenne Sacred Arrows, also favored breaking camp and seeking Crazy Horse's village. Aligned Oglalas and Cheyennes could withstand any soldier attack, he declared. Many of the council chiefs knew too well of the enormous threat posed by any soldiers as close as these, already having suffered the calamity of an attack on one of their own camps at the start of this war, and then the Rosebud and Little Big Horn fights, and the constant flight since then. But they knew too of an ominous ending at their agency, if somehow they did submit. "We were not allowed to live in peace," Iron Teeth lamented.[9]

In the midst of the morning's difficult exchange Last Bull, chief of the Kit Fox Society, weighed in. "No! We will stay here and fight," he insisted, and declared that if people attempted to leave, his Kit Fox warriors would slash their saddle cinches. Warrior society chiefs like Last Bull normally sat quietly during council deliberations. Their role afterward was simply enforcing the chiefs' decisions. Besides, some noted that because those soldiers had already advanced beyond any normal straight-line course to this village, they were surely seeking Crazy Horse. Plainly browbeaten by Last Bull's tirade, the assembled chiefs raised no objections but merely instructed the society chiefs to continue to watch for soldiers. Beaver Heart, a nineteen-year-old warrior who had joined the camp with Morning Star and his followers, reflected on the matter years later. "So we stayed," he observed plaintively, and "spent the night dancing."[10]

But there were other ominous signs, as well. That morning during the great deliberation, Box Elder, the eighty-one-year-old nearly blind mystic who had prophesied the recovery of the ponies after the Powder River fight, and the imminence of an attack at the Little Big Horn, spent time in prayer and again had a vision. He saw soldiers and enemy scouts attacking the village and killing people. He summoned his son, Medicine Top, to warn the families that this camp would be attacked early on the morrow. Women, now, should go to the high cliffs and build breastworks and stay there, he said, and then they will be saved. As criers spread the word of Box Elder's vision families began assembling belongings and saddling horses, but Kit Fox warriors intervened, Last Bull and other society chiefs shouting warnings that "No one will go away! The people will dance the victory dance all night." Again, Last Bull and the Kit Foxes prevailed.[11]

Indeed, through the night the camp danced. In the weeks before, the Cheyennes had ranged the Big Horn River country widely, hunting buffalo mostly, and Last Bull and the Kit Foxes themselves falling upon a Shoshone hunting party and killing thirty of those enemies, taking scalps and other bounty (thus explaining Many Beaver Dams telling Gray Fox Crook that the Cheyennes were on the other side of the Big Horns). Last Bull and the Kit Foxes were determined that the village should celebrate this victory. A great bonfire was built in the center of the camp, and the exultant victors, many with Shoshone scalps bobbing from the tips of willow wands, danced through the night with other men and women.[12]

The drumming and dancing ceased at dawn, and some had just gone to sleep when gunfire reverberated through the Red Fork canyon just downstream of the camp, first a single shot, and then many guns. Some in the village quickly recalled Box Elder's vision. Others had been at Powder River in wintery circumstances just like this and remembered that horror. Some had just come from the Indian Territory and had no personal experiences of this sort at all, but had heard the stories. But no words of caution, or consciousness, or experience prepared anyone for the sheer terror of the moment.[13]

A herder was the first to encounter the attackers. Sits in the Night had driven horses down the Red Fork late the day before, and in the predawn rode to check on them. Before quite reaching his ponies he spotted people driving them off. "He could hear the blows as they struck them," he told an interviewer in 1908. Sits in the Night gazed puzzlingly at the intruders for a few moments, realized their character and threat, and shot at them, and then hurriedly turned and made off like a deer. William Garnett, a Red Cloud Agency mixed-blood scouting for the blue coats, watched the moment intently, too, and yelled to those around him: "He fired first; now fire." Those scattered shots were the opening salvo in the Battle of the Red Fork of the Powder River, November 25, 1876.[14]

The downstream gunfire was trailed almost immediately by another commotion disrupting the camp in the day's breaking light. Some villagers were startled when Indian ponies ran straight through the camp, until quickly realizing that they were being driven by enemy scouts, who also flew through the tipis determinedly driving those animals away. Shots were fired. Frightened Cheyenne fighters tumbled half naked from their lodges, with little in their hands but rifles and belts of ammunition. Panicked women and children fled westward and northward beyond the upper bounds of the camp, where the flanks of the mountains rose abruptly and offered immediate security. Few had any time to save anything from the lodges more than themselves. Behind the vulnerable ones some watched as soldier scouts and blue coats fanned into a standard frontal line and charged the camp, some headed for the village directly and others crossing the open ground to the north, aiming for the ravines crowded now with fleeing people.[15]

Black White Man recalled the shock of those first moments, with bullets sounding like hailstones striking the lodges around him. He had horses tied up at his lodge and saddled one for his wife and son and watched as they rode to safety. He then ran toward the attackers and fired at them, but in turning about he glanced at his own lodge, which stood near the river, and saw other tethered ponies running back and forth straining to break their ties. He ran to his lodge, cut the animals loose, and drove them to the heights. On his way he overtook a little boy who he helped to safety. That neither he nor the boy was hit by the spray of bullets puzzled him ever after. Beaver Heart, a vibrant old man in 1934, remembered having danced through the night, but then the tumult of the attack. "I rush from my lodge. I am naked. It is very cold. I run for my life. Soldiers everywhere. There is no time to snatch up even a robe. Pawnees and Shoshones shoot at me. I run faster up the canyon toward the mountainside. Many of my people dead. Others run with me."[16]

Indeed, people were already dying. As the young Hunkpapa boy, Deeds, retrieving horses on the day of the Little Big Horn battle, was the first of the traditionals to die in that engagement, here, similarly, a young Cheyenne herder, Walking Coyote, was the first Cheyenne killed, shot through the neck as he attempted to retrieve ponies at the lower end of the camp. In the village early in the attack Iron Teeth shepherded two sons and three daughters to safety, but her husband, Red Ripe, and an older son remained behind and fought the soldiers. He had his horse with him but fought afoot believing he might shoot better, she remembered. "Suddenly, I saw him fall. I started to go back to him," she said, "but my sons made me go on, with my three daughters. The last time I ever saw Red Ripe, he was lying there dead in the snow."[17]

Lone Wolf, known to some as Red Bird, was also chasing family horses in those opening moments and remembered bullets crackling tipi poles and watching as warriors fired at the attackers. With army scouts chasing him, he raced back to his lodge. He saw Burns Red trying to drive his ponies away from the village. "The enemy stopped chasing me and turned toward him," he recalled. Burns Red's pony fell. "That was the last time I ever saw him." Lone Wolf remembered, too, a young man, Scabby, struggling to mount a horse. It jumped and Scabby fell every time. Others around Lone Wolf told him to flee, and as he started his own pony got excited, jumped, and fell, throwing him. Lone Wolf made it afoot to the high rocks beyond the camp. Looking back he recalled seeing young Cheyenne warriors fighting like birds and singing like cranes, hawks, and owls.[18]

Little Wolf, one of the venerated Old Man Chiefs and perhaps the most renowned fighter among all the Northern Cheyennes, gathered a handful of warriors and positioned them in a group of rocks at the upper end of the camp, forming a shield between the helpless ones and the advancing soldiers. In the ensuing exchange he often stood out prominently and was noticeably hit several times, as were others with him. Still the warriors maintained their fire and provided an effective cover. Garnett, advancing with the soldier scouts, remembered witnessing those heroics and particularly bullets striking one individual among the defenders. He later learned that this was Little Wolf, who was wounded, the chief acknowledged, six times that day. One of Garnett's cohorts, the Grabber, Frank Grouard, guiding on yet another of Gray Fox Crook's campaigns, claimed he was the one who shot Little Wolf.[19]

Even in the worst of the assault, individual Cheyennes found opportunities for distinctive personal gallantry, reflecting for their part the timeless valor of a Plains warrior, and actions, too, invariably capturing the admiring eye of soldier witnesses. Early in the engagement a warrior emerged from one of the boulder-strewn inclines beyond the camp crowded now with women and children. He rode a white horse. An eagle feather bonnet draped to his horse's feet and he carried a buffalo hide shield. Riding toward the soldiers he hurled insults at the enemy, even while "bullets struck the ground before him, behind him, beside him," until one "knocked him lifeless from his charger." The fearless warrior may have been Walking Whirlwind, Little Wolf's son-in-law.[20]

That tragic killing spurred a second rider who emerged from the same rocky cover. He, too, as a soldier later recounted, was ornamented with feathers, carried a thick buffalo hide shield, and sat astride a spirited pony. He charged recklessly to the body of his fallen kinsman, dismounted, lifted the lifeless warrior onto the back of his pony, and carried the fallen man back to the distant rocks. Soldiers were visibly astonished. That brave man's name is lost to history.[21]

The soldiers, who greatly outnumbered the Cheyenne warriors, steadily advanced their own lines beyond the margins of the village and toward the boulder strewn inclines north and west. That same broad rocky interface had at first provided protection for noncombatants as they fled the assault, but now it was occupied mostly by warriors. One line of boulders in the northwest drew inordinate soldier attention after warriors there shot and killed a mounted blue coat and snatched his gun and cartridge belt. Soldiers fell back, dismounted, but maintained a continual fire into the rocks. Soon other soldiers came on. Young Two Moon watched from afar and thought to himself: "My friends are in a very bad place. I fear they will all be killed."[22]

Others sensed their predicament. Yellow Nose, repeatedly heroic on the Little Big Horn battlefield, watched those movements on horseback and rode to Young Two Moon and those with him. "If those soldiers reach the top of the hill they will kill those men lying behind it," he cried out. "We must protect them." Yellow Nose and some twenty others charged toward the soldiers, drawing their attention and fire before scattering to safety. Most of the challenging warriors escaped unharmed, although Brave Bear's horse was shot and he necessarily fled afoot. During it all, Young Two Moon rode to the people cornered in the rocks. He recognized many. They all escaped the fix safely.[23]

Elsewhere west of the village warriors noted another of their own, a man named Crawling, wounded in the leg and lying in the open. Braided Locks, returned from the charge on the soldier line east of there, with Hairy Hand dashed forward on foot and carried their wounded kinsman to safety. But for others, heroism came at a price. Braided Locks was later shot through the body and Yellow Nose through the breast. Both survived.[24]

The Cheyennes were not the only ones suffering such agonies. Elsewhere on the plain north of the village and early in the attack soldiers, evidently drawn by a gathering of Indian ponies, ran headlong onto warriors shielding noncombatants fleeing through a deep gulch northward away from the camp. Almost at point-blank range Cheyennes rose from the ravine and fired into the attackers and notably struck the blue coat's young leader, shot through the head and body. Yellow Eagle ever after asserted that it was he who shot the young officer. He rushed forward, counted first coup, and claimed the officer's gun. Two Bulls, at Yellow Eagle's side, counted second coup, and Bull Hump counted third and also collected ammunition from the officer's saddlebags, and then, as he ran off, saw a soldier pistol on the ground and grabbled it as well. Around the officer five other soldiers were wounded, but all were carried to safety.[25]

With soldiers and their Indian allies in complete control of the camp by midmorning, the destruction of the lodges began. Officers hailed the richness of the village, its 173 lodges variously of government-issue canvas and buffalo skin filled with ammunition, saddles, foodstuffs, everyday tools and equipment, blankets, war shields, clothing, and some twelve hundred buffalo robes. Everything was thrown into what one eyewitness called "the funeral pyres of Cheyenne glory." But the soldiers were equally intrigued by many unusual items and invariably retained them, especially those bearing testimony to these Cheyennes having been in the Rosebud fight and at the Little Big Horn. In the horde were such objects as a guard roster belonging to one of the luckless Seventh Cavalry companies and already transformed by High Bull into a drawing book documenting personal prowess. The buckskin jacket worn by Captain Thomas Custer—noted by an identification mark on the coat and affirming perhaps Yellow Nose's claim to have killed *the* officer commanding on Last Stand Hill—was a particular treasure. Soldiers also seized a pillow case fashioned from one of the stars and bars flags captured in that battle along with many other irresistible Seventh Cavalry relics. Equally intriguing items were discovered from the Rosebud battle, including the hat worn by Sergeant William Allen (identified by the name on the band), and the scalp of a Shoshone warrior killed there and identified now by kinsman who recognized unique ornaments in the hair. The scalp and the discovery of a little buckskin bag containing the severed hands of ten or twelve little Indian children, cut off at the wrists and still very fresh, greatly distressed the Shoshones who wailed in mourning throughout the night. Meantime, the Cheyennes could only watch the destruction of their camp in abject horror when, in the dead of winter, everything they owned was commandeered or disappeared in flames.[26]

Sickening, too, was the loss of many Cheyenne ponies. Contemporary accounts suggest that the army's Indian allies gathered six or seven hundred animals, mostly consolidated smaller family herds that grazed the hillsides east, north, and south of the camp. The army's first contacts had been with herders, often younger boys, ranging downriver to check on family stock in that direction. Doubtless, too, Cheyenne survivors watched in disgust as Pawnee scouts loaded nearly a hundred of those captured ponies "with such plunder as appealed to their fancy," during the camp's destruction. But a number of ponies escaped the army's surround. Some one hundred were grazing in the deep pockets of the Red Fork above the camp. The captured animals were mostly distributed among the army's Indian allies, but seventy-five or eighty were recaptured from the Pawnees the next day. Every surviving pony would soon be crucial as survivors fled the scene.[27]

By midday the fighting had all but ended. Cheyenne warriors held advantageous high ground to the north and west and maintained a desultory fire, but shortages of ammunition hindered their aggressiveness. The soldiers and their Indian allies, meanwhile, remained active in torching the camp. They retained the captured ponies, and manned the high ground to the south and along their own avenue of withdrawal to the east. In this relative lull, the soldier commander sensed a moment to extend a peace overture to the Cheyennes, perhaps thinking he might induce their surrender, and sent William Rowland, a Kentuckian married to a Cheyenne woman and a noted sign talker, plus Hard Robe, Rowland's Cheyenne brother-in-law, and the Grabber, Frank Grouard, to confer with the chiefs. The three soon enough singled-out Morning Star, and over the span of a safe distance opened a compelling exchange. The Old Man Chief, a late arrival to this war and not one of its most ardent supporters, told them that two of his sons had been killed that morning along with many of his followers. Yes, he was willing to surrender, he allowed, but he was unable to influence others around him, including Old Man Chiefs Little Wolf and Old Bear, who, with so many more, were plainly ready to die in a continuing fight. Anyway, the Whites could not be trusted, he asserted. Those with the chief were far less amenable, one of them screaming out: "Go home! You have no business here! We can whip the White soldiers alone but can't fight you, too." In light of such reluctance, the soldier commander decided simply to let hunger and the winter elements finish his work and the next morning he withdrew to rejoin the Gray Fox.[28]

In the day's waning moments, one other episode etched itself in the lore of the Red Fork fight. Young Two Moon remembered recognizing one of the Cheyennes fighting alongside the blue coats, a man named Old Crow, or Crow, who in fact was one of their own Council Chiefs. In a moment late in the engagement Old Crow rode quietly toward the northwest beyond the camp and hailed kinsman shielded in the rocks. In a remorseful tone he explained that he was obliged to fight them, but as atonement he would leave for them a pile of ammunition. That any of their own, no less an esteemed Council Chief, was now scouting for the army and trying to kill them angered the people and they scoffed and told him so. But later, survivors found a heap of cartridges on a knoll near where the exchange had occurred.[29]

Red Fork was another costly fight in this Indian war, a conflict brought on by the American government for the sole purpose of driving these last free-roaming native peoples from the northern plains. And it was distinctly a Cheyenne fight. Those Northern Cheyennes, the followers of Old Bear, Little Wolf, Two Moon, and Morning Star, hidden away in a nook of the Big Horn Mountains, were merely attempting to avoid further contact with the American army, at least this season. But on November 25 in the Cheyenne season of the hard frost moon, soldiers discovered and attacked them. It was the sixth major fight of Sitting Bull's War. The Red Fork people may have preferred thinking of this as a Cheyenne War, or Old Bear's and Little Wolf's War—they had been in the midst of four of its engagements—but the Americans simply saw the Cheyennes as more of the buffalo hunting people aligned with the figurehead Sitting Bull. To Whites, they were purposefully resisting treaties, avoiding the agencies, and impeding progress. Some forty Cheyennes were killed at Red Fork, mostly protecting women, children, and the old ones, with Crow Split Nose, chief of the Elk Scrapers Society, the most prominent casualty among them. Other victims including Scabby, valiant in the Rosebud fight, and Red Ripe and Gathering His Medicine, husband and son of the extraordinary Cheyenne woman Iron Teeth, among others. Additionally, as many as sixty-five Cheyennes were wounded. Soldiers noted seven of their own killed and twenty-two wounded.[30]

One overriding horrific legacy of the Red Fork fight shrouds its memory: the perverse reality that some Cheyennes had turned against their kin and now guided and fought alongside their enemy. The fact weighed heavily on Old Crow, a Council Chief, when he attempted an apology and delivered cartridges in recompense late in the fight. A foremost Cheyenne chronicler clouds the action, explaining that the White River Cheyennes who volunteered knew uniquely the near hopelessness of the Northerners' destiny, and that the officer commanding those attacking troops, Ranald S. Mackenzie, was a soldier much like the bulldog Miles who had already led a successful war against kin in the Buffalo South the year before (Miles was engaged there, too.) Others have focused on the harsh realities of acculturation at work at the Lakota and Cheyenne agencies, where conformance and cattle were becoming the accepted norm. By whatever measure, and whether softened by cartridges or insights or compliance, the Red Fork Cheyennes saw only betrayal. Years later Cheyenne elders noted that nearly all those who sided with the *ve'ho'es* that late winter season of 1876 were dead by 1885, surely killed by the power of *Maahótse*, the people's Sacred Arrows, objects of great comfort and retribution.[31]

The Cheyennes did not flee far that evening of November 25, and no *ve'ho'es* hounded their trail. With little for clothing or cover, the surviving villagers fled through the snowpack into the Big Horns. They followed the Red Fork into its headlands where a camp of sorts was made in the dark. No one had lodges or shelters, and people merely huddled around small fires and endured the cold. Coverings were almost nonexistent, although Young Two Moon had stolen his way back into the camp as it was being burned and picked up three buffalo robes. The need was a thousandfold. Horse meat was the simplest and only food, the meat roasted over the coals of the nightly fires. In recounting the horror nearly sixty years later, Beaver Heart's eyes welled up as he told of those several nights, "alive with the cries of men tortured with wounds and women and children dying of cold." In several instances, children were stuffed into the paunches of freshly butchered horses. Despite all efforts, eleven Cheyenne babies reportedly perished that night from the intense cold.[32]

Over the next several days the Cheyennes skirted the snowy Big Horn Mountain highlands, crossing from the Red Fork headwaters to the Lodge

Pole Creek drainage, today's Clear Creek. All along, young men went ahead and built large warming fires and the people walked from fire to fire, warming themselves at each stop while others continued on and arranged this unique survivor's trail. The people were several days in returning to the prairie. Hunters managed to kill a few buffalo along the way to sustain the weakest among them. From Lodge Pole Creek where it emerged from the Big Horns, the Cheyenne's course took them northward along or past a series of streams and landmarks already etched in the saga of Sitting Bull's War—Lake De Smet, Prairie Dog Creek, the Tongue River to near the mouth of Otter Creek, and Otter Creek to Beaver Creek. There they found Crazy Horse's camp. They were eleven days in reaching the Oglalas. For many of these Cheyennes, this odyssey of travel began on this same Beaver Creek, a small Tongue River tributary, the previous July when the great summer coalition of Lakotas and Cheyennes began to shatter.[33]

Wooden Leg was not among the Cheyennes caught on the Red Fork. Instead, he trailed with a small band that hunted in the favored Rosebud and Tongue River drainages during that time. When his party learned of Indians descending the Tongue Valley, his band advanced to meet them. Who were those people, the hunters wondered? To their utter surprise, as Wooden Leg recounted, they "were our Cheyennes, the whole tribe." His memory of the scene was haunting. "They had but little food. Many of them had no blankets or robes. They had no lodges. Only here and there was one wearing moccasins. The others had their feet wrapped in loose pieces of skin or cloth. Women, children, and old people were straggling along over the snow-covered trail down the valley. The Cheyennes were very poor."[34]

On Beaver Creek Wooden Leg remembered that Crazy Horse and the Lakotas received the beleaguered people hospitably. It was a pathetic redo of these same Oglalas welcoming Cheyennes after the Powder River fight in March. But the Oglalas were impoverished also, the war having so thoroughly disrupted normal hunting and trading cycles and the routines of agency contact, when additional staples were always abundant. Still, the Lakota camps fitted the Cheyennes with foodstuffs, lodges, robes, and other critical matter. Young Black Elk remembered Oglala men going from camp to camp to collect clothes and tipis for the Cheyennes. For the first time in many nights no one went to bed hungry or cold. Yet many years later some Cheyennes carped over notions that the Sioux were stingy with aid. Short Bull, an Oglala, was asked about this and dismissed the thought. "There is nothing to that story," he told an interviewer. "We helped the Cheyennes the best we could. We hadn't much ourselves." There, too, the Red Fork Cheyennes reunited with the small band of Cheyennes belonging to Black Moccasin, the fourth of the Old Man Chiefs. He and his followers had gone their own way in midsummer, variously hunting and then aligning with Crazy Horse.[35]

Since the time of the Slim Buttes fight in Dakota in September, Crazy Horse and a mixed lot of Lakotas—Oglalas mostly with a smattering of Brulés and Cheyennes—had trailed from the Little Missouri country west to the Powder River and then to the upper reaches of the Tongue. He and his followers remained stridently committed to a life on the buffalo prairie despite the year's threats, challenges, and bloodshed. Additionally aligned with him now were Miniconjous under Touch the Clouds, Roman Nose, and Hump, and Sans Arcs under Fast Bull. The latter were those who more recently had inquired of surrender terms at Cheyenne River Agency, but when learning fully of the government's loathsome dictates, fled westward instead.[36]

Touch the Clouds, standing at a widely noticed six feet seven inches tall, was something of a shadow figure through the course of Sitting Bull's War. A moderate who embraced traditional values but also understood the realities of agency life, he was a close confidant of Crazy Horse and also his cousin. The war chief's mother, Rattle Blanket Woman, and Touch the Clouds's father, Lone Horn, were sister and brother. He left no known accounts of the war, and yet figured in many of its most critical events, presently and yet to come. With Crazy Horse, too, were the scattered remnants of Miniconjous and Sans Arcs who had negotiated a unique if vaporous surrender with Bear Coat Miles in October. Those people, as with the Cheyennes now, had lost virtually everything in the Cedar Creek fight north of the Yellowstone. Once aligned with Sitting Bull, indeed some of those traditionals submitted at Cheyenne River afterward but the majority quietly disappeared onto the trail and to hunt.[37]

The encampment's growth in this time of flux was rather dramatic. In late November, before the arrival of refugee Miniconjous, Sans Arcs, and then Cheyennes, Crazy Horse rallied some 230 lodges of committed traditionals, mostly southern people. But with the coming of Miniconjous and Sans Arcs from several sectors, a scattering of Blackfeet and Hunkpapa Sioux, and now another 150 lodges of Cheyennes, the camp ballooned to a soon reported five hundred lodges, counting in its midst some 735 warriors. Those were astonishing if fragile numbers in a village nearly comparable in size to the one on Rosebud Creek at Sun Dance time the previous May.[38]

The mere existence of threatening armies both north and south was but one stress bedeviling the Northerners on the Tongue as they slowly drifted the river southward in conventional quests for wood, grazing, and hunting, even in this harshest of seasons. Buffalo were proving scarce. The major herds south of the Yellowstone now ranged east of the Powder and up the Little Powder, or with other herds north of the river in the almost inaccessible Big Open. During this time, kinsmen from the agencies repeatedly visited Crazy Horse and the chiefs, invariably bearing gifts of tobacco and more directly and intentionally heartfelt pleas to submit and end this war. The visits greatly annoyed many of the traditionals and most particularly the eminent war chief himself because they sowed dissent in an already war-weary coalition. But increasing numbers did keep wondering how many villages had to burn before the Lakotas sought peace with the *wasicus*? The season came to be known as the time of the peace-talkers.[39]

Shortly after the Cheyennes joined Crazy Horse the first of these peace-talkers, a small but notable contingent of Oglalas from Red Cloud

Agency, appeared in the camp. Among them were Horn Chips, the chief's revered spiritualist, and Sitting Bull of the South, a legendary warrior in the days of the Platte River and Bozeman Trail wars of the 1860s. He was an effective full-blood middleman now, much like Red Cloud and Spotted Tail. This same Sitting Bull had prominently intervened in 1875 when Little Big Man threatened to kill the Black Hills commissioners, almost alone saving the White men's lives. He drew attention again just months later when he stormed out of the duplicitous follow-up proceedings that ultimately signed away the Black Hills. The party carried word now from the Red Cloud agent who hoped to coax Crazy Horse and his followers in. Come for food and blankets and peace, the emissaries boomed. Some elders countered that that was a long distance to travel in the wintertime, and, anyway, Bear Coat Miles was offering the same things right here in their own country.[40]

If what was said about the Bear Coat was true, however, some thought to confirm it, and Crazy Horse, in an apparent nod to the war-weary in his camp, agreed to send messengers to confer with the soldier chief. Besides, this presented an opportunity to trade, the camp possessing stolen American horses that might be returned and exchanged for things badly needed. Fifteen or twenty warriors led by Spotted Elk, a seasoned, fifty-year-old Miniconjou chief, departed the Hanging Woman Creek camp bound for the bustling Tongue River post. Sitting Bull of the South and four others from the Red Cloud Agency rode with them. On the crest of the Yellowstone Valley just above the post the party halted. Sitting Bull and those from the south continued on, believing perhaps that because they were agency Indians they would be well received. None of them knew Bear Coat Miles but rode forward unafraid, carrying a large white flag of passage. The remainder of the party watched from afar as the five emissaries slipped from view. And then Spotted Elk and the others heard shooting.[41]

Sitting Bull's party closed within view of the cantonment's sprawl of log huts and its imposingly tall flagpole and large stars and bars flag fluttering at the top. They also noticed a Crow camp pitched along the frozen Tongue. Hereditary enemies, a number of Crow army scouts rode out to meet them, advancing as if they were friends, and shook hands. But in an unforeseen instant they pulled the five from their ponies and shot and stabbed them to death. The white flag of truce fell to the ground, saturated with blood. One of the Crows attempted to hide it and another grabbed Sitting Bull's engraved Henry rifle given to him by President Grant just that spring for his valor when interceding in the so-called flag pole affair at Red Cloud Agency. The attackers then fled west.[42]

Only later did the Crows learn that their victims were delegates from a Sioux camp far up the Tongue and that they had come to explore the prospects of surrendering. History has speculated evermore whether a successful mission might have brought an end to Sitting Bull's War sooner. One introspective officer almost in the moment confided to his diary the shame and consequence of the event. "The death of this chieftain, Sitting Bull of the South, was a heavy blow to our national credit with the plains Indians: it shook their faith in our professions of good will and satisfied them that we were not to be trusted and that the Indians who, bearing white flags, entered our forts and reservations should [be] like the victims descending into Hell." Indeed, shame hung heavily. In this own way, White Bull was equally blunt. "This unlucky chance made further efforts at peace unpopular in Sitting Bull's camp, for the young men killed had relatives in all the bands."[43]

Bear Coat Miles learned of the murders almost immediately and was furious. He dismissed the scouts on the spot and seized their horses and personal property, including the Henry rifle, but the damage was done. The prospective peace mission was instantly dashed. Those watching from afar turned and fled to the Hanging Woman Creek camp in abject disgust and horror. Crazy Horse was likewise enraged and succeeded in swaying most of the moderates to sustain his aggressive, war-ready stance. Perhaps now, he thought, Miles could be drawn into a fight on the chief's terms, and on the chief's ground, in a battle that might win back the buffalo prairie. In the last week of December Crazy Horse sent fifty Oglala and Cheyenne warriors to steal cattle and horses and harry the soldiers at the Tongue River cantonment and to draw Miles out. As one in the Indian camp later reported, the whole village was prepared to fight.[44]

Even as the Spotted Elk mission and Oglala deaths enlivened the soldier camp on the Yellowstone, a second peace-talker chapter opened in the Hanging Woman Creek camp. This particular overture involved two Miniconjous, Important Man and Foolish Bear, dispatched by the Cheyenne River agent in early December in an effort uniquely encouraged by the five Miniconjou and Sans Arc hostages then held at the agency. Those five had surrendered to Bear Coat Miles in October and served as surety that their kinsmen would submit at that agency in due course. A few did, but most of that sizeable element—Lakotas once aligned with Sitting Bull on Cedar Creek when that village was attacked—spurned turning themselves in and trailed toward Crazy Horse instead.[45]

Important Man and Foolish Bear were several weeks in finding Crazy Horse's camp. Heavy, persistent snows impeded their travel and obscured any sense of old trails. When they arrived, the chiefs and elders assembled and listened thoughtfully as the two described in detail recent events at Cheyenne River, including the general unhorsings and disarmings occurring in the fall. They were candid about circumstances, too. While returnees would similarly lose ponies and firearms they would be treated fairly and properly cared for, affirming most particularly that they would receive adequate provisioning.[46]

Some among the Miniconjous and Sans Arcs remained quite sympathetic to the notion of surrendering, but for most this outcome remained highly objectionable, particularly in light of the killings at the Tongue River post. One elder avowed that "they would never submit as long as they lived." Another declared: "I see they are determined to destroy all our peace and happiness, and my advice will be to my people, as long as I live, never to submit to the Whites." Important Man and Foolish Bear went separately to the Miniconjou and Sans Arc circles hoping to induce at least some to return. But they were dogged by an angered Crazy Horse who taunted the effort. On two succeeding occasions small family groups attempted to flee but were intercepted by Oglala *akicitas* and forced to return. The two emissaries were permitted to leave, alone however, several weeks later. Hardline elders scorned them both dismissively. "They came from the Whites."[47]

Even while the Important Man and Foolish Bear overtures were being rebuffed in Crazy Horse's camp, the deputation of warriors sent by the chief downriver to harass the Tongue River army camp was achieving its intended purpose. In a series of pestering raids, warriors ran off horses and mules and several hundred cattle from a contractor's herd. On December 27 some 400 of Miles's complement, slightly more than half the soldier garrison, commenced a search for the marauders and stolen livestock. Bear Coat Miles knew intuitively that he was chasing Crazy Horse, the figurehead Lakota still roaming freely south of the Yellowstone. But in the moment one might wonder who was chasing whom when in fact it was Crazy Horse who had so consciously triggered the ploy, plainly hoping to draw the Bear Coat and his despised foot soldiers into what might well be a conclusive fight for the buffalo prairie. Each protagonist smugly believed he controlled the other's fate.[48]

Upriver, the camp on Hanging Woman Creek was again preparing to move, and in two directions. The Cheyennes were intent on traveling the Tongue River valley, while the principal body of Lakotas and some Cheyennes favored ascending the Hanging Woman drainage. Widespread food deficiencies largely drove the decision. Meat and berry stocks were all but exhausted, depleted through sharing among refugees or lost in the wholesale village destructions at Slim Buttes, Cedar Creek, and Red Fork. The peace-talkers knew this, too, and consciously focused their surrender appeals on food—trading the abhorrence of relinquishing weapons and ponies in exchange for full stomachs. Most of these Lakotas and Cheyennes had not known a routine season of hunting and gathering in the buffalo country for nearly a year. Larders were empty and hunting presently was barely meeting daily family needs. An axiom was again holding true in Indian country, particularly in time of war. Whatever the context, wherever the war, in the end the story was always about food.[49]

The Lakotas and Cheyennes aligned with Crazy Horse were aware of soldiers approaching on the Tongue, having baited them to the field. But not everyone was completely wary of the threat. Slightly below the mouth of Hanging Woman Creek, soldier scouts encountered and seized a small party of Cheyennes, seven women and children returning from a buffalo hunt. A trailing Cheyenne warrior, Big Horse, witnessed the capture and rushed the news to the greater camp, then on the verge of separating. Swelled Face, a Miniconjou in the village, described the commotion when Big Horse's news spread from circle to circle. The move up the Tongue was hastened, but collectively, and the elders turned the matter of the imminent threat over to the military societies where the war chiefs immediately elected to rescue the women and children and prepare for a general fight. "We expected to have a great battle," Red Horse later recalled. Crazy Horse's conclusive fight for the buffalo prairie seemed about to ignite.[50]

In a near reflection of the response on Rosebud Creek in mid-June when soldiers from the south imminently threatened Sitting Bull's ascendant village, as many as four hundred Lakotas and Cheyennes streamed from their Tongue River camp in the darkness of January 8 to confront the blue coats again. The soldiers were camped slightly above the mouth of Hanging Woman Creek. The Tongue River valley in the soldier's fore narrowed distinctively as it passed through the Wolf Mountains, with the icy stream twisting along the bottom. Wooded hills rose abruptly on either side. In the fore at this point was a distinguishing landform straddling the valley floor, a prominence widely known among Indian people then as Belly Butte—Battle Butte today—a feature aptly reflecting the native name. Deep snows and ice glazed everything.[51]

As the warriors approached Belly Butte they divided. Crazy Horse and Little Big Man rallied Lakotas on the high ground west of the river, and Cheyennes led by White Bull, or Ice, and Two Moon occupied similar high ground in the east. Red Sack, an Oglala from Crazy Horse's circle, later told authorities at Red Cloud Agency that this approach was by design, the chiefs hoping to lure the blue coats up the Tongue and into their clutches. To trigger the surprise, decoys advanced and at daybreak opened fire on the soldiers. The startled doughboys responded, meeting the attackers with disciplined rifle fire and several times charging and dispersing warrior concentrations. But they walked into no trap.[52]

All morning long warriors fought afoot and availed the lofty rocks, crags, and pine-clad bluffs east and west. "We had the advantage of them," Wooden Leg believed, "because of our position on the high and rocky ledge." From a roost early in the fight some among the blue coats remembered an Indian memorably shouting out in faulty English that they "would eat no more fat meats," which they construed to mean that they had eaten their last breakfast. Soldiers and soldier scouts hurled epithets of their own. Throughout the early attack, Crazy Horse's voice was heard above the din, urging warriors on to battle and valor in their attempts to pierce or flank the soldier lines. But quickly the battle stalemated and turned into yet another long-range desultory fight much as occurred in the later phases of the Slim Buttes engagement. Here, it lasted through the rest of the morning.[53]

The day's clash was foremost punctuated by the heroics of a Cheyenne, Big Crow, who boasted that no bullet could go through him. A Sioux warrior, Swelled Face, and many Whites called him a medicine man, while others simply remembered him as the bravest warrior they ever knew. More likely he was, as one remembered, simply a transfixed determined fighter angered over the loss of kin in the Red Fork fight and again among Bear Coat's current hostages. However motivated, many across the field watched as Big Crow, bedecked in an elaborate feather bonnet with tails so long they dragged in the snow, prominently exposed himself on a high ridge on the right. With Cheyennes watching in dread, he zigged and zagged along the ridge—some called it dancing—all the while plainly firing a cavalry carbine collected among the spoils of the Little Big Horn fight. Soldier bullets ricocheted in the rocks around him, but Big Crow was untouched. When he ran out of cartridges he dropped back to the rocks behind him and asked friends for more. Each offered one or two or three, enough to fill his belt, and he strutted forward again, those behind pleading with him to not expose himself so recklessly. But this time a soldier bullet struck him in the midsection and knocked him to the ground, mortally wounded. Three friends, Wooden Leg among them, crawled out. Big Crow was dying. "Just leave me here where there is shelter," he implored. "I will die anyhow. Go on home." His rescuers covered him with a buffalo robe and scampered to cover.[54]

Bear Coat Miles entrenched some of his foot soldiers on critical perches above the stream, and alarmingly wheeled an artillery piece to the western flank of Belly Butte. Despite the difficulties of the deep snow, he trailed two guns on this movement, and his makeshift artillerymen soon found their range, battering concentrations of Lakotas and Cheyennes with lethal shrapnel. Miles had used one of those same guns advantageously against Sitting Bull's coalition at Cedar Creek, although here Young Black Elk's recollection of cannon fire somewhat obscures its deadliness. He and other boys watched the fight from afar and at one point plainly saw a cannon ball whistling their way. It did not explode but simply skidded through the snow. One of the boys chased it down, picked it up, and took the odd curiosity home. Miles's Napoleon gun fired several types of projectiles, including highly sensitive exploding shells, as here, and canister rounds, which were cannon-sized projectiles resembling enormous shotgun shells. Both targeted living enemies. Perhaps the fuse on the particular shell Black Elk mentioned did not ignite and the boy was simply lucky.[55]

A snowstorm settled across the battlefield in the midmorning and by noon turned into a raging blizzard that brought closure to the Wolf Mountains fight. Throughout the morning both sides scrapped valiantly, with warriors probing the ranks of the hated infantry and soldiers effectively holding their lines and using their long-range rifles to great effect. But in the blinding snow the protagonists turned about, warriors withdrawing to the Upper Tongue and the soldiers, retaining the eight Cheyenne captives, returning to the Tongue River post. The conclusive victory Crazy Horse and Miles each had imagined was purely illusionary, whether for Miles the immediate capitulation of Crazy Horse and his followers, or the great chief's even loftier notion of destroying an army and forcing the soldiers' abandonment of the buffalo country. Indian losses at Belly Butte were three killed, including a young Sioux boy, an Oglala warrior

Runs the Bear, and Big Crow, the Cheyenne showoff, with several dozen wounded. Bear Coat reported three killed and eight wounded.[56]

The Wolf Mountains fight was neither victory nor defeat for either side, but it was quickly seen as a turning in this nearly yearlong open war forced upon the traditionals living in the northern buffalo country. But for one more clash four months hence, the days of fighting were all but over. No one grasped such a striking fact as yet, but the indications were abundant. Council leaders recognized the peoples' shortages of ammunition, a nagging issue always but exacerbated now in the ruggedness and isolation of winter. Equally daunting, Bear Coat Miles had again proven his ability to hunt down his enemy regardless of season and wherever they might take refuge. Just as critical were the barely met day-to-day subsistence needs of the camp, whether foods for the people or forage for their animals. Crazy Horse and other militants had succeeded in holding this coalition of Lakotas and Cheyennes together, sometimes with brute force and through yet another fight with the blue coats. But the appeals from the peace-talkers, the nagging hunger, despondent morale, and general weariness of war were inescapable. In the days ahead Crazy Horse's coalition traveled farther up the Tongue and at the confluence with Prairie Dog Creek again found buffalo, enough to meet immediate needs. All the while, the pressures to submit were unrelenting.[57]

While in the Prairie Dog Creek camp near the end of January, Sitting Bull joined the southern coalition. The stalwart Hunkpapa had been roused by Miles's troops in mid-December on Ash Creek, just beyond the Cedar Creek divide north of the Yellowstone. That village lay in ruin, and his coalition of Northern Lakotas was mostly shattered. Some one hundred lodges clung to the great chief now as they ventured south of the

Yellowstone in search of Crazy Horse. Sitting Bull brought and shared ammunition and tobacco acquired from a prairie Métis caravan trading south of the Canadian line and saved from the Ash Creek destruction. The nightly councils were raucous. Some elders wanted to submit unhesitatingly. Others argued for a continuation of the war. Sitting Bull added the discordant option of fleeing the country for British America, the land of the Grandmother, and home of the Blackfoot, Cree, and Métis. His was a Northern Lakota's view, people who were comfortable in that border country. Already spiritual kin like the Santees lived there almost continuously. More recently, Sitting Bull reported having sent some of his allies north for yet more ammunition and to induce the Red River Métis to join in the fight. But the Oglalas and Cheyennes found the British America option objectionable. They were open to continuing the war, perhaps, but they were people of the south. In truth, there was little unity in the Prairie Dog Creek camp. The old Lakota World and the buffalo prairie were turned upside down.[58]

13
CRUEL FATE OF THE CHEYENNES

"My two sons said it was the only thing our family could do."
—Iron Teeth, Northern Cheyenne

The war was not going well for any of the traditionals still clinging to the buffalo country. After successfully campaigning against Sitting Bull's alliance north of the Yellowstone that winter of 1876–1877, Bear Coat Miles turned his attention to the people aligned with Crazy Horse south of the river. Their fight in the Wolf Mountains on January 8, 1877, had proved an impasse, but those foot soldiers demonstrated again their ability to maneuver aggressively in the cold and snow. From his Tongue River outpost, Bear Coat remained an uncaged threat. Elsewhere, a mixed force of cavalry and infantry was still maneuvering in the Upper Powder River Basin, the same blue coats that had decimated the Cheyenne village on the Red Fork of the Powder. While no longer particularly threatening Crazy Horse's coalition, their presence north of the Black Hills blocked normal pathways to the south, and some of those soldiers remained busily engaged constructing another military outpost—the eventual Cantonment Reno—on the Middle Powder River, and a place by now having all the appearances of a permanent installation.

Sitting Bull's meeting with Crazy Horse at the end of January was brief, and, from the Great Chief's perspective, disappointingly unproductive. Crazy Horse's loose federation on Prairie Dog Creek was large and the Hunkpapa had hoped to integrate the remaining traditionals. But Sitting Bull stepped instead into the intractable debate among the Oglalas, Cheyennes, Miniconjous, and Sans Arcs over whether to continue fighting or quit the war altogether. His own resolute voice was not persuasive, and neither was the prospect of flight northward, despite now his generous distribution of cartridges, blankets, beads, and tobacco, precious commodities recently obtained in the north from the Métis, and with allusions to more. Finding no common ground, Sitting Bull departed, crossed over to the Powder, and trailed the river to its mouth, determined to again cross the Yellowstone and seek out what one informant, a Miniconjou named Swelled Face, called the Red River Indians. He was hopeful of trade and perhaps even inducing those Indians to join him in this agonizing war. In hindsight, one sees Sitting Bull's departure as the most crippling blow yet to any prospective success in the conflict. A lifeway on the buffalo prairie swung precariously in the balance, yet the war's most prominent figureheads would never see each other again.

On Prairie Dog Creek, the loose confederation of Lakotas and Cheyennes aligning with Crazy Horse struggled to determine their own course, whether indeed to remain allied in the buffalo country, be lured apart simply by the incessant need to hunt, or, so weary of war, heed the appeals of the agency peace-talkers. In other times, Crazy Horse, normally an introspective and diffident individual, rarely participated in daily councils. Now, however, in light of the army's relentless assaults and his own futile attempt at entrapping and destroying the Bear Coat's foot soldiers in the Wolf Mountains, he was thoroughly roused and argued forcefully for war. But the dissention surrounding him was insurmountable, and Sitting Bull's departure its own visible blow. Many times already Crazy Horse's *akicitas* forcibly intercepted small Lakota bands as they too attempted to separate, and the Cheyennes were also considering going their own way. Crazy Horse's grip was growing untenable.[1]

Even as the Crazy Horse camp trailed eastward to the Powder in search of buffalo, individual parties and small bands parted, sometimes challenging the *akicitas* and sometimes the war chief himself. Notably, Spotted Elk and Red Horse led Miniconjou kinsman eastward to Cheyenne River. Other small bands successfully departed for the Red Cloud and Spotted Tail agencies in the Pine Ridge. Even greater blows came in early February when Spotted Eagle led 150 lodges of Sans Arcs, Hunkpapas, and Miniconjous northward to reunite with Sitting Bull; and the Cheyennes separated for the west, intending to hunt in the Big Horn country and perhaps even open communications with Bear Coat Miles and surrender at his post. As one chronicler aptly noted, "the Sioux might talk, but the war was ended," or so it seemed to some anyway.[2]

Crazy Horse was not alone in confronting camp dissention. Elders, too, were exercising independence and leadership. Near the end of January they invited a young Oglala, Red Sack, married to Crazy Horse's sister, to visit Red Cloud Agency, inquire of surrender conditions there, and report back as quickly as circumstances might allow. None of the elders doubted the odious burden of surrendering ponies and weapons but questioned whether they would have to confront additional conditions and infringements. Red Sack's arrival at Camp Robinson thirty days later drew widespread attention, but he fed officers there a careful report, offering a glossed-over account of the recent Wolf Mountains fight and telling of dire circumstances in the camp, but not much more. Meanwhile, he quietly went about his own reconnaissance. In due course, agents allowed him to return to Crazy Horse's camp, believing he would convey surrender inducements much as the peace-talkers were doing.[3]

Red Sack indeed returned to the Oglalas in late February. Mostly his news was commonly understood, but he also forecast that the great Brulé chief Spotted Tail was organizing his own peace initiative. That news was startling, more so than any other peace initiative before this. These Lakotas and Cheyennes alike knew Spotted Tail well. Some decried his friendliness with the Whites, but no one doubted his legacy as a fierce warrior or his genuine resolve now for the well-being of not just the Brulés but all Lakotas. For Crazy Horse, the news was personal. Spotted Tail was Crazy Horse's uncle. His stepmother, Worm's second wife, was a sister of the Brulé chief. As a boy, Crazy Horse had often lived in Spotted Tail's camp, but in the years since no one had traveled the White man's road more visibly, and that had not been Crazy Horse's road.[4]

All the while, the defections continued, including some fifteen lodges of Brulés and Oglalas led by Eagle Pipe and Spider, bound for Spotted Tail Agency. Miniconjous and Sans Arcs under Touch the Clouds and Roman Nose departed for the Cheyenne River Agency. Most startling of all, the Cheyennes departed for the headwaters of the Little Big Horn.

That wars have unforeseen and unintended victims is an axiom as old as human conflict. The Northern Cheyenne followers of the great Old Man Chiefs, Old Bear, Little Wolf, Black Moccasins, and Morning Star, embraced the same northern plains as did their far more numerous friends, the Lakotas, and they had their own unique spiritual and cultural ties to many of its landmarks—the Black Hills, Bear Butte, the Big Horns. They hunted the same buffalo, and before Sitting Bull's War had fought alongside their friends in many struggles for a homeland and lifeway.

The debate now over the destiny of a people was every bit as heated in the Northern Cheyenne circle as elsewhere in the Crazy Horse confederation. One thing was certain. The Northern Cheyennes had suffered immensely in this war, the price of a deep allegiance with the Oglalas. They wanted now simply to hunt and avoid further White contact. They were still recovering from the horrific destruction of their village on the Red Fork barely two months earlier, and traveled west to the familiar ground of the Upper Little Big Horn, their place of sanctuary immediately after the Custer fight. "Almost the entire Northern Cheyenne tribe was in this winter camp,"

Wooden Leg recalled, and so were their esteemed counsellors, the Old Man Chiefs. In all, the camp tallied some 175 lodges and about 1,200 people. There in the headlands of the Little Big Horn and adjacent Lodge Grass and Rotten Grass creeks the hunting was good and soldiers did not bother them.[5]

But by now, regrettably, nothing went unnoticed. In late January word passed from wolfers and Crows aligned with the not-so-distant Crow Agency on the Yellowstone of encounters with the Cheyennes, and Miles was quickly informed. Rather than mustering his foot soldiers he dispatched Johnnie Bruguier to the Cheyenne camp. The perplexing run-away from the law—turned Sitting Bull interpreter—turned interpreter and middleman now for Miles, was accompanied by one of the prisoners Miles retained from the time of the Wolf Mountains episode, a Cheyenne woman named Sweet Taste. She was a widow and oldest captive of that lot, and Miles had befriended her. Each led a pack horse laden with tobacco, foodstuffs, and other gifts as they bounded south toward the Big Horns. The pair readily located the Cheyenne camp on the Little Big Horn. Bruguier approached fearing for his safety—he did not speak the language—but the two were hospitably received, and the camp showed considerable surprise at the well-being of the captive. Sweet Taste Woman reported that the others were being treated equally as well at the Tongue River post, where they had been given shelter, warm clothing, and plenty of food. The two distributed their gifts to the principal chiefs, and Sweet Taste Woman implored the elders and all to accept the government's terms.[6]

The chiefs deliberated for several days. The particulars of surrender were timeworn and still generally upsetting, and the leading warrior societies were plainly divided. The Kit Foxes favored surrendering to Miles, but the Elk Scrapers, remembering particularly the devastation on the Red Fork, argued against submission. The principal chiefs were likewise divided, not necessarily by the notion of submitting and ending the war but over where such a surrender ought to occur. Little Wolf and Morning Star favored doing so at the White River Agency. Standing Elk agreed. They had kin and allegiances in the south. Two Moon pushed equally hard for surrendering to Miles. At best the counsellors agreed to defer any decision until learning more from Miles and only then would they decide their fate. Meanwhile, they agreed that it would be well to move in that direction.[7]

The Cheyennes crossed back to the Tongue and slowly descended the river. Bruguier and Sweet Taste Woman remained with the camp. When approaching the mouth of Hanging Woman Creek, Wooden Leg and several others combed the eastern hillsides of the Belly Butte battlefield seeking out the remains of Big Crow, who they had abandoned on the field—at his insistence—that morning of the fight. Big Crow's body was readily located, found propped against a bush in a thin group of small pines. The men stretched him out and covered him with stones. Wooden Leg recalled years later that "his people felt better when we told them what we had done." Meanwhile, from the mouth of Hanging Woman Creek a delegation of nineteen from the camp, men and women combined, advanced ahead of the others, bound directly for the soldier fort. Among them were Old Wolf and Little Chief, and Two Moon and White Bull, variously representing the chief's council and warrior societies, and also Johnnie Bruguier.[8]

As the Cheyenne peace delegation neared the Tongue River fort, Bruguier rode ahead to report their intent and assuring those behind that he would meet them as they approached and guide them into the post. Recalling the terrible bloodletting occurring when Sitting Bull of the South similarly approached the fort two months earlier, this doubtless was an intentional surety. Bruguier, as promised, soon returned with a message from Miles assuring the delegates that they should not fear anything but should come in and talk.[9]

In a measure of pomp on February 19, minutes before the Cheyennes arrived, Miles mustered his garrison, forming his soldiers ceremonially in front of their quarters and greeted the arriving Indians. Recognizing and shaking hands with Two Moon and White Bull and calling them by name, Bear Coat escorted the delegation into the cantonment. After pausing first for a meal, Miles ushered most of the emissaries into his quarters, an unassuming log home in the midst of a welter of similar unpretentious log buildings and tents. Suspicions lingered, but the officers with Miles had no visible firearms and the edginess soon turned to talk. Miles continually assured the Cheyennes that he would treat them justly if they surrendered, but he dosed his remarks with the same almost brutal frankness he used with Sitting Bull on Cedar Creek in October. "I want you people to come here and surrender to me," he said, "to give up your arms and your horses, and turn them over to me. If you do as I tell you I will be a good man to you, but if you do not do this I will be mean to you." Sitting Bull had been outright offended by Miles's jarring tone and his village had been attacked and destroyed, a consequence these Cheyennes well understood. Little Chief and Two Moon spoke on behalf of their people, Little Chief telling Miles that "you have not lied yet, and I am going to try you and am coming in here. I am going to surrender to you."[10]

As if to sweeten the prospect, Miles reportedly also told the Cheyennes that they would "be allowed to choose your own place for a reservation—anywhere from Yellowstone River south." He was referring plainly to the Cheyennes' revered Powder River country, broadly described. Several days after their arrival and reassured again of obtaining subsistence, the emissaries departed, still retaining their arms and ponies and pledging to bring their people in within a few days. As collateral, several compliant chiefs from the delegation remained behind with Miles.[11]

Behind them meanwhile, the Cheyenne camp had moved east to the Powder where they momentarily reunited with the Oglalas. They camped at the mouth of the Little Powder, the Cheyennes remaining separate on the west side of the river. The cantonment delegation found them there and the difficult talk of surrender resumed.[12]

While on the Powder, the Cheyennes were also visited by seven of their kin from the White River Agency. That effort, promoted by agents at Camp Robinson, was yet another iteration of the peace-talker initiative. The seven carried gifts of tobacco and came expressly to encourage the Cheyennes to surrender there and reunite with kin. They and all the Indians in the south, the emissaries assured, were being bounteously fed and treated well in every respect. Moreover, no one was being punished in any manner for past conduct in warfare against the soldiers. For most, particularly those favoring the south, such talk was enough. "To my father and most of the Cheyennes this sounded more attractive than the invitation to go to the Elk River fort," Wooden Leg recalled. The debate intensified, dwelling not just on whether the Cheyennes should surrender, but where. In the end, as Wooden Leg explained to his biographer, "it was decided to let every Cheyenne choose for himself."[13]

At that, the Cheyennes divided. The four Old Man Chiefs, Little Wolf, Morning Star, Dirty Moccasins, and Old Bear, and the band leaders drawn by allegiances in the south, upward of nine hundred people in all, commenced the trail to the Pine Ridge country. That sizeable body, in turn, quickly divided again. Little Wolf's followers, largely unencumbered by any elderly or battle wounded and mounted on stronger ponies, steadily and consciously pushed southward on the all-too-familiar Powder River Trail, and by February 28 had reached the environs of the White River Agency. After preliminary contact with intermediaries at Camp Robinson, Little Wolf and 385 others, mostly Cheyennes but also some Sioux, mustering pride and pomp and donning the best clothing surviving the fires of the Red Fork, paraded before an audience of government agents and soldiers at Camp Robinson and then relinquished firearms and ponies. In their eyes, while this submission was unconditional, this was no surrender. The lands of the north were theirs but they were destitute and simply no longer able to resist the soldiers. Forecasting that others were behind them, a few retained their weapons and mounts and were permitted to return and hurry them along.[14]

Morning Star's followers, shielding many of the vulnerable ones, trailed south on a much more deliberate pace, a journey variously hampered by late winter snows, mud, and the extreme impoverishment of the people. Upon descending the final bluffs and reaching the White River fort and agency on April 21, they too marshaled considerable pride as 524 people likewise paraded before an audience of agents and soldiers, including now no less than Gray Fox Crook and Ranald Mackenzie. Mackenzie was the very officer who had destroyed their village on the Red Fork on November 25,

1876. Like Little Wolf's people, they were an extremely destitute lot, often living on horse meat, and their surviving mounts were bony and stumbled along. After yielding firearms, a small number of bows and arrows, and more than six hundred animals, they were carefully counted and led off and fed. Most worrisome among the people were those who were seriously wounded and otherwise ailing. Almost immediately the incapacitated ones were led to the care of the army's Camp Robinson surgeons, who spent many days tending suppurating and infected gunshot wounds and victims of frostbite.[15]

For the many Cheyennes aligned with Little Wolf and Morning Star, the war seemed over. Many of those people had seen it all from the very start, more than a year earlier at Powder River. Since then Cheyennes had fought in almost every major engagement of the war. Twice, entire Cheyenne villages had been destroyed. Scores of Cheyennes were killed and countless others wounded. Now they were impoverished to the point of utter starvation. In surrendering they had assumed the best, abundant food foremost, and that they would be allowed to stay on the northern plains, their traditional homeland. And yet entirely unforeseen at the moment, travails of an even more horrific sort loomed.

Meanwhile, one other smaller concentration of Cheyennes remained in the Powder River camp after the departure of the Old Man Chiefs, and it too divided. While notions of surrender dominated the thinking of those heading south and the majority of those remaining in this camp, intending to head north, some Cheyennes were not ready to surrender at any place. Fourteen or fifteen men, half of them with women and children, led by White Hawk of the Elk warriors, separated and turned westward. They proposed, they said, to join Miniconjou Sioux then camped on Rosebud Creek. The others in the camp, the followers of Crazy Head, Old Wolf, and Two Moon, some 291 people, plus ten kindred Sioux led by the Miniconjou, Hump, some forty-five lodges in all, commenced the trail northward to the Tongue River post, lured by Bear Coat Miles's overtures. On April 22, a raw and disagreeable day with snow squalls every few hours, Miles learned of their approach and delivered cattle to feed them and directed his soldiers to erect tents for the needy in a camping place in the cottonwood bottoms along the Yellowstone above the post. The next day the Cheyennes were ushered into the center of the cantonment where, on the same parade ground that had witnessed soldiers lining-up to welcome the peace delegates a month earlier, they surrendered weapons and horses. Miles then directed them to the selected camping place, and uniquely allowed each family to retain two ponies for procuring wood and ordinary camp uses.[16]

By allowing the Cheyennes to retain a few of their ponies, Miles had stretched his prerogative considerably. The edict from Washington in October directed that the war's protagonists surrender all firearms and ponies, and it allowed agents no local discretion. Already some had complained that without firearms their charges would be unable even to kill agency beeves, which were a standard fare in the ration allowance. Miles was not the only commanding officer who had twisted this seemingly inflexible dictate. During the reservation-wide confiscations occurring in the fall, when the edict was rather broadly and stridently enforced, Crook had not imposed it at the Spotted Tail Agency. Sheridan howled but Crook stood his ground, asserting that Spotted Tail and his Brulé followers had not taken up arms against the army (an eyes-closed half-truth) and, more important, the chief himself was friendly and generally useful to the government. Miles almost certainly knew of this. The greater point now was that the Cheyennes surrendering to Miles did, indeed, receive a more enlightened treatment than those surrendering in the Pine Ridge, a matter of earlier consideration as the Cheyennes deliberated their future. The Cheyennes separating on the Powder did so for many reasons, however, and for many, loyalties and kinfolk were as important as ponies.

When reporting the surrender to his superior in Saint Paul, Miles also made a case that those Cheyennes remain under his charge at Tongue River. They were fearful of agency control, some had told him, and others complained of near starvation at the agencies. Miles was sure they could be fed and clothed economically at Tongue River, and he furthermore planned on making good use of some of the warriors. In conversations with the Cheyenne delegation a month earlier, Miles had already proposed enlisting some of them to assist his soldiers in quieting and even pursuing other Northern Indians. But Miles's superior, Alfred Terry, worried that the retention of any Cheyennes at Tongue River, in favorable country, would be unsettling to Indians already at the agencies or those still in the buffalo country. In turn, when Miles's commendation reached Chicago, Phil Sheridan was adamantly opposed to it, charging that it would be disruptive and foment unrest at the agencies. Moreover, he noted that the Tongue River post was not on or near any Indian reservation. He intended, he foretold, to order those Cheyennes removed from Tongue River to Fort Randall on the Middle Missouri, where they could be kept inexpensively until they rejoined their kin. Sheridan's superior, William T. Sherman, Commanding General of the Army, also weighed in and agreed with moving the Cheyennes to a Missouri River agency. The army could ill afford to feed prisoners at such expensive points like Tongue River, he asserted. At the moment, a Cheyenne future with Miles lasting any longer than a few weeks and the arrival of the first steamboats seemed doubtful.[17]

Camped along the river above their White River Agency the newly arrived Cheyennes agonized over their own uncertain future. In councils with Crook and their agent in the days since appearing, they well sensed their own precariousness. Crook was pushing several options, whether perhaps joining kinsmen in the Indian Territory, or relocating to the Shoshone and Arapaho Agency at Fort Washakie in central Wyoming, or remaining in the Pine Ridge a while longer while others, meaning distant government officials, decided their fate. Crook plainly advocated moving the Cheyennes to the Indian Territory. Debate in nightly councils was painfully inconclusive. Most of the White River Cheyennes favored an eventual return to the Powder River country, a generations-long homeland speckled with cultural landmarks and the graves of their ancestors, but some indeed preferred joining kinsmen in the south. The quandary was not unlike the painful deliberations in the southern Big Horns on the eve of the horrendous attack on November 25, where many had argued to flee and thereby save themselves from threatening soldiers, but others browbeating and favoring doing nothing. In the Pine Ridge, meanwhile, the Cheyennes paid little heed to the continuing parades of arriving Oglalas, submissively waited their turn during ration distribution cycles, and mostly tended to themselves amid the uncertainly.[18]

Crook was not present when Crazy Horse surrendered on May 6, the penultimate capitulation in the Pine Ridge that spring. He had traveled to Chicago and then Washington to take up the issue of a northern homeland for the Sioux. In those places, the fate of the Cheyennes was also sealed. When he returned to Camp Robinson on May 23, he immediately sought-out Cheyenne chiefs and elders. Some gathered with Crook the next morning to hear him announce that it was the government's will that they be moved to the Indian Territory, and virtually immediately. Standing Elk, an eloquent individual chosen by the council to speak for the Cheyennes and make their case for remaining in the Pine Ridge, instead puzzlingly spoke of the people's willingness to move to the south. The chiefs around him, Little Wolf and Morning Star among them, were stunned but no one spoke up, and then inexplicably agreed to accept what Standing Elk said. Crook needed no more.[19]

Around Cheyenne campfires, the attitude was one of simple resignation. "None of us wanted to go," Iron Teeth remembered. She had lost her husband and a son in the Red Fork fight. "We liked best the northern country," she continued, "but one of our chiefs, Red Sash, or Standing Elk, made friends with the White men soldier chiefs by lying to them and telling them we were willing to go. My two sons then said it was the only thing our family could do."[20]

Four days after the Cheyenne headmen met with Crook, the confused, astonished, half-forced and half-persuaded people, 973 men, women, and children in all, commenced an arduous overland trail to the Cheyenne-Arapaho Agency in western Indian Territory. They were squired by a small contingent of cavalry, a few supply wagons, and a small cattle herd. Theirs was a seventy-day journey to a faraway place that few people knew and to a future that no one at the moment could possibly imagine.[21]

14
SHOCK AND DESPAIR IN THE PINE RIDGE

"Look out, watch your step. You are going into a dangerous place."
—He Dog, Oglala Lakota

The future of Crazy Horse and his fragile, ever-shrinking alliance of Oglalas and close allies was fraught with confusion as winter turned to spring, 1877. Bands were peeling off repeatedly. Most were bound for an agency, even as the core alliance trailed down the Powder to the mouth of the Little Powder, slightly ahead of the arrival of the Cheyennes. The nightly deliberations were not unlike those occurring in the Cheyenne camp behind them. No longer was there meaningful will to continue this war, only the question now of where to surrender and when. As with the Cheyennes, the Oglalas were also an impoverished lot. The continual tension, ceaseless movement, and destructive fighting throughout the previous seasons were emotionally and physically exhausting, and had thoroughly disrupted normal hunting routines. No food reserves existed at all, and daily hunting was barely meeting family needs. Even Crazy Horse, ever the most strident of the Oglalas before this, was acknowledging the simple fact that limits had been reached. The fundamental well-being of his followers always dominated his thinking. And, like the Cheyennes who were visited by kindred emissaries from the White River Agency, Crazy Horse's alliance also welcomed a succession of peace-talkers from the south.[1]

To this very camp at the mouth of the Little Powder came a sizeable group of envoys from Red Cloud Agency, thirty men and a handful of women led by Hunts the Enemy (Sword or George Sword of a later day) and Few Tails. Hunts the Enemy, a nephew of Red Cloud who was twice wounded in the Fetterman fight in 1866 and a signer of the 1868 Fort Laramie Treaty, was an agency moderate now, and well known to these Oglalas. The two men brought gifts of tobacco and foodstuffs and renewed the calls for peace and solidarity. In two days of talks a new consensus emerged, largely by sidestepping the insurmountable issues of the war's origins, the theft of the Black Hills, and the pony and arms confiscations. Instead they focused on the needs and wishes of the people. The envoys assured the elders that the Red Cloud agent was aware of their suffering and offered abundant provisioning, blankets, and clothing if they came in. They further offered assurances from Gray Fox Crook himself that "nothing untoward [would be] done to them," implying amnesty for all that had happened in the recent past. The elders saw this as better than what Bear Coat was offering, and few Oglalas trusted Miles anyway after the devious murders of kin that winter. Upon his return to Red Cloud Agency, Hunts the Enemy reported that the northerners were showing great favor for ending the fighting.[2]

Barely had Hunts the Enemy's party departed when runners from the Spotted Tail envoy reached the camp, announcing that the renowned Brulé chief himself would soon be there and that he sought an open council with all the Northerners. The chief's visit had been anticipated since the time of Red Sack's return, he the Oglala emissary who recently visited Red Cloud Agency and had learned of this mission. Indeed, the esteemed fifty-three-year-old Brulé led north some 250 Brulés and Oglalas, families included. With them were Jose Merrivale and Francis Boucher, the chief's problematic relative. Both came along as interpreters charged with conveying reports of progress along the way and able to intervene in the event that this peace delegation encountered Whites or soldiers who might see them as enemy Northerners. The scale of the mission was intentional. Among the peace-talkers were fathers, uncles, and grandfathers whose own quiet word with family members and kin carried every bit the weight as the esteemed chief himself. It was mid-March, in the Lakota month of the Sore Eyes moon.[3]

Spotted Tail's mission yielded promising results almost immediately. When passing Bear Lodge Butte, the Brulé chief encountered Touch the Clouds, leading some seventy lodges of mostly Miniconjous. After hearing the same moderate surrender terms that Hunts the Enemy and Few Tails had announced, he agreed to submit at the Brulé agency in the Pine Ridge. Touch the Clouds was familiar with the White River agencies and had learned from Spotted Elk that terms at Cheyenne River were not nearly as generous. Farther up the trail when reaching the headwaters of the Little Powder, Spotted Tail encountered and likewise convinced Roman Nose and Black Shield and their ninety lodges of Miniconjous and Sans Arcs to surrender. They were already bound for Spotted Tail Agency.[4]

To Spotted Tail's dismay, his nephew was not in the Oglala camp when he arrived. Faced with the overwhelming burdens of not only deciding his own fate but also that of the friends and families who revered him, Crazy Horse had disappeared into the Blue Mountains east of the Powder to fast, pray, and seek guidance that might steer him in this difficult time. The war chief occasionally sought such enlightenment but also recognized the importance of his uncle's mission, and in his stead asked his father, Worm, to speak for him. The old man accepted Spotted Tail's tobacco and pledged that his son wanted peace and would soon come into the agency. As a small token of assurance, Worm presented Merrivale with one of Crazy Horse's ponies, symbolic of this intent to come in. Any inferred connection between the chief and the aged Mexican interpreter, someone so long aligned with the people of the Pine Ridge country and himself married to a Brulé woman, was never explained.[5]

In nightly councils over the next number of days, Spotted Tail repeated the same inducements the camp's elders had heard from Hunts the Enemy and Few Tails, but served-up now by one of the most distinguished of Pine Ridge chiefs. To this, Spotted Tail added an additional truth. Do this, and do it now, he implored, before the grass was high enough to support soldier horses, because they would otherwise come and fight you. As one chronicler aptly noted, those were "hard words but true."[6]

Spotted Tail apparently also seasoned his inducements with one additional and even more compelling reason for submitting now. The chief openly, and with consent from Crook himself, suggested that once this war was over, these Northerners might be allowed to occupy a reservation in the hunting ground. Notions of an agency somewhere north of the Black Hills in or proximate to the buffalo country had spiced conversations for a long while, and indeed any such genuine prospect would have been an enormous enticement now. Miles, not coincidentally, was offering much the same hope to the Cheyennes. The Cheyenne treaty in 1868 had at least suggested such a possibility, but not so with the Lakotas, whose reservation bounds were formalized in their own 1868 treaty and already served with distinct agencies for each of the *oyates*. Still, the Oglalas and Brulés in the Pine Ridge were something of an anomaly. Crook and Spotted Tail both knew of and understood the widespread political distaste for those two agencies, located in Nebraska and not in the Dakota Territory, and the feverish desire to move them beyond the state boundary. But government officials imagined new agencies along the White River or even eastward as far as the White's confluence with the Missouri. Still, to these war-weary Lakotas clinging to the buffalo prairie, such talk of an agency north of the Black Hills, however manipulative, only meant north, not east, and Spotted Tail knew so.[7]

Spotted Tail and his delegation returned to the Pine Ridge on April 5 after fifty days in the Powder River country, having faithfully served his accepted role as an emissary but also seizing the opportunity to hunt buffalo while coming and going. In the worst of weather, he had put the interests of the Lakota people ahead of his own *oyate*, and he rightly declared his mission a success, forecasting the imminent arrivals of Miniconjous, Sans Arcs, and Crazy Horse, too, who was coming in and prepared to accept peace. And yet an air of pessimism clouded the Indian camps at the Pine Ridge agencies. Crazy Horse's aversion to forts, camps, and agencies was well-known and a turn from the free life now remained nearly impossible to fathom.[8]

Throughout March and April the surrender of Northern Indians was striking. Individuals, small family groups, and larger bands of Miniconjous, Sans Arcs, Blackfeet, Brulés, and Oglalas made their way through difficult winter conditions to submit and join kinfolk at one agency or another on the sprawling Great Sioux Reservation. Already in late February, in the frigid Lakota month of the popping trees, the mostly Miniconjou followers of Red Horse, Spotted Elk, and White Eagle, some 229 people, submitted at Cheyenne River Agency. In an interview soon after their arrival, Red Horse pleaded an all too familiar case, reminding the local army commander that this had been a war of principle. "The hostile Indians . . . never ceded any of the Big Horn country or the Black Hills and [yet] the Whites continued to trespass in that country. Our council men told us that we would have to fight for our country, that that would be the only way to retain it." A war for the buffalo country. Nearly every Lakota coming in now could say the same thing.[9]

Circumstances in the Pine Ridge were even more hectic. On March 6 fifteen lodges of Northern Indians submitted at the Spotted Tail Agency. They had encountered Spotted Tail himself on Rapid Creek north of there "who urged them to come right in." But the most striking arrivals since the first of the Cheyennes appeared were 130 Oglalas led by No Water and another 133 Cheyennes, with Left Hand and Black Moon the most notable of that lot. The bands trickled into Red Cloud Agency over several days beginning on March 10. They quickly fell in with the array of Lakota, Cheyenne, and Arapaho circles scattered along the White and its local tributaries, both above and below the agency.[10]

Downstream on Beaver Creek, another of the White's tributaries, the Miniconjou followers of Touch the Clouds and Roman Nose, and Sans

Arcs with Red Bear and High Bear, some 917 individuals, reached Spotted Tail Agency on April 14. Spotted Tail and his ever-faithful companion, Boucher, had ridden out that morning to the mouth of Beaver Creek to meet the newcomers and guide them into the camp. Prominent Miniconjou and Sans Arc warriors took the lead as the bands paraded by and headed to a nearby camping place. Later that morning thirty of the principal chiefs rode into the little post nearby and approached a cluster of government agents and soldiers, including Gray Fox Crook, Ranald Mackenzie, and several of their aides, who themselves had hurriedly crossed the forty-five miles separating the Pine Ridge army camps to monitor these surrenders. The chiefs presented the general with a symbolic surrender firearm, laying it on the ground before him, and each then shook his hand. The day was then taken up with speech-making and a feast offered by the local Brulés. Spotted Tail himself tended the surrender of ponies and firearms, gathering some 1,430 animals and a paltry number of weapons. Crook protested that so few guns were given up and admonished Spotted Tail to do it again or he would have soldiers scour the lodges. But the firearms matter was then quietly ignored. Spotted Tail's wintertime effort was delivering compelling results and attention turned elsewhere, particularly to the whereabouts of Crazy Horse, the great Oglala chief himself, and the prime target of Spotted Tail's mission.[11]

Trouble arose at Spotted Tail Agency almost immediately. The peace-talkers, one and all, including Spotted Tail, promised the Northern Indians that in exchange for the humiliation of surrendering and the loss of ponies and firearms, they would be bounteously fed. And yet the local agent, Jesse M. Lee, reassigned to the duty from line service with one of the local infantry companies, was immediately confronted with shortages of rations and pled for a hurried resupply to tend not only his normal charges but also the many new arrivals and the two or three hundred *Wajaje* Brulés soon to be transferred from Red Cloud Agency. He understood well the political sensitivity of his predicament and in his official appeal reminded the Commissioner of Indian Affairs of the inadvisability of failing to deliver these vital issuances. Lee's situation did not improve immediately. In June and

July he again sent imploring letters and was repeatedly told that supplies of every sort had been shipped and ought to have been received by now. Lee knew well that most of the Indians in his charge were there only because they were receiving full issuances of every sort. The matter remained dire, but that no band bolted suggests the agent somehow surmounted his challenge.[12]

North and west of the Black Hills the lingering coalition of Crazy Horse's people were slowly making their way toward Red Cloud Agency, variously resting and attempting to hunt en route and still agonizing over the distasteful prospect of quitting the war and yielding the buffalo country. Smaller bands that had scattered before now, principally to hunt, joined again, and the circle had swelled to some 155 lodges of mostly Oglalas, but with Brulés, Miniconjous, and Sans Arcs also in the mix. Principal elders included Little Hawk, Little Big Man, Old Hawk, and Big Road, with He Dog recognized as the camp's head *akicita*. Almost unspoken was the continued general deference paid to Crazy Horse, the esteemed and broadly revered war chief, who had fallen again into the quiet, introspective mode so common to his character. To those nearest him, he was listless and filled with despair, repeatedly lamenting that "all is lost . . . the country is lost . . . the freedom is lost."[13]

But Crazy Horse remembered promises, too. On the trail south in the days from the time of Spotted Tail's visit, the great war chief actually marked the location where he wished to have his agency, later telling the general and others at Camp Robinson, including newspaper correspondents, that "in coming this way I picked out a place where I wish to live hereafter. I put a stake in the ground to mark the spot. There is plenty of game in that country." Spotted Tail's promise of a northern agency—Crook's promise—resonated, and the war chief reacted, at one point telling a warrior in his camp that they were agreeing to go in, get rations and clothing, "and return west of the Black Hills again." On some occasions things might appear so simple. Young Black Elk's father paid particular heed to this thinking and recalled Crazy Horse's thoughtful explanation of this critical moment in Northern Oglala history. In relating essences to his son, who in turn in 1931 shared them with his biographer, the boy was told: "I am making plans for the good of my people," the chief asserted. "This country is ours, therefore I am doing this." Those words and actions would haunt the principals for the rest of their days.[14]

For those awaiting the great chief at Camp Robinson, the air of doubt and wait prompted Crook to organize and dispatch yet another peace envoy, this one led no less than by Red Cloud, the lordly Oglala, whom Crook charged now with locating and personally escorting Crazy Horse to the agency. Even at age fifty-five and averse to this war, Red Cloud was open to the challenge, particularly in light of the obvious attention his rival, Spotted Tail, received during and after his own peace initiative. Rivalries aside, simple pragmatism also figured in the effort. Since the time of the Fort Laramie Treaty and Red Cloud's coming over to the Whites, he and his people had lived the vagaries of an agency existence, with the quirks of ever-changing agents, and the realities of government provisioning, heavy or lean depending on supply and budgetary conditions, and where beef substituted for buffalo. But there was generally a sufficiency of meat, coffee, beans, corn, flour, soda, salt, sugar, and tobacco. Assurances of such provisioning now, particularly in light of the well-known and widespread destitution of the northern people, would be vital but easy to convey.[15]

But Gray Fox Crook also advised Red Cloud to express in plain terms that each day of delay was one day closer to the movement of troops, who at that very moment, in fact, were again preparing for the field and assuming to advance against any lingering Northerners. Crook also coyly authorized Red Cloud to sweeten the surrender in two additional ways. Once the surrenders were complete, Crazy Horse would be permitted to organize a buffalo hunt in the favored country, and he could also personally visit the Great Father if he wished, adding a twist to the notion of an agency in the north and therewith offering an opportunity for Crazy Horse to help make the case for himself.[16]

Red Cloud was several days organizing his delegation, which ultimately numbered some eighty individuals from the agency, warriors mostly but some accompanied by wives, and led by several principal band chiefs including Yellow Bear and Slow Bull and the lately surrendered No Water. The party also included several agency interpreters, Antoine Ladeau, Antoine Janis, and Jose Merrivale. A month earlier it was Merrivale who had received one of Crazy Horse's ponies, given by the chief's father as an assurance of this surrender. Red Cloud's destination was plain enough. Crazy Horse's people were last noted near Bear Lodge Butte, along the timeworn Red Cloud-Powder River Trail.[17]

As the great body of Cheyennes had separated while on their own journey to the Pine Ridge, the Oglalas splintered too. Red Cloud met several smaller bands as he progressed northward and hurried them along. With one he sent along one of his couriers, chiefly to procure a dispatch of foodstuffs from Camp Robinson to feed the oncoming forlorn ones. Red Cloud was soon welcomed into the Northerners' camp. Days were spent in conversations with headmen and elders and in due course Red Cloud had his face-to-face meeting with the great war chief, Crazy Horse. The fearless warrior and victor at the Little Big Horn and the aged mastermind of the Bozeman Trail War had not met like this for years, but the younger man spread a buffalo robe for the two to sit on and they counseled. The conversation was amicable and ran the usual gamut of firearms, ponies, and foodstuffs, as well as news that a delegation of Oglalas would soon go to Washington to discuss with the Great Father the prospect of a northern agency. Crazy Horse assured his Oglala mentor that he was coming in, and in an affirming gesture placed his extravagantly beaded, painted, and hair fringed war shirt on Red Cloud's shoulders. Red Cloud again dispatched a courier to Camp Robinson to forecast their arrival in eight or nine days. The Northerners' travel had been hindered by snow and the weakness of their ponies. Fortunately, the seasons were changing and springtime warmth and rains were again yielding nourishing grasses.[18]

Behind them at Camp Robinson a striking young army lieutenant, William P. Clark, known widely as White Hat by the Sioux for the broad-brimmed Stetson he favored, was now standing in for Crook. The general had departed for Chicago and Washington to personally take up the thorny matter of a new home—a northern home—for these people. White Hat hurriedly dispatched a relief train westward, commanded by a fellow junior officer and aided by an interpreter, William Garnett. The wagons were topped with rations, and one hundred beeves were pushed alongside by a complement of Indian scouts led by American Horse the younger, Red Cloud's son-in-law. The precious cargo reached the oncomers on Sage Creek, some forty miles west of Camp Robinson, on May 1. The site was a mere three miles downstream of the Hat Creek stage station, the scene of much travail and bloodshed during the course of the war. There the foodstuffs were distributed and wholly devoured. The young officer in charge approached Crazy Horse and shook his hand, allegedly the first time since childhood that the great Oglala had touched the hand of a White man. But this was no moment for pomp. The people spent three days on Sage Creek eating and resting.[19]

Word of Crazy Horse's approach animated the Camp Robinson garrison. This little outpost in the Pine Ridge had witnessed more than its share of intense excitement in its bare three-year existence, from the days of attempting to purchase or strong arm away the Black Hills from the Lakotas to the recent massive surrenders of Northern Cheyennes. Coming now were the very people and their war chief who six months earlier had killed Custer and where he, like Sitting Bull, had emerged as a figurehead of the war. Through most of this war-time period, Camp Robinson bristled with soldiers drawn from the farthest corners of the country, always many more than any ordinary infantry garrison. Most remained and were now on high alert, attentive though intentionally exhibiting an outward nonchalance as a dust cloud rose in the west. A complement of Indian scouts were also marshaled and secreted in the broken high country north of the post, likewise observant and ready to respond at a moment's call. But none of this proved necessary.[20]

It was Sunday, May 6, a day as memorable in the saga of Sitting Bull's War as the brutal soldier attack on the Cheyenne village in March 1876, or the bloody fight on the Little Big Horn. That morning Clark, with twenty Indian scouts and several interpreters, plus a correspondent from the *Chicago Times*, rode west to meet these last holdouts. About five miles west of the post Clark's party passed the returning wagons that had been dispatched some days earlier with foodstuffs. Not far behind, Clark could see Crazy Horse, mounted. The officer stopped and watched as the chief came on. Crazy Horse rode a spotted white pony. He and his principal lieutenants, Little Hawk, Little Big Man, and He Dog, all approached and dismounted. Other warriors clustered and watched from a short distance behind. Red Cloud, with those in the fore, led the chiefs forward to meet the officer.[21]

Crazy Horse, the focus of attention, was thirty-seven. Clark opposite him was thirty-one. The solemn occasion belonged to two able young warriors. For a moment they stared at one another pensively and then sat on the ground and ritualistically smoked. Only then did they shake hands. Crazy Horse did so with his left hand, telling Clark through an interpreter, that he shook with that hand because his heart was on that side, a point speaking to the solemnity of the occasion. Clark expressed a general desire for peace, and detailed the protocols to come, including the surrendering of arms and ponies and a headcount. Crazy Horse acknowledged Clark's words and said that he too wanted this peace, a peace to last forever. Before concluding, Crazy Horse seized the moment to describe for Clark the place where he wanted his people to live, near the Tongue River in the revered buffalo country. The intent of fixating on that point may have been lost on Clark, but it was obviously foremost in Crazy Horse's consciousness, he ever mindful of promises made. On that He Dog, likely on Crazy Horse's nod, advanced and flung his lavishly beaded and ornamented buckskin war shirt on Clark's shoulders and placed his feather headdress on his head, signs of submission and good will. Crazy Horse doubtless would have done the same had he not given his own status-imparting war shirt to Red Cloud just days before.[22]

The brief but momentous encounter complete, Crazy Horse motioned to advance. Red Cloud and his peace-talker delegation and Clark and his scouts led the strung-out cavalcade, ultimately advancing a quarter mile ahead of the Oglalas. At this point Red Cloud and his peace-talkers were anxious simply to get out of the way. The procession neared the army camp around 2:00 P.M. With none of the charging on horseback and firing of guns and pistols that had characterized some surrenders, the chiefs in their finery led the nearly two-mile-long spectacle as it bypassed the post. A simple measured chant, what one newsman called a "Peace Song," rose above the din. Behind the chiefs trailed other headmen and warriors, and then old men, families, dogs, seemingly countless travois, and the pony herd, all skirting the northern margins of the post to designated campsites along the White, midway between Camp Robinson and Red Cloud Agency. None of the *wasicu* onlookers had been at the Little Big Horn, where surviving soldiers had watched as that massive village departed upriver after the battle. The spectacle now was nearly the same, aside perhaps for relative size. These were proud, unconquered people who fought for their country and a lifeway, and were coming now to make peace, not surrender. One observant officer in the camp proclaimed to those around him, "By God! This is a triumphal march, not a surrender."[23]

Quickly at the designated campsite five distinct band circles rose. At 4:00 P.M. Crazy Horse, Little Big Man, He Dog, and other chiefs gathered at a small crescent on an edge of the circles and laid guns on the grass at Clark's feet. Warriors from behind did so as well. Clark had come alone and huddled merely with interpreters, Mackenzie and other officers of the post having deferred the proceedings to him. Clark noted the weapons and was sure that the camp held more. With little fuss he directed the Indian scouts to search the lodges and also conduct a headcount. By nightfall 117 firearms were collected, including three Winchesters belonging to Crazy Horse. The headcount tallied 145 lodges, 217 men, 312 women, 186 boys, and 184 girls, a sum of 899 people. Separately Red Cloud's peace-talkers and the enrolled scout confiscated 2,200 ponies, US mules, and cavalry horses, and after separating the government stock a day later, the animals were distributed to those who had helped bring the great war chief to the Pine Ridge. It was a perplexing reward because in effect it meant the remounting of peoples who had lost their own horses the previous fall. Besides, many of those animals would be gifted back to Crazy Horse's people in due course.[24]

Not lost on the gawkers who came to the camp that evening and in the next few days was the forlorn condition of the people, their lodges, and their surrendered animals. Susan Bordeaux Bettelyoun, a mixed blood living at Camp Robinson then, remembered the people being extremely poor and destitute, some having lost lodges and camp equipage to the soldiers, and all having been subjected to the army's endless chase. John Bourke, another of Crook's aides present during the surrender, likewise thought the lodges were small and badly tattered and the number and weight of buffalo robes meager. He had been in the villages destroyed at Powder River, Slim Buttes, and Red Fork, and had a perspective on such things. Bourke commented, too, on the camp's dogs. One normally saw packs of dogs running and yipping through Indian camps, he recalled, but not here, where only an occasional furtive mutt was seen. Most, Bourke guessed, had been eaten.[25]

Many had longed for years so see this day, and then it was over. Crazy Horse, the remarkable warrior who fought Gray Fox Crook at Rosebud Creek, Long Hair Custer at the Little Big Horn, and Bear Coat Miles in the Wolf Mountains, had led his followers in. In the moment, it mattered not whether it was to surrender, or submit, or merely make a peace and be fed and clothed. "We had enough to eat now," remembered young Black Elk, "and we boys could play without being afraid of anything." And yet for Crazy Horse, the days ahead were difficult and often frustrating as he obligingly confronted a bewildering new world, with a confounding celebrity status, incessant pressures to indeed join a delegation bound for Washington to meet the Great Father, the unconscionable handling of the Oglala's closest friends, the Cheyennes, and the doubletalk of a promised hunt and an agency of his own. None of this could be foreseen. The outlook at sunset on May 6 was simply of peace and foodstuffs for the people.[26]

When Crazy Horse started for the Pine Ridge at Spotted Tail's beckoning, one small band of devout traditionals remained behind in the Powder River country. Two Miniconjous, Lame Deer and Fast Bull, steadfastly insisted that peace with the Whites was impossible as long as miners remained in the Black Hills and Miles's soldiers occupied the buffalo country. So, they struck off on their own. With perhaps thirty lodges the band headed west, benefitting by the emergent springtime grasses and the periodic attachment of other disaffected holdouts, all vowing never to surrender. By early May Lame Deer's camp had grown to fifty-one lodges, with the coming of some fifteen belonging to Cheyennes under an Elk Society chief named White Hawk. Through the early spring the small lot of resolute holdouts ambled westward, hunting buffalo in the familiar country of the Upper Tongue and Rosebud. By early May they paused on Muddy Creek (today's Lame Deer Creek), an eastern affluent of Rosebud Creek just above the Medicine Rocks.[27]

Miles was fully aware of these holdouts. Bear Coat first heard of them from White Bull, one of the Cheyennes who had just surrendered at Tongue River, who told of Indians, probably Sioux, chasing buffalo on the Rosebud. Bear Coat, ever eager to advance on any such isolated band, again first dispatched Big Leggins Bruguier to locate them, determine their intentions, and ensure that they understood fully Miles's own offerings and capabilities. Bruguier readily located the camp, but his subsequent report to Miles was discouraging for he described determined Indians that were well provisioned, well mounted, and fully alert to surprises coming from that direction. Lame Deer, in fact, boldly told Bruguier that "no White man could get near his camp." The report infuriated Miles and predictably spurred his action.[28]

Bear Coat led twelve companies of infantry and cavalry and a complement of Indian scouts, Cheyennes mostly but also including the Miniconjou Hump and several of his followers, southward from his cantonment, up the Tongue, across to the Rosebud by way of Greenleaf Creek, and up the

Rosebud. What particularly struck Miles as he commenced his sortie were the welcoming conditions of the seasonally transformed buffalo prairie. "In striking contrast to former campaigns," he penned in his memoir, "at this time the prairies were covered with green grasses, the trees were in full foliage, the air filled with the odor of flowers, and the birds were singing. If we had been going to some peaceful festival, the scene could not have been more propitious."[29]

Miles was not drawn by flowers and or chirping birds, however. He went to the field again to corral Indians. On May 7, the day after Crazy Horse's surrender at Red Cloud Agency, he struck Lame Deer's small camp, and the results were predictable from the start. The leading force of cavalry, some 225 horsemen, alone greatly outnumbered the collective tally of warriors in the village, amounting perhaps to seventy-five. Miles's mounted troops swept the village in the breaking light, catching it completely unaware and driving its occupants largely into the steep hillsides to the west. Some of his soldiers pursued them for a considerable distance in the pine-covered highlands. From the camp and its margins nearly 500 ponies and mules were also driven off. The shooting soon turned desultory. In the morning light Lame Deer was spotted in the distance and hailed by Hump, who had come up with Miles's scouts and infantry and now occupied high ground in the northeast. Pressed by Miles, Hump urged Lame Deer to surrender. Lame Deer drew a white cloth and he and several others rode forward, plainly it seemed willing to talk, and Hump likewise rode over. Lame Deer and Hump talked matters through and the chief agreed to confer with Miles.[30]

When word reached Bear Coat. he too rode out, accompanied by several staff members and an orderly carrying a white flag. When Miles reached the chief the two dismounted and shook hands. Bear Coat had no visible weapons, but Lame Deer carried a rifle. His nephew at his side, Big Ankle, was also armed. Miles asked them to put their weapons down. Lame Deer laid his rifle on the ground, but the nephew, plainly agitated, paced and blurted out: "I am a soldier walking on my own land. I will give up my gun to no man. They have already killed my grandmother." He kept repeating this. Indeed, an old woman, reportedly Lame Deer's mother-in-law, was killed in the initial assault. White Bull, another Cheyenne standing alongside Miles, tried to calm the nephew, but they scuffled and Big Ankle's weapon discharged. The bullet passed through White Bull's coat. Lame Deer also attempted to calm his nephew, but the moment exploded, and Lame Deer picked up his own rifle and fired at Bear Coat. The bullet missed the colonel but killed a soldier behind him and triggered an immediate resumption of general shooting. The chief and those around him turned and attempted to flee to the hillside. Big Ankle was struck several times, and then Lame Deer too was wounded as he labored to carry off his relative. Both died at the creek.[31]

Miles's troops occupied the camp through the remainder of the day and evening, and the next morning burned the lodges and nearly all their contents, including some two hundred saddles and caches of dried meats. Fifty Indian weapons, mostly magazine rifles, were carried off as were a trove of relics from the Little Big Horn battle. After culling and shooting the poorest of the ponies, the command commenced its return to the Yellowstone, pushing with it nearly 450 captured animals. In coming weeks Miles mounted four companies of his infantry on those same Indian ponies, an enterprising experiment with payoffs later that year. Indian casualties in the Muddy Creek fight were fourteen killed, including Lame Deer, his animated nephew, Big Ankle, another of the camp's chiefs, Iron Star (the Miniconjou, not the Hunkpapa of that name), plus Heart Ghost and Shorty. An equal number were wounded. The attackers recorded four killed and eight wounded.[32]

In the battle's wake, the Lame Deer refugees, now led by Fast Bull, one of the chief's sons, refused to submit. Despite other attempts at forcing his hand, he and his followers successfully eluded other sorties mounted against them and roamed the buffalo country well into the fall. The Lame Deer fight was the last formal armed engagement of Sitting Bull's War, bringing to a close a string of nearly twenty such episodes in which Indian blood was shed in 1876 and 1877. Sheridan's Army had deployed twenty-eight distinct times during the course of the war. In the wake of the Lame Deer fight, Sheridan concluded openly that "the Sioux war was now over," and those words have tantalized contemporary and modern chroniclers ever since. One salty storyteller living in Omaha, Nebraska, expressed much the same thing some years after, but with a sly twist. So ended, he asserted, "Inspector Watkins's little scheme for sending out a few soldiers to run the wild Sioux onto the reservation." The writer referred to Erwin C. Watkins, the Indian Service inspector, who made the government's case in November 1875 for what he predicted then would be a simple, quick little war.[33]

Was Sheridan on the mark? On the battlefield, perhaps so. But most everyone then understood that wars have consequences well beyond the hallowed fields, where tempers continued to flare, bullets flew, and indecision (or decision) reigned. And nowhere was that more apparent than in the Pine Ridge as spring turned to summer, 1877.

When Crook returned to Camp Robinson on May 23 his primary objective was seizing the chance, at last, to meet his long-time nemesis, Crazy Horse. On May 25, the day after consulting with and announcing the Cheyennes' fate, White Hat Clark, for Crook's benefit, orchestrated a grand pageant with the Sioux. At his instigation nearly eight hundred Oglala and Brulé chiefs and warriors gathered and paraded before the general and other assembled officers and agents. As one chronicler aptly observed, these were not men who had been crushed, broken, or whipped, but people who glistened with sweat, courage, pride, and even anger. The leading chiefs advanced to meet Crook and shake his hand. For Crazy Horse, this too was the first time he met, let alone shook hands with this man of promises, the man who controlled his fate. They had been on the same battlefields before, at Rosebud and Slim Buttes, but this was different and heady.[34]

The round of handshaking was followed by a general council that consumed the better part of the afternoon. With Leon Palladay and William

Garnett interpreting and two newspaper correspondents penning eyewitness accounts, Red Cloud, ever the statesman, opened the proceedings, pleading as always for the government's help in caring for his people. Other chiefs followed, variously repeating all-too-familiar homilies of broken promises and continual upheavals throughout the Indian country. But sometimes they touched upon the central issue of the day: a new homeland for these people, one presumably somewhere in the Powder River country. And then, the normally reticent war chief joined in, and this time was unrestrained.[35]

> You sent tobacco to my camp and invited me to come in. When the tobacco reached me I started and kept moving till I reached here. I have been waiting ever since arriving, for Gen. Crook, and now my heart has been made happy. In coming this way I picked out a place where I wish to live hereafter. I put a stake in the ground to mark the spot. There is plenty of game in that country. All of my relatives here approve of my choice. I want them to go back with me and always live there together.[36]

Crook had the last word and spoke carefully, fully cognizant of the near hopelessness of the cause célèbre. "You asked," he said, "for a reservation in the upper country. This is taken down and will be sent to Washington. I cannot decide these things myself. They must be decided in Washington. The commissioner promised he would let some of you go and talk to him at Washington . . . I had rather you would hear for yourselves . . . I will try and be in Washington myself, so I can hear both sides."[37]

The Pine Ridge people had come to trust Crook. He knew that country and their cause, and he was as honest now as his own circumstances allowed. Already his pleadings in Chicago and Washington for a northern homeland for these people had come to naught. He knew that reality and had he been completely forthright now he knew that most of these people would have bolted for the north and in doing so crush this long-labored peace effort. But perhaps the envisioned visit by the chiefs to

Washington—that delegation now presumably including one of the war's eminent figures—might prove persuasive yet.[38]

—∿—

The saga of Crazy Horse's surrender had been followed carefully by the nation's newspapers. Their editors and reporters fed readers colorful details on what may have indeed been a closing episode of a costly war. But a voice no one had yet heard belonged to Crazy Horse, a leading figurehead and perhaps the one most perfectly suited to unlock the Custer mystery. The two correspondents on the scene recognized the opportunity. One got close. The other got a scoop.

George Wallihan, writing as "Rapherty" for the *Cheyenne Daily Leader*, tried hard. He had been in the gold country that spring where he penned a series of intriguing accounts of the booming Deadwood. At the behest of his editor, he turned south and reached Red Cloud Agency in the middle of May, just after Crazy Horse's surrender. His editor wanted a Crazy Horse story. At the agency Wallihan shrewdly connected with two individuals he believed would introduce him to the chief. They were John W. Dear, one of the well-connected and licensed traders at Red Cloud Agency, and Frank Grouard, the everywhere mixed-blood who had once lived in Crazy Horse's camp and more recently had visibly guided Gray Fox Crook on each of his successive campaigns against these very Indians. Grouard's time as a scout for the enemy seemed irrelevant now. With Dear's and Grouard's assistance and Grouard interpreting, Wallihan and a small entourage, including a beguiling young woman who would soon become Wallihan's wife, spent part of an afternoon with Crazy Horse and several other prominent Oglalas, including Red Cloud and Little Big Man. They all shook hands and smoked. During the afternoon Little Big Man was quite talkative, but not so the chief. Wallihan thought him "ungracious" and "sullen," and the opportunity to inquire about the Little Big Horn fight never presented itself.[39]

Also seizing the moment was John W. Ford, the well-known Fort Laramie telegrapher and occasional correspondent for the *Chicago Times*.

He arrived with Crook on May 23 to report on the general's meetings with the Cheyennes and Oglalas. Ford was with Crook when Touch the Clouds surrendered at Spotted Tail Agency in April and he, like Wallihan, eyed a Crazy Horse story and believed that he had perfect entrées, including White Hat Clark, whom he had lately befriended, and Crook himself. Their relationship spanned not just the Touch the Clouds episode but the entire course of the war. The moment seemed propitious.[40]

At Ford's prompting, on May 24 Clark arranged a meeting with Crazy Horse. William Garnett from the agency interpreted. Present with the chief were Horned Horse, who fought at the Little Big Horn and whose son was killed there, and Red Dog, an agency Oglala. Ford coyly suggested that the details he gathered came from Crazy Horse himself, and that this was truly Crazy Horse's own story, but all along Horned Horse did most of the talking, apparently with Crazy Horse and Red Dog confirming the details (even though Red Dog was not at the Little Big Horn). Questions about the Custer fight led the conversation, and Horned Horse touched upon the attack, which was "a surprise and totally unlooked for." He also told of the enormous sprawl of the Indian village, Custer dividing his force, and the warriors themselves dividing, with some getting between Custer and the fleeing noncombatants and others getting onto his rear. "Outnumbering him as they did, they had him at their mercy, and the dreadful massacre ensued." But for the timely arrival of General Terry, the Indians would have wiped Reno out too. Ford's interview ranged through other episodes of the war, including the Rosebud fight, and the already so-called Sibley Scout affair occurring just after the Little Big Horn. The sum amounted to a dramatic narrative, made all the more compelling when bearing as it did Crazy Horse's imprimatur, even if never composed of his own words.[41]

A slow summer pace quickly enveloped the Northerners as they transitioned to agency life, one of beef and flour not buffalo and tipsin, duck cotton instead of skin lodges, and conformance and stability, not the sauntering days of old, or the exasperations and terror of war. In keeping with a long-held tradition among the Lakotas, the Crazy Horse people Sun Danced in late June on a prairie bench along the White River just beyond Crazy Horse's camp. The selected field was ironically almost within sight of another broad grassy swale where in September 1875 government commissioners attempted to purchase the Black Hills. The landscape was crowned still by a singular tall cottonwood tree, an ever-after heralded Council Tree. The four-day Sun Dance culminated, as always, with the shedding of blood as a handful of dancers offered themselves in sacrifice to *Wakan Tanka*. The pleadings this time were simple enough. They prayed for survival and renewal.[42]

Unanswered questions still burdened the people, however. When would their summer hunt be permitted, and what about moving? Crazy Horse pushed the former matter repeatedly. He and everyone easily remembered that when Spotted Tail and Red Cloud trailed north that spring hoping to lure those people to the Pine Ridge both had promised such a hunt. Buffalo remained at the center of everyday Lakota life, a food source, skins for moccasins and lodges, robes for trade, and a ritualistic, prideful labor. Crook was away, but his aides fielded hunting requests in June and July and at one point reported to Crook that nearly *every* Pine Ridge resident wished to go. The herds remained robust in the distant Powder and Tongue River country. The residents could care little that such a hunt posed political and administrative challenges for Crook, even as they watched him and his emissaries conveniently sidestep the issue for half the summer. But the time came when Crook could avoid it no longer.

At the end of July seventy chiefs and headmen, including Red Cloud, Crazy Horse, Little Big Man, and Young Man Afraid of His Horses, were summoned to a council at Red Cloud Agency. There, White Hat Clark delivered two messages from the Gray Fox. The hunt would be permitted as quickly as arrangement could be made. Lasting about twenty nights, Spotted Tail would lead and keep everyone within bounds. He "can be trusted," a newspaper reported. Following the hunt, Clark continued, come mid-September, a delegation of eighteen leading men would go to

Washington and make the case for a new agency. The news was joyously received. Agent James Irwin delivered three beeves to the council that were butchered on the spot and the attendees feasted.[43]

And then Pine Ridge politics exploded. The prospect of hundreds of Oglalas, Brulés, and Arapahos parading north to hunt buffalo brought cries of White dissent locally and regionally. No sooner had White Hat Clark announced Crook's approval for the hunt than two Red Cloud Indians visited Irwin to offer a stark warning. Crazy Horse was not to be trusted, they said. He was an "unreconstructed Indian" who, if allowed to lead away well-armed and equipped men, would never return but instead go on the "warpath" or even break and join Sitting Bull, who was by then known to be in Canada. Irwin found the report credible and passed it through channels to the Commissioner of Indian Affairs. Then Spotted Tail announced his own opposition to the hunt, questioning his ability to control such a disparate lot. Within days of having approved the hunt, Crook withdrew his permission.[44]

The breaking of Crook's promise opened, as one chronicler observed, a fissure between Crazy Horse and the very military officers he had allowed himself to trust. When the hunt was canceled, Crazy Horse reversed himself about the planned Washington trip. Friends counseled caution anyway, suggesting that were he to go he would be imprisoned. Through most of the summer the war chief had been openly willing to travel east and had even discussed the matter with Garnett, who had accompanied a similar trip in 1875 and endorsed this one now. Furthermore, Crazy Horse knew precisely where he wanted his new agency and the detail was virtually his alone to advocate and describe. But not now.[45]

Compounding the state of confusion at Red Cloud Agency, Crook, in late August, sought scouts from the Lakota camps to join the campaign he was organizing against the Nez Perce Indians. The Nez Perces were then enmeshed in their own war in the northwest and headed lately for the same plains country that Crazy Horse and Sitting Bull coveted. White Hat Clark already had his own complement of Indian scouts who largely functioned as policemen in the camps, but they refused to join Gray Fox in this new movement, many believing that the true objective was the capture of Sitting Bull. Clark pressured the chiefs individually and slowly brought some around, including the cautious Crazy Horse, even while the chief openly wondered why it was, after having pledged at Hat Creek that he would not go on the warpath anymore, he was being urged "to go and kill men again." Still, he would do so. "He would go," he told Clark, "and camp beside the soldiers and fight with them till all the Nez Perces were killed."[46]

But is that what the war chief really said? Two conflicting versions of Crazy Horse's response cloud the story, and Louie Bordeaux is at the center of both. Bordeaux was a respected twenty-nine-year-old mixed-blood interpreter normally engaged at Camp Sheridan and Spotted Tail Agency. He had no apparent political or social difficulties with the war chief and was present when Crazy Horse told Clark and others of his willingness to assist the soldiers, "to fight with them until all the Nez Perces were killed." But Bordeaux went on to witness another telling of the chief's commitment, where Touch the Clouds and other chiefs who were present related the same story but where the interpreter then was Frank Grouard. Grouard, according to Bordeaux, willfully misinterpreted Crazy Horse's words, saying that "he was going back to his country in the north and would take the warpath and fight the soldiers till they were all killed." Puzzlingly, Bordeaux did not object to the apparent misinterpretation, at lease on the spot, and by the time he did so later the damage was done. On hearing Grouard's version of Crazy Horse's response, the officers at Camp Robinson were understandably shaken. Luther Bradley, the new senior officer succeeding Ranald Mackenzie, immediately notified Crook, then in Omaha and about to embark by train for the Nez Perce campaign, and to Sheridan in Chicago, warning both of a potential emergency at Red Cloud Agency.[47]

Believing that the Nez Perce affair was "but a small matter" compared to these Pine Ridge Indians, Sheridan diverted Crook to Camp Robinson. When reaching there on September 2, Gray Fox was briefed on the recent turn of events, including Grouard's puzzling translation of Crazy Horse's words. Crook knew that only Crazy Horse himself could set this matter straight. He instructed Clark to assemble some of the principals, including the war chief, to clear the matter, and even suggested that a small feast be offered to secure the war chief's presence. But Crazy Horse spurned the invitation, telling his friend He Dog that "people over there have said too much. I don't want to talk to them any more. No good would come of it." He Dog, aware of the various rumors swirling about and the explosiveness of the moment, pleaded with his friend to attend, but to no avail. Spurned but not deterred, Crook intended to proceed with the council and, if necessary, go straight to Crazy Horse's camp himself and meet him there.[48]

Then matters turned even more perverse. The next morning as two interpreters, Garnett and Baptiste Pourier, prepared to escort Crook to the council, Woman Dress, an Indian scout and Red Cloud's nephew, ventured by. Woman Dress asked of their doings. Alarmed by what he heard, he blurted: "Don't you go there with General Crook. When you hold this council at White Clay, Crazy Horse is going to come in there with sixty Indians, and catch General Crook by the hand, like he is going to shake hands, and he is going to hold on to him, and those sixty Indians are going to kill Crook and whoever he has with him." Stunned, Garnett pressed Woman Dress on how had he learned of this plot and was told that two other scouts, Lone Bear and his brother Little Wolf, both Oglalas, had been in Crazy Horse's camp the night before and overheard it. Garnett and Pourier brought Woman Dress to Crook and Clark. Pourier was related to Woman Dress through marriage and vouched for his trustworthiness, and the scout warned the general not to go.[49]

Crook was perplexed and instructed Garnett to bring in Red Cloud and eight or nine of his followers for a private council. When the chief, Little Wound, Red Dog, Man Afraid, American Horse, and others learned of the alleged assassination plot they too were astonished and alarmed. Crook informed them that Crazy Horse should be arrested, and he wished for them to do it. They agreed, one even suggesting killing the war chief, but Crook objected strenuously to that, declaring that that "must not be done as it would be murder." Crook insisted that the war chief be taken prisoner. Clark added that he would give the man who arrested the chief a bounty of three hundred dollars and a fine racing pony. Crook, believing his business at Red Cloud was finished (or perhaps grounded in sheer prudence should matters go awry), departed for Sidney, intent on continuing to the Nez Perce campaign.[50]

Word of the intended arrest leaked and Bradley, a practical man, fretted over the possibility of trouble in the Crazy Horse camp. He insisted that the action be done not in the dark but in broad daylight and that the arresting party be reinforced with troops. He, like Crook, wanted the arrest executed quickly and without inciting an incident. He also wanted no harm to come to the war chief nor did he want Crazy Horse to take flight and resume the abhorrent war.[51]

Since early summer, Crazy Horse remained steadfastly camped on the White near the mouth of Little White Clay Creek, five miles from the post. As the arresting party and its soldier complement approached in the breaking light of September 4, Little Big Man appeared. The stalwart disruptor of the Black Hills purchase proceedings of 1875 and one who stood always at the war chief's side, even as recently as their surrender in May, had had a falling out with his old friend and now worked with the Whites. He brought word that Crazy Horse had fled, taking with him his wife and two friends east to the Spotted Tail Agency. Behind him, the camp was in disarray and on the verge of breaking apart.[52]

Crazy Horse sought an ally. Touch the Clouds, his cousin and longtime confidant, was camped on Beaver Creek, three miles below Camp Sheridan. There, as well, was Crazy Horse's father, Worm, and stepmother, and his spiritual mentor, Horn Chips. Touch the Clouds, two years older than Crazy Horse, was deeply alarmed by his cousin's story and that matters had spiraled uncontrollably at Red Cloud Agency. Crazy Horse knew that he had been followed to the Miniconjou village, and now even it, too, was disassembling. Word of these troubles quickly reached Camp Sheridan. There, the local commander, Daniel Burke, dispatched old man Jose Merrivale and Charlie Tackett with a few Brulé scouts northward to encourage Crazy Horse to come to the post and talk. The pair soon returned and reported that Touch the Clouds had calmed things, but he too was upset and leading his warriors to the army station. In the interval, Burke received couriers from Camp Robinson, reporting on the morning's botched arrest and asking him to arrest the war chief and deliver him there.[53]

Forewarned, Burke assembled a few cohorts, no more than himself, Jesse Lee, the military agent at the agency, Louie Bordeaux, the interpreter, and the post's doctor, and rode out intent on meeting Touch the Clouds and presumably Crazy Horse and lead them to the post. They rode an army ambulance and quickly encountered the Miniconjous a mile and a half down Beaver Creek where they drew up opposite each other. The Indians were of a fighting mind, Bordeaux remembered, but surprisingly Crazy Horse rode forward and extended his hand in friendship. Lee, the local agent, assured him that Camp Sheridan's officers were of a different mind, and the war chief and Touch the Clouds agreed to continue to the post and talk.[54]

Spotted Tail, leading his own sizeable complement of followers and annoyed that this "load of trouble" had been "dumped" at his door, awaited their arrival. As the Miniconjous reached the center of the post, Spotted Tail stepped forward and addressed Crazy Horse directly, less now as a blood uncle but as the cautious patriarch of the Brulés, telling the war chief that there is never trouble here. "We keep the peace. We, the Brulés, do this. They obey me, and every Indian who comes here must listen to me! You say you want to come to this agency and live peaceably. If you stay here you must listen to me. That is all!" "*Haus!*" resonated across the grounds.[55]

Spotted Tail joined Touch the Clouds and Crazy Horse and the army officers as they adjourned to the adjutant's office. Crazy Horse was pressed on why it was he had fled to Touch the Clouds's camp and why there was general upheaval behind him now, and he opened up. There were "bad winds blowing" at Red Cloud, he said, and he poured out how he had watched soldiers and scouts advance on his camp this morning, but that he wanted no more war. He had promised that he would not fight against any nation anymore but then had been called into a council at Camp Robinson and asked to fight the Nez Perces. He reluctantly agreed but found the notion appalling. As to the rumors circulating, Crazy Horse called them all falsehoods, all bad interpretations. He sought Touch the Clouds's camp because it was peaceful there.[56]

When Crazy Horse had about finished, he looked directly at Burke and Lee and told them that he wanted his band transferred to Spotted Tail Agency, where there was a better opportunity to live in peace. The outpouring in this late afternoon was moving and convincing. The great war chief recognized his hopelessness. At best, Burke, Lee, and Spotted Tail, sensing the sorrow and anxiety in the war chief's countenance, urged him to return to Camp Robinson and give the officers there his side of these events. "No harm would come to him; he would be protected," they assured, even though they knew well that Crook had ordered his arrest and likely deportment to a distant prison. The destination was almost certainly Fort Marion in Saint Augustine, Florida, although some thought it was Fort Jefferson in the Dry Tortugas, a place that had been abandoned some years earlier. Before departing for Touch the Clouds's camp, Crazy Horse consented to return to Camp Robinson in the morning. Quietly, Touch the Clouds assured Burke that he would not let Crazy Horse get away.[57]

Late that evening, Crazy Horse talked with Touch the Clouds. He had earlier prayed for guidance and figured that he was at the end of his trail, that something was going to happen. He talked of death, and how his bones would turn to rock and his joints to flint. To Touch the Clouds it seemed as though Crazy Horse was looking to die. There was no sleep this night for the troubled man.[58]

When Crazy Horse arrived at Lee's quarters at Camp Sheridan the next morning, September 5, he was apprehensive and vacillating over the notion of returning to Camp Robinson. Burke and Lee again assured him that no harm would come to him. He was dressed plainly in a white cotton shirt with faint blue stripes, simple buckskin leggings, and beaded moccasins. Around his waist was cinched a leather belt with a sheathed, well-worn trade knife—a tobacco knife in day-to-day use—that now was mostly concealed by a red wool trade blanket draped over one shoulder and wrapped around his waist. A small red medicine bag with powders Chips had prepared for him was suspended around his neck. Lee, Bordeaux, Touch the Clouds, High Bear, and several others climbed into an ambulance, and the party departed around 9:00 A.M. The war chief preferred riding alongside, with Chips, Standing Bear, and a handful of other allies at his side. The two Pine Ridge army posts were forty-five miles apart, normally a six to eight hour journey, but the little caravan went by way of Touch the Clouds's camp, adding some minutes to allow Crazy Horse a few final words with his wife and parents. In all, the entourage numbered about twenty individuals.[59]

About an hour into the travel, other riders appeared, first a group of Brulés sent by Spotted Tail, and behind them the same Oglala scouts who had followed Crazy Horse from the White Clay Creek camp to Touch the Clouds's village. Initially the two groups kept their distance, but by midday the riders had mostly closed on the ambulance. Lee, reflecting later, was certain that by now "Crazy Horse . . . realized that he was practically a prisoner."[60]

When about fifteen miles from Camp Robinson, Lee sent a note ahead by Indian courier questioning whether his destination should be the agency or the post, and begging consideration for the war chief. Crazy Horse, he said, was not being delivered by force but by persuasion, and had been promised that he would have an occasion to state his case. At about four miles out, Lee received a response from White Hat Clark. Bradley wanted the chief delivered to the adjutant's office, the post's headquarters building on the west side of the military compound. The adjutant's office stood alongside the post's guardhouse.[61]

Only when the entourage passed the agency did Oglalas faithful to Red Cloud begin crowding the scene. Soon, they outnumbered those riding with the war chief. From their midst, He Dog rode up and shook Crazy Horse's hand, apparently both admonishing him: "You ought to take that trip to Washington; now you are in a jam," but also offering a forewarning: "Look out, watch your step. You are going into a dangerous place." The war chief did not look right, He Dog later recalled. Lee was dismayed when they crossed the Robinson parade ground late that afternoon and pulled up in front of the adjutant's office. Bradley was nowhere to be seen. They stopped as he had been instructed and a young officer emerged and announced simply that Crazy Horse was to be turned over to the Officer of the Day, who in turn would usher him under soldier escort to the guardhouse. Thus and simply, arrested and confined.[62]

Lee protested. What about those few words with Bradley first, he pleaded? The officer told him to take the matter up with Bradley directly. Lee ushered Crazy Horse, Touch the Clouds, and his other companions into the adjutant's office and rushed across the grounds to Bradley's quarters, located at the southern end of officer's row, believing that perhaps he might straighten things out. Bradley, attentive to the bustle on the parade ground but consciously apart from it, heard Lee out but was unsympathetic. His orders were preemptory, he explained. Lee objected strenuously, almost to the point of insubordination, he remembered, but Bradley declared that his hands were tied. Deliver Crazy Horse to the Officer of the Day, he ordered, and tell him that "not a hair of his head should be harmed."[63]

Frustrated and incensed, Lee returned to Crazy Horse and with the best massaging possible told the chief that it was too late in the evening for a talk. Bradley would see him in the morning, but he should go now with the Officer of the Day. He would be taken care of, and "not a hair of his head would be harmed." Those around him uttered "*hau!*" Resigned, the chief looked to the door. The promises, always the promises kept coming, he doubtless thought. The Officer of the Day, a seasoned, bearded, older man named James Kennington, stepped forward and the two went outside. There, two other soldiers stood attentively and filed behind them as they stepped off to the building next door, some sixty feet away. Little Big Man, the chief's erstwhile friend, sidled up to him, boxing him in on one shoulder with the officer on the other, and kept "assuring him that wherever he was taken he would go with him and stand by him."[64]

The guardhouse next door was slightly larger than the adjutant's office. Its windows were barred, hinting at a function a world apart from the adjutant's office with its desks and chairs and papers. This was purposefully a jail. Outside, a single sentry shouldering a rifle with a sharp, eighteen-inch-long bayonet extending from its end, snapped to attention as the tightly reined war chief approached the door. Once inside, Crazy Horse grasped the differences immediately. Ten other guardsmen, all off duty soldiers, lined a back wall and jumped to attention. Scattered about were the trappings of confinement—large iron balls, chains, iron cuffs. To his right was an inside door with a barred window, and through it the prison room where inside were small barred cells and several prisoners shackled in irons, the chains clinking and rattling on the wood floor every time one stirred.[65]

In that instant, Crazy Horse grasped that he was being jailed. He exploded with rage, lunging backward toward the outside door. Little Big Man grabbed him and the two swung wildly at each other. Kennington attempted to separate the pair, but the sinewy warrior lunged again. The chief tore away Little Big Man's cotton shirt and then reached for his own knife, slashing his attacker's left wrist. The fight exploded out the door, Kennington on their heels. Outside, onlookers, Indians and Whites alike, watched in horror. Many heard guns being cocked. Kennington screamed out: "Don't shoot! Don't shoot!" The officer tried to get at Crazy Horse with his sword, but the chief, still thrashing wildly, pushed him away. As the tempest whirled in the direction of the sentry outside, the man reflexively lowered his rifle to an infantryman's well-engrained *charge* position, his right hand grasping the weapon at the small of the stock and pressing it against his right hip, his left hand gripping the piece tightly at the lower barrel band, with the point of the long bayonet raised to the height of his chin. Louic Bordeaux, one of the interpreters in the mix, heard Kennington shriek: "Stab the son-of-a-bitch! Stab the son-of-a-bitch!" The guard lunged, and in an instant Crazy Horse crumpled to the ground. It had happened in seconds, and then an eerie silence wrapped the crowd.[66]

The wound was fatal. The sentry's bayonet lunge penetrated Crazy Horse's back right side and punctured both kidneys. Within moments Indians around him placed him on his red blanket. A small debate ensued over whether to haul him inside the guardhouse or next door but in due course he was carried to the adjutant's office. A cot was available, but the war chief insisted on being placed on the floor. He convulsed in pain. One of the post's doctors in the throng of observers pushed his way through to the office and examined the bloody wound. The chief was frothing at the mouth and his pulse was weak. Blood seeped from the penetration in his lower back. The doctor administered hypodermics of morphine to ease the pain, but he could see that life was short.[67]

A few friends huddled with Crazy Horse into the evening and in the background Kennington and another officer stood watch, as did the interpreters, Bordeaux and then Baptiste Pourier, and the doctor who was always close. Through it all, Touch the Clouds crouched faithfully at his cousin's side, at one point asking for permission to remove him to an Indian lodge so that he might die there, but Kennington refused. He Dog was present for a long while as well. Outside he had examined the wound. At that early moment Crazy Horse told his friend that he could "feel the blood flowing." He Dog lifted his bloody shirt and saw two wounds, one the fatal strike and the other a stab of sorts. Whether the latter was inflicted by Little Big Man, Kennington, or the sentry, whose bayonet may simply have run the body, will never be known. Inside, Crazy Horse was rarely lucid, the morphine relieving him of all pain but also dulling him to sleep. Later in the evening, Crazy Horse's parents appeared, having departed Touch the Clouds's camp earlier in the day plainly conscious of their son's foreboding as he headed out that morning. Father and son exchanged a few words. Mother cried. Both remained in the room to the last.[68]

A few others stopped by as well: the post's primary doctor, Lee, Bradley, Clark, but the pauses were scattered and brief. What is well confirmed is that death came quietly, just before midnight. Touch the Clouds had remained at his side and was especially moved. When the chief's breathing ceased, the extraordinary Miniconjou laid his hand on Crazy Horse's breast and said: "It is good. He has looked for death, and it has come."[69]

The army had not intended to kill Crazy Horse. Instead, they wished simply to separate him and his influence from the politically charged Pine Ridge, where allegiances between *oyates* and people seemed endlessly at odds. Through the long course of Sitting Bull's War, from the days of the railroad surveys along the Yellowstone, through the theft of the Black Hills, and clashes with Crook, Custer, and Miles, Crazy Horse had loomed as one of the central figures in the cause of preserving a people's lifeway and their independence on the buffalo prairie. He was a middle-aged man at the time of death. He had signed no treaties. He distanced himself from agencies and forts throughout his life. He was introverted most of the time, but not always, yet by the sheer magnitude of his battlefield heroics he rallied an extraordinary alliance of Lakotas, Southerners from the land of his and their birth, and other sectors, and often including Northern Cheyennes. Cumulative numbers aligning with the chief occasionally exceeded those with Sitting Bull. He persevered to the fullest extent possible and as long as his people could sustain themselves. His destiny was different from Sitting Bull's. They came from different ends of Sioux Country, and their futures inevitably took them in opposite directions. But their cause was the same, borne in a reverence for the land, the creatures of that land, and a lifeway held free.

Stillness fell across the Pine Ridge after Crazy Horse's killing. Whites feared the worst. The people who gathered on the Camp Robinson parade ground that late afternoon and witnessed the killing, Indians and Whites alike, departed stunned. Each had a story to tell, shaped by individual perspective, proximity, and personal character. The army shuddered predicting a mass exodus of Northerners, and in the days to come that partly occurred. Perhaps, despite Sheridan's enticing proclamation, this war was not over at all.

15
DEFIANCE

> "They told us that this line was considered holy. On one side you are perfectly free to do as you please. On the other you are in danger."
>
> —High Eagle, Hunkpapa Lakota

The people surrendering in the Pine Ridge had no sense of the Far North, no real way of comprehending Sitting Bull's hopes for the unique sanctuary beckoning from beyond the Medicine Line. But the Hunkpapas were indeed familiar with that borderlands region of the Upper Missouri and Milk rivers. They had traded often at Fort Union and Fort Peck in the long years those fur outposts were active, and traded more recently with the Métis from farther north. Importantly, buffalo herds north of the rivers were every bit as robust as the herds ranging the Big Open or south of the Yellowstone. Some had watched, too, the laying of the stone heaps a few years past, which for the first time formally marked two distinctive lands. Already they grasped, if superficially, the different political geospheres operating in the north and south. In the south lay the land of the blue coats, steamboats, prospectors, railroaders, and a Great Father, all seemingly bent against them now and forcing them out of the buffalo prairie. To the north lay a prairieland quite apart, with untrammeled grasses, abundant buffalo, native peoples—some friendly and some not—and but few Whites, and all within the intangible realm of a Grandmother. Importantly, kindred Santees had fled there, and the Métis people, increasingly essential Hunkpapa trading partners, resided there. Both groups described a north country very much resembling the buffalo prairie of Sitting Bull's native land, but a world not at war.

The lands beyond the boundary were the farthest northerly projection of the North American Great Plains. Like the land it was a part of, there too one saw vast rolling mixed- and short-grass prairies, speckled with eroded badlands, wind-swept buttes, inviting timbered uplands, lakes, and bisecting water courses. And as with the land it adjoined, it witnessed dramatic weather extremes, with temperatures fluctuating from summertime highs of 100°F to wintery lows of -50°F. Most importantly, it was land rich indeed with familiar game, creatures as varied as prairie dogs, antelope, and deer, and dominated wholly by buffalo, a species knowing no boundary but merely drifting north or south with the grasses, winds, and water.

Two distinctive oases further defined this beckoning land. In the east, due north of Fort Peck and some twenty miles beyond the border, lay the Wood Mountain uplands, a twenty-mile-long swath of hills, sheltering coulees, aspen and ash groves, springs, and good grazing, in all a dramatic feature rising distinctly above the surrounding prairie. One hundred miles to the west across rolling prairie lay an even more expansive landscape, the Cypress Hills, a sinewy one-hundred-mile-long, twenty-mile-wide upland rising nearly two thousand feet above the adjacent prairie. The Hills were heavily forested, including with desirable lodge pole pine, and rich with game. Native cultures had long flourished there, particularly embracing a wintertime haven. More recently, Whites likened the Cypress Hills to the Black Hills of Dakota, though without the feverish mining chaos of the south. Scoring the grasslands between was the Frenchman's River, the White Mud River to some, heading in the Cypress Hills and flowing eastward and then bending south near Pinto Horse Butte and draining into Montana and the Milk River. In the United States, the stream was and is still known as Frenchman's Creek. By volume, it resembled Rosebud Creek, south of the Yellowstone.[1]

One other critical attribute distinguished the lands of the north. Law enforcement was dramatically different. In the United States, Indians endured a mish-mash of laws and codes imposed on them that in many instances were different or even nonexistent in adjacent White culture. Matters of liquor, access to guns, and trespass on Indian lands always drew ire and never aligned with Indian perspectives. Moreover, enforcement in Indian country south of the border generally fell to the US army and civilian courts, where relations were sour and justice rare. The sordid invasion of the Black Hills was itself the most recent egregious manifestation. This disparity of US law and a free-for-all Wild West was borne in trespass, liquor, and guns. And so much of it played out on Indian land, until that land was summarily taken from them.[2]

On the Canadian frontier the North-West Mounted Police, established in 1873 and euphemistically referred to simply as the Red Coats for the scarlet jackets they commonly wore, functioned as the relative counterpart to the US army. But they embraced unique doctrines and methodologies that were distinctly Canadian. Sent west initially to address the influx of illicit American whiskey traders in the Cypress Hills, the force also confronted Indian affairs in the prairie country almost immediately. With Indians, the Red Coats benefitted enormously from the even-handed legacy of the mighty Hudson's Bay Company. Hudson's Bay had ministered a vast fur trading empire whose domain across the Canadian interior, called Rupert's Land, spanned those same prairielands until 1869. In that year the Canadian Confederation acquired Rupert's Land, which hence was recognized as a corner of the nation's North-West Territories.[3]

In the world of the fur trade, friendly relations with native peoples was of a critical value, and often achieved through intermarriage with native women. The emergence of the Métis, peoples of mixed native and European heritage, was one consequence of this self-serving alliance. Like their predecessors, the NWMP also stressed friendly relations with the natives, a necessity borne in part by the modest size of the Red Coat force, barely three hundred men, scattered across a vast area dotted with small stations throughout the western hinterlands. Two such stations were a post in the Cypress Hills due north of Fort Benton, Montana, and another in the Wood Mountain uplands, north of Fort Peck. From those stations the force achieved its ends with small patrols and an open dialog. The Red Coats confronted the US Sioux immediately after they crossed the Medicine Line and consistently served notice that the interlopers must obey Canadian law and not use the Territory to stage raids against the United States. Jeopardize that trust and they would lose their status as refugees and be removed. Remarkably, this simple, open, up-front strategy succeeded admirably.[4]

When Sitting Bull and his followers, some one hundred lodges, broke from Crazy Horse's camp in late January 1877, they were determined to go north. Sitting Bull had attempted one final time to consolidate the remaining traditionals in the Yellowstone country and continue the war but instead ran headlong into that camp's overwhelming desire to quit fighting and surrender. He then openly embraced an alternative vision of escaping the torment of Bear Coat Miles and his soldiers by fleeing to the north, an option that was not supported by those whose allegiances lay so decidedly in the south. The influential Hunkpapa struck for the north himself, crossing the Yellowstone at the mouth of the Powder and trailing ground from there that was all too familiar—the courses of Cedar Creek, Ash Creek, and Big Dry Creek, all scenes of confrontation in recent months, as he headed for Fort Peck.

Already elements of Sitting Bull's Hunkpapa coalition preceded him on much the same course. All had crossed the Medicine Line, including fifty-two lodges of his cousin Black Moon's people in December, fifty-seven lodges of Four Horns's followers in mid-March, and Gall's small band that crossed and immediately aligned with a Yanktonai camp in the Wood Mountain. For most of those Hunkpapas, the crossing was spiritual.

Among them was High Eagle, who recalled years later that "they told us that this line was considered holy." He added: "They called that a holy trail. They believed things are different when you cross from one side to another. You are altogether different. On one side you are perfectly free to do as you please. On the other you are in danger."[5]

Sitting Bull's Hunkpapas crossed the wide Missouri on March 17, gingerly picking their way over still frozen but soft ice and camping on the river's north side. It was nearing the dangerous time of the river's spring breakup, when in a split second the ice and waters would surge in a dramatic cacophony of release and sound. River rats knew to steer clear of the bottomlands in this precarious time, but Sitting Bull's people were caught unaware and pathetically trapped by a wall of water that swept their camp and destroyed many possessions. A bad omen perhaps, or, as likely, a statement of passing from a troubled land to a beckoning freedom.[6]

The Hunkpapas continued the trail north, following the Milk and then Frenchman's Creek. They crossed the Medicine Line on April 30 intent on finding his revered uncle Four Horns's camp. While still in the United States the resolute Sitting Bull wavered one last time, pondering at one evening council whether to stay and fight the White soldiers until *they* surrendered. The notion was almost delusional and the other chiefs were by then committed. They had had enough of war. Their future, they recognized, lay in the north. The Hunkpapas stayed their course and a week later Sitting Bull and his followers, now numbering 135 lodges and upward of nine hundred people, reached Pinto Horse Butte, a landmark aside Frenchman's River. It lay sixty miles north of the line and was in the midst of a Canadian prairie then in spectacular springtime bloom.[7]

Twice earlier and again now when bands of war-weary US Sioux reached Canada they were visited by a mounted police officer, usually traveling with two or three interpreters but otherwise alone. The officer confronted the refugees and made clear the conditions of their exile. The Red Coat was Inspector James M. Walsh, a dogged thirty-seven-year-old whom US acquaintances remembered as almost Custer-like in appearance, mannerism, and even dress. Unlike Custer, however, he brought to his mission an informed and sympathetic view of Indians. Most importantly, Walsh was renowned for keeping his word, and he would henceforth loom large in the affairs of these Lakotas, and Sitting Bull particularly. The Lakotas often referred to him as Long Lance because policemen with him when on parade commonly carried long lances tipped with red and white pennons. But Sitting Bull had his own unique name for Walsh, calling him the Lean Red Coat.[8]

In reporting his conferences to superiors, Walsh assured all that there was no quibbling over the stated conditions. The chiefs pledged that they sought only peace. The inspector at first was not so sure. Walsh was particularly struck by the battlefield bounty evident in the camps: Seventh Cavalry horses, US mules, cavalry accoutrements, and an array of fine weapons, including Winchesters. But he also noted the general dearth of ammunition. Some people were hunting buffalo with spears fabricated from their own camp knives; others were killing their horses for food. The chiefs asked for ammunition and Walsh, conscious of the sensitivity of providing these war-time exiles with munitions, issued permits for limited purchases but carefully cautioned them that this was for hunting purposes alone. Jean Louis Legaré, operator of a trading post near the Red Coat's own Wood Mountain station, was prepared to handle the business and rose to the occasion.[9]

An auspicious series of councils occurred almost within days of Sitting Bull having settled into camp at Pinto Horse Butte. The first occurred on the occasion of an appearance of a Catholic priest, Martin Marty, a zealous missionary from the Standing Rock Agency. Marty had traveled north with two interpreters, William Halsey from the Poplar River Agency, and John Howard from Bear Coat Miles's Tongue River Cantonment, plus eight Indian guides. He was here expressly to convince the Hunkpapas to return to their home country. Marty carried letters of introduction from the head of the Catholic Bureau of Indian Missions and the Commissioner of Indian Affairs, the latter having apprised him of the standard US surrender terms. Sitting Bull found the overture offensive. He easily remembered similar visits years earlier by Father Pierre De Smet in the days of treaty making. He had dismissed De Smet, too, but had taken a liking to the Jesuit. He viewed Father Marty as a "disguised Yankee," however, who had come to deceive. He bristled, moreover, at the prelate's interpreters, quietly telling a mounted police surgeon that were they south of the Medicine Line he would know what to do with them, but not here where such an action would have compromised his exile.[10]

Another council occurred the following day, this one joined by four mounted police officers. The force's assistant commissioner, Acheson G. Irvine, commander of the police detachment at Fort Macleod, west of the Cypress Hills, was eager to meet the famous Hunkpapa. With Walsh at his side, on June 1 the Red Coats, Abbot Marty, and the Hunkpapa chiefs again deliberated the priest's appeal. Sitting Bull, still plainly incensed at having been followed by the three Americans, again scoffed at Marty's overture, at one point turning to Irvine and asking: "Will the White Mother protect us if we remain here?" Irvine remembered that the Hunkpapas seemed greatly relieved when assured that they would be protected while on this side. Sitting Bull then issued a sharp retort to the prelate. "What would I return for? To have my horses and arms taken away? What have the Americans to give me? They have no lands. Once I was rich, plenty of money, but the Americans stole it all in the Black Hills. I have come to remain with the White Mother's children." Noisily, the assembled chiefs agreed. Not wishing for raised tempers, Walsh adjourned the meeting. Marty retired to Dakota the next day, flustered though still convinced of the righteousness of the American demands.[11]

Late that evening Sitting Bull joined Irvine in the officer's tent and told in a calm and deliberate manner of his many grievances against the United States. Irvine was completely taken with the chief, whom he remembered as "a man of somewhat short stature, but with a pleasant face, a mouth showing great determination, and a fine high forehead. When he smiled, which he often did, his face brightened up wonderfully." Sitting Bull was likewise calmed after having discovered for the first time White officials who seemed genuinely trustworthy and prepared to protect them. And the land was equally welcoming. Buffalo were plentiful on the prairie this season, and trader Legaré was patient and even-handed and almost always at their disposal. Then, too, friendly Santees and Yanktonais in the Wood Mountain were equally welcoming. Some had been with the chief at the Little Big Horn, an event all were coming to recognize as a defining moment in this painful war. Sitting Bull held a Sun Dance that summer in the Wood Mountain, near a Métis village, the event yet another semblance of normalcy. "They lived good," remembered Legaré. For the Hunkpapas and aligned US Sioux, crossing the Medicine Line was bringing tremendous satisfaction.[12]

Whatever the satisfaction enjoyed in the Lakota circles on Frenchman's River, a storm of another sort was brewing in Ottawa, Washington, and London at that same time. The Canadian government was plainly unable and unwilling to tolerate forever this influx of US asylum seekers, estimated that summer at nearly three thousand people. Canada managed native relations in the lands west of the Great Lakes quite differently than the Americans south of the border. Treaties existed in the north, too, insuring the Canadian government's access to the western lands. The nation had its own westering ambitions, including a national railroad, but accorded its native peoples large tracts of land, intentionally set aside to allow for a high degree of self-sufficiency, whether by farming or hunting, just as in the heady days of the fur trade. The Canadians added no overlaying structure of agencies, government administrators, or the provision of amenities like clothing and foodstuffs, although it provided varieties of financial inducements to those who signed. The US Indians had come to the lands of the Métis, Plains Cree, Plains Ojibwa, Assiniboine, Blackfoot, and others, all variously occupying the same crowning uplands, prairies, and watersheds discovered by the Sioux. They all hunted the same small game and buffalo that provided now that good life, as Legaré put it, enjoyed by the interlopers. But sheer proximity of natives and newcomers alone foreshadowed trouble ahead.[13]

Notwithstanding the simple kindnesses and understandings characterizing the labors of the Mounted Police, the Canadian government's efforts at handling the intruders were feeble. They offered no inducements to stay, had no outward capacity of their own to drive those Indians back onto US soil, and were concerned that US troops might cross the border and handle matters themselves. They held at the onset to the rather simple belief that the United States might soften the surrender terms, and that that alone would prompt the refugees to go back south. But one Canadian official candidly acknowledged the shallowness of this thinking and implored the US Government "to use their best endeavors to induce those Indians to return to their own country."[14]

William T. Sherman, commanding general of the American army, summarized his government's initial views of the matter in a letter forwarded by the Secretary of War to the Secretary of State and Great Britain's chargé d'affaires in Washington. Sherman acknowledged that the United States should meet the overtures of the Canadian authorities and arrive at some general understanding of the matter, but allowed as well that Miles stood ready to lead a sufficient force to the border and force that hand. Preferably, in Sherman's view, the English authorities should elect to adopt those refugee Indians as their own, but the general also worried that, if permitted to recuperate, Sitting Bull's people would use British soil as a base of operations against US interests. Before such matters got out of hand, Sherman suggested that the US Interior Department, in cooperation with Canadian authorities, send a commission to meet with the Indians and offer safe conduct to Fort Buford and the Missouri River agencies. This would still be regarded as a surrender, of course, and the Indians would still necessarily forfeit firearms and ponies. The notion of a commission, a timeless echo in American Indian relations, was quickly embraced.[15]

Word of a US commission passed quickly through Canadian channels, and authorities in Ottawa clarified their government's own desires on the matter. An official in the Canadian Department of State made clear that the commission's general purpose was to induce Sitting Bull's people to return to the United States, and advised Inspector James F. Macleod, commissioner of the North-West Mountain Police, to cooperate. But "do not duly press the Indians," he said. "Our action should be persuasive, not compulsory." Another Canadian official, fearing failure almost from the onset, worried that the United States would indeed demand access to the borderlands, but, "based upon the principles of international law, that foreign territory cannot be made the basis of hostile operations." Yet another official in the Canadian Department of the Interior feared that the United States would insist that Canada assume responsibility for these Indians, plus any reparations for injury or damages they might inflict in the United States or on its citizens. The handwringing was magnificent. Canadian authorities had pressed the issue to begin with, but were ill prepared to greatly help achieve a satisfactory outcome.[16]

Even while politicians in Washington and Ottawa grappled with the unpleasant prospects of this influx of US Sioux north of the border, another crisis in the United States threatened the Canadian calm. Some in the north were aware of the exodus of the Nez Perce Indians, people fleeing their own homeland in the Idaho-Oregon border country and making their way eastward through mountainous Montana and Yellowstone National Park, and hounded at every step by the US Army. The Nez Perces had apparently intended at the onset to simply join friends in the buffalo country, but of late had continued their flight north across the Yellowstone River and toward the Medicine Line. Bear Coat Miles's troops surrounded most of them forty-five miles short of the border in early October, but as many as fifty men, women, and children, some seriously wounded, escaped the cordon and reached Sitting Bull's Lakotas, some even straggling in while Walsh was present. The Sioux camp was outraged. Walsh had come to lure Sitting Bull to Fort Walsh to meet with American peace commissioners but was instead berated by the Sioux. "Why have you come to seek us to go and talk with men who are killing our own race? You can see these men, women, and children, wounded and bleeding. We cannot talk with men who have blood on their hands. They have stained the grass of the White Mother with it."[17]

—~—

The Sitting Bull Commission, organized in Saint Paul, traveled by rail westward through Omaha, Cheyenne, and Ogden, and by stage from Utah to Helena. The commissioners' journey was impeded at several points in northern Montana by the Nez Perce crisis then exploding across the heart of that territory. The somewhat ironic head of the new commission was General Alfred Terry of Saint Paul, a veteran of this Sioux war who was Bear Coat Miles's immediate superior and had been on the Custer field when those dead were buried. Joining Terry's small complement in Omaha were two newspaper correspondents—Jerome Stillson of the *New York Herald*, and Charles Diehl of the *Chicago Times*. Like George Wallihan of the *Cheyenne Daily Leader* and John Ford, also writing for the *Chicago Times*, in the Pine Ridge at the time of Crazy Horse's surrender, Stillson and Diehl were eager to interview the war's foremost protagonist, Sitting Bull. Yet a third reporter, John J. Healy of the *Fort Benton Record* joined the complement when passing through that riverside community. Particulars of Terry's mission were detailed in a directive from the Secretaries of War and Interior. Do what was possible, they implored, to induce the chief and his followers to return to the United States. Assure them that they would be pardoned for any acts of hostility committed during the war, but they must, of course, surrender arms and ammunition and all their horses and ponies.[18]

Inspector Macleod and a small detachment of pennon and lance toting red-coated mounted policemen awaited Terry at the border near the Kennedy Crossing of the Milk River on the afternoon of October 15. They took to the trail immediately, routing across the prairie and through the Cypress Hills to Fort Walsh, reaching the post the next day. A Union Jack fluttered above the small stockaded compound, its whitewashed outer walls and interior log buildings glistening in the late autumn sun. Though long-gone by Terry's time, the Hunkpapas present would have instantly remembered a parallel. Old Fort Union at the confluence of the Yellowstone and Missouri had been likewise a small, whitewashed trading post and a favorite from a decade past. Sibley tents were pitched on the fort's south side for the US commissioners. Sitting Bull's delegation of about twenty mostly Hunkpapas arrived several days before and were provided lodging and fed in one of the interior barracks. The chief, however, preferred to camp apart, outside, off the north wall along an adjacent stream known as Battle Creek, partly, some acknowledged, because he was in mourning over the loss of a nine-year-old son who died two weeks earlier. These Lakotas were reluctant participants in this or any meeting with US army officers, and present now only through the dogged intercessions of Long Lance Walsh and several trusted Métis interpreters at Wood Mountain. Most remembered too well the meetings with Bear Coat Miles on Cedar Creek a year earlier that ended with his outright attacking them.[19]

Preconference preparations involved convening three interpreters on the morning of October 17, including Baptiste Shane, representing the United States, Constant Provost, the official interpreter at Fort Walsh, and André Larivée, a Métis interpreter from Wood Mountain who was friendly to Sitting Bull and designated to represent his interests. Terry's address was read through and its meaning fully explained. That afternoon, Baptiste Shane would interpret and the others were to listen and ensure that what was said was accurate. Misinterpretation would not be a cause of failure.[20]

The conference convened that afternoon at 3:00 P.M. in Fort Walsh's officer's mess, an accommodating building adjacent to Walsh's quarters. It was a simple, functional space, ornamented chiefly by a Union Jack suspended on one wall, and set for the occasion with two long tables and a few scattered chairs. Terry's staff, the police officers, and the three newspapermen crowded the room, mostly lining several of its walls. The various scribes were seated at one of the tables. Macleod seated himself at the other. Forty-nine-year-old Terry, bearded, a Yale law school graduate and experienced litigator, and a veteran Indian affairs commissioner, seated himself in another of the chairs, this one positioned in front of the Macleod's table. Interpreters hovered at his sides. Lost but to history was the fact that Terry had been present at Fort Laramie in 1868 with another commission. That one had negotiated the close of a different war with the Sioux and laid the foundation in a grand treaty for a reservation, agencies, and the presumed assimilation of the Sioux people. These Northerners had roundly rejected all those terms from the outset.

Walsh escorted Sitting Bull and the other chiefs to the room. When they entered most likewise ushered themselves to walls opposite the uniformed blue coated and red coated *wasicus* and mostly seated themselves on the floor. The great chief, swaddled in a navy blue blanket, was shown a chair opposite Terry, but he slid it aside and instead spread a buffalo robe on the plank floor where he seated himself, filled his pipe, and commenced smoking. There was no pipe ceremony, a normal requirement before such auspicious occasions, but likely an intentional slight now. *New York Herald* correspondent Stillson thought Sitting Bull exuded a contemptuous attitude, as much suggesting to the US delegation that they could "go to the devil."[21]

The proceedings at the opening belonged to Terry, and he dished-up an oration that was, by now, exceedingly timeworn to these Indians. He solemnly extended the heartfelt wishes of the president for a lasting peace, and told the chief and others in the room that if they would return to their country the United States was fully willing to pardon them and all the Sioux for their past deeds. Yes, they would need to give up their arms and horses, but the animals would be sold and the proceeds used to purchase cattle, enabling them to take up the occupation of cattle breeding. Terry repeated himself several times, varying the reasonings slightly, and one time stressing the clothing and foodstuffs the people would receive when the wild game of the prairie had disappeared. The translations took time and he wanted what was said to be plainly understood. Doubtless his closing point was plainly understood also. They had no choice in this matter. "Should you attempt to return with arms in your hands you must be treated as enemies of the United States."[22]

Sitting Bull sat stone-faced throughout Terry's long oration, invariably maintaining eye contact but impenetrable, and always smoking. The others behind were equally stilled, although once, Stillson, recalled, "the right eye of Spotted Eagle actually winked derision toward Colonel Macleod." And they too continuously smoked. Finally, after an awkward-seeming pause, Sitting Bull rose and offered a blunt Lakota response.[23]

> For sixty-four years you have kept me and my people and treated us bad. What have we done that you should want us to stop? We have done nothing. It is all the people on your side that have started us to do all these depredations. We could not go anywhere else, and so we took refuge in this country. . . . I was born and raised in this country with the Red River half-breeds, and I intend to stay with them. . . . You have got ears, and you have got eyes to see with them, and you see how I live with these people. You see me? Here I am! If you think I am a fool you are a bigger fool than I am. This house is a medicine house. You come here to tell us lies, but we don't want to hear them. I don't wish any such language used to me; that is, to tell me such lies in my Great Mother's house. Don't you say two more words. Go back home where you came from. This country is mine and I intend to stay here.[24]

Once during his response, Sitting Bull paused and shook hands with the Canadian officers, and he did so again at the end. From time to time "*hau, hau*" from the Indians behind interrupted his comments and showed their perfect sympathy with what was said. The chief returned to his buffalo robe and several from behind stepped forward and offered remarks much like his, all defiant. Terry listened stoically. When all had spoken, the American delegation rose and prepared to leave the room, but the general interrupted, asking an interpreter to pose one more question. "Shall I say to the president that you refuse the offers that he has made to you? Are we to understand from what you have said that you refuse those offers?"[25]

A long pause followed. The chief looked at Macleod and Walsh, but they gave him no responsive sign. He looked toward the interpreters but they, too, were emotionless. Then he said: "I could tell you more, but that is all that I have to tell you. If we told you more, you would not pay any attention to it. That is all I have to say. This part of the country does not belong to your people. You belong on the other side. This side belongs to us."

Terry looked at Macleod and said: "I think we can have nothing more to say to them, Colonel."

Macleod replied: "Well, I suppose you are right."[26]

Terry turned on his heels and walked out. The conference had been ill-fated from the start, doomed by ten years of bloodletting and broken promises. In truth, the Americans were glad that these troublesome Lakotas had come to Canada and that they somehow were now swearing a resolve to live peaceably north of the Medicine Line. If in the south, their presence would only have obliged continued campaigning and bloodshed lasting until the government had achieved its intent of sweeping the buffalo country clean of roaming Indians. And there indeed was the crux. Stillson was right in his observation of Sitting Bull. The great chief was telling Terry and his government to "go to the devil."

But the Canadians had no wish for these Lakotas either, fearful of difficulties between their own natives and these interlopers, and a political imbroglio should they cross the border to raid or hunt. After the council adjourned, Macleod met separately with the chiefs and impressed upon them the importance of the decision they had just made. The Queen's government looked upon them as US Indians taking refuge from their enemies. Macleod reminded them that their only hope was the buffalo, and once that source of supply was gone they could expect nothing whatever from the Queen's government except protection as long as they behaved themselves. The warning was prescient. Macleod fully understood that buffalo ranged at will, simply following grass and water. To the beasts, boundaries were meaningless, and therein lay the potential for trouble. As well, he recognized the extraordinary pressures those animals faced as a critical food source for not only these interloping American Indians but for all of Canada's prairie natives. He reminded the chiefs that their decision not only affected themselves but also their children. They were unmoved. They trusted the Canadians and were content to stay.[27]

As the meeting closed, Charles Diehl of the *Chicago Times* cornered Walsh and asked if he could interview Sitting Bull. Walsh inquired and the chief at first said no, telling the inspector that he had no interest in talking with a reporter representing the United States. But Walsh persisted and his friend relented and welcomed into his lodge the reporter, an interpreter, and a stenographer. With Walsh looking on, Diehl, a deft interviewer, almost immediately sensed that the weight of recent days was released, if at least for the moment. Sitting Bull sat relaxed and conversed in a natural manner, looking at Diehl directly when speaking, smiling occasionally, and even laughing heartily. The newsman coaxed him into talking about family, his birthplace, his desire for peace, and his intent to stay in Canada. Naturally, Diehl pressed about the Custer fight, the subject most Americans wanted to read about. Sitting Bull added nothing new to that story. He was asleep in his tipi when the attack began, and he saw very little of the fight itself. Mostly, he knew only what others had told him. Those few questions seemed enough, but Diehl asked whether he could talk with him again after he returned to the Wood Mountain. The chief, seemingly aware that he had given the reporter his moment, coyly replied that he, Diehl, had come with Terry and company and could return with them.[28]

Jerome Stillson also cornered Walsh about interviewing the chief, and the inspector arranged a private gathering that evening in the reporter's quarters. Present with the inspector were two interpreters and a stenographer. Stillson was at first struck by the chief's visage, upright, loose black hair hanging freely, a simple calico shirt and cloth leggings, and moccasins, magnificently beaded and quilled. He removed a fox skin cap when he entered the room, "with the dignity and grace of a natural gentleman." The two shook hands. Stillson turned first to one of the interpreters. "Explain again to Sitting Bull that he is with a friend." The chief smiled and shook the reporter's hand again. The ensuing conversation lasted about an hour. As with Diehl, here the two ranged through the chief's background, his long enmity with the United States, and his contentment now with the Great Mother. "Do you expect to live here by hunting," Stillson posed? "Are there buffaloes enough?" The chief was candid. "I don't know; I hope so."[29]

Stillson grasped the importance of buffalo. "How long do you think the buffaloes will last," he pressed? "We know that on the other side the buffaloes will not last very long," Sitting Bull replied. "We kill buffaloes, as we kill other animals, for food and clothing and to make our lodges warm. Your young men shoot for pleasure. All they take from a dead buffalo is his tail, or his head, or his horns. You call us savages. What are they?"

Sitting Bull was at his best when telling of the Custer battle, softened perhaps by Diehl's probings that afternoon. With little evident prompting he described the early moments of the attack, and the second attack, meaning when Custer struck. "The village by this time was thoroughly aroused," he explained. "The squaws were like flying birds; the bullets were like humming bees. Our young men rained lead across the river and drove the White braves back. . . . Your people were killed. I tell no lies about dead men. These men who came with the Long Hair were as good men as ever fought." Stillson pushed the chief. "How long did this big fight continue?" But Walsh interrupted, "You cannot certainly depend upon Sitting Bull's or any other Indian's statement in regard to time or numbers." The chief answered simply: "The sun was there," pointing to within two hours from the western horizon. By now he plainly had had enough. He rose, wrapped himself in his blanket, shook Stillson's hand, placed his fox skin cap upon his head, and stepped into the night.[30]

Something remarkable had occurred. The Diehl and Stillson interviews, first published in their respective Chicago and New York City newspapers, were reprinted widely. Each reporter had succeeded in introducing to local and then national audiences a man with a personality, a man also with background and a family, and one who was a leader with a clear vision for his people. They had successfully humanized a traditional who before this was but a scorned, faceless enemy. His cause was still not wholly understood or embraced and never would be, and he was still foreseen as a potential borderlands threat, but he no longer was a shadowless unknown. And while the visage was fresh, Stillson sketched a portrait of the chief, his hair hanging loose, the fox skin cap upon his head. A month later the image graced the cover page of *Harper's Weekly*, one of the nation's illustrated newspapers. It was and is a striking likeness of a humble, holy one, and the first ever to appear in public print.[31]

Sitting Bull and fellow chiefs embarked for their camps at Pinto Horse Butte on the morning of October 18, accompanied by Inspector Walsh. All were glad for the simple conclusion of a contentious meeting. While the US delegation and Canadians immediately reported that little had been accomplished at Fort Walsh, plainly the chief had stood his ground, affirming his resolve to remain north of the Medicine Line now and perhaps forever. And yet even while the camps of US Sioux settled in for a rugged northern plains winter, forces beyond them brought continued disruptions to their circles.[32]

The arrival of a handful of Nez Perce refugees from the Bear's Paw engagement below the Medicine Line had perplexed Sitting Bull before setting off with Walsh to meet with the US commissioners. Their plight angered him and doubtless sharpened his temperament when confronting Terry and suffering his sanctimonious pleadings for peace. When he returned he discovered that as many as one hundred forlorn Nez Perce stragglers, largely under their chiefs White Bird and Yellow Wolf, had settled into his camp. The chief was customarily cordial. "You can stay with us here as long as you please," he told them. "The red coats say that as long as we obey their law, we can stay. All I want is to be at peace." The refugees were feasted, the many wounded carefully treated, and all easily fell into the simple routines of camp life. "The Sioux were having a good time," one of them remembered, "and we joined in."[33]

Many of the Nez Perces remained in the Sioux camp in the coming years. One married a Sioux woman. Another, an odd, compelling figure in his own unique way, was an individual named Cut Off or No Feet or Steps. Steps was likely in his early thirties, probably a Yakama and aligned now by way of contact with the Bannock-Shoshones. It was not his bloodline that drew attention, however, but the fact that when in his teens both feet and his right hand were horribly frozen and he hobbled now on his knees. But when mounted, Steps was also an exceptional rider who possessed a unique ability to communicate with horses—in another day one might call him a horse whisperer. He easily caught Sitting Bull's attention, and the chief, with his own innate ability to recognize and embrace forlorn ones, welcomed him into his personal household as his family's herder, providing his newfound wrangler with his own lodge and a young Hunkpapa woman to care for it, and him. Steps remained with the Hunkpapas forevermore, is seen in numerous later photographs with the chief, and died on Oak Creek on the Standing Rock Reservation in 1903.[34]

Bedraggled Nez Perces were not the only war-weary, deceit-frazzled Indians embracing the belief that Sitting Bull and Canada were a last hope for independence in the buffalo country. In the Pine Ridge in the days surrounding the killing of Crazy Horse, Lame Deer's long-hunted coalition of mostly Miniconjous surrendered at Spotted Tail Agency, some seventy-five people appearing on September 4 and another 250 on September 11. Since their clash with Miles on Muddy Creek on May 7, those holdouts, led principally after Lame Deer's death by Fast Bull, one of his sons, had eluded the US troops flooding the northern buffalo range throughout the summer. But the murder of Crazy Horse weighed heavily upon these new arrivals, and on the night of September 23 Fast Bull led forty lodges—some 192 people—northward again, this time boldly declaring the intent to take refuge with Sitting Bull.[35]

The Lame Deer coalition was not the only distraught body of Pine Ridge people embracing Canada as a possible haven. That fall the government formally denied the long hoped-for agency in the buffalo country even while successfully inducing the relocation of the two Nebraska agencies from the Pine Ridge to the Missouri River in Dakota and failing to grasp or accept the reluctance of those Oglalas and Brulés, people of the old Buffalo South, to move that far to the east. When meeting with the president in

September the chiefs succeeded in gaining yet another concession, a move somewhere else on the White in the coming spring. But in the meantime, supplies had already been stockpiled on the Missouri and an interim move to the river was obliged. In due course, in October the western *oyates* were forcibly trailed eastward out of Nebraska, with the Brulés eventually reaching the old Ponca Agency on Ponca Creek just below Fort Randall (the Poncas themselves having been relocated to the Indian Territory earlier that year), and the Oglalas trailing the White but stopping well short of the Missouri. Along the way small bands broke free from both caravans and consolidated in what eventually resembled a Northerners camp of old at the forks of the Cheyenne River, joining there many of Crazy Horse's followers who likewise had trailed off after the chief's death. Their intent at the moment was not a flight to Canada but merely stepping beyond the immediate grasp of agency officials.[36]

In daily councils, the allied Pine Ridge refugees, Oglalas and Miniconjous mostly, concluded to flee to Canada, one among them telling government agents that "they belong to the North and not to either Spotted Tail or Red Cloud Agency." Skunk Horse, an Oglala in Big Road's band, interviewed several years later, put the matter in pragmatic terms. "Our band concluded that they did not wish to eat beef anymore, but would prefer to go north, live in a big country, hunt buffalo and be free to do as we pleased." Big Road had been away when that consensus was reached. He had been one of the Washington delegates who actually spoke with and shook the Great Father's hand. When he returned, he pleaded with his followers to turn back, but they were firm. Instead of resisting, Big Road joined the flight. Young Black Elk remembered that "we traveled fast and soldiers did not follow us." The refugees trailed northward in two separate parties, skirting the Slim Buttes, safely crossing the Yellowstone and Missouri rivers, and eventually following Frenchman's Creek straight to the Medicine Line and to Sitting Bull's people. Reports of raiding in the northern Black Hills country and Yellowstone Valley circulated among military authorities, but conscious haste and inclement weather made troop sorties inconsequential.[37]

In Canada, Big Road emerged as the most influential leader of the exiled southern people, amidst such other notables as He Dog, Red Bear, Low Dog, and Little Hawk. By the spring of 1878 some 200 lodges of Pine Ridge people had aligned with Sitting Bull, whose own immediate coalition then numbered some 109 lodges, bringing the tally of recent refugees to just short of two thousand people, about half the size of the great Sun Dance camp of early June 1876. Not far off were 150 lodges of Canadian Santee Sioux led by White Eagle, refugees of another day who were now well-settled in the Wood Mountain uplands. And buried within that camp were Inkpaduta and his small lot of followers, survivors in their own way of a second American Indian war.[38]

The exiled Lakotas found their first winter in Grandmother's Land appealing. For the first time they were beyond the reach of the hated blue coats. Some still worried that US soldiers might cross the border and attack them, but the Red Coats calmed them. That could not happen, Walsh and others assured, and if it did the Red Coats would protect them. And while the weather was rugged in the prairie country along Frenchman's River, the essentials—buffalo, wood, water, access to trade—were at hand. "Our relatives . . . took care of us," Black Elk remembered. "They had made plenty of meat, for there were many buffalo in that country, and it was a good winter."[39]

Appealing too were the long-standing relationships the Lakotas enjoyed with the Métis, people whose services as facilitators, interpreters, and important trading partners were invaluable during this unique sojourn in Canada. One trader in particular, Jean Louis Legaré, had operated a thriving trading post in the Wood Mountain country since 1871. The tall, bearded mixed-blood had a gentle, courteous mien and cultivated these Lakotas, who quickly saw that he was a man of fair play. Some knew him already from the days of the borderland surveys, and he and the chief particularly developed a sympathetic and productive rapport. From Legaré, especially now, came the munitions Walsh authorized and that were much needed to hunt the buffalo that sustained the people, with buffalo robes again the natural denominator of trade.[40]

But even in this apparent calm occasional ominous signs were noted. In late November the US commanding officer at Fort Shaw, located between Fort Benton and Helena, reported that "large parties of Sioux from across the line" were hunting buffalo in the Sweet Grass Hills southwest of the Cypress Hills, and the Piegan Indians in that locale were frightened away from their natural hunting grounds. Those intruders may or may not have been newly arrived US Sioux, but such reports soon became commonplace and affirmed several borderland realities: buffalo paid no heed to the stone heaps, and intertribal conflicts were rife and endlessly explosive.[41]

In this unique period when hundreds of US Sioux were flocking to Sitting Bull's camp, it also became apparent, at least to some, that this otherwise seemingly becalmed spiritual one had not surrendered all hope for regaining his traditional Lakota homeland and a lifeway in the familiar Buffalo North. In fact, perhaps an opportunity was presenting itself to renew this war with the United States. The new arrivals had stories to tell of the fervor in the south. Some recounted the death of Lame Deer and the incessant hounding suffered by those survivors since then. Those from the Pine Ridge shared stories of promises made and betrayed, including the commitments to allow them to hunt buffalo and to have a northern agency. From Pine Ridge they also heard of the forced uprooting now of the Oglalas and Brulés from home country and their being forced toward the Missouri. Topping all, of course, was the most egregious twist yet, the outright killing of Crazy Horse, a revered, tradition-bound ally, the great chief's alter-ego in this war. One in the camps, Eagle Elk, among the few Oglalas accompanying Sitting Bull when he first went north, remembered that "bad stories came to us that summer, and just before winter we heard that the *wasicus* had murdered Crazy Horse at the Soldier's Town. We did not go home."[42]

Quietly, Sitting Bull momentarily renewed his call for others to join him, dispatching couriers to the south with news and encouragement. There were plenty of buffalo and game in the British Possessions, the couriers told, and already seven different Indian nations had joined the chief's camp. Small bands of Assiniboines and Yanktonais were also joining. While such words, in truth, were greatly overdrawn, Sitting Bull's avowed intention, they insisted, was to lead this coalition south in the middle of winter and make war on the United States.[43]

Word of Sitting Bull's invitation not only circulated among agency people but also among the borderlands people, Americans *and* Canadians, and while an edginess tempered relations that winter so did countering news that spread equally quick and wide. Inspector Walsh visited with Colonel John Gibbon at Fort Shaw in late January 1878. He had just come from Sitting Bull's camp and gained from him assurances that neither he nor any of his people had any idea of coming south of the line. Inspector A. G. Irvine of the mounted police likewise quickly passed word through Canadian channels of having recently visited the chief's camp, and learned that there was no foundation whatsoever for rumors that Assiniboines and Yanktonais were joining him or that he intended to move south. In truth, a reality had settled across the Indian camps north of the Medicine Line. The buffalo country of old was indeed lost. The Black Hills were lost. *Wasicus* controlled the rivers. New army forts dotted the buffalo range and more were foretold. In the United States, an existence on the Great Sioux Reservation was a central fact of life now for all Lakotas, save these in Canada.[44]

An interloper in this period of seeming calm provided an interesting perspective on the chief's thinking. Father Jean Baptiste Marie Genin, a Catholic priest long active in mission work in northern Minnesota and Dakota who in an earlier day had frequented Hunkpapa camps on the Missouri, spent twenty-five days that fall proselytizing among the Plains Indians in Canada. Where Father Martin Marty's intercessions six months earlier were expressly intent on convincing the Hunkpapas to submit at their agency, Genin's simple ambitions were baptizing and preaching the bible. (Whites also suspected him of trafficking in munitions, charges which were disproved.) He was fluent in the Dakota language, and at an appropriate moment he expressly sought out the chief. Sitting Bull, perhaps remembering those contacts from long ago, was receptive. The two smoked together and talked at length, in part even about the Custer battle and considerably on the glowing prospects of the Grandmother's Land.

Sitting Bull admitted to being particularly harsh with Father Marty on the occasion of that visit, thinking that he was a disguised Yankee there only to deceive him. As their conversation drew to a close, Sitting Bull spoke openly of his hopes for the future.[45]

> My brother, Black Gown, when you go back to my lands in Dakota, the White people will ask you what Sitting Bull says, and what he means to do. Please tell them that I want none of their gold or silver, none of their goods, but that I desire to come back and live upon my lands; for there is plenty of game and grass, and we can live well if they will only let us alone. As to my going to war again they need not be troubled, for I never fight except when I cannot avoid it.[46]

Winter count keepers documented several key episodes that recall a traumatic year, 1877. Many in the Pine Ridge country, Oglalas and Brulés mostly but also the Miniconjous residing there, commonly remembered this as the year when Crazy Horse was killed. Their glyphs were sometimes striking. Oglala chief American Horse's winter count, for instance, showed an army rifle fixed with a long bayonet on its end and penetrating the great war chief. Cloud Shield, another Oglala, uniquely remembered this as the year when Crazy Horse's band fled the agency and went north.[47] But Northern Lakotas more commonly remembered this as the year when Sitting Bull made an agreement with the Red Coats at Fort Walsh, ensuring their ability to stay safely north of the Medicine Line. At year's end, the flight to Canada was proving itself a glowing triumph after years of struggle. It all seemed so wholly righteous.[48]

16
THE STARVING YEARS

"I cannot help but like it, if they are going to treat us this way."
—Old Bull, Hunkpapa Lakota

War never returned to the Lakotas, scattered that winter of 1877–78 from Pinto Horse Butte to the Wood Mountain uplands, and when the cold season gave way to spring a sense of the old ways seemed largely intact. Life as always centered on buffalo, and the herds seemed yet substantial. The people were soon in motion, family groups and bands scattering across the prairielands north of the Medicine Line, some even venturing to the grasslands north and west of the Cypress Hills, and others hovering dangerously close to the border, and even momentarily crossing beyond the stone heaps.

Hunting put the Lakotas in steady contact with Canadian natives, and that itself brought a certain unease to life and its routines. But such was daily existence throughout the lands of the buffalo. The herds of the Big Open and Powder River country in United States were similarly preyed upon by various groups of people, some friendly, some not friendly at all. Canadian authorities fretted provincially, of course, since these Lakota interlopers were hunting Canadian animals, the primary food source for their own native peoples. While more northerly herds existed in Canada, the animals under the greatest pressures now were those that paid no heed to the stone heaps and roamed freely from the Canadian prairies to the Milk River, a cross-border meander mirrored by the native peoples of the north and south who hunted them. The real issue increasingly focused on how long those buffaloes could last.[1]

—∿∿—

The Lakota people north and south of the Medicine Line were plainly aware of the many forces intent on killing buffalo. All knew of the mindless slaughter of buffaloes occurring throughout the United States' Buffalo South, and some had even witnessed it, triggered as it was by the influx of railroads and White hunters seemingly intent solely on taking tongues and hides. Some among them acknowledged similar forces poised to strike the animals of the Buffalo North. They may not have acknowledged or understood that their own hunting demands contributed to this fateful demise. Since the coming of the fur traders, their own seasonal take had well exceeded that needed for daily consumption, and this in a world where buffalo robes—tanned skins—were money, a point evident even now in the free trade occurring at Legaré's post. The Hunkpapas, moreover, commonly stepped through the crushed-bone detritus scoring countless Métis hunting camps dotting the entire Upper Missouri country. Those people were "market hunters," taking skins and crushing bones to render fats. When seen on an even larger scale, with a world-wide demand for buffalo hides—untanned skins—that were now being commercially tanned and fashioned into clothing, lap robes, and industrial leathers, one was witnessing the unconscionable destruction of a core North American animal species.

But that mass slaughter, while looming, had not yet reached the far northern plains, where steamboats plied navigable waters but as yet no railroad crossed the land, and agents still reported, as did Fort Buford's commanding officer in January 1878, that "the whole country" north and west of Wolf Point "is full of buffalo." But how full? The well-traveled

Inspector Walsh, for one, understood this native dependency on those animals, but also plainly witnessed the intense robe trade at hand, evident in the trading houses at Fort Benton, and north of the border in the realm of Forts Macleod and Walsh and in the Wood Mountain. At one point he even dared to admonish Sitting Bull not to kill buffaloes less than one year of age. The chief scoffed. "Who gave you this land and all the buffalo in it? You have not as much right here as we have, and the Americans put all these mischief making laws in your head. I will cross the line and kill what I like." Walsh, it seems, was an ironic voice for buffalo reproductive and self-sustaining health, at a time when most of the world did not care.[2]

Simple routines, a traditional Sun Dance and cycles of hunting, marked the Lakota's first year in British America. And so did a general calm. In midsummer 1878 MacLeod at Fort Walsh was visited by Whirlwind Bear, one of the Oglala chiefs with Sitting Bull at the time of the Commission, who came solely, the inspector believed, to express his satisfaction with the protection afforded his people since crossing the border. Macleod was gratified. The Red Coats had indeed been paying close heed to the Lakotas, Macleod having gone so far as to place a trusted informant in their camps, charging him with reporting from time to time their locations and temperament. A short while later Macleod wrote again, providing his government with a clear sense of the general sprawl of US Sioux on British soil. Sitting Bull with eighty lodges was noted at Pinto Horse Butte. Black Moon with 200 lodges was on Frenchman's River just downstream. Two hundred and fifty lodges of Miniconjous were moving toward Old Wives' Lake, north of Wood Mountain, while Spotted Eagle, the dynamic Sans Arc chief with fifty lodges, was then headed from Old Wives' Lake toward Pinto Horse Butte, intent on linking with Sitting Bull. Separately, A. G. Irvine at Fort Macleod reported a camp of two hundred lodges of Crazy Horse's people north of that post west of the Cypress Hills. Both agents also acknowledged other Indians in those same margins, Plains Cree, Santee Sioux, Assiniboine, Blackfoot, Yanktonai, Nez Perce, and Métis, all somehow peaceably crowding an utterly unique prairieland in a truly distinctive summer. But sadly, it was nearly all an illusion.[3]

The Frenchman's River buffalo herd was a simple extension, a northerly finger of sorts, of the once sprawling mass of animals filling the Buffalo North. Never itself particularly large and always heavily hunted, the herd's instinctive meander that late summer led them easterly, with hunters close behind. Inspector Irvine reported in August that the robust herd seen that spring was now apparently thick in the Wood Mountain countryside east of the prairie, with Sitting Bull, Spotted Eagle, and three hundred lodges of US Sioux moving in that direction too, and Oglalas from the Cypress Hills not far behind.

And then the unimaginable happened. In November, Inspector Irvine reported to Ottawa that the buffalo north of the line had all but disappeared. Informants told of an almost immediate unsettlement in the Lakota camps and that some were considering following the buffalo south into Montana. "The women are urging the men to cross and save their children from starving," Irvine wrote. Walsh, at the Wood Mountain Post, purposefully challenged those chiefs in his proximity and mostly gained assurances that the Hunkpapas, Oglalas, and Sans Arcs had no intention of moving south of the line. But Sitting Bull, for one, confessed that in order to feed his children he had indeed crossed the line in search of meat. Ever the spiritualist, Sitting Bull also allowed that "he was certain the Great Spirit would pity them and send the buffalo into the White Mother's country." Any movement across the line, no less for the sake of the children, was audacious and dangerous. In this long story of unwanted war and a people clinging to yesterday, buffalo remained central to their everyday functional and spiritual lives. And hunger was again proving itself the ultimate driving force.[4]

The American Sioux were trapped in an improbable political nightmare. In this apparent buffalo vacuum, the refugees for the most part clung faithfully to the British side of the line, even when learning of and sometimes watching Canadian Indians trail the herds south of the stone heaps. For the British natives, hunting of the sort was a natural course.

For the Lakotas, that prospect was fraught with danger. They knew that US troops monitored the line, adding to the jeopardy of quiet incursions. Indeed, Bear Coat Miles at his Tongue River Post, now the newly christened Fort Keogh, and a counterpart, John Brooke, commander of the newly established Fort Assinniboine west of the Bear's Paw Mountains, were both paying careful heed to this borderland traffic. Miles, in fact, had quietly beseeched Sherman, commanding general of the US army, for consent "to advance north to the British line, drive back Sitting Bull & Co., and if necessary follow them across the border." Sherman quickly cut Miles short. Both northern commanders were clearly instructed to distinguish the hunters and give British Indians the way. This was no time for aggression, Sherman scowled.[5]

The cold season exasperated circumstances all the more. Winters across the northern borderlands are notoriously long and difficult, with snows and bitter temperatures typically arriving in September and lasting through March. "That was a very cold winter," Young Black Elk, an Oglala, remembered. "There were many blizzards, game was hard to find, and afterwhile the papa (dried meat) that we had made in the summer was all eaten. It looked as though we might starve to death if we did not find some game soon. Everybody was downhearted." The brutal winter was particularly difficult for the people from the south. They knew cold and snow, too, but conditions in the Pine Ridge country and throughout the central plains were rarely as severe and prolonged as they were experiencing now in Canada.[6]

The food crisis turned all the more exasperating and further strained the political order as spring turned to summer 1879. Inspector Macleod summarized the predicament succinctly. "The Sioux invasion and their continued residence in our territory have entirely changed the Indian situation," he observed, "and completely upset the calculations upon which the different treaties were based, viz., that the Indians could subsist on buffalo until they became self-supporting." The Canadian government's tolerance for the Lakotas and their followers, reluctant always but permissive, was eroding. US authorities grumbled, too, observing that British Indians and some of Sitting Bull's people, in fact, were coming south to hunt. Fort Peck Indians complained that the Sioux were scattering the buffalo and running off other game and stealing horses. US agents wanted the interlopers restrained north of the line. Buffalo remained the key. One Canadian chronicler put the matter almost poetically. "Robins, ducks and wild flowers came in their own good time in 1879 but the buffalo herds did not." That summer remnants of the Canadian herd roamed the Milk River drainage and Little Rocky and Bear's Paw countryside well south of the Medicine Line. The herd never returned. [7]

Hunger also softened attitudes, at least momentarily. Two well-known Cheyenne River Indians, Black Wolf, an Oglala married to a Miniconjou woman and living among her people, and Fox, a Miniconjou, among those who had fled the agency at the height of the war, returned in January. They told of the sizeable camps of aligned refugees, representing nearly all the Lakota *oyates*, and of recent councils among the head men. One council was so large, in fact, that a special lodge was needed. On that occasion, Sitting Bull, Black Shield, Spotted Eagle, and Big Road were principal speakers, and each embraced favorably the prospect of quitting the war and returning to their country. Black Wolf thought the speeches were well received by the onlookers. Sitting Bull and the counsellors furthermore agreed to send runners to the different agencies to tell of this desire for peace and learn of the terms that would be imposed when coming in. Thirteen runners were selected. Sitting Bull's last words to Black Wolf were heartfelt. "I believe you will have a great difficulty in making the officers believe in your good intentions, but act like a man and then they may believe you." [8]

Struggling through the snow and cold, the couriers paused at Fort Peck and then Wolf Point, where one of their number remained. The others continued through the Big Open, across the Yellowstone, and separated at the Slim Buttes, with two bound for Standing Rock, eight for Spotted Tail and Red Cloud. Black Wolf and Fox headed for Cheyenne River. At each of the agencies, the runners told of this desire to return. They all acknowledged that there was no game in British America, and the people were suffering for want of food. Word of this moderated, almost imploring tone, passed from local agents to the civil and military hierarchies in Washington, where the government's response was quick, and not only disappointingly inflexible but also seemingly spiteful. Old War Horse Sheridan in Chicago set the tone, demanding the surrender of guns, ammunition, and ponies, but also vindictively proclaiming that "steps should be taken to arrest the runners who occasionally come in. In most cases they are spies or messengers sent to find out what is going on and breeders of disinformation." In course, agents at Cheyenne River conveyed this response to Black Wolf and Fox and both quietly slipped away on the night of February 15, bound, it was supposed, for Sitting Bull's camp.[9]

Word of this American inflexibility merely roused further anxiety and anger, and Sitting Bull, for one, was enraged. On March 23 he led members of his own family and most of the chiefs of the Hunkpapas and Miniconjous to Inspector Walsh's quarters at Wood Mountain Post, where he vented, and revealed his soul.

> I have but one heart and it is the same today as when I first shook your hand, what I wish to say to the White Mother is, that when I first entered her country, I told you that my heart was pale and how my people had been persecuted by the Americans, and that I come to the White Mother's country to sleep sound and ask her to have pity [on] me—that I would never again shake the hand of an American.
>
> I am looking to the north for my life, and hope the White Mother will never ask [me] to look to the country I left, although mine, and not even the dust of it did I sell, but the Americans can have it.
>
> Those who wish to return to the Americans can go, and those who wish to remain here, if the White Mother wishes to give them a piece of land, can farm, but I will remain what I am until I die, a hunter, and when there are no more buffalo or game, I will send my children to hunt and live on prairie mice.[10]

The utterance was profound, and Walsh was deeply moved. But he was also beset by Ottawa to bring a closure to this ongoing crisis. The Canadians were growing increasingly intolerant of these refugees and had no intention of providing land or any other inducement to stay. Walsh understood this but also recognized that he was nearly the only government agent on either side of the line that the chief trusted, and his response now was necessarily guarded. He agreed with the chief that there was no country superior to the Cypress Hills region, but told him and the others that they would have an easier time on the US reservation where they would be supplied with seeds and tools and taught how to farm. Walsh also spoke frankly about the wild game. It was getting scarce, not only in Canada but in Montana. The railroads were coming—the Northern Pacific line had already reached Sitting Bull's beloved Little Missouri badlands—and trains would bring more settlers, and if the Sioux dared to cross the border to hunt or make war they would be chased down.[11]

Walsh heard one conciliatory note from Sitting Bull at their meeting. If any of those with him wished to return to the United States they would be free to do so. In the border country small bands from the Sitting Bull alliance were indeed crossing, not merely to hunt, but some inquiring about submitting. At the Fort Peck Agency at Poplar River, the local agent was confused by this and pressed his superiors. The bands were asking, he noted, whether the Sitting Bull Indians would be received at that agency, and rations issued to them just as to the agency Indians? The agent trusted their sincerity and was positive that if they were tended they would remain and live peaceably. At the same time border crossings to hunt were increasing. That same agent in June reported that Sitting Bull Indians were now roaming across the reservation and on both sides of the Missouri, hunting buffalo. He felt threatened and sought protection, despite assertions earlier from Spotted Eagle and others that the crossings were merely to hunt, not commit depredations, for Walsh and others had warned them of repercussions if such transgressions persisted.[12]

The borderlands were indeed overrun. Despite pleadings from those like Skunk Horse, an Oglala in Big Road's band, who asserted that "we came over there to hunt buffalo, did not intend to fight, did not wish to fight," the incursions drew Miles to the Medicine Line. And this time, he was fully encouraged by his superiors. "Drive the hostile Sioux over the line," one directive admonished. Ever the dutiful operative, Bear Coat Miles assembled columns of blue coats from his own Fort Keogh and from the new Fort Custer, located at the mouth of the Little Big Horn River, only fifteen miles from the Custer battlefield. He led them to the Milk River and to Frenchman's Creek, intent on stemming the open traffic occurring there.[13]

On July 17 a few miles north of the Milk River on Frenchman's Creek soldiers from Miles's column encountered hunters. Presuming them to belong to Sitting Bull's camp, the soldiers gave chase. The drainage was a rugged badlands ideal for buffalo. The soldiers and their scouts far outnumbered the hunters, Red Hawk, an Oglala, later recalled. Red Hawk also confirmed that Sitting Bull was present and had particularly ensured the safe flight of the women and children. Casualties were few during the chase, and most of the Indians slipped beyond the border. Miles's scouts reported that the main Indian camp was just north of the stone heaps on Little Rocky Creek, almost within sight. Miles knew not to cross the line. Terry had been admonished by the president and secretary of war to ensure that that did not occur. Their caution had been conveyed westward by telegraph. The episode, loosely dubbed the Milk River or Beaver Creek fight, amounted to the final armed exchange of Sitting Bull's War, occurring fully four years after the first bloodshed at Powder River.[14]

Miles continued to the border and camped just south of the stone heaps. A newsman with the column remembered the border's simplicity, "a rude heap of stones, with a small trench dug around it, which we knew to be 'the line' because three other structures of similar appearance were visible, a couple of miles apart, on a direct line east and west." Several days later Major Walsh visited Bear Coat. He had been alerted by his government of the soldiers' sortie and had his own vested interest both in the sanctity of the line and his friend, Sitting Bull.[15]

Unlike Miles, Walsh was not restrained from crossing into the United States. The two exchanged cordialities. The newsman admired Walsh, eying "a right pleasant man, with a strong love for Sitting Bull and his Sioux tribe." On the occasion the inspector was dressed not in his distinctive red coat but in a buckskin suit. The two officers were a year apart in age, Walsh thirty-nine and Miles forty, and although not quite equals in respective rank and service, and no way alike in temperament, their demeanors that day suggested otherwise. Both officers declared their interests. Miles was plainly intent on driving the Indian hunters over the line. Walsh told of his own orders to notify his government of any hostile proceedings on the part of the Sioux, but confessed that he did not know whether hunting buffalo could be called a hostile act or not. "The people were hungry," he declared matter-of-factly. Miles allowed that he had orders to obey. They talked about the murders occurring along the Yellowstone that were being blamed on these Sioux, and the seeming free trade of ammunition benefiting these Indians. Walsh brushed off the matter of depredations, declaring simply that if somehow they involved these Sioux and not Yanktonais, Gros Ventres, or others, the matter should be taken up with the Dominion government. And he explained that any ammunition sales occurring in Canada were for hunting purposes only. Despite simple differences, most of the exchange was good natured and productive.[16]

The newsman covering this campaign with Miles was John Finerty of the *Chicago Times*. Finerty was a veteran of this Sioux War, having been in the field three years earlier with Crook at the Rosebud and Slim Buttes. Like Stillson and Diehl before him, he recognized a unique opportunity to interview Sitting Bull in person. Eyeing a moment, he sought Walsh's intercession. Nearly two years had elapsed since Stillson and Diehl had succeeded in meeting the chief at Fort Walsh. Circumstances had changed and here again was an opportunity to talk face-to-face with the war's most intriguing, near mythic figure. Walsh consented and told Finerty that he would return in several days and take him to Sitting Bull's camp. When he returned, Walsh was accompanied by Long Dog, one of the chief's favorite lieutenants who was along merely as a becalmed representative of the refugees. When Long Dog was asked which side of the line he preferred to live on, he looked at Walsh and replied simply: "We intend to remain with him."[17]

Finerty's account of the journey across the border to meet Sitting Bull was a colorful travelogue. He described touring through one of the finest grasslands he said he had ever seen, and then through the Wood Mountain countryside, which amounted, he thought, to ample well-watered, gentle bluffs. Finally, he reached a cluster of rude wooden structures in the western periphery occupied by Walsh's police contingent and Legaré. Traces of Sitting Bull's camp ran northward from there almost as far as the Chicagoan could see.[18]

What awaited Finerty on the morrow was an eye-opener. He confessed believing when leaving the US side that the numbers of Indians in Canada had been greatly exaggerated, and he said as much to Walsh. "Very well," Walsh replied. "You shall soon see for yourself." After traveling a short distance beyond the police and trader outpost, he crested a hill to see an American Indian camp stretching almost endlessly before him. A slow throb from a buffalo-hide drum pierced the air, and Finerty learned that Big Road's Oglalas were hosting a dance. Red River carts were scattered about. Walsh pointed out prominent leaders, again Long Dog, and Low Dog, Big Road (who Finerty consistently called Broad Trail), Gall, No Neck, Rain in the Face, Spotted Eagle.[19]

Walsh and Finerty came at last to a council arena where chiefs were already gathered and seated in a semicircle. Behind were warriors, women, and children who had come to watch the proceedings. Two chairs stood opposite, awaiting the White men. Sitting Bull was not present at first but shortly appeared from behind the assembled mass. Mounted, he was stolid and carried an eagle wing fan. Finerty assumed he would come forward, but Walsh explained that he would hear everything first but say nothing until the elders called upon him.[20]

When all was quiet Walsh motioned to André Larivée, the Wood Mountain Métis interpreter friendly to Sitting Bull, to convey Walsh's greetings. Lean Red Coat then proceeded to tell of his visit with the White chief, Bear Coat. Foremost, he cautioned them not to cross the boundary in search of buffalo. "Wait until they, the buffalo, come here. They are headed this way now," he asserted. Walsh knew that meat in the camp was nearly exhausted and that if buffalo did not cross the line soon he did not know what could be done for their benefit. But one thing was certain. They could not violate the laws. “I am willing to do all I can to aid you, within the law.”[21]

The assembled chiefs were curious about the man seated alongside the inspector, concerned particularly that he was a soldier. The Red Coat introduced him as a friend who writes for White men’s newspapers. “My father and his came from the same country,” he shared, and he will “tell the straight truth about you.” Several chiefs sprang forward to shake Finerty’s hand, and another seized the moment to speak of the buffalo. But others wanted to hear Finerty speak. Pressed, the newsman good-naturedly complemented the chiefs for their eloquence and said he had not come to fight or spy but only to see how they lived. He acknowledged the danger beyond the stone heaps but repeated that he was not an agent of the government or a soldier but merely here now to put what he saw and heard before his people. Chiefs again stepped forward and told of the injustices they had suffered and the treachery of Bear Coat and his soldiers. How long would the Bear Coat remain on the Milk, one of them wondered? Walsh interjected, telling them that it might be all summer if the young men kept crossing the line. Through it all, Finerty was most interested in Sitting Bull, whose face he noted lighted up from time to time but who remained all the while in the background, plainly unapproachable. Despite not talking with the chief for now, Finerty and Walsh retired from the camp with the newsman writing that the council was the most singularly enriching experience of his life.[22]

The next day Finerty and Walsh returned. On the hilltop they again paused and surveyed the scene. Without actually counting, Finerty was certain that he was looking upon a thousand, maybe eleven hundred lodges, occupied by 2,500 fighting men. Alas, for history’s sake, this was a unique moment and he might well have actually counted. Ammunition was plentiful, he noted, but food of any sort was scarce. Indian leaders acknowledged their presence but this time mostly left them alone. Again, Finerty spotted Sitting Bull in the distance. The chief knew he was there and instructed Larivée to convey his thoughts, telling the reporter through his intermediary that he wanted nothing to do with him. "I never seek anybody. Least of all do I seek any Americans," Larivée related. Two years in the Grandmother's Land had hardened him, and his burdens were many. While Walsh remained his friend and traders were accessible, there was no interplay with the old agencies, and those routine contacts were sorely missed. Miles's stridency furthermore had set its own inflexible tone. And most critically, the buffalo had all but disappeared and his people were famished. The message was clear. Finerty grasped this essential nature of buffalo and Indians, but also an ominous future, telling his readers: "The buffalo is, beyond doubt, fast disappearing, and, with the annihilation of that animal, the independence of the wild Sioux nation must come to an end. The Indians, I think, are beginning to recognize this stubborn fact themselves. When Sitting Bull himself is asked what his people will do when no more buffalo are left, he answers: 'Then the Great Spirit will send something else.'"[23]

The chief's dismissal nettled Finerty, but he later wrote that he could not deny that Sitting Bull had some great, mysterious power over the Sioux, and especially over his own Hunkpapas. Finerty departed for the American line on August 2. For five weeks his stories filled columns of the *Chicago Times* and thrilled readers with great scenes from the far northern plains, even if not conveying any of the great chief's actual words.[24]

Sitting Bull's stridency indeed stymied the eager reporter and reflected an exasperating frustration over the lack of buffalo and the inability of a people to adequately feed themselves. The chief and his followers had come unsuspectingly to a land where buffalo were already in peril. Canadian natives overhunted them, and the herd was not self-sustaining. It migrated at will, as Sitting Bull's people had witnessed that fall and winter, and then disappeared across the Medicine Line. Sitting Bull's people had also stepped into a different political world. When Canadian Indians needed buffalo and the herd in the north was thin or by seasonal migration all but nonexistent, they conveniently trailed to the south and hunted the Milk and Missouri River countryside and Big Open. But that option did not exist for the US Sioux. While momentarily pleasuring in bountiful hunting in the second half of 1877, they were merely living a dream. Buffalo were present, until they were gone.[25]

Historians tell us that the Canadian herd was all but wiped out by the summer of 1879, and thereafter existed no more. As in the United States, the Canadian range shrank continually even as intertribal harvests increased. In Canada, like the United States, robes were money, but so, too, was a second buffalo byproduct—pemmican, produced from dried meats and fats and comprising a critical staple in segments of the Canadian economy. Ever competitive markets and marketers also played roles. Where the Hudson's Bay Company was long the sole avenue to national and European marketplaces, by midcentury routes spawned by enterprising US and Canadian traders diverted robes to Saint Paul, transported there by Métis in long trains of Red River carts, or sent them to Saint Louis, shipped down the Missouri from the trading posts dotting the upper river. Compounding the Canadian prairieland dilemma was the simple entrée of the Métis people from the Red River valley, and the arrival of refugee Santee Sioux from Minnesota after 1862. Both had entered a landscape already overpopulated and fully exploiting the buffalo. When buffalo disappeared in the north, Indians concluded they had merely migrated to the south, into the United States. When the buffalo disappeared in the south a few years later, Indians and voracious White hide hunters merely exclaimed that the animals had gone north. Neither was true. No one could quite fathom that the buffalo herds that once blackened the prairies from Mexico to Canada were disappearing wholly from the North American Great Plains.[26]

For those most dependent on buffalo as a food source, hunger trumped everything. Oglalas and Brulés were among the first to quietly break from the northern alliance. They were abandoning Canada barely a year after fleeing the chaos in the south following the killing of Crazy Horse and the forced relocations of the Pine Ridge agencies. Sitting Bull held faithful to what he told Walsh in March. The bands could decide such matters for themselves, and if they chose to return to the United States they were free to do so. Those departing now were conscious of Bear Coat's soldiers and sidestepped them carefully, but, as one Canadian newspaper noted, "The Sioux chiefs say they don't want to fight particularly, but their children cry for meat and they must have it. They will fight any force that gets between them and the buffalo."[27]

Agents paid heed to the occasional arrival of scattered small bands, refugees presumably from "Sitting Bull's camp" and some already known at the agencies. One was Skunk Horse, an Oglala from Big Road's band, who with several others fled south in mid-September. Traveling by night and hiding by day, they encountered no White men until reaching the Cheyenne River east of the Black Hills. They arrived at the Pine Ridge Agency, the renamed and relocated Red Cloud Agency, in early October. Ushered to the agent's office and interviewed, Skunk Horse's accounting of buffalo and war was revealing. There were plenty of buffalo in the north, Skunk Horse observed, but they moved from place to place. When in the White Mother's country, there was plenty to eat. But when they went south of the Medicine Line, they could not be gotten. "The Great Father got mad about the fight we had with General Custer and drove us out of our own country," Skunk Horse said. "He made the attack on us to compel us to go and live on a reservation and eat beef but we wanted to live in our own country and eat buffalo meat." Agents across the Great Sioux Reservation would hear variations of this lament repeatedly in the coming months.[28]

Barely a week later, Water Spout, another Oglala from Big Road's band, leading twenty people from Wood Mountain appeared at the Pine Ridge Agency in late September 1879. He had been noticed in Montana as he crossed the Yellowstone between Glendive and Fort Buford, but had then quietly disappeared. Upon reaching the agency he, too, was immediately questioned by the curious operative. Buffalo were scarce north of the line, the agent reported, and the approaching cold weather and hunger will likely force a great number of other Northern Indians to return. Water Spout and his followers possessed a pass given to them by Superintendent Walsh, affirming their desire to return to Red Cloud Agency and that they were entering the United States with no "hostile intent." A written copy of that unique document was forwarded to the Commissioner of Indian Affairs.[29]

A short while later at the new Rosebud Agency an even larger band of Brulés under the guidance of Good Bird, some eighty-seven people in all, appeared in midwinter. The Rosebud agent listened to a similar account of discontent in Sitting Bull's camp. The majority of those returnees had fled north in 1878 during the continuous upheavals in the south, but now they expressed their willingness to abide by the laws and live in peace with the Whites. "They had had enough of the hostile camp," one of them confessed. The Rosebud agent was new to the scene but immediately grasped that tending the wants of these new arrivals was imperative, especially when Good Bird's people told of others following a like course.[30]

Hunting conditions were turning dire along the Missouri too. Skunk Horse and others told of encountering buffalo as they crossed the Medicine Line and made their way to the agencies, but others suggested trouble. The wholesale attack on the buffalo herds in the Red Water and Big Dry country south of the Missouri had begun. White men were killing buffalo merely for their hides, and those hunters were also reaching north of the river into the southern span of the Fort Peck Reservation, home of Assiniboine and Yanktonai people. Friendly Indians across that landscape dependent on those animals likewise expressed alarm. When the matter reached Chicago and the War and Interior Departments in Washington, government officials acknowledged the essential nature of that traditional food source and ordered that the wholesale slaughter of buffalo north of the river be stopped. Enforcement was wanting, however, and the situation only worsened.[31]

Through those early departures, Sitting Bull remained steadfastly committed to Walsh and his chosen life in the north. He affirmed the point in

October when Abbott Martin Marty, the Catholic cleric from Dakota, visited him again. Marty had tried to induce Sitting Bull's surrender in the summer of 1877, shortly after the chief crossed into Canada, but the chief had brushed him aside, thinking the priest was merely a disguised government agent. Marty believed his mission would succeed this time. Hearing of widespread hunger in the camps, he had secured an endorsement from Ottawa that willingly assented to any scheme that might return the Sioux to their own country. A contingent of Red Coats escorted the cleric as he made his way from Fort Walsh into the Frenchman's River countryside. This time he encountered Spotted Eagle, the Sans Arc chief, who organized a council for the priest. The chiefs and elders there told Marty they understood their plight but were still unwilling to trust the US government. Anyway, the buffalo would return, they said with a complete, if almost blind conviction. Sitting Bull ignored the proceedings entirely. Abbott Marty had no meaningful rejoinder and returned to Dakota.[32]

But the buffalo did not return and the hunger persisted. Surreptitious border crossings continued, particularly along Frenchman's Creek, and remained ever irksome to the authorities in the States. The pervasive hunger, meanwhile, gnawed at Sitting Bull's resolve. In midwinter the Fort Assinniboine commander reported an exchange with a Milk River mixed-blood who had recently visited the chief's camp on Frenchman's and learned that Sitting Bull was considering returning to his own country, permanently. But he expressed concerns for his people and himself. They had killed others, he fretted, and some one or many in the United States may wish to take revenge. Would his people be safe, he worried? But the chief also faced a day-to-day reckoning. His determination to sustain an independent life had been central to this war—and to this flight to Canada—but his people had to eat. He could plainly see that buffalo were disappearing. Was the chief's uncertainty a sign of genuine apprehension or an honest acceptance of fate? From a distance, the alternatives seem indisputable. But on Frenchman's River at midwinter 1879–80, one only senses agonizing apprehension and confusion.[33]

—~—

The winter of 1879–80 was long and difficult. Heavy snows blanketed the borderlands and effectively pushed the buffalo of the Milk and Upper Missouri even farther south into the Big Dry country, and straight into the guns of White hunters. The predicament not only handicapped agency Assiniboine and Yanktonai peoples dependent upon those animals but also stretched the access of the trans-border peoples. That quietly included Sitting Bull's Sioux. With no buffalo, starvation and suffering gripped all natives alike. At Wood Mountain, Walsh, in flagrant disregard to orders, raided company stocks to aid the desperate Indians hovering at his door. Others provided table scraps, and rations. However well-intended, the efforts were not enough. At Walsh's urging, some took to fishing, but buffalo hunters had no natural knowledge of the art of catching fish. Horses, even in their own diminished condition, ultimately provided the only practical food alternative.[34]

The remaining American Sioux camps on Frenchman's River were divided into four sizeable circles, Hunkpapas under Sitting Bull, Black Moon, Gall, and Long Dog; Miniconjous under Black Eagle; Sans Arcs under Spotted Eagle; and Oglalas under Big Road. Young Black Elk in Big Road's circle remembered those desperate times. "We [were] homesick for our own country where we used to be happy. The old people talked much about it and the good days before the trouble came. Sometimes I felt like crying when they did that."[35]

For many, the pitiable condition soon overtook any resolve to sustain a traditional and independent life. On January 29, 1880, the agent at Poplar River on the Missouri, Nathan S. Porter, reported the arrival of White Gut, a Sitting Bull stalwart, with forty-one families, some 284 people, Hunkpapas mostly, and many with relations among the Yanktonais. All were in an "almost starving condition," Porter noted. He exacted the standard surrender conditions, ponies and guns, and immediately added the refugees to the agency rolls and issued rations. Within days, other Indians followed, bringing the agent's tally of surrendered people on February 17 to 398.[36]

During this time Porter also had a quizzical interview with Gall. The agent understood Gall's stature among the Northern Indians and particularly his relationship with Sitting Bull, and when the two were face-to-face he simply listened to the chief's harangue over the surrender terms. If the standard was not the relinquishment of ponies and guns, people would come immediately, Gall asserted, or if they were "fed enough to support life" they also would come and comply with conditions. But he told the agent that from what he could see at the agency there was scarcely food enough on hand to tend agency Indians, let alone others. And he was right. The disappearance of buffalo affected everyone, and the agents on this remote northern reservation were still openly augmenting food issuances with the hunting of local buffalo. Eager to achieve such a noteworthy surrender as Gall, Porter put the chief on his rolls and gave him a ration ticket. "He comes to see what can be done for his people," Porter assured.[37]

Still, the people kept coming. In early March the Poplar River agent reported the arrival of another 222 Northerners who gave up ponies and arms. They were added to the rolls and issued rations. Even the ponies were in a starving condition, the agent noted. The Poplar River and Fort Belknap Agencies on the Fort Peck Reservation tirelessly welcomed newcomers. Neither place had oppressive military contingents in their proximities, a matter of considerable importance to some in Canada. That and food were matters of particular relevance now.[38]

The aligned people north of the border continued to dwindle as bands large and small either crossed the line or deliberated doing so. In late March Brave Bear, a Miniconjou, led 116 followers to Fort Keogh on the Yellowstone where they surrendered arms and ponies and were fed. At that same time Bull Dog, a Brulé, inquired through an intermediary, Louis Riel, about surrendering at Fort Assinniboine on the Upper Milk. Riel, a Métis activist and of late a local Missouri River roustabout, played a coy hand, insisting that the surrender terms be softened. He urged the commanding officer to feed and clothe the people, give them ammunition so that they might hunt small game, and let them retain their weakened ponies. He was betting that such liberal terms would yield the return of not just Bull

Dog and fifty-seven lodges of Brulés but also Sitting Bull and all the Sioux. "Would it not be better to bring the whole tribe at once, as there are chances to do it now, under the control of the government? Riel asked. "Sitting Bull and the others would be treated liberally and at the same time watched very closely?" The commanding officer at Fort Assinniboine was inexperienced in such matters and sought guidance. The ploy ultimately yielded nothing. American agents across the border country had been reminded repeatedly throughout the winter that the surrender terms were inflexible.[39]

Sitting Bull was conscious of these movements. He spent the late winter on Frenchman's River near the Mud Houses, the old borderlands trading establishment just north of the Medicine Line that some remembered as Fort N. J. Turney from the days of the border surveys. He also looked to the north, frantic it seems, to do something to comfort his people. Walsh had urged that they take to fishing. Riel told the Fort Assinniboine commander that he had learned that Sitting Bull contemplated going to the lakes of the northwest to subsist as long as possible on fish. It was, in all, a reflection of a desperate time.[40]

And yet matters worsened even more. Authorities in the United States had long questioned the influence of the North-West Mounted Police in prolonging the inevitable. The Canadian government's official position was consistently clear. US Indians would be tolerated north of the line but they would never be accepted or accommodated as British Indians. But often local agents wished otherwise. By now some half dozen police officers had married Sioux women, and a former Red Coat, James H. Thompson, lived among them, had adopted Indian habits and dress, and continually worked against the interests of US officials. And Walsh, more than any other individual in the force, offered benevolence and hope that plainly swayed Sitting Bull, lately even promising to take up the chief's case personally with officials in Ottawa and Washington.[41]

This obvious compassion confounded Walsh's superiors to such an extent that on July 13, 1880, he was relieved of his assignment at Wood Mountain, dispatched east on extended leave, and then reassigned to the command of Fort Qu'Appelle, a quiet station some 140 miles northeast of the Wood

Mountain uplands. With that, Sitting Bull lost his most important ally, and the blow was irreconcilable. Moreover, Walsh's successor at Wood Mountain, Lief Crozier, a distinguished officer in the force, ignored Sitting Bull and traveled among the camps talking to the minor chiefs and warriors, encouraging them to surrender. He told them frankly that if they did not return to the United States they would starve.[42]

The defections of Northerners continued. Oglalas and Brulés particularly eyed Fort Keogh on the Yellowstone. That they favored such a formidable military complex, commanded no less by Bear Coat Miles, one of the great thorns of this war, is curious. In recent years Northern Cheyennes had surrendered there and so had Brave Bear's Miniconjous in March. The likely draw now was simply the opportunity to hunt buffalo in the Big Open country, a land they would necessarily and pleasurably traverse when traveling south. Miles tallied the many surrenders occurring at his station during this late phase of the war, and the record for midyear 1880 was striking. On June 14 eighty-two lodges aligned with the Oglala Little Hawk surrendered. His band tallied some 585 people. Few if any noted the irony here. Little Hawk was Crazy Horse's uncle, and these were largely the same Crazy Horse people who had surrendered to White Hat Clark at Camp Robinson three years earlier.[43]

The officer overseeing the confiscation of arms and ponies reported learning from Little Hawk's people that two hundred additional lodges were not far behind, hunting and awaiting assurances of fair treatment for Little Hawk's band. Within days another 132 individuals, Oglalas under Iron Thunder mostly, surrendered at the post. The great unknown had been concerns over fair treatment and the delivery of sufficient foodstuffs but neither were problems at Keogh or anywhere else just then. A month later on September 8, Big Road and He Dog led their followers into Keogh, bringing with them some two hundred people and upping Miles's tally of surrendered Sioux to 830.[44]

The country took heed. Observers believed almost universally that this protracted Indian war was truly nearing an end. In the nation's view, and at the cost of Civil War hero Custer and the heart of a US cavalry regiment, not to mention millions of dollars spent in executing this war, the northern plains were opened to settlement. The gold-rich Black Hills were secure. Buffalo, the Indians' prime foodstuff and sole lingering motive for clinging to the open grasslands, were being wiped out. And a second transcontinental railroad was pushing to completion. Even then graders for the Northern Pacific had reached the Yellowstone and were advancing up that valley toward the Powder River. In the early 1870s survey work on this railroad had been a leading factor igniting this war.[45]

Lakota chiefs, elders, and warriors did not grasp or seem even to care about the Great Father's self-righteousness. This was a war thrust upon them by a thoughtless government and its people who collectively placed no value whatever on buffalo—beyond its usefulness as a crass commodity—or lands and hills sacred for generations, or a traditional way of Indian life. Little could they comprehend the simple freedom of the plains in the manner and spirit of Indian forebearers. That had all been erased by forces greater than their own, leaving the traditionals, band by band, family by family, individual by individual, reduced to hunger, the humiliation of submission, the loss of ponies and firearms, and an uncertain future at an agency in Dakota.

By fall 1880 the once mighty alliance of Northerners beyond the Medicine Line had been reduced to the camps of Sans Arcs and Miniconjous aligned with Spotted Eagle, a sizeable body of Hunkpapas aligned with Black Moon, Rain in the Face, and Gall, and the oft-times independent smaller circle of Hunkpapas tightly clinging to Sitting Bull. Soon the great chief would find himself alone. Hunting across the borderlands remained bleak. Confronting the inescapable gnawing impoverishment of their people and the dispirited counsel of Crozier and other Red Coats, the remaining chiefs turned to the south. Returnees drifted both to Poplar River and Fort Keogh, ever cautious and often anxious to argue the odious surrender terms, or, of late, the destiny of the people once the rivers opened again to downstream boat traffic. Some postured to stay at Poplar River among the Yanktonais.[46]

The surrender at Fort Keogh on October 30 of Spotted Eagle and his Sans Arc and Miniconjou followers, and of Rain in the Face and his small band of Hunkpapas, signaled the near collapse of the old alliance. Those 495 people in 110 lodges had long been stalwart allies of Sitting Bull. They had been in his fold almost continuously since the days when the Northerners were more commonly referred to as the non-treaty people fighting railroad surveyors on the Yellowstone. When coming south they lingered momentarily at Poplar River but indicated their intent to continue to Keogh farther south, hunting buffalo as they crossed the Big Open. When closing on the Yellowstone in late October Spotted Eagle asked for wagons to bring in part of his impoverished lot. Miles was accommodating. Both chiefs railed incessantly at the officer accompanying the wagons, recalling the injustices of the Whites and how the United States always treated Indian people poorly. The officer assured them that Miles was different, but Rain in the Face spat back, recalling what had happened to Joseph of the Nez Perce when they surrendered. Miles had told Joseph that he and his people would be taken to their old home in Idaho, but instead they were shipped off to the sickest place in the Indian Territory, where they were dying now. The new arrivals were ushered to a burgeoning Indian camp nestled along the Yellowstone, a short distance above the post. Conditions for a while were tense, but beef on the hoof and army rations soon calmed everyone.[47]

By early winter only the camps of Black Moon, Gall, and Sitting Bull remained north of the Medicine Line, sprawling along Frenchman's River near the old Mud Houses. The impetus to surrender was strong. Black Moon and Gall visited Poplar River from time to time, taking friendly meals, discussing surrender prospects with the agent, and suggesting their willingness to do so. Even Sitting Bull might cross the line if circumstances were right, they said. What the situation lacked, it seemed, was a triggering event or figure.[48]

Circumstances, as if on call, delivered a new intermediary. That individual was not another Catholic priest, army officer, or Red Coat, but rather an unprepossessing, well-known Upper Missouri Plainsman of the Isaiah Dorman–Johnny Bruguier sort. His name was Edwin H. Allison. Indians called him "Fish." The thirty-three-year-old knew the tradition-minded Sioux well, having worked the river agencies and forts for years. He was fluent in their tongue, and of late had been interpreting at Fort Belknap on the Milk. That fall cattlemen pushing twelve hundred steers from western Montana's Sun River country to Bismarck—still the functional end-of-track for the Northern Pacific Railroad—brought Allison into their employ. The cowmen knew the country east of Fort Belknap to be dangerous, but Allison professed to know the land and the Indian people crowding it now.[49]

Near the mouth of Frenchman's Creek the drovers indeed ran headlong into Indian hunters, a party led no less than by Gall. Allison knew Gall from his days at Grand River Agency. Allaying the cattlemen's concerns, Allison rode among the hunters and surprised the chief. Gall inquired about the cattle. The quick-witted interpreter declared that they belonged to the Queen of England and had been purchased for her army. The answer sufficed, Gall admitting that they were unwilling to molest persons or property under the protection of the Grandmother's government. Allison shared tobacco and coffee and invited the chief and others to eat beef that night with the cowmen. During dinner the conversation ranged widely, including the current nightmarish dilemma of holdouts above the line. In the moment, Allison conceived the notion, or so he later wrote, of visiting Sitting Bull and his people and convincing them to surrender. Gall offered to assist if somehow possible.[50]

The drovers continued to Fort Buford where Allison sought out the post commander, Major David Brotherton. He reported his encounter with Gall and the prospect of talking with the great chief himself. With so many failures before this, Brotherton endorsed the action, and so did his superior, Alfred Terry. Allison set out immediately, backtrailing along the Missouri. At Wolf Point he bounded north to Wood Mountain, where, in its western prairie fringe, he encountered the Sioux. Some recognized him from his days at the Dakota agencies, and one led him to Gall's lodge.[51]

The meeting was convivial and Gall fed him buffalo tongue and fried cake. Sitting Bull was away, but when he returned a day later a council was convened and the scout and great chief spoke face to face. Allison explained later that he could see that the Americans and their intentions confused these people, but also, he thought, the British had "grossly deceived" them, and Walsh particularly, who was promising much more than he could deliver. Allison attempted to set the record straight, and believed, he said, that the facts were a "severe blow to Sitting Bull and his hopes." Allison lingered in the camp for three days, all the while tended by Gall's people. When he departed, Sitting Bull was nowhere to be seen but Allison was pleased when Gall and a sizeable lot of Hunkpapas fell in with him, crossed the line, and trailed to Poplar River, commencing there a protracted if difficult engagement with the agent.[52]

Continuing to Buford, Allison again offered to return to Sitting Bull's camp, and Terry, by telegraphic exchange, endorsed the effort again. Traveling this time with a wagon heaped with hard bread, sugar, bacon, and tobacco, and a sidekick, an enlisted soldier dressed in citizen's clothes, Allison reached Sitting Bull's camp on Frenchman's River on October 30. But other matters had the immediate attention of the people. An internal squabble and killing had occurred over a horse, the consequences of a horse raid by the Blackfoot. Soon, however, an opportunity arose to gather the principal chiefs and elders, distribute the gifts, and explain again the terms of surrender. By now, the surrender of ponies and arms were time-worn threads, but they still touched a chord. Sitting Bull admitted that, as Allison reported, "the severity of the winters and the scarcity of game in the country he now occupied are facts he cannot overlook," but he then balked at the word "surrender." "He was not in arms against the United States," the chief declared, but merely defending himself against troops "when he was hunting buffalo in his own country. And he had never, by word or act, relinquished his claim to that country."[53]

Sitting Bull's outburst partly reflected the anxiety pervading the camp, but mostly signaled his own tangled countenance. Above all he held to the belief that Walsh offered prospects of a reserve in Canada and anxiously awaited his return, even while Crozier repeatedly told the chief that Walsh was never coming back. During his stay, Allison had other opportunities to talk with Sitting Bull and learned of other "dreads." Were he to come to Fort Buford, Sitting Bull dreaded any military display upon his arrival. He dreaded the presence of troops in his camp searching for arms. He feared that a strict guard would be placed over his camp, and he feared foremost for his own close confinement. This war, he knew, had consequences, just or unjust, and those consequences seemed poisonous. Allison could only promise to refer such matters to Brotherton. But he could also see that the chief had barely enough meat to last his people a few weeks. Eventually, he wrote, "he will have to make a hasty march to Buford to keep from starving or killing his ponies for food."[54]

Obstructive counsel from the ex-red coat "renegade" in Sitting Bull's camp, the man remembered dismissively as Thompson, only complicated matters. An informant reached the Poplar River Agency shortly after Allison's departure and told how Thompson countered all that Allison had said. They were all lies, he asserted. Furthermore, any such action talked of would be an insult to the Queen. Sitting Bull assured the man that he had no intention of surrendering.[55]

After separating from Allison in October Gall did continue to the Poplar River Agency, not necessarily intending to surrender but again merely to avail himself of agency largess. This time he noted the presence of a newly arrived army contingent, which doubtless sharpened his tone. As he told the officer commanding the little garrison, neither he nor Sitting Bull had any intention of surrendering. The officer noted that Gall was well armed, though he was apparently in need of ammunition, and he had already seized the munition stocks possessed by the local traders. Gall's small band lingered on the margins of the agency for weeks and watched as his camp was joined by some of Spotted Eagle's Sans Arcs who had slipped away from Fort Keogh, and Black Moon and his Hunkpapas from Canada, growing the circle from twenty-three to seventy-three lodges in a very short while. They remained unapproachable about surrendering, however, and generally intimidating enough to keep the soldiers and agents at bay. The local officer had little experience in such matters and pleaded with superiors for reinforcements. He also suggested sending a military force against the Northerners. Terry would hear nothing of the latter. But Gall did acknowledge that Sitting Bull was angry at him for having separated from the northern camp. Indeed, his and Black Moon's presence south of the line severely diminished the remnant northern alliance.[56]

Much of Gall's rhetoric was bluster. Others could see that he posed no warlike threat whatsoever and that he and his people were more ragged and destitute than ever. When conferring with the officer a second time his tone changed. He admitted that he liked the Poplar River locale. It had wood and buffalo. He conceded that he would surrender there, but he would not submit if forced to go to Buford or Keogh where there was neither wood nor buffalo and too many Whites. The officer sought approval to permit a surrender at Poplar River, suggesting that otherwise "they will remain without surrendering, hunt buffalo, and get what they want from the Yanktonais this winter, and be prepared for anything but surrendering in the spring." The officer's pleadings reached deaf ears. Terry and Brotherton had already agreed that any surrender must occur at Fort Buford, a place much better suited to handle so many people.[57]

While Gall and the Poplar River officer sparred over the nuances of surrender, the intrepid Edwin Allison returned to Sitting Bull's camp at Wood Mountain for yet a third time. Again, he hoped to cajole the holdouts to cross the line and end this war. He traveled this time with Fort Buford's post interpreter, serving primarily as a courier to keep Brotherton and Terry informed of any progress or need. Sitting Bull's camp was visited simultaneously by Inspector Acheson Irvine, the assistant commissioner of the NWMP, and several of his subordinates who had also come to induce the chief's surrender. Sitting Bull told Gall earlier that he chafed at "these scouts running to his camp all the time," but he begrudgingly allowed Allison and Irvine to have their say. The operatives had quietly talked beforehand and agreed that Irvine would make his case first, and alone. Irvine's message was straight-forward and consistent. There could be no reserve for the Sioux in Canada. They must surrender to the United States Government. Allison had his say when the inspector finished, and in his presence. His message was consistent. Sitting Bull asked for four days to deliberate the terms.[58]

When the chiefs gathered again several days later the agents repeated themselves. Sitting Bull told Irvine that he would go over to the United States. But then he immediately found excuses for not doing so. The weather was cold, he said, his people were poorly clad, and their supply of meat was all but exhausted. It was obvious, Allison thought, that while the chief's capacity to resist these endless overtures was weak, he held to a lingering belief that Walsh would somehow return and present him with new options, including staying in Canada. Meanwhile, the camp continued to dwindle. Seven additional lodges of Hunkpapas departed for Poplar River and thirty lodges of Sans Arcs headed to Fort Keogh to join kin.[59]

When Allison returned to United States several days later, another defection accompanied him, people led by Low Dog and Crow King. Those stalwart Oglalas and Hunkpapas had crossed the vaunted line many times in recent years, surreptitiously to hunt buffalo, and the people traveled south now only until buffalo were encountered. Allison concluded that he was merely a guise so that they might come south and lay in a supply of meat. He intended to proceed directly to Fort Buford, but before departing he cajoled three of them to accompany him, seize the opportunity to talk with Brotherton, and assess circumstances at the fort for themselves. They would be free to return and do so, in all likelihood, Allison was sure, with a favorable report. Among the delegates was no less than Crow King, one of the band leaders and a long-time intractable foe of the Whites. The riders reached Fort Buford on Christmas Eve.[60]

Allison judged the matter correctly. The Indians were hospitably treated. They liked what they saw and said so when they returned to their people a week later. But on their return the messengers encountered new circumstances. Major Guido Ilges and additional troops from Forts Keogh and Buford had arrived to augment the slender, near powerless Poplar River contingent. The presence of so many soldiers was disconcerting and greatly changed the nature of the place. Furthermore, Ilges was another no-nonsense soldier like Bear Coat Miles (who unknown to those Sioux had recently been transferred away from Montana). Like Miles, Ilges saw only one outcome, the unconditional surrender of the Indians. On December 31 the major convened a council of chiefs and band leaders from the many Hunkpapas and allies now crowding the Missouri and Poplar River bottoms to hear Crow King's story. About forty attended, including Gall. As Allison had imagined, Crow King's tale of an amenable place and seemingly abundant foodstuffs brought about an agreement among the chiefs to lead their people to Buford and give up. Ilges pressed for a date. The chiefs adeptly implored him for time to consider the action. Ilges gave them two days.[61]

Ilges was visited by a lesser chief the next morning. He came to argue. The people would move in the spring, he declared, and in the meantime wanted only to hunt. Furthermore, they were tired of talking to soldiers, and some were prepared to fight. Ilges feared that the Indians might decamp and return to Canada. He brusquely told the chief that they would move the next day. To ensure it, in the morning light he deployed nearly all of his command, an overkill of nearly three hundred well-armed infantry and cavalry, plus a rifled artillery piece known as a Rodman Gun. In day-long maneuvering Ilges's troops effectively corralled those Sioux, who were mostly nestled in the Missouri River bottoms above the Poplar River confluence. As the chief had foretold, some were indeed prepared to fight, and in the fracas one warrior was killed and an old woman wounded. But the resistance melted quickly, and soon a white flag fluttered from a lodge pole.[62]

Gall and his impoverished followers surrendered, yielding on the spot two hundred ponies and sixty-nine guns. On January 6 some seventy-five men and 230 dependents commenced a four-day, sixty mile trek to Fort Buford, escorted by one of Ilges's cavalry companies. Behind them, their tattered lodges were burned. Most of the woman and children rode in wagons. Gall and nearly all of the men walked. The temperature was bitterly cold, one day alone dropping to twenty-eight below zero, with deep snow. Many suffered from frostbite. Upon reaching Fort Buford Brotherton immediately sheltered the oncomers in a vacant warehouse near the steamboat landing and issued clothing, plenty to eat, wood stoves, and ample firewood. The reception and provender were calming. "I am glad I am here now," Gall confessed to a newsman a short while later. "Major Brotherton and Captain Clifford both treat me well."[63]

Crow King's and Low Dog's people were camped well beyond the Missouri River entanglement that snared Gall. Through part of the morning when Ilges attacked, Crow King had been at the Poplar River Agency, standing atop one of its buildings and watching as the scene unfolded. Allison stood with him and was dismayed by this unbridled military display. It threatened to disrupt everything. Allison urged Crow King to race to his camp and assure his people that the action was not directed at them and that the Americans, as he had personally seen at Buford, had only good intentions toward them. Crow King's salve partly worked. Low Dog and his followers were spooked by Ilges's action and fled to the north, but Crow King allayed the concerns of his own people, and he led them on their own trek eastward to the Yellowstone-Missouri Confluence. Allison traveled with Gall's party to Buford but encountered Crow King's people on his own return to Poplar River, and they, too, were hurriedly provided with wagons and sleighs dispatched by Brotherton. Crow King and his people, some 350 in fifty-one lodges, reached Fort Buford on February 10 where they surrendered guns and ponies to Brotherton. They were fed immediately, and then sheltered with Gall's people.[64]

—~—

By year's end, 1880, the coalition of tradition-bound Lakotas clinging to Sitting Bull had diminished to a few hundred people, largely the followers of Low Dog and the great chief himself. Canadian ambivalence, the disappearance of the northern-most plains buffalo, the onset of an endless hunger, and the cycles of US emissaries promising foodstuffs and clothing if only they would surrender, had shredded the alliance. And yet even then the seeming inevitable end was somehow filled with drama.

In desperation, Sitting Bull implored the Red Coats for help, but Crozier at the Wood Mountain Post had no mind for it. He was as resolute as the chief, though each espousing entirely different courses. Crozier's message never wavered. The Canadian government would never allow the Sioux a permanent home in Canada. Nor would they ever receive a food ration. Their only recourse was to surrender to the United States, just as Big Road, Spotted Eagle, Gall, and Crow King had done. The Métis trader Jean Louis Legaré, another Canadian whom the chief had come to trust, said the same thing, even while compassionately doing his best to make provisions available. Sitting Bull, meanwhile, held to the lingering hope that he would receive good treatment from the mounted police as long as possible, and that he would hear from Walsh, who had promised to return. Perhaps he would bring different options. The chief knew of Walsh's new assignment at Fort Qu'Appelle, 140 miles distant, though apparently he was not there yet. Perhaps alternatively Sitting Bull would go there himself.[65]

But Crozier's stern council and the fragile conditions north of the line resonated with Low Dog and his Oglalas. In the earliest days of the springtime thaw Low Dog led twenty lodges, some 135 people, south on a direct course to Fort Buford, where they surrendered on April 11, 1881. Crozier particularly took note. Within days he was in communication with the *Toronto Globe* newspaper, where he noted that "every lodge which leaves Sitting Bull weakens his power. I believe before a month has elapsed this doughty chieftain will have bid adieu to the White Mother's dominions."[66]

Distraught, Sitting Bull held firm while pondering options both in the United States and to the northeast in the Canadian lakes country and Fort Qu'Appelle. Again he turned to Red Coat Crozier. He wished, he told him, to send his own representatives to Fort Buford and learn the truth, and he wanted a policeman to go with them, "for I know what a red coat says is true." Crozier was elated and quickly agreed to the proposition.[67]

Four men, including Sitting Bull's trusted nephew and adopted son, One Bull, and Bone Club, a son of Four Horns, as well as Inspector Alex Macdonell, Crozier's newly assigned second in command at Wood Mountain Post, and an interpreter, reached Fort Buford on April 12, the day after Low Dog's surrender. Brotherton feasted them and allowed them to mingle with the others who had come in, now numbering nearly eleven hundred Lakotas. The emissaries plainly saw that those Indians at Buford were well fed and clothed, and had been provided with tents, stoves, and fuel. But One Bull was also forthright with Brotherton, explaining Sitting Bull's reluctance about returning to the United States. "They killed us when we are over there and we don't want to stay," plainly remembering such episodes as the killing of Crazy Horse. The delegation returned to Wood Mountain on April 17 and reported that the people in the south were indeed well treated and fed and would soon be moved to Standing Rock. But an unconvinced Sitting Bull cried out at one point, "I do not believe a word that is said." Crozier was furious and told the chief to "go to hell." Before spinning on his heels and leaving the room, Crozier ordered the chief away from the Wood Mountain Post.[68]

Sitting Bull moved his camp, a semblance now of perhaps sixty lodges. He went twenty-five miles east to Willow Bunch in the heart of the Wood Mountain, where his friend Jean Louie Legaré had recently relocated his trading post. Earlier, Crozier sent a note imploring Legaré to do what he could to induce the Sioux to return to America. The trader knew and liked these people. His years of experience on the plains had taught him to deal with the most pressing problem first, and address causes later. The people were starving. Recalling the conditions he witnessed, Legaré said, "Many of them had not even a pony, and those who had, possessed very lean ones; and as the ponies died either of leanness or sickness, they ate it at once."

The trader's immediate impulse was to organize a bounteous feast, and in due course he dished five hundred pounds of pemmican, fifteen sacks of flour, four bales of dried meat, thirty pounds of sugar, ten pounds of tea, and three pounds of tobacco, worth to him $350. And on full stomachs he dispensed some hard advice. He could not do this again, he warned, and the Queen was not willing to help. You are very poor. For the sake of your children, go back to the other side. The chief and his people agreed but confessed to a fearsome concern. "I trust you, but not the Americans," Sitting Bull allowed. "They are only waiting to get us all together, and then slaughter us." Legaré offered to lead a delegation to Buford personally. And he needed to do so soon to replenish his stocks. He would introduce them to Major Brotherton and allow them to assess circumstances for themselves. He would stay with them throughout, he assured.[69]

On April 26, Legaré led a string of Red River carts south to the timeless and now greening Yellowstone-Missouri Confluence, 150 miles distant. Thirty Sioux men started with him. Fourteen turned back almost immediately, but the trader and the others continued to the fort. Prominent among them was Old Bull, another of Sitting Bull's extended family, who was intrigued by Legaré's description of Fort Buford. Again the Hunkpapas found conditions at Buford favorable, Old Bull noting that families were receiving all the food they could eat. At one point an interpreter asked, "Well, how do you like it?" to which Old Bull admitted, "I cannot help but like it, if they are going to treat us this way." When it was time to return to Willow Bunch several days later, only Old Bull and three others chose to go. The rest found conditions so much to their liking they folded in with their well-tended kin.[70]

When Legaré reached Willow Bunch, he found that the chief and most of his people, perhaps two hundred in forty lodges, were gone, torn by the hope of seeing Walsh again and bound now for Fort Qu'Appelle. Barely eighty people remained on the margins of Legaré's operation, mostly women, children, and elderly. Hoping to save as much of his food stock as possible he offered to lead those willing on a second trip to Buford. Almost immediately thirty-two agreed to go, including, remarkably, Many Horses, Sitting Bull's sixteen-year-old daughter, who was quietly running off with a suitor. Within days Legaré was on the trail again and when his train reached Buford in May 31, an amazing scene animated the riverfront. Three steamboats had reached the post and were preparing to move the assembled Lakotas—the Gall, Crow King, and Low Dog people—downriver to Standing Rock Agency. Even then, lodges and possessions were being loaded onto the boats. Everyone at riverside went peaceably, including Many Horses and those just arriving with Legaré.[71]

Sitting Bull's exile in Canada ultimately closed quickly. The chief's journey to Qu'Appelle brought only heartbreak. Walsh had not returned to the little police post on Qu'Appelle Lake, and the chief would never see him again. There, two men awaited, the well-known and recently promoted Police Commissioner Acheson Irvine, whom the chief had dealt with repeatedly during his exile, and Edgar Dewdney, the Canadian Commissioner of Indian Affairs. The officials merely repeated the government's well-worn admonishments. Canada would not help the Lakotas by providing either a reserve of land or foodstuffs. And Irvine waved-off Walsh. The chief's trusted friend would not return. The Canadian view all along had been consistent and unalterable. It had already achieved the surrender of most of the wartime refugees, and without bloodshed. Canada would let hunger do its work, and, as Dewdney observed, that condition was fast approaching. The Sioux were then living off duck eggs and roots, he noted.[72]

Broken in spirit, the chief and his people returned to Willow Bunch and the only friend remaining, Jean Louis Legaré. Almost immediately upon arriving on July 2, Sitting Bull learned that forty-eight of his people had gone south with the trader on his two recent trips to Buford. Among them was his precious daughter, Many Horses. Legaré understood that the people were hungry, and he fed them yet again. Later that day the trader announced that he was bound for Buford once again, in seven days, and if they chose to come, he would take them along. The days passed slowly. Legaré offered no other feasts, although on one occasion he laid out twelve sacks of flour on the floor of his store and they all quickly disappeared. On the seventh day, July 11, Legaré and a cadre of Métis laborers loaded thirty-seven Red River carts and wagons with the wares of the remaining people and commenced the trail to the confluence. Sitting Bull, Four Horns, and a few others trailed separately, seemingly aimlessly, and suggesting even their own destination of Milk River or Poplar River. But the next day they folded in with Legaré. After four years in Canada, the final two hundred Lakota exiles were coming home.[73]

America's war horse general, Philip Henry Sheridan, the mastermind of this Indian war, had announced the end of the Great Sioux War nearly four years earlier, in the immediate wake of Miles's fight with Lame Deer. That was a White man's name for this Indian war, bestowed by newspapers, and a White man's view of war. The Lakotas and Northern Cheyennes had no particular name for the conflict they had endured, merely then or ever after remembering a war forced upon them by the Whites, over a railroad, the Black Hills, and a lifeway on the buffalo prairie. Indeed, the episode on Muddy Creek in June 1877 more or less closed Sheridan's shooting war. But the end of bullets only brought the beginning of three more years of frustrating diplomacy, cat-and-mouse chases in the hunting lands of the border country, and an ultimately devastating privation and starvation, where hunger proved the most powerful persuader of all. At stake, indeed, was a free life on the buffalo prairie—the core essence of every tradition-bound Lakota and Northern Cheyenne. And that ideal was stripped bare. Sheridan's war succeeded in bringing all the Sioux people onto the reservation, but what lay ahead was an unimaginable future of continued privation, death, a duplicitous government, land theft, the complete annihilation of the last of the once mighty buffalo herds, and Indian lives inexorably transformed.

The great days were quashed. But in light of vitality and memory in Sioux Country, then and even now, how does one define an end to a war when in legacy there is no end?

EPILOGUE

The labors of such newsmen as John Ford, Charles Diehl, Jerome Stillson, John Finerty, and others in the field during the long course of this 1870s Indian war—Sitting Bull's War—had helped turn the saga into a national event. Newspaper readers throughout the land were fully aware of an ambitious railroad, gold in the Black Hills, a pragmatic president, the crushing defeat of Custer at the Little Big Horn, and the continual press of Sheridan's Army to sweep the northern plains clean of its Indians, all in the cause of American Manifest Destiny. Readers were aware, too, of that humble day in 1881 when Sitting Bull surrendered his rifle at Fort Buford to end it all. Whites viewed it all as progress, one more near final step in the settlement of a vast continent.

Reactions around Indian campfires through those same years told a different story. The people aligning with Old Bear, Little Wolf, Sitting Bull, Crazy Horse, Gall, Spotted Eagle, and so many other illustrious traditional Lakota and Northern Cheyenne chiefs had not necessarily been bested by Sheridan's Army at all, formidable though it was with its seemingly endless numbers and unmatched matériel superiority, or the odious labors of government commissioners bearing contrived diplomatic solutions, but by simple, pervasive hunger. What awaited Sitting Bull and the last few

Lakotas aligning with him as they made their way from Willow Bunch to the confluence of the Yellowstone and Missouri in July 1881 was food. A newsman on the scene from Saint Paul aptly captured that essence in a story his paper poignantly headlined "The End of a Romance." In the reporter's eyes, for all of Sitting Bull's "fierce spirit" and that "carnival of slaughter and vengeance in the ravines of the Little Big Horn," in the final tally, this war story and its ending amounted to two simple truths. The buffalo were all but gone, and "hunger was a more powerful persuader than Allison or Legaré in inducing Sitting Bull and his followers to surrender to the rations of Major Brotherton." Hunger. Another keen observer touched a parallel but connected chord. The end was "for the sake of the children."[1]

Within days of Sitting Bull's arrival at Fort Buford, and after all its essential formalities, including his uttering an infamous line wishing to be remembered as the last man of his tribe to surrender his rifle, he confronted yet another reality. He and his people were soon to be ushered to Fort Yates and the Standing Rock Agency. The chief was despondent over the simple fact that he no longer controlled his own fate. He was indeed well treated by Brotherton and his soldiers, but would that continue at Yates? And what about the rest of his people who remained at Wood Mountain and Willow Bunch? Even then, Legaré was headed north and upon his return would presumably come back with the others. On the evening of July 28 many of the Hunkpapas walked the short distance to the Buford landing to eye a riverboat just docking from upriver. They had seen those massive sternwheelers before. Some among them had even fired on such vessels. But now they were to be passengers. The next morning after eating, the chief and his followers, 188 people in all, and all of their worldly possessions were ushered aboard and the steamer commenced a three-day journey to family and friends at Standing Rock. The Hunkpapas were going home.[2]

Sitting Bull's concern for those who remained in Canada was apt. Some 250 Lakotas, Hunkpapas mostly but a few from each of the other *oyates* as well, consciously retained their guns and ponies and chose to remain in the north, most living at first in the proximity of Legaré's store at Willow Bunch, but some in course making their way to Fort Qu'Appelle, and others around 1882 relocating to Moose Jaw, a budding railroad hamlet seventy-five miles north. The collective number dwindled through the years to about 120 people by the turn of the century as family after family quietly returned to relatives at one or another of the Sioux agencies in Dakota. Through the years those who remained suffered the unshakable indifference of the Canadian government. Finally, in 1910, a campaign led by a Presbyterian clergyman led to creation by the Canadian Department of Indian Affairs of a small reserve for the Lakotas west of the old Wood Mountain police post. Descendants live there yet today and remember the legacy of Sitting Bull's War. Of the old people, on November 12, 1956, Julia Lethbridge died at Fort Qu'Appelle, at the age of ninety. She was believed to be the last of those who followed Sitting Bull across the Medicine Line so many years earlier.[3]

The Northern Cheyennes led by Old Bear, Little Wolf, and Morning Star who were summarily transferred from the Pine Ridge to the Indian Territory at the time of Crazy Horse's surrender in 1877, faced their own grim fate during the ensuing years. Despite the general embrace of southern kin, conditions in the south were appalling. Sickness alone claimed sixty lives in the first year, and indifference and food shortages plagued the rest. Increasingly, many eyed a return to the north, despite the risks and difficulties likely with such a flight. Local agents in what became Oklahoma were wary of that possibility and posted troops to watch over the Cheyennes. A breakaway occurred in the darkness of September 9, 1878, when some three hundred Northern Cheyennes led by Morning Star and Little Wolf fled the Darlington Agency. In the moment, they consciously left lodges standing and home fires burning to deceive agency authorities and blue coats. They too were going home.[4]

What followed was a dogged chase through Kansas and into the Sand Hills of central Nebraska where the people reluctantly divided. Morning Star preferred to reunite with friendly Oglalas in the Pine Ridge. Little Wolf wished to hold the Cheyennes together and continue to the familiar haunts of the Yellowstone. Neither chief had any firm sense of the changed circumstances prevailing on the northern plains, where Oglalas and Brulés no longer resided in the Pine Ridge. Indian peoples no longer roamed the lands south of the Yellowstone freely either. Both landscapes instead were well-traveled by soldiers.[5]

Morning Star's followers were trapped first, on October 23, in the Niobrara River valley, and taken to Fort Robinson and domiciled in an unoccupied barrack. Basic amenities were provided but seventy-five bleak days followed. The Cheyennes seemed, at least at first, to be unaware of the political maelstrom trailing them. Sheridan wanted the people returned to the Indian Territory and the ringleaders exiled to Florida. Kansans wanted them transferred to civilian authorities for trial on charges of murder, theft, and the destruction of property occurring when they passed through that state. Indecision and obstinacy prevailed as winter set in and where the rhetoric at the fort turned increasingly antagonistic. Under incessant pressure to be returned to the south, Morning Star at one point told the commander that he was on his own ground. "I will never go back. You may kill me here; but you cannot make me go back." In a perverse effort to induce compliance, heating, water, and foodstuffs were withheld. At a breaking point, in the darkness of January 9, 1879, with temperatures hovering below freezing, the imprisoned Cheyennes broke free en masse and fled through the snow west up the White River.[6]

The flight proved a bloodbath from the start as troops hounded the Cheyennes through the timbered, broken ground of the Pine Ridge and into the badlands of the Hat Creek Breaks, often using artillery to dislodge secreted bands. Soldiers eventually trapped the last few Cheyennes in a deep draw along Indian Creek (today's Antelope Creek), twenty-seven miles northwest of the post. They fought and more died until the Cheyennes fired their last cartridge. In the end, sixty-four Northern Cheyenne men, women, and children were killed in the break-out, seventy-eight were captured and reconfined, and seven others were unaccounted for, including Morning Star. The carnage enraged the nation and worked to counter the enmity in Kansas where charges were eventually dismissed. At month's end, the survivors were moved from Fort Robinson to the Pine Ridge Agency. Morning Star and his small party appeared there several weeks later, having successfully eluded troops and surviving on little more than dried rosehips.[7]

Little Wolf and his followers similarly eluded troops successfully, finding haven first along the Niobrara during part of that winter and then continuing their own long journey to Montana, skirting the Black Hills and Bear Butte while trailing to the Yellowstone. But on March 25, he and his people ran headlong into a detail led by Lieutenant William Philo "White Hat" Clark, whom they remembered from their time at Camp Robinson. Clark, conscious of the mismanagement and bloodshed shrouding Morning Star's break-out from Fort Robinson, induced Little Wolf's surrender and led them to Fort Keogh on the promise of a provisional asylum while the government resolved Northern Cheyenne affairs. Morning Star and many of his survivors joined them that fall. The Cheyennes lived in exile at Keogh for three years while investigations of all manner ensued, and where their camp ironically was joined by hundreds of surrendering Sioux people returning from Canada. The Sioux at Keogh were moved downriver to Standing Rock in June 1881, shortly after Gall's people were moved there from Fort Buford. Finally, in November 1884, President Chester A. Arthur signed an executive order creating a permanent reservation for the homesick Cheyennes, astride their beloved Tongue and Rosebud rivers. Descendants of the two headstrong illustrious Cheyenne chiefs and their followers reside there today.[8]

The exiled Cheyennes at Fort Keogh witnessed yet another indignity in November 1881 when Northern Pacific Railroad tracklayers reached Miles City and continued west across the Fort Keogh grounds within plain sight of the detained people. Many of them had joined the Lakotas in the early 1870s to resist railroad surveyors when they first plied the Yellowstone Valley, and were incensed even then by any manner of trespass into their intact and revered buffalo country. Ominously now, arriving by rail in Miles City were buffalo hide hunters and the literal death knell of the once mighty Buffalo North.[9]

The story of the destruction of the buffaloes occurring in Dakota and Montana was a mere echo of that occurring in the Buffalo South a decade earlier. The wanton killing of the sprawling Great Plains buffalo herd was plainly enabled by the coming of these railroads, first across the central plains in the late 1860s and then spanning the southern plains shortly thereafter, and now throughout the north. The iron rails conveniently linked robust buffalo herds, single-minded hide hunters, and receptive marketplaces, and gave rise to plains communities like Dodge City and Fort Griffin in the south, both notoriously known as "hide towns," and Dickinson, Glendive, and Miles City in the north that boomed as centers of this feverish, thoughtless slaughter. In Montana and Dakota the prime killing lasted through the winter of 1882–83 and then plummeted. One fur buyer noted that by "1885 the collection of hides amounted to little or nothing." A smug Montana hide hunter expressed it another way: "when we got through the hunt there was not a hoof left."[10]

Many in the north had seen vestiges of the slaughter. A Fort Peck agent bemoaned Whites ruthlessly killing buffaloes in the Red Water and Big Dry country south of the Missouri in October 1879 and hunters even then eying opportunities north of the river, where those same animals were yet a vital foodstuff for local Assiniboines and Yanktonais. In a cruel irony, a steamboat transporting 12,037 buffalo hides from the Yellowstone country arrived in Bismarck in July 1881, docking hours ahead of another stern-wheeler carrying Sitting Bull's people. Then there was William T. Hornaday, chief taxidermist of the Smithsonian Institution, who, seeking buffalo in Montana in 1886, killed a few final specimens that he might mount and exhibit so Americans of another day could see what their nation's most iconic mammal once looked like. Hornaday's hunt was a perversity:

killing a few final survivors so that they might be mounted as museum specimens. The very heart and soul of the northern plains, the focus of a people's lifeway, and the reason for a fitful, bloody Indian war, disappeared with the few final shots.[11]

But in fact a few animals did survive, scattered in places like Yellowstone National Park, created only a few years before, and small private herds dotting the plains. They survived even in the show stock of the most celebrated buffalo hunter of all, William F. "Buffalo Bill" Cody, who paraded a small group with his Wild West show. That sum, small and scattered as it was, provided a genetically diverse-enough rootstock for the eventual regeneration of America's most iconic mammal, a groundswell that took hold at the turn of the twentieth century. Today, nearly a half million buffalo thrive in major public, private, and Indian herds throughout the land. For a bleak moment, the alternative was but a few magnificent Great Plains beasts, stuffed and exhibited behind glass in museums.[12]

Difficult days lay ahead for the Lakotas and Northern Cheyennes who were now plainly reservation-bound people. For a culture wedded to the freedom of the open plains for multiple generations, weekly allowances of beef, pork, and flour, and a secondary lifeway in log cabins were painful adjustments. Yet life went on. The Northern Cheyenne woman Iron Teeth, Susan Iron Teen in her later years, who suffered pitiably during the long course of Sitting Bull's War, spoke humbly and gracefully in 1926, two years before her death. She told of those times to Thomas Marquis, a physician on the Northern Cheyenne Reservation. Her husband and son were killed on the Red Fork of the Powder River in November 1876. She was among those ushered to the Indian Territory in 1877 and also one who escaped the Fort Robinson confinement in 1879. Decades later she told Marquis that "I used to cry every time anything reminded me of the killing of my husband and my son. But I have become old enough to talk quietly of them. I used to hate all White people, especially their soldiers. But my heart has become changed to softer feelings. Some of the White people are good, maybe as good as Indians."[13]

Iron Teeth lived many years beyond the war. So did some of the prominent chiefs who led and fought valiantly to sustain a traditional life on the buffalo prairie. Little Wolf, a revered Northern Cheyenne Old Man Chief who was valiant and inspirational in many of the war's critical episodes, lived a humble life in the years that followed, partly in a self-imposed exile after a regrettable altercation and killing of a fellow Cheyenne. He had played a central part in the flight of the Cheyennes to Montana and the creation there of a reservation in the old haunts of the Tongue and Rosebud. He was seldom photographed and never interviewed, and died alone in 1904 at the approximate age of sixty.[14]

Big Road, the Northern Oglala pragmatist led followers through most of the critical episodes of the war, including the Little Big Horn fight, Crazy Horse's surrender, and the subsequent flight to Canada. Afterward, he partnered at Fort Yates with an unknown artist and created an extraordinary list of Oglala families that had been with him in Canada and throughout most of the war. Today, the so-called Big Road Roster reveals the identities of eighty-four family heads and helps put names to the invariably silent tallies of lodges and warriors participating in the war. Big Road continued to advocate for his people after they were released from Fort Yates in 1882, fiercely defended Lakota land rights during the fateful Crook Commission discussions in 1888–89, and embraced the Ghost Dance when it swept the Pine Ridge Agency in 1890. But in that fractious time, he had a change of heart and helped lead his people and others out of the Pine Ridge Stronghold as the crisis worsened. Big Road was occasionally photographed, including on that crucial visit to Washington in September 1877, the one spurned by Crazy Horse, where the Pine Ridge chiefs and head men implored government officials to grant a much-promised agency in the buffalo country. Big Road seems never to have been interviewed and died in 1894 at the approximate age of sixty.[15]

The stalwart Sans Arc chief Spotted Eagle was in the mix of Sitting Bull's War at nearly every stage, from resisting railroad surveyors in the early 1870s, in the days of the great ascendancy after the surprise attack on the Cheyennes at Powder River, and through most of the war's great battles thereafter. He came separately to join Sitting Bull in Canada in 1877 and was among those who reproached Terry at the raucous Fort Walsh conference. He also welcomed forlorn Nez Perce refugees into his camp after some of them, too, crossed the Medicine Line. Of his several appearances at the Cheyenne River Agency in the later days of the war, he somehow sidestepped any confrontation with the inquisitive Colonel William H. Wood, commander of the Cheyenne River military post. Wood had sought out many other similarly visible Sans Arcs and Miniconjous whenever they appeared and closely interrogated them on the current happenings in the buffalo country. Wood's interviews are an unheralded archive of revealing wartime dialogues. Although Spotted Eagle lived until 1898, it seems that he was never interviewed, though he was well photographed. He, too, visited Washington during the time of the great reservation land severances occurring in the late 1880s. Spotted Eagle was approximately sixty-four years old at the time of his passing.

Gall was another of Sitting Bull's closest allies who endured the long course of the war. Born in 1838, the Hunkpapa had also fought courageously in the wars of the 1860s, including the Sully campaign and Killdeer Mountain fight in 1864 in the wake of the Minnesota Dakota War, and Red Cloud's War in the revered buffalo country of Wyoming and Montana in the mid-1860s, where he was particularly prominent in the Fetterman fight. Gall boldly confronted Stanley and Custer in the years of the railroad surveys, and was something of an "everywhere warrior" on the Little Big Horn battlefield. No one lost more on the field that day than Gall, where two wives and three children were slain in a fusillade from Reno's troops at the opening of the fight. Gall went to Canada with Sitting Bull and proved an exasperation to government officials when he returned to Montana in the winter of 1880–81, bent on surrender but fearful of consequences.[16]

In 1886 Gall returned to Montana for festivities associated with the tenth anniversary of the Custer battle. At the several-day-long event, the chief was talkative and enjoyed widespread notoriety, and at one point led a tour of the battlefield. But a newsman early on caught a glimpse of Gall that uniquely revealed his private self. Upon arriving at Fort Custer at the start of the affair, Gall, upon alighting from the carriage delivering him from the Yellowstone River railroad station, stepped several paces away, sat down in the grass, and gazed long and intently at the surrounding hills and mountains. He then rose from his contemplation and remarked to an interpreter: "When I look at this country, which was mine so long, where the game was plentiful and where was the glory of constant war between the White man and the Indian, I feel like a woman." Pondering a lifeway and a land lost, Gall's inner pain was wrenching. In his final years at Standing Rock, Gall remained influential among his people. He warmed to the precepts of the Episcopal faith, agreed with the land severances of the late 1880s, and advised caution during the days of the Ghost Dancing. He died in 1894 at the age of fifty-six.[17]

Easily the most enigmatic individual rising to prominence during the course of Sitting Bull's War was the Northern Oglala Little Big Man, a fervent traditional and lifelong friend of Crazy Horse. Born about 1840, Little Big Man had a distinctive physical presence, with a noticeable short stature, sinewy lines, scarred chest, and riveting eyes. An officer remembered him as "a nervy, earnest little devil that would take hold of your hand and would squeeze the blood out of it when he shook hands with you." Little Big Man first drew notice in the early 1870s when he and others, Crazy Horse among them, terrorized Whites along the North Platte in the proximity of the first Red Cloud Agency and Fort Laramie. He gained special notoriety in 1875 when his disruptive behavior before the Allison Commission, then at Red Cloud Agency attempting to secure purchase the Black Hills, thoroughly chilled the proceedings. Some months later he was among messengers dispatched from the north after the Powder River fight carrying Sitting Bull's call to all traditionals to join him on Rosebud Creek. And he was alongside Crazy Horse when the Oglalas surrendered at Camp Robinson in May 1877.[18]

But then came Little Big Man's puzzling transformation, a near total conversion to the side of the Whites, attributable some said to a souring of his relationship with the war chief over a woman, or, as others have suggested, because he had been "worked" by local agents at Red Cloud Agency and Camp Robinson, notably the headstrong White Hat Clark. Little Big Man stood beside his old friend when the war chief made his final appearance at Camp Robinson, but tussled with him during the botched arrest, and was himself wounded by the chief moments before Crazy Horse was stabbed by the soldier.[19]

Whites subsequently presented Little Big Man with a silver medal for his involvement in the sordid Crazy Horse affair. He seems never to have been bedeviled by what he did, and perhaps as a reflection of having been so empowered, offered in August 1878 to travel to Canada and bring back his friend Big Road and his people. The local agent endorsed the offer and encouraged the Commissioner of Indian Affairs to approve it. But trust was a fragile thing. The Interior Department passed the proposal to the War Department, which in turn forwarded it to Sheridan in Chicago, where the general's sour response killed the prospect. Little Big Man is thought to have died near the Pine Ridge Agency in 1887, at the age of forty-seven and is buried in the Holy Cross Cemetery on the reservation.[20]

By 1881, no Indian who had participated in Sitting Bull's War faced an enviable future, but no one suffered the indignities more than the implacable Hunkpapa Sitting Bull, the spiritual heart of this war for the buffalo prairie and still an unwavering traditional. After surrendering at Fort Buford and obligingly boating to Fort Yates, Sitting Bull, fifteen members of his immediate family, and 157 others were again ushered aboard a steamboat in mid-September 1881, and whisked downriver to Fort Randall to an exile in the farthest southeastern corner of the Dakota Territory. It was a common fate. In the wake of other Indian wars influential chiefs like him were commonly separated from impressionable kinsmen. Such was the simple intent in the Crazy Horse debacle, and it was no different now. Sitting Bull and his followers, mostly those who had clung closely to him throughout the long war, and now ironically including even Steps, the odd Yakima who had come north with the Nez Perce, endured a near two-year-long exile at Randall. They were well fed and had the run of the post, but they were never far from the watchful eye of guards.[21]

Sitting Bull complained bitterly and often about this injustice, usually to seemingly sympathetic but invariably unmoved local officers. But it was the intercessions of outsiders that ultimately altered the chief's fate. Martin Marty, the Catholic prelate now living in Yankton who had twice before attempted to intercede on the chief's behalf, particularly rallied to his cause, mounting an aggressive, attention-getting letter writing campaign. Marty was joined by concerned citizens and even James McLaughlin, the current Standing Rock agent, who petitioned the Commissioner of Indian Affairs to resettle the Randall exiles in the Grand River country. It took some while, and the realization of sweeping change across the northern plains to finally enable that logical and just outcome. By then, the buffaloes, the burly beacons of all plains Indians, were all but gone. And the Northern Pacific Railroad had indeed proved a harbinger of settlement, providing regular train service across all of Dakota and Montana. Plainly, the northern plains had been transformed, and the army relented. On April 28, 1883, Sitting Bull and 160 Lakotas boarded a steamboat and headed upriver, where the chief removed himself to the farthest corner of the Standing Rock environs, up Grand River twenty miles beyond his birthplace, and to his final home.[22]

The following months were heady for the devout traditional and many Hunkpapas. While the northern plains buffaloes had been all but decimated in the intervening years, not every last animal was wiped out. Shortly after Sitting Bull's return to Standing Rock, a small herd of perhaps one thousand animals was discovered in the rugged drainage of the Little Missouri, straight west, and the Standing Rock people were invited to hunt them. That fall a chase ensued in the spirit of yesterday, but this one tinged with the overtones of today's reality as White hunters killed what few animals the Sioux families left behind. Even still, a notable calm pervaded the Indian camp at the close of that last evening on Hidden Wood

Creek as Hunkpapas, Blackfeet, and Upper and Lower Yanktonais feasted as friends.[23]

In coming years, the chief traveled often to eastern cities, frequently accompanied by McLaughlin or his wife. In 1885 he spent the summer touring with Buffalo Bill Cody's Wild West and on their pause in Washington met no less than his old war-time nemesis, General Sheridan, and President Grover Cleveland. And yet always his fundamental beliefs in Lakota customs and culture, and a reverence for what remained of Lakota land, never wavered. Matters took a nightmarish turn in 1889 when yet another government commission set upon the Lakotas and sought to apportion away much of the Great Sioux Reservation. Sitting Bull was outraged and on August 3 he led twenty likeminded men, all mounted on horseback and wearing their finest war apparel, to the Standing Rock council grounds to protest. The traditionals were waved off by McLaughlin's Indian police, but they showered the proceedings with epithets. It made no difference. The commissioners obtained the necessary signatures at Standing Rock and at each of the other Sioux agencies that shredded the vast Great Sioux Reservation prescribed in the 1868 Fort Laramie Treaty. The last of the old lands were now all but gone.[24]

The land theft was unconscionable. So too was the continual badgering to educate the children in the White man's ways, the unrelenting pressures to take up farming and stock raising, and the ceaseless push to embrace White man's Christianity. Cultural values were demonized. Sacred rituals like the Sun Dance were banned. And the wild game was all but gone and agency food issuances sometimes late or fraudulently reduced. Into this societal and cultural upheaval came word from other reservations of a new religion sweeping across Indian Country, one that promised the return of the halcyon days when the land was free of White people and buffalo again filled the prairie. All one needed do, subscribers learned, was embrace the tenets of this new faith, and mostly simply dance. Throughout the summer and fall of 1890 all of Sioux Country was swept up by this new Ghost Dance craze. Sitting Bull embraced it, too, and McLaughlin was horrified.[25]

Sitting Bull refused to heed McLaughlin's repeated admonishments to stop the dancing when the movement swept the chief's small community. Even Bear Coat Miles, now commanding the army's Military Division of the Missouri in Chicago, took heed, and offered the services of Buffalo Bill Cody to intercede. Cody, like Red Coat Walsh, was one of the few *wasicus* the great chief respected. But Cody was intercepted as he attempted to reach the Grand River, and nobody stemmed the fervor. In sheer panic, and in an already fractious relationship, McLaughlin ordered his Indian police to arrest Sitting Bull. On Monday, December 15, in a break-of-day confrontation at Sitting Bull's log cabin on the Grand, a policeman, Red Tomahawk, scuffled with and killed the great chief. Indian Country had seen this before, in the Pine Ridge thirteen years earlier, where in a similar botched arrest another of the lustrous chiefs lay dead. Custer's death was twice atoned. Such seemed the pathetic legacy of this war, as was the equally unthinkable tragedy occurring on Wounded Knee Creek two weeks later.[26]

—⁓—

And yet within such tragic endings there was still dignity. In the years after, in the becalmed, ever-humble back corners of the Sioux reservations dotting North and South Dakota, on the Northern Cheyenne Reservation in Montana, and even on the Shoshone-Arapaho Reservation in central Wyoming, traditionals lived on. In 1919, Left Hand, one of the Arapahos nestled in the Cheyenne camp at the Little Big Horn in 1876, told Colonel Tim McCoy, then the Adjutant General of the State of Wyoming, his story of the Custer fight and closed with a perspective that spoke volumes for aging traditionals like him. "The Indian is like a prisoner on his reservation," Left Hand intoned. "The buffalo are all gone, the antelope are gone, and now we old men can only sit by the fire, sing our war songs and dream of the past."[27]

The words were more revealing and profound than McCoy probably grasped. Left Hand was speaking for the bygone days when buffalo, the paramount species in a healthy prairie environment, and every other creature great and small, and the grasses and brush and flowers, flourished in unison, and that rich tapestry in turn sustained the prairie people. And then in the wake of a war it was all gone. But McCoy and so many others like him captured that spirit. They took copious jottings and notes, and in the process of recording the voices and memories of those old white-haired traditionals, diverse and scattered as they were, a legacy was preserved, and writers of yet another day are enabled to tell their stories. *Sitting Bull's War* is one of them.

ACKNOWLEDGMENTS

Historians do not write books in vacuums. We scrutinize reams of source material, query widely, seek favors continually, and at project's end are ever grateful to librarians, archivists, museum specialists, and friends who endured the course with us. Yet again I am the beneficiary of abundant good grace, warm encouragement, and humor as I stepped through the most complicated and challenging project of my writing career. My simple payback is open gratitude expressed in these few paragraphs.

Among librarians and archivists, Martha Grenzeback, Omaha Public Library; Cindy Hagen, Little Bighorn Battlefield National Monument; Crow Agency, Montana; Cyndie Harlan, Hearst Library, Lead, South Dakota; Laura Jolley, State Historical Society of Missouri, Columbia; Zoe Ann Stolz, Montana Historical Society, Helena; Keli Brings Three White Horses, Sicangu Heritage Center, Mission, South Dakota; Kim Ostermyer, Sheridan Public Library, Wyoming; Abby Hoverstock, Denver Public Library; Lauren Gray, Kansas Historical Society, Topeka; Starr Zabel, Fort Phil Kearny/Bozeman Trail Association, Banner, Wyoming; Matt Piersol, Nebraska State Historical Society, Lincoln; Tawa Ducheneaux, Oglala Lakota College, Kyle, South Dakota; and Linda Allen, Willow Bunch Museum, Saskatchewan, cordially facilitated interlibrary loans and copy materials from the vast collections in their hands, often repeatedly.

Friends are often archivists, too, and I acknowledge Gary Clayton Anderson, University of Oklahoma, Norman; Philip Burnham, Baltimore, Maryland; Kingsley Bray, Manchester, England; C. Lee Noyes, Morrisonville, New York; Marc Abrams, Brooklyn, New York; the late William Lass, Mankato, Minnesota; Michel Hogue, Carleton University, Ottawa, Ontario; Rich Clow, University of Montana, Missoula; Dale Kozman, Lombard, Illinois; Bob Kolbe, Sioux Falls, South Dakota; Darrell Linthacum, Hardin, Montana; Frank Robertson, Apple Valley, Minnesota; Sandy Barnard, Wake Forest, North Carolina; Jim Donovan,

Dallas, Texas; John Doerner, Hardin, Montana; Dennis Hagen, Denver, the late John Monnett, Lafayette, Colorado; Claire Thomson, Wood Mountain, Saskatchewan; Vince Heier, Robertsville, Missouri, and Janet Milburn, Fort Walsh National Historic Site, Saskatchewan, who provided leads and often copy matter from their respective personal and public collections and files.

Thomas Powers, South Royalton, Vermont, repeatedly provided materials from his own extensive Crazy Horse collection and offered continual reassurances, usually when they were needed most. So too did David Wolff, Spearfish, South Dakota; Jerry Greene, Arvada, Colorado; Doug Scott, Grand Junction, Colorado; and Paul Hutton, Albuquerque.

Throughout the project, Mike Cowdrey of San Luis Obispo, California, proved an inspiring correspondent with a keen eye on all manner of northern plains Indian history and culture. He proved a tireless font of minutiae that invariably proved relevant, on subjects as diverse as *taureaux*, Sitting Bull imagery, and Crazy Horse's war shirt. Likewise two other friends, Mark Gardner of Cascade, Colorado, and Eli Paul, Kansas City, Missouri, maintained a similar continual chatter as my story evolved, variously reacting to or adding to the discovery of the moment, testing my thinking and conclusions, and always kicking me forward. The imprint on the story by these fine fellows was invaluable.

Sometimes simple good advice is critical. Steven Baker, an editor friend at the University of Oklahoma Press, was my go-to guy with questions on matters of difficult grammar. Early on, I leaned, too, on the now late Robert Utley of Scottsdale, Arizona, who corroborated details on Sitting Bull and was quick with sage counsel. Bob's email name was "oldbison" for charming good reason. And Joe Jackson of Virginia Beach, Virginia, was particularly encouraging at late stages of the project, offering his own insights on courses of action when all I saw before me were stumbling blocks.

Michael Donahue, Little Bighorn Battlefield ranger, pointed me in the right direction to the Sitting Bull prayer site overlooking the Little Big Horn Valley; and Randy Kane, Crawford, Nebraska; Todd Harburn, Twin Lake, Michigan; Charles "Chip" Haas, Omaha; and John Hedren, Deephaven, Minnesota ventured there with me one hot June afternoon. Some fifteen decades later, the place still exudes an aura.

At a critical moment late in the project, Gerard Baker, Miles City, Montana; Dayton Duncan, Rindge, New Hampshire; Dakota Goodhouse, Bismarck, North Dakota; and Emily Levine of Lincoln, Nebraska, rallied to address a Sitting Bull riddle. We never quite answered the question but the exchange demonstrated yet again the value of good friends.

As my manuscript progressed, I'd send chapters for review and comment to Jo Ann Hajek of Omaha, Randy Kane, and Mike Cowdrey, and they'd scrub the typos and invariably argue details. Always were their observations helpful if sometimes exceedingly challenging. In later stages selected chapters and larger segments were read by David Wolff, Ephriam Dickson of Carlsbad, New Mexico, Eli Paul, and Mike Meloy of Helena, and again the story is better for their thoughtful commentary. The completed manuscript was read by a tireless old friend, Charles Rankin of Helena, editor of many of my previous works, and chasing now a parallel story of his own. I've long-known Chuck, moreover, as a virtuoso wordsmith and he willingly took on my narrative. He'd always preface himself with a careful line that this was my story and I should embrace his suggestions as I wished, but no one has ever been more efficient at untangling my run-on sentences or suggesting appropriate alternative or rearranged words. I didn't dispute much.

I am especially grateful to my agent, Christopher Rogers, of the Dunow, Carlson & Lerner Literary Agency who took a chance with me as I dared enter a book world I knew very little about. Chris proved a tireless font of sound advice and encouragement. He, in turn, put me in the good hands of Pegasus Books, whose fine editors and artisans transformed my raw words into this unique product. At Pegasus, Claiborne Hancock, Jessica Case, Maria Fernandez, and Meghan Jusczak eased me through publication labors that were at once familiar but in the independent world also refreshingly unique.

And, finally, a special nod to Tom Jonas, of Phoenix, Arizona, a gifted cartographer who produced the two vibrant maps in the book

I dedicated this book to Marv Kaiser, of Prescott, Arizona, and formerly Williston, North Dakota. We befriended early in my Fort Union years and in those days saddled through plenty, professionally and personally. In the many years since, Marv still connects regularly, and beyond sharing family chatter and charming gossip we beat this project and its prospects to a pulp. His encouragement and good humor has never flagged. Hats off to you, Marv.

I sign off always with a nod to my girls, daughters Ethne and Whitney, daughter-in-law Alicia, and dear wife Connie. They know me best, suffer me graciously, and are grateful, I am sure, that I surface for air at least once in a while.

To one and all, thank you very much.

BIBLIOGRAPHY

Abbreviations

BYU, Brigham Young University
CBHMA, Custer Battlefield Historical & Museum Association
CCA, Crow Creek Agency
CRA, Cheyenne River Agency
DS, Dakota Superintendency
GRA, Grand River Agency
LBA, Lower Brule Agency
LBHA, Little Big Horn Associates
MMWH, *Montana The Magazine of Western History*
MS, Montana Superintendency
NA, National Archives
OU, University of Oklahoma
RCA, Red Cloud Agency
STA, Spotted Tail Agency
SWP, Sioux War Papers
USAMHI, U.S. Army Military History Institute
WA, Whetstone Agency

Manuscripts and Archival Collections

George Bent Papers. Beinecke Rare Book and Manuscript Library, Yale University, New Haven, CT.

Walter M. Camp Papers. Harold B. Lee Library, Brigham Young University, Provo, UT.

Walter Stanley Campbell Collection. Western History Collections, University of Oklahoma Libraries, Norman, OK.

John Colhoff and Joseph Balmer correspondence. Kingsley Bray Collection, Manchester, England.

Lewis F. Crawford Papers. State Historical Society of North Dakota, Bismarck, ND.

Crazy Horse Papers. Museum of the Fur Trade, Chadron, NE.

Doris Duke Collection. Western History Collections, University of Oklahoma Libraries, Norman, OK.

Fort Laramie National Historic Site Archives. National Park Service, Fort Laramie, WY.
Fort Laramie Telegrams Sent, 1876
Names File

Joseph Gallio Masters Collection. Kansas Historical Society, Topeka, KS.
Francis Vinton Greene Papers. New York Public Library, New York, NY.
Jerome A. Greene Papers. Arvada, CO.
George Bird Grinnell Manuscript Collection. Braun Research Library, Autry National Center of the American West, Los Angeles, CA.
Eleanor Hinman Papers. Nebraska State Historical Society, Lincoln, NE.
James Boyd Hubbell Papers. Minnesota Historical Society, Saint Paul, MN.
Edmond S. Meany Papers. University of Washington Libraries, Special Collections, Seattle, WA.
Nelson A. Miles Papers. U.S. Army Heritage and Education Center, Carlisle Barracks, PA.
David Humphreys Miller Collection. McCracken Research Library, Buffalo Bill Center of the West, Cody, WY.
National Archives, Kansas City, KS.
Record Group 75, Bureau of Indian Affairs, Rosebud Indian Agency, Census Roll of Indians at Spotted Tail Agency, 1877.
National Archives, Washington, DC.
Record Group 75, Letters Received by the Office of Indian Affairs, 1821–1881, Microcopy 234, Cheyenne and Arapaho Agency, Roll 121; Cheyenne River Agency, Rolls 127–31; Crow Creek Agency, Roll 249; Dakota Superintendency, Rolls 252–258, 261–62, 266, 270, 273; Fort Berthold Agency, Roll 295; Grand River Agency, Roll 306; Lower Brule Agency, Roll 401; Montana Superintendency, Rolls 491–92, 495–98, 500, 503–505, 509, 511, 513, 515–18; Red Cloud Agency, Rolls 715, 717–21, 723–25; Spotted Tail Agency, Rolls 840–41, 843; Standing Rock Agency, Rolls 845–47, 850; Whetstone Agency, Rolls 925–27.
Record Group 94, Adjutant General's Office Letters Received, 1876; Microcopy 666, Sioux War Papers, Rolls 280, 284–85.
Record Group 125, Records of the United States Court of Claims, General Jurisdiction, Legaré v. United States, no. 15713.
Record Group 393, Records of United States Army Continental Commands, Department of Dakota Letters Received, 1876; Department of the Platte Letters Received, 1876; Department of the Platte Telegrams Sent, 1875.
Record Group 533, Records of United States Army Continental Commands, Microcopy 1495. Military Division of the Missouri Special Files, Roll 605.
John G. Neihardt Collection. University of Missouri Libraries, Columbia, MO.
Samuel O'Connell Papers. Montana Historical Society Archives, Helena, MT.
Thomas Powers Collection, South Royalton, VT.
Crazy Horse Papers; Sioux Names Index.

Record Group 7, Records of the Governor General's Office. Library and Archives Canada, Ottawa, Ontario.
Frank Robertson Papers, Apple Valley, MN.
Mari Sandoz Collection (MS 0080). Archives & Special Collections, University of Nebraska Lincoln Libraries, Lincoln, NE.

Newspapers

Army and Navy Journal (New York City), 1871, 1873, 1876–77, 1880–81
Billings Gazette, 1934
Bismarck Tribune, 1876–77, 1881, 1886
Black Hills Weekly Pioneer, 1876
Brooklyn Daily Eagle, 1880
Cheyenne Daily Leader, 1876–78
Cheyenne Daily Sun, 1877
Chicago Inter-Ocean, 1874, 1876
Chicago Times, 1877–79
Chicago Tribune, 1876, 1881
Cincinnati Commercial, 1876
Daily Oklahoman (Oklahoma City), 1930
Deseret News (Salt Lake City), 1878, 1881
Detroit Free Press, 1877
Fort Dodge Messenger, 1875
New York Herald, 1875–77, 1879
New York Times, 1874, 1876–77, 1879–81, 1884, 1945
New York Tribune, 1873, 1876–77
New York World, 1876
Omaha Bee, 1876, 1903
Omaha Herald, 1876
Rapid City Daily Journal, 1951
Riverton Review (Wyoming), 1919
Rocky Mountain Husbandman (Diamond City, Montana), 1881
Saint Paul Pioneer Press, 1876–77, 1881, 1883, 1886
Sheridan Post (Wyoming), 1911
Washington National Republican, 1877
Weekly Rocky Mountain News (Denver), 1876
Winners of the West (Saint Joseph, Missouri), 1932–33

Books and Articles

Abrams, Marc, ed. *Newspaper Chronicle of the Indian Wars*, 15 vols., 1844–1969. Brooklyn, NY: Abrams Publications, 2010.

Adjutant General's Office. *Chronological List of Actions, &, With Indians from January 15, 1837 to January, 1891.* Fort Collins, CO: Old Army Press, 1979.

Agonito, Rosemary and Joseph. "Resurrecting History's Forgotten Women: A Case Study from the Cheyenne Indians." *Frontiers: A Journal of Women Studies* 6 (Autumn 1981): 8–16.

Albers, Patricia C. *The Home of the Bison: An Ethnographic and Ethnohistorical Study of Traditional Cultural Affiliations to Wind Cave National Park.* [Minneapolis, MN]; National Park Service and Department of American Indian Studies, University of Minnesota, 2003.

Allison, [E. H.] *The Surrender of Sitting Bull.* Dayton, OH: Walker Litho. and Printing Co., 1891.

Anderson, Gary Clayton. *Massacre in Minnesota: The Dakota War of 1862, The Most Violent Ethnic Conflict in American History.* Norman: University of Oklahoma Press, 2019.

———. *Sitting Bull and the Paradox of Lakota Nationhood.* New York: Pearson Longman, 2007.

Anderson, Grant K. "Samuel D. Hinman and the Opening of the Black Hills." *Nebraska History* 60 (Winter 1979): 520–42.

Anderson, Harry H. "Cheyennes at the Little Big Horn—A Study of Statistics." *North Dakota History* 27 (Spring 160): 81–93.

———. "A History of the Cheyenne River Indian Agency and its Military Post, Fort Bennett, 1868–1891." In *South Dakota Report and Historical Collections,* Vol. 28. Pierre: South Dakota Historical Society, 1957.

———. "Indian Peace-Talkers and the Conclusion of the Sioux War of 1876." *Nebraska History* 44 (December 1963): 233–54.

———. "A Sioux Pictorial Account of General Terry's Council at Fort Walsh, October 17, 1877." *North Dakota History* 22 (July 1955): 93–116.

———. "The War Club of Sitting Bull the Oglala." *Nebraska History* 42 (March 1961): 55–62.

Aquila, Richard. "Plains Indian War Medicine." *Journal of the West* 13 (April 1974): 19–43.

Bad Heart Bull and Helen H. Blish. *A Pictographic History of the Oglala Sioux.* Lincoln: University of Nebraska Press, 1967.

Baird, George W. "A Winter Campaign in Montana and Its Results." In *Personal Recollections of the War of the Rebellion,* ed. A. Noel Blakeman, 421–37. New York: G. P. Putnam's Sons, 1907.

Barbour, Barton H. *Fort Union and the Upper Missouri Fur Trade.* Norman: University of Oklahoma Press, 2001.

Barnard, Sandy. *Custer's First Sergeant John Ryan.* Terre Haute, IN: AST Press, 1996.

Barrett, Carole. "One Bull: A Man of Good Understanding." *North Dakota History* 66 (Summer–Fall 1999): 3–16.

Bear Nose, Roy. "Shout At, Her Autobiography." *Chicago Westerners Brand Book* (March 1962): 2–3, 7.

Beck, Paul N. *Inkpaduta: Dakota Leader.* Norman: University of Oklahoma Press, 2008.

Benham, D. J. "The Sioux Warrior's Revenge." *Canadian Magazine* 43 (Sept. 1914): 455–63.

Berg, Francie M. *Buffalo Heartbeats Across the Plains.* Hettinger, ND: Dakota Buttes Visitors Council, 2018.

Bettelyoun, Susan Bordeaux, and Josephine Waggoner. *With My Own Eyes: A Lakota Woman Tells Her People's Story.* Ed. Emily Levine. Lincoln: University of Nebraska Press, 1998.

Bigart, Robert, ed. *Letters from the Rocky Mountain Missions: Father Philip Rappagliosi.* Lincoln: University of Nebraska Press, 2003.

Bordeaux, William J. *Custer's Conqueror.* N.p.: Smith and Company, [1944].

Bourke, John G. *The Diaries of John Gregory Bourke, Vol. 1, November 20, 1872–July 28, 1876.* Ed. Charles M. Robinson III. Denton: University of North Texas Press, 2003.

———. *The Diaries of John Gregory Bourke, Vol. 2, July 29, 1876–April 7, 1878.* Ed. Charles M. Robinson III. Denton: University of North Texas Press, 2005.

———. John G. *The Diaries of John Gregory Bourke, Vol. 3, June 1, 1878–June 22, 1880.* Ed. Charles M. Robinson III. Denton: University of North Texas Press, 2007.

———. *On the Border With Crook.* New York: Charles Scribner's Sons, 1891.

———. *Mackenzie's Last Fight with the Cheyennes: A Winter Campaign in Wyoming and Montana.* Governor's Island, NY: Military Service Institution, 1890; reprint, Bellevue, NE: Old Army Press, 1970.

Bradley, James H. *The March of the Montana Column: A Prelude to the Custer Disaster.* Ed. Edgar I. Stewart. Norman: University of Oklahoma Press, 1961.

Brady, Cyrus Townsend. *Indian Fights and Fighters.* New York: Doubleday, Page & Company, 1904.

Bray, Kingsley M. *Crazy Horse: A Lakota Life.* Norman: University of Oklahoma Press, 2006.

———. "Crazy Horse and the End of the Great Sioux War." *Nebraska History* 79 (Fall 1998): 94–115.

———. "Pine Ridge Letters Shed New Light on the Battle of the Little Bighorn." *Ghost Herder, Journal of the Friends of the Little Bighorn Battlefield* 1 (May 2011): 37–48.

———. "Teton Sioux Population History, 1655–1881." *Nebraska History* 75 (Summer 1994): 165–88.

———. "'We Belong to the North': The Flights of the Northern Indians from the White River Agencies, 1877–1878." *MMWH* 55 (Summer 2005): 28–47.

Brininstool, E. A. *Crazy Horse: The Invincible Ogalalla Sioux Chief.* Los Angeles, CA: Wetzel Publishing Co., 1949.

Brink, Jack W. "A Hunter's Quest for Fat Bison." In *Bison and People on the North American Great Plains: A Deep Environmental History*, ed. Geoff Cunfer and Bill Weiser, 90–121. College Station: Texas A&M University Press, 2016.

Brown, Franz K. *Thunder Visions: The Crazy Horse Wotawe of the Lakota Medicine Man Woptuha.* Hot Springs, SD: [Franz Brown], 2010.

Brown, Jesse, and A. M. Willard. *The Black Hills Trails: A History of the Struggles of the Pioneers in the Winning of the Black Hills.* Rapid City, SD: Rapid City Journal Company, 1924.

Brown, Joseph Epes. *The Sacred Pipe: Black Elk's Account of the Seven Rites of the Oglala Sioux.* Norman: University of Oklahoma Press, 1953.

Brown, Mark H. *The Plainsmen of the Yellowstone: A History of the Yellowstone Basin.* New York: G. P. Putnam's Sons, 1961.

Buechel, Eugene, and Paul I. Manhart. *Lakota Tales & Texts*, vol. 2. Chamberlain, SD: Tipi Press, 1998.

Buecker, Thomas R. *Fort Robinson and the American West, 1874–1899.* Lincoln: Nebraska State Historical Society, 1999.

———. "Gold in the Hills: Rumors, Reports and Innuendo." *Museum of the Fur Trade Quarterly* 52 (Winter 2016): 6–14.

———. "Lt. William Philo Clark's Sioux War Report and Little Big Horn Map." *Greasy Grass* 7 (May 1991): 11–21.

———. ed. "A Surgeon at the Little Big Horn: The Letters of Dr. Holmes O. Paulding." *MMWH* 32 (Autumn 1982): 34–49.

Buecker, Thomas R., and Charles E. Hanson, "Spotted Tail's Agency on Wheels." In *Spotted Tail: Renaissance Man of the Lakotas*, ed. James A. Hanson, 127–41. Chadron, NE: Museum of the Fur Trade, 2020.

Buecker, Thomas R., and R. Eli Paul. *The Crazy Horse Surrender Ledger.* Lincoln: Nebraska State Historical Society, 1994.

Burdick, Usher L., ed. *David F. Barry's Indian Notes on "The Custer Battle."* Baltimore, MD: Wirth Brothers, 1949.

———. *The Last Battle of the Sioux Nation.* Stevens Point, WI: Worzalla Publishing Co., [1929].

———. *Tales from Buffalo Land: The Story of Fort Buford.* Baltimore, MD: Wirth Brothers, 1940.

Burnham, Philip. *Song of Dewey Beard: Last Survivor of the Little Bighorn.* Lincoln: University of Nebraska Press, 2014.

Campbell, Archibald, and W. J. Twining. *Reports Upon the Survey of the Boundary Between the Territory of the United States and the Possessions of Great Britain.* [Washington, DC: Government Printing Office], 1878.

Carroll, John M., ed. *The Eleanor H. Hinman Interviews on the Life and Death of Crazy Horse*. N.p.: Garry Owen Press, 1976.

Charger, Samuel. "Chronology of the Sioux Indians from an Early Period." *Sunshine Magazine* 10 (September 1928): 3–8.

Cheney, Roberta Carkeek. *Sioux Winter Count: A 131-Year Calendar of Events*. Happy Valley, CA: Naturegraph, 1998.

Chronological List of Action, &c., With Indians from January 15, 1837 to January, 1891. [Washington, DC]: Adjutant General's Office, 1891; reprint, Fort Collins, CO: Old Army Press, 1979.

Clark, Robert A., ed. *The Killing of Chief Crazy Horse*. Lincoln: University of Nebraska Press, 1988.

Clow, Richmond L. "General Philip Sheridan's Legacy: The Sioux Pony Campaign of 1876." *Nebraska History* 57 (Winter 1976): 461–76.

———. *Spotted Tail: Warrior and Statesman*. Pierre: South Dakota Historical Society Press, 2019.

Collins, John S. *Across the Plains in '64*. Omaha, NE: National Printing Company, 1904.

Colpitts, George. "A Metis View of the Summer Market Hunt on the Northern Plains." In *Bison and People on the North American Great Plains: A Deep Environmental History*, ed. Geoff Cunfer and Bill Weiser, 201–24. College Station: Texas A&M University Press, 2016.

Commissioner of Indian Affairs. *Report of the Commissioner of Indian Affairs to the Secretary of the Interior for the Year 1871*. Washington, DC: Government Printing Office, 1872.

———. *Report of the Commissioner of Indian Affairs to the Secretary of the Interior for the Year 1873*. Washington, DC: Government Printing Office, 1874.

———. *Report of the Commissioner of Indian Affairs to the Secretary of the Interior for the Year 1874*. Washington, DC: Government Printing Office, 1874.

———. *Report of the Commissioner of Indian Affairs to the Secretary of the Interior for the Year 1875*. Washington, DC: Government Printing Office, 1875.

———. *Report of the Commissioner of Indian Affairs to the Secretary of the Interior for the Year 1876*. Washington, DC: Government Printing Office, 1876.

———. *Report of the Commissioner of Indian Affairs to the Secretary of the Interior, 1877–78*. Washington, DC: Government Printing Office, 1878.

———. *Report of the Commissioner of Indian Affairs to the Secretary of the Interior, 1879–80*. Washington, DC: Government Printing Office, 1880.

Coues, Elliott, ed. *Forty Years a Fur Trader on the Upper Missouri: The Personal Narrative of Charles Larpenteur, 1833–1872*, two vols. New York: Francis P. Harper, 1898.

Cowdrey, Mike, and Ned & Jody Martin. *Horses & Bridles of the American Indians*. Nicasio, CA: Hawk Hill Press, 2012.

Cowie, Isaac. *The Company of Adventurers*. Toronto, Ontario: William Briggs, 1913; reprint, Lincoln: University of Nebraska Press, 1993.

Cozzens, Peter. *The Earth Is Weeping: The Epic Story of the Indian Wars of the American West*. New York: Alfred A. Knopf, 2016.

Crawford, Lewis F. *Rekindling Camp Fires: The Exploits of Ben Arnold (Connor)*. Bismarck, ND: Capital Book Co., 1926.

Cunfer, Geoff, and Bill Weiser, eds. *Bison and People on the North American Great Plains: A Deep Environmental History*. College Station: Texas A&M University Press, 2016.

DeBarthe, Joe. *The Life and Adventures of Frank Grouard, Chief of Scouts, U.S.A.* St. Joseph, MO: Combe Printing Company, 1894.

DeMallie, Raymond J. "The Sioux in Dakota and Montana Territories: Cultural and Historical Background of the Ogden B. Read Collection." In *Vestiges of a Proud Nation: The Ogden B. Read Northern Plains Indian Collection*, ed. Glenn E. Markoe, 18–69. Burlington, VT: Robert Hull Fleming Museum, 1986.

———. "'These Have No Ears': Narrative and the Ethnohistorical Method." *Ethnohistory* 40 (Fall 1991): 515–38.

———. *The Sixth Grandfather: Black Elk's Teachings Given to John G. Neihardt*. Lincoln: University of Nebraska Press, 1984.

———. "Teton." In *Handbook of North American Indians, Plains*, Vol. 13, Part 2 of 2, ed. Raymond J. DeMallie, 794–820. Washington, DC: Smithsonian Institution, 2001.

Dempsey, Hugh A., ed. *Men in Scarlet*. Calgary: Historical Society of Alberta/ McClelland and Stewart West, [1974].

Denig, Edwin Thompson. *Five Indians Tribes of the Upper Missouri*. Norman: University of Oklahoma Press, 1961.

Densmore, Frances. *A Collection of Specimens from the Teton Sioux*, Vol. 11, no. 3, *Indian Notes and Monographs*. New York: Museum of the American Indian, Heye Foundation, 1948.

———. *Teton Sioux Music*. Washington, DC: Government Printing Office, 1918.

Dickson III, Ephriam D. "The Big Road Roster." *CBHMA 21st Annual Symposium Proceedings*. Hardin, MT: CBHMA, 2007, 47–56.

———. "Black Moon: The Minneconjou Leader." *LBHA Newsletter* (December 2006): 4–5.

———. "Prisoners in the Indian Camp: Kill Eagle's Band at Little Big Horn." *Greasy Grass* 27 (May 2011): 3–11.

———. "Reconstructing the Indian Village on the Little Bighorn: The Cankahuhan or Soreback Band, Oglala." *Greasy Grass* 22 (May 2006): 2–14.

———. "Reconstructing the Little Big Horn Indian Village: The Oglala Tribal Circle." *CBHMA 20th Annual Symposium Proceedings*. Hardin, MT: CBHMA, 2006, 65–72.

———. *The Sitting Bull Surrender Census*. Pierre: South Dakota State Historical Society Press, 2010.

Diehl, Charles Sanford. *The Staff Correspondent*. San Antonio: Clegg Company, 1931.

Dillon, Robert. *Pute Tiyośpaye (Lip's Camp): A History and Culture of a Sioux Indian Village*. Wanblee, SD: Crazy Horse School, 1978.

Dixon, Chris. "Foley's Horse—Reflections on the Drawings of Amos Bad Heart Bull and Other Lakota Sources." *CBHMA 34th Annual Symposium Proceedings*. Hardin, MT: CBHMA, 2021, 18–31.

Dixon, Joseph K. *The Vanishing Race: The Last Great Indian Council*. Garden City, NY: Doubleday, 1913; reprint New York: Bonanza Books, 1975.

Dobak, William A. "Killing the Canadian Buffalo, 1821–1881." *Western Historical Quarterly* 27 (Spring 1996): 33–52.

Dodge, Richard Irving. *The Plains of North America and Their Inhabitants*. New York: G. P. Putnam's Sons, 1877.

Donahue, Michael N. *Drawing Battle Lines: The Map Testimony of Custer's Last Fight*. El Segundo, CA: Upton and Sons, Publishers, 2008.

———. "The Maps of John Stands In Timber." *Greasy Grass* 30 (May 2014): 20–29.

———. *Where the Rivers Ran Red: The Indian Fights of George Armstrong Custer*. Montrose, CO: San Juan Publishing Group, 2018.

Donovan, James. *A Terrible Glory, Custer and the Little Bighorn: The Last Great Battle of the American West*. New York: Little Brown and Company, 2008.

Douaud, Patrick C., ed. *The Western Metis: Profile of a People*. Regina, Saskatchewan: Canadian Plains Research Center/University of Regina, 2007.

Duncan, Dayton, and Ken Burns. *Blood Memory: The Tragic Decline and Improbable Resurrection of the American Buffalo*. New York: Alfred A. Knopf, 2023.

Eastman, Charles A. *Indian Heroes and Great Chieftains*. Boston, MA: Little, Brown, and Company, 1929.

———. "Rain in the Face: The Story of a Sioux Warrior." *The Outlook*, Oct. 27, 1906, 507–12.

Eckroth, David, and Harold Hagen. *Baker's Battle on the Yellowstone, Aug. 14, 1872: The Battle of Poker Flat*. Sheridan, WY: Frontier Heritage Alliance, 2004.

Eckroth, David, and Harold Hagen, with Mike Penfold. "Baker's Battle on the Yellowstone, August 14, 1872." *Greasy Grass* 31 (May 2015): 26–47.

Ege, Robert J. "Braves of all Colors: The Story of Isaiah Dorman, Killed at the Little Big Horn." *MMWH* 16 (January 1966): 35–40.

Eggleston, Wilfrid. "The Cypress Hills." *Canadian Geographical Journal* 42 (February 1951): 52–67.

Ens, Gerhard J. "The Border, the Buffalo, and the Metis of Montana." In *The Borderlands of the American and Canadian Wests: Essays on Regional History of the Forty-ninth Parallel*, ed. Sterling Evans, 139–54. Lincoln: University of Nebraska Press, 2006.

Everett, John P. "Bullets, Boots, and Saddles." In *The Sunshine Magazine Articles,* ed. John M Carroll, 1–27. Bryan, TX: privately printed, n.d.

Ewers, John C. *Indian Life on the Upper Missouri*. Norman: University of Oklahoma Press, 1968.

Finerty, John F. *War-Path and Bivouac, or, The Conquest of the Sioux*. Chicago, IL: Donohue & Henneberry, 1890.

Flores, Dan. "The Great Contraction: Bison and Indians in Northern Plains Environmental History." In *Legacy: New Perspectives on the Battle of the Little Bighorn*, ed. Charles E. Rankin, 2–22. Helena: Montana Historical Society, 1996.

———. "Reviewing an Iconic Story: Environmental History and the Demise of the Bison," In *Bison and People on the North American Great Plains: A Deep Environmental History*, ed. Geoff Cunfer and Bill Weiser, 30–47. College Station: Texas A&M University Press, 2016.

Forsyth, James W., and F. D. Grant. *Report of an Expedition Up the Yellowstone River, Made in 1875*. Washington, DC: Government Printing Office, 1875.

Fox, Richard A. *Archaeology, History, and Custer's Last Battle: The Little Big Horn Reexamined*. Norman: University of Oklahoma Press, 1993.

———. "The Value of Oral History: White Eagle's Account." In *CBHMA 9th Annual Symposium Proceedings*. Hardin, MT: CBHMA, 1996, 1–27.

———. "West River History: The Indian Village on Little Bighorn River, June 25–26, 1876." In *Legacy: New Perspectives on the Battle of the Little Bighorn*, ed. Charles E. Rankin, 139–65. Helena: Montana Historical Society, 1996.

Franklin, Catharine R. "Black Hills and Bloodshed: The U.S. Army and the Invasion of Lakota Land, 1868–1876." *MMWH* 63 (Summer 2013): 26–41.

Froiland, Sven G. *Natural History of the Black Hills*. Sioux Falls, SD: Center for Western Studies, Augustana College, 1978.

Garavaglia, Louis A., and Charles G. Worman. *Firearms of the American West, 1866–1894*. Albuquerque: University of New Mexico Press, 1985.

Gardner, Mark Lee. *The Earth Is All That Lasts: Crazy Horse, Sitting Bull, and the Last Stand of the Great Sioux Nation*. New York: Mariner Books, 2022.

Gatchell, T. J. "The Battle on the Red Fork." In *Powder River Country: The Papers of J. Elmer Brock*, ed. Margaret Brock Hanson, 88–94. Kaycee, WY: self-published, 1981.

Gilbert, Hila. *"Big Bat" Pourier*. Sheridan, WY: Mills Company, 1968.

Godfrey, E. S. *An Account of Custer's Last Campaign and the Battle of the Little Big Horn*. Palo Alto, CA: Lewis Osborne, 1968.

Goplen, Arnold O. *The Historical Significance of Fort Lincoln State Park*. Bismarck: State Historical Society of North Dakota, n.d.

Grabill, Andrew W. *Policing the Great Plains: Rangers, Mounties, and the North American Frontier, 1875–1910*. Lincoln: University of Nebraska Press, 2007.

Grafe, Ernest, and Paul Horsted. *Exploring With Custer: The 1874 Black Hills Expedition*. Custer, SD: Golden Valley Press, 2002.

Graham, W. A. *The Custer Myth: A Source Book of Custeriana*. Harrisburg, PA: Stackpole Company, 1953.

Grange, Jr., Roger T. "The Garnier Oglala Winter Count." *Plains Anthropologist* 8 (May 1963): 74–79.

Gray, John S. *Centennial Campaign, The Sioux War of 1876*. Fort Collins, CO: Old Army Press, 1976.

———. *Custer's Last Campaign: Mitch Boyer and the Little Bighorn Reconstructed*. Lincoln: University of Nebraska Press, 1991.

———. "Frank Grouard: Kanaka Scout or Mulatto Renegade." *Chicago Westerners Brand Book* (October 1959): 57–59, 62–64.

———. "The Lame Deer Fight Ends the Sioux War." *Chicago Westerners Brand Book* (May 1974): 17–19, 23–24.

———. "News from Paradise: Charley Reynolds Rides from the Black Hills to Fort Laramie." *By Valor & Arms* 3 (no. 3): 37–45.

———. "Peace-talkers from Standing Rock Agency." *Chicago Westerners Brand Book* (May 1966): 17–19.

———. "Sitting Bull Strikes the Glendive Supply Trains." *Chicago Westerners Brand Book* (June 1971): 25–27, 31–32.

———. "What Made Johnnie Bruguier Run?" *MMWH* 14 (April 1964): 34–49.

Greene, Candace S., and Russell Thornton, eds. *The Year the Stars Fell: Lakota Winter Counts at the Smithsonian*. Washington, DC: Smithsonian Institution, 2007.

Greene, Jerome A. *American Carnage: Wounded Knee, 1890*. Norman: University of Oklahoma Press, 2014.

———. *Beyond Bear's Paw: The Nez Perce Indians in Canada*. Norman: University of Oklahoma Press, 2010.

———. *Fort Randall on the Missouri, 1857–1892*. Pierre: South Dakota State Historical Society, 2005.

———. *January Moon: The Northern Cheyenne Breakout from Fort Robinson, 1878–1879*. Norman: University of Oklahoma Press, 2020.

———, ed. *Lakota and Cheyenne: Indian Views of the Great Sioux War, 1876–1877*. Norman: University of Oklahoma Press, 1994.

———. *Morning Star Dawn: The Powder River Expedition and the Northern Cheyennes, 1876*. Norman: University of Oklahoma Press, 2003.

———. *Nez Perce Summer, 1877: The U.S. Army and the Nee Me Poo Crisis*. Helena: Montana Historical Society Press, 2000.

———. "Out With a Whimper: The Little Missouri Expedition and the Close of the Great Sioux War." *South Dakota History* 35 (Spring 2005): 1–39.

———. *Slim Buttes, 1876: An Episode of the Great Sioux War*. Norman: University of Oklahoma Press, 1982.

———. *Yellowstone Command: Colonel Nelson A. Miles and the Great Sioux War, 1876–1877*. Lincoln: University of Nebraska Press, 1991.

Grinnell, George Bird. *The Fighting Cheyennes*. New York: Charles Scribner's Sons, 1915.

Haag, Larry, and Lawrence Barkwell. *The Boundary Commission's Metis Scouts—The 49th Rangers*. Winnipeg, Manitoba: Louis Riel Institute, 2009.

Hagen, Dennis. "Major Brisbin's Fort Pease Relief: Was the First Military Operation of the Great Sioux War a Necessary Humanitarian Effort?" *Greasy Grass* 35 (May 2019): 30–38.

Hämäläinen, Pekka. *Lakota America: A New History of Indigenous Power*. New Haven, CT: Yale University Press, 2019.

Hammer, Kenneth, ed. *Custer in '76: Walter Camp's Notes on the Custer Fight*. Provo, UT: Brigham Young University Press, 1976.

Hanna, Oliver Perry. *An Old Timer's Story of the Old Wild West*. [Big Horn, WY]: Big Horn City Historical Society, 2018.

Hanson, Jr., Charles E. "The Post-War Indian Gun Trade." *Museum of the Fur Trade Quarterly* 4 (Fall 1968): 1–11.

———, ed. "Red Cloud's Mission to Crazy Horse, 1877." *Museum of the Fur Trade Quarterly* 22 (Spring 1986): 9–13.

Hanson, James A., ed. "The F. C. Boucher Trade Token." *Museum of the Fur Trade Quarterly* 41 (Winter 2005): 16–18.

———. "Field Glasses." *Museum of the Fur Trade Quarterly* 47 (Summer 2011): 12–13.

———, ed. *Spotted Tail: Renaissance Man of the Lakotas*. Chadron, NE: Museum of the Fur Trade, 2020.

Hanson, Jeffrey R., and Sally Chirinos. *Ethnographic Overview and Assessment of Devils Tower National Monument, Wyoming*. Denver, CO: National Park Service, Intermountain Region, 1997.

Hanson, Joseph Mills. *The Conquest of the Missouri: Being the Story of the Life and Exploits of Captain Grant Marsh*. Chicago, IL: A. C. McClurg & Co., 1909.

Hantz, Joan. "The Girl Who Saved Her Brother." In *We, The Northern Cheyenne People: Our Land, Our History, Our Culture*, ed. Richard Little Bear, 67–70. Lame Deer, MT: Chief Dull Knife College, 2008.

Hardorff, Richard G. "Baliran, Honzinger, and the Custers: The Facts and Fictions of the Rain-in-the-Face Myth." *LBHA Research Review* 2 (December 1988): 2–19.

———, ed. *Camp, Custer, and the Little Bighorn: A Collection of Walter Mason Camp's Research Papers on General Custer's Last Fight*. El Segundo, CA: Upton and Sons, Publishers, 1997.

———, ed. *Cheyenne Memories of the Custer Fight: A Source Book*. Spokane, WA: Arthur H. Clark Company, 1995.

———. *The Custer Battle Casualties, II: The Dead, The Missing, and a Few Survivors.* El Segundo, CA: Upton and Sons, Publishers, 1999.

———. *Hokahey! A Good Day to Die! The Indian Casualties of the Custer Fight.* Spokane, WA: Arthur H. Clark Company, 1993.

———, ed. *Indian Views of the Custer Fight: A Source Book.* Spokane, WA: Arthur H. Clark Company, 2004.

———, ed. *Lakota Recollections of the Custer Fight: New Sources of Indian-Military History.* Spokane, WA: Arthur H. Clark Company, 1991.

———, ed. *The Surrender and Death of Crazy Horse.* Spokane, WA: Arthur H. Clark Company, 1998.

Hassrick, Royal B. "The Culture of the Sioux." In *Vestiges of a Proud Nation: The Ogden B. Read Northern Plains Indian Collection*, ed. Glenn E. Markoe, 71–77. Burlington, VT: Robert Hull Fleming Museum, 1986.

———. *The Sioux: Life and Customs of a Warrior Society.* Norman: University of Oklahoma Press, 1964.

Hedren, Paul L. *After Custer: Loss and Transformation in Sioux Country.* Norman: University of Oklahoma Press, 2011.

———. "Buffalo South and the Fort Laramie Treaties." In *Spotted Tail: Renaissance Man of the Lakotas*, ed. James A. Hanson, 75–105. Chadron, NE: Museum of the Fur Trade, 2020.

———. "The Crazy Horse Medal: An Enigma from the Great Sioux War." *Nebraska History* 75 (Summer 1994): 195–99.

———. *First Scalp for Custer: The Skirmish at Warbonnet Creek, Nebraska, July 17, 1876.* Rev. ed. Lincoln: Nebraska State Historical Society, 2005.

———. *Fort Laramie in 1876: Chronicle of a Frontier Post at War.* Lincoln: University of Nebraska Press, 1988.

———. "Garrisoning the Black Hills Road: The United States Army's Camps on Sage Creek and Mouth of Red Canyon, 1876–1877." *South Dakota History* 37 (Spring 2007): 1–45.

———. *Great Sioux War Orders of Battle: How the United States Army Waged War on the Northern Plains, 1876–1877.* Norman, Okla.: Arthur H. Clark Company, 2011.

———, ed. *Ho! For the Black Hills: Captain Jack Crawford Reports the Black Hills Gold Rush and Great Sioux War.* Pierre: South Dakota State Historical Society Press, 2012.

———. *John Finerty Reports the Sioux War.* Norman: University of Oklahoma Press, 2020.

———. "Persimmon Bill Chambers: The 'Scourge of the Black Hills.'" *Annals of Wyoming* 81 (Autumn 2009): 2–10.

———. *Powder River: Disastrous Opening of the Great Sioux War.* Norman: University of Oklahoma Press, 2016.

———. *Rosebud, June 17, 1876: Prelude to the Little Big Horn*. Norman: University of Oklahoma Press, 2019.

———. "Sitting Bull's Surrender at Fort Buford: An Episode in American History." *North Dakota History* 62 (Fall 1995): 2–15.

———. "'three cool, determined men': The Sioux War Heroism of Privates Evans, Stewart, and Bell." *MMWH* (Winter 1991): 14–27.

———. "Who Killed Crazy Horse? A Historiographical Review and Affirmation." *Nebraska History* 101 (Spring 2020): 2–17.

Heski, Tom. "Trailing the Lakota, Cheyenne, Custer & Reno: An On the Ground Synopsis." In *CBHMA 19th Annual Symposium Proceedings*. Hardin, MT: CBHMA, 2005, 9–18.

Hildebrandt, Walter, and Brian Hubner. *The Cypress Hills: The Land and Its People*. Saskatoon, Saskatchewan: Purich Publishing, 1994.

Hilger, H. Inez. "The Narrative of Oscar One Bull." *Mid-America* 28 (July 1946): 147–72.

Hill, Christina Gish. *Webs of Kinship: Family in Northern Cheyenne Nationhood*. Norman: University of Oklahoma Press, 2017.

Hogue, Michel. *Metis and the Medicine Line: Creating a Border and Dividing a People*. Chapel Hill: University of North Carolina Press, 2015.

Hornaday, William T. *The Extermination of the American Bison*. Washington, DC: Government Printing Office, 1889.

———. "The Passing of the Buffalo." *Cosmopolitan* 4 (October 1887): 85–98.

Horsted, Paul. *The Black Hills Yesterday and Today*. Custer, SD: Golden Valley Press, 2006.

Horsted, Paul, with Ernie Grafe and Jon Nelson. *Crossing the Plains with Custer*. Custer, SD: Golden Valley Press, 2009.

Howard, James H. "Two Teton Dakota Winter Count Texts." *North Dakota History* 27 (Spring 1960): 67–79.

———, ed. *The Warrior Who Killed Custer: The Personal Narrative of Chief Joseph White Bull*. Lincoln: University of Nebraska Press, 1968.

Howard, Joseph Kinsey. *Strange Empire: A Narrative of the Northwest*. New York: William Morrow and Company, 1952.

Hunt, Frazier and Robert Hunt. *I Fought with Custer: The Story of the Last Survivor of the Battle of the Little Big Horn*. New York: Charles Scribner's Sons, 1950.

Hunt, Fred A. "The Crumbling of Crazy Horse's Command." *Overland Monthly* 59 (February 1912): 159–63.

———. "The Punishment of Pi-zi's People," *Overland Monthly* 55 (March 1910): 299–316.

Hutchins, James S. *Boot & Saddles at the Little Bighorn*. Fort Collins, CO: Old Army Press, 1976.

———. *The Papers of Edward S. Curtis Relating to Custer's Last Battle*. El Segundo, CA: Upton & Sons, 2000.

———. "Poison in the Pemmican: The Yellowstone Wagon-Road & Prospecting Expedition of 1874." *MMWH* 8 (July 1958): 8–25.

Hutton, Paul Andrew, ed. *The Custer Reader*. Lincoln: University of Nebraska Press, 1992.

———. *Phil Sheridan and His Army*. Lincoln: University of Nebraska Press, 1985.

Hyde, George E. *Red Cloud's Folk: A History of the Oglala Sioux Indians*. Norman: University of Oklahoma Press, 1937.

———. *A Sioux Chronicle*. Norman: University of Oklahoma Press, 1956.

———. *Spotted Tail's Folk: A History of the Brulé Sioux*. Norman: University of Oklahoma Press, 1961.

Isenberg, Andrew C. *The Destruction of the Bison*. New York: Cambridge University Press, 2000.

Jackson, Donald. *Custer's Gold: The United States Cavalry Expedition of 1874*. New Haven, CT: Yale University Press, 1966.

Jackson, Joe. *Black Elk: The Life of an American Visionary*. New York: Farrar, Straus and Giroux, 2016.

Jenney, Walter P. *The Mineral Wealth, Climate and Rain-Fall, and Natural Resources of the Black Hills of Dakota*. Washington, DC: Government Printing Office, 1876.

Jennings, John. "The Plains Indians and the Law." In *Men in Scarlet*, ed. Hugh A. Dempsey, 50–65. Calgary: Historical Society of Alberta-McClelland and Stewart West, [1974].

Jensen, Richard E., ed. *The Indian Interviews of Eli S. Ricker, 1903–1919*. Lincoln: University of Nebraska Press, 2005.

Johnson, Virginia W. *The Unregimented General: A Biography of Nelson A. Miles*. Boston, MA: Houghton Mifflin Company, 1962.

Joyner, Christopher C. "The Hegira of Sitting Bull to Canada: Diplomatic Realpolitic, 1876–1881." *Journal of the West* 13 (April 1974): 6–18.

Kadlecek, Edward and Mabell Kadlecek. *To Kill an Eagle: Indian Views on the Last Days of Crazy Horse*. Boulder, CO: Johnson Books, 1981.

Kane, Randy. "The 'Flagpole Affair' at Red Cloud Agency: An Incident in the Cultural Transition of the Oglala Sioux." *Nebraska History* 97 (Fall 2016): 117–26.

———. "Who Killed Crazy Horse? Politics at Red Cloud Agency, Summer 1877." *Nebraska History* 101 (Fall 2020): 94–105.

Kappler, Charles J., ed. *Indian Affairs, Laws and Treaties, Vol. 1 (Laws)*. Washington, DC: Government Printing Office, 1904.

———, ed. *Indian Treaties, 1778–1883*. Mattituck, NY: Amereon House, 1972.

Karolevitz, Robert F. *Bishop Martin Marty: "The Black Robe Lean Chief."* Yankton, SD: privately printed, 1980.

Kelly, Carla. *Fort Buford: Sentinel at the Confluence*. Williston, ND: Fort Union Association, 2009.

Kime, Wayne R., ed. *The Powder River Expedition Journals of Colonel Richard Irving Dodge*. Norman: University of Oklahoma Press, 1997.

King, Charles. *Campaigning With Crook and Stories of Army Life*. New York: Harper & Brothers, 1890.

Knight, Oliver. "War or Peace: The Anxious Wait for Crazy Horse." *Nebraska History* 54 (Winter 1973): 521–44.

Krause, Herbert and Gary D. Olson. *Prelude to Glory: A Newspaper Accounting of Custer's 1874 Expedition to the Black Hills*. Sioux Falls, SD: Brevet Press, 1974.

LaPointe, Ernie. *Sitting Bull: His Life and Legacy*. Salt Lake City, UT: Gibbs Smith, 2009.

Larned, Charles W. "Expedition to the Yellowstone River in 1873: Letters of a Young Cavalry Officer." In *The Custer Reader*, ed. Paul Andrew Hutton, 180–200. Lincoln: University of Nebraska Press, 1992.

Larpenteur, Charles. *The Original Journal of Charles Larpenteur: My Travels to the Rocky Mountains Between 1833 and 1872*. Ed. Michael M. Casler. Chadron, NE: Museum Association of the American Frontier, 2007.

Larson, Robert W. *Gall: Lakota War Chief*. Norman: University of Oklahoma Press, 2007.

———. *Red Cloud: Warrior-Statesman of the Lakota Sioux*. Norman: University of Oklahoma Press, 1997.

Lass, William E. "The North Dakota-Canada Boundary." *North Dakota History* 63 (Fall 1996): 2–23.

———. "Steamboats on the Yellowstone." *MMWH* 35 (Autumn 1985): 26–41.

Lazarus, Edward. *Black Hills, White Justice: The Sioux Nation Versus the United States, 1775 to the Present*. New York: HarperCollins Publishers, 1991.

Lee, Jesse M. "The Capture and Death of an Indian Chieftain." *Journal of the Military Service Institution* 54 (May–June 1914): 323–40.

Leiker, James N., and Ramon Powers. *The Northern Cheyenne Exodus in History and Memory*. Norman: University of Oklahoma Press, 2011.

Leonard, Gary. *Black Twin: Dark Lord of the Oglala*. London: English Westerners Society, 2005.

Libby, O. G., ed. *The Arikara Narrative of the Campaign Against the Hostile Dakotas, June 1876*. Glorieta, NM: Rio Grande Press, 1976.

Liddic, Bruce R. *I Buried Custer: The Diary of Pvt. Thomas W. Coleman, 7th U.S. Cavalry*. College Station, TX: Creative Publishing Company, 1979.

Liddic, Bruce R., and Paul Harbaugh, eds. *Camp on Custer: Transcribing the Custer Myth*. Spokane, WA: Arthur H. Clark Company, 1995.

Linderman, Frank B. *American: The Life Story of a Great Indian*. New York: John Day Company, 1930.

Little Bear, Richard. *We, The Northern Cheyenne People: Our Land, Our History, Our Culture*. Lame Deer, MT: Chief Dull Knife College, 2008.

Lubetkin, M. John. *Before Custer: Surveying the Yellowstone, 1872*. Norman, OK: Arthur H. Clark Company, 2015.

———. "Clash on the Yellowstone: Monday, August 3, 1873." *LBHA Research Review* 17 (Summer 2003): 12–31.

———. *Custer and the 1873 Yellowstone Survey: A Documentary History*. Norman, OK: Arthur H. Clark Company, 2013.

———. "Jay Cooke, The Northern Pacific, and Custer on the Yellowstone," In *CBHMA 20th Annual Symposium*. Hardin, MT: CBHMA, 2006, 1–12.

———. *Jay Cooke's Gamble: The Northern Pacific Railroad, The Sioux, and the Panic of 1873*. Norman: University of Oklahoma Press, 2006.

———. *Road to War: The 1871 Yellowstone Surveys*. Norman, OK: Arthur H. Clark Company, 2016.

———. "Strike Up Garryowen,' August 11, 1873: Custer's Second Battle on the Yellowstone." *LBHA Research Review* 20 (Summer 2006): 2–16, 30–31.

Ludlow, William. *Report of a Reconnaissance of the Black Hills of Dakota, Made in the Summer of 1874*. Washington, DC: Government Printing Office, 1875.

MacEwan, Grant. *Sitting Bull: The Years in Canada*. Edmonton, Alberta: Hurtig Publishers, 1973.

MacLean, French L. *Sitting Bull, Crazy Horse, Gold, and Guns: The 1874 Yellowstone Wagon Road and Prospecting Expedition and the Battle of Lodge Grass Creek*. Atglen, PA: Schiffer Publishing, Ltd., 2016.

Madsen, William B. *Crazy Horse: The Lakota Warrior's Life & Legacy*. Layton, UT: Gibbs Smith, 2016.

Magid, Paul. *The Gray Fox: George Crook and the Indian Wars*. Norman: University of Oklahoma Press, 2015.

Mallery, Garrick, ed. *The Dakota and Corbusier Winter Counts,* Reprints in Anthropology, Vol. 36. Lincoln, NE: J & L Reprint Company, 1987.

Manypenny, George W. *Our Indian Wards*. Cincinnati, OH: Robert Clarke & Co., 1880.

Manzione, Joseph. *"I Am Looking to the North for My Life," Sitting Bull, 1876–1881*. Salt Lake City: University of Utah Press, 1991.

Marino, Cesare. "Lingering Clouds at the Greasy Grass: Numbers, Casualties, and Identity of the Indians Who Fought There in 1876." *LBHA Research Review* 19 (Summer 2005): 2–12.

Markoe, Glenn E., ed. *Vestiges of a Proud Nation: The Ogden B. Read Northern Plains Indian Collection*. Burlington, VT: Robert Hull Fleming Museum, 1986.

Marquis, Thomas B. *The Cheyennes of Montana*. Ed. Thomas D. Weist. Algonac, MI: Reference Publications, 1978.

———. *Memoirs of a White Crow Indian*. New York: The Century Co., 1928.

———. *She Watched Custer's Last Battle*. Hardin, MT: Hardin Tribune-Herald Printing, 1933.

———. *A Warrior Who Fought Custer.* Minneapolis, MN: Midwest Company, 1931.

Marshall III, Joseph M. *The Day the World Ended at the Little Bighorn: A Lakota History*. New York: Viking, 2007.

Marshall, Robert A. "How Many Indians Were There?" In *Custer and His Times, Book Two,* eds., John M. Carroll and Jay Smith, 207–224. Fort Worth, TX: Little Big Horn Associates, 1984.

Masters, Joseph G. *Shadows Fall Across the Little Horn*. Laramie: University of Wyoming Library, 1951.

Matthiessen, Peter. *In the Spirit of Crazy Horse.* New York: Viking, 1991.

McChristian, Douglas C. *Fort Laramie: Military Bastion of the High Plains*. Norman, OK: Arthur H. Clark Company, 2008.

McClernand, Edward J. *With the Indian and the Buffalo in Montana, 1870–1878*. Glendale, CA: Arthur H. Clark Company, 1969.

McClintock, John S. *Pioneer Days in the Black Hills*. Deadwood, SD: self-published, 1939.

McCrady, David G. *Living with Strangers: The Nineteenth-Century Sioux and the Canadian-American Borderlands*. Lincoln: University of Nebraska Press, 2006.

———. "Louis Riel and Sitting Bull's Sioux: Three Lost Letters." In *The Western Metis: Profile of a People*, ed. Patrick C. Douaud, 203–12. Regina, Saskatchewan: Canadian Plains Research Center/University of Regina, 2007.

McCreight, M. I. *Chief Flying Hawk's Tales: The True Story of Custer's Last Fight*. New York: Alliance Press, 1936.

———. *Firewater and Forked Tongues: A Sioux Chief Interprets U.S. History*. Pasadena, CA: Trail's End Publishing Co., 1947.

McDermott, John D. *Circle of Fire: The Indian War of 1865*. Mechanicsburg, PA: Stackpole Books, 2003.

———. *Gen. George Crook's 1876 Campaigns*. Sheridan, WY, Frontier Heritage Alliance, 2000.

———. *Red Cloud: Oglala Legend*. Pierre: South Dakota Historical Society Press, 2015.

———. *Red Cloud's War: The Bozeman Trail, 1866–1868*, two vols. Norman, OK: Arthur H. Clark Company, 2010.

McGillycuddy, Julia B. *McGillycuddy Agent: A Biography of Dr. Valentine B. McGillycuddy*. Stanford University, CA: Stanford University Press, 1941.

McGinnis, Anthony R. *Counting Coup and Cutting Horses: Intertribal Warfare on the Northern Plains, 1738–1889*. Lincoln: University of Nebraska Press, 1990.

McLaughlin, Castle. *A Lakota War Book from the Little Bighorn: The Pictographic "Autobiography of Half Moon."* Cambridge, MA: Peabody Museum Press, 2013.

McLaughlin, James. *My Friend the Indian*. Boston, MA: Houghton Mifflin Company, 1910.

McLemore, Clyde. "Fort Pease: The First Attempted Settlement in Yellowstone Valley." *MMWH* 2 (January 1952): 16–31.

Medicine Crow, Joe. "Custer and His Crow Scouts." In *Little Bighorn Remembered: The Untold Indian Story of Custer's Last Stand*, ed. Herman J. Viola, 104–23. New York: Times Books, 1999.

Mekeel, Scudder. "A Short History of the Teton-Dakota." *North Dakota History* 10 (July 1943): 137–205.

Michno, Gregory F. "Crazy Horse, Custer, and the Sweep to the North." *MMWH* 43 (Summer 1993): 42–53.

———. *Lakota Noon: The Indian Narrative of Custer's Defeat*. Missoula, MT: Mountain Press Publishing Company, 1997.

———. "Revision at the Little Bighorn: The Fall of Gall." *LBHA Research Review* 10 (June 1996): 19–25.

Miles, Nelson A. *Personal Recollections and Observations of General Nelson A. Miles*. Chicago, IL: Werner Company, 1897.

Miller, David, and others, eds. *The History of the Assiniboine and Sioux Tribes of the Fort Peck Indian Reservation: 1600–2012*. Poplar, MT: Fort Peck Community College, 2012.

Miller, David Humphreys. *Custer's Fall: The Indian Side of the Story*. New York: Duell, Sloan and Pearce, 1957.

———. "Echoes of the Little Bighorn." *American Heritage* 22 (June 1971): 28–39.

Monaghan, Leila. "Cheyenne and Lakota Women at the Battle of the Little Bighorn." *MMWH* 67 (Autumn 2017): 3–21.

Monnett, John H. *Tell Them We are Going Home: The Odyssey of the Northern Cheyennes*. Norman: University of Oklahoma Press, 2001.

———. *Where a Hundred Soldiers Were Killed: The Struggle for the Powder River Country in 1866 and the Making of the Fetterman Myth*. Albuquerque: University of New Mexico Press, 2008.

Monson, Paul G. "From Swiss Monk to Lakota Missionary: How Sitting Bull Transformed Bishop Martin Marty." *South Dakota History* 50 (Spring 2020): 4–24.

Moore, John H., Margot Liberty, and A. Terry Straus. "Cheyenne." In *Handbook of North American Indians, Plains*, Vol. 13, Part 2 of 2, ed. Raymond J. DeMallie, 863–85. Washington, DC: Smithsonian Institution, 2001.

Murray, Robert A. *Military Posts in the Powder River Country of Wyoming, 1865–1894*. Lincoln: University of Nebraska Press, 1968.

Neihardt, John G. *Black Elk Speaks, Being the Life Story of a Holy Man of the Oglala Sioux*. New York: William Morrow & *Company*, 1932.

———. *When the Tree Flowered: An Authentic Tale of the Old Sioux World*. New York: Macmillan Company, 1951.

Nelson, Marilyn Dear, and Christopher Nelson. *Red Cloud and the Indian Trader: The Remarkable Friendship of the Sioux Chief and JW Dear in the Last Days of the Frontier.* Essex, CT: TwoDot, 2023.

Nelson, Mark J. *White Hat: The Military Career of Captain William Philo Clark.* Norman: University of Oklahoma Press, 2018.

Nichols, Ronald H., ed. *Reno Court of Inquiry: Proceedings of a Court of Inquiry in the Case of Major Marcus A. Reno.* Hardin, MT: CBHMA, 2007.

Nohl, Jr., Lessing H. "Mackenzie Against Dull Knife: Breaking the Northern Cheyennes in 1876." In *Probing the American West: Papers from the Santa Fe Conference,* ed. K. Ross Toole and others, 86–92. Santa Fe: Museum of New Mexico Press, 1962.

Noyes, C. Lee. "Valley Fight Overview." In *CBHMA 24th Annual Symposium Proceedings.* Hardin, MT: CBHMA, 2010.

Olson, James C. *Red Cloud and the Sioux Problem.* Lincoln: University of Nebraska Press, 1965.

Olstad, Tyra A. *Zen of the Plains: Experiencing Wild Western Places.* Denton: University of North Texas Press, 2014.

Opening Up the West, Being the Official Reports to Parliament of the Activities of the Royal North-West Mounted Police Force from 1874–1879. Toronto, ON: Coles Publishing Company, 1973.

Papandrea, Ronald J. *They Never Surrendered: The Lakota Sioux Band That Sayed in Canada.* Warren, MI: self-published, 2003.

Parker, Watson. *Gold in the Black Hills.* Norman: University of Oklahoma Press, 1966.

Pearson, Jeffrey V. "Nelson A. Miles, Crazy Horse, and the Battle of Wolf Mountains." *MMWH* 51 (Winter 2001): 52–67.

———. "Tragedy at Red Cloud Agency: The Surrender, Confinement, and Death of Crazy Horse." *MMWH* 55 (Summer 2005): 14–27.

Pengra, Lilah Morton. "Five Questions About Isaiah Dorman & the 1876 Yellowstone Expedition." *CBHMA 31st Annual Symposium Proceedings.* Hardin, MT: CBHMA, 2017: 50–61.

———. *Isaiah Dorman: Interpreting the Evidence.* Buffalo Gap, SD: Lune House Publishing, 2016.

Pennanen, Gary. "Sitting Bull: Indian Without a Country." *Canadian Historical Review* 51 (June 1970): 123–40.

Peterson, Frances Y. "Dewey Iron Hail." *Frontier Times* 35 (Fall 1961): 37–38.

Pope, Dennis C. *Sitting Bull: Prisoner of War.* Pierre: South Dakota State Historical Society Press, 2010.

Potter, James E., ed. *From Our Special Correspondent: Dispatches from the 1875 Black Hills Council at Red Cloud Agency, Nebraska.* Lincoln: Nebraska State Historical Society Books, 2016.

Powell, Peter J. "High Bull's Victory Roster." *MMWH* 25 (Winter 1975): 14–21.

———. "Ox'zem: Box Elder and His Sacred Wheel Lance." *MMWH* 20 (April 1970): 30–41.

———. *People of the Sacred Mountain: A History of the Northern Cheyenne Chiefs and Warrior Societies, 1830–1879*, two vols. San Francisco: Harper & Row, 1981.

———. *Sweet Medicine: The Continuing Role of the Sacred Arrows, the Sun Dance, and the Sacred Buffalo Hat in Northern Cheyenne History*, two vols. Norman: University of Oklahoma Press, 1969.

Powers, Thomas. *The Killing of Crazy Horse.* New York: Alfred A. Knopf, 2010.

Powers, William K. *Winter Count of the Oglala.* Kendall Park, NJ: Lakota Books, [1962].

Price, Catherine. *The Oglala People, 1841–1879: A Political History.* Lincoln: University of Nebraska Press, 1996.

Quivey, Addison M. "The Yellowstone Expedition of 1874." In *Contributions to the Historical Society of Montana*, Vol. 1, Helena: Independent Publishing Company, 1902.

Rankin, Charles E., ed. *Legacy: New Perspectives on the Battle of the Little Bighorn.* Helena: Montana Historical Society, 1996.

Red Shirt, Delphine. *George Sword's Warrior Narratives.* Lincoln: University of Nebraska Press, 2016.

Report of the Sitting Bull Indian Commission. Washington, DC: Government Printing Office, 1877.

Richard, Gordon. "Was Touch the Clouds at the Little Bighorn?" *CBHMA Battlefield Dispatch*, 40 (Summer 2021): 7, 9.

Riggs, Thomas Lawrence. "Sunset to Sunset: A Lifetime with My Brothers, The Dakotas," *South Dakota Historical Collections*, Vol. 29. Pierre: South Dakota State Historical Society, 1958.

Riley, Paul D. "The Battle of Massacre Canyon." *Nebraska History* 54 (1973): 220–249.

Roberts, Gary L. "The Shame of Little Wolf." *MMWH* 28 (July 1978): 36–47.

Robertson, Francis B. "We Are Going to Have a Big Sioux War: Colonel David S. Stanley's Yellowstone Expedition, 1872." *MMWH* 34 (Autumn 1984): 2–15.

Robinson, Charles M. *The Buffalo Hunters.* Austin, TX: State House Press, 1995.

Rodenbough, Theo F. *Uncle Sam's Medal of Honor.* New York: G. P. Putnam's Sons, 1886.

Roe, Frank G. "The Extermination of the Buffalo in Western Canada." *Canadian Historical Review* 15 (March 1934): 1–23.

Russell, Don *The Lives and Legends of Buffalo Bill.* Norman: University of Oklahoma Press, 1960.

Saindon, Robert A. *Old Fort Peck & Its Neighborhood.* N.p.: self-published, 2011.

Sandburg, Carl. *Smoke and Steel.* New York: Harcourt, Brace and Company, 1920.

Sandoz, Mari. *Crazy Horse: The Strange Man of the Oglalas*. New York: Hastings House, 1942.

———. *Hostiles and Friendlies: Selected Short Writings of Mari Sandoz*. Lincoln: University of Nebraska Press, 1959.

Schneider, George A., ed. *The Freeman Journal: The Infantry in the Sioux Campaign of 1876*. San Rafael, CA: Presidio Press, 1977.

Schultz, James Willard. *William Jackson, Indian Scout*. Boston: Houghton Mifflin, 1926; reprint, Springfield, IL: William K. Cavanaugh, 1976.

Scott, Douglas D. "Ammunition Components from the Rosebud Battlefield and Their Relationship to the Battle of the Little Bighorn." In *CBHMA 28th Annual Symposium Proceedings*. Hardin, MT: CBHMA, 2015, 102–25.

Scott, Douglas D. and others. *Archaeological Perspectives on the Battle of the Little Bighorn*. Norman: University of Oklahoma Press, 1989.

Scott, Hugh Lenox. *Some Memories of a Soldier*. New York: Century Co., 1928.

Secretary of War. *Annual Report of the Secretary of War for the Year 1874*. Washington, DC: Government Printing Office, 1874.

———. *Annual Report of the Secretary of War for the Year 1877*. Washington, DC: Government Printing Office, 1877.

———. *Annual Report of the Secretary of War* for the Year 1881. Washington, DC: Government Printing Office, 1881.

Seminole, Mina. "Northern Cheyenne Sacred Sites and Objects." In *We, The Northern Cheyenne People: Our Land, Our History, Our Culture*, ed. Richard Little Bear, 85–88. Lame Deer, MT: Chief Dull Knife College, 2008.

Simons, John Y., ed. *The Papers of Ulysses S. Grant, Vol. 26: 1875*. Carbondale: Southern Illinois University Press, 2003.

———, ed. *The Papers of Ulysses S. Grant, Vol. 28: November 1, 1876–September 30, 1878*. Carbondale: Southern Illinois University Press, 2005.

Slaughter, Linda W. "Leaves from Northwestern History." In *Collections of the State Historical Society of North Dakota*, Vol. 1. Bismarck, ND: Tribune, State Printers and Binders, 1906.

Smalley, Eugene V. *History of the Northern Pacific Railroad*. New York: G. P. Putnam's Sons, 1883.

Smalley, Vern G. "The Lone Tepees Along Reno Creek." In *CBHMA 12th Annual Symposium Proceedings*. Hardin, MT: CBHMA, 1998, 1–11.

Smith, Dennis J. "Convergence: Fort Peck Assiniboine and Sioux Arrive in the Fort Peck Region, 1800–1871." In *The History of the Assiniboine and Sioux Tribes of the Fort Peck Indian Reservation: 1600–2012*, ed. David Miller and others, 43–65. Poplar, MT: Fort Peck Community College, 2012.

———. "The Starving Years, 1878–1888." In *The History of the Assiniboine and Sioux Tribes of the Fort Peck Indian Reservation: 1600–2012*, ed. David

Miller and others, 113–30, 147–54. Poplar, MT: Fort Peck Community College, 2012.

Smith, Sherry L. *Sagebrush Soldier: Private William Earl Smith's View of the Sioux War of 1876*. Norman: University of Oklahoma Press, 1989.

Smith, Victor Grant. *The Champion Buffalo Hunter: The Frontier Memoirs of Yellowstone Vic Smith*. Ed. Jeanette Prodgers. Helena, MT: TwoDot, 1997.

Spindler, Will. "The Scout Who Saved the Sioux," *Frontier Times* 42 (June–July 1968): 13, 44–45.

Sprague, Donovin. "Hump & Crazy Horse: Defending the Lakota & Cheyenne, 1876–1877." *CBHMA 24th Annual Symposium Proceedings*. Hardin, MT: CBHMA, 2010: 57–73.

Standing Bear, Luther. *My People the Sioux*. Boston, MA: Houghton Mifflin Company, 1923.

Stands In Timber, John. "Last Ghastly Moments at the Little Bighorn." *American Heritage* 17 (April 1966): 14–21, 72.

Stands In Timber, John, and Margot Liberty. *Cheyenne Memories*. New Haven, CT: Yale University Press, 1967.

———. *A Cheyenne Voice: The Complete John Stands In Timber Interviews*. Norman: University of Oklahoma Press, 2013.

Stewart, Edgar I. *Custer's Luck*. Norman: University of Oklahoma Press, 1955.

Stewart, Edgar I. and Jane R. Stewart, eds. *The Field Diary of Lt. Edward Settle Godfrey*. Portland, OR: Champoeg Press, 1957.

Sundstrom, Linea. "The Sacred Black Hills, An Ethnohistorical Review." *Great Plains Quarterly* 17 (Summer–Fall 1997): 185–212.

Svingen, Orlan J. *The Northern Cheyenne Indian Reservation, 1877–1900*. Niwot: University Press of Colorado, 1993.

Szabo, Joyce M. *Howling Wolf and the History of Ledger Art*. Albuquerque: University of New Mexico Press, 1994.

Taylor, Joseph Henry. *Kaleidoscopic Lives*. Washburn, ND: self-published, 1902.

Thomas, Rodney G. *Rubbing Out Long Hair, Pehin Hanska Kasota*. Spanaway, WA: Elk Plains Press, 2009.

Topping, E. S. *The Chronicles of the Yellowstone*. Saint Paul: Pioneer Press, 1883; reprint, Minneapolis, MN: Ross & Haines, Inc., 1968.

Trinque, Bruce A. "The Fight in Fishing Woman Ravine." In *Custer and His Times, Book Four*, ed. John P. Hart, 213–26. LaGrange Park, IL: LBHA, 2002.

Turchen, Lesta V., and James D. McLaird. *The Black Hills Expedition of 1875*. Mitchell, SD: Dakota Wesleyan University Press, 1975.

Turner, C. Frank. "Sitting Bull Tests the Mettle of the Redcoats." In *Men in Scarlet*, ed. Hugh A. Dempsey, 66–76. Calgary: Historical Society of Alberta/McClelland and Stewart West, [1974].

Utley, Robert M. *Frontiersmen in Blue: The United States Army and the Indians, 1848–1865*. New York: Macmillan Publishing Co., 1967.

———. *The Lance and The Shield: The Life and Times of Sitting Bull.* New York: Henry Holt and Company, 1993.

———. *The Last Sovereigns: Sitting Bull and the Resistance of the Free Lakotas.* Lincoln: University of Nebraska Press, 2020.

Vaughn, J. W. *Indian Fights: New Facts on Seven Encounters*. Norman: University of Oklahoma Press, 1966.

———. *The Reynolds Campaign on Powder River.* Norman: University of Oklahoma Press, 1961.

———. *With Crook at the Rosebud*. Harrisburg, PA: Stackpole Company, 1956.

Vestal, Stanley. "The Man Who Killed Custer." *American Heritage* 8 (February 1957): 4–9, 90–91.

———. *New Sources of Indian History, 1850–1891*. Norman: University of Oklahoma Press, 1934.

———. *Sitting Bull: Champion of the Sioux*. Norman: University of Oklahoma Press, 1932, new edition, 1957.

———. *Warpath and Council Fire: The Plains Indians' Struggle for Survival in War and in Diplomacy*. New York: Random House, 1948.

———. *Warpath: The True Story of the Fighting Sioux Told in a Biography of Chief White Bull.* Boston, MA: Houghton Mifflin Company, 1934.

Viola, Herman J. *Little Bighorn Remembered: The Untold Indian Story of Custer's Last Stand*. New York: Times Books, 1999.

Wade, F. C. "The Surrender of Sitting Bull." *The Canadian Magazine* 24 (Fall 1910): 335–44.

Waggoner, Josephine. *Witness: A Húnkpapȟa Historian's Strong-Heart Song of the Lakotas*. Ed. Emily Levine. Lincoln: University of Nebraska Press, 2013.

Walker, James R. *Lakota Society*. Lincoln: University of Nebraska Press, 1982.

Webb, Walter Prescott. *The Great Plains*. New York: Ginn and Company, 1931.

Wedel, Waldo R. "Notes on the Prairie Turnip (Psoralea esculenta) Among the Plains Indians." *Nebraska History* 59 (Summer 1978): 155–79.

Werts, Keith T. *The Crazy Horse and Colonel Nelson Miles Fight of 1877: New Discoveries at the Battle of the Butte*. Spokane, WA: Werts Publishing, 2014.

West, Elliott. *Last Indian War: The Nez Perce Story*. New York: Oxford University Press, 2009.

Wheeler, Homer W. *Buffalo Days: Forty Years in the Old West*. New York: A. L. Burt Company, 1923.

Williams, Thomas Benton. *The Soul of the Red Man*. N.p.: privately printed, 1937.

Wilson, Garrett. *Frontier Farewell: The 1870s and the End of the Old West*. Regina, Saskatchewan: University of Regina Press, 2014.

Wiltsey, Norman B. "The Great Buffalo Slaughter." In *The American West*, ed. Raymond Friday Locke, 109–40. Los Angeles, CA: Mankind Publishing Company, 1971.

———. "We Killed Custer." *Real West* 11 (June 1968): 25–27.

Wishart, Bruce. "Grandmother's Land: Sitting Bull in Canada, Part I, Arrival of the Warrior." *True West* 37 (May 1980): 14–20.

———. "Grandmother's Land: Sitting Bull in Canada, Part II, The Time of Power." *True West* 37 (June 1980): 26–32.

———. "Grandmother's Land: Sitting Bull in Canada, Part III, The Time of Defeat." *True West* 37 (July 1980): 20–27.

———. "Grandmother's Land: Sitting Bull in Canada, Part IV, Surrender." *True West* 37 (August 1980): 28–32.

Wolff, David A. *The Savior of Deadwood: James K. P. Miller on the Gold Frontier.* Pierre: South Dakota Historical Society Press, 2021.

Woodhead, Henry, ed. *The Buffalo Hunters.* Alexandria, VA: Time-Life Books, 1993.

"Yellow Nose Tells of Custer's Last Stand," *Big Horn-Yellowstone Journal*, 1 (Summer 1992): 14–17.

Young, Harry. *Hard Knocks: A Life Story of the Vanishing West.* Portland, OR: Wells & Company, 1915.

Special Reports

Belitz, Larry. "Chips Collection of Crazy Horse Medicines." 2010.

Cowdrey, Mike. "A Winter Count of the *Wajaje* Lakota, 1758–59 to 1885–86." 2014.

Scott, Douglas D. "Searching the Battle of the Rosebud for the Soldier Burials: Historic Records Research and Archaeological Investigations." 2022.

On-line Resources

Akta Lakota Museum and Cultural Center, Chamberlin, South Dakota, "Thirteen Lakota Moons," aktalakota.stjo.org.

Boucher, Francis. findagrave.com.

Cowdrey, Mike. "A Letter from Sitting Bull." Heritage Auctions, Lot 70401, Nov. 20, 2020, fineart/ha.com.

Goodhouse, Dakota. "The Blue Thunder Winter Count," thefirstscout.blogspot.com.

———. High Dog and Long Soldier Winter Counts, thefirstscout.blogspot.com.

Henry Model 1840 .44 caliber rifle, americanindian.si.edu.

"Steps—Seeskoomkee—Bannock/Shoshone and Nez Perce," American-Tribes.com.

Thomson, Claire. "Lakota Place Names in Southwestern Saskatchewan." skhistory.ca.

NOTES

Preface

1 Carl Sandburg, "Buffalo Dusk," in *Smoke and Steel* (New York: Harcourt, Brace and Company, 1920), 235.

1. A Time in the West

1 "Incidents of the Surrender," *Saint Paul and Minneapolis Pioneer Press*, Aug. 3, 1881.

2 "Piping Times of Peace," *Saint Paul and Minneapolis Pioneer Press*, Aug. 3, 1881; "Sitting Bull," *Army and Navy Journal*, Aug. 13, 1881 (quotation); "Sitting Bull's Surrender," *Saint Paul and Minneapolis Pioneer Press*, Aug. 14, 1881.

3 "Sitting Bull," *Army and Navy Journal*, Aug. 13, 1881; "Sitting Bull's Surrender," *Saint Paul and Minneapolis Pioneer Press*, Aug. 14, 1881 (quotation).

4 "Piping Times of Peace," *Saint Paul and Minneapolis Pioneer Press*, Aug. 3, 1881; "The Surrender of Sitting Bull," *Army and Navy Journal*, July 23, 1881.

5 "Bagged by Brotherton," *Saint Paul and Minneapolis Pioneer Press*, July 20, 1881.

6 "Story of the Surrender," *Saint Paul and Minneapolis Pioneer Press*, July 21, 1881.

7 John C. Ewers, "When Sitting Bull Surrendered His Winchester," in *Indian Life on the Upper Missouri* (Norman: University of Oklahoma Press, 1968), 178–79; Louis A. Garavaglia and Charles G. Worman, *Firearms of the American West, 1866–1894* (Albuquerque: University of New Mexico Press, 1985), 370; "Sitting Bull's Surrender," *Saint Paul and Minneapolis Pioneer Press*, Aug. 14, 1881 (quotation); Jean Legaré to Walter Camp, Oct. 27, 1910, W. M. Camp Papers, Harold B. Lee Library, BYU, Provo, UT; Usher L. Burdick, *Tales from Buffalo Land: The Story of Fort Buford* (Baltimore, MD: Wirth Brothers, 1940), 46, 48; Carole Barrett, "One Bull: A Man of Good Understanding," *North Dakota History* 66 (Summer–Fall 1999): 9, quoting the Campbell Papers, University of Oklahoma, Norman. The next day Fort Buford's post trader offered Mrs. Clifford $500 for the horse, but she kept it and it became the pet of Clifford's son until it was stolen by a soldier deserter, who fled with it to Canada.

8 "Bull at Buford," *Saint Paul and Minneapolis Pioneer Press*, July 21, 1881; Garavaglia and Worman, *Firearms of the American West*, 369.

9 "Bull at Buford," *Saint Paul and Minneapolis Pioneer Press*, July 21, 1881.

10 "Bull at Buford."

11 "Bull at Buford."

12 "Piping Times of Peace," *Saint Paul and Minneapolis Pioneer Press*, Aug. 3, 1881. Despite considerable effort the identity of the lone newsman remains a mystery. See Paul L. Hedren, "Sitting Bull's Surrender at Fort Buford: An Episode in American History," *North Dakota History* 62 (Fall 1995): 7n19.

13 The characterization is drawn from Robert M. Utley, *The Lance and The Shield: The Life and Times of Sitting Bull* (New York: Henry Holt and Company, 1993), 11, 21, 32–33; Peter Cozzens, *The Earth Is Weeping: The Epic Story of the Indian Wars of the American West* (New York: Alfred A. Knopf, 2016), 191–92; and Mark Lee Gardner, *The Earth Is All That Lasts: Crazy Horse, Sitting Bull, and the Last Stand of the Great Sioux Nation* (New York: Mariner Books, 2022), 20, 72–75.

14 Utley, *The Lance and The Shield*, 20, 100–101, 143–44, 166, 193, 226; Ernie LaPointe, *Sitting Bull: His Life and Legacy* (Salt Lake City, UT: Gibbs Smith, 2009), frontispiece; Ephriam D. Dickson III, *The Sitting Bull Surrender Census* (Pierre: South Dakota State Historical Society Press, 2010), 23.

15 For two rather distinctive examinations of the plains, both by American geographers, see Walter Prescott Webb, *The Great Plains* (New York: Ginn and Company, 1931); and Tyra A. Olstad, *Zen of the Plains: Experiencing Wild Western Places* (Denton: University of North Texas Press, 2014).

16 Webb, *Great Plains*, 43–44; Richard Irving Dodge, *The Plains of North America and Their Inhabitants* (New York: G. P. Putnam's Sons, 1877), 120; Andrew C. Isenberg, *The Destruction of the Bison* (New York: Cambridge University Press, 2000), 23.

17 Dan Flores, "The Great Contraction: Bison and Indians in Northern Plains Environmental History," in *Legacy: New Perspectives on the Battle of the Little Bighorn*, ed. Charles E. Rankin (Helena: Montana Historical Society Press, 1996), 13, 17–18; Paul L. Hedren, "Buffalo South and the Fort Laramie Treaties," in *Spotted Tail: Renaissance Man of the Lakotas*, ed. James A. Hanson (Chadron, NE.: Museum of the Fur Trade, 2020), 76–77, 102n1; John G. Neihardt, *When the Tree Flowered: An Authentic Tale of the Old Sioux World* (New York: Macmillan Company, 1951), 137 (quotation).

18 Patricia C. Albers, *The Home of the Bison: An Ethnographic and Ethnohistorical Study of Traditional Cultural Affiliations to Wind Cave National Park* ([Minneapolis, MN]: National Park Service and Department of American Indian Studies, University of Minnesota, 2003), 49, 78; Royal B. Hassrick, "The Culture of the Sioux," in *Vestiges of a Proud Nation: The Ogden B. Read Northern Plains Indian Collection*, ed. Glenn E. Markoe (Burlington, VT: Robert Hull Fleming Museum, 1986), 71.

19 Albers, *Home of the Bison*, 79, 82; Joseph M. Marshall III, *The Day the World Ended at the Little Bighorn: A Lakota History* (New York: Viking, 2007), 44; Raymond J. DeMallie, "Teton," in *Handbook of North American Indians, Plains*, Vol. 13, Part 2 of 2, ed. Raymond J. DeMallie (Washington, DC: Smithsonian Institution, 2001), 794; Kingsley M. Bray, "Teton Sioux Population History, 1655–1881," *Nebraska History* 75 (Summer 1994): 175.

20 Albers, *Home of the Bison*, 79; Marshall, *Day the World Ended at the Little Bighorn*, 45; DeMallie, "Teton," 794.

21 Albers, *Home of the Bison*, 77, 79–80; Marshall, *Day the World Ended at the Little Bighorn*, 45; DeMallie, "Teton," 794; Barton H. Barbour, *Fort Union and the Upper Missouri Fur Trade* (Norman: University of Oklahoma Press, 2001), 98, 232.

22 Mari Sandoz, *Crazy Horse: The Strange Man of the Oglalas* (New York: Hastings House, 1942), 98–99; Albers, *Home of the Bison*, 92; Catherine Price, *The Oglala People, 1841–1879: A Political History* (Lincoln: University of Nebraska Press, 1996), 5; DeMallie, "Teton," 807; Thomas Powers, *The Killing of Crazy Horse* (New York: Alfred A. Knopf, 2010), 70.

23 Mike Cowdrey and Ned & Jody Martin, *Horses & Bridles of the American Indians* (Nicasio, CA: Hawk Hill Press, 2012), 15; Stanley Vestal, *Sitting Bull: Champion of the Sioux* (Norman: University of Oklahoma Press, 1932, new edition, 1957), 26.

24 Stanley Vestal, *New Sources of Indian History—1850–1891* (Norman: University of Oklahoma Press, 1934), 164; Josephine Waggoner, *Witness: A Húnkpapȟa Historian's Strong-Heart Song of the Lakotas*, ed. Emily Levine (Lincoln: University of Nebraska Press, 2013), 108 (quotation), 109.

25 Powers, *The Killing of Crazy Horse*, 78; Edwin Thompson Denig, *Five Indians Tribes of the Upper Missouri* (Norman: University of Oklahoma Press, 1961), 5–6; DeMallie, "Teton," 794; Sven G. Froiland, *Natural History of the Black Hills* (Sioux Falls, SD: Center for Western Studies, Augustana College, 1978), 11; Peter Matthiessen, *In the Spirit of Crazy*

Horse (New York: Viking, 1991), 4; He Dog interview, Crazy Horse Papers, Museum of the Fur Trade, Chadron, NE, (quotation). The matter of the sacredness of the Black Hills is well defended by Linea Sundstrom, "The Sacred Black Hills, An Ethnohistorical Review," *Great Plains Quarterly* 17 (Summer–Fall 1997): 185–212.

26 Mina Seminole, "Northern Cheyenne Sacred Sites and Objects," in *We, The Northern Cheyenne People: Our Land, Our History, Our Culture*, ed. Richard Little Bear (Lame Deer, MT: Chief Dull Knife College, 2008), 85–88; Henry Woodhead, ed., *The Buffalo Hunters* (Alexandria, VA: Time-Life Books, 1993), 44–47; Jeffrey R. Hanson and Sally Chirinos, *Ethnographic Overview and Assessment of Devils Tower National Monument, Wyoming* (Denver, CO: National Park Service, Intermountain Region, 1997), 13; Peter John Powell, *People of the Sacred Mountain: A History of the Northern Cheyenne Chiefs and Warrior Societies, 1830–1879*, two vols. (San Francisco, CA: Harper & Row, 1981), vol, 1: xxxvii; Thomas Odell to George Hyde, October 23, 1939, Thomas Powers Papers, South Royalton, VA; Waggoner, *Witness*, 62, 109.

27 Thomas B. Marquis, "Iron Teeth, A Cheyenne Old Woman," in *The Cheyennes of Montana*, ed. Thomas D. Weist (Algonac, MI: Reference Publications, 1978), 57; Utley, *The Lance and The Shield*, 39.

28 "Arming the Sioux," *Army and Navy Journal*, July 29, 1876, discussing illegal trading carried on in the proximity of Fort Peck, Montana, in 1873. The gamut of Indian firearms is perfectly exemplified by the two weapons Sitting Bull surrendered at Fort Buford in 1881, an aged Northwest trade gun and a modern Winchester carbine. Indian weapons of the era are carefully detailed by Charles E. Hanson, Jr., "The Post-War Indian Gun Trade," *Museum of the Fur Trade Quarterly* 4 (Fall 1968): 1–11; and Garavaglia and Worman, *Firearms of the American West*, ch. 6, "Postwar Indian Guns." Archaeological studies of cartridges and bullets unearthed on the Rosebud and Little Big Horn battlefields provide additional specifics. See Douglas D. Scott, "Ammunition Components from the Rosebud Battlefield and Their Relationship to the Battle of the Little Bighorn," in *CBHMA 28th Annual Symposium Proceedings*, (Hardin, MT: CBHMA, 2015), 102–25; and Douglas D. Scott and others, *Archaeological Perspectives on the Battle of the Little Bighorn* (Norman: University of Oklahoma Press, 1989).

29 Michel Hogue, *Metis and the Medicine Line: Creating a Border and Dividing a People* (Chapel Hill: University of North Carolina Press, 2015), 53, 74–75, 85; Gerhard J. Ens, "The Border, the Buffalo, and the Metis of Montana," in *The Borderlands of the American and*

Canadian Wests: Essays on Regional History of the Forty-ninth Parallel, ed. Sterling Evans (Lincoln: University of Nebraska Press, 2006), 140–41, 144–45.

30 David G. McCrady, *Living with Strangers: The Nineteenth-Century Sioux and the Canadian-American Borderlands* (Lincoln: University of Nebraska Press, 2006), 12–13; Denig, *Five Indians Tribes of the Upper Missouri*, 31 (quotation); Vestal, *New Sources of Indian History*, 234; James H. Howard, ed., *The Warrior Who Killed Custer: The Personal Narrative of Chief Joseph White Bull* (Lincoln: University of Nebraska Press, 1968), 65.

31 The 1862 Minnesota War is carefully detailed in Gary Clayton Anderson, *Massacre in Minnesota: The Dakota War of 1862, The Most Violent Ethnic Conflict in American History* (Norman: University of Oklahoma Press, 2019). The battles fought in the Dakota Territory in 1863 and 1864 are summarized by Robert M. Utley, *Frontiersmen in Blue: The United States Army and the Indians, 1848–1865* (New York: Macmillan Publishing Co., 1967), 272–78; and Gardner, *The Earth Is All That Lasts*, 84–97.

32 On this Platte River war see John D. McDermott, *Circle of Fire: The Indian War of 1865* (Mechanicsburg, PA: Stackpole Books, 2003); and Gardner, *The Earth Is All That Lasts*, 118–24.

33 George Bird Grinnell, *The Fighting Cheyennes* (New York: Charles Scribner's Sons, 1915), 229 (quotation).

34 Literature on the Red Cloud or Bozeman Trail War is abundant. Particularly recommended is John D. McDermott, *Red Cloud's War: The Bozeman Trail, 1866–1868*, two vols. (Norman, OK: Arthur H. Clark Company, 2010); and John H. Monnett, *Where a Hundred Soldiers Were Killed: The Struggle for the Powder River Country in 1866 and the Making of the Fetterman Myth* (Albuquerque: University of New Mexico Press, 2008).

35 "Treaty with the Sioux—Brulé, Oglala, Miniconjou, Yanktonai, Hunkpapa, Blackfeet, Cuthead, Two Kettles, Sans Arcs, and Santee—and Arapaho, 1868," in Charles J. Kappler, ed., *Indian Treaties, 1778–1883* (Mattituck, N.Y.: Amereon House, 1972), 998–1007; George W. Manypenny, *Our Indian Wards* (Cincinnati, OH: Robert Clarke & Co., 1880), 296; Hedren, "Buffalo South and the Fort Laramie Treaties," 92–94.

36 "Treaty with the Sioux," 1003–1007; McDermott, *Red Cloud's War*, Vol. 2, 501–508. Other individuals signed the document, as on May 2 at Fort Laramie when thirteen signatures are noted but only two names documented.

37 Raymond J. DeMallie, "The Sioux in Dakota and Montana Territories: Cultural and Historical Background of the Ogden B. Read Collection," in Markoe, *Vestiges of a Proud Nation*, 30; Utley, *The Lance and The Shield*, 90–91.

38 Carla Kelly, *Fort Buford: Sentinel at the Confluence* (Williston, ND: Fort Union Association, 2009), 6, 13–19; Nelson A. Miles, *Personal Recollections and Observations of General Nelson A. Miles* (Chicago: Werner Company, 1897), 194–95.

39 Elliott Coues, ed., *Forty Years a Fur Trader on the Upper Missouri: The Personal Narrative of Charles Larpenteur, 1833–1872*, two vols. (New York: Francis P. Harper, 1898), Vol. 2, 428, 429–30 (quotations). For context, see Charles Larpenteur, *The Original Journal of Charles Larpenteur: My Travels to the Rocky Mountains Between 1833 and 1872*, ed. Michael M. Casler (Chadron, NE: Museum Association of the American Frontier, 2007), 180. The confrontation occurred on October 15, 1867.

40 Charles W. Hoffman affidavit, December 3, 1902, James Boyd Hubbell Papers, Minnesota Historical Society, Saint Paul; Miles, *Personal Recollections and Observations of General Nelson A. Miles*, 194–95.

41 Scudder Mekeel, "A Short History of the Teton-Dakota," *North Dakota History* 10 (July 1943): 187–88; DeMallie, "Teton," 797.

42 Thomas B. Marquis, *Warrior Who Fought Custer* (Minneapolis, MN: Midwest Company, 1931), 35 (quotation); "Memorandum of Council held with Cheyennes at Fort Fetterman, W. T., August 29 and 31, 1871," NA M234, RCA, Roll 715, 55.

43 James N. Leiker and Ramon Powers, *The Northern Cheyenne Exodus in History and Memory* (Norman: University of Oklahoma Press, 2011), 33; John H. Moore, Margot Liberty, and A. Terry Straus, "Cheyenne," in DeMallie, *Handbook of North American Indians, Plains*, Vol. 13, Part 2, 865, 880; "Treaty with the Northern Cheyenne and Northern Arapaho, 1868," in Kappler, *Indian Treaties*, 1012–15; Bray, "Teton Sioux Population History," 175.

44 J. Q. Smith, "Report of the Commissioner of Indian Affairs," in *Annual Report of the Commissioner of Indian Affairs to the Secretary of the Interior for the Year 1876* (Washington, DC: Government Printing Office, 1876), xiv (quotation). See also Utley, *The Lance and The Shield*, 88; and Joe Jackson, *Black Elk: The Life of an American Visionary* (New York: Farrar, Straus and Giroux, 2016), 69.

45 Utley, *The Lance and The Shield*, 86, 87 (quotation), 88–89, and 351n12, where he acknowledges the potential of a different date and place for

this pivotal event and differentiates the meanings of war chief and supreme chief, which were distinct bestowals in Sitting Bull's life. Vestal, *Sitting Bull*, 86–91, places the event in 1867 ahead of Father Pierre-Jean De Smet's treaty advocacy in 1868, but adds critical Oglala and Cheyenne voices to the proceedings. Gardner, *The Earth Is All That Lasts*, 140–41, also accepts the 1867 date. Cumulative evidence—distinctions between war chief and supreme chief—post, not pre De Smet—Oglala and Cheyenne participation—appears to favor Utley's assessment, as does this writer.

46 Denig, *Five Indians Tribes of the Upper Missouri*, 25; Royal B. Hassrick, *The Sioux: Life and Customs of a Warrior Society* (Norman: University of Oklahoma Press, 1964), 185; Flying Hawk Narrative, in *Firewater and Forked Tongues: A Sioux Chief Interprets U.S. History*, by M. I. McCreight (Pasadena, CA: Trail's End Publishing Co., 1947), 4–5; Pekka Hämäläinen, *Lakota America: A New History of Indigenous Power* (New Haven, CT: Yale University Press, 2019), 194.

2. Railroaders on the Yellowstone

1 F. D. Pease ltr., [Dec. 24, 1870], NA M234, MS, Roll 491, 406 (read National Archives, Microcopy 234, Montana Superintendency, Roll 491, frame 406); W. H. Lewis ltr., July 18, 1871, NA M234, DS, Roll 252, 208; Joseph Kinsey Howard, *Strange Empire: A Narrative of the Northwest* (New York: William Morrow and Company, 1952), 305; Isaac Cowie, *The Company of Adventurers* (Toronto: William Briggs, 1913; reprint, Lincoln: University of Nebraska Press, 1993), 422 (quotation); Hogue, *Metis and the Medicine Line*, 77. The disquieting story of market hunting and pemmican production is well told by George Colpitts, "A Metis View of the Summer Market Hunt on the Northern Plains," in Geoff Cunfer and Bill Weiser, eds., *Bison and People on the North American Great Plains: A Deep Environmental History* (College Station: Texas A&M University Press, 2016), 201–24.

2 Vestal, *New Sources of Indian History*, 235; McGrady, *Living With Strangers*, 46.

3 A. J. Simmons ltr., May 12, 1871, NA M234, MS, Roll 491, 638; Robert A. Saindon, *Old Fort Peck & Its Neighborhood* (n.p.: self-published, 2011), 69; Dennis J. Smith, "Convergence: Fort Peck Assiniboine and Sioux Arrive in the Fort Peck Region, 1800–1871," in David Miller and others, *The History of the Assiniboine and Sioux Tribes of the Fort Peck Indian Reservation: 1600–2012* (Poplar, MT: Fort Peck Community College, 2012), 72.

4 J. A. Viall ltrs., Oct. 18 and Oct. 28, 1871, A. J. Simmons ltr., Oct. 15, 1871 (quotation), all NA M234, MS, Roll 491, 994; Smith, "Convergence," in Miller, *History of the Assiniboine and Sioux Tribes*, 56–57.

5 J. A. Viall ltr., Nov. 16, 1871, H. B. Freeman rpt., Nov. 6, 1871, A. J. Simmons ltr., Nov. 6, 1871, all NA M234, MS, Roll 491, 1030; McGrady, *Living With Strangers*, 47.

6 J. A. Viall ltr., Aug. 21, 1871, NA M234, MS, Roll 491, 874; A. J. Simmons ltr., Dec. 5, 1871, NA M234, MS, Roll 492, 638 (quotation).

7 Eugene V. Smalley, *History of the Northern Pacific Railroad* (New York: G. P. Putnam's Sons, 1883), 381–85.

8 J. C. O'Connor rpt., Sept. 9, 1871, in *Report of the Commissioner of Indian Affairs to the Secretary of the Interior for the Year 1871* (Washington, DC: Government Printing Office, 1872), 526 (quotation); Theo. M. Koues ltr., Aug. 12, 1871, NA M234, CRA, Roll 127, 272; D. S. Stanley ltr., July 30, 1871, NA M234, DS, Roll 252, 45.

9 D. S. Stanley ltrs., May 13, 1871 and July 30, 1871, both NA M234, DS, Roll 252, 36 (first quotation), 45 (second quotation).

10 J. A. Viall ltr., Aug. 21, 1871, NA M234, MS, Roll 491, 874.

11 "From Fort Buford, D.T.," *Army and Navy Journal*, June 24, 1871.

12 Robert W. Larson, *Gall: Lakota War Chief* (Norman: University of Oklahoma Press, 2007), 81; M. John Lubetkin, *Jay Cooke's Gamble: The Northern Pacific Railroad, The Sioux, and the Panic of 1873* (Norman: University of Oklahoma Press, 2006), 89–93, 99, 112–13; M. John Lubetkin, *Road to War: The 1871 Yellowstone Surveys* (Norman, OK: Arthur H. Clark Company, 2016), 214, 256; R. E. A. Crofton ltr., Apr. 19, 1872, NA M234, DS, Roll 252, 231.

13 William Quinton rpt., May 19, 1871, NA M234, MS, Roll 491, 1107 (quotations); "Crook's Chief Scout," *Bismarck Weekly Tribune*, Oct. 18, 1876; Joe DeBarthe, *The Life and Adventures of Frank Grouard, Chief of Scouts, U.S.A.* (St. Joseph, MO: Combe Printing Company, 1894).

14 H. B. Freeman rpt., Nov. 6, 1871, NA M234, MS, Roll 491, 1030; DeBarthe, *Life and Adventures of Frank Grouard*, 93, 110–11. Grouard awaits a modern biographer, but see also John Gray, "Frank Grouard: Kanaka Scout or Mulatto Renegade," *Chicago Westerners Brand Book* (October 1959); Utley, *The Lance and The Shield*, 94; and Gardner, *The Earth Is All That Lasts*, 189–91.

15 Vestal, *New Sources of Indian History*, 160–61; Stanley Vestal, *Warpath: The True Story of the Fighting Sioux Told in a Biography of Chief White Bull* (Boston, MA: Houghton Mifflin Company, 1934), 137.

16 Waggoner, *Witness*, 108.

17 Theo. M. Koues ltr., Mar. 30, 1872, NA M235, CRA, Roll 127, 624; D. S. Stanley ltr., Apr. 7, 1872, NA M235, CRA, Roll 127, 769.
18 D. S. Stanley ltr., Apr. 7, 1872, NA M235, CRA, Roll 127, 769.
19 D. S. Stanley ltr., Apr. 7, 1872 (first quotation); Theo. M. Koues ltr., Apr. 20, 1872, NA M235, CRA, Roll 127, 642; Theo M. Koues rpt., Aug. 15, 1872, in *Report of the Commissioner of Indian Affairs, 1872*, 262 (second quotation).
20 R. E. A. Crofton ltr., Apr. 19, 1872, NA M234, DS, Roll 252, 231.
21 Robert W. Larson, *Red Cloud: Warrior-Statesman of the Lakota Sioux* (Norman: University of Oklahoma Press, 1997), 150 (quotation); Gardner, *The Earth Is All That Lasts*, 215.
22 Vestal, *New Sources of Indian History*, 169; Vestal, *Warpath*, 137; Carlisle Boyd ltr., Sept. 6, 1872, NA M235, CRA, Roll 127, 786; A. J. Simmons ltr., Dec. 8, 1872, NA M234, MS, Roll 495, 753.
23 Vestal, *New Sources of Indian History*, 169–70; David Eckroth and Harold Hagen, *Baker's Battle on the Yellowstone, Aug. 14, 1872: The Battle of Poker Flat* (Sheridan, WY: Frontier Heritage Alliance, 2004), 41–42; Kingsley M. Bray, *Crazy Horse: A Lakota Life* (Norman: University of Oklahoma Press, 2006), 162; Carlisle Boyd ltr., Sept. 6, 1872, NA M235, CRA, Roll 127, 786.
24 Vestal, *Warpath*, 141.
25 Vestal, *Warpath*, 142.
26 Vestal, *Warpath*, 142.
27 Vestal, *Warpath*, 142.
28 Vestal, *Warpath*, 143.
29 Utley, *The Lance and The Shield*, 109; E. M. Baker rpt., Oct. 18, 1872, NA M234, DS, Roll 252, 378; A. J. Simmons ltr., Dec. 8, 1872, NA M234, MS, Roll 495, 753; Vestal, *New Sources of Indian History*, 169–70; Carlisle Boyd ltr., Sept. 6, 1872, NA M235, CRA, Roll 127, 786.
30 M. John Lubetkin, *Before Custer: Surveying the Yellowstone, 1872* (Norman, OK: Arthur H. Clark Company, 2015), 151; Eckroth and Hagen, *Baker's Battle on the Yellowstone*, 63–64; David Eckroth and Harold Hagen with Mike Penfold, "Baker's Battle on the Yellowstone, August 14, 1872," *Greasy Grass* 31 (May 2015): 34–35.
31 Francis B. Robertson, "'We Are Going to Have a Big Sioux War': Colonel David S. Stanley's Yellowstone Expedition, 1872," *Montana The Magazine of Western History* 34 (Autumn, 1984): 11; Lubetkin, *Jay Cooke's Gamble*, 123; Larson, *Gall*, 83–84.
32 Utley, *The Lance and The Shield*, 22, 82; Larson, *Gall*, 15, 17.
33 Larson, *Gall*, 84; Lubetkin, *Jay Cooke's Gamble*, 130 (first and second quotations); Lubetkin, *Before Custer*, 125, 126 (third quotation), 130; Utley, *The Lance and The Shield*, 110.

34 Robertson, "We Are Going to Have a Big Sioux War," 13.

35 Robertson, "We Are Going to Have a Big Sioux War," 13–14; Lubetkin, *Before Custer*, 196, 216–17; Linda W. Slaughter, "Leaves from Northwestern History," in *Collections of the State Historical Society of North Dakota*, Vol. 1 (Bismarck, ND: Tribune, State Printers and Binders, 1906), 200.

36 Robertson, "We Are Going to Have a Big Sioux War," 14; Lubetkin, *Before Custer*, 203, 211, 220; D. S. Stanley ltr., Oct. 12, 1872, NA M234, DS, Roll 252, 366.

37 Arnold O. Goplen, *The Historical Significance of Fort Lincoln State Park* (Bismarck: State Historical Society of North Dakota, n.d.), 57; J. B. Fry tele., Oct. 17, 1872, NA M234, DS, Roll 252, 249; W. P. Carlin rpt., Nov. 4, 1872, NA M234, DS, Roll 252, 412 (quotation).

38 Robertson, "We Are Going to Have a Big Sioux War," 15.

39 J. W. Daniels ltr., Jan. 28, 1873, NA M234, RCA, Roll 717, 90.

40 J. W. Daniels ltr., Jan. 28, 1873, 90.

41 J. W. Daniels ltr., Jan. 28, 1873, 90.

42 A. J. Simmons ltr., Dec. 8, 1872, NA M234, MS, Roll 495, 753.

43 A. J. Simmons ltrs., Dec. 8, 1872 and Dec. 15, 1872, both NA M234, MS, Roll 495, 753.

44 Clarence Bennett ltr., Aug. 26, 1872, Frank Robertson Papers, Apple Valley, Minn.

45 For useful overviews of this agency finagling, see Thomas R. Buecker, *Fort Robinson and the American West, 1874–1899* (Lincoln: Nebraska State Historical Society, 1999), 2–3; and Thomas Buecker and Charles E. Hanson, "Spotted Tail's Agency on Wheels," in Hanson, *Spotted Tail*, 135–38. Regarding the Cheyennes, see Marquis, *Warrior Who Fought Custer*, 20.

46 Vestal, *Warpath*,157–58, 159 (quotation); Howard, *Warrior Who Killed Custer*, 65.

47 Vestal, *Warpath*, 154, 160.

48 Edward Collins ltr., Apr. 27, 1873, D. S. Stanley endorsement, May 3, 1873 (dead letter), both NA M234, MS, Roll 497, 297; "Arming the Sioux," *Army and Navy Journal*, July 29, 1876 (second quotation).

49 A. J. Simmons ltrs., Sept. 30, 1873, and Oct. 11, 1873, both NA M234, MS, Roll 496, 90 and 122 respectively.

50 Edmond Palmer ltr., July 11, 1873, NA M234, GRA, Roll 306, 182.

51 Adjutant General's Office, *Chronological List of Actions, &c, With Indians from January 15, 1837 to January, 1891* (Fort Collins, CO: Old Army Press, 1979), 54–55; W. P. Carlin rpts., May 9, 1873, and June 15, 1873, both NA M234, DS, Roll 252, 740 and 823 respectively;

M. John Lubetkin, "Jay Cooke, The Northern Pacific, and Custer on the Yellowstone," in *CBHMA 20th Annual Symposium Proceedings* (Hardin, MT: CBHMA, 2006), 5.

52 Charles W. Larned, "Expedition to the Yellowstone River in 1873: Letters of a Young Cavalry Officer," in *The Custer Reader*, ed. Paul Andrew Hutton (Lincoln: University of Nebraska Press, 1992), 194; Joseph Mills Hanson, *The Conquest of the Missouri: Being the Story of the Life and Exploits of Captain Grant Marsh* (Chicago, IL: A. C. McClurg & Co., 1909), 166, 174, 178–79.

53 M. John Lubetkin, "Clash on the Yellowstone: Monday, August 3, 1873," *LBHA Research Review* 17 (Summer 2003): 16–20.

54 Vestal, *Warpath*, 163; "The Big Horn Fight," *Army and Navy Journal*, Nov. 8, 1873; Lubetkin, "Clash on the Yellowstone," 16–20.

55 Richard G. Hardorff, "Baliran, Honzinger, and the Custers: The Facts and Fictions of the Rain-in-the-Face Myth," *LBHA Research Review* 2 (December 1988): 8; Lubetkin, "Clash on the Yellowstone," 24; Usher L. Burdick, ed., *David F. Barry's Indian Notes on "The Custer Battle"* (Baltimore, MD: Wirth Brothers, 1949), 39; Waggoner, *Witness*, 437; Frank Zahn note, undated, George Gallio Masters Collection, Kansas Historical Society, Topeka.

56 Lubetkin, "Clash on the Yellowstone," 21–22; "The Yellowstone War," *New York Tribune*, September 8, 1873; Michael N. Donahue, *Where the Rivers Ran Red: The Indian Fights of George Armstrong Custer* (Montrose, CO: San Juan Publishing Group, 2018), 72; M. John Lubetkin, *Custer and the 1873 Yellowstone Survey: A Documentary History* (Norman, OK: Arthur H. Clark Company, 2013), 228, 232.

57 Lubetkin, *Jay Cooke's Gamble*, 254–55; "The Yellowstone War," *New York Tribune*, Sept. 9, 1873.

58 DeBarthe, *Life and Adventures of Frank Grouard*, 114; Larned, "Expedition to the Yellowstone River in 1873," 196–97.

59 "The Yellowstone War," *New York Tribune*, Sept. 9, 1873 (first quotation); Edward Collins ltr., Oct. 7, 1873, NA M234, MS, Roll 497, 625 (second quotation); DeBarthe, *Life and Adventures of Frank Grouard*, 115.

60 "The Big Horn Fight," *Army and Navy Journal*, Nov. 8, 1873.

61 M. John Lubetkin, "Strike Up Garryowen,' August 11, 1873: Custer's Second Battle on the Yellowstone," *LBHA Research Review* 20 (Summer 2006): 14–16.

62 Neihardt, *When the Tree Flowered*, 137; Charles A. Eastman, "Rain in the Face: The Story of a Sioux Warrior," *The Outlook*, Oct. 27, 1906, 510.

63 Smalley, *History of the Northern Pacific Railroad*, 198–202, 388.

64 William K. Powers, *Winter Count of the Oglala* (Kendall Park, NJ: Lakota Books, [1962]), 33. Regarding Spotted Tail and the Republican River buffalo country, see Hedren, "Buffalo South and the Fort Laramie Treaties," in Hanson, *Spotted Tail*, ch. 4.

65 Mike Cowdrey, "A Winter Count of the *Wajaje* Lakota 1758–59 to 1885–86," 2014, 41; Roberta Carkeek Cheney, *Sioux Winter Count: A 131-Year Calendar of Events* (Happy Valley, CA: Naturegraph, 1998), 36. The standard account of the Massacre Canyon event is Paul D. Riley, "The Battle of Massacre Canyon," *Nebraska History* 54 (1973), but see also Richmond L. Clow, *Spotted Tail: Warrior and Statesman* (Pierre: South Dakota Historical Society Press, 2019), 82–85.

66 White Bull interview, Walter Stanley Campbell Collection, box 105, folder 24, University of Oklahoma, Norman; J. W. Daniels rpt., Aug. 18, 1873, in *Annual Report of the Commissioner of Indian Affairs to the Secretary of the Interior for the Year 1873* (Washington, DC: Government Printing Office, 1874), 244 (quotation). Crazy Horse's involvement at Massacre Canyon is discussed by Gardner, *The Earth Is All That Lasts*, 206–207, 449–50n201.

3. Buffalo and Borders

1 James C. Olson, *Red Cloud and the Sioux Problem* (Lincoln: University of Nebraska Press, 1965), 162–63; J. J. Saville rpt., Aug. 31, 1874, in *Annual Report of the Commissioner of Indian Affairs to the Secretary of the Interior for the Year 1874* (Washington, DC: Government Printing Office, 1874), 251.

2 J. J. Saville rpt., Nov. 2, 1874, NA M234, RCA, Roll 718, 1184; Larson, *Red Cloud*, 156; Buecker, *Fort Robinson and the American West*, 6; P. H. Sheridan tele., Mar. 25, 1874, NA M234, RCA, Roll 718, 1400 (quotation); *New York Times*, Feb. 21, 1874; Olson, *Red Cloud and the Sioux Problem*, 164; J. W. Daniels rpt., Aug. 18, 1873, in *Annual Report of the Commissioner of Indian Affairs, 1873*, 244.

3 Douglas C. McChristian, *Fort Laramie: Military Bastion of the High Plains* (Norman, OK: Arthur H. Clark Company, 2008), 340–41; *New York Times*, Feb. 21, 1874.

4 McChristian, *Fort Laramie*, 341–43; John E. Smith tele., Feb. 11, 1874, NA M234, DS, Roll 253, 566; Harry Young, *Hard Knocks: A Life Story of the Vanishing West* (Portland, OR: Wells & Company, 1915), 104; Alex Chambers tele., Feb. 18, 1874, NA M234, DS, Roll 253, 478.

5 William Garnett interview, in *The Indian Interviews of Eli S. Ricker, 1903–1919*, ed. Richard E. Jensen (Lincoln: University of Nebraska Press, 2005), 7, hereafter *Ricker Indian Interviews*; Kingsley M. Bray,

"Pine Ridge Letters Shed New Light on the Battle of the Little Bighorn," *Ghost Herder, Journal of the Friends of the Little Bighorn Battlefield* 1 (May 2011): 38–39; Buecker, *Fort Robinson and the American West*, 6–7; Jackson, *Black Elk* 70; Powers, *The Killing of Crazy Horse*, 57–58; Young, *Hard Knocks*, 150. Some sources including Saville himself assert that the killer was a Miniconjou of Lone Horn's band and furthermore that Spotted Tail's Brulés found and killed him a short while later. See J. J. Saville tele., Feb. 9, 1874, NA M234, RCA, Roll 718, 610; J. J. Saville rpt., Aug. 31, 1874, in *Annual Report of the Commissioner of Indian Affairs, 1874*, 251; George E. Hyde, *Spotted Tail's Folk: A History of the Brulé Sioux* (Norman: University of Oklahoma Press, 1961), 195; and Clow, *Spotted Tail*, 89.

6 John E. Smith ltr., May 5, 1874, NA M234, RCA, Roll 718, 1440; McChristian, *Fort Laramie*, 343–45; J. J. Saville tele., Feb. 20, 1874, NA M234, RCA, Roll 718, 637.

7 J. J. Saville rpt., Aug. 31, 1874, in *Annual Report of the Commissioner of Indian Affairs, 1874*, 252.

8 Wm. W. Alderson ltr., Jan. 15, 1874, NA M234, MS, Roll 498, 56; W. H. Fanton ltr., Aug. 5, 1874, NA M234, MS, Roll 498, 1024.

9 Addison M. Quivey, "The Yellowstone Expedition of 1874," *Contributions to the Historical Society of Montana*, Vol. 1, 2nd ed. (Helena: Independent Publishing Company, 1902), 237; James S. Hutchins, "Poison in the Pemmican: The Yellowstone Wagon-Road & Prospecting Expedition of 1874," *MMWH* 8 (July 1958): 10–11.

10 Hutchins, "Poison in the Pemmican," 8–9; Quivey, "The Yellowstone Expedition of 1874," 236; Mark H. Brown, *The Plainsmen of the Yellowstone: A History of the Yellowstone Basin* (New York: G. P. Putnam's Sons, 1961), 214–16; Oliver Perry Hanna, *An Old Timer's Story of the Old Wild West* ([Big Horn, WY]: Big Horn City Historical Society, 2018), 46.

11 Hutchins, "Poison in the Pemmican," 13; Hanna, *Old Timer's Story of the Old Wild West*, 47; Statement of Spotted Bear, Campbell Collection, OU; Statement of Stands With Horns In Sight, Campbell Collection, OU.

12 N. B. Sweitzer rpt., Feb. 14, 1874, NA M234, MS, Roll 500, 684. French L. MacLean, *Sitting Bull, Crazy Horse, Gold, and Guns: The 1874 Yellowstone Wagon Road and Prospecting Expedition and the Battle of Lodge Grass Creek* (Atglen, PA: Schiffer Publishing, Ltd., 2016), 17–29. MacLean posits that many prominent Northern Indians *may* have taken part in this episode, but evidence of that is purely speculative.

13 Hutchins, "Poison in the Pemmican," 15–16; Quivey, "The Yellowstone Expedition of 1874," 243.

14 Statement of Stands With Horns In Sight, Campbell Collection, OU (quotations); Hutchins, "Poison in the Pemmican," 17.

15 Hanna, *Old Timer's Story of the Old Wild West*, 48–49; E. S. Topping, *The Chronicles of the Yellowstone* (Saint Paul, MN: Pioneer Press, 1883; reprint, Minneapolis, MN: Ross & Haines, Inc., 1968), 108–109; Statement of Stands With Horns In Sight, Campbell Collection, OU; Hutchins, "Poison in the Pemmican," 17–18; James Gourley narrative, in MacLean, *Sitting Bull, Crazy Horse, Gold, and Guns*, 149; Utley, *The Lance and The Shield*, 119.

16 James Gourley narrative, in MacLean, *Sitting Bull, Crazy Horse, Gold, and Guns*, 148; Hutchins, "Poison in the Pemmican," 18–20; Hanna, *Old Timer's Story of the Old Wild West*, 45, 51; Joe E. Cook narrative, in *The Black Hills Trails: A History of the Struggles of the Pioneers in the Winning of the Black Hills*, by Jesse Brown and A. M. Willard (Rapid City, SD: Rapid City Journal Company, 1924), 561.

17 Hutchins, "Poison in the Pemmican," 20–21; Hanna, *Old Timer's Story of the Old Wild West*, 51.

18 Hanna, *Old Timer's Story of the Old Wild West*, 54 (quotation); Hutchins, "Poison in the Pemmican," 22.

19 George Herendeen interview, Kenneth Hammer, ed., *Custer in '76: Walter Camp's Notes on the Custer Fight* (Provo, UT: Brigham Young University Press, 1976), 220; Quivey, "The Yellowstone Expedition of 1874," 250.

20 Hutchins, "Poison in the Pemmican," 23, 25; Statement of Stands With Horns In Sight, Campbell Collection, OU (quotations).

21 Quivey, "The Yellowstone Expedition of 1874," 246, 247–48. The Expedition's unique artillery pieces and distinctive handmade oyster can rounds are discussed by MacLean, *Sitting Bull, Crazy Horse, Gold, and Guns*, 82–104, 193.

22 J. J. Saville ltr., Jan. 16, 1874, NA M234, RCA, Roll 718, 509 (quotation). For typical monthly reports see J. J. Saville ltr., Aug. 29, 1874, NA M234, RCA, Roll 718, 1007, and Durfee & Peck rpt., Aug. 31, 1874, NA M234, MS, Roll 498, 216.

23 H. W. Bingham ltr., Nov. 14, 1873, NA M234, CRA, Roll 128, 155 (quotation); Durfee & Peck letter, Nov. 14, 1873, NA M234, CRA, Roll 128, 171; H. W. Bingham tele., Mar. 8, 1874, NA M234, CRA, Roll 128, 341.

24 Geo. Clendenin ltr., Jan. 1, 1874, NA M234, MS, Roll 498, 565 (first quotation); W. W. Alderson ltr., Mar. 30, 1874, NA M234, MS, Roll 498, 82 (second and third quotations).

25 W. W. Alderson ltr., Feb. 3, 1874, NA M234, MS, Roll 498, 87; W. W. Alderson ltr., May 1, 1874, NA M234, MS, Roll 498, 119.

26 W. W. Alderson ltr., June 1, 1874, Chas. D. Hard rpt., May 16, 1874, and Good Dog stmt., May 14, 1874, all in NA M234, MS, Roll 498, 147.

27 John E. Smith ltr., May 5, 1874, NA M234, RCA, Roll 718, 1440.

28 "Report of Capt. W. J. Twining," in *Reports Upon the Survey of the Boundary Between the Territory of the United States and the Possessions of Great Britain*, by Archibald Campbell and W. J. Twining ([Washington, DC: Government Printing Office], 1878), 68.

29 McCrady, *Living with Strangers*, 49; "Report of Capt. W. J. Twining," in *Reports Upon the Survey of the Boundary Between the Territory of the United States and the Possessions of Great Britain*, 69; William E. Lass, "The North Dakota-Canada Boundary," *North Dakota History* 63 (Fall 1996): 10–14; Larry Haag and Lawrence Barkwell, *The Boundary Commission's Metis Scouts—The 49th Rangers* (Winnipeg, MB: Louis Riel Institute, 2009), 3–4.

30 "Report of Captain James F. Gregory," in *Reports Upon the Survey of the Boundary Between the Territory of the United States and the Possessions of Great Britain*, 278–84; McCrady, *Living with Strangers*, 49–50, 52–53.

31 George M. Dawson diary, July 13, 1874, in Haag and Barkwell, *Boundary Commission's Metis Scouts*, 29; Colpitts, "A Metis View of the Summer Market Hunt on the Northern Plains," in Cunfer and Weiser, eds., *Bison and People on the North American Great Plains*, 201–24.

32 "Report of Captain James F. Gregory," 281; F. V. Greene ltr., July 12, 1874, Francis Vinton Greene papers, New York Public Library (quotation); McCrady, *Living with Strangers*, 54–55.

33 F. V. Greene ltr., July 12, 1874, Francis Vinton Greene papers, New York Public Library.

34 Vestal, *New Sources of Indian History*, 162; Vestal, *Warpath*, 169; B. F. Potts ltr., July 11, 1874, NA M234, MS, Roll 500, 167; DeBarthe, *Life and Adventures of Frank Grouard*, 163.

35 Raymond J. DeMallie, ed., *The Sixth Grandfather: Black Elk's Teachings Given to John G. Neihardt* (Lincoln: University of Nebraska Press, 1984), 158; He Dog interview, Crazy Horse Papers, Museum of the Fur Trade, Chadron, NE (quotation).

4. Black Hills Mayhem

1 For useful summaries see Thomas R. Buecker, "Gold in the Hills: Rumors, Reports and Innuendo," *Museum of the Fur Trade Quarterly* 52 (Winter 2016): 6–14; and James E. Potter, ed., *From Our Special Correspondent: Dispatches from the 1875 Black Hills Council at Red Cloud*

Agency, Nebraska (Lincoln: Nebraska State Historical Society Books, 2016), 12.

2 Paul Andrew Hutton, *Phil Sheridan and His Army* (Lincoln: University of Nebraska Press, 1985), 290–91; "Report of Lieut. Gen. P. H. Sheridan, Oct. 1, 1874," in *Annual Report of the Secretary of War for 1874* (Washington, DC: Government Printing Office, 1874), 24; Jackson, *Black Elk*, 81; Catharine R. Franklin, "Black Hills and Bloodshed: The U.S. Army and the Invasion of Lakota Land, 1868–1876," *MMWH* 63 (Summer 2013): 33–34.

3 William Ludlow, *Report of a Reconnaissance of the Black Hills of Dakota, Made in the Summer of 1874* (Washington, DC: Government Printing Office, 1875), 7; "Treaty with the Sioux," Article 2, Kappler, *Indian Treaties*, 998.

4 G. A. Custer tele., Aug. 2, 1874, in Senate Executive Documents, 43d Congress, 2nd Session., no. 32, 3–4; Powers, *The Killing of Crazy Horse*, 82–83; Slow Bull stmt., Aug. 3, 1876, NA M234, RCA, Roll 718, 945.

5 Long Bear stmt., Aug. 3, 1876, NA M234, RCA, Roll 718, 945; Donald Jackson, *Custer's Gold: The United States Cavalry Expedition of 1874* (New Haven, CT: Yale University Press, 1966), 93.

6 DeMallie, *The Sixth Grandfather*, 158.

7 DeMallie, *The Sixth Grandfather*, 155–57, 159.

8 Custer tele., Aug. 2, 1874, in Senate Executive Documents, 43d Congress, 2nd Session, no. 32, 5.

9 Ludlow, *Report of a Reconnaissance of the Black Hills of Dakota*, 14; Ernest Grafe and Paul Horsted, *Exploring With Custer: The 1874 Black Hills Expedition* (Custer, SD: Golden Valley Press, 2002), 78–79, 85–87; Jackson, *Custer's Gold*, 84–85; David A. Wolff, *The Savior of Deadwood: James K. P. Miller on the Gold Frontier* (Pierre: South Dakota Historical Society Press, 2021), 34–35.

10 Jackson, *Custer's Gold*, 85–90; Grafe and Horsted, *Exploring With Custer*, 90–91; John S. Gray, "News from Paradise: Charley Reynolds Rides from the Black Hills to Fort Laramie," *By Valor & Arms* 3 (no. 3): 39–42; "Gold!" *Chicago Inter-Ocean*, Aug. 27, 1874, in Herbert Krause and Gary D. Olson, *Prelude to Glory: A Newspaper Accounting of Custer's 1874 Expedition to the Black Hills* (Sioux Falls, SD: Brevet Press, 1974), 126.

11 Ludlow, *Report of a Reconnaissance of the Black Hills of Dakota*, 17; Paul Horsted with Ernie Grafe and Jon Nelson, *Crossing the Plains with Custer* (Custer, SD: Golden Valley Press, 2009), 71.

12 H. W. Bingham ltr., Aug. 17, 1874, NA M234, CRA, Roll 128, 416.

13 Bray, *Crazy Horse*, 180–81; James Wright ltr., July 27, 1874, NA M234, MS, Roll 500, 1029; Utley, *The Lance and The Shield*, 115–17: "Standing Bear Tells About the Black Hills," in DeMallie, *The Sixth Grandfather*, 163–64 (quotations).

14 "Gold!" *Chicago Inter-Ocean*, Aug. 27, 1874 (quotation); Powers, *The Killing of Crazy Horse*, 87–88; Franklin, "Black Hills and Bloodshed," 32–33.

15 "Report of the Sioux Commission," *Annual Report of the Commissioner of Indian Affairs, 1874* (Washington, DC: Government Printing Office, 1874), 87–97; Grant K. Anderson, "Samuel D. Hinman and the Opening of the Black Hills," *Nebraska History* 60 (Winter 1979): 525–26.

16 P. H. Sheridan ltr., Sept. 3, 1874, NA M234, DS, Roll 253, 668 (quotation); Thomas W. Vincent tele., July 12, 1875, NA M234, DS, Roll 255, 699 (Grant's directive); B. R. Cowen ltr., Sept. 8, 1874, in "Message on the Black Hills Country," Senate Ex. Doc. no. 2, 44th Cong., Spec. Sess., (1875), 3–15; Franklin, "Black Hills and Bloodshed," 36–37.

17 H. W. Bingham ltrs., Oct. 31, 1874, Dec. 5, 1874, NA M234, CRA, Roll 128, 445 (quotations) and 462.

18 J. J. Saville ltr., Mar. 29, 1875, and "Proceedings of a Council with the Indians at the Red Cloud Agency," Mar. 29, 1875, NA M234, RCA, Roll 719, 765. An edited variant of the "Proceedings" appears in John Y. Simons, ed., *The Papers of Ulysses S. Grant, Vol. 26: 1875* (Carbondale: Southern Illinois University Press, 2003), 122.

19 Simons, *Papers of Ulysses S. Grant, 1875*, 122–23.

20 Candace S. Greene and Russell Thornton, eds., *The Year the Stars Fell: Lakota Winter Counts at the Smithsonian* (Washington, DC: Smithsonian Institution, 2007), 274; Randy Kane, "The 'Flagpole Affair' at Red Cloud Agency: An Incident in the Cultural Transition of the Oglala Sioux," *Nebraska History* 97 (Fall 2016): 120–25; Dakota Goodhouse, "The Blue Thunder Winter Count," thefirstscout.blogspot.com; Charles A. Eastman, *Indian Heroes and Great Chieftains* (Boston, MA: Little, Brown, and Company, 1929), 140–41.

21 James W. Forsyth, and F. D. Grant, *Report of an Expedition Up the Yellowstone River, Made in 1875* (Washington, DC: Government Printing Office, 1875), 3, 7–8; William E. Lass, "Steamboats on the Yellowstone," *MMWH* 35 (Autumn, 1985): 30.

22 Hanson, *Conquest of the Missouri*, 203, 218; Forsyth and Grant, *Report of an Expedition Up the Yellowstone River*, 11.

23 Clyde McLemore, "Fort Pease: The First Attempted Settlement in Yellowstone Valley," *MMWH* 2 (January 1952): 18, 20–21; Dennis

Hagen, "Major Brisbin's Fort Pease Relief: Was the First Military Operation of the Great Sioux War a Necessary Humanitarian Effort?" *Greasy Grass* 35 (May 2019): 32–33; Brown, *Plainsmen of the Yellowstone*, 221–22; Hanson, *Conquest of the Missouri*, 222; D. W. Benham ltr., June 29, 1874, NA M234, MS, Roll 503, 493.

24 Geo. L. Tyler ltr., [June 29, 1874], NA M234, MS, Roll 503, 493; "The Siege of Fort Pease," *New York Herald*, Mar. 8, 1876; Hagen, "Major Brisbin's Fort Pease Relief," 34; Benham ltr., June 29, 1874, NA M234, MS, Roll 503, 493.

25 White Bull narrative, envelope 497, Grinnell Papers, Southwest Museum/Autry National Center, Los Angeles; Utley, *The Lance and The Shield*, 122.

26 White Bull narrative, envelope 497; Utley, *The Lance and The Shield*, 123.

27 White Bull narrative, envelope 497.

28 White Bull narrative, envelope 497.

29 White Bull narrative, envelope 497 (quotation); Powell, *People of the Sacred Mountain*, Vol. 2, 929.

30 Olson, *Red Cloud and the Sioux Problem*, 176–77, 186–88; J. J. Saville teles., Apr. 13, 1875, and Apr. 24, 1875, NA M234, RCA, Roll 719, 803 and 805 respectively; Larson, *Red Cloud*, 163.

31 Clow, *Spotted Tail*, 103; Edward P. Smith, "Report of the Commissioner of Indian Affairs," in *Annual Report of the Commissioner of Indian Affairs to the Secretary of the Interior for the Year 1875* (Washington, DC: Government Printing Office, 1875), 8.

32 Watson Parker, *Gold in the Black Hills* (Norman: University of Oklahoma Press, 1966), 63; C. Delano ltr., Mar. 26, 1875, NA M234, DS, Roll 254, 869.

33 Ibid., 64–65; Walter Jenney tele., June 17, 1875, NA M234, DS, Roll 254, 988; Walter P. Jenney, *The Mineral Wealth, Climate and Rain-Fall, and Natural Resources of the Black Hills of Dakota* (Washington, DC: Government Printing Office, 1876), 56; "The Black Hills," *New York Herald*, June 23, 1875 (quotations).

34 E. A. Howard ltr., Aug. 14, 1874, NA M234, STA, Roll 840, 347.

35 E. A. Howard ltr., Aug. 14, 1874, 347; "The Gold Seekers," *New York Herald*, Aug. 26, 1875; Potter, *From Our Special Correspondent*, 82; Lesta V. Turchen and James D. McLaird, *The Black Hills Expedition of 1875* (Mitchell, SD: Dakota Wesleyan University Press, 1975), 99–100; Paul Horsted, *The Black Hills Yesterday & Today* (Custer, SD: Golden Valley Press, 2006), 24–25.

36 "The Gold Seekers," *New York Herald*, Aug. 26, 1875.

37 "The Gold Seekers," *New York Herald*, Aug. 26, 1875.

38 Potter, *From Our Special Correspondent*, 81–82.

39 "Report of the Commission Appointed to Treat with the Sioux Indians for the Relinquishment of the Black Hills," in *Annual Report of the Commissioner of Indian Affairs, 1875*, 184, 186; E. P. Smith ltr., June 16, 1875, NA M234, DS, Roll 254, 77; E. P. Smith ltr., June 18, 1875, NA M234, DS, Roll 256, 370; John S. Collins, *Across the Plains in '64* (Omaha, NE: National Printing Company, 1904), 91.

40 DeBarthe, *Life and Adventures of Frank Grouard*, 173; J. J. Saville ltr., Aug. 16, 1875, NA M234, RCA, Roll 719, 1012; "The Wild Sioux," *New York Herald*, Aug. 20, 1875; "The Grand Council," *New York Herald*, Sept. 22, 1875.

41 DeBarthe, *Life and Adventures of Frank Grouard*, 173 (first quotation), 174; Hila Gilbert, *"Big Bat" Pourier* (Sheridan, WY: Mills Company, 1968), 43 (second quotation).

42 "The Wild Sioux," *New York Herald*, Aug. 20, 1875; Powell, *People of the Sacred Mountain*, Vol. 2, 930.

43 "The Wild Sioux," *New York Herald*, Aug. 20, 1875; J. J. Saville ltr., Aug. 16, 1875, NA M234, RCA, Roll 719, 1012; Bray, *Crazy Horse*, 189–90.

44 "The Big Talk," *New York Herald*, Sept. 12, 1875; Potter, *From Our Special Correspondent*, 15; Sandoz, *Crazy Horse*, 296; William Garnett interview, in Jensen, *Ricker Indian Interviews*, 85.

45 J. J. Saville ltr., Sept. 23, 1875, NA M234, RCA, Roll 719, 1096; H. W. Bingham tele., Aug. 6, 1874, NA M234, CRA, Roll 128, 820; "Report of the Commission," 186; "The Black Hills," *New York Herald*, Oct. 7, 1875; Collins, *Across the Plains in '64*, 93; Samuel Charger, "Chronology of the Sioux Indians from an Early Period," *Sunshine Magazine* 10 (September 1928): 6; John D. McDermott, *Red Cloud: Oglala Legend* (Pierre: South Dakota Historical Society Press, 2015), 75.

46 "The Council Fire," *New York Herald*, Sept. 13, 1875; "The Grand Council/Spotted Tail's Price," *New York Herald*, Sept. 22, 1875; "The Indians," *Fort Dodge Messenger*, Sept. 30, 1875, and "Possible Trouble Ahead," *New York Tribune*, Sept. 13, 1875, both in Potter, *From Our Special Correspondent*, 148, 157; Charger, "Chronology of the Sioux Indians from an Early Period," 6; Bray, *Crazy Horse*, 190.

47 "The Black Hills," *New York Herald*, Oct. 6, 1875; "Report of the Commission," 187; Cozzens, *The Earth Is Weeping*, 218 (quotation).

48 J. J. Saville ltr., Jan. 8, 1875, NA M234, RCA, Roll 719, 682; Sandoz, *Crazy Horse*, 297–98; "The Black Hills," *New York Herald*, Oct. 7, 1875; Gilbert, *"Big Bat" Pourier*, 43 (first quotation); Collins, *Across the Plains in '64*, 94, 95 (second quotation); George E. Hyde, *Red Cloud's Folk: A*

History of the Oglala Sioux Indians (Norman: University of Oklahoma Press, 1937), 243.

49 Mari Sandoz, "The Lost Sitting Bull," in *Hostiles and Friendlies: Selected Short Writings of Mari Sandoz* (Lincoln: University of Nebraska Press, 1959), 101–102; Harry H. Anderson, "The War Club of Sitting Bull the Oglala," *Nebraska History* 42 (March 1961): 55; Powers, *The Killing of Crazy Horse*, 120; *Cheyenne Daily Leader*, Sept. 29, 1876 (quotation).

50 "Report of the Commission," 188–89 (quotations), 190; William Garnett interview, Jensen, *Ricker Indian Interviews*, 86; Olson, *Red Cloud and the Sioux Problem*, 208–209.

51 "Report of the Commission," 188. 190, 194; William Garnett interview, Jensen, *Ricker Indian Interviews*, 87; McDermott, *Red Cloud*, 79.

52 Singing Bear narrative, Eugene Buechel and Paul I. Manhart, *Lakota Tales & Texts*, Vol. 2 (Chamberlain, SD: Tipi Press, 1998), 613; Black Elk, quoting Lone Horn, DeMallie, *The Sixth Grandfather*, 169 (first quotation); Iron Hawk, quoting Sitting Bull, DeMallie, *The Sixth Grandfather*, 171–72 (second quotation).

53 DeMallie, *The Sixth Grandfather*, 172n13; Sandoz, *Crazy Horse*, 294; John G. Neihardt, *Black Elk Speaks, Being the Life Story of a Holy Man of the Oglala Sioux* (New York: William Morrow & *Company*, 1932), 81 (quotation).

54 Jensen, *Ricker Indian Interviews*, 449n104; Black Elk narrative, DeMallie, *The Sixth Grandfather*, 164–65.

55 J. J. Saville ltr., Oct. 11, 1875, NA M234, RCA, Roll 719, 1137; F. Van Vliet tele., Nov. 5, 1875, NA M234, RCA, Roll 719, 1380; "Report of the Commission," 189 (quotation).

56 On Eagle Elk and the shrinking island, see Neihardt, *When the Tree Flowered*, 202; and He Dog interview, Crazy Horse Papers, Museum of the Fur Trade, Chadron, NE, (quotation). George Hyde, *Red Cloud's Folk*, 258, makes the opposite case, that the Northerners were so incensed by these persistent threats that they were telling their agency kin that they meant to do something about it, maybe next year. Hyde, however, offers no supporting evidence.

57 This segment is a reworking of a larger discussion of the White House conference appearing in Paul L. Hedren, *Powder River: Disastrous Opening of the Great Sioux War* (Norman: University of Oklahoma Press, 2016), 42–45.

58 Simon, *Papers of Ulysses S. Grant, 1875*, 163; Department of the Platte Telegrams Sent, Nov. 8, 1875, NA RG 393, Washington, DC.

59 J. Q. Smith, "Report of the Commissioner of Indian Affairs," in *Annual Report of the Commissioner of Indian Affairs to the Secretary of*

the Interior for the Year 1876 (Washington, DC: Government Printing Office, 1876), xiv, xv; John G. Bourke, *The Diaries of John Gregory Bourke, Vol. 1, November 20, 1872–July 28, 1876*, ed. Charles M. Robinson III (Denton: University of North Texas Press, 2003), 273 (quotation).

60 E. C. Watkins rpt., Nov. 9, 1875, NA M234, DS, Roll 255, 832; N. B. Switzer ltr., Mar. 8, 1875, NA M234, MS, Roll 503, 312.

61 E. C. Watkins rpt., Nov. 9, 1875, 832.

62 E. C. Watkins rpt., Nov. 9, 1875, 832.

63 E. C. Watkins rpt., Nov. 9, 1875, 832 (quotations); Manypenny, *Our Indian Wards*, 302–303, 304 (fiction).

64 Smith, "Report of the Commissioner of Indian Affairs," *Annual Report of the Commissioner of Indian Affairs, 1876*, xv.

5. War Comes to the Cheyennes First

1 E. C. Watkins report, Nov. 9, 1875, NA M234, DS, Roll 255, 832; Z. Chandler ltr., Dec. 3, 1875, NA M234, DS, Roll 255, 72.

2 H. W. Bingham ltr., Dec. 22, 1875, NA M234, CRA, Roll 129, 31 (quotation); E. A. Howard ltr., Jan. 6, 1876, NA M234, STA, Roll 840, 899; John Burke ltr., Dec. 22, 1875, NA M234, SRA, Roll 846, 8; T. M. Reily ltr., Dec. 27, 1875, NA M234, LBA, Roll 401, 59; Henry Livingston ltr., Dec. 23, 1875, NA M234, CCA, Roll 249, 157; Wm. W. Alderson ltr., Jan. 21, 1876, NA M234, MS, Roll 504, 38.

3 H. W. Bingham ltr., Dec. 22, 1875, NA M234, CRA, Roll 129, 31 (quotation); E. A. Howard ltr., Jan. 6, 1876, NA M234, STA, Roll 840, 899; T. M. Reily ltr., Dec. 27, 1875, NA M234, LBA, Roll 401, 59; Henry Livingston ltr., Dec. 23, 1875, NA M234, CCA, Roll 249, 157; Wm. W. Alderson ltr., Jan. 21, 1876, NA M234, MS, Roll 504, 38.

4 "White Bull Interview," Richard G. Hardorff, ed., *Indian Views of the Custer Fight: A Source Book* (Spokane, WA: Arthur H. Clark Company, 2004), 162.

5 J. S. Hastings ltr., Jan. 28, 1876, NA M234, RCA, Roll 720, 212; Short Buffalo (Short Bull) interview, John M. Carroll, ed., *The Eleanor H. Hinman Interviews on the Life and Death of Crazy Horse* (n.p.: Garry Owen Press, 1976), 39 (first quotation); Gary Leonard, *Black Twin: Dark Lord of the Oglala* (London, UK: English Westerners Society, 2005), 5–6; Neihardt, *Black Elk Speaks*, 90 (second quotation); Powell, *People of the Sacred Mountain*, Vol. 2, 934.

6 H. W. Bingham ltr., Feb. 12, 1876, NA M234, CRA, Roll 129, 92.

7 Powell, *People of the Sacred Mountain*, Vol. 2, 934; Stanley Vestal, *Warpath and Council Fire: The Plains Indians' Struggle for Survival in War and in Diplomacy* (New York: Random House, 1948), 210.

8 Burke tele., Jan. 30, 1876, NA M234, SRA, Roll 846, 806; Vestal, *Warpath*, 217; "Abstract of Letter from John E. Brughuiere," *Winners of the West*, Oct. 30, 1932.

9 Waggoner, *Witness*, 124–25. Waggoner asserted furthermore that Bruguier remained in Sitting Bull's camp through the time of the great Sun Dance in early June 1876 (125), but contradicts herself earlier in her narrative when relating that Big Leggins reported to Custer after returning to the Missouri River (124). Custer, immersed in political squabbles in the East during much of this time, returned to Fort Abraham Lincoln on May 10 and commenced his fateful campaign on May 17. James Donovan, *A Terrible Glory, Custer and the Little Bighorn: The Last Great Battle of the American West* (New York: Little Brown and Company, 2008), 115, 134–35. No Indian accounts support the contention that a White man or mixed-blood was present in Sitting Bull's camp during that extended period from February to early June.

10 Z. Chandler ltr., Feb. 1, 1876, NA M234, DS, Roll 258, 223; W. W. Belknap ltr., Feb. 3, 1876, NA M234, DS, Roll 258, 220.

11 Manypenny, *Our Indian Wards*, 308; J. S. Hastings ltr., Jan. 24, 1876, NA M234, RCA, Roll 720, 194; H. W. Bingham ltr., Jan. 26, 1876, NA M234, CRA, Roll 129, 61.

12 Geo. W. Felt ltr., Jan. 29, 1876, NA M234, CRA, Roll 129, 533 (first quotation); Wm. Vandever ltr., Nov. 1, 1875, NA M234, SRA, Roll 846, 549 (second quotation); George Ruhlen ltr., Apr. 19, 1876, RG 393, Series 1173, Department of Dakota Letters Received, NA.

13 M. H. Day ltr., Feb. 4, 1876, NA M234, LBA, Roll 401, 103.

14 Shave Elk (Thomas Disputed) interview, Bruce R. Liddic and Paul Harbaugh, eds., *Camp on Custer: Transcribing the Custer Myth* (Spokane, WA: Arthur H. Clark Company, 1995), 124; He Dog interview, Hammer, *Custer in '76*, 205; Marquis, *Warrior Who Fought Custer*, 159 (quotations), 160.

15 Utley, *The Lance and The Shield*, 128; Hagen, "Major Brisbin's Fort Pease Relief," 35–36; Hedren, *Powder River*, 49.

16 He Dog interview, Hammer, *Custer in '76*, 205; Vestal, *Warpath and Council Fire*, 210; White Bull interview, Hardorff, *Indian Views*, 161–62; Weasel Bear interview, Frazier and Robert Hunt, *I Fought with Custer: The Story of the Last Survivor of the Battle of the Little Big Horn* (New York: Charles Scribner's Sons, 1950), 216. Old Bear biographical references are scattered throughout Hedren, *Powder River.*

17 Neihardt, *When the Tree Flowered*, 209; J. S. Hastings ltr., Jan. 28, 1876, NA M234, RCA, Roll 720, 212; Jackson, *Black Elk*, 92; Bray, *Crazy Horse*, 193.

18 Tall Bull interview, Hammer, *Custer in '76*, 212; George Ruhlen ltr., Apr. 19, 1876, RG 393, Series 1173, Department of Dakota Letters Received, NA; White Bull interview, Hardorff, *Indian Views*, 161–62; One Bull interview, Richard G. Hardorff, ed., *Camp, Custer, and the Little Bighorn: A Collection of Walter Mason Camp's Research Papers on General Custer's Last Fight* (El Segundo, CA: Upton and Sons, Publishers, 1997), 87.

19 Wm. W. Alderson ltr., Jan. 21, 1876, and tele., Mar. 16, 1876, NA M234, MS, Roll 504, 38 and 117 respectively; Larson, *Gall*, 104; White Bull interview, Hardorff, *Indian Views*, 161; Vestal, *New Sources of Indian History*, 162–63.

20 Marquis, *Warrior Who Fought Custer*, 156.

21 Powell, *People of the Sacred Mountain*, Vol. 2, 939; Marquis, *Warrior Who Fought Custer*, 161. On the size of the Powder River village, this is a reconfiguration from Hedren, *Powder River*, 50, where I reported 105 lodges and wickiups and 735 people. On the matter of individual tipi populations throughout this war, a point of considerable interest and study, see Paul L. Hedren, *Rosebud, June 17, 1876: Prelude to the Little Big Horn* (Norman: University of Oklahoma Press, 2019), 393n27, and Robert A. Marshall, "How Many Indians Were There?" in John M. Carroll and Jay Smith, eds., *Custer and His Times, Book Two* (Fort Worth, TX: Little Big Horn Associates, 1984), 211.

22 Peter J. Powell, *Sweet Medicine: The Continuing Role of the Sacred Arrows, the Sun Dance, and the Sacred Buffalo Hat in Northern Cheyenne History*, two vols. (Norman: University of Oklahoma Press, 1969), Vol. 1, 92–93; Gary L. Roberts, "The Shame of Little Wolf," *MMWH* 28 (July 1978): 39; Hedren, *Powder River*, 52.

23 DeBarthe, *Life and Adventures of Frank Grouard*, 154–55 (first quotation), 193 (second quotation); Mari Sandoz ltr., Oct. 7, 1958, Archives & Special Collections, University of Nebraska-Lincoln.

24 Marquis, *Warrior Who Fought Custer*, 164 (first quotation); Black Eagle account, Jerome A. Greene, ed., *Lakota and Cheyenne: Indian Views of the Great Sioux War, 1876–1877* (Norman: University of Oklahoma Press, 1994), 9 (second quotation).

25 Marquis, *Warrior Who Fought Custer*, 165–66; Hedren, *Powder River*, 210–11.

26 Marquis, *Warrior Who Fought Custer*, 165; Thomas B. Marquis, *She Watched Custer's Last Battle* (Hardin, MT: Hardin Tribune-Herald Printing, 1933), [2]; Powell, *People of the Sacred Mountain*, Vol 2: 941–92.

27 Bourke, *Diaries, Vol. 1*, 255 (quotation); Hedren, *Powder River*, 212.

28 Powell, *People of the Sacred Mountain*, vol. 2: 943; Marquis, *Warrior Who Fought Custer*, 167; Hedren, *Powder River*, 212–13.

29 Bourke, *Diaries, Vol. 1*, 253; "The Fight With Crazy Horse," *Weekly Rocky Mountain News*, April 12, 1876; Marquis, *Warrior Who Fought Custer*, 167–68 (quotations); "The Story of Chief Two Moons," Joseph K. Dixon, *The Vanishing Race: The Last Great Indian Council* (Garden City, NY: Doubleday, 1913, reprint, New York: Bonanza Books, 1975), 184 (final quotation).

30 Bourke, *Diaries, Vol. 1*, 255; DeBarthe, *Life and Adventures of Frank Grouard*, 193 (quotation).

31 Black Eagle account, Greene, *Lakota and Cheyenne*, 11; Marquis, *Warrior Who Fought Custer*, 168.

32 Marquis, *She Watched Custer's Last Battle*, [2] (quotation); Powell, *People of the Sacred Mountain*, Vol. 2, 944; Marquis, *Warrior Who Fought Custer*, 92; Hedren, *Powder River*, 214–15, 359.

33 Two Moon interview, Richard G. Hardorff, ed., *Lakota Recollections of the Custer Fight: New Sources of Indian-Military History* (Spokane, WA: Arthur H. Clark Company, 1991), 132; Black Eagle account, Greene, *Lakota and Cheyenne*, 11; Peter J. Powell, "Ox'zem: Box Elder and His Sacred Wheel Lance," *MMWH* 20 (April 1970): 36; Hedren, *Powder River*, 215–16.

34 Marquis, *Warrior Who Fought Custer*, 169 (quotation); Hedren, *Powder River*, 217–18.

35 Bull Hump interview, Richard G. Hardorff, ed., *Cheyenne Memories of the Custer Fight: A Source Book* (Spokane, WA: Arthur H. Clark Company, 1995), 84; Hedren, *Powder River*, 218, 240. Jesse Vaughn tells of local settlers encountering masses of horse bones, none with horseshoes, at the mouth of Joe Creek, south of the army's Lodge Pole Creek camp. J. W. Vaughn, *The Reynolds Campaign on Powder River* (Norman: University of Oklahoma Press, 1961), 154n7.

36 Marquis, *Cheyennes of Montana*, 250–51; Marquis, *Warrior Who Fought Custer*, 168–69; Powell, *People of the Sacred Mountain*, Vol. 2, 945; Black Eagle account, Greene, *Lakota and Cheyenne*, 12.

37 Black Eagle account, Greene, *Lakota and Cheyenne*, 12 (quotation); Marquis, *Warrior Who Fought Custer*, 169.

38 Marquis, *Warrior Who Fought Custer*, 170; Utley, *The Lance and The Shield*, 132.

39 He Dog interview, July 7, 1930, Carroll, *Eleanor H. Hinman Interviews*, 23 (first quotation); Short Bull interview, Carroll, *Eleanor H. Hinman Interviews*, 43 (second quotation).

40 Two Moon interview, Hardorff, *Lakota Recollection*, 133; Bray, *Crazy Horse*, 200; Hamlin Garland's Two Moon interview, Hardorff, *Cheyenne Memories*, 100.

41 Marquis, *Warrior Who Fought Custer*, 170; Powell, *People of the Sacred Mountain*, Vol. 2, 945; John S. Gray, *Centennial Campaign, The Sioux War of 1876* (Fort Collins, CO: Old Army Press, 1976), 325.

42 Vestal, *Warpath*, 182–83; Marquis, *Warrior Who Fought Custer*, 170–71, 172 (quotation).

43 Marquis, *Warrior Who Fought Custer*, 177.

44 "Tales of the Sioux," *Saint Paul and Minneapolis Pioneer Press*, Aug. 14, 1881.

45 Marquis, *Warrior Who Fought Custer*, 178.

46 Two Moon interview, Hardorff, *Lakota Recollection*, 133 (quotation); Donovan, *A Terrible Glory*, 84.

47 Marquis, *Warrior Who Fought Custer*, 179–80; James R. Walker, *Lakota Society* (Lincoln: University of Nebraska Press, 1982), 19; Sandoz, *Crazy Horse*, 36.

48 Short Bull interview, Carroll, *Eleanor H. Hinman Interviews*, 39.

49 John Colhoff ltr., Apr. 17, 1952, Colhoff-Balmer Letters, Kingsley Bray Collection.

6. The Great Ascendancy

1 Marquis, *Warrior Who Fought Custer*, 180.

2 Bray, *Crazy Horse*, 201; "Spotted Tail Reserve," *Omaha Bee*, May 15, 1876; He Dog interview, June 30, 1931, Sandoz Papers, UNL; Paul L. Hedren, "Persimmon Bill Chambers: The 'Scourge of the Black Hills,'" *Annals of Wyoming*, 81 (Autumn 2009): 6–7.

3 Marquis, *Warrior Who Fought Custer*, 181–83; Powell, *People of the Sacred Mountain*, Vol. 2, 949; David H. Miller, *Custer's Fall: The Indian Side of the Story* (New York: Duell, Sloan and Pearce, 1957), 66.

4 Marquis, *Warrior Who Fought Custer*, 182 (quotation); Donovan, *A Terrible Glory*, 69; Paul N. Beck, *Inkpaduta: Dakota Leader* (Norman: University of Oklahoma Press, 2008), 135.

5 One Bull recollection, John P. Everett, "Bullets, Boots, and Saddles," in *The Sunshine Magazine Articles*, Sept. 1930, ed. John M. Carroll (Bryan, TX: privately printed, n.d.), 7; Young Two Moon interview, Hardorff, *Cheyenne Memories*, 160 (quotation); Vestal, *Warpath*, 183–84.

6 Marquis, *Warrior Who Fought Custer*, 183.

7 Rain in the Face narrative, Eastman, *Indian Heroes and Great Chieftains*, 143; Young Two Moon interview, Hardorff, *Cheyenne Memories*, 160; Hyde, *Red Cloud's Folk*, 256–57.

8 Geo. Ruhlen ltr., Apr. 19, 1876, RG 393, Series 1173, Department of Dakota Letters Received, NA; William B. Madsen, *Crazy Horse: The Lakota Warrior's Life & Legacy* (Layton, UT: Gibbs Smith, 2016), 94; White Bull interview, Hardorff, *Indian Views*, 164; Sandoz, *Crazy Horse*, 308.

9 Census Roll of Indians at Spotted Tail Agency, 1877, Rosebud Indian Agency, Bureau of Indian Affairs, RG 75, National Archives at Kansas City; James A. Hanson, "F. C. Boucher Trade Token," *Museum of the Fur Trade Quarterly* 41 (Winter 2005): 16–17; J. H. Pratt ltr., Feb. 25, 1875, NA M234, STA, Roll 840, 547.

10 Sam O'Connell, "Juneaux's Trading Post on Milk River," Samuel O'Connell Papers, MS 597, Montana Historical Society, Helena (first quotation); John Burke tele., July 24, 1876, NA M234, SRA, Roll 847, 27 (hostile camp); Jackson, *Black Elk*, 93; Neihardt, *Black Elk Speaks*, 92 (final quotation).

11 Kill Eagle's statement, R. E. Johnston ltr., Sept. 17, 1876, NA M234, SRA, Roll 847, 241–3 (quotation); "The Indian Battles," *New York Herald*, Sept. 24, 1876; Ephriam D. Dickson, "Prisoners in the Indian Camp: Kill Eagle's Band at Little Big Horn," *Greasy Grass* 27 (May 2011): 6–10; "Kill Eagle Map," Michael N. Donahue, *Drawing Battle Lines: The Map Testimony of Custer's Last Fight* (El Segundo, CA.: Upton and Sons, Publishers, 2008), 138–43. The Kill Eagle interview is an important source shedding considerable light on the spring and summer plight of the Northern Indians and their Rosebud and Little Big Horn fights. Cited here and throughout is the original report, in forty-seven holographic pages. Useful published versions exist including "Kill Eagle's Story," *New York Herald*, Oct. 6, 1876, and W. A. Graham, *The Custer Myth: A Source Book of Custeriana* (Harrisburg, PA: Stackpole Company, 1953), 48–56, though each have slight transcription errors and excisions.

12 James H. Bradley, *The March of the Montana Column: A Prelude to the Custer Disaster*, ed. Edgar I. Stewart (Norman: University of Oklahoma Press, 1961), 87.

13 Marquis, *Warrior Who Fought Custer*, 184 (quotation); Powell, *People of the Sacred Mountain*, Vol. 2, 949.

14 Marquis, *Warrior Who Fought Custer*, 184–86; Utley, *The Lance and The Shield*, 135; Powell, *People of the Sacred Mountain*, Vol. 2, 949–50.

15 "Bad Indians on the Sidney Route," *Cheyenne Daily Leader*, May 30, 1876; Paul L. Hedren, ed., *Ho! For the Black Hills: Captain Jack Crawford Reports the Black Hills Gold Rush and Great Sioux War* (Pierre: South Dakota State Historical Society Press, 2012), 126, 132, 137–39.

16 "Going to War," *New York Herald*, June 9, 1876.

17 John G. Bourke, *On the Border With Crook* (New York: Charles Scribner's Sons, 1891), 288–89; "Crook's 'Close Shave,'" *Cheyenne Daily Leader*, May 18, 1876; Paul L. Hedren, *Fort Laramie in 1876: Chronicle of a Frontier Post at War* (Lincoln: University of Nebraska Press, 1988), 92–94. The notion that this somehow had been Red

Cloud's doing appears in McDermott, *Red Cloud*, 86, citing "Red Cloud Becomes Civilized," *Indian School Journal* 5 (Feb. 1905): 18–19.

18 Neihardt, *Black Elk Speaks*, 92 (quotation); J. S. Hastings tele., June 5, 1876, NA M234, RCA, Roll 720, 314; [E. F.] Townsend tele., May 29, 1876, Fort Laramie Telegrams Sent, Vol. 2, May 29, 1876, Archives, Fort Laramie National Historic Site, Wyoming; James Egan report, June 8, 1876, Dept. of the Platte Letters Received, RG393, Entry 3731, NA.

19 Neihardt, *Black Elk Speaks*, 92–95; Black Elk narrative, DeMallie, *The Sixth Grandfather*, 170–71; James Egan report, June 8, 1876, Dept. of the Platte Letters Received, RG393, Entry 3731, NA; Hedren, *Fort Laramie in 1876*, 100–101.

20 Marquis, *Warrior Who Fought Custer*, 186–87; "Thirteen Lakota Moons," Akta Lakota Museum and Cultural Center, atkalakota.stjo.org. Custer trail student Thomas Heski asserts that the village's first camp on the Rosebud was not eight but as many as eighteen miles above its mouth. Wooden Leg, who grew up in that country, knew that campsite's later owners, and told his biographer specifically eight miles seems irrefutable. Tom Heski, "Trailing the Lakota, Cheyenne, Custer & Reno: An On the Ground Synopsis," in *CBHMA 19th Annual Symposium Proceedings* (Hardin, MT: CBHMA, 2005), 15.

21 Marquis, *Warrior Who Fought Custer*, 187; Powell, *People of the Sacred Mountain*, Vol. 2, 950; Miller, *Custer's Fall*, 230.

22 Marquis, *Warrior Who Fought Custer*, 188.

23 One Bull, "Sitting Bull's prophesy," Campbell Collection, box 110, folder 8, OU (quotation); Utley, *The Lance and The Shield*, 136; Hämäläinen, *Lakota America*, 357–58.

24 One Bull, "Sitting Bull's prophesy," Campbell Collection, OU.

25 Eastman, "Rain in the Face," 511 (quotation); Bradley, *March of the Montana Column*, 119–20.

26 Marquis, *Warrior Who Fought Custer*, 188–90.

27 Neihardt, *Black Elk Speaks*, 94–95; Marquis, *Warrior Who Fought Custer*, 191 (quotation).

28 Red Horse interview, W. H. Wood ltr., Feb. 27, 1877, NA M234, DS, Roll 262, 246.

29 "The Sioux War/Threatened Defections of the Indians," *New York Herald*, July 9, 1876 (first quotation); M. A. Reno tele., April 27, 1876, NA M234, SRA, Roll 847, 562 (second quotation).

30 White Bull narrative, Campbell Collection, box 105, folder 24, OU.

31 Utley, *The Lance and The Shield*, 137; Gardner, *The Earth Is All That Lasts*, 230–31; Vestal, *Sitting Bull*, 148; Kill Eagle's statement, R. E. Johnston ltr., Sept. 17, 1876, NA M234, SRA, Roll 847, 241/13.

32 LaPointe, *Sitting Bull*, 63 (quotation); Vestal, *Sitting Bull*, 149; Powell, *People of the Sacred Mountain*, Vol. 2, 951. On pipe etiquette, I refer to the Colhoff-Balmer ltr, Jan. 21, 1950, Kingsley Bray Collection; and Eagle Elk, Neihardt, *When the Tree Flowered*, 46.

33 Vestal, *Sitting Bull*, 149; Colhoff-Balmer ltr, Oct. 25, 1949, Kingsley Bray Collection; Delphine Red Shirt, *George Sword's Warrior Narratives* (Lincoln: University of Nebraska Press, 2016), 217; Joseph Epes Brown, *The Sacred Pipe: Black Elk's Account of the Seven Rites of the Oglala Sioux* (Norman: University of Oklahoma Press, 1953), 71–72; Coleman diary, June 22, 1876, Bruce R. Liddic, *I Buried Custer: The Diary of Pvt. Thomas W. Coleman, 7th U.S. Cavalry* (College Station, TX: Creative Publishing Company, 1979), 14; "Standing Bear Tells About the Sun Dance," DeMallie, *The Sixth Grandfather*, 173–74.

34 White Bull narrative, Campbell Collection, box 105, folder 24, OU; Vestal, *Sitting Bull*, 150; Utley, *The Lance and The Shield*, 137–38; Gardner, *The Earth Is All That Lasts*, 231; Powell, *People of the Sacred Mountain*, Vol. 2, 952.

35 Vestal, *Sitting Bull*, 150 (quotations); Utley, *The Lance and The Shield*, 137–38; Gardner, *The Earth Is All That Lasts*, 231–32; One Bull interview, Hardorff, *Indian Views*, 141.

36 One Bull interview, Hardorff, *Indian Views*, 141; One Bull interview, Campbell Collection, box 105, folder 19, OU; Vestal, *Sitting Bull*, 150–51; Bray, *Crazy Horse*, 204 (second quotation); Jackson, *Black Elk*, 99. Virtually every word of Sitting Bull's dream has been analyzed carefully. For compelling insight on the notion of "having no ears," see Raymond J. DeMallie, "'These Have No Ears': Narrative and the Ethnohistorical Method," *Ethnohistory* 40 (Fall 1991): 515–38. On the notion of "coming with heads down," see H. Inez Hilger, "The Narrative of Oscar One Bull," *Mid-America* 28 (July 1946): 165. On the subtle variations of interpreting Sitting Bull's dream, see Gardner, *The Earth Is All That Lasts*, 455n232 "like so many grasshoppers."

37 Hunt and Hunt, *I Fought With Custer*, 73; Edgar I. and Jane R. Stewart, eds., *The Field Diary of Lt. Edward Settle Godfrey* (Portland, OR: Champoeg Press, 1957), 9, 10 (quotation); John S. Gray, *Custer's Last Campaign: Mitch Boyer and the Little Bighorn Reconstructed* (Lincoln: University of Nebraska Press, 1991), 212; "Red Star's Story," O. G. Libby, ed., *The Arikara Narrative of the Campaign Against the Hostile Dakotas, June 1876* (Glorieta, NM: Rio Grande Press, 1976), 78–79; Miller, *Custer's Fall*, 15–16. The Muddy Creek of 1876–77, today's Lame Deer Creek, is not to be confused by today's Muddy Creek, the

next upstream affluent of Rosebud Creek. See George B. Grinnell, *The Fighting Cheyennes* (New York: Charles Scribner's Sons, 1915), 374, 379.

38 Marquis, *Warrior Who Fought Custer*, 190–91, 193. The dramatic pony recovery is recounted in the preceding chapter and in Hedren, *Powder River*, 217–19.

39 Marquis, *Warrior Who Fought Custer*, 193–94.

40 Marquis, *Warrior Who Fought Custer*, 194.

41 Marquis, *Warrior Who Fought Custer*, 194–95.

42 Marquis, *Warrior Who Fought Custer*, 195–96.

43 Marquis, *Warrior Who Fought Custer*, 196.

44 Marquis, *Warrior Who Fought Custer*, 197; Greene, *Lakota and Cheyenne*, 21.

45 Runs the Enemy account, Dixon, *Vanishing Race*, 65.

46 Bourke, *On the Border With Crook*, 296; Little Hawk reminiscence, Greene, *Lakota and Cheyenne*, 23 (quotation).

47 Little Hawk reminiscence, Greene, *Lakota and Cheyenne*, 23.

48 Foolish Elk interview, Hammer, *Custer in '76*, 197; Marquis, *Warrior Who Fought Custer*, 179 (quotation); Stands In Timber interview, Hardorff, *Cheyenne Memories*, 167.

49 Marquis, *Warrior Who Fought Custer*, 207. These soldier movements, the Ball Scout, Bradley's several forays, and the Reno Scout are well chronicled and documented in Edgar I. Stewart, *Custer's Luck* (Norman: University of Oklahoma Press, 1955), and Donovan, *A Terrible Glory*.

7. Stopping the Gray Fox

1 Young Two Moon interview, Hardorff, *Cheyenne Memories*, 138.

2 Marquis, *Cheyennes of Montana*, 255; Thomas B. Marquis, *Memoirs of a White Crow Indian* (New York: The Century Co., 1928), 241; Miller, *Custer's Fall*, 7.

3 Marquis, *Warrior Who Fought Custer*, 182; Thos. J. Mitchell ltr., July 29, 1876, NA M234, MS, Roll 505, 433; "Moving on the Sioux," *New York Herald*, Aug. 19, 1876.

4 "The Black Hills/Mr. Bear Stands Up's Statement," *Saint Paul Pioneer Press*, July 15, 1876; Manypenny, *Our Indian Wards*, 315.

5 Vestal, *Warpath*, 185; Marquis, *Warrior Who Fought Custer*, 197 (quotation).

6 Little Hawk reminiscence, Greene, *Lakota and Cheyenne*, 23–24; John Stands In Timber and Margot Liberty, *Cheyenne Memories* (New Haven, CT: Yale University Press, 1967), 183.

7 Little Hawk reminiscence, Greene, *Lakota and Cheyenne*, 24–25.

8 Stands In Timber and Liberty, *Cheyenne Memories*, 183; Little Hawk reminiscence, Greene, *Lakota and Cheyenne*, 25; Grinnell, *Fighting Cheyennes*. Cheyennes, 318.

9 Marquis, *Warrior Who Fought Custer*, 197–98; Vestal, *New Sources of Indian History*, 163; White Man Runs Him recollection, James S. Hutchins, *The Papers of Edward S. Curtis Relating to Custer's Last Battle* (El Segundo, CA: Upton & Sons, 2000), 153; Feather Earring account, Graham, *Custer Myth*, 98; Eagle Elk, Neihardt, *When the Tree Flowered*, 213.

10 Little Hawk reminiscence, Greene, *Lakota and Cheyenne*, 25 (first quotation); Standing Bear narrative, DeMallie, *The Sixth Grandfather*, 174 (second quotation).

11 Young Two Moon account, Greene, *Lakota and Cheyenne*, 26 (quotation); Grinnell, *Fighting Cheyennes*, 220; Vestal, *Warpath*, 185.

12 Marquis, *Warrior Who Fought Custer*, 198 (first quotation); Sandoz, *Crazy Horse*, 313 (second quotation); Eastman, "Rain in the Face," 511 (third quotation).

13 High Dog recollection, Buechel and Manhart, *Lakota Tales & Texts*, Vol. 1, 298; Marquis, *Warrior Who Fought Custer*, 199 (quotation). Particulars on battle preparation and dress are discussed in Eastman, "Rain in the Face," 508; J. W. Vaughn, *With Crook at the Rosebud* (Harrisburg, PA: Stackpole Company, 1956), 44; Grinnell, *Fighting Cheyennes*, 323; and more broadly in Geo. Bent to Geo. Hyde ltr., January 24, 1906, George Bent Papers, Beinecke Rare Book and Manuscript Library, Yale University; Frances Densmore, *Teton Sioux Music* (Washington, DC: Government Printing Office, 1918), 350; Hassrick, *The Sioux*, 86; and Richard Aquila, "Plains Indian War Medicine," *Journal of the West* 13 (April 1974): 24–28.

14 Vestal, *Warpath*, 186 (quotation); Howard, *Warrior Who Killed Custer*, 23 plate 13, 48.

15 He Dog interview, Carroll, *Eleanor H. Hinman Interviews*, 23 (first quotation); Red Feather interview, Carroll, *Eleanor H. Hinman Interviews*, 36; Eagle Elk interview, November 27, 1942, John Neihardt Papers, University of Missouri, Columbia; White Bull statement, Vestal, *New Sources of Indian History*, 320; Chips interviews, Richard G. Hardorff, ed., *The Surrender and Death of Crazy Horse* (Spokane, WA: Arthur H. Clark Company, 1998), 77, 85; Chips interview, Jensen, *Ricker Indian Interviews*, 277 (second quotation). Crazy Horse's spiritual beliefs and customs, explained within the religious contexts of the Lakotas, are summarized here. It is a critically important element of the story and no better told than by Thomas

Powers, *The Killing of Crazy Horse*, 176–81, who, moreover, places his discussion within the context of the looming Rosebud battle. Crazy Horse's ear and heart stones and other battle medicines survive and are carefully described by Larry Belitz, "Chips Collection of Crazy Horse Medicines," 2010, 101–108; and are pictured in Franz K. Brown, *Thunder Visions: The Crazy Horse Wotawe of the Lakota Medicine Man Woptuha* (Hot Springs, SD: [Franz Brown], 2010).

16 Young Two Moon account, Greene, *Lakota and Cheyenne*, 26–27; Hyde, *Red Cloud's Folk*, 263; Weasel Bear interview, Hunt and Hunt, *I Fought with Custer*, 216.

17 Eagle Elk, Neihardt, *When the Tree Flowered*, 213 (quotation); Vestal, *Warpath*, 187; Vestal, *Sitting Bull*, 153.

18 Runs the Enemy account, Dixon, *Vanishing Race*, 66; Shave Elk (Thomas Disputed) interview, Liddic and Harbaugh, *Camp on Custer*, 125 (quotation); Jackson, *Black Elk*, 101.

19 Powers, *The Killing of Crazy Horse*, 175–76. The warrior number at Rosebud is a disputed detail. Old Bull told his interviewer, Walter Campbell, that over 1000 Indians fought at the Rosebud (Old Bull notes, Campbell Collection, OU), a number Campbell (Vestal) repeated in *Warpath*, 187. Charles A. Eastman, a turn-of-the-twentieth century Santee Sioux physician and scholar, studied many of the same sources, conducted his own original interviews, and concluded that 700 warriors met soldiers that day. "Was It a Massacre?" *Red Man and Helper*, August 17, 1900, in *Gen. George Crook's 1876 Campaigns*, John D. McDermott (Sheridan, WY, Frontier Heritage Alliance, 2000), 206. The conclusion here follows methodologies described earlier and embraced throughout this narrative, and align with Eastman's assessment.

20 John Stands In Timber and Margot Liberty, *A Cheyenne Voice: The Complete John Stands In Timber Interviews* (Norman: University of Oklahoma Press, 2013), 438; "The End of the Cheyenne Trail," *The Daily Oklahoman*, November 23, 1930; Richard A. Fox, "The Value of Oral History: White Eagle's Account," in *CBHMA 9th Annual Symposium Proceedings* (Hardin, MT: CBHMA, 1996), 7–8.

21 Vestal, *Warpath*, 187; Grinnell, *Fighting Cheyennes*, 325; Stands In Timber and Liberty, *A Cheyenne Voice*, 433; Sandoz, *Crazy Horse*, 317.

22 Stands In Timber and Liberty, *A Cheyenne Voice*, 416; Eagle Elk, Neihardt, *When the Tree Flowered*, 214.

23 Grinnell, *Fighting Cheyennes*, 320.

24 Grinnell, *Fighting Cheyennes*, 320; Jack Keenan, "Wrinkled Cheyenne Warrior Tells of Battle With Crook," *Billings Gazette*, June 17, 1934; Powell, *People of the Sacred Mountain*, Vol. 2, 959.

25 Iron Hawk recollection, DeMallie, *The Sixth Grandfather*, 174–75. There are two Iron Hawks in this timeframe, a father and son, and both Oglala. The father's narrative was collected by Eli Ricker (Iron Hawk interview, Jensen, *Ricker Indian Interviews*, 314–15). The Iron Hawk of this story is the elder's son, better known then as Runs in Circle, or Runs Around. See Ephriam D. Dickson III, "Reconstructing the Indian Village on the Little Bighorn: The Cankahuhan or Soreback Band, Oglala," *Greasy Grass* 22 (May 2006): 14; and Dickson, *Sitting Bull Surrender Census*, 148n96.

26 For additional particulars on this physiographically complex battlefield, see Interlude, "Notes on Rosebud Geography," Hedren, *Rosebud, June 17, 1876*, 178–84.

27 Marquis, *Warrior Who Fought Custer*, 119–20 (first quotation); Bear Soldier interview, Lewis Crawford Papers, State Historical Society of North Dakota, Bismarck (second quotation).

28 Vestal, *Sitting Bull*, 153 (quotation); Eagle Elk, Neihardt, *When the Tree Flowered*, 214.

29 Sandoz, *Crazy Horse*, 318–19; James Chase in the Morning, Edward and Mabell Kadlecek, *To Kill an Eagle: Indian Views on the Last Days of Crazy Horse* (Boulder, CO: Johnson Books, 1981), 91 (first quotation); Eagle Elk, Neihardt, *When the Tree Flowered*, 215 (second quotation). Crazy Horse's memorable lines have been studied carefully. See Hedren, *Rosebud, June 17, 1876*, 416–17n9. In good probability the words, repeated by others then and later, were indeed originally his.

30 Hedren, *Rosebud, June 17, 1876*, 186 (first quotation), 189 (second quotation).

31 Baptiste Pourier interview, Edmond S. Meany Papers, University of Washington, Seattle (first quotation); "Noted Oglala Medicine Man Kept Crazy Horse's Secret," *Rapid City Daily Journal*, Feb. 11, 1951 (second quotation).

32 Young Two Moon interview, Greene, *Lakota and Cheyenne*, 28.

33 Louis Dog recollection, Stands In Timber and Liberty, *A Cheyenne Voice*, 423, 430; Grinnell, *Fighting Cheyennes*, 323–24; Little Hawk reminiscence, Greene, *Lakota and Cheyenne*, 25; Powell, *Sweet Medicine*, Vol. 1, 102; Stands In Timber and Liberty, *Cheyenne Memories*, 188–89; Rosemary and Joseph Agonito, "Resurrecting History's Forgotten Women: A Case Study from the Cheyenne Indians," *Frontiers: A Journal of Women Studies* 6 (Autumn 1981): 8; Joan Hantz, "The Girl Who Saved Her Brother," in Richard Little Bear, *We, The Northern Cheyenne People*, 67.

34 Vestal, *Warpath*, 188; Howard, *Warrior Who Killed Custer*, 49, 50 (quotation); White Bull account, Greene, *Lakota and Cheyenne*, 20.

35 Lewis F. Crawford, *Rekindling Camp Fires: The Exploits of Ben Arnold (Connor)* (Bismarck, ND: Capital Book Co., 1926), 251–52.

36 Marquis, *Warrior Who Fought Custer*, 200 (first quotation); Iron Hawk recollection, DeMallie, *The Sixth Grandfather*, 175 (second quotation).

37 Marquis, *Warrior Who Fought Custer*, 200; Joe Medicine Crow, "Custer and His Crow Scouts," in *Little Bighorn Remembered: The Untold Indian Story of Custer's Last Stand*, ed. Herman J. Viola (New York: Times Books, 1999), 109. Charging Girl narrative, James H. Cook Collection, Powers, *The Killing of Crazy Horse*, 489n18.

38 Marquis, *Warrior Who Fought Custer*, 199–200 (quotation); Cowdrey, Martin, and Martin, *Horses & Bridles of the American Indians*, 107.

39 William Garnett interview, Jensen, *Ricker Indian Interviews*, 46, 84; Sandoz, *Crazy Horse*, 318–19; Miller, *Custer's Fall*, 62–63; Powers, *The Killing of Crazy Horse*, 186 (quotation).

40 Anthony R. McGinnis, *Counting Coup and Cutting Horses: Intertribal Warfare on the Northern Plains, 1738–1889* (Lincoln: University of Nebraska Press, 1990), 135; Hedren, *Rosebud, June 17, 1876*, 281.

41 Hedren, *Rosebud, June 17, 1876*, 217–18.

42 Bourke, *On the Border With Crook*, 314 (quotation); Hedren, *Rosebud, June 17, 1876*, 218.

43 Neihardt, *When the Tree Flowered*, 214; Keenan, "Wrinkled Cheyenne Warrior."

44 Runs the Enemy account, Dixon, *Vanishing Race*, 66.

45 Louis Dog recollection, Stands In Timber and Liberty, *Cheyenne Voice*, 423.

46 Keenan, "Wrinkled Cheyenne Warrior."

47 Powell, *People of the Sacred Mountain*, Vol. 2, 995; Limpy recollection, Stands In Timber and Liberty, *Cheyenne Voice*, 417, 426–27, 431.

48 Limpy recollection, Stands In Timber and Liberty, *Cheyenne Voice*, 417–18, 431, 435; Keenan, "Wrinkled Cheyenne Warrior"; Powell, *People of the Sacred Mountain*, Vol. 2, 995.

49 Stands In Timber and Liberty, *A Cheyenne Voice*, 436, 438.

50 "Vengeance of Indian Maid," *Sheridan Post*, Aug. 22, 1911; Cyrus Townsend Brady, *Indian Fights and Fighters* (New York: Doubleday, Page & Company, 1904), 198; Hedren, *Rosebud, June 17, 1876*, 262.

51 Neihardt, *When the Tree Flowered*, 214.

52 Young Two Moon interview, Greene, *Lakota and Cheyenne*, 28–29. Accounts of Scabby's demise vary. Some report him as a casualty of the Rosebud fight (Hedren, *Rosebud, June 17, 1876*, 285), while others count him as a casualty of the Red Fork battle on November 25, 1876 (Grinnell, *Fighting Cheyennes*, 352).

53 Red Hawk interview, Edmond S. Meany Papers, University of Washington; Hedren, *Rosebud, June 17, 1876*, 268–69.

54 Stands In Timber and Liberty, *A Cheyenne Voice*, 425, 432 (quotation); J. M. Thralls Two Moon interview, Hardorff, *Cheyenne Memories*, 121.

55 Stands In Timber and Liberty, *A Cheyenne Voice*, 432; Runs the Enemy account, Dixon, *Vanishing Race*, 67; Neihardt, *When the Tree Flowered*, 215.

56 Tall Bull interview, Hammer, *Custer in '76*, 212 (first quotation); Plenty Coups (Crow), Frank B. Linderman, *American: The Life Story of a Great Indian* (New York: John Day Company, 1930), 166–67; Iron Hawk recollection, DeMallie, *The Sixth Grandfather*, 176 (second quotation); White Bull (Cheyenne) interview, Hammer, *Custer in '76*, 211. The severely wounded officer was Captain Guy V. Henry, Third Cavalry, Hedren, *Rosebud, June 17, 1876*, 263–64.

57 Grinnell, *Fighting Cheyennes*, 323; Neihardt, *When the Tree Flowered*, 215.

58 Horned Horse interview, "Doves and Devils," *Chicago Times*, May 26, 1877; John G. Bourke, *The Diaries of John Gregory Bourke, Vol. 2, July 29, 1876–April 7, 1878*, ed. Charles M. Robinson III (Denton: University of North Texas Press, 2005), 287; Kill Eagle's statement, R. E. Johnston ltr., Sept. 17, 1876, NA M234, SRA, Roll 847, 241/27.

59 Vestal, *Sitting Bull*, 154; LaPointe, *Sitting Bull*, 65.

8. We Wish to Live!

1 Louis Dog account, Keenan, "Wrinkled Cheyenne Warrior." Soldier estimates of warrior numbers varied widely, from one thousand to nearly three thousand. See Hedren, *Rosebud, June 17, 1876*, 305–306.

2 Hamlin Garland's Two Moons interview, Hardorff, *Cheyenne Memories*, 100 (first quotation); Howard, *Warrior Who Killed Custer*, 49 (second quotation); Neihardt, *When the Tree Flowered*, 215 (third quotation); Eagle Elk interview, November 29, 1942, John G. Neihardt Collection, State Historical Society of Missouri; Jackson, *Black Elk*, 451–52; Iron Hawk recollection, DeMallie, *The Sixth Grandfather*, 175 (fourth quotation).

3 Sandoz, *Crazy Horse*, 321.

4 Ibid. (first quotation); Weasel Bear interview, Hunt and Hunt, *I Fought with Custer*, 216 (second quotation); Runs the Enemy account, Dixon, *Vanishing Race*, 67 (third quotation).

5 Shave Elk (Thomas Disputed) interview, Liddic and Harbaugh, *Camp on Custer*, 123; He Dog interview, Hammer, *Custer in '76*, 205.

6 Standing Bear narrative, DeMallie, *The Sixth Grandfather*, 177 (quotation); Louis Dog recollection, Stands In Timber and Liberty, *A Cheyenne Voice*, 402, 423; Respects Nothing interview, Hardorff, *Lakota Recollections*, 32; Vestal, *Warpath*, 190. Rosebud's lone mass

grave remains one of the story's greatest enigmas. Despite considerable effort, it has never been found. See Douglas D. Scott, "Searching the Battle of the Rosebud for the Soldier Burials: Historic Records Research and Archaeological Investigations," 2022, TMs. Accounts of a watch and diamond ring taken from the Rosebud dead seem questionable and in greater probability are recoveries associated with the Little Big Horn battle.

7 Marquis, *Warrior Who Fought Custer*, 92, 203, 252–53.

8 Feather Earring account, Graham, *Custer Myth*, 98; He Dog interview, Hammer, *Custer in '76*, 205; Old Eagle account, Miller, *Custer's Fall*, 75–76, 238; Red Bear (Arikara) story, Libby, *Arikara Narrative,121*; Donahue, *Where the Rivers Ran Red*, 310n90; Young Hawk (Arikara) interview, Hammer, *Custer in '76*, 192; Cannonball Woman interview, Hardorff, *Camp, Custer, and the Little Bighorn*, 85, 85–86n4. The so-called "lone tipi" is one of the minor intrigues of the Little Big Horn saga in which battle enthusiasts tie themselves in knots arguing the location of a single tipi, when in fact Indian testimony points to several tipis. A compelling examination of the lone tipi phenomenon is made by Vern G. Smalley, "The Lone Tepees Along Reno Creek," in *CBHMA 12th Annual Symposium Proceedings* (Hardin, MT: CBHMA, 1998): 1–11.

9 American Horse reminiscence, Greene, *Lakota and Cheyenne*, 49 (quotation) (Greene mistakenly identifies this informant as an Oglala); Marquis, *Warrior Who Fought Custer*, 202–203.

10 Marquis, *Warrior Who Fought Custer*, 203; Mrs. Spotted Horn Bull account, "Tales of the Tatankas," *Saint Paul Pioneer Press*, May 19, 1883; Castle McLaughlin, *A Lakota War Book from the Little Bighorn: The Pictographic "Autobiography of Half Moon"* (Cambridge, MA: Peabody Museum Press, 2013), 18.

11 Runs the Enemy account, Dixon, *Vanishing Race*, 67; Marquis, *Warrior Who Fought Custer*, 203 (quotation).

12 Marquis, *Warrior Who Fought Custer*, 25, 204; Marquis, *Cheyennes of Montana*, 254–55; "Mrs. Spotted Horn Bull's View," James McLaughlin, *My Friend the Indian* (Boston, MA: Houghton Mifflin Company, 1910), 166 (quotation).

13 Thomas B. Marquis, *She Watched Custer's Last Battle* (Hardin, MT: Hardin Tribune-Herald, 1933), [2]; Eastman, "Rain in the Face" 511 (quotation).

14 "An Illustrious Sioux," *Rocky Mountain Husbandman* (Diamond City, MT), May 5, 1881; Usher L. Burdick, *The Last Battle of the Sioux Nation* (Stevens Point, WI: Worzalla Publishing Co., [1929]),

39; Larson, *Gall*, 110–11; Joseph Henry Taylor, *Kaleidoscopic Lives* (Washburn, ND: self-published, 1902), 143; Marshall, "How Many Indians Were There?" 215.

15 Hollow Horn Bear interview, Hardorff, *Lakota Recollections*, 178–79.

16 Marquis, *Warrior Who Fought Custer*, 205; Two Moon interview, Hardorff, *Lakota Recollections*, 134 (first quotation); Lone Man's story, Will Spindler, "The Scout Who Saved the Sioux," *Frontier Times* 43 (June–July 1968): 44 (second quotation); Densmore, *Teton Sioux Music*, 91.

17 Sandoz, *Crazy Horse*, 322; Utley, *The Lance and The Shield*, 142.

18 Waterman (Arapaho) account, Graham, *Custer Myth*, 109; Young Two Moon account, Greene, *Lakota and Cheyenne*, 67; Powell, *People of the Sacred Mountain*, Vol. 2, 1004 (quotation). The five were named; see Hedren, *Rosebud, June 17, 1876*, 345.

19 Foolish Elk interview, Hammer, *Custer in '76*, 197–98; Foolish Elk recollection, William J. Bordeaux, *Custer's Conqueror* (n.p.: Smith and Company, [1944]), 57; Bourke, *Diaries, Vol. 2*, 30.

20 Marquis, *Warrior Who Fought Custer*, 204–205; "Custer Battle Cheyennes," in Marquis, *Cheyennes of Montana*, 255.

21 Marquis, *Warrior Who Fought Custer*, 214.

22 Black Elk interview, DeMallie, *The Sixth Grandfather*, 178; Beard recollection, Viola, *Little Bighorn Remembered*, 44; Respects Nothing interview, Hardorff, *Lakota Recollections*, 31; Donovan, *Terrible Glory*, 187–87.

23 The layout of the Little Big Horn village has been studied exhaustively. This simple construction considered several dozen Indian mentions, particularly Joseph White Cow Bull (Miller, "Echoes of the Little Big Horn," *American Heritage* 22 (June 1971): 32), Red Horse (Hardorff, *Indian Views*, 71–72), Black Elk (Neihardt, *Black Elk Speaks*, 106), Respects Nothing (Donahue, *Drawing Battle Lines*, 177, 179), Shave Elk, (Liddic and Harbaugh, *Camp on Custer*, 121), and Wooden Leg (Marquis, *Warrior Who Fought Custer*, 208–209). Also critical are the assessments of Gregory F. Michno, *Lakota Noon: The Indian Narrative of Custer's Defeat* (Missoula, MT: Mountain Press Publishing Company, 1997), 5, 6, 12; Richard A. Fox, Jr., "West River History: The Indian Village on Little Bighorn River, June 25–26, 1876," in Rankin, *Legacy*, 147–49: and William Clark's maps (Donahue, *Drawing Battle Lines*, 96, 99), Clark gaining his sense of the field from people surrendering at Red Cloud Agency in 1877. People were invariably specific about the locations of their own camps, but imprecise about the locations of others.

24 Kill Eagle's statement, R. E. Johnston ltr., Sept. 17, 1876, NA M234, SRA, Roll 847, 241–43; Utley, *The Lance and The Shield*, 143–44; One

Bull and White Bull interview, Hardorff, *Camp, Custer, and the Little Bighorn*, 86; Vestal, *Sitting Bull*, 159.

25 White Bull interview, Hardorff, *Indian Views*, 163; McLaughlin, *My Friend the Indian*, 167.

26 "Tales of the Tatankas," *Saint Paul Pioneer Press*, May 19, 1883; Julia Face interview, Hardorff, *Lakota Recollections*, 188, 192. This Plenty Lice is not to be confused by a warrior of the same name killed in the Arrow Creek fight in 1872.

27 Powell, *People of the Sacred Mountain*, Vol. 2, 1006, referencing communications with John Stands In Timber.

28 Young Little Wolf interview, Hardorff, *Cheyenne Memories*, 91; Marquis, *Warrior Who Fought Custer*, 205.

29 Marquis, *Warrior Who Fought Custer*, 204. A foremost exponent of the "summer roamers" notion is John Gray, whose repeated mentions of it in *Centennial Campaign* (as on 333) have been echoed widely by prominent historians. All do so offering no particular substantiation. For thoughtful analyses, see Stewart, *Custer's Luck*, 309–12n15, and Marshall, "How Many Indians Were There?"

30 Kill Eagle's statement, R. E. Johnston ltr., Sept. 17, 1876, NA M234, SRA, Roll 847, 241–44; Kill Eagle map, Donahue, *Drawing Battle Lines*, 141; Stands In Timber and Liberty, *A Cheyenne Voice*, 365, 380; Runs the Enemy account, Dixon, *Vanishing Race*, 170; Thomas Disputed interview, Liddic and Harbaugh, *Camp on Custer*, 125 (quotation).

31 Marquis, *Warrior Who Fought Custer*, 211, 383 (first quotation); Dewey Beard interview, David Humphreys Miller, "Echoes of the Little Bighorn," 37 (second quotation).

32 Sandoz, *Crazy Horse*, 324; Red Feather interview, Hardorff, *Lakota Recollections*, 81 (first quotation); Marquis, *Warrior Who Fought Custer*, 214–15 (second quotation), 216; Powell, *People of the Sacred Mountain*, Vol. 2, 1007; John Stands In Timber, "Last Ghastly Moments at the Little Bighorn," *American Heritage* 17 (April 1966): 19; Brave Bear account, Dec. 1, 1905, George Bent Papers, Beinecke Rare Book and Manuscript Library, Yale University, New Haven, CT.

33 Wolf Tooth narrative, Stands In Timber and Liberty, *A Cheyenne Voice*, 365, 382; Donovan, *A Terrible Glory*, 189–90.

34 Young Two Moon interview, Hardorff, *Cheyenne Memories*, 152; Powell, *People of the Sacred Mountain*, Vol. 2, 1008 (quotation).

35 An army officer described this site and helps us locate it. Three days after the Custer fight Charles Varnum explored Custer's trail in that proximity and remembered a high hill off of Cedar Coulee with a "pile of stones and Indian medicine bags and other things on it." Charles A. Varnum testimony, in Ronald H. Nichols, ed., *Reno Court of Inquiry:*

Proceedings of a Court of Inquiry in the Case of Major Marcus A. Reno (Hardin, MT: CBHMA, 2007), 158. One Bull and some subsequent writers placed the site on today's Last Stand Hill, a prominence whose importance obviously grew through the years. But on reflection, that pinpointing seems improbable, is far too distant, and lacks an equivalent to Varnum's certainty.

36 One Bull narrative, Miller, "Echoes of the Little Bighorn," 30. Such a prayer stick survives. See Frances Densmore, *A Collection of Specimens from the Teton Sioux*, Vol. 11, no. 3, *Indian Notes and Monographs* (New York: Museum of the American Indian, Heye Foundation, 1948), plate xvii(b).

37 Robert P. Higheagle, "Twenty-five Songs Made by Sitting Bull," Campbell Collection, OU. One Bull later offered a slight variation of the words, but the essence is identical. One Bull narrative, Miller, "Echoes of the Little Bighorn," 30; Vestal, *Sitting Bull*, 158; Gardner, *The Earth Is All That Lasts*, 2.

9. One Day in June

1 White Bull recollection, Paul A. Hutton, ed., *The Custer Reader* (Lincoln: University of Nebraska Press, 1992), 336–37; Jackson, *Black Elk*, 106; Powers, *The Killing of Crazy Horse*, 302; Two Moon interview, Hardorff, *Cheyenne Memories*, 101.

2 Emily Standing Bear recollection, Robert Dillon, *Pute Tiyośpaye (Lip's Camp): A History and Culture of a Sioux Indian Village* (Wanblee, SD: Crazy Horse School, 1978), 13; White Shield interview, Hardorff, *Cheyenne Memories*, 50; Marquis, *Warrior Who Fought Custer*, 216.

3 Powers, *The Killing of Crazy Horse*, 303; Little Soldier statement, Joseph G. Masters, *Shadows Fall Across the Little Horn* (Laramie: University of Wyoming Library, 1951), 33; Miller, *Custer's Fall*, 52-53; Waldo R. Wedel, "Notes on the Prairie Turnip (*Psoralea esculenta*) Among the Plains Indians," *Nebraska History* 59 (Summer 1978): 155.

4 Stands In Timber, "Last Ghastly Moments at the Little Bighorn," 20 (quotation); Powell, *People of the Sacred Mountain*, Vol. 2, 1009; Michno, *Lakota Noon*, 198–99.

5 Black Bear interview, Hammer, *Custer in '76*, 203; Miller, *Custer's Fall*, 62–63. The seven Red Cloud Oglalas are named in Hardorff, *Indian Views*, 51n20. Young Red Cloud's probable departure is complicated. Miller, above, asserted that the young man merely contemplated joining Black Bear but did not do so. Two Moon suggested that he, in fact, did depart the camp, but rapidly returned that same day (Two Moon story, Hutchins, *Papers of Edward S. Curtis*, 57). But Jack Red Cloud "and others" were specifically acknowledged at Red Cloud

Agency on August 3, the notice observing that "they were in the Rosebud fight" but with no mention of the Little Big Horn (P. H. Sheridan tele., Aug. 3, 1876, NA M234, DS, Roll 258, 365). Jack Red Cloud's only known account of the Little Big Horn episode is so vague that it does not confirm his presence in the climactic fight (Dixon, *Vanishing Race*, 168–70).

6 White Bull interview, Hardorff, *Indian Views*, 152; Frances Y. Peterson, "Dewey Iron Hail," *Frontier Times* 35 (Fall 1961): 38; Feather Earring account, Graham, *Custer Myth*, 97; Bear Soldier interview, Lewis Crawford Collection, series 10058, notebook 25, box 2, State Historical Society of North Dakota, Bismarck; Powers, *The Killing of Crazy Horse*, 303.

7 Luther Standing Bear, *My People the Sioux* (Boston, MA: Houghton Mifflin Company, 1923), 82; Horny Horse account, Bourke, *Diaries, Vol.* 2, 268; Powers, *The Killing of Crazy Horse*, 305; Bordeaux, *Custer's Conqueror*, 54 (quotations).

8 Red Bird (Little Wolf) interview, Hardorff, *Cheyenne Memories*, 91; Hammer, *Custer in '76*, 212n2; Marquis, *Warrior Who Fought Custer*, 249–50; Bull Hump and White Bird interview, Hardorff, *Cheyenne Memories*, 86.

9 Marquis, *Warrior Who Fought Custer*, 250; Roberts, "The Shame of Little Wolf," 39; White Man Runs Him story, Graham, *Custer Myth*, 21; Gray, *Custer's Last Campaign*, 240; Donovan, *Terrible Glory*, 207–208.

10 Standing Bear interview, Hammer, *Custer in '76*, 214; He Dog interview, Hammer, *Custer in '76*, 206; Black Bear interview, Hammer, *Custer in '76*, 203 (quotation).

11 Wolf Tooth narrative, Stands In Timber and Liberty, *A Cheyenne Voice*, 366, 382 (first quotation); Powell, *Sweet Medicine*, Vol. 1, 115; L. R. Hare testimony, Nichols, *Reno Court of Inquiry*, 277 (second quotation); Daniel Kanipe account, Hammer, *Custer in '76*, 97 (third quotation). This episode has also been interpreted in an entirely different manner but that interpretation does not comport well with some key geographical references in Wolf Tooth's own narrative. See Michael Donahue, "The Maps of John Stands In Timber," *Greasy Grass* 30 (May 2014): 21-25.

12 Feather Earring account, Graham, *Custer Myth*, 97.

13 Moving Robe Woman (Mary Crawler) statement, Hardorff, *Indian Views*, 186; Masters, *Shadows Fall Across the Little Big Horn*, 30–31; Little Soldier interview, Hardorff, *Indian Views*, 174; Iron Hawk recollection, DeMallie, *The Sixth Grandfather*, 190; Little Soldier account, Joseph Gallio Masters Collection, MS 1225, ser. B, folder

15, Kansas Historical Society, Topeka; One Bull map, Donahue, *Drawing Battle Lines*, 214, 217. Much about the Deeds episode is conflicting but the simple facts, as presented here, can be distilled. For more, see Richard G. Hardorff, *Hokahey! A Good Day to Die! The Indian Casualties of the Custer Fight* (Spokane, WA: Arthur H. Clark Company, 1993), 17ff.

14 Long Sioux recollections, Bent to Hyde ltr., Sept. 11, 1905, George Bent Papers, Yale University.

15 Runs the Enemy account, Dixon, *Vanishing Race*, 171.

16 Little Soldier interview, Hardorff, *Indian Views*, 175.

17 "Mrs. Spotted Horn Bull's View," McLaughlin, *My Friend the Indian*, 168–69 (first quotation); Moving Robe Woman interview, Hardorff, *Lakota Recollections*, 93 (second quotation); Leila Monaghan, "Cheyenne and Lakota Women at the Battle of the Little Bighorn," *MMWH* 67 (Autumn 2017): 15–16.

18 Walking Hunter interview, David Humphreys Miller Collection, "Indians Who Fought Custer," McCracken Research Library, MS007, Buffalo Bill Center of the West, Cody, Wyo.; White Bull interview, Hardorff, *Indian Views*, 150; Miller, *Custer's Fall*, 87.

19 "Bull, the Braggart," *Saint Paul Pioneer Press*, July 25, 1881; One Bull narrative, Miller, "Echoes of the Little Bighorn," 31; White Bull interview, Hardorff, *Indian Views*, 150, 153 (quotation).

20 Black Elk interview, DeMallie, *The Sixth Grandfather*, 181; Little Soldier interview, Hardorff, *Indian Views*, 174; Masters, *Shadows Fall Across the Little Big Horn*, 31–32; Marquis, *She Watched Custer's Last Battle*, [2].

21 Hardorff, *Hokahey!* 35, 41, 134; Rodney G. Thomas, *Rubbing Out Long Hair, Pehin Hanska Kasota* (Spanaway, WA: Elk Plains Press, 2009), 100–101); "The Story of Chief Gall," *Saint Paul Pioneer Press*, July 18, 1886 (quotation); Larson, *Gall*, 127.

22 Vestal, *Warpath*, 193; Foolish Elk interview, Hammer, *Custer in '76*, 198–99. Foolish Elk told William Bordeaux that his Rosebud injury kept him out of this Big Horn fight, but he told others of his many actions throughout the day (Bordeaux, *Custer's Conqueror*, 57). The varied and sometimes complex, sometimes hasty, warrior preparations are well summarized by Powers, *The Killing of Crazy Horse*, 307–308.

23 C. Lee Noyes, "Valley Fight Overview," *CBHMA 24th Annual Symposium Proceedings* (Hardin, MT: CBHMA, 2010): 45; Kill Eagle's statement, R. E. Johnston ltr., Sept. 17, 1876, NA M234, SRA, Roll 847, 241/31; White Bird map, Donahue, *Drawing Battle Lines*, 156–57; Stewart, *Custer's Luck*, 354.

24 Vestal, *Sitting Bull*, 162 (first quotation); Charging Bear recollection, Norman B. Wiltsey, "We Killed Custer," *Real West* 11 (June 1968): 26 (second quotation).

25 Strikes Two (Arikara) interview, Hardorff, *Camp, Custer, and the Little Bighorn*, 52–53; Gall interview, Burdick, *David F. Barry's Indian Notes on "The Custer Battle,"* 21 (quotation); Powers, *The Killing of Crazy Horse*, 306.

26 Brave Bear account, Dec. 1, 1905, George Bent Papers, Yale University (quotation); Hardorff, *Hokahey!* 34, 57.

27 Eagle Elk interview, Hardorff, *Lakota Recollections*, 103; Soldier Wolf interview, Hardorff, *Cheyenne Memories*, 42; White Bull, Brave Wolf, and Hump narrative, Oscar Long report, Hardorff, *Indian Views*, 48; Grinnell, *Fighting Cheyennes*, 344; Iron Hawk interview, Hardorff, *Lakota Recollections*, 65 (quotation).

28 Thunder Bear narrative, Hardorff, *Indian Views*, 88 (first quotation); One Bull recollection, Everett, "Bullets, Boots, and Saddles," in Carroll, *The Sunshine Magazine Articles*, 7; Charging Bear recollection, Wiltsey, "We Killed Custer," 26 (second quotation); Black Elk narrative, DeMallie, *The Sixth Grandfather*, 182; Good White Buffalo Woman, "Tales of the Tatankas," *Saint Paul Pioneer Press*, May 19, 1883 (third quotation); Marquis, *Warrior Who Fought Custer*, 220, 221 (fourth quotation).

29 Vestal, *Warpath*, 194 (quotation); Thunder Bear narrative, Hardorff, *Indian Views*, 88; American Horse interview, Hardorff, *Cheyenne Memories*, 28.

30 Good White Buffalo Woman, "Tales of the Tatankas," *Saint Paul Pioneer Press*, May 19, 1883; Moving Robe Woman interview, Hardorff, *Lakota Recollections*, 94; M. I. McCreight, *Chief Flying Hawk's Tales: The True Story of Custer's Last Fight* (New York: Alliance Press, 1936), 27 (first quotation); Marquis, *Warrior Who Fought Custer*, 223 (second quotation); Red Feather interview, Hardorff, *Lakota Recollections*, 84; Brave Bear narrative, Hardorff, *Indian Views*, 84.

31 Stands In Timber, "Last Ghastly Moments at the Little Bighorn," 21; Black Elk narrative, DeMallie, *The Sixth Grandfather*, 183; Powell, *People of the Sacred Mountain*, Vol. 2, 1016; Powers, *The Killing of Crazy Horse*, 311; Noyes, "Valley Fight Overview," 54–55; Hardorff, *Hokahey!* 57.

32 Two Moon narrative, Hardorff, *Indian Views*, 109; Soldier Wolf interview, Hardorff, *Cheyenne Memories*, 42; Tall Bull interview, Hammer, *Custer in '76*, 212.

33 Two Moon's story, Hutchins, *Papers of Edward S. Curtis*, 58; James A. Hanson, "Field Glasses," *Museum of the Fur Trade Quarterly* 47

(Summer 2011): 12–13; Yellow Nose interview, Hardorff, *Indian Views*, 102; White Shield interview, Hardorff, *Cheyenne Memories*, 50 (quotations).

34 White Bull recollection, Hutton, *Custer Reader*, 338–39; White Bull interview, Hardorff, *Indian Views*, 155; Flying Hawk interview, Hardorff, *Lakota Recollections*, 51; Marquis, *Warrior Who Fought Custer*, 227; Pine interview, Miller, *Custer's Fall*, 133, 247.

35 Charging Bear recollection, Wiltsey, "We Killed Custer," 27 (first quotation); Neihardt, *When the Tree Flowered*, 219 (second quotation).

36 Runs the Enemy account, Dixon, *Vanishing Race*, 174.

37 "General Godfrey's Comment on Gall's Story," Graham, *Custer Myth*, 94–95; Greg Michno, "Revision at the Little Bighorn: The Fall of Gall," *LBHA Research Review* 10 (June 1996): 23.

38 White Cow Bull narrative, Miller, "Echoes of the Little Bighorn," 33; Soldier Wolf interview, Hardorff, *Cheyenne Memories*, 43 (first quotations); Horned Horse story, John F. Finerty, *War-Path and Bivouac, or, The Conquest of the Sioux* (Chicago, IL: Donohue & Henneberry, 1890), 191 (second quotation).

39 Bear's Ghost interview, Campbell Collection, OU; Utley, *The Lance and The Shield*, 152–53; Donovan, *Terrible Glory*, 243.

40 Lilah Morton Pengra, *Isaiah Dorman: Interpreting the Evidence* (Buffalo Gap, SD: Lune House Publishing, 2016), 1, 10–11, 62, 82–83; Robert J. Ege, "Braves of all Colors: The Story of Isaiah Dorman, Killed at the Little Big Horn," *MMWH* 16 (January 1966): 37–38; Crawford, *Rekindling Camp Fires*, 154–55.

41 Pengra, *Isaiah Dorman*, 210–11; Runs the Enemy account, Dixon, *Vanishing Race*, 173; Bear's Ghost interview, Campbell Collection, OU; Lilah Morton Pengra, "Five Questions About Isaiah Dorman & the 1876 Yellowstone Expedition," *CBHMA 31st Annual Symposium Proceedings* (Hardin, MT: CBHMA, 2017): 58-59; Michno, *Lakota Noon*, 88–89.

42 Bear's Ghost interview, Campbell Collection, OU (first quotation); Crawford, *Rekindling Camp Fires*, 155; Eagle Elk interview, Hardorff, *Lakota Recollections*, 101; Pengra, "Five Questions About Isaiah Dorman & the 1876 Yellowstone Expedition," 52–53; Michno, *Lakota Noon*, 88–89; Henry Jones statement, Richard G. Hardorff, *The Custer Battle Casualties, II: The Dead, The Missing, and a Few Survivors* (El Segundo, CA: Upton and Sons, Publishers, 1999), 124 (second quotation), 125.

43 Wolf Tooth narrative, Stands In Timber and Liberty, *Cheyenne Voice*, 382; Marquis, *Warrior Who Fought Custer*, 229 (first quotation); "The

Story of Chief Gall," *Saint Paul Pioneer Press*, July 18, 1886 (second quotation); Stewart, *Custer's Luck*, 313.

44 "Low Dog's Story of the Custer Fight," *Army and Navy Journal*, Aug. 13, 1881; Red Feather interview, Hardorff, *Lakota Recollections*, 87.

45 Horned Horse story, "Doves and Devils," *Chicago Times*, May 26, 1877; Samuel Miller recollection, R. G. Carter ltr., July 27, 1926, Graham, *Custer Myth*, 322 (herding); Rain in the Face narrative, Eastman, *Indian Heroes and Great Chieftains*, 148 (quotation).

46 Shave Elk interview, Liddic and Harbaugh, *Camp on Custer*, 123.

47 White Thunder account, Thomas Lawrence Riggs, "Sunset to Sunset: A Lifetime with My Brothers, The Dakotas," *South Dakota Historical Collections*, Vol. XXIX (Pierre: South Dakota State Historical Society, 1958), 187.

48 Gall interview, Burdick, *David F. Barry's Indian Notes*, 27 (quotation); Two Moon narrative, Hardorff, *Indian Views*, 111; Donahue, *Drawing Battle Lines*, 221; Grinnell, *Fighting Cheyennes*, 339.

49 Red Hawk interview, Hardorff, *Lakota Recollections*, 43, 44 (quotation); Red Feather interview, Hardorff, *Lakota Recollections*, 87; Richard Allan Fox, *Archaeology, History, and Custer's Last Battle: The Little Big Horn Reexamined* (Norman: University of Oklahoma Press, 1993), 147.

50 Grinnell, *Fighting Cheyennes*, 339 (quotation); Red Hawk interview, Hardorff, *Lakota Recollections*, 44.

51 J. W. Pope letter, 1892, Graham, *The Custer Myth*, 115; "The Story of Chief Gall," *Saint Paul Pioneer Press*, July 18, 1886; Hardorff, *Hokahey!* 61.

52 Two Moon narrative, Hardorff, *Indian Views*, 111.

53 White Bull recollection, Hutton, *Custer Reader*, 340; Howard, *Warrior Who Killed Custer*, 56 (quotations).

54 Red Hawk interview, Hardorff, *Lakota Recollections*, 44 (first quotation); "The Story of War Chief Gall of the Uncpapas," unnamed Chicago newspaper, June 26, 1886, Graham, *Custer Myth*, 88–89 (second quotation); Yellow Nose interview, Hardorff, *Indian Views*, 103; Bent to Hyde ltr., April 2, 1912, George Bent Papers, Yale University.

55 Tactical cohesion and disintegration are thoroughly explored by Fox, *Archaeology, History, and Custer's Last Battle*, who makes this a central premise in this compelling book. Notions of a battle lost are well espoused by Hardorff, *Hokahey!* 60; and Powers, *The Killing of Crazy Horse*, 319.

56 Marquis, *She Watched Custer's Last Battle*. [4] (first quotation); Marquis, *Warrior Who Fought Custer*, 231 (second quotation); White Bull interview, box 105, notebook 5, Campbell Collection, OU (third quotation); Donohue, *Where the Rivers Ran Red*, 192; Donovin Sprague, "Hump & Crazy Horse: Defending the Lakota & Cheyenne,

1876–1877," *CBHMA 24th Annual Symposium Proceedings* (Hardin, MT: CBHMA, 2010): 67.

57 White Shield interview, Hardorff, *Cheyenne Memories*, 53, 54n10; Yellow Nose interview, Hardorff, *Indian Views*, 104; "Yellow Nose and the Flag," Stands In Timber and Liberty, *Cheyenne Voice*, 375.

58 McCreight, *Chief Flying Hawk's Tales*, 28–29.

59 Vestal, *Warpath*, 195; Red Feather interview, Hardorff, *Lakota Recollections*, 87, 88 (quotation); Mark Spider recollection, Masters, *Shadows Fall Across the Little Big Horn*, 41–42; He Dog interview, Hammer, *Custer in '76*, 207; Powers, *The Killing of Crazy Horse*, 320. Reports of Crazy Horse and White Bull goading one another are discussed by Gardner, *The Earth Is All That Lasts*, 411–12n17 *through the gauntlet*, and Gregory F. Michno, "Crazy Horse, Custer, and the Sweep to the North," *MMWH* 43 (Summer 1993): 51.

60 Waterman account, Graham, *Custer Myth*, 110 (first quotation); Vestal, *Warpath*, 196 (second quotation); Powers, *The Killing of Crazy Horse*, 321.

61 "Truth About Custer," *Saint Paul Pioneer Press*, June 26, 1886 (first and third quotations); Gall interview, Burdick, *David F. Barry's Indian Notes*, 27 (second quotation). Gall boasted of his achievements boldly in 1886 and they've been derided ever since. But quiet resolve, born perhaps in the grief of his enormous family loss this day, achieved great ends too.

62 Red Hawk interview, Hardorff, *Lakota Recollections*, 43; Eagle Elk interview, Hardorff, *Lakota Recollections*, 104; Roy Bear Nose, "Shout At, Her Autobiography," *Chicago Westerners Brand Book* (March 1962): 7; Marquis, *Warrior Who Fought Custer*, 234 (second quotation); Stands In Timber and Liberty, *Cheyenne Memories*, 400.

63 Roan Bear recollection, Hardorff, *Indian Views*, 114; Big Beaver interview, Hardorff, *Cheyenne Memories*, 148. The farthest extent of this soldier advance is a contested point in Little Big Horn lore. This halt is almost certainly located somewhere within today's Custer National Cemetery.

64 Wolf Tooth testimony, Stands In Timber and Liberty, *Cheyenne Memories*, 199; Flying Hawk interview, Hardorff, *Lakota Recollections*, 52; Two Moon story, Dixon, *Vanishing Race*, 181; Shot in the Eye account, Donahue, *Drawing Battle Lines*, 165 (quotation); Standing Bear interview, Hardorff, *Lakota Recollections*, 59; Donovan, *Terrible Glory*, 267–68.

65 White Bull interview, Hardorff, *Indian Views*, 155; Iron Hawk recollection, DeMallie, *The Sixth Grandfather*, 191 (quotations).

66 Stands In Timber, "Last Ghastly Moments at the Little Bighorn," 21, 72 (quotations); "Wolf Tooth's Story," Stands In Timber and Liberty, *A Cheyenne Voice*, 368.

67 Marquis, *She Watched Custer's Last Battle.* [7]; Young Two Moon interview, Hardorff, *Cheyenne Memories*, 161–62n22; Monaghan, "Cheyenne and Lakota Women at the Battle of the Little Bighorn," 15.

68 Two Moon interview, Hardorff, *Cheyenne Memories*, 103; Stanley Vestal, "The Man Who Killed Custer," *American Heritage* 8 (February 1957): 8; Two Eagles interview, Hardorff, *Lakota Recollections*, 146 (first quotation); Iron Hawk recollection, DeMallie, *The Sixth Grandfather*, 191 (second quotation).

69 Little Hawk and White Shield interviews, Hardorff, *Cheyenne Memories*, 63 and 56 respectively; McCreight, *Chief Flying Hawk's Tales*, 29; Turtle Rib interview, Hammer, *Custer in '76*, 202; Grinnell, *Fighting Cheyennes*, 341; Donahue, *Where the Rivers Ran Red*, 199–200; Powell, *People of the Sacred Mountain*, Vol. 2, 1027; Chris Dixon, "Foley's Horse—Reflections on the Drawings of Amos Bad Heart Bull and Other Lakota Sources," *CBHMA 34th Annual Symposium Proceedings* (Hardin, MT: CBHMA, 2021): 18–31. This soldier's name was John Foley, a trooper revered in the lore of the Little Big Horn as the last man killed. In truth, of course, the truly last killed were those soldiers lying wounded on the field or pretending to be dead. See Two Moon interview, Hardorff, *Cheyenne Memories*, 103, and Powers, *The Killing of Crazy Horse*, 325.

70 Two Eagles interview, Hardorff, *Lakota Recollections*, 148; "Yellow Nose Tells of Custer's Last Stand," *Big Horn-Yellowstone Journal*, 1 (Summer 1992): 16 (first quotation); Howard, *Warrior Who Killed Custer*, 62; Runs the Enemy account, Dixon, *Vanishing Race*, 175, 176 (second quotation).

71 Standing Bear narrative, DeMallie, *The Sixth Grandfather*, 186 (first quotation); D. J. Benham, "The Sioux Warrior's Revenge," *Canadian Magazine* 43 (Sept. 1914): 462 (second quotation); Hollow Horn Bear interview, Hardorff, *Lakota Recollections*, 183.

72 Eagle Bear interview, Hardorff, *Indian Views*, 189 (first quotation); White Shield interview, Hardorff, *Cheyenne Memories*, 56 (second quotation); Low Dog's Story of the Custer Fight," *Army and Navy Journal*, Aug. 13, 1881; "Stories of thc Sioux," *Saint Paul Pioneer Press*, Aug. 14, 1881 (third quotation); Gall interview, Burdick, *David F. Barry's Indian Notes*, 21 (fourth quotation).

73 Acker Standing Crane narrative, Bruce A. Trinque, "The Fight in Fishing Woman Ravine," in *Custer and His Times, Book Four*, ed. John P. Hart (LaGrange Park, IL: LBHA, 2002), 215, 220. Buckskin suits were the distinctive attire worn a number of Seventh Cavalry officers on that campaign, including not the least George Armstrong Custer,

his brother Thomas W. Custer, a troop captain, another troop captain George W. Yates, and the regimental adjutant William W. Cooke. All would have been clustered with that distinctive flag and all died on Last Stand Hill. James S. Hutchins, *Boot & Saddles at the Little Bighorn* (Fort Collins, CO: Old Army Press, 1976), 15.

74 "Yellow Nose Tells of Custer's Last Stand," *Big Horn-Yellowstone Journal*, 1 (Summer 1992): 17; Yellow Nose interview, Hardorff, *Indian Views*, 104 (first quotation), 105; "Yellow Nose's Story," Ralph Goodman interview, T-436-14, Doris Duke Collection, Western History Collections, OU (second and third quotations); Grinnell, *Fighting Cheyennes*, 341 (final quotation). Tom Custer was likely the last of the buckskin soldiers. He had T.W.C. tattooed on an arm: Edward Godfrey interview, Hammer, *Custer in '76*, 77; Sandy Barnard, *Custer's First Sergeant John Ryan* (Terre Haute, IN: AST Press, 1996), 197.

75 Stands In Timber, "Last Ghastly Moments at the Little Bighorn," 21; Big Beaver interview, Hardorff, *Cheyenne Memories*, 150 (first quotation); Red Horse interview, Hardorff, *Indian Views*, 75 (second quotation). For useful summaries and analyses of this closing episode, another of the many ponderables of the Little Big Horn, see Michno, *Lakota Noon*, 270–73, and Scott, *Archaeological Perspectives on the Battle of the Little Bighorn*, 39–43.

76 Marquis, *A Warrior Who Fought Custer*, 237.

77 Philip Burnham, *Song of Dewey Beard: Last Survivor of the Little Bighorn* (Lincoln: University of Nebraska Press, 2014), 33.

78 Two Eagles interview, Hardorff, *Lakota Recollections*, 150; Marquis, *She Watched Custer's Last Battle*, [5].

79 Neihardt, *Black Elk Speaks*, 131 (first quotation); Black Elk recollection, DeMallie, The *Sixth Grandfather*, 194 (second quotation); Jackson, *Black Elk*, 120.

80 Charging Bear recollection, Wiltsey, "We Killed Custer," 27. This Charging Bear, a Miniconjou who figures in an episode to come, is not to be confused with the also well-known Oglala Charging Bear.

81 Little Knife interview; Hardorff, *Indian Views*, 55; "Sitting Bull Talks," *New York Herald*, Nov. 16, 1877 (first quotation); One Bull interview, box 110, Campbell Collection, OU (second quotation); Utley, *The Lance and The Shield*, 161 (third quotation).

82 Marquis, *Warrior Who Fought Custer*, 257; Stewart, *Custer's Luck*, 397; Marquis, *She Watched Custer's Last Battle*, [7]; Red Horse account, W. H. Wood ltr., Feb. 27, 1877, NA M234, DS, Roll 262, 247.

83 Stands In Timber interview, Hardorff, *Cheyenne Memories*, 172, 172n14; "Wolf Tooth's Story," Stands In Timber and Liberty, *A*

Cheyenne Voice, 369; Standing Bear narrative, DeMallie, *The Sixth Grandfather*, 187 (second quotation); White Bull (Cheyenne) interview, Hammer, *Custer in '76*, 211 (third quotation).

84 Bull Hump interview, Hardorff, *Cheyenne Memories*, 84; Miller, *Custer's Fall*, 176 (quotation), 238; Marquis, *Warrior Who Fought Custer*, 248–49.

85 Standing Bear narrative, DeMallie, *The Sixth Grandfather*, 189 (first quotation); Young Two Moon interview, Hardorff, *Cheyenne Memories*, 154; Vestal, *Warpath*, 201; Marquis, *She Watched Custer's Last Battle*, [6] (second quotation); Marquis, *Warrior Who Fought Custer*, 254–55.

86 Young Two Moon interview, Hardorff, *Cheyenne Memories*, 154; Moving Robe Woman interview, Masters Collection, MS 1225, ser. B, folder 15, Kansas Historical Society, Topeka (first quotation); "Mrs. Spotted Horn Bull's View," McLaughlin, *My Friend the Indian*, 176 (second quotation); E. S. Godfrey, *An Account of Custer's Last Campaign and the Battle of the Little Big Horn* (Palo Alto, CA: Lewis Osborne, 1968), 60.

87 Hardorff, *Hokahey!* 121ff; Cesare Marino, "Lingering Clouds at the Greasy Grass: Numbers, Casualties, and Identity of the Indians Who Fought There in 1876," *LBHA Research Review* 19 (Summer 2005): 5–6; Godfrey, *Account of Custer's Last Campaign*, 60.

88 Marquis, *She Watched Custer's Last Battle*, [8]. The veracity of this identification of Custer by Cheyenne women is another of the enduring Little Big Horn debates. For assessments, see Michno, *Lakota Noon*, 293; Powers, *The Killing of Crazy Horse*, 326–27; and Powell, *Sweet Medicine*, Vol. 1, 119–22.

89 He Dog interview, Hardorff, *Lakota Recollections*, 77; Young Little Wolf interview, Hardorff, *Cheyenne Memories*, 90; Marquis, *Warrior Who Fought Custer*, 377.

10. A Dangerous Time

1 Standing Bear narrative, DeMallie, *The Sixth Grandfather*, 189 (first quotation); Hollow Horn Bear interview, Hardorff, *Lakota Recollections*, 185 (second quotation).

2 Hardorff, *Hokahey!* 87–89; Godfrey, *Account of Custer's Last Campaign*, 62.

3 White Bull interview, Hardorff, *Indian Views*, 165; Old Bull statement; Hardorff, *Indian Views*, 122 (quotation); Standing Bear narrative, DeMallie, *The Sixth Grandfather*, 189.

4 Kill Eagle account, R. E. Johnston ltr., Sept. 17, 1876, NA M234, SRA, Roll 847, 241/42; Red Horse account, W. H. Wood ltr., Feb. 27, 1877, NA M234, DS, Roll 262, 247.

5 Marquis, *Warrior Who Fought Custer*, 269 (quotation); Lights interview, Hardorff, *Lakota Recollections*, 172; "Low Dog's Story of Custer's Fight," *Army and Navy Journal*, Aug. 13, 1881.

6 White Bull interview, Hardorff, *Lakota Recollections*, 123; Vestal, *Warpath*, 204–205; Miller, *Custer's Fall*, 189.

7 Turning Hawk interview, Hardorff, *Indian Views*, 146; "Low Dog's Story of Custer's Fight," *Army and Navy Journal*, Aug. 13, 1881; Red Horse account, W. H. Wood ltr., Feb. 27, 1877, NA M234, DS, Roll 262, 247.

8 Little Soldier interview, Hardorff, *Indian Views*, 177; Two Moon narrative, Hardorff, *Indian Views*, 112; Flying Hawk narrative, Hardorff, *Indian Views*, 126; He Dog interview, Hammer, *Custer in '76*, 208; Red Hawk interview, Hardorff, *Lakota Recollections*, 46.

9 Marquis, *Warrior Who Fought Custer*, 270; Kill Eagle account, R. E. Johnston ltr., Sept. 17, 1876, NA M234, SRA, Roll 847, 241/43.

10 Edward J. McClernand, *With the Indian and the Buffalo in Montana, 1870–1878* (Glendale, CA: Arthur H. Clark Company, 1969), 59, 146 (quotation); Paulding ltr., July 2, 1876, Thomas R. Buecker, ed., "A Surgeon at the Little Big Horn: The Letters of Dr. Holmes O. Paulding," *MMWH* 32 (Autumn 1982): 43; Burdick, *Tales from Buffalo Land*, 52.

11 Respects Nothing interview, Hardorff, *Lakota Recollections*, 29; Marquis, *Warrior Who Fought Custer*, 270–71; Marquis, *She Watched Custer's Last Battle*, [7]; Miller, *Custer's Fall*, 190.

12 Marquis, *Warrior Who Fought Custer*, 273–74.

13 Marquis, *Warrior Who Fought Custer*, 274; Miller, *Custer's Fall*, 190.

14 Waterman and Left Hand accounts, Graham, *Custer Myth*, 110–11; Powell, *People of the Sacred Mountain*, Vol. 2, 1043; R. S. McKenzie tele., Aug. 1, 1876, NA M234, Cheyenne and Arapaho Agency, Roll 121, 510; J. D. Miles ltr., Aug. 4, 1876, NA, War Department, Office of the Adjutant General, Consolidated File 3770, AGO, 1876.

15 Stands In Timber and Liberty, *Cheyenne Voice*, 438; Marquis, *Warrior Who Fought Custer*, 275; Marquis, *She Watched Custer's Last Battle*, [7]; Harry Anderson, "A Sioux Pictorial Account of General Terry's Council at Fort Walsh, October 17, 1877," *North Dakota History* 22 (July 1955): 101.

16 Stands In Timber and Liberty, *A Cheyenne Voice*, 372, 377; Peterson, "Dewey Iron Hail," 38; Feather Earring account, Graham, *Custer Myth*, 98; Black Elk narrative, DeMallie, *The Sixth Grandfather*, 196 (quotations); Two Moon narrative, Hardorff, *Indian Views*, 112; Charger, "Chronology of the Sioux Indians from an Early Period," 3.

17 Feather Earring account, Graham, *Custer Myth*, 98; Two Moon interview, Hardorff, *Cheyenne Memories*, 105 (quotation).

18 George A. Schneider, ed., *The Freeman Journal: The Infantry in the Sioux Campaign of 1876* (San Rafael, CA: Presidio Press, 1977), 59; "Custer's Death/Gibbon's Movement," *New York Herald*, July 8, 1876.

19 "The Story of War Chief Gall of the Unkpapas," Graham, *Custer Myth*, 89, reprinting an unnamed Chicago newspaper dated June 26, 1886; Hyde, *Red Cloud's Folk*, 274; White Bull interview, Hardorff, *Indian Views*, 160; Bray, *Crazy Horse*, 235–36; Black Elk narrative, DeMallie, *The Sixth Grandfather*, 197–98; John S. Poland report, July 24, 1876, NA M234, DS, Roll 258, 390; One Bull recollection, Everett, "Bullets, Boots, and Saddles," 7.

20 Little Sun account, Greene, *Lakota and Cheyenne*, 75; Bull Hump interview, Hardorff, *Cheyenne Memories*, 84; Red Bird (Young Little Wolf) interview, Hardorff, *Cheyenne Memories*, 90.

21 Little Sun account, Greene, *Lakota and Cheyenne*, 75; Bull Hump interview, Hardorff, *Cheyenne Memories*, 84–85.

22 Little Sun account, Greene, *Lakota and Cheyenne*, 75, 77; Little Hawk remembrance, Greene, *Lakota and Cheyenne*, 77; Bull Hump interview, Hardorff, *Cheyenne Memories*, 85; Red Bird (Young Little Wolf) interview, Hardorff, *Cheyenne Memories*, 91; Fox, "The Value of Oral History: White Eagle's Account," 13. Frank Grouard misidentified the deceased Cheyenne, calling him White Antelope. DeBarthe, *Life and Adventures of Frank Grouard*, 273; Paul L. Hedren, *John Finerty Reports the Sioux War* (Norman: University of Oklahoma Press, 2020), 118, 241n14; Hardorff, *Lakota Recollections*, 29n15.

23 Hedren, *John Finerty Reports the Sioux War*, 119.

24 Black Elk narrative, DeMallie, *The Sixth Grandfather*, 198; Gall narrative, "Truth About Custer," *Saint Paul Pioneer Press*, June 26, 1886; White Bull interview, Hardorff, *Indian Views*, 158; Shoots Walking statement, Hardorff, *Indian Views*, 169; Kill Eagle account, R. E. Johnston ltr., Sept. 17, 1876, NA M234, SRA, Roll 847, 241/36; Feather Earring account, Graham, *Custer Myth*, 98; Red Hawk interview, Hardorff, *Lakota Recollections*, 46–47.

25 Marquis, *Warrior Who Fought Custer*, 276–77 (quotation); Tall Bull interview, Hammer, *Custer in '76*, 213.

26 Theo F. Rodenbough, "A Soldier-Scout's Story," chap. in *Uncle Sam's Medal of Honor* (New York: G. P. Putnam's Sons, 1886), 313: Paul L. Hedren, "'three cool, determined men': The Sioux War Heroism of Privates Evans, Stewart, and Bell," *MMWH* (Winter 1991): 21–23.

27 Black Elk narrative, DeMallie, *The Sixth Grandfather*, 198–99; Charles King, *Campaigning With Crook and Stories of Army Life* (New York:

Harper & Brothers, 1890), 72 (first quotation); Neihardt, *Black Elk Speaks*, 137 (second quotation).

28 Black Elk narrative, DeMallie, *The Sixth Grandfather*, 198–99; Respects Nothing interview, Hardorff, *Lakota Recollections*, 29; Marquis, *Warrior Who Fought Custer*, 278.

29 Waggoner, *Witness*, 336.

30 Afraid of Eagles statement, R. E. Johnston ltr., Sept. 17, 1876, NA M234, SRA, Roll 847, 241/48; Kill Eagle account, R. E. Johnston ltr., Sept. 17, 1876, NA M234, SRA, Roll 847, 241/16–18, 36; "The Hostile Red Men," *New York Herald*, Sept. 20, 1876; "Kill Eagle," *Saint Paul and Minneapolis Pioneer Press and Tribune*, Sept. 29, 1876; "What Kill Eagle Saw," *Army and Navy Journal*, Sept. 30, 1876; "Kill Eagle's Story," *New York Herald*, Oct. 6, 1876.

31 Marquis, *Warrior Who Fought Custer*, 278; Powell, *People of the Sacred Mountain*, Vol. 2, 1050.

32 Respects Nothing interview, Hardorff, *Lakota Recollections*, 29; Black Elk narrative, DeMallie, *The Sixth Grandfather*, 199; Masters, *Shadows Fall Across the Little Horn*, 54, 55 (fire boats).

33 Hollow Horn Bear interview, Hardorff, *Lakota Recollections*, 186; Thos. J. Mitchell ltr., July 29, 1876, NA M234, MS, Roll 505, 433 (quotation).

34 John Burke ltr., J. S. Poland ltr., both Aug. 11, 1876, NA M234, SRA, Roll 847, 71.

35 Iron Teeth narrative, Marquis, *Cheyennes of Montana*, 70n39; John H. Monnett, *Tell Them We are Going Home: The Odyssey of the Northern Cheyennes* (Norman: University of Oklahoma Press, 2001), 16–17 (quotation).

36 J. D. Miles ltr., July 11, 1876, NA M234, Cheyenne and Arapaho Agency, Roll 121, 465; Iron Teeth narrative, Marquis, *Cheyennes of Montana*, 70; Powell, *People of the Sacred Mountain*, Vol. 2, 1048.

37 James S. Hastings ltr., July 14, 1876, NA M234, RCA, Roll 720, 351.

38 Beaver Heart narrative, Greene, *Lakota and Cheyenne*, 81–82; Josie Tangle Yellow Hair statement, Greene, *Lakota and Cheyenne*, 83–84; Harry H. Anderson, "Cheyennes at the Little Big Horn—A Study of Statistics," *North Dakota History*, 27 (Spring 160): 90.

39 "The Indian War," *New York Herald*, July 23, 1876; Paul L. Hedren, *First Scalp for Custer: The Skirmish at Warbonnet Creek, Nebraska, July 17, 1876*, rev. ed. (Lincoln: Nebraska State Historical Society, 2005), 20–21.

40 P. H. Sheridan tele., July 19, 1876, NA M234, RCA, Roll 720, 1006; Beaver Heart narrative, Greene, *Lakota and Cheyenne*, 82; Iron Teeth narrative, Marquis, *Cheyennes of Montana*, 71 (quotation).

41 "Merritt's March," *Cheyenne Daily Leader*, July 20, 1876; "The Indians," *Chicago Inter-Ocean*, July 20, 1876; "Telegraphic," and "The Indian Campaign," *Omaha Bee*, July 20 and 24, 1876 respectively; "Indian Affairs," *Cincinnati Commercial*, July 20, 1876; "The Indian War," *New York Herald*, July 23, 1876. Cody's stage show was called *The Red Right Hand; or Buffalo Bill's First Scalp for Custer*, a tale thoroughly analyzed by Don Russell, *The Lives and Legends of Buffalo Bill* (Norman: University of Oklahoma Press, 1960), 253–57; and also told through the career of his stage partner that season, Captain Jack Crawford, in Paul L. Hedren, ed. *Ho! For the Black Hills*, 237–47.

42 P. H. Sheridan teles., Aug. 3 and 5, 1876, NA M234, DS, Roll 258, 365 and 380 respectively; Hedren, *Fort Laramie in 1876*, 139–40; Paul L. Hedren, "Garrisoning the Black Hills Road: The United States Army's Camps on Sage Creek and Mouth of Red Canyon, 1876–1877," *South Dakota History* 37 (Spring 2007): 20–21; J. W. Vaughn, "The Burning of Heck Reel's Wagon Train," chapter in *Indian Fights: New Facts on Seven Encounters* (Norman: University of Oklahoma Press, 1966), 172–74.

43 John S. McClintock, *Pioneer Days in the Black Hills* (Deadwood, SD: self-published, 1939), 83, 86, 121, 135–36; Wolff, *Savior of Deadwood*, 72, 76.

44 Anderson, "A Sioux Pictorial Account," 101.

45 Black Elk narrative, DeMallie, *The Sixth Grandfather*, 199; Marquis, *She Watched Custer's Last Battle*, [7]; One Bull account, Greene, *Lakota and Cheyenne*, 58; "Trip of the Steamer Carroll," *New York Herald*, Aug. 7, 1876; Topping, *Chronicles of the Yellowstone*. 193.

46 "Steamers Carroll and Far West Attacked by Indians Who Line the Banks," *New York Herald*, Aug. 8, 1876; Black Elk narrative, DeMallie, *The Sixth Grandfather*, 199 (quotation); Gray, *Centennial Campaign*, 210–11. Black Elk refers to Runs Fearless by his nickname, Yellow Shirt, Bray, *Crazy Horse*, 446n14.

47 Marquis, *Warrior Who Fought Custer*, 280; Gabriel Solomon affidavit, Aug. 18, 1876, in "Papers Relating to the Sioux Indians of the United States Who Have Taken Refuge in Canadian Territory," RG 7, Governor General's Office, G21, Vol. 323, File 2001-1, Prints 1875–1879, Ottawa, Ontario, Library and Archives Canada (quotation); McCrady, *Living with Strangers*, 66; Vestal, *Sitting Bull*, 182; Neihardt, *Black Elk Speaks*, 136.

48 Respects Nothing interview, Hardorff, *Lakota Recollections*, 29; White Bull interview, Hardorff, *Indian Views*, 158; Tall Bull interview, Hammer, *Custer in '76*, 213; Beck, *Inkpaduta*, 139; Utley, *The Lance*

and The Shield, 209; Dickson, *Sitting Bull Surrender Census*, 38; Gray, *Centennial Campaign*, 344.

49 Flying By interview, Hardorff, *Camp, Custer, and the Little Bighorn*, 90; White Bull interview, Hardorff, *Indian Views*, 158; Anderson, "A Sioux Pictorial Account," 101; Neihardt, *When the Tree Flowered*, 223 (quotation); Powers, *The Killing of Crazy Horse*, 204–205. Flying By insisted that the major break-up occurred on Beaver Creek. In that locale, Beaver Creek and the Little Missouri River are parallel drainages.

50 White Bull interview, Hardorff, *Indian Views*, 158; Geo. P. Buell ltr., Sept. 9, 1876, NA M234, DS, Roll 262, 208; John Colhoff to Helen Blish, Apr. 7, 1929, Hinman Notebook, Sandoz Papers, University of Nebraska, Lincoln; Powers, *The Killing of Crazy Horse*, 204–205.

51 Eagle Shield account, Geo. P. Buell and W. H. Wood ltrs., Feb. 19, 1877, NA M234, DS, Roll 262, 208; Red Horse account, Greene, *Lakota and Cheyenne*, 86; Respects Nothing interview, Hardorff, *Lakota Recollections*, 30; Hyde, *Red Cloud's Folk*, 275.

52 H. W. Bingham tele., Aug. 5, 1876, and ltr., July 29, 1876, NA M234, CRA, Roll 129, 230 and 239 respectively; P. H. Sheridan tele., Aug. 9, 1876, W. T. Sherman tele, Aug. 12, 1876, both NA M234, CRA, Roll 129, 685; R. E. Johnston ltr., Sept. 7, 1876, NA M234, SRA, Roll 847, 220; W. P. Carlin rpt., Aug. 26, 1876, NA M234, SRA, Roll 847, 616.

53 Geo. P. Buell ltr., Sept. 9, 1876, NA M234, DS, Roll 262, 208.

54 Black Bear account, "An Indian Interviewed," *Cheyenne Daily Leader*, Nov. 1, 1876; "Against Sitting Bull," *New York Herald*, Aug. 15, 1876; "Indian Arms and Ammunition," *Cheyenne Daily Leader*, July 14, 1876.

55 Potter, *From Our Special Correspondent*, 107, 254; "Personal Paragraphs," *Cheyenne Daily Leader*, June 10, 1876; *Cheyenne Daily Leader*, June 11, 1876.

56 "An Army Officer's View," *New York Times*, July 13, 1876 (quotation); W. R. Steele ltr., July 28, 1876, NA M234, STA, Roll 841, 208; M. C. Foot ltr, Aug. 15, 1876, NA M234, STA, Roll 841, 211; "Carrying Ammunition to the Hostiles," *Black Hills Weekly Pioneer*, July 29, 1876; "Spotted Tail Reserve," *Omaha Daily Bee*, Sept. 13, 1876.

57 Medicine Cloud statement, Thos. J. Mitchell rpt., [Aug. 1, 1876], NA M234, DS, Roll 258, 504 (quotation); Little Buck Elk interview, Thos. J. Mitchell ltr., Sept. 26, 1876, NA M234, MS, Roll 505, 538; [W. P.] Carlin ltr., Aug. 22, 1876, NA M234, DS, Roll 258, 486; "Hunting Bull's Braves," *Omaha Herald*, Aug. 19, 1876; "The Sentiments and Opinions of Sitting Bull," *New York Herald*, Aug. 19, 1876; "Sitting Bull," *Bismarck Weekly Tribune*, Oct. 18, 1876.

58 C. W. Darling ltr., Aug. 22, 1876, NA M234, Fort Berthold Agency, Roll 295, 929.

11. The Hunted

1 "Gen. Terry on the March," *New York Tribune*, Sept. 5, 1876; "Camping With Crook," *New York World*, Sept. 17, 1876; "Up the Yellowstone," *New York Herald*, Sept. 17, 1876.

2 Thos. J. Mitchell ltr., Sept. 14, 1876, NA M234, MS, Roll 505, 522; Jerome A. Greene, *Yellowstone Command: Colonel Nelson A. Miles and the Great Sioux War, 1876–1877* (Lincoln: University of Nebraska Press, 1991), 58.

3 Thos. J. Mitchell ltr., Sept. 14, 1876, NA M234, MS, Roll 505, 522; McCrady, *Living with Strangers*, 66.

4 Swelled Face statement, W. H. Wood ltr., Feb. 21, 1877, NA M234, DS, Roll 262, 197; Geo. P. Buell ltr., Sept. 9, 1876, NA M234, DS, Roll 262, 208; P. H. Sheridan tele., Sept. 8, 1876, NA M234, DS, Roll 262, 534; P. H. Sheridan ltr., Aug. 8, 1876, NA M234, CRA, Roll 129, 674; Charger, "Chronology of the Sioux Indians from an Early Period," 3.

5 Red Horse account, W. H. Wood ltr., Feb. 27, 1877, NA M234, DS, Roll 262, 246; Tall Bull statement, Greene, *Lakota and Cheyenne*, 92; Swelled Face statement, W. H. Wood ltr., Feb. 21, 1877, NA M234, DS, Roll 262, 197 (quotation); Eagle Shield account, W. H. Wood ltr., Feb. 19, 1877, NA M234, DS, Roll 262, 208.

6 "An Indian Interviewed," *Cheyenne Daily Leader*, Nov. 1, 1876; Sandoz, *Crazy Horse*, 339n1; Red Horse account, W. H. Wood ltr., Feb. 27, 1877, NA M234, DS, Roll 262, 246; Anderson, "A Sioux Pictorial Account," 102; Hedren, *John Finerty Reports the Sioux War*, 194; Jerome A. Greene, *Slim Buttes, 1876: An Episode of the Great Sioux War* (Norman: University of Oklahoma Press, 1982), 49. White Bull was positive that Iron Plume was a Sans Arc. White Bull notes, Group 1, Box 2, Camp Papers, BYU, Provo, Utah. The number of lodges in this small camp was almost immediately disputed. Red Horse asserted a camp of forty-eight lodges. Many Shields, a Sans Arc, said forty lodges (Greene, *Lakota and Cheyenne*, 89). White accounts consistently stated thirty-seven lodges, plus another four that did not have covers stretched over them, and those numbers based on actual field counts. Bourke, *Diaries, Vol. 2*, 108.

7 "Crook's Campaign," *New York Herald*, Oct. 2, 1876; Greene, *Slim Buttes, 1876*, 63.

8 Bourke, *Diaries, Vol. 2*, 108; Short Bull interview, Carroll, *Eleanor H. Hinman Interviews*, 41 (first quotation); "Crook's Campaign," *New York Herald*, Oct. 2, 1876; Hedren, *John Finerty Reports the Sioux War*,

193 (second quotation); Greene, *Slim Buttes, 1876*, 73. The guidon and a buffalo skin tipi collected on the scene were celebrated trophies soon photographed and eventually donated to museums where they are seen yet today. Vaughn, "The Buckskin Lodge at Slim Buttes," chapter in *Indian Fights*, 185–86.

9 Bourke, *Diaries, Vol. 2*, 109–10; Hedren, *John Finerty Reports the Sioux War*, 183 (first quotation); Black Bear account, "An Indian Interviewed," *Cheyenne Daily Leader*, Nov. 1, 1876; Short Bull interview, Carroll, *Eleanor H. Hinman Interviews*, 41; Bray, *Crazy Horse*, 244.

10 King, *Campaigning With Crook and Stories of Army Life*, 119, 131; Short Bull interview, Carroll, *Eleanor H. Hinman Interviews*, 41; Hedren, *John Finerty Reports the Sioux War*, 188; Powers, *The Killing of Crazy Horse*, 212. Sources differ on the matter of the morphine injection. Doctor Valentine McGillycuddy asserted that he did, in fact, administer a hypodermic of morphine. Julia B. McGillycuddy, *McGillycuddy Agent: A Biography of Dr. Valentine B. McGillycuddy* (Stanford, CA: Stanford University Press, 1941), 58.

11 Red Horse account, W. H. Wood ltr., Feb. 27, 1877, NA M234, DS, Roll 262, 246; Charger, "Chronology of the Sioux Indians from an Early Period," 4; Neihardt, *Black Elk Speaks*, 137; He Dog interview, Hammer, *Custer in '76*, 208; Sandoz, *Crazy Horse*, 340; "The Indian Campaign," *New York Times*, Sept. 17, 1876; King, *Campaigning With Crook and Stories of Army Life*, 104.

12 "Indians," *Chicago Tribune*, Sept. 19, 1876; Hedren, *John Finerty Reports the Sioux War*, 197; Charger, "Chronology of the Sioux Indians from an Early Period," 4.

13 "Indians," *Chicago Tribune*, Sept. 19, 1876; Vestal, *Sitting Bull*, 187–88.

14 Short Bull interview, Carroll, *Eleanor H. Hinman Interviews*, 41 (first quotation); He Dog interview, Crazy Horse Papers, Museum of the Fur Trade, Chadron, NE, (second quotation).

15 "The Sioux Commission," *Report of the Secretary of the Interior, 1877–78* (Washington, DC: Government Printing Office, 1878), 413; "Instructions for Commissioners," Sept. 1, 1876, NA M234, DS, Roll 257, 101; Forty-Fourth Congress, 2d Session, 19 Stat., 254, Chap. 72, Feb. 28, 1877, Charles J. Kappler, ed., *Indian Affairs, Laws and Treaties, Vol. 1 (Laws)* (Washington, DC: Government Printing Office, 1904), 254–57; Red Cloud interview, Jensen, *Ricker Indian Interviews*, 345.

16 Charger, "Chronology of the Sioux Indians from an Early Period," 4; McDermott, *Red Cloud*, 87–91; Edward Lazarus, *Black Hills, White Justice: The Sioux Nation Versus the United States, 1775 to the Present* (New York: HarperCollins Publishers, 1991), 110.

17 Forty-Fourth Congress, 2d Session, 19 Stat., 254, Chap. 72, Feb. 28, 1877, Kappler, *Indian Affairs, Laws and Treaties*, Vol. 1, 259; "The Council at Red Cloud," *New York Times*, Sept. 21, 1876.

18 "The Sioux Commission," *New York Herald*, Sept. 27, 1876 (quotation); Powers, *The Killing of Crazy Horse*, 219–21; Sandoz, "The Lost Sitting Bull," in *Hostiles and Friendlies*, 102–103; Gardner, *The Earth Is All that Lasts*, 264–65; William Garnett interview, Jensen, *Ricker Indian Interviews*, 87–88.

19 Forty-Fourth Congress, 2nd Sess., 19 Stat., 254, Chap. 72, Feb. 28, 1877, Kappler, *Indian Affairs, Laws and Treaties*, Vol. 1, 259–60, 262–64; Yellow Horse recollection, Jensen, *Ricker Indian Interviews*, 325; "Last Surviving Signer of Indian Treaty," *Sunshine Magazine*, September 1929, 29; John Y. Simons, ed., *The Papers of Ulysses S. Grant, Vol. 28: November 1, 1876-September 30, 1878* (Carbondale: Southern Illinois University Press, 2005), 97; Cozzens, *The Earth Is Weeping*, 278–79.

20 Cozzens, *The Earth Is Weeping*, 281–82.

21 Red Horse account, W. H. Wood ltr., Feb. 27, 1877, NA M234, DS, Roll 262, 246; McCrady, *Living with Strangers*, 32, 65.

22 Little Buck Elk account, Thomas J. Mitchell ltr., Sept. 25, 1876, NA M234, MS, Roll 505, 538.

23 Ibid.; Red Horse account, W. H. Wood ltr., Feb. 27, 1877, NA M234, DS, Roll 262, 246; George Boyle ltr., Oct. 8, 1876, within W. B. Hazen ltr., Oct. 11, 1876, NA M234, DS, Roll 258, 701.

24 Waggoner, *Witness*, 122–23; John S. Gray, "What Made Johnnie Bruguier Run?" *MMWH* 14 (April 1964): 37, 42; "Standing Rock News," *Bismarck Tribune*, Dec. 22, 1876; "Johnny Brughiere," *Winners of the West*, Aug. 20, 1932; Bourke, *Diaries, Vol. 2*, 346.

25 "Abstract of Letter from John E. Brughuire," *Winners of the West*, Oct. 30, 1932; Waggoner, *Witness*, 124–25; Vestal, *Warpath*, 218; Spotted Bear statement, Campbell Collection, OU; He Dog interview, Hardorff, *Lakota Recollections*, 77 (quotation).

26 Thos. J. Mitchell tele., Oct. 13, 1876, NA M234, MS, Roll 505, 548 (Mitchell reported that the crossing occurred at the mouth of the Big Horn River); Bear Face interview, John S. Gray, "Peace-talkers from Standing Rock Agency," *Chicago Westerners Brand Book* (May 1966): 17–18; N. A. Miles rpt., Oct. 25, 1876, NA M234, DS, Roll 258, 790.

27 Vestal, *Warpath*, 219, 221 (first quotations); Greene, *Yellowstone Command*, 81–88; White Bull interview, Hardorff, *Indian Views*, 158–59; John S. Gray, "Sitting Bull Strikes the Glendive Supply Trains," *Chicago Westerners Brand Book* (June 1971): 26; "Indian Warfare,"

Chicago Tribune, Dec. 7, 1876 (fight); Howard, *Warrior Who Killed Custer*, 50 (final quotations), 51.

28 Vestal, *Warpath*, 221–22; Greene, *Yellowstone Command*, 260n37. We have from Bruguier's nephew, John E. Brughière, the Lakota text of the message, plus a literal translation, and the rendition tied to the stake, Vestal, *Warpath*, 222, 222n1.

29 Vestal, *Sitting Bull*, 192–93; Bear Face interview, Gray, "Peace-talkers from Standing Rock Agency," 18; Gray, "Sitting Bull Strikes the Glendive Supply Trains," 31; "The Indian Campaign," *New York Herald*, Nov. 27, 1876; Greene, *Yellowstone Command*, 89–90.

30 "Sitting Bull," *New York Herald*, Nov. 6, 1876; Gardner, *The Earth Is All that Lasts*, 266.

31 "Winter Campaigning Against Indians in Montana in 1876," *Winners of the West*, Sept. 30, 1933; Bear Face interview, Gray, "Peace-talkers from Standing Rock Agency," 18; "Sitting Bull," *New York Herald*, Nov. 6, 1876; Greene, *Yellowstone Command*, 90–91.

32 Spotted Elk interview, W. H. Wood ltr., Mar. 1, 1877, NA M234, DS, Roll 262, 268; Greene, *Yellowstone Command*, 93–94; Utley, *The Lance and The Shield*, 171.

33 White Bull interview, Greene, *Lakota and Cheyenne*, 112 (first quotation); Bear Face interview, Gray, "Peace-talkers from Standing Rock Agency," 18–19; Nelson A. Miles rpt., Oct. 25, 1876, NA M234, DS, Roll 258, 790 (second quotation); Utley, *The Lance and The Shield*, 171–72.

34 Spotted Elk interview, W. H. Wood ltr., Mar. 1, 1877, NA M234, DS, Roll 262, 268; Bear Face interview, Gray, "Peace-talkers from Standing Rock Agency," 19; Bear Face, Waggoner, *Witness*, 394–95; Utley, *The Lance and The Shield*, 172.

35 N. A. Miles rpt., Oct. 25, 1876, NA M234, DS, Roll 258, 790; Waggoner, *Witness*, 676n36.3; Greene, *Yellowstone Command*, 95–96; Vestal, *Sitting Bull*, 198; Miles, *Personal Recollections*, 226 (quotation); Utley, *The Lance and The Shield*, 172.

36 Miles, *Personal Recollections*, 225 (quotation); James Willard Schultz, *William Jackson, Indian Scout* (Boston, MA: Houghton Mifflin, 1926; reprint, Springfield, IL: William K. Cavanaugh, 1976), 182–83; Vic Smith, *The Champion Buffalo Hunter: The Frontier Memoirs of Yellowstone Vic Smith* (Helena, MT: TwoDot, 1997), 68 (one hundred lodges); Greene, *Yellowstone Command*, 100–104.

37 Vestal, *Warpath*, 223 (quotation); Wm. Hazen rpt., Oct. 27, 1876, within R. C. Drum tele., Oct. 31, 1876, NA M234, DS, Roll 256, 101; Schultz, *William Jackson*, 184.

38 Waggoner, *Witness*, 151, 424; Bear Face interview, Gray, "Peace-talkers from Standing Rock Agency," 19; Spotted Elk interview, W. H. Wood ltr., Mar. 1, 1877, NA M234, DS, Roll 262, 268; Schultz, *William Jackson*, 184.

39 Gray, "What Made Johnnie Bruguier Run?" 45; Utley, *The Lance and The Shield*, 172–73.

40 Spotted Elk account, Greene, *Lakota and Cheyenne*, 109; Schultz, *William Jackson*, 184–85; Greene, *Yellowstone Command*, 107–108.

41 Miles, *Personal Recollections*, 228; Anderson, "A Sioux Pictorial Account," 102; Greene, *Yellowstone Command*, 108. Miles's numbers appear misleading and perhaps intentionally so. The established Miniconjou and Sans Arc lodge counts at Little Big Horn were seventy-five and sixty-five, respectively, and even while continually splitting and realigning, those numbers had not risen appreciably since, with an exception perhaps of the arrival of the Bull Eagle and Red Skirt bands, who most regarded as agency people. See Harry H. Anderson, "A History of the Cheyenne River Indian Agency and its Military Post, Fort Bennett, 1868–1891," *South Dakota Report and Historical Collections*, Vol. 28 (Pierre: South Dakota Historical Society, 1957), 470–71.

42 Schultz, *William Jackson*, 185; E. H. Hyat, "Report of the Commissioner of Indian Affairs," Nov. 1, 1877, *Report of the Secretary of the Interior, 1877–78*, 411; Geo. D. Ruggles note, Nov. 7, 1876, and N. A Miles rpt., Oct. 27, 1876 (quotation), both within J. D. Cameron ltr., Nov. 16, 1876, NA M234, DS, Roll 258, 800; Anderson, "A History of the Cheyenne River Indian Agency and its Military Post," 470; Greene, *Yellowstone Command*, 108–109.

43 Anderson, "A Sioux Pictorial Account," 103; Spotted Elk interview, W. H. Wood ltr., Mar. 1, 1877, NA M234, DS, Roll 262, 268.

44 Thos. J. Mitchell ltrs., Oct. 23, Nov. 11 (two), Nov. 13, 1876, all NA M234, MS, Roll 505, 631, 600, 641, and 604 respectively; George Boyle ltr., Oct. 8, 1876, within W. B. Hazen ltr., Oct. 11, 1876, NA M234, DS, Roll 258, 701; "A Report from Indian Agent Mitchell," *New York Herald*, Dec. 2, 1876; McCrady, *Living with Strangers*, 66–68; Utley, *The Lance and The Shield*, 176; Gray, "What Made Johnnie Bruguier Run?" 44.

45 George Boyle ltr., Oct. 8, 1876, within W. B. Hazen ltr., Oct. 11, 1876, NA M234, DS, Roll 258, 701; Thos. J. Mitchell ltr., Nov. 11, 1876, NA M234, MS, Roll 505, 600; McCrady, *Living with Strangers*, 68; Schultz, *William Jackson*, 185; Anderson, "A Sioux Pictorial Account," 105; Utley, *The Lance and The Shield*, 176 (quotations), 203.

46 Miles, *Personal Recollections*, 221; Schultz, *William Jackson*, 185–86; Nelson A. Miles ltr., Oct. 26, 1876, NA M234, DS, Roll 258, 790.

47 "Winter Campaigning Against Indians in Montana in 1876," *Winners of the West*, Sept. 30, 1932; Greene, *Yellowstone Command*, 122ff; Cozzens, *The Earth Is Weeping*, 299–300.

48 "Winter Campaigning Against Indians in Montana in 1876," *Winners of the West*, Sept. 30, 1932; Joseph Culbertson, "Fighting Sitting Bull After Custer Battle Described by Scout for Miles," *Winners of the West*, Nov. 30, 1933; R. C. Drum tele., Jan. 16, 1877, NA M234, DS, Roll 259, 10; *Chronological List of Action, &c., With Indians from January 15, 1837 to January, 1891* ([Washington, DC]: Adjutant General's Office, 1891; reprint, Fort Collins, Colo.: Old Army Press, 1979), 63; Joseph Manzione, *"I Am Looking to the North for My Life," Sitting Bull, 1876–1881* (Salt Lake City: University of Utah Press, 1991), 26; Greene, *Yellowstone Command*, 140–41.

49 "Mrs. Spotted Horn Bull's View," McLaughlin, *My Friend the Indian*, 177.

50 The pony confiscation policy is well studied. See particularly Richmond L. Clow, "General Philip Sheridan's Legacy: The Sioux Pony Campaign of 1876," *Nebraska History* 57 (Winter 1976): 461–76; and Hutton, *Phil Sheridan and His Army*, 322–27.

51 Waggoner, *Witness*, 132; "Indians Disarmed," *New York Herald*, Oct. 27, 1876; "Red Cloud Disarmed and Deposed," "Disarmament at Standing Rock," *Army and Navy Journal*, Oct. 28, and Nov. 4, 1876 respectively; Paul L. Hedren, *Great Sioux War Orders of Battle: How the United States Army Waged War on the Northern Plains, 1876–1877* (Norman, OK: Arthur H. Clark Company, 2011), 132–37; Clow, "General Philip Sheridan's Legacy," 462–63; Olson, *Red Cloud and the Sioux Problem*, 234–35.

52 Hämäläinen, *Lakota America*, 373; Alfred H. Terry tele., Oct. 26, 1876, NA M234, SRA, Roll 847, 692; Waggoner, *Witness*, 132 (first quotation); Charger, "Chronology of the Sioux Indians from an Early Period," 3 (second quotation); Little No Heart ltr., Dec. 11, 1877, M234, CRA, Roll 130, 676 (third quotation); Hugh Lenox Scott, *Some Memories of a Soldier* (New York: Century Co., 1928), 37.

53 Alfred H. Terry rpt., Nov. 16, 1878, NA M234, SRA, Roll 850, 307; J. F. Cravens rpt., Aug. 18, 1877, *Report of the Secretary of the Interior, 1877–78*, 448–49; Theo. Schwan rpt., Aug. 20, 1879, *Report of the Secretary of the Interior, 1879–80* (Washington, DC: Government Printing Office, 1880), 126–27; Manypenny, *Our Indian Wards*, 319–20, 360–61; Alfred H. Terry tele., Oct. 26, 1876, NA M234, SRA, Roll 847, 692; Anderson, "A History of the Cheyenne River

Indian Agency and its Military Post," 466–68; Clow, "General Philip Sheridan's Legacy," 466–67, 470, 472–74; Waggoner, *Witness*, 134; Bourke, *Diaries, Vol. 2*, 152; "U.S. to Pay Sioux Indians for Ponies Taken in 1876," *New York Times*, July 4, 1945.

54 George W. Baird, "A Winter Campaign in Montana and Its Results," in *Personal Recollections of the War of the Rebellion*, ed. A. Noel Blakeman (New York: G. P. Putnam's Sons, 1907), 431.

12. Red Fork and Belly Butte

1 Manypenny, *Our Indian Wards*, 330; "Indian Talk," *New York Herald*, Nov. 27, 1876; Jerome A. Greene, *Morning Star Dawn: The Powder River Expedition and the Northern Cheyennes, 1876* (Norman: University of Oklahoma Press, 2003), 78–79; William Garnett interview, Jensen, *Ricker Indian Interviews*, 22 (quotation). The identities of Crook's Cheyenne, Sioux, and Arapaho scouts are known, and also some Shoshones. See McDermott, *Gen. George Crook's 1876 Campaigns*, 92–94, 331.

2 Robert A. Murray, *Military Posts in the Powder River Country of Wyoming, 1865–1894* (Lincoln: University of Nebraska Press, 1968), 110–11.

3 Marquis, *Warrior Who Fought Custer*, 278–79, 282–83; Grinnell *Fighting Cheyennes*, 346; Powell, *People of the Sacred Mountain*, Vol. 2, 1050; Iron Teeth narrative, Marquis, *Cheyennes of Montana*, 70.

4 Marquis, *Warrior Who Fought Custer*, 283, 284 (quotation), 285; Weasel Bear interview, Hunt and Hunt, *I Fought with Custer*, 217; Powell, *Sweet Medicine*, Vol. 1, 151; Iron Teeth narrative, Marquis, *Cheyennes of Montana*, 71 (quotation). The Red Fork lodge count varies dramatically and one sees variously from 65 to 205 in the primary sources. I cite Bourke, who was there and careful about such details. Bourke, *Diaries, Vol. 2*, 185.

5 William Garnett interview, Jensen, *Ricker Indian Interviews*, 24–25; Bourke, *Diaries, Vol. 2*, 177; "General Mackenzie's Fight," *New York Herald*, Dec. 11, 1876.

6 William Garnett interview, Jensen, *Ricker Indian Interviews*, 25–26; Bourke, *Diaries, Vol. 2*, 177, 179; "General Mackenzie's Fight," *New York Herald*, Dec. 11, 1876; Richard I. Dodge diary, *The Powder River Expedition Journals of Colonel Richard Irving Dodge*, ed. Wayne R. Kime (Norman: University of Oklahoma Press, 1997), 82.

7 John G. Bourke, *Mackenzie's Last Fight with the Cheyennes: A Winter Campaign in Wyoming and Montana* (Governor's Island, N.Y.: Military Service Institution, 1890; reprint, Bellevue, NE: Old Army Press, 1970), 13.

8 Grinnell, *Fighting Cheyennes*, 356–59; Greene, *Morning Star Dawn*, 90–91.

9 Grinnell, *Fighting Cheyennes*, 355, 359 (first quotation); Peter J. Powell, "High Bull's Victory Roster," *MMWH* 25 (Winter 1975): 14–15; Powell, *People of the Sacred Mountain*, Vol. 2, 1054; Iron Teeth narrative, Marquis, *Cheyennes of Montana*, 71 (second quotation).

10 Grinnell, *Fighting Cheyennes*, 355; Powell, "High Bull's Victory Roster," 14–15; Powell, *People of the Sacred Mountain*, Vol. 2, 1054; Beaver Heart account, Greene, *Lakota and Cheyenne*, 119 (quotation). Insight on Last Bull's arrogance is offered by Sherry L. Smith, *Sagebrush Soldier: Private William Earl Smith's View of the Sioux War of 1876* (Norman: University of Oklahoma Press, 1989), 68–69.

11 Powell, "Ox'zem," 36; Powell, "High Bull's Victory Roster," 14–15; Powell, *People of the Sacred Mountain*, Vol. 2, 1057 (quotation).

12 Powell, *People of the Sacred Mountain*, Vol. 2, 1057; Powell, "High Bull's Victory Roster," 15.

13 Stands In Timber and Liberty, *A Cheyenne Voice*, 167, 173; Bourke, *Mackenzie's Last Fight with the Cheyennes*, 22.

14 Powell, *People of the Sacred Mountain*, Vol. 2, 1057 (first quotation); William Garnett interview, Jensen, *Ricker Indian Interviews*, 30 (second quotation).

15 Grinnell, *Fighting Cheyennes*, 351.

16 Black White Man account, Greene, *Lakota and Cheyenne*, 121, 124; Powell, *People of the Sacred Mountain*, Vol. 2, 1059; Keenan, "Wrinkled Cheyenne Warrior" (quotation).

17 Stands In Timber and Liberty, *A Cheyenne Voice*, 167; Bourke, *Mackenzie's Last Fight with the Cheyennes*, 23; Iron Teeth narrative, Marquis, *Cheyennes of Montana*, 71; Iron Teeth account, Greene, *Lakota and Cheyenne*, 114 (quotation).

18 "Stacy Riggs (Red Bird)—Lone Wolf Describes Battle," Thomas Benton Williams, *The Soul of the Red Man* (n.p.: privately printed, 1937), 242–43.

19 Powell, *People of the Sacred Mountain*, Vol. 2, 1059–61; William Garnett interview, Jensen, *Ricker Indian Interviews*, 31–32; DeBarthe, *Life and Adventures of Frank Grouard*, 328.

20 Bourke, *Mackenzie's Last Fight with the Cheyennes*, 25–26; Powell, *People of the Sacred Mountain*, Vol. 2, 1062; Homer W. Wheeler, *Buffalo Days: Forty Years in the Old West* (New York: A. L. Burt Company, 1923), 133–34; McDermott, *Gen. George Crook's 1876 Campaigns*, 107.

21 Bourke, *Mackenzie's Last Fight with the Cheyennes*, 26; McDermott, *Gen. George Crook's 1876 Campaigns*, 107, 127n64. Wheeler, *Buffalo Days*, 134, asserts that this warrior too was killed by soldier fire.

22 Grinnell, *Fighting Cheyennes*, 362; Powell, *People of the Sacred Mountain*, Vol. 2, 1061.

23 Grinnell, *Fighting Cheyennes*, 362, 364–65; Powell, *People of the Sacred Mountain*, Vol. 2, 1062, 1068–69; Stands In Timber and Liberty, *A Cheyenne Voice*, 168.

24 Grinnell, *Fighting Cheyennes*, 366–67; McDermott, *Gen. George Crook's 1876 Campaigns*, 106.

25 Grinnell, *Fighting Cheyennes*, 361–62; Powell, *People of the Sacred Mountain*, Vol. 2, 1061; Bull Hump account, item 348, Grinnell Papers, Southwest Museum; Lessing H. Nohl, Jr., "Mackenzie Against Dull Knife: Breaking the Northern Cheyennes in 1876," ed. K. Ross Toole and others, *Probing the American West: Papers from the Santa Fe Conference* (Santa Fe: Museum of New Mexico Press, 1962), 88–89. The officer, First Lieutenant John A. McKinney, Fourth Cavalry, was hit six times but lived long enough to warn off his command and mumble a few words about his mother.

26 Bourke, *Mackenzie's Last Fight with the Cheyennes*, 28–31 (quotation on 29); Bourke, *Diaries, Vol. 2*, 188–90, 196; "General Mackenzie's Fight," *New York Herald*, Dec. 11, 1876; Manypenny, *Our Indian Wards*, 328; Grinnell, *Fighting Cheyennes*, 353–54; Powell, "High Bull's Victory Roster," 16–17, 20–21; Greene, *Morning Star Dawn*, 134–39.

27 Bourke, *Mackenzie's Last Fight with the Cheyennes*, 29 (quotation), 33; Luther North statement, T. J. Gatchell, "The Battle on the Red Fork," in *Powder River Country: The Papers of J. Elmer Brock*, ed. Margaret Brock Hanson (Kaycee, WY: self-published, 1981), 94; Grinnell, *Fighting Cheyennes*, 354, 367; Greene, *Morning Star Dawn*, 161.

28 Bourke, *Diaries, Vol. 2*, 187 (quotation); Hard Robe statement, T. J. Gatchell, "The Battle on the Red Fork," 93; Wheeler, *Buffalo Days*, 134; Cozzens, *The Earth Is Weeping*, 289. Some sources say three of Morning Star's sons were killed. See William Garnett interview, Jensen, *Ricker Indian Interviews*, 32, and Powell, *Sweet Medicine*, Vol. 1, 164n11.

29 Grinnell, *Fighting Cheyennes*, 365–66; Powell, *People of the Sacred Mountain*, Vol. 2, 1065; Stands In Timber and Liberty, *A Cheyenne Voice*, 169.

30 Powell, *Sweet Medicine*, 163–64; Powell, *People of the Sacred Mountain*, Vol. 2, 1062–63; Bourke, *Mackenzie's Last Fight with the Cheyennes*, 27; Iron Teeth narrative, Marquis, *Cheyennes of Montana*, 81; McDermott, *Gen. George Crook's 1876 Campaigns*, 104, 111–12; Greene, *Morning Star Dawn*, 139–40.

31 Powell, *People of the Sacred Mountain*, Vol. 2, 1060; Joyce M. Szabo, *Howling Wolf and the History of Ledger Art* (Albuquerque: University of New Mexico Press, 1994), 125.

32 Keenan, "Wrinkled Cheyenne Warrior"; Greene, *Morning Star Dawn*, 160.

33 Stands In Timber and Liberty, *A Cheyenne Voice*, 169; Grinnell, *Fighting Cheyennes*, 368; Marquis, *Warrior Who Fought Custer*, 287.

34 Marquis, *Warrior Who Fought Custer*, 286.

35 Marquis, *Warrior Who Fought Custer*, 287; Black Elk narrative, DeMallie, *The Sixth Grandfather*, 201; Short Bull interview, Carroll, *Eleanor H. Hinman Interviews*, 41–42; Grinnell, *Fighting Cheyennes*, 369; Powell, *People of the Sacred Mountain*, Vol. 2, 1071; Kingsley M. Bray, "Crazy Horse and the End of the Great Sioux War," *Nebraska History* 79 (Fall 1998): 96.

36 Eagle Shield account, W. H. Wood ltr., Feb. 19, 1877, NA M234, DS, Roll 262, 208; Short Bull interview, Carroll, *Eleanor H. Hinman Interviews*, 41; Anderson, "A Sioux Pictorial Account," 102; Spotted Elk interview, W. H. Wood ltr., Mar. 1, 1877, NA M234, DS, Roll 262, 268.

37 Powers, *The Killing of Crazy Horse*, 243, 280. Touch the Clouds' participation in the Little Big Horn fight is disputed. See Gordon Richard, "Was Touch the Clouds at the Little Bighorn?" *CBHMA Battlefield Dispatch*, 40 (Summer 2021): 7.

38 The sum of five hundred was reported by Miles at the time of the Tongue River fight, and also by William Philo Clark, who was with Crook then at Red Cloud Agency. Gray, *Centennial Campaign*, 350; Thomas R. Buecker, "Lt. William Philo Clark's Sioux War Report and Little Big Horn Map," *Greasy Grass* 7 (May 1991): 19. Of the Red Fork survivors as many as eighteen lodges of Southern Cheyennes fled southward, skirting mountains, plains, and people, and eventually reaching the Darlington Agency in the Indian Territory. A few others quietly submitted at the White River Agency in Nebraska. Powell, *People of the Sacred Mountain*, Vol. 2, 1065, referencing John Stands In Timber. Other accounts, unsupported, suggest eight hundred lodges with Crazy Horse at this time, a mistaken tally exceeding even the cumulative size of the Little Big Horn village.

39 W. H. Wood ltr., Dec. 28, 1876, NA M234, DS, Roll 261, 907; Eagle Shield account, W. H. Wood ltr., Feb. 16, 1877, NA M234, DS, Roll 262, 222; Gardner, *The Earth Is All That Lasts*, 271; Harry H. Anderson, "Indian Peace-Talkers and the Conclusion of the Sioux War of 1876," *Nebraska History* 44 (December 1963): 233–36.

40 Sandoz, "The Lost Sitting Bull," in *Hostiles and Friendlies*, 103, 106; Horn Chips interview, Hardorff, *Surrender and Death of Crazy Horse*, 79. Impetus for the Sitting Bull peace effort is variously ascribed to

the Red Cloud agent, the military, and Crook himself. Most likely the immediate effort originated with the Red Cloud agent, although perhaps inspired by the War Department, operating through the Secretary of War, the Secretary of the Interior, and the Commissioner of Indian Affairs, and explaining as well similar efforts originating at other Sioux agencies.

41 Spotted Elk interview, W. H. Wood ltr., Mar. 1, 1877, NA M234, DS, Roll 262, 268; Foolish Bear and Important Man interview, W. H. Wood ltr., Jan. 24, 1877, NA M1495, Spec. Files., Mil. Div. Mo., Roll 605; Swelled Face statement, W. H. Wood ltr., Feb. 21, 1877, NA M234, DS, Roll 262, 197; Report of the Commissioner of Indian Affairs, Nov. 1, 1877, in *Report of the Secretary of the Interior, 1877–78* (Washington, DC: Government Printing Office, 1878), 412; "The Corbusier Winter Counts," in *The Dakota and Corbusier Winter Counts*, Reprints in Anthropology, Vol. 36, ed. Garrick Mallery (Lincoln, NE: J & L Reprint Company, 1987), 146; Powers, *The Killing of Crazy Horse*, 244.

42 Foolish Bear and Important Man interview, W. H. Wood ltr., Jan. 24, 1877, NA M1495, Spec. Files., Mil. Div. Mo., Roll 605, naming the five: Sitting Bull the Good, Red Skirt No. 2, The Yearling, Fat Hide, and Bad Leg; Eagle Shield account, W. H. Wood ltr., Feb. 16, 1877, NA M234, DS, Roll 262, 222, similarly naming all except Bad Leg; N. A. Miles ltr., Dec. 17, 1876, NA M234, DS, Roll 262, 64; "Winter Campaigning," *New York Herald*, Feb. 19, 1877; Powell, *Sweet Medicine*, Vol. 1, 172. The matter of the Henry Model 1860 .44 caliber rifle is a story onto itself. It survives and is now in the collections of the Smithsonian and can be seen at americanindian.si.edu. William Garnett interview, Jensen, *Ricker Indian Interviews*, 84; Powers, *The Killing of Crazy Horse*, 245.

43 Marquis, *Memoirs of a White Crow Indian*, 270; John G. Bourke, *The Diaries of John Gregory Bourke, Vol. 3, June 1, 1878–June 22, 1880*, ed. Charles M. Robinson III (Denton: University of North Texas Press, 2007), 64 (first quotation); "Young-Sitting Bull is Killed December 17, 1876," Vestal, *New Sources of Indian History*, 182–83 (second quotation).

44 Foolish Bear and Important Man interview, W. H. Wood ltr., Jan. 24, 1877, NA M1495, Spec. Files., Mil. Div. Mo., Roll 605; Swelled Face statement, W. H. Wood ltr., Feb. 21, 1877, NA M234, DS, Roll 262, 197; Red Horse account, W. H. Wood ltr., Feb. 27, 1877, NA M234, DS, Roll 262, 246; Powell, *Sweet Medicine*, Vol. 1, 173; Anderson, "The War Club of Sitting Bull the Oglala," 55, 59; Bray, "Crazy Horse and the End of the Great Sioux War," 97.

45 Foolish Bear and Important Man interview, W. H. Wood ltr., Jan. 24, 1877, NA M1495, Spec. Files., Mil. Div. Mo., Roll 605.

46 Foolish Bear and Important Man interview, W. H. Wood ltr., Jan. 24, 1877, NA M1495, Spec. Files., Mil. Div. Mo., Roll 605.

47 Foolish Bear and Important Man interview, W. H. Wood ltr., Jan. 24, 1877, NA M1495, Spec. Files., Mil. Div. Mo., Roll 605 (first quotations); Eagle Shield account, W. H. Wood ltr., Feb. 16, 1877, NA M234, DS, Roll 262, 222 (final quotation); Bray, "Crazy Horse and the End of the Great Sioux War," 97.

48 Swelled Face statement, W. H. Wood ltr., Feb. 21, 1877, NA M234, DS, Roll 262, 197; Fred A. Hunt, "The Crumbling of Crazy Horse's Command," *Overland Monthly* 59 (February 1912): 160; Powers, *The Killing of Crazy Horse*, 248; Jeffrey V. Pearson, "Nelson A. Miles, Crazy Horse, and the Battle of Wolf Mountains," *MMWH* 51 (Winter 2001): 57–58.

49 Marquis, *Warrior Who Fought Custer*, 289; Powell, *Sweet Medicine*, Vol. 1, 172.

50 Red Horse account, W. H. Wood ltr., Feb. 27, 1877, NA M234, DS, Roll 262, 246 (quotation); Marquis, *Memoirs of a White Crow Indian*, 271; Swelled Face statement, W. H. Wood ltr., Feb. 21, 1877, NA M234, DS, Roll 262, 197; Eagle Shield account, W. H. Wood ltr., Feb. 19, 1877, NA M234, DS, Roll 262, 208; Powell, *Sweet Medicine*, Vol. 1, 174–76; Powell, *People of the Sacred Mountain*, Vol. 2, 1075; Greene, *Yellowstone Command*, 153. Wooden Leg identified the captives, Marquis, *Warrior Who Fought Custer*, 293.

51 Powell, *People of the Sacred Mountain*, Vol. 2, 1075–76; "The Indian War," *Detroit Free Press*, Feb. 14, 1877.

52 Eagle Shield account, W. H. Wood ltr., Feb. 19, 1877, NA M234, DS, Roll 262, 208; Red Sack account, "Miles' Fight on Tongue River," *Cheyenne Daily Sun*, Feb. 14, 1877; Powell, *People of the Sacred Mountain*, Vol. 2, 1074–75; Hunt, "The Crumbling of Crazy Horse's Command," 162.

53 Marquis, *A Warrior Who Fought Custer*, 290 (first quotation); Nelson Miles to Mary Miles, Jan. 11, 1877, in Virginia W. Johnson, *The Unregimented General: A Biography of Nelson A. Miles* (Boston, MA: Houghton Mifflin Company, 1962), 150 (second quotation); Baird, "A Winter Campaign in Montana and Its Results," 432–33; "The Indian War," *Detroit Free Press*, Feb. 14, 1877; [Miles's Indian Campaign,] *Army and Navy Journal*, May 5, 1877.

54 Swelled Face statement, W. H. Wood ltr., Feb. 21, 1877, NA M234, DS, Roll 262, 197; Sandoz, *Crazy Horse*, 353; Wooden Leg narrative,

in Keith T. Werts, *The Crazy Horse and Colonel Nelson Miles Fight of 1877: New Discoveries at the Battle of the Butte* (Spokane, WA: Werts Publishing, 2014), 145; Powell, *People of the Sacred Mountain*, Vol. 2, 1076–77; Marquis, *Warrior Who Fought Custer*, 290–91; Stands In Timber and Liberty, *Cheyenne Memories*, 221 (quotation). The location today is still marked with a cairn. See Werts, *The Crazy Horse and Colonel Nelson Miles Fight of 1877*, 145, 51n65, 114–15.

55 Black Elk narrative, DeMallie, *The Sixth Grandfather*, 202; Bray, "Crazy Horse and the End of the Great Sioux War," 98–99; Schultz, *William Jackson*, 190–91. Stands In Timber and Liberty, *Cheyenne Memories*, 220, relate a similar story of a Cheyenne warrior who carried home an unexploded cannonball, drilled a hole in it, and poured out powder and little round balls. He too chanced death and was purely lucky.

56 N. A. Miles tele., Jan. 20, 1877, NA M234, DS, Roll 262, 81; N. A. Miles rpt., Jan. 23, 1877, NA M234, DS, Roll 262, 112; Eagle Shield account, W. H. Wood ltr., Feb. 19, 1877, NA M234, DS, Roll 262, 208; Marquis, *Warrior Who Fought Custer*, 293; Powers, *The Killing of Crazy Horse*, 248–49.

57 Bray, *Crazy Horse*, 259; Jackson, *Black Elk*, 140; Miles, *Personal Recollections*, 238–39; Sandoz, *Crazy Horse*, 354.

58 Eagle Shield account, W. H. Wood ltr., Feb. 16, 1877, NA M234, DS, Roll 262, 222; Swelled Face statement, W. H. Wood ltr., Feb. 21, 1877, NA M234, DS, Roll 262, 197; Larson, *Gall*, 154; Manzione, *"I Am Looking to the North for My Life,"* 33; Bray, *Crazy Horse*, 259–60; Utley, *The Lance and The Shield*, 180.

13. Cruel Fate of the Cheyennes

1 White Eagle statement, within Red Horse account, W. H. Wood ltr., Feb. 27, 1877, NA M234, DS, Roll 262, 246; Swelled Face statement, W. H. Wood ltr., Feb. 21, 1877, NA M234, DS, Roll 262, 197; Eagle Shield account, W. H. Wood ltr., Feb. 16, 1877, NA M234, DS, Roll 262, 222; Bray, "Crazy Horse and the End of the Great Sioux War," 101–102.

2 Red Horse account, W. H. Wood ltr., Feb. 27, 1877, NA M234, DS, Roll 262, 246; Swelled Face statement, W. H. Wood ltr., Feb. 21, 1877, NA M234, DS, Roll 262, 197; Bray, *Crazy Horse*, 262–63; Hyde, *Spotted Tail's Folk*, 242 (quotation).

3 Bray, "Crazy Horse and the End of the Great Sioux War," 101, 106; Powers, *The Killing of Crazy Horse*, 253; Red Sack account, "Miles' Fight on Tongue River," *Cheyenne Daily Sun*, Feb. 14, 1877; "The Hostile Sioux," *New York Herald*, Feb. 14, 1877.

4 Bray, *Crazy Horse*, 267.

5 Marquis, *Warrior Who Fought Custer*, 293 (quotation), 294; Powell, *People of the Sacred Mountain*, Vol. 2, 1078; Anderson, "Cheyennes at the Little Big Horn," 91.

6 Jas. S. Brisbin ltr., Feb. 14, 1877, NA M234, DS, Roll 262, 190; Miles, *Personal Recollections*, 239–40; Marquis, *Warrior Who Fought Custer*, 295; Stands In Timber and Liberty, *Cheyenne Memories*, 222; Powell, *Sweet Medicine*, Vol. 1, 182; Christina Gish Hill, *Webs of Kinship: Family in Northern Cheyenne Nationhood* (Norman: University of Oklahoma Press, 2017), 134–35; Powell, *People of the Sacred Mountain*, Vol. 2, 1087, 1089, and 1380n1, where the author counters Miles's mention of sending not one but two Cheyennes with Bruguier.

7 Powell, *People of the Sacred Mountain*, Vol. 2, 1089–90; Powell, *Sweet Medicine*, Vol. 1, 186; Marquis, *Warrior Who Fought Custer*, 296.

8 Marquis, *Warrior Who Fought Custer*, 296 (quotation), 297; Miles, *Personal Recollections*, 240.

9 Grinnell, *Fighting Cheyennes*, 370.

10 Grinnell, *Fighting Cheyennes*, 371 (first quotation); Powell, *Sweet Medicine*, Vol. 1, 188; Miles, *Personal Recollections*, 243 (second quotation).

11 Powell, *Sweet Medicine*, Vol. 1, 189.

12 Marquis, *Warrior Who Fought Custer*, 297; Powell, *People of the Sacred Mountain*, Vol. 2, 1124.

13 Marquis, *Warrior Who Fought Custer*, 298 (quotations); Powell, *People of the Sacred Mountain*, Vol. 2, 1124.

14 Powell, *Sweet Medicine*, Vol. 1, 192; Powell, *People of the Sacred Mountain*, Vol. 2, 1125, 1128, 1141–44; Bourke, *Diaries, Vol. 2*, 250–51; P. H. Sheridan tele., Mar. 23, 1877, NA M234, DS, Roll 262, 307; Bourke, *Diaries, Vol. 3*, 58; "The Surrendered Hostiles," *New York Herald*, May 11, 1877.

15 Powell, *People of the Sacred Mountain*, Vol. 2, 1144–45; Bourke, *Diaries, Vol. 2*, 273–75; "Surrender of More Indians," *New York Times*, Apr. 22, 1877; "The Conquered Cheyennes," *Chicago Times*, Apr. 22, 1877; "The Indian Campaign," *New York Tribune*, Apr. 23, 1877; P. H. Sheridan tele., Mar. 23, 1877, NA M234, DS, Roll 262, 307; Greene, *Morning Star Dawn*, 189–90; Buecker, *Fort Robinson and the American West*, 93. Many of the surrendering Cheyennes, particularly heads of families, were recorded by the local agents. See Thomas R. Buecker and R. Eli Paul, *Crazy Horse Surrender Ledger* (Lincoln: Nebraska State Historical Society, 1994), 101–106.

16 Marquis, *Warrior Who Fought Custer*, 299; Nelson A. Miles ltr., Apr. 22, 1877, NA M234, DS, Roll 262, 413; "Report of Indians That Surrendered or Were Captured Through the Exertions of the Troops of the District of the Yellowstone," Nelson A. Miles Papers, Box T-2, U.S. Army Military History Institute, Carlisle Barracks, PA; Grinnell, *Fighting Cheyennes*, 373; Greene, *Yellowstone Command*, 198.

17 Stands In Timber and Liberty, *Cheyenne Memories*, 224; Nelson A. Miles ltr., Apr. 26, 1877, Alfred H. Terry 1st end., May 9, 1877, P. H. Sheridan 2nd end., May 14, 1877, all NA M234, DS, Roll 262, 421; W. T. Sherman tele., May 12, 1877, NA M234, DS, Roll 262, 403.

18 Powell, *Sweet Medicine*, Vol. 1, 195.

19 "Red Cloud Agency," *Cheyenne Daily Leader*, May 27, 1877; Powell, *Sweet Medicine*, Vol. 1, 195; Powell, *People of the Sacred Mountain*, Vol. 2, 1149–51.

20 Iron Teeth narrative, Marquis, *Cheyennes of Montana*, 72.

21 E. A. Hayt, Report of the Commissioner of Indian Affairs, Nov. 1, 1877, in *Report of the Secretary of the Interior, 1877–78*, 415.

14. Shock and Despair in the Pine Ridge

1 Bray, *Crazy Horse*, 265.

2 Garnett interview, Jensen, *Ricker Indian Interviews*, 45; Red Shirt, *George Sword's Warrior Narratives*, 60; Sword interview, Jensen, *Ricker Indian Interviews*, 327–28; Hardorff, *Surrender and Death of Crazy Horse*, 79n15; Hyde, *Spotted Tail's Folk*, 243; Bray, *Crazy Horse*, 265–66; Powers, *The Killing of Crazy Horse*, 251 (quoting Hunts the Enemy), 253; "Report of Brigadier General Crook," in *Annual Report of the Secretary of War for the Year 1877* (Washington, DC: Government Printing Office, 1877), 84; Sandoz, *Crazy Horse*, 354–55.

3 Susan Bordeaux Bettelyoun and Josephine Waggoner, *With My Own Eyes: A Lakota Woman Tells Her People's Story*, ed. Emily Levine (Lincoln: University of Nebraska Press, 1998), 106–107; [Geo.] Crook ltr., Feb. 5, 1877, NA M234, STA, Roll 843, 696; Bourke, *Diaries, Vol. 2*, 245; Clow, *Spotted Tail*, 153–54; Bray, *Crazy Horse*, 267; Greene, *Yellowstone Command*, 187.

4 "The Reds in Rags," *Chicago Times*, Apr. 19, 1877; Bray, "Crazy Horse and the End of the Great Sioux War," 107–108.

5 Louis Bordeaux interview, Liddic and Harbaugh, *Camp on Custer*, 137–38; J. M. Lee rpt., Apr. 5, 1877, NA M234, STA, Roll 841, 1150; Hyde, *Spotted Tail's Folk*, 243–44; Clow, *Spotted Tail*, 156; Bray, *Crazy Horse*, 269–70; "Census Roll of Indians at Spotted Tail Agency, 1877," Rosebud Indian Agency, Bureau of Indian Affairs, RG 75, National Archives at Kansas

City. The enigmatic Merrivale was a trapper and trader about forty-eight years old. He hailed from New Mexico and was long among the shadow figures at Fort Laramie and along the North Platte River, pivotal early locales of the Brulés. McDermott, *Red Cloud's War*, Vol. 1, 19.

6 Neihardt, *Black Elk Speaks*, 142; Anderson, "Indian Peace-Talkers and the Conclusion of the Sioux War of 1876," 247; Cozzens, *The Earth Is Weeping*, 304 (quotation).

7 Sandoz, *Crazy Horse*, 355; Anderson, "Indian Peace-Talkers and the Conclusion of the Sioux War of 1876," 243; Powers, *The Killing of Crazy Horse*, 259–60; Bray, *Crazy Horse*, 266, 270.

8 J. M. Lee rpt., Apr. 5, 1877, NA M234, STA, Roll 841, 1150; Red Feather interview, Carroll, *Eleanor H. Hinman Interviews*, 24; Hyde, *Red Cloud's Folk*, 290; Clow, *Spotted Tail*, 156–57; Bray, "Crazy Horse and the End of the Great Sioux War," 111.

9 Red Horse account, W. H. Wood ltr., Feb. 27, 1877, NA M234, DS, Roll 262, 246 (quotation); P. H. Sheridan tele., Feb. 27, 1877, NA M234, CRA, Roll 129, 1274.

10 J. M. Lee ltr., Mar. 6, 1877, Hinman Papers, Nebraska State Historical Society, Lincoln (quotation); W. P. Clark ltr., Mar. 3, 1877, NA M666, SWP, Roll 280, 217; P. H. Sheridan tele., Mar. 23, 1877, NA M666, SWP, Roll 280, 234, 101–104; Hyde, *Spotted Tail's Folk*, 243; Buecker and Paul, *Crazy Horse Surrender Ledger*, 101–104.

11 George Crook tele., Apr. 19, 1877, Hinman Papers, Nebraska State Historical Society, Lincoln; J. M. Lee ltr., Apr. 19, 1877, NA M234, STA, Roll 841, 728; "Surrender of the Sioux Bands," *New York Times*, Apr. 18, 1877; Bourke, *Diaries, Vol. 2*, 253, 256–60; Hyde, *Spotted Tail's Folk*, 245.

12 J. M. Lee ltrs., Apr. 19, 1877, NA M234, STA, Roll 841, 724 and 728; J. M. Lee rpt., Aug. 2, 1877, NA M234, STA, Roll 841, 926.

13 Bray, *Crazy Horse*, 275; Matthew King interview, Edward and Mabell Kadlecek, *To Kill an Eagle*, 125 (quotation).

14 "Grand Pow-Wow," *Cheyenne Daily Leader*, May 26, 1877 (first quotation); Red Feather interview, Carroll, *Eleanor H. Hinman Interviews*, 33 (second quotation); Black Elk narrative, DeMallie, *The Sixth Grandfather*, 202–203; Powers, *The Killing of Crazy Horse*, 256.

15 Hyde, *Red Cloud's Folk*, 290; Bray, "Crazy Horse and the End of the Great Sioux War," 111–12; The noted ration was detailed by Agent Lee at Spotted Tail in his pleas for resupply. J. M. Lee ltrs., Apr. 19, 1877, NA M234, STA, Roll 841, 724 and 728.

16 Bourke, *Diaries, Vol. 2*, 266; Garnett, interview, Jensen, *Ricker Indian Interviews*, 46–47; Paul Magid, *The Gray Fox: George Crook and the*

Indian Wars (Norman: University of Oklahoma Press, 2015), 358; Bray, "Crazy Horse and the End of the Great Sioux War," 112; Cozzens, *The Earth Is Weeping*, 304.

17 Charles E. Hanson, Jr., ed., "Red Cloud's Mission to Crazy Horse, 1877," *Museum of the Fur Trade Quarterly* 22 (Spring, 1986): 9–13, detailing the delegate's names; F. C. Boucher communique, Mar. 25, 1877, Hinman Papers, Nebraska State Historical Society, Lincoln; R. C. Drum ltr., Apr. 27, 1877, NA M234, DS, Roll 262, 390; Bray, *Crazy Horse*, 274–75.

18 "Hard Up," *Cheyenne Daily Leader*, May 5, 1877; Bray, *Crazy Horse*, 278–79.

19 Magid, *Gray Fox*, 360–61; Garnett, interview, Jensen, *Ricker Indian Interviews*, 47; Sandoz, *Crazy Horse*, 366; Buecker, *Fort Robinson and the American West*, 92; Powers, *The Killing of Crazy Horse*, 260–61; Oliver Knight, "War or Peace: The Anxious Wait for Crazy Horse," *Nebraska History* 54 (Winter 1973): 538. He Dog asserted that Crazy Horse would not speak to the officer, let alone shake his hand. He Dog interview, Hardorff, *Lakota Recollections*, 79.

20 Bourke, *Diaries, Vol. 3*, 67; "Crazy Horse's Band," *New York Herald*, May 28, 1877; Mark J. Nelson, *White Hat: The Military Career of Captain William Philo Clark* (Norman: University of Oklahoma Press, 2018), 51–53, particularly here detailing the evolution of Clark's scouts.

21 "Crazy Horse With Us," *Chicago Times*, May 7, 1877; "Crazy Horse's Surrender," *New York Herald*, May 7, 1877; "Crazy Horse's Band," *New York Herald*, May 28, 1877; He Dog interview, Crazy Horse Papers, Museum of the Fur Trade, Chadron, NE.

22 Nelson, *White Hat*, 3; He Dog interview, Hardorff, *Lakota Recollections*, 79; "Crazy Horse With Us," *Chicago Times*, May 7, 1877; "Crazy Horse's Surrender," *New York Herald*, May 7, 1877; Bourke, *Diaries, Vol. 2*, 297; "Crazy Horse's Band," *New York Herald*, May 28, 1877; Short Bull interview, Carroll, *Eleanor H. Hinman Interviews*, 42; Powers, *The Killing of Crazy Horse*, 263. The dramatic, ornate war shirts belonging to Crazy Horse and He Dog survive and today are exhibited respectively in the Plains Indian Museum at the Buffalo Bill Center of the West, Cody, Wyoming (where it is known as the Red Cloud shirt), and in the Morris County Historical Society Museum, Morristown, New Jersey, and this with a thankful nod to Mike Cowdrey for alerting me to these particulars.

23 "Crazy Horse With Us," *Chicago Times*, May 7, 1877; "Crazy Horse's Surrender," *New York Herald*, May 7, 1877; "Surrender of Crazy Horse," *New York Tribune*, May 7, 1877; Bourke, *Diaries, Vol. 2*,

297; "Crazy Horse's Band," *New York Herald*, May 28, 1877 (first quotation); Powers, *The Killing of Crazy Horse*, 262; Sandoz, *Crazy Horse*, 361 (second quotation).

24 "Surrender of Crazy Horse," *New York Tribune*, May 7, 1877; "Crazy Horse With Us," *Chicago Times*, May 7, 1877; Bourke, *Diaries, Vol. 2*, 298; C. A. Johnson ltr., May 6, 1877, NA M234, RCA, Roll 721, 313; Bray, *Crazy Horse*, 283–84; Magid, *Gray Fox*, 354. The surrendering people were recorded in a key volume published as *Crazy Horse Surrender Ledger*, Buecker and Paul, eds.

25 Susan Bordeaux Bettelyoun narrative, Hardorff, *Surrender and Death of Crazy Horse*, 125; Bourke, *Diaries, Vol. 2*, 297; Powers, *The Killing of Crazy Horse*, 263.

26 Jeffrey V. Pearson, "Tragedy at Red Cloud Agency: The Surrender, Confinement, and Death of Crazy Horse," *MMWH* 55 (Summer 2005): 14; Neihardt, *Black Elk Speaks*, 143; Jackson, *Black Elk*, 145.

27 Bray, "Crazy Horse and the End of the Great Sioux War," 108–110; Powell, *People of the Sacred Mountain*, Vol. 2, 1129; John S. Gray, "The Lame Deer Fight Ends the Sioux War," *Chicago Westerners Brand Book* 31 (May 1974): 18; White Bull account, Greene, *Lakota and Cheyenne*, 139; Grinnell, *Fighting Cheyennes*, 378.

28 White Bull account, Greene, *Lakota and Cheyenne*, 139; Grinnell, *Fighting Cheyennes*, 373; R. C. Drum ltr., Apr. 27, 1877, NA M234, DS, Roll 262, 390; Miles, *Personal Recollections*, 244; Greene, *Yellowstone Command*, 202 (quotation).

29 Gray, "The Lame Deer Fight Ends the Sioux War," 18; Miles, *Personal Recollections*, 249 (quotation).

30 Grinnell, *Fighting Cheyennes*, 375–76; White Bull accounts, Greene, *Lakota and Cheyenne*, 136, 144; A. M. Fuller acct., "Gen. Miles' Victory," *Saint Paul and Minneapolis Pioneer Press*, June 1, 1877; Powell, *People of the Sacred Mountain*, Vol. 2, 1132. Other Sioux remember Lame Deer's nephew killed alongside him in the fight, calling him Fool Heart. Bad Heart Bull, in Helen H. Blish, *A Pictographic History of the Oglala Sioux* (Lincoln: University of Nebraska Press, 1967), 163. Hump called him simply Ankle. Hump reminiscence, Greene, *Lakota and Cheyenne*, 147.

31 Grinnell, *Fighting Cheyennes*, 376, 377 (quotation); White Bull accounts, Greene, *Lakota and Cheyenne*, 137, 143; Lame Deer sketch, Waggoner, *Witness*, 364; Powell, *People of the Sacred Mountain*, Vol. 2, 1132–33. Regarding Big Ankle, see Emily Levine, Waggoner, *Witness*, 669n3.

32 A. M. Fuller account, "Gen. Miles' Victory," *Saint Paul and Minneapolis Pioneer Press*, June 1, 1877; Buecker, "Lt. William Philo

Clark's Sioux War Report," 20; Miles, *Personal Recollections*, 255; White Bull notes, Group 1, Box 2, Camp Papers, BYU, Provo, UT. Greene, *Yellowstone Command*, 212, 214.

33 Miles, *Personal Recollections*, 253; Jerome A. Greene, "Out With a Whimper: The Little Missouri Expedition and the Close of the Great Sioux War," *South Dakota History* 35 (Spring 2005): 1–39; Hedren, *Great Sioux War Orders of Battle*, 211–12; P. H. Sheridan rpt., Oct. 25, 1877, *Annual Report of the Secretary of War, 1877*, 56 (first quotation); "Wars in the West," *Chicago Times*, Nov. 17, 1877; Baird, "A Winter Campaign in Montana and Its Results," 436; Schultz, *William Jackson*, 201; Hyde, *Red Cloud's Folk*, 292 (second quotation).

34 Powers, *The Killing of Crazy Horse*, 274, 288.

35 Garnett interview, Jensen, *Ricker Indian Interviews*, 52–53; Powers, *The Killing of Crazy Horse*, 274–75.

36 "Grand Pow-Wow," *Cheyenne Daily Leader*, May 26, 1877, repeated nearly word for word in the *Chicago Times* account, "Doves and Devils," May 26, 1877.

37 "Doves and Devils," *Chicago Times*, May 26, 1877.

38 Magid, *Gray Fox*, 365.

39 "'Lo' at Home," *Cheyenne Daily Leader*, May 23, 1877; "Red Cloud Agency," *Cheyenne Daily Leader*, May 27, 1877; Powers, *The Killing of Crazy Horse*, 268–70, 272–73; Marilyn Dear Nelson and Christopher Nelson, *Red Cloud and the Indian Trader: The Remarkable Friendship of the Sioux Chief and JW Dear in the Last Days of the Frontier* (Essex, CT: TwoDot, 2023), 217–18.

40 Powers, *The Killing of Crazy Horse*, 273–74, 293; "Doves and Devils," *Chicago Times*, May 26, 1877.

41 "Doves and Devils," *Chicago Times*, May 26, 1877 (quotations); "The Custer Massacre," *Saint Paul and Minneapolis Pioneer Press*, May 29, 1877, repeating the *Chicago Times* account; Powers, *The Killing of Crazy Horse*, 293–95; Bray, *Crazy Horse*, 302.

42 Garnett interview, Jensen, *Ricker Indian Interviews*, 54–56; Powers, *The Killing of Crazy Horse*, 283–88. A second major Lakota Sun Dance was held by the Red Cloud and Spotted Tail people on Chadron Creek ten days later. Garnett interview, Jensen, *Ricker Indian Interviews*, 56–57.

43 Benj. J. Shopp rpt., Aug. 15, 1877, Hardorff, *Surrender and Death of Crazy Horse*, 168–69; "Going After Buffalo," *Cheyenne Daily Leader*, Aug. 7, 1877 (quotation); Powers, *The Killing of Crazy Horse*, 343–44.

44 Shopp, rpt., Aug. 15, 1877, Hardorff, *Surrender and Death of Crazy Horse*, 169–70 (quotations); Powers, *The Killing of Crazy Horse*, 345.

45 Powers, *The Killing of Crazy Horse*, 345; Garnett interview, Jensen, *Ricker Indian Interviews*, 59–60; Gardner, *The Earth Is All That Lasts*, 289; Pearson, "Tragedy at Red Cloud Agency," 17.

46 Louis Bordeaux interview, Jensen, *Ricker Indian Interviews*, 296 (quotations); Garnett interview, Jensen, *Ricker Indian Interviews*, 60–61; Pearson, "Tragedy at Red Cloud Agency," 20.

47 Louis Bordeaux interview, Jensen, *Ricker Indian Interviews*, 296 (quotation), 297; Jesse Lee ltr., c1914, in E. A. Brininstool, *Crazy Horse: The Invincible Ogalalla Sioux Chief* (Los Angeles, CA: Wetzel Publishing Co., 1949), 36; Powers, *The Killing of Crazy Horse*, 359. Bordeaux went on to explain Grouard's reasoning, as he saw it anyway. See Powers, *The Killing of Crazy Horse*, 352–53. Red Cloud's first major biographer, George Hyde, relatively exonerates Grouard and while acknowledging the possibility of a mistranslation shifts the blame to Crazy Horse directly, *Red Cloud's Folk*, 295–97.

48 Magid, *Gray Fox*, 378 (first quotation); P. H. Sheridan tele., Sept. 1, 1877, NA M234, RCA, Roll 721, 780; He Dog interview, Carroll, *Eleanor H. Hinman Interviews*, 31 (second quotation); Powers, *The Killing of Crazy Horse*, 373.

49 William Garnett account, Robert A. Clark, ed., *Killing of Chief Crazy Horse* (Lincoln: University of Nebraska Press, 1988), 77 (quotation); Garnett interview, Jensen, *Ricker Indian Interviews*, 66; Powers, *The Killing of Crazy Horse*, 374–75. Only much later was it revealed that Little Wolf's account was a fabrication, its reasoning lost, as Garnett attempted to explain it, "in the secret corners and crevices of the human mind." But in the moment Little Wolf's statement, as reported by Woman Dress, sounded dire and was accepted as fact. Garnett interview, Jensen, 67; Bray, *Crazy Horse*, 356.

50 He Dog interview, Carroll, *Eleanor H. Hinman Interviews*, 29; Billy Hunter (William Garnett) statement, Hardorff, *Surrender and Death of Crazy Horse*, 59, 62 (quotation); Magid, *Gray Fox*, 383–84.

51 Garnett interview, Jensen, *Ricker Indian Interviews*, 62–63; L. P. Bradley ltr., Sept. 7, 1877, Hardorff, *Surrender and Death of Crazy Horse*, 184; Chips interview, Hardorff, *Surrender and Death of Crazy Horse*, 86; Randy Kane, "Who Killed Crazy Horse? Politics at Red Cloud Agency, Summer 1877," *Nebraska History* 101 (Fall 2020): 97; Gardner, *The Earth Is All That Lasts*, 288; Powers, *The Killing of Crazy Horse*, 382–83, 387.

52 Garnett interview, Jensen, *Ricker Indian Interviews*, 62–63; Chips interview, Hardorff, *Surrender and Death of Crazy Horse*, 86; Kane, "Who Killed Crazy Horse?" 97; Gardner, *The Earth Is All That Lasts*, 288; Powers, *The Killing of Crazy Horse*, 382–83, 387.

53 Garnett interview, Jensen, *Ricker Indian Interviews*, 65, 68; Horned Chips interview, Jensen, *Ricker Indian Interviews*, 276; Louis Bordeaux interview, Jensen, *Ricker Indian Interviews*, 293, 297; Powers, *The Killing of Crazy Horse*, 389–90, noting among other matters that this was not the same Beaver Creek in the Tongue River country, where Crazy Horse hoped to have his agency, and reminding us that Beaver Creek is a ubiquitous stream name in the American West.

54 Louis Bordeaux interview, Jensen, *Ricker Indian Interviews*, 293–94; Jesse M. Lee, "The Capture and Death of an Indian Chieftain," *Journal of the Military Service Institution* 54 (May–June 1914): 332; Powers, *The Killing of Crazy Horse*, 391; Clow, *Spotted Tail*, 161.

55 Hyde, *Spotted Tail's Folk*, 252 ("load of trouble" and "dumped"); Lee, "The Capture and Death of an Indian Chieftain," 332 (final quotations).

56 Louis Bordeaux interview, Liddic and Harbaugh, *Camp on Custer*, 143 (quotation); Gardner, *The Earth Is All That Lasts*, 301.

57 Louis Bordeaux interview, Jensen, *Ricker Indian Interviews*, 296–96, 297 (quotation); Magid, *Gray Fox*, 385; Lee, "The Capture and Death of an Indian Chieftain," 334. Lee mentions the Dry Tortugas, 339, as does Sandoz, *Crazy Horse*, 410.

58 Sandoz, *Crazy Horse*, 404; James Chase in Morning statement, Kadlecek and Kadlecek, *To Kill an Eagle*, 93; Bray, *Crazy Horse*, 373.

59 Horn Chips interview, Jensen, *Ricker Indian Interviews*, 276; White Calf interview, Carroll, *Eleanor H. Hinman Interviews*, 45; Lee, "The Capture and Death of an Indian Chieftain," 335; Powers, *The Killing of Crazy Horse*, 400, 403, 528n2.

60 Lee, "The Capture and Death of an Indian Chieftain," 335.

61 Lee, "The Capture and Death of an Indian Chieftain," 336.

62 He Dog interview, Crazy Horse Papers, Museum of the Fur Trade, Chadron, NE (first quotation); He Dog interview, Carroll, *Eleanor H. Hinman Interviews*, 29 (second quotation); Lee, "The Capture and Death of an Indian Chieftain," 336.

63 Lee, "The Capture and Death of an Indian Chieftain," 336–37.

64 Lee, "The Capture and Death of an Indian Chieftain," 337 (first quotation); Garnett interview, Jensen, *Ricker Indian Interviews*, 69, 70 (second quotation).

65 Paul L. Hedren, "Who Killed Crazy Horse? A Historiographical Review and Affirmation," *Nebraska History* 101 (Spring 2020): 4–5.

66 Garnett interview, Jensen, *Ricker Indian Interviews*, 70; Powers, *The Killing of Crazy Horse*, 412 (first quotation, referencing William Garnett's interview with Hugh Scott); Louie Bordeaux interview, Jensen, *Ricker Indian Interviews*, 300 (second quotation); Jackson, *Black Elk*, 156. Almost from

the start, the individual who stabbed Crazy Horse has been misidentified and conveniently forgotten. But his name is known, a red-whiskered older soldier named William Gentles. See Hedren, "Who Killed Crazy Horse?" 9–15, and "Light on Border Mystery," *Omaha Daily Bee*, Apr. 11, 1903.

67 Lee, "The Capture and Death of an Indian Chieftain," 338; V. T. McGillycuddy ltr, June 24, 1927, Clark, *Killing of Chief Crazy Horse*, 125–26; McGillycuddy, *McGillycuddy Agent*, 85; Powers, *The Killing of Crazy Horse*, 420.

68 Lee, "The Capture and Death of an Indian Chieftain," 338; He Dog interview, Carroll, *Eleanor H. Hinman Interviews*, 30; Baptiste Pourier interview, Hardorff, *Surrender and Death of Crazy Horse*, 92; Powers, *The Killing of Crazy Horse*, 422.

69 Lee, "The Capture and Death of an Indian Chieftain," 338; Powers, *The Killing of Crazy Horse*, 422–23; L. P. Bradley ltr., Sept. 7, 1877, Hardorff, *Surrender and Death of Crazy Horse*, 184.

15. Defiance

1 Wilfred Eggleston, "The Cypress Hills," *Canadian Geographical Journal* 42 (February 1951): 58–59; Walter Hildebrandt and Brian Hubner, *The Cypress Hills: The Land and Its People* (Saskatoon, Saskatchewan: Purich Publishing, 1994), 11, 17–18.

2 John Jennings, "The Plains Indians and the Law," in *Men in Scarlet*, Hugh A. Dempsey, ed., (Calgary: Historical Society of Alberta/ McClelland and Stewart West, [1974]), 57–58.

3 Jennings, "The Plains Indians and the Law," 55, 57–58; Garrett Wilson, *Frontier Farewell: The 1870s and the End of the Old West* (Regina, Saskatchewan: University of Regina Press, 2014), 32.

4 Andrew W. Grabill, *Policing the Great Plains: Rangers, Mounties, and the North American Frontier, 1875–1910* (Lincoln: University of Nebraska Press, 2007), 29, 38; Jerome A. Greene, *Beyond Bear's Paw: The Nez Perce Indians in Canada* (Norman: University of Oklahoma Press, 2010), 18-20; Manzione, *"I Am Looking to the North for My Life,"* 42–43.

5 J. M. Walsh ltrs., Dec. 31, 1876, Mar. 15, 1877, "Papers Relating to the Sioux Indians of the United States Who Have Taken Refuge in Canadian Territory," Governor General's Office, Governor General's Numbered Files, RG 7, G 21, Vol. 323, file 2001-1, prints 1875–1879, Library and Archives of Canada, Ottawa, Ont., 9 and 12; James F. Macleod ltr., May 30, 1877, NA M234, DS, Roll 261, 575; Gall narrative, "An Illustrious Story," *Rocky Mountain Husbandman* (Diamond City, MT), May 5, 1881; Robert Higheagle narrative, box 104, folder 22, Campbell Collection, OU (quotation).

6 Robert M. Utley, *The Last Sovereigns: Sitting Bull and the Resistance of the Free Lakotas* (Lincoln: University of Nebraska Press, 2020), 19–20.

7 "Latest from Sitting Bull," *Cheyenne Daily Leader*, June 10, 1877; McGrady, *Living With Strangers*, 73.

8 E. A. Hayt, Report of the Commissioner of Indian Affairs, Nov. 1, 1877, in *Report of the Secretary of the Interior, 1877–78*, 412; "Sitting Bull," *New York Herald*, Oct. 22, 1877; Utley, *The Last Sovereigns*, 21–22; Manzione, *"I Am Looking to the North for My Life,"* 44; Utley, *The Lance and The Shield*, 185; Mike Cowdrey, "A Letter from Sitting Bull," Heritage Auctions, Lot 70401, Nov. 20, 2020, fineart/ha.com.

9 A. G. Irvine ltr., May 23, 1877, "Papers Relating to the Sioux Indians," 16; James F. Macleod ltr., May 30, 1877, "Papers Relating to the Sioux Indians," 18; "Sitting Bull," *Saint Paul and Minneapolis Pioneer Press*, June 12, 1877.

10 McGrady, *Living With Strangers*, 76–77; Utley, *The Lance and The Shield*, 188; Slaughter, "Leaves from Northwestern History," 280 (quotation); Robert F. Karolevitz, *Bishop Martin Marty: "The Black Robe Lean Chief"* (Yankton, SD: privately printed, 1980), 66.

11 Utley, *The Lance and The Shield*, 188; A. G. Irvine ltr., June 6, 1877, "Papers Relating to the Sioux Indians," 21, 22 (first quotation); E. Dalrymple Clark rpt., June 2, 1877, "Papers Relating to the Sioux Indians," 27 (second quotation); "Father Martin's Visit to Sitting Bull," *Bismarck Tri-Weekly Tribune*, June 18, 1877; Paul G. Monson, "From Swiss Monk to Lakota Missionary: How Sitting Bull Transformed Bishop Martin Marty," *South Dakota History* 50 (Spring 2020): 15–17.

12 A. G. Irvine ltr., June 6, 1877, "Papers Relating to the Sioux Indians," 21 (first quotation); Vestal, *Sitting Bull*, 210; Jean Legaré narrative, Walter Camp Papers, box 1, folder 14, BYU (second quotation); Utley, *The Lance and The Shield*, 189.

13 James F. Macleod ltr., May 30, 1877, "Papers Relating to the Sioux Indians," 18; Wilson, *Frontier Farewell*, 148–51; Utley, *The Lance and The Shield*, 191.

14 F. R. Plunkett ltrs., July 34, June 20, 1877, "Papers Relating to the Sioux Indians," 32–33, 21 respectively; C. Frank Turner, "Sitting Bull Tests the Mettle of the Redcoats," in Dempsey, *Men in Scarlet*, 71.

15 W. T. Sherman ltr., July 17, 1877, NA M234, DS, Roll 261, 616; Utley, *The Last Sovereigns*, 37–38.

16 R. W. Scott ltrs, Aug. 13 and 15, 1877, "Papers Relating to the Sioux Indians," 34, 35 (first quotation); "Papers Relating to the Sioux Indians," 39, citing the *Washington National Republican*, Aug. 15, 1877 (second quotation); David Mills ltr., Aug. 29, 1877, "Papers Relating to the Sioux Indians," 40.

17 Greene, *Beyond Bear's Paw*, 38, quoting an unnamed individual, *New York Herald*, Oct. 22, 1877. Sources on the Nez Perce War are voluminous. Commended are Elliott West, *Last Indian War: The Nez Perce Story* (New York: Oxford University Press, 2009); and Jerome A. Greene, *Nez Perce Summer, 1877: The U.S. Army and the Nee Me Poo Crisis* (Helena: Montana Historical Society Press, 2000).

18 "Sitting Bull," *New York Herald*, Oct. 22, 1877; "After Sitting Bull," *Army and Navy Journal*, Sept. 22, 1877; *Report of the Sitting Bull Indian Commission* (Washington, DC: Government Printing Office, 1877), 3–4; Charles Sanford Diehl, *The Staff Correspondent* (San Antonio, TX: Clegg Company, 1931), 127; Utley, *The Lance and The Shield*, 372–73n19.

19 "Sitting Bull," *New York Herald*, Oct. 22, 1877; "The Saucy Sioux," *Chicago Times*, Oct. 22, 1877; *Report of the Sitting Bull Indian Commission*, 6; James F. Macleod ltr., Oct. 27, 1877, "Papers Relating to the Sioux Indians," 77; Utley, *The Lance and The Shield*, 192; McCrady, *Living With Strangers*, 77–78.

20 *Report of the Sitting Bull Indian Commission*, 6; Paul L. Hedren, *After Custer: Loss and Transformation in Sioux Country* (Norman: University of Oklahoma Press, 2011), 157; Christopher C. Joyner, "The Hegira of Sitting Bull to Canada: Diplomatic Realpolitic, 1876–1881," *Journal of the West* 13 (April 1974): 12.

21 "The Saucy Sioux," *Chicago Times*, Oct. 22, 1877; "Sitting Bull," *New York Herald*, Oct. 23, 1877 (quotation); Wilson, *Frontier Farewell*, 332; Vestal, *Sitting Bull*, 215.

22 *Report of the Sitting Bull Indian Commission*, 7, 8 (quotation); "Sitting Bull," *New York Herald*, Oct. 23, 1877.

23 "Sitting Bull," *New York Herald*, Oct. 23, 1877.

24 *Report of the Sitting Bull Indian Commission*, 8 (quotation); "Sitting Bull," *New York Herald*, Oct. 23, 1877.

25 "Sitting Bull," *New York Herald*, Oct. 23, 1877 (*hau*); *Report of the Sitting Bull Indian Commission*, 8, 9 (final quotation).

26 *Report of the Sitting Bull Indian Commission*, 9 (first quotation); "Sitting Bull," *New York Herald*, Oct. 23, 1877 (final quotations).

27 *Report of the Sitting Bull Indian Commission*, 10; James F. Macleod ltr., Oct. 17, 1877, "Papers Relating to the Sioux Indians," 81; Alfred H. Terry and A. G. Lawrence tele., Oct. 20, 1877, NA M234, DS, Roll 262, 923; Utley, *The Lance and The Shield*, 198.

28 Diehl, *Staff Correspondent*, 129–30; Utley, *The Last Sovereigns*, 50, citing the *Chicago Times*, Nov. 19, 1877.

29 "Sitting Bull Talks," *New York Herald*, Nov. 14, 1877.

30 "Sitting Bull Talks," *New York Herald*, Nov. 14, 1877.

31 "Custer's Last Fight," *Army and Navy Journal*, Nov. 24, 1877; *Harper's Weekly*, Dec. 8, 1877; Utley, *The Lance and The Shield*, opposite 143.

32 "Sitting Bull," *New York Herald*, Oct. 23, 1877; Cozzens, *The Earth Is Weeping*, 310.

33 Greene, *Beyond Bear's Paw*, 63, 65; West, *Last Indian War*, 296–97; Vestal, *New Sources of Indian History*, 242–43 (quotations).

34 Waggoner, *Witness*, 151–53, 621n6; West, *Last Indian War*, 298; "Steps—Seeskoomkee—Bannock/Shoshone and Nez Perce," www.American-Tribes.com.

35 P. H. Sheridan teles., Sept. 5 and Sept. 12, 1877, NA M234, DS, Roll 262, 781 and 798 respectively; [J. M.] Lee tele., Sept. 13, 1877, NA M234, STA, Roll 841, 984; Greene, "Out With a Whimper," 4-38; Kingsley M. Bray, "'We Belong to the North': The Flights of the Northern Indians from the White River Agencies, 1877–1878," *MMWH* 55 (Summer 2005): 34; Slaughter, "Leaves from Northwestern History," 276.

36 Olson, *Red Cloud and the Sioux Problem*, 250–51; Bray, "We Belong to the North," 32–35, 40.

37 James Irwin ltr., Nov. 5, 1877, NA M234, RCA, Roll 721, 589 (first quotation); Skunk Horse interview, V. T. McGillycuddy rpt., Oct. 7, 1879, NA M234, RCA, Roll 724, 1048 (second quotation); "The Indian Pow-Wow," *Washington National Republican*, Sept. 2, 1877, "Papers Relating to the Sioux Indians," 61; Neihardt, *Black Elk Speaks*, 150 (third quotation); Chas. G. Bartlett ltrs., Dec. 19, 1877, Jan. 6, 1878, NA M234, DS, Roll 266, 598 and 647; N. A. Miles ltr., [undated but Jan. 1878], NA M234, DS, Roll 266, 660; Bray, "We Belong to the North," 34–35, 41–43, 45.

38 Powers, *The Killing of Crazy Horse*, 430–31; G. W. Baird ltr., Dec. 16, 1877, NA M234, DS, Roll 266, 588; Manzione, *"I Am Looking to the North for My Life,"* 44.

39 Neihardt, *Black Elk Speaks*, 151.

40 McGrady, *Living With Strangers*, 76–79, 84; Grant MacEwan, *Sitting Bull: The Years in Canada* (Edmonton, Alberta: Hurtig Publishers, 1973), 99–100; Utley, *The Lance and The Shield*, 190.

41 Guido Ilges ltr., Nov. 22, 1877, NA M234, DS, Roll 266, 535; Gary Pennanen, "Sitting Bull: Indian Without a Country," *Canadian Historical Review* 51 (June 1970): 130; Anderson, "A Sioux Pictorial Account of General Terry's Council at Fort Walsh," 113.

42 Neihardt, *When the Tree Flowered*, 224.

43 G. W. Baird ltr., Dec. 16, 1877, NA M234, DS, Roll 266, 588; Baird ltr., Dec. 16, 1877, "Papers Relating to the Sioux Indians," 100–101; Bull Eagle, in Chas. G. Bartlett ltr., Jan. 29, 1878, NA M666, SWP,

Roll 284, 207; "Bull Eagle's Bulletin," *Chicago Times*, [Jan. 31, 1878,] NA M666, SWP, Roll 284, 417; "R. C. and S. T./Bull Eagle's Story," *Cheyenne Weekly Leader*, Feb. 21, 1878.

44 [John] Gibbon tele., Jan 28, 1878, NA M234, DS, Roll 266, 703; A. G. Irvine tele., Feb. 2, 1878, "Papers Relating to the Sioux Indians," 106; Bray, "We Belong to the North," 44, 47.

45 Slaughter, "Leaves from Northwestern History," 245–47, 250, 277, 283–84; Robert Bigart, ed., *Letters from the Rocky Mountain Missions: Father Philip Rappagliosi* (Lincoln: University of Nebraska Press, 2003), 102; "Taurus the Red," *Deseret News* (Salt Lake City, UT), June 19, 1878.

46 Slaughter, "Leaves from Northwestern History," 280.

47 Greene and Thornton. *Year the Stars Fell*, 35, 278–79; Howard, *Warrior Who Killed Custer*, 22; James H. Howard, "Two Teton Dakota Winter Count Texts," *North Dakota History* 27 (Spring 1960): 75; Roger T. Grange, Jr., "The Garnier Oglala Winter Count," *Plains Anthropologist* 8 (May 1963): 77; Vestal, *Warpath*, 270; Levine, "Lone Dog Winter Count," in Waggoner, *Witness*, 557; Powers, *Winter Count of the Oglala*, 33.

48 Dakota Goodhouse, thefirstscout.blogspot.com, referencing the High Dog and Long Soldier winter counts; Vestal, *New Sources of Indian History*, 350.

16. The Starving Years

1 W. Bird ltr., Oct. 3, 1878, NA M234, MS, Roll 509, 490; Utley, *The Lance and The Shield*, 201–202.

2 Dan'l Huston ltr., Jan. 9, 1878, NA M234, DS, Roll 266, 708 (first quotation); James Walsh in Nelson Miles ltr., Jan. 12, 1878, NA M234, DS, Roll 266, 688 (second quotation); Frank G. Roe, "The Extermination of the Buffalo in Western Canada," *Canadian Historical Review* 15 (March 1934): 15.

3 James Macleod ltrs., June 26 and July 9, 1879, "Papers Relating to the Sioux Indians," 117–18; A. G. Irvine ltr., July 14, 1878, "Papers Relating to the Sioux Indians," 119–20; Dickson, *Sitting Bull Surrender Census*, 133.

4 A. G. Irvine ltrs., Aug. 11 and Nov. 10, 1878, "Papers Relating to the Sioux Indians," 121, 125 (quotation); Manzione, *"I Am Looking to the North for My Life,"* 129.

5 W. T. Sherman tele., Aug. 6, 1878, NA M234, MS, Roll 511, 891; Utley, *The Lance and The Shield*, 204 (quotation); Greene, *Yellowstone Command*, 226–27.

6 Neihardt, *Black Elk Speaks*, 154–55.

7 Greene, *Beyond Bear's Paw*, 77 (first quotation); Pennanen, "Sitting Bull," 131; MacEwan, *Sitting Bull*, 153 (second quotation); Roe, "The Extermination of the Buffalo in Western Canada," 17.

8 Black Wolf and Fox interview, Theo. Schwan ltrs., Jan. 10, Jan. 12, 1879, NA M234, DS, Roll 270, 176, 386 (quotation); "Suing for Peace," *New York Herald*, Jan. 25, 1879; "Sitting Bull's Plea for Mercy," *New York Times*, Jan. 28, 1879. Interestingly, the runners to Cheyenne River Agency, Black Wolf and Fox, carried with them a two-sided drawing by Sitting Bull depicting this council of chiefs and identifying the participants, the document authenticating these pleas for peace. Mike Cowdrey, "A Letter from Sitting Bull," Heritage Auctions, Lot 70401, Nov. 20, 2020, fineart/ha.com.

9 Black Wolf and Fox interview, W. H. Wood ltr., Jan. 12, 1879, NA M234, DS, Roll 270, 386; Red Cloud and head chiefs ltr., Feb. 5, 1879, NA M234, RCA, Roll 725, 849; P. H. Sheridan tele., Jan. 21, 1879, NA M666, SWP, Roll 285, 368; Theo. Schwan ltr., Feb. 17, 1879, NA M234, CRA, Roll 131, 286.

10 Manzione, *"I Am Looking to the North for My Life,"* 133, quoting Walsh to Irvine, Mar. 23, 1879; Utley, *The Lance and The Shield*, 206, 376n16, dating the letter March 24, citing National Archives of Canada, RG 7, G21, Vol. 318, file 2001, pt. 3b (NAC F1386, f124).

11 John A. Macdonald memo., Feb. 28, 1879, "Papers Relating to the Sioux Indians," 139–41; Manzione, *"I Am Looking to the North for My Life,"* 133; Hedren, *After Custer*, 78.

12 W. Bird ltr., Apr. 7, 1879, NA M234, MS, Roll 513, 318; W. Bird ltr., June 6, 1879, NA M234, MS, Roll 515, 779; A. H. Terry tele., June 28, 1879, NA M234, MS, Roll 515, 740; A. G. Irvine ltr., Feb. 23, 1879, "Papers Relating to the Sioux Indians," 131–32.

13 Skunk Horse interview, V. T. McGillycuddy rpt., Oct. 7, 1879, NA M234, RCA, Roll 724, 1048 (first quotation); E. D. Townsend ltr., July 1, 1879, NA M234, MS, Roll 515, 740 (second quotation).

14 N. A. Miles tele., July 9, 1879, NA M234, MS, Roll 515, 809; N. A. Miles tele., July 18, 1879, NA M234, MS, Roll 515, 812; Red Hawk interview, Edmond S. Meany Papers, box 13, folder 27, University of Washington; Miles, *Personal Recollections*, 309; "The Reds' Refuge," *Chicago Times*, Aug. 19, 1879; Finerty, *War-Path and Bivouac*, 346; W. T. Sherman tele., July 24, 1879, NA M234, MS, Roll 515, 796; Utley, *The Lance and The Shield*, 208.

15 "Report of Superintendent Walsh," Dec. 16, 1879, in *Opening Up the West, Being the Official Reports to Parliament of the Activities of the Royal North-West Mounted Police Force from 1874–1879* (Toronto, Ontario: Coles Publishing Company, 1973), 14 ; "Walsh's Wards," *Chicago Times*, Aug. 8, 1879 (quotation); Finerty, *War-Path and Bivouac*, 346.

16 Finerty, *War-Path and Bivouac*, 347–48 (quotations), 349; Walsh's Wards," *Chicago Times*, Aug. 8, 1879; Utley, *The Lance and The Shield*, 209; Utley, *The Last Sovereigns*, 69–70. In fact, murderous episodes were occurring along the Yellowstone, involving other Indians but not these Sioux. "A March in Montana," *Chicago Times*, May 17, 1879.

17 "The Devil's Den," *Chicago Times*, Aug. 9, 1879; Finerty, *War-Path and Bivouac*, 353; Pennanen, "Sitting Bull," 133 (quotation).

18 "The Reds' Refuge," *Chicago Times*, Aug. 19, 1879; Finerty, *War-Path and Bivouac*, 354–55, 357.

19 "The Reds' Refuge," *Chicago Times*, Aug. 19, 1879 (quotation); Finerty, *War-Path and Bivouac*, 356–58, 361–62.

20 Finerty, *War-Path and Bivouac*, 359–60.

21 "The Reds' Refuge," *Chicago Times*, Aug. 19, 1879; Finerty, *War-Path and Bivouac*, 363, 364 (quotations).

22 Finerty, *War-Path and Bivouac*, 365 (quotation), 366–67; "The Reds' Refuge," *Chicago Times*, Aug. 19, 1879.

23 Finerty, *War-Path and Bivouac*, 371, 372 (first quotation); "The Terrible Tetons," *Chicago Times*, Aug. 22, 1879 (second quotation); Utley, *The Lance and The Shield*, 210; Utley, *The Last Sovereigns*, 72.

24 Finerty, *War-Path and Bivouac*, 372, 382; "The Terrible Tetons," *Chicago Times*, Aug. 22, 1879.

25 Jack W. Brink, "A Hunter's Quest for Fat Bison," in Cunfer and Waiser, *Bison and People on the North American Great Plains*, 114.

26 William A. Dobak, "Killing the Canadian Buffalo, 1821–1881," *Western Historical Quarterly* 27 (Spring 1996): 47–52; Geoff Cunfer, "Overview: The Decline and Fall of the Bison Empire," in Cunfer and Waiser, *Bison and People on the North American Great Plains*, 23–25.

27 Jackson, *Black Elk*, 169; Utley, *The Last Sovereigns*, 68, quoting Winnipeg's *Manitoba Free Press*, Aug. 8, 1879.

28 V. T. McGillycuddy ltr., Oct. 7, 1879, NA M234, RCA, Roll 724, 1048.

29 A. H. Terry tele., Oct. 9, 1979, NA M234, DS, Roll 270, 718; V. T. McGillycuddy ltr., Oct. 22, 1879, and J. M. Walsh pass, Sept. 23, 1879, both NA M234, RCA, Roll 724, 1028.

30 Cicero Newell ltr., Feb. 27, 1880, NA M234, STA, Roll 845, 731.

31 P. H. Sheridan tele., Oct. 31, 1879, NA M234, MS, Roll 515, 895.

32 Wilson, *Frontier Farewell*, 364–66; Karolevitz, *Bishop Martin Marty*, 74, quoting the *Yankton Press and Dakotaian*, Nov. 18, 1879; Monson, "From Swiss Monk to Lakota Missionary," 20–21.

33 H. M. Black rpt., Dec. 27, 1879, NA M234, DS, Roll 273, 622; W. L. Lincoln ltr., Feb. 4, 1880, NA M234, MS, Roll 516, 879.

34 "Report of Superintendent J. M. Walsh," Dec. 31, 1880, in *Opening Up the West*, 25; Dennis J. Smith, "The Starving Years, 1878–1888," in Miller, et al., *History of the Assiniboine and Sioux Tribes of the Fort Peck Indian Reservation*, 122; Wilson, *Frontier Farewell*, 381–84.

35 Wilson, *Frontier Farewell*, 384; Neihardt, *Black Elk Speaks*, 159.

36 N. S. Porter ltr., Feb. 6, 1880, NA M234, MS, Roll 517, 293.

37 N. S. Porter ltr., Feb. 6, 1880, NA M234, MS, Roll 517, 293 (first quotation); N. S. Porter ltr., Feb. 17, 1880, NA M234, MS, Roll 517, 301 (final quotations); "The Indian Situation," *Brooklyn Daily Eagle*, Feb. 9, 1880; DeMallie, "The Sioux in Dakota and Montana Territories," in Markoe, *Vestiges of a Proud Nation*, 47.

38 N. S. Porter ltr., Mar 4, 1880, NA M234, MS, Roll 517, 308.

39 "Report of Indians That Surrendered or Were Captured Through the Exertions of the Troops of the District of the Yellowstone," Nelson A. Miles Papers, Box T-2, USAMHI, Carlisle Barracks, PA; H. M. Black ltr., Mar. 19, 1880, Louis Riel ltr., Mar. 18, 1880 (quotation), both NA M234, DS, Roll 273, 678; Howard, *Strange Empire*, 340-41; David G. McCrady, "Louis Riel and Sitting Bull's Sioux: Three Lost Letters," in *The Western Metis: Profile of a People*, ed. Patrick C. Douaud (Regina, Saskatchewan: Canadian Plains Research Center/University of Regina, 2007), 204.

40 Louis Riel ltr., Mar. 18, 1880, NA M234, DS, Roll 273, 678; A. G. Irvine ltr., Nov. 6, 1880, NA M234, DS, Roll 273, 959.

41 McCrady, "Louis Riel and Sitting Bull's Sioux," in Douaud, *Western Metis*, 207; [N. A.] Miles tele., Nov. 14, 1880, NA M234, DS, Roll 273, 945; Manzione, *"I Am Looking to the North for My Life,"* 138, 142.

42 "Report of Superintendent L. N. F. Crozier," Dec. 1880, in *Opening Up the West*, 32; Manzione, *"I Am Looking to the North for My Life,"* 142; Utley, *The Lance and The Shield*, 214; Turner, "Sitting Bull Tests the Mettle of the Redcoats," in Dempsey, *Men in Scarlet*, 74; "Personal Items," *Army and Navy Journal*, Oct. 1, 1881.

43 "Report of Indians Surrendered," Miles Papers, Box T-2, USAMHI; [J. N. G.] Whistler teles., June 14 and June 15, 1880, both NA M234, DS, Roll 273, 761; N. A. Miles tele., Aug. 20, 1880, NA M234, MS, Roll 518, 388.

44 "Report of Indians Surrendered," Miles Papers, Box T-2, USAMHI; N. A. Miles tele., Aug. 20, 1880, NA M234, MS, Roll 518, 388; Geo. A. Forsyth tele., Sept. 10, 1880, NA M234, DS, Roll 273, 841; Dickson, "Reconstructing the Indian Village on the Little Bighorn," 11.

45 "The Surrender of the Sioux," *New York Times*, Aug. 21, 1880; "Indian Affairs," *Army and Navy Journal*, Aug. 28, 1880; Hedren, *After Custer*, 81.

46 N. A. Miles tele., Oct. 23, 1880, NA M234, DS, Roll 273, 878; Utley, *The Lance and The Shield*, 215.

47 N. A. Miles tele., Oct. 23, 1880, NA M234, DS, Roll 273, 892; N. A. Miles tele., Oct. 28, 1880, NA M234, DS, Roll 273, 899; [A. H.] Terry tele., Oct 31, 1880. NA M234, DS, Roll 273, 906; "Report of Indians Surrendered," Miles Papers, Box T-2, USAMHI; DeMallie, "The Sioux in Dakota and Montana Territories," in Markoe, *Vestiges of a Proud Nation*, 48–49; McCrady, *Living With Strangers*, 101.

48 A. G. Irvine ltr., Nov. 6, 1880, NA M234, DS, Roll 273, 959.

49 [E. H.] Allison, *The Surrender of Sitting Bull* (Dayton, OH: Walker Litho. and Printing Co., 1891), 9–10, 22, 24; "Bagged by Brotherton," *Saint Paul and Minneapolis Pioneer Press*, July 20, 1881; Manzione, *"I Am Looking to the North for My Life,"* 142.

50 Allison, *Surrender of Sitting Bull*, 11–15.

51 Allison, *Surrender of Sitting Bull*, 17–18, 22, 24; E. A. Allison rpt., Oct. 12, 1880, NA M234, DS, Roll 273, 881; Manzione, *"I Am Looking to the North for My Life,"* 143–44; Utley, *The Last Sovereigns*, 83.

52 Allison, *Surrender of Sitting Bull*, 25–26; E. A. Allison rpt., Oct. 12, 1880, NA M234, DS, Roll 273, 881 (quotations); Manzione, *"I Am Looking to the North for My Life,"* 143–44; Utley, *The Last Sovereigns*, 83.

53 A. H. Terry tele., Oct. 20, 1880, NA M234, DS, Roll 273, 860; Allison, *Surrender of Sitting Bull*, 31–36; [D. H.] Brotherton rpt., Nov. 7, 1880, NA M234, DS, Roll 273, 926 (quotations).

54 [D. H.] Brotherton rpt., Nov. 7, 1880, NA M234, DS, Roll 273, 926 (quotation); "Bagged by Brotherton," *Saint Paul and Minneapolis Pioneer Press*, July 20, 1881; "Sitting Bull Nearly Starved," *New York Times*, Nov. 11, 1880.

55 [N. A.] Miles tele., Nov. 14, 1880, NA M234, DS, Roll 273, 945.

56 [O. B.] Read tele., Nov. 26, 1880, [Samuel] Breck tele., Nov. 27, 1880, both NA M234, DS, Roll 273, 965; O. B. Read tele., Dec. 9, 1880, NA M234, MS, Roll 518, 446; Smith; "The Starving Years, 1878–1888," 126; "Bagged by Brotherton," *Saint Paul and Minneapolis Pioneer Press*, July 20, 1881; Utley, *The Lance and The Shield*, 218.

57 [D. H.] Brotherton tele., Nov. 27, 1880, NA M234, DS, Roll 273, 965; [O. B.] Read tele., Dec. 4, 1880, [Samuel] Breck tele., Dec. 6, 1880, both NA M234, DS, Roll 273, 982; "Poplar Creek Agency," *Deseret News* (Salt Lake City, UT), Jan. 12, 1881.

58 J. Culbertson communication, J. N. G. Whistler ltr., Dec. 11, 1880, NA M234, DS, Roll 273, 1003; Vestal, *New Sources of Indian History*, 249; [D. H.] Brotherton ltr., Dec. 4, 1880, NA M234, DS, Roll 273, 990.

59 Allison, *Surrender of Sitting Bull*, 48; [D. H.] Brotherton ltr., Dec. 4, 1880, NA M234, DS, Roll 273, 990; [J. N. G.] Whistler ltr., Dec. 16, 1880, NA M234, DS, Roll 273, 996.

60 Alfred Terry tele., Dec. 20, 1880, NA M234, DS, Roll 273, 996, 1001; Allison, *Surrender of Sitting Bull*, 68–70; "Sitting Bull at Milk River," *New York Times*, Dec. 28, 1881; "Bagged by Brotherton," *Saint Paul and Minneapolis Pioneer Press*, July 20, 1881; Utley, *The Lance and The Shield*, 219.

61 Fred A. Hunt, "The Punishment of Pi-zi's People," *Overland Monthly* 55 (March 1910): 304; Allison, *Surrender of Sitting Bull*, 72–73; Vestal, *New Sources of Indian History*, 251–52; Utley, *The Lance and The Shield*, 219.

62 Hunt, "The Punishment of Pi-zi's People," 305–308; Allison, *Surrender of Sitting Bull*, 79; "Fighting Obstinate Indians," *New York Times*, Jan. 5, 1881; Vestal, *New Sources of Indian History*, 252–53.

63 Hunt, "The Punishment of Pi-zi's People," 305–308; Allison, *Surrender of Sitting Bull*, 79; "Fighting Obstinate Indians," *New York Times*, Jan. 5, 1881; Vestal, *New Sources of Indian History*, 252–53; Larson, *Gall*, 3; "Chief Gall," *Chicago Tribune*, Feb. 2, 1881 (quotation).

64 Allison, *Surrender of Sitting Bull*, 76–77, 83–84; Vestal, *New Sources of Indian History*, 254; A. H. Terry report, Oct. 9, 1881, in *Annual Report of the Secretary of War* (Washington, DC: Government Printing Office, 1881), 107; Utley, *The Lance and The Shield*, 220.

65 J. L. Legaré ltr., Oct. 27, 1910, Camp Papers, BYU, Provo; F. C. Wade, "The Surrender of Sitting Bull," *The Canadian Magazine* 24 (Fall 1910): 338; Larson, *Gall*, 171; Utley, *The Last Sovereigns*, 90.

66 "The Death of General Custer," *New York Times*, May 7, 1881, quoting the *Toronto Globe*; Utley, *The Lance and The Shield*, 222.

67 Wade, "The Surrender of Sitting Bull," 338; Utley, *The Lance and The Shield*, 222 (quotation).

68 Utley, *The Lance and The Shield*, 222; Pennanen, "Sitting Bull," 138; Barrett, "One Bull," 9 (first quotation); Vestal, *New Sources of Indian History*, 256 (second quotation); Wilson, *Frontier Farewell*, 404 (third quotation).

69 MacEwan, *Sitting Bull*, 185; J. L. Legaré ltr., Oct. 27, 1910, Camp Papers, BYU; Wilson, *Frontier Farewell*, 404–405; Greene, *Beyond Bear's Paw*, 91 (first quotation); Wade, "The Surrender of Sitting Bull," 339–40; Vestal, *Sitting Bull*, 225 (second quotation); Utley, *The Last Sovereigns*, 108.

70 J. L. Legaré ltr., Oct. 27, 1910, Camp Papers, BYU; Wilson, *Frontier Farewell*, 405; Utley, *The Last Sovereigns*, 108–109; Vestal, *New Sources of Indian History*, 259 (quotation).

71 J. L. Legaré ltr., Oct. 27, 1910, Camp Papers, BYU; J. L. Legaré deposition, Aug. 17, 1881, NA RG 123, Records of the United States Court of Claims, General Jurisdiction, *Legaré v. United States*, No.

15713; Pennanen, "Sitting Bull," 138; Wade, "The Surrender of Sitting Bull," 341; "Disposing of Troublesome Indians," *New York Times*, May 29, 1881; Utley, *The Last Sovereigns*, 109–110.

72 Pennanen, "Sitting Bull," 137, 139; Manzione, *"I Am Looking to the North for My Life,"* 147–48.

73 J. L. Legaré deposition, Aug. 17, 1881, NA RG 123, Records of the U.S. Court of Claims, General Jurisdiction, *Legaré v. United States*, no. 15713; "The End of a Romance," *Saint Paul and Minneapolis Pioneer Press*, July 21, 1881; Wade, "The Surrender of Sitting Bull," 341; Utley, *The Last Sovereigns*, 111–13.

Epilogue

1 "The End of a Romance," *Saint Paul and Minneapolis Pioneer Press*, July 21, 1881 (first quotations); "Sitting Bull's Surrender," *Saint Paul and Minneapolis Pioneer Press*, Aug. 14, 1881 (final quotation).

2 "Sitting Bull's New Quarters," *Saint Paul and Minneapolis Pioneer Press*, July 27, 1881; "Sitting Bull," *Bismarck Tribune*, Aug. 5, 1881; "Piping Times of Peace," *Saint Paul and Minneapolis Pioneer Press*, Aug. 3, 1881; [D. H.] Brotherton tele., July 29, 1881, NA M666, SWP, Roll 288; Utley, *The Lance and The Shield*, 233; Dennis C. Pope, *Sitting Bull: Prisoner of War* (Pierre: South Dakota State Historical Society Press, 2010), 14–15.

3 Ronald J. Papandrea, *They Never Surrendered: The Lakota Sioux Band That Stayed in Canada* (Warren, MI: self-published, 2003), 5–7, 17, 25; Pennanen, "Sitting Bull," 139; Ephriam D. Dickson III, "Black Moon: The Minneconjou Leader," *LBHA Newsletter* (December 2006): 4; Miller, *Custer's Fall*, 250.

4 Grinnell, *Fighting Cheyennes*, 386–89; Monnett, *Tell Them We are Going Home*, 41–42.

5 Grinnell, *Fighting Cheyennes*, 394–95; Hedren, *After Custer*, 140; Monnett, *Tell Them We are Going Home*, 109–10.

6 Hedren, *After Custer*, 141; Grinnell, *Fighting Cheyennes*, 399–402, 403 (quotation); Monnett, *Tell Them We are Going Home*, 120; Jerome A. Greene, *January Moon: The Northern Cheyenne Breakout from Fort Robinson, 1878–1879* (Norman: University of Oklahoma Press, 2020), 42.

7 Grinnell, *Fighting Cheyennes*, 410; Greene, *January Moon*, 136–42, 145, 165–67; Monnett, *Tell Them We are Going Home*, 156; Hedren, *After Custer*, 141–43.

8 Hedren, *After Custer*, 142–43; Monnett, *Tell Them We are Going Home*, 168; Orlan J. Svingen, *The Northern Cheyenne Indian Reservation, 1877–1900* (Niwot: University Press of Colorado, 1993), 26n12, 44;

Larsen, *Gall*, 173. For thoughtful reflections on this painful odyssey, see Leiker and Powers, *The Northern Cheyenne Exodus in History and Memory.*

9 Hedren, *After Custer*, 84.

10 "The End of the Buffalo," *New York Times*, Dec. 26, 1884; Charles M. Robinson, *The Buffalo Hunters* (Austin, TX: State House Press, 1995), 116 (hide towns); William T. Hornaday, *The Extermination of the American Bison* (Washington, DC: Government Printing Office, 1889), 440 (second quotation), 512 (third quotation, echoing the notorious hunter Vic Smith); Hedren, *After Custer*, 96–97, 101–102.

11 P. H. Sheridan tele., Oct. 31, 1879, NA M234, MS, Roll 515, 895; "Rivers and Lakes," *Saint Paul and Minneapolis Pioneer Press*, July 27, 1881; William T. Hornaday, "The Passing of the Buffalo," *Cosmopolitan*, 4 (October 1887): 85.

12 The heartening restoration of the buffalo is a story told by many, but see particularly Dayton Duncan and Ken Burns, *Blood Memory: The Tragic Decline and Improbable Resurrection of the American Buffalo* (New York: Alfred A. Knopf, 2023), chapters 11 and 12; and the analysis of Dan Flores, "Reviewing an Iconic Story: Environmental History and the Demise of the Bison," in Cunfer and Waiser, *Bison and People on the North American Great Plains*, ch. 2.

13 Iron Teeth narrative, Marquis, *Cheyennes of Montana*, 81.

14 Roberts, "The Shame of Little Wolf," 39–47.

15 Ephriam Dickson III, "Reconstructing the Little Big Horn Indian Village: The Oglala Tribal Circle," *CBHMA 20th Annual Symposium Proceedings* (Hardin, MT: CBHMA, 2006), 65–72; Ephriam D. Dickson III, "The Big Road Roster," *CBHMA 21st Annual Symposium Proceedings* (Hardin, MT: CBHMA, 2007), 47–56; George E. Hyde, *A Sioux Chronicle* (Norman: University of Oklahoma Press, 1956), 234–35, 247, 251, 282.

16 Larson, *Gall*, 127.

17 "The Story of Chief Gall," *Saint Paul Pioneer Press*, July 18, 1886; "Upon his arrival," *Bismarck Weekly Tribune*, July 9, 1886 (quotation); "Phizi/Gall," Waggoner, *Witness*, 423–26.

18 Powers, *The Killing of Crazy Horse*, 107–108, 443 (quotation).

19 Powers, *The Killing of Crazy Horse*, 347, 442–43.

20 Paul L. Hedren, "The Crazy Horse Medal: An Enigma from the Great Sioux War," *Nebraska History* 75 (Summer 1994): 195–99; James R. O'Beirne ltr., Aug. 2, 1878, Little Big Man ltr., Aug. 1, 1878, both NA M234, RCA, Roll 723, 265; Geo. McCrary ltr., Sept. 28, 1878, NA M234, RCA, Roll 725, 1028; Powers, *The Killing of Crazy Horse*, 442; Gardner, *The Earth Is All That Lasts*, 389.

21 Jerome A. Greene, *Fort Randall on the Missouri, 1857–1892* (Pierre: South Dakota State Historical Society, 2005), 140–41; Pope, *Sitting Bull*, 44–47.

22 Pope, *Sitting Bull*, 95, 122, 124–25; Greene, *Fort Randall on the Missouri*, 147.

23 Hornaday, *Extermination of the American Bison*, 511–12; Victor Grant Smith, *The Champion Buffalo Hunter: The Frontier Memoirs of Yellowstone Vic Smith*, ed. Jeanette Prodgers (Helena, MT: TwoDot, 1997), 190; Francie M. Berg, *Buffalo Heartbeats Across the Plains* (Hettinger, ND: Dakota Buttes Visitors Council, 2018), 54–55; McLaughlin, *My Friend the Indian*, 116.

24 Gardner, *The Earth Is All That Lasts*, 324–38, 346; Jerome A. Greene, *American Carnage: Wounded Knee, 1890* (Norman: University of Oklahoma Press, 2014), 48; Hedren, *After Custer*, 164–68.

25 Gardner, *The Earth Is All That Lasts*, 346; Hedren, *After Custer*, 168–70.

26 Gardner, *The Earth Is All That Lasts*, 357, 366–70; Greene, *American Carnage*, 173–74, 179–81.

27 "Adjutant General McCoy Gets Information on Custer Massacre from Arapaho Indians," *Riverton Review*, Oct. 8, 1919; "The Story of Left Hand," Graham, *Custer Myth*, 112 (quotation).

INDEX

A

Above Man. *See* Red Cloud, Jack
Adair, Lewis, 42–43
agencies. *See* Indian agencies; *specific agencies*
agency Indians, 46, 97, 253; Black Hills and, 91, 258; confiscation of ponies and firearms from, 274–276; on Great Sioux Reservation, 23; joining of Indian coalition by, 123, 181–182; as messengers, 295–297; railroads and, 32; rations for, 56; in Sitting Bull's camp, 125–126; summons communication and, 101–104; traditionals and, 25, 35–37; warning from, 246; in Washington delegation, 85
akicitas, 118, 143, 149, 151, 237, 298, 306–307
Alderson, William, 65–66, 101
Allen, William, 289
Allison, Edwin H., 397–403, 410
Allison, William, 88, 90–93, 98
Allison Commission, 88, 90–93, 418
American Horse, 19, 80, 173, 245, 327, 341, 373
ammunition: from dead soldiers, 206–207; from Rosebud Creek battle, 171; supply of, 16, 70, 123–124, 246–249, 261, 264–265, 271, 303, 355, 370, 383; trade of, 17, 48, 64–66, 104, 105
amnesty, 319
Antelope Creek, 412–413
Antelope Woman. *See* Big Head, Kate
Appleton, Frank, 58
Arapahos, 47, 176, 230–231, 238, 239
Arikaras, 227, 249
arms trade. *See* firearms
army. *See* US Army
Arrow Creek, battle of, 38–40, 45, 58, 81
Arthur, Chester A., 413
Articles of Agreement, 258–260
Ash Creek, 63, 126, 178; camp on, 145–146, 149, 169–185
Ash Creek, fight on, 275, 276, 303–304
assimilation, 23–24, 292, 362, 421
Assiniboines, 22, 28, 30, 49, 143, 252, 371, 372, 389

B

Battle Butte, 300–303
battle preparations, by warriors, 147–149, 195–196
Battle Ridge, 204
battles. *See specific battles*
battle tactics, 78, 153–154
Bear Butte, 14, 105, 242, 308
Bear Coat. *See* Miles, Nelson A.
Bear Face, 264, 265, 267, 269
Bear Lodge Butte, 14, 93, 242, 320, 326
Bear's Ghost, 203
Bear Soldier, 154
Bear Stands Up, 143–144
Bear Walks on a Ridge, 111
Bear With Horns, 195
Beaver Creek, 236, 237, 244, 261–262, 293, 382
Beaver Heart, 240, 278, 283, 285, 292
Belknap, William, 95–96
Belly Butte, battle of, 300–303, 305
Bennett, Clarence, 45–46
Bettelyoun, Susan Bordeaux, 330
Big Ankle, 332–333
Big Beaver, 218
Big Breast, 89
Big Crow, 301–303, 310
Big Dry Creek, 263, 264, 271
Big Foot, 183, 188, 191, 204
Big Head, Kate (Antelope Woman), 110–111, 113, 219, 223
Big Horn Mountains, 10–11, 19, 91, 131, 133, 146, 174, 234, 280–281, 291–293, 308
Big Horn River, 51–52, 81, 82
Big Horse, 300
Big Open country, 3, 21, 76, 81, 251, 260, 276, 278, 295, 350, 387, 394
Big Road, 107, 129, 189, 245, 324; agency summons and, 102; in Black Hills, 74; in Canada, 369, 370, 384, 391; at Crazy Horse's camp, 94, 115; joining of Indian coalition by, 133, 134, 174–175, 277; post-war, 416; Sitting Bull and, 123, 125; surrender by, 394
Big Road Roster, 416
Bingham, H. W., 65, 78, 102
Bismarck, 53
Bissonette, Joseph, 144
Black Bear, 187–188, 190–191, 194, 239, 246–247
Black Coyote, 214
Black Crane, 84
Black Eagle, 89, 103, 110, 112, 115, 270, 391
Black Elk, 74, 94, 102, 125, 127, 133, 149, 219, 220
Black Elk Peak, 14
Blackfeet, 11, 18, 21

Blackfeet Sioux, 121, 125–126, 149; in Sitting Bull's camp, 179, 194, 236–237; surrender of, 322
Black Hairy Dog, 283
Black Hills, 10–14, 20, 58, 70, 308; army foray into, 70, 72–99, 257; attempts to purchase, 36, 257–258, 338; commission on, 90–93; confrontations in, 242; gold in, 71, 74–78, 79, 85–87, 96, 127–128, 238; internal council on, 88–92; loss of, 257–260, 296, 319, 395; Newton-Jenney Expedition in, 85–87; prospectors in, 78, 79, 84–87, 94, 96, 127–128, 331; sale of, 79–80, 87–94, 181; Washington delegation on, 85; White House conference on, 95–97; Whites invasion of, 67, 120, 127–128, 133, 225, 238–239, 258, 352, 395
Black Kettle, 18
Black Moccasins, 126, 294, 308, 312
Black Moon, 26, 37, 38, 136, 245, 269, 322, 353; in Canada, 376, 391, 396; discussions with agents by, 31, 45; at Fort Peck, 45; at Little Big Horn, 194; at Poplar River Agency, 400
Black Shield, 320
Black Sun, 172
Black Twin, 85, 102, 107
Black White Man, 285
Black Wolf, 379, 380
Blue Earth Hills, 261–262, 269
Blue Mountains, 116
Blue Thunder, 80
Bone Club, 405
Bordeaux, Louie, 340, 343, 347, 348
borderlands surveyors, 67–69
Boucher, Francis, 124–125, 144, 247–248, 254, 261, 319–320, 323
Bourke, John, 330
Box Elder (Maple Tree), 89, 102, 109, 111, 113, 116, 184, 283–284
Bozeman, Montana, 60, 63
Bozeman Trail, 20, 63, 167, 279
Bozeman Trail War, 19, 20, 88, 150, 296, 326
Bradley, Luther, 340, 342, 345, 346
Braided Locks, 288
Brave Bear, 183, 192, 197, 199, 288, 392
Breech Cloth, 221
British America. *See* Canada
Brooke, John, 378
Brotherton, David, 1–6, 20, 397–400, 403, 405, 406
Brown Back, 188, 192
Bruguier, Johnnie, 103–104, 107, 262–264, 266, 267, 269, 271–273, 309, 310, 331
Brulés, 12, 18, 38, 238; agencies and, 46, 143–144, 275; buffalo hunting and, 54; defections by, 308; fighting between Pawnees and, 55; forced to move East, 368–369, 371; Fort Laramie Treaty and, 21, 24–25; joining of Indian coalition by, 133; in Pine Ridge, 321; return to US by, 387–388, 389, 394; at Rosebud Creek battle, 173; in Sitting Bull's camp, 179; surrender by, 322, 392–393; territory of, 10
buffalo: in Canada, 356, 374–379, 388–389; destruction of, by railroads, 32, 414; dwindling population of, 45, 295, 364, 365–366, 375, 377–379, 386–389, 392; in Far North, 350; of Great Plains, 9–10, 32; hunting of, 25, 28–29, 47–49, 54–56, 59, 61, 68, 76, 125, 127, 131, 135, 137, 144–145, 252, 259–260, 321, 338, 371, 374–375, 377, 381–383, 394; migration of, 28, 386; near extinction of, 3, 375, 387, 395, 410, 414–415, 420; overhunting of, 386–387, 389, 414–415
Buffalo Calf Trail Woman, 156, 176, 214
buffalo country: agency in, 324–327, 335, 339, 358, 368–369, 416; intrusions into, 6, 35, 64, 67, 80, 82–84, 128, 225; lifeways of, 99, 119, 131, 142; loss of, 372; reservation in, 321; soldiers in, 19, 50, 141, 145, 150, 175, 177, 189–190, 249, 265, 302, 331. *See also* Great Plains; Indian Country; Sioux Country
buffalo culture, 11, 16
Buffalo North, 9, 15, 239, 258, 371, 375, 377, 414
Buffalo Road, 240
buffalo robes, 16, 29, 43, 48, 375, 376, 387
Buffalo South, 9, 15, 259, 292, 368, 375, 414
Bull Doesn't Fall Down, 158
Bull Dog, 392–393
Bull Eagle, 269–270, 271
Bull Hump, 288
burials, 172–173, 180, 223, 229
Burke, Daniel, 342–343, 344
Burke, John, 103, 125
"Burning Grounds," 124, 247, 248, 261
Burns Red, 286
Burnt Thigh, 256

C

Calhoun Hill, 206, 207, 211, 212
Camel-Back Ridge, 152, 154, 155, 159, 160, 167
camp police. See *akicitas*
camp procession, 118
Camp Robinson, 155, 239, 240, 256, 311, 312, 326, 342–343, 413; bolstering of troops at, 258; commander of, 66, 73; Crazy Horse at, 324, 327–330, 334, 344–345; Crook at,

316, 325, 334; establishment of, 58; Red Sack's arrival at, 307
Camp Sheridan, 58, 344
Canada, 3, 6; allure of, 351–352; buffalo in, 374–379, 386–389; food shortages in, 378–380, 386–388, 390; Great Plains in, 351; Indian refugees in, 357–359, 361–411; law enforcement in, 352–353; plan to flee to, 251–252, 260–261, 304, 306, 350–352, 369; relations between US and, 357–367; Santee in, 261, 351, 357, 370; Sitting Bull and followers in, 3, 339, 353–367, 370–373, 377, 380–381, 389–390, 393–408; treatment of Indians in, 357–358, 378–379, 404, 407, 411; weather conditions in, 378; winter of 1879-80 in, 389–393
cannon fire, at Belly Butte battle, 302
Cantonment Reno, 279–280, 305
Carroll (steamboat), 247
causalities: at Belly Butte, 302–303; at Cedar Creek, 268; at Little Big Horn, 192, 195, 197, 199, 205, 207, 209, 212, 223, 229; at Rosebud Creek, 166, 167, 169–170, 172, 180; at Slim Buttes, 256–257
Cedar Creek, 265, 267, 275, 276, 295
Centennial Valley, 242
Chalk Buttes, 118, 120–121
Chambers, "Persimmon Bill," 121
Chandler, Zachariah, 95–96, 99, 100, 101
Charcoal Bear, 131, 134
Charger, Martin, 253, 275
Charging Bear, 196, 198, 201, 219–220, 255, 256
Cheyenne, Wyoming, 59
Cheyenne-Arapaho Agency, 317
Cheyenne Daily Leader, 336
Cheyenne River Agency, 36, 52, 78, 105, 245, 252–253, 256, 270–271; confiscation of ponies and firearms at, 275, 276; surrender at, 322; surrender terms at, 294; weapons sales at, 65
Cheyenne River stage station, 241
Cheyennes, 10, 15, 38, 89; allied with US Army, 291–292; attack on, at Powder River, 109–120, 142, 225; at Battle of Little Big Horn, 202, 210, 213, 220; Black Hills and, 14, 94–95; camps of, 52, 233–234; departure of, from Sitting Bull's camp, 231, 232, 237; divisions among, 312, 313, 316; homeland of, 143, 174, 313; joining of Indian coalition by, 120–122, 126, 130, 131; at Little Big Horn, 224; move to Indian Territory of, 316–317; Platte River troubles of, 18–19; reaction to agency summons by, 102–103; Red Fork attack on, 282–294; reservation for, 413; at Sitting Bull's camp, 179, 180, 189, 225, 236–237; Southern, 18, 24, 121–122, 150, 239; suffering endured by, 313; surrender by, 311–317; surrender terms for, 321; transferred to Indian Territory, 411; at White River Agency, 315–316; winter camps of, 106–109. *See also* Northern Cheyennes
Chicago Times, 336, 360, 365, 383, 386
Chief Eagle, 113
Christianity, 421
Circling Bear, 38
Civil War, 54, 203, 250, 257
Clark, William P., 327–329, 334, 337–339, 413; Crazy Horse and, 345; Nez Perce campaign and, 339–341
Cleveland, Grover, 421
Clifford, Harriet, 4
Clifford, Walter, 1–2, 6
Cody, William F. "Buffalo Bill," 241, 415, 421, 422
Collins, John, 79–80, 85, 88, 90
Comes in Sight, 156, 162, 209
Commissioner of Indian Affairs, 76, 78, 90, 94, 101, 339, 389
communal councils, 25
company traders, 16
Congress, US, 258, 259, 260
Conical Hill, 156, 159–160, 166
Corn Indians, 227
Cottonwood Creek, 57
Council Tree, 90, 338
Cowie, Isaac, 29
Crawling, 288
Crazy Head, 313
Crazy Horse, 14, 58–59, 61, 70, 89, 97, 102, 142; after Little Big Horn battle, 253, 256; alliance led by, 277; arrest of, 341–347; at Arrow Creek, 38, 39–40; at Battle of Little Big Horn, 188–189, 197–198, 201, 206, 210–211, 215; at Belly Butte battle, 300–303; Black Hills Expedition and, 76–77; buffalo hunt and, 338, 339; campaigns against, 278–280; camp of, 93, 94, 107, 115–116, 281, 293–295, 298–299, 318–319, 326, 327; coalition of, 278, 305–307, 318–319, 324, 326; Crook and, 278–279, 281–282, 334–336, 340–342, 344; departure of, from Sitting Bull's camp, 245; dissention at camp of, 306–308; killing of, 347–349, 368, 371, 373, 405, 418–419; leadership of, 115–116, 306–307, 320, 324–325, 349; Metz Massacre and, 121; move to Spotted Tail Agency by, 344; Nez Perce campaign and, 340–341, 343; notoriety of, 19, 103, 111; Pawnee killings

and, 55; peace negotiations with, 295–297, 319–320, 325–326; Powder River attack and, 115–116; at Prairie Dog Creek camp, 304, 306–307; press coverage of, 336–337; Red Cloud and, 326; at Rosebud Creek battle, 148, 149, 154, 155, 158, 160; search for, 274, 281–283, 299, 323; Sitting Bull and, 306; Spotted Tail and, 308, 319–320, 343; surrender by, 316–317, 321–322, 327–330, 336–337; war preparations by, 148, 195; Washington delegation and, 85
Crook, George, 96, 97, 99, 128–129, 275, 278–280, 312; Crazy Horse and, 278–279, 281–282, 334–336, 340–342, 344; departure of, 327; Iron Plume and, 255–257; Lakota buffalo hunting and, 338–339; Nez Perce campaign and, 339–342; peace negotiations by, 315–316, 319, 324–326, 335–336; Red Fork battle and, 282; at Rosebud Creek battle, 167; surrender terms and, 314, 321, 323
Crook Commission, 416
Crooked Nose, 139
Crosby, Eben, 42
Crow Buttes, 90
Crow Foot, 4, 5, 8
Crow King, 174, 175, 194, 206, 216, 401–403
Crow Necklace, 282
Crow Reservation, 49
Crows, 7, 10–12, 25, 27, 28; buffalo hunting by, 81; fighting between Sioux and, 45, 81–83, 126; land occupied by, 143; railroads and, 34; at Rosebud Creek battle, 151, 153, 156, 158, 165; as soldier scouts, 151, 153, 158, 165, 171, 177, 279, 296–297
Crow Split Nose, 291
Crozier, Lief, 394, 399, 404, 405
Custer, George Armstrong, 54, 72, 73, 175–176; attack on Cheyennes by, 150; Black Hills Expedition of, 72–77; death of, at Little Big Horn, 2, 3, 224, 230, 239, 249, 263, 394; gold discovery and, 14, 75, 77, 85
Custer, Thomas, 289
Custer City, 121
Cut Off, 367–368
Cypress Hills, 351, 353, 374, 381

D

Dakota Sioux, 18
Dakota Territory, 3, 10, 12, 20, 321, 414, 419; railroad construction in, 32; surveying of, 67–68
Darlington Agency, 411
Davis Creek, 143, 144, 190, 235
Deadwood, 242, 256, 336
Dear, John W., 336
Deeds, 192, 203–204, 285–286
Deer Medicine Rocks, 14, 83–84, 131, 135
Department of the Platte, 96
De Smet, Pierre, 41, 71, 355–356
Devils Tower, 14
Dewdney, Edgar, 407
Dewey Beard, 183, 219
Dickinson, 414
Diehl, Charles, 360, 365, 366, 409
Dirty Moccasins. *See* Black Moccasins
Dodge City, 414
Dog, 162, 169
Dog's Backbone, 227
Dorman, Isaiah, 203–204, 224
Dull Knife. *See* Morning Star
Durfee & Peck Company, 29, 59, 65

E

Eagle Bear, 216
Eagle Elk, 10, 95, 187, 244; at Ash Creek, 149, 160, 164, 166; at Battle of Little Big Horn, 201, 212; on Crazy Horse, 148, 160; at Rosebud Creek battle, 170; survey stakes pulled by, 28, 53
Eagle Pipe, 308
Eagle Shield, 245
Elbow Woman, 111
Elk Scrapers Society, 291, 309
Esevone, 131

F

Far North, 350. *See also* Canada
Fast Bull, 294, 331, 333, 368
Fat Bear, 194
Fetterman Massacre, 19, 417
Few Tails, 319, 320, 321
fighting tactics, 169
Finerty, John, 383–386, 409
firearms, 29, 30; access to, 48; confiscation of, 4, 5, 274–276, 312–314, 319, 323, 329, 394; from dead soldiers, 206–207, 208; supply of, 123–124; trade of, 16–17, 48–49, 64–67, 104–105, 124–125, 246–249; of Whites, 64. *See also* ammunition; Henry rifles; Winchester rifles
Fire Thunder, 259
fishing, 391, 393
flag pole affair, 92, 297
Flying Hawk, 198–199, 206, 210, 228
food shortages, 56–59, 89, 257–259, 267, 299, 303, 323–324, 377–380, 386–390, 392, 405–406, 411
Foolish Bear, 298, 299
Foolish Elk, 140, 176–177, 195–196

Foolish Thunder, 270
Ford, John W., 336–337, 360, 409
Fort Abraham Lincoln, 49, 72, 80, 134, 275
Fort Assinniboine, 378, 392–393
Fort Belknap Agency, 392
Fort Benton, 17, 68, 82
Fort Benton Record, 360
Fort Berthold, 2, 107
Fort Berthold Arikara Agency, 249
Fort Browning, 29, 30
Fort Buford, 1–2, 31, 33, 67, 68, 82, 358, 399, 402; attacks on, 22, 23, 29, 43; commander of, 272; Indian surrenders at, 400, 402–403, 404; Sitting Bull's delegation to, 405–407; Sitting Bull's surrender at, 1–7, 409–410
Fort C. F. Smith, 19, 63
Fort Connor, 19
Fort Custer, 382
Fort Ellis, 37, 97
Fort Fetterman, 57
Fort Griffin, 414
Fort Jefferson, 344
Fort Keogh, 378, 382, 392, 394, 413
Fort Laramie, 11, 12, 15, 16, 19, 47, 57, 58; peace negotiations at, 20–21
Fort Laramie Treaty, 23–24, 25, 37, 41, 46, 54, 57, 59, 71–72, 77, 86, 91, 96–97, 258, 319, 325, 421
Fort Macleod, 356, 376
Fort Marion, 344
Fort McKeen, 43, 49
Fort N. J. Turney, 69, 393
Fort Pease, 82–83, 88, 106
Fort Peck, 29, 31, 37, 43–45, 48–49, 59, 101, 269, 271–273, 350, 379
Fort Peck Agency, 271–272, 389
Fort Peck Reservation, 252, 392
Fort Phil Kearny, 19
Fort Pierce, 16
Fort Pierre, 12
Fort Qu'Appelle, 393–394, 404, 405, 407, 411
Fort Randall, 315, 369, 419–420
Fort Reno, 19, 279
Fort Rice, 21, 40
Fort Ridgely, 203
Fort Robinson, 412, 413
Fort Shaw, 371, 372
Fort Stevenson, 37
Fort Sully, 33, 36, 78
Fort Union, 12, 16, 22, 23, 82, 350, 360–361
Fort Walsh, 360–362, 373, 376
Fort Yates, 5, 6, 117, 275, 410, 416
Foster Creek, 126
Four Horns, 4, 26, 37, 44, 245, 269, 353, 354, 408
Four Robes, 8
Four Sacred Arrows, 14
Fox, 379, 380
French Creek, 85, 86, 87
Frenchman's Creek, 30, 66, 352, 354, 382, 390, 397
Frenchman's River, 68–69, 351–352, 376, 396
fur trade, 16, 17, 48, 352–353, 375

G

Gall, 41–43, 48–50, 107, 129, 189, 269; Allison and, 397, 398; at Big Horn River, 52; in Canada, 384, 391, 396; joining of Indian coalition by, 174, 175, 353; at Little Big Horn, 195, 196, 201–202, 204, 206, 207, 208, 211–212, 216, 417; at O'Fallon Creek, 40–41; at Poplar River Agency, 399–401; post-war life of, 417–418; stature of, 392; surrender by, 400–401, 403
Gap, 151–152, 155, 159, 160, 163
Garnett, William, 284–287, 327, 334–335, 337, 339, 341
Gathering His Medicine, 291
Gatling guns, 227, 243
Genin, Jean Baptiste Marie, 372–373
Gets the Best of Them, 39
Ghost Dance movement, 416, 418, 421–422
Gibbon, John, 30, 372
Girl Who Saved Her Brother. *See* Buffalo Calf Trail Woman
Glendive Creek, 50, 251–252, 414
gold, 14, 18; in Black Hills, 71, 74–75, 77–79, 85–87, 96, 127–128, 238; discovery of, 19, 74–75; prospectors, 60, 62, 78, 80, 83–87, 94, 96, 127–128, 238–239, 331
Gold Exchange, 54
gold rush, 75, 77, 78, 96, 127–128, 238
Good Bird, 389
Good Dog, 66
Good White Buffalo Woman, 174, 180, 193, 223, 273–274
Goose Creek, 233
government rations, 56, 89, 272, 275, 276, 323–324, 327, 391, 392
Grabber. *See* Grouard, Frank
Grand River Agency, 49
Grant, Ulysses S., 79, 80, 88, 90, 92, 95–97, 99–100, 260
Gray Eagle, 179
Grease People, 17
Great Mystery, 7
Great Plains, 8–9; buffalo of, 9–10, 32; northern boundary of, 351; Sioux Country of, 10–15; springtime on, 81; White settlement of, 395, 420. *See also* buffalo country

Great Sioux Reservation, 3, 46, 97, 372; agencies on, 23, 35–36, 101, 322; boundaries of, 72; creation of, 15, 56, 72; exodus of Indians from, 134; gold discovery and, 77; government edict to relocate to, 99–104, 106–108, 129, 142, 225; miners on, 257; Pony Campaign on, 274–276; reapportionment of, 421; solders on, 257; Whites invasion of, 257. *See also* Sioux Country
Great Sioux War. *See* Sitting Bull's War
Greene, Francis, 68–69
Greenleaf Creek, 133, 134, 137
Gregory, James, 68–69
Gros Ventre Indians, 48–49, 124
Grouard, Frank, 34, 70, 88, 89, 104, 109–110, 112, 203, 234, 255, 286–287, 290, 336, 340

H

Hail, 282
Hairy Hand, 288
Halsey, William, 355
Hanging Woman Creek camp, 293–295, 297–299
Hard Robe, 290
Harney Peak, 14
Harper's Weekly, 366–367
Harris, Stephen, 42
Hastings, James, 101–102
Hat Creek Breaks, 14
Hawk Dog, 40
Healy, John J., 360
Heart Butte, 42
Heart Ghost, 333
Heart River attack, 49
He Dog, 102, 106, 228, 256, 263, 318; attack at Powder River and, 110, 112, 114, 115, 119; on the Black Hills, 14, 70; in Canada, 370; Crazy Horse and, 148, 211, 324, 328, 341, 345, 348; government summons and, 107, 119; on Rosebud Creek battle, 171; surrender by, 394
Hell Roaring Rapids, 81
Henry rifles, 16, 66, 92, 246, 297
Hidatsas, 249
hide towns, 414
High Back Bone, 19
High Bear, 234, 323
High Eagle, 350, 354
High Wolf, 282
Hinman, Samuel, 77–78
Hollow Horn Bear, 175, 177, 182, 216, 226
Holy Bald Eagle, 85, 102
Honsinger, John, 51
Hornaday, William T., 414–415
Horn Chips, 148, 296, 342
Horned Horse, 202, 337
horse culture, 11, 12, 16
horses: confiscation of, 274–276, 312–314, 319, 323, 329–330, 394; eating of, 391; of soldiers, 155–156, 159, 161, 206; stealing, 12, 22, 27, 144
Howard, Edwin, 86
Howard, John, 355
Howling Wolf, 166
Hudson's Bay Company, 17, 352, 387
Hump, 294, 331, 332
"hundred in the hand" battle, 19
hunger, 257, 267, 303, 377, 379, 386–388, 390–393, 399, 405–406, 408, 410. *See also* food shortages
Hunkpapa Sioux, 5, 18, 24, 26, 32, 38; alliances of, 249; in Battle of Little Big Horn, 196; camps of, 51–52, 69–70; in Canada, 353–359, 361–367, 389–393; firearms trade and, 123–124; Fort Laramie Treaty and, 21; homeland of, 11; joining of Indian coalition by, 143; lodges of, 44–45; Métis and, 29–30; movement of, 35; remaining in Canada, 410–411; at Rosebud Creek battle, 173; in Sitting Bull's camp, 179, 196; at Standing Rock Agency, 6; surrender by, 396; trade with, 66; travel north by, 350–351, 353–354. *See also* Lakotas; Sitting Bull's camp
Hunkpapa Sun Dance, 135–137
hunting lands, 258, 259
Hunts the Enemy, 319–321

I

Ice. *See* White Bull
Ilges, Guido, 402–403
Important Man, 298, 299
Indian agencies, 3, 23; communication of Grant's ultimatum by, 101–104; conditions at, 246, 315; firearms and, 64–65, 105; fluidity of movement on and off, 25–26; food supplies at, 392; on Great Sioux Reservation, 23, 35–36, 101, 322; military posts and, 72, 182; promise of northern, 324–327, 335, 339, 368–369, 371; for Southern Lakotas, 46–47; traditionals and, 35–37, 80; troops deployed to, 58. *See also* agency Indians; *specific agencies*
Indian attacks, on Whites, 41–43
Indian children, education of, 421
Indian Country: army encroachment into, 37–38, 177; Ghost Dance movement in, 421–422; railroad construction in, 30–34, 36–37; White encroachment into, 31, 32,

71, 77, 225. *See also* Black Hills; buffalo country; Great Plains
Indian Creek, 412–413
Indian independence, 23–24
Indian lands, 15, 133; loss of, 258–260, 352; theft of, 421
Indian raiders, 56–58
Indian reservations, 15, 20–21, 24–25, 97; in buffalo country, 321, 335, 339, 368–369; for Cheyennes, 413; food shortages on, 56–57, 59; for Lakotas, 321. *See also specific reservations*
Indian Territory, 24, 97, 279, 315–317; Indians sent to, 369, 396, 411; Southern Cheyennes in, 24, 102, 231, 239
Indian tribes: alliances among, 10; allied with US Army, 279, 291–292; conflicts among, 17, 55; fighting between army and, 49–53; fighting between White settlers and, 61–63; resistance by, 56–59. *See also specific tribes*
Indian wars, 10, 100, 419
Inkpaduta, 18, 122, 179, 244–246, 251, 370
Inyan Kara, 14
Iron Cedar, 201
Iron Dog, 37, 269, 271, 272
Iron Hail (Dewey Beard), 183, 219
Iron Hawk, 153, 157, 166, 170, 197, 213, 215
Iron Horn, 37
Iron Plume, 245, 254–257
Iron Star, 333
Iron Teeth, 280, 281, 283, 286, 291, 305, 316–317, 415–416
Iron Thunder, 394
Irvine, Acheson G., 356, 372, 376, 377, 401, 407
Irwin, James, 339

J
Janis, Antoine, 326
Jay Cooke & Company, 54
Jenney, Walter P., 85–86, 98
Julia Face, 180
Jumping Bull, 134, 136

K
Kansas, 10, 412, 413
Kansas Pacific Railroad, 32
Kennington, James, 346, 347, 348
Kicking Bear, 58, 256
Killdeer Mountain, 18, 22, 120, 245, 248–249, 262, 417
Kill Eagle, 125–126, 149, 167, 179, 194, 236–237
Kiowas, 10
Kit Fox Society, 283, 284, 309
Kollmar Creek, 159, 161–163, 165–166

L
Ladeau, Antoine, 326
Lakotas, 10–11, 18; camps of, 51–52; in Canada, 353–357, 361–367, 370–371, 374–379; cardinal virtues of, 7; coalition and, 182; confiscation of ponies and firearms from, 274–276; fighting between Whites and, 19–20; at Fort Buford, 405; gatherings of, 26; land ownership and, 15; leadership of, 12; leaving of Yellowstone country by, 243–244; at Little Big Horn, 202, 220, 224; movement of, 25–26; peace negotiations with, 19; at Pine Ridge, 337–350; relations between Métis and, 28–31, 47–48, 370; remaining in Canada, 410–411; reservation for, 321, 415–416; resistance by, 53; sale of Black Hills and, 91; seasonal migration of, 28, 35; in Sitting Bull's camp, 225, 237; surrender by, 322–324, 402–403; territory of, 13–14, 20–21; traditions of, 23–24; transfer to Standing Rock Agency, 410; treaty with, 321
Lame Deer, 26, 40, 107, 117, 331–333, 368, 408
Lame Deer Creek, 83–84, 331
Lame Sioux, 138
Lame White Man, 121–122, 208–209, 212
Larivée, André, 361, 384, 386
Larpenteur, Charles, 22
Last Bull, 106, 108, 109, 283, 284
Last Stand Hill, 211, 214–218, 224, 226, 289
Lee, Jesse M., 323–324, 343–346
Left Hand, 322, 422–423
Legaré, Jean Louis, 1, 355–357, 370, 384, 404–408, 410, 411
Lethbridge, Julia, 411
Lewis and Clark expedition, 10
Limpy, 160–162
Little Big Horn, battle of, 3, 8, 186–225, 357; battlefield, 235, 280; camp after, 222–224; causalities, 192, 195, 197, 199, 205, 207, 209, 212, 223, 229; consequences of, 225–226; fighting in, 196–221; Gall at, 417; plunder from, 220; Sitting Bull's description of, 366; Sitting Bull's visions about, 188–189; soldier attack on camp in, 192–196; stories about, 337
Little Big Horn River, 173
Little Big Horn Valley, 144, 146, 174, 178
Little Big Horn Valley Fight, 199
Little Big Man, 58–59, 94, 245, 324; arrest of Crazy Horse and, 342, 346–347; at Belly Butte battle, 300; Black Hills Commission and, 89–90, 91–93, 96–97, 257, 296; buffalo hunt and, 338; Crazy Horse and,

328, 336, 418–419; notoriety of, 55, 57, 103; post-war life of, 418–419; siding with Whites by, 418–419; Sitting Bull's call to action and, 125, 127, 129, 130, 133; during war, 418; on Whites' encroachment, 71
Little Buck Elk, 248, 261
Little Chief, 310, 311
Little Hawk, 55, 324, 328; alert by, about soldiers, 142, 144–146, 150, 184; in Canada, 370; discovery of soldiers by, 139, 140, 151; at Rosebud Creek battle, 149, 152; surrender by, 394
Little Missouri River, 244
Little No Heart, 275
Little Red Horn, 43
Little Soldier, 193
Little Voice, 192
Little Wolf, 19, 89, 181, 222, 227, 239, 280, 308, 316, 341; Allison Commission and, 94–95; at Battle of Little Big Horn, 189–190; joining of Indian coalition by, 109; post-war, 416; post-war life of, 411, 412, 413; at Powder River attack, 111, 116; at Red Fork, 286–287, 290; at Sun Dance, 83; surrender by, 309, 312
Little Wound, 259, 341
Lodge Grass Creek, 231, 235
Lodge Pole Creek, 114
Lodge Pole Trail, 146
Lone Antelope, 44, 45
Lone Bear, 341
Lone Dog, 188, 191
Lone Horn, 93, 94, 294
Lone Man, 176
Lone Tree, 90
Lone Wolf, 286
Long Bear, 73
Long Dog, 31, 37, 45, 244–246, 251–252, 261, 383–384, 391
Long Feather, 264, 265, 267, 269
Long Road, 227
Long Sioux, 192
Lost Leg, 166
Low Dog, 117, 204, 216, 228, 370, 384, 401, 403, 404
Lower Yellowstone, 11, 21, 26–27, 28, 35, 50, 60, 63, 69, 76, 82, 129

M

Macdonell, Alexander, 6, 405
Mackenzie, Ranald S., 292, 312–313, 323, 329, 340
Macleod, James F., 358, 360, 363, 364, 376, 378
Mad Wolf, 200
Magpie Eagle, 144, 145, 150, 180, 231, 239
Makes Room, 26
Man Afraid of His Horse, 19, 341
Mandans, 249
Manifest Destiny, 409
Man that Goes in the Middle. *See* Gall
Many Beaver Dams, 281, 282
Many Caches, 7
Many Horses, 8, 406–407
Many Lice, 228
Marquis, Thomas, 415
Marty, Martin, 355–356, 372, 373, 390, 420
Massacre Canyon, 55
McCoy, Tim, 422, 423
McLaughlin, James, 420–422
Medicine Cloud, 143, 238, 248
Medicine Line, 3, 69, 350, 353–354, 382. *See also* US–Canada border
Medicine Rocks, 331
Medicine Tail Coulee, 178, 185, 200, 201, 204, 205, 209, 212, 221
Medicine Top, 283
Merrivale, Jose, 319–320, 326, 342
Métis: buffalo hunting by, 17, 21, 59, 68, 375, 387; in Canada, 304, 351, 352–353, 370, 387; fighting between Sioux and, 17, 27; military intervention against, 30–31; relations between Lakotas and, 28–31, 47–48; trade by, 16–17, 29–31; trade with, 47–48, 49, 59, 69, 105, 124, 246, 261, 350, 370
Metz Massacre, 121
Miles, J. D., 231
Miles, Nelson A., 265–274, 276–278, 292, 298, 299; attack by, at Cedar Creek, 268–270; at Belly Butte battle, 302–303; Crazy Horse and, 297, 305; at Fort Keogh, 394, 396; Ghost Dance movement and, 422; monitoring of border traffic by, 378, 382; Muddy Creek and, 331–334; Nez Perce campaign and, 359; peace negotiations with, 296–297, 309–311, 314, 319; Sitting Bull and, 266–268; surrender terms and, 314–315, 321; transfer of, 402; Walsh and, 382–383
Miles City, 413, 414
Milk River, 29, 30, 31
Milk River Agency, 59
Milk River fight, 382
Milk River Reservation, 48–49, 69
miners. *See* prospectors
Miniconjou Sioux, 26, 32, 38, 52, 70, 73–74, 117, 242, 313; after Little Big Horn battle, 252–254; aligned with Crazy Horse, 294; arrest of, 252–253; Black Hills Expedition and, 76; in Canada, 376, 391; defections by, 308; departure of, from Sitting Bull's

camp, 245, 252; Fort Laramie Treaty and, 21; homeland of, 11–12; joining of Indian coalition by, 139; return to US by, 392; at Rosebud Creek battle, 173; surrender by, 269–271, 320, 322–323, 368, 394, 396; winter camps of, 107
Minnesota, 11, 18, 32, 67, 203, 261, 262, 274, 287, 372
Minnesota Dakota War, 18, 417
Missouri River, 11, 13
Missouri River agencies, 315, 358
Missouri River Progressives, 236
Mitchell, Thomas, 252
mixed-bloods, 16–17, 23, 66–67. *See also* Métis
Mizpah Creek, 122
Montana, 3, 10–11, 17, 19, 20, 29, 60, 413, 414, 417. *See also* Big Open country
Moose Jaw, 411
Morning Star, 89, 239, 240, 280, 290, 308–309, 312–313, 316, 411–413
Moving Robe Woman, 173, 193, 195, 203–204, 223
Muddy Creek, 137, 235
Muddy Creek fight, 331–334, 408
Mud Houses, 393
Musselshell River, 29
Musselshell trading post, 31, 65–66

N
Newton, Henry, 85
Newton-Jenney Expedition, 85–87
New York Herald, 360, 362
New York Stock Exchange, 54
Nez Perce Indians: crisis with, 360; Crook's campaign against, 339–343; fleeing of, to Canada, 359, 367; joining of Sitting Bull's camp by, 367–368; surrender by, 396
night trading, 16–17
Niobrara Valley, 57, 412, 413
No Clothing People. *See* Santee Sioux
No Feet, 367–368
No Flesh, 62
No Neck, 44, 245, 384
non-treaty Indians, 25, 26, 65, 96–97, 142. *See also* Northern Indians; traditionals
Northern Arapahos, 47
Northern Cheyenne Reservation, 422
Northern Cheyennes, 24–25, 47, 80, 238; attack on, at Powder River, 109–119, 225; escape from Indian Territory by, 411–413; Fort Laramie Treaty and, 24–25; government summons and, 102–103; homeland of, 308, 313; movement of, after Little Big Horn, 280–281; peace negotiations by, 309–311; reservation-bound, 415–416; in Sitting Bull's camp, 126–127, 131, 225, 231; suffering endured by, 308–309, 313; at Sun Dance, 83; surrender by, 311–313, 394; transferred to Indian Territory, 411. *See also* Cheyennes
northern herd. *See* Buffalo North
Northern Indians: arms trading by, 49, 66–67; arrest of, 252–253; attitudes toward Whites by, 117–118; Black Hills sale and, 90–93; camps of, 69–70; captured, 255–256; clearing of, from Big Open country, 276–278; coalition of, 120–142, 181–182, 244–245; confiscation of ponies and firearms from, 274–276, 312–314, 319, 329–330; fleeing of, to Canada, 251–252, 260–261, 304, 306, 350–352, 369; government attitudes toward, 97–99; government summons to, 99–108, 119, 129, 142, 225; holdouts, 331–334; lifeways of, 3, 6–7, 12, 15, 101, 119, 131, 141, 142, 168, 225, 306, 308, 329, 349, 371, 408, 415; reaction of, to Powder River attack, 116–118; return to US by, 387–389, 394–395, 401–402, 404; southern agencies and, 58; surrender by, 263, 322–326; war weariness of, 303, 306–307; White House conference and, 96–97; winter camps of, 60–61, 105–108; in Yellowstone country, 88–90. *See also* traditionals; *specific tribes*
Northern Pacific Railroad, 105, 420; construction of, 30–34, 36–37, 43–44, 53–54, 381, 413–414; end of, 397; Indian opposition to, 36–37, 39, 43–45; survey work for, 31–34, 40–42, 49, 52–53, 67–69, 72, 210, 395
Northern Sioux, 18
North-West Mounted Police, 68, 352–356, 376, 393, 404
North-West Territories, 17, 352
No Water, 322, 326

O
O'Fallon Creek, 40–41
Oglalas, 12, 37, 238; agencies and, 46–47, 57, 89; Black Hills sale and, 89–90; camps of, 44–45, 52, 70; in Canada, 391; defections by, 308; departure of, from Sitting Bull's camp, 245; divisions among, 318; encounters between army column and, 73–74; fighting between Pawnees and, 55; forced move East of, 368–369, 371; Fort Laramie Treaty and, 21; homeland of, 10–11; joining of Indian coalition by, 130, 133, 174–177; led by

Crazy Horse, 27, 38, 70, 76, 277; lodges of, 45; movement of, 129; Northern Cheyennes and, 24–25; peace negotiations with, 319–321; Platte River wars and, 18–19; return to US by, 387–388, 394; in Sitting Bull's camp, 179, 187–188; splintering of, 326; suffering endured by, 318–319, 330; surrender by, 318–319, 322, 327–330, 404; welcoming of Cheyennes by, 293–294; winter camps of, 105–108. *See also* Crazy Horse; Lakotas; Red Cloud; Sioux people
Oklahoma, 24, 411
Old Bear, 89, 102, 106–108, 110, 114–116, 119, 215, 280, 290, 308, 312, 411
Old Bozeman Road, 63
Old Bull, 149, 154, 374, 406
Old Crow, 290–291
Old Hawk, 324
Old Man Chiefs, 107, 109, 126, 182, 189, 239, 280, 286, 290, 294, 308, 309, 312, 416. *See also* Black Moccasins; Little Wolf; Morning Star; Old Bear; Sitting Bull
Old She Bear, 172–173
Old Two Moon, 176
Old Wolf, 310, 313
One Bull, 4, 122, 131, 132, 149, 154, 179, 185, 198, 233, 405
One Horn, 93, 94
Otter Creek, 93, 106
Overland Trails, 19, 32
Ox'zem, 109, 113
oyates, 10–12, 14, 20, 23–24, 80, 258, 321, 348, 369, 379, 410–411

P
Palladay, Leon, 334
Panic of 1873, 53–54, 77, 96
Pawnees, 55
peace negotiations, 20–21, 264–269, 295–299, 307–314, 319–321, 325–326
peace-talkers, 295–299, 303, 306–307, 311, 319–320, 323, 325–326, 329
Pease, Fellowes, 23, 82–83
Pease Bottom, 82
pemmican, 28–29, 387
Piegan Indians, 371
Pine Ridge, 10, 14, 238, 239, 241, 322
Pine Ridge Agency, 46–47, 257–259, 322, 337–349, 350, 388, 413, 416
Pinto Horse Butte, 354–356, 367, 376
Pioneer Press, 1, 4, 5, 6, 7
Plains Métis. *See* Métis
Platte River, 18
Plenty Lice, 38, 40
Pompeys Pillar, 52
Ponca Agency, 369
ponies. *See* horses
Pony Campaign, 274–276
Poplar River Agency, 355, 391–392, 398–400, 402–403
Porter, Nathan S., 391, 392
Potts, Benjamin, 60
Pourier, Baptiste, 155, 341, 348
Powder Face, 111
Powder River, 60, 93
Powder River, battle of, 100, 109–119, 120, 142, 225
Powder River Basin, 11, 44–45, 76, 258, 278–279
Powder River Trail, 47, 94, 189, 240, 312
Prairie Chicken, 51
Prairie Dog Creek, 152, 293; Indian camp at, 303–307; soldier camp at, 138, 140, 152
press coverage: of Crazy Horse surrender, 336–337; of Sitting Bull Commission, 360, 365–367; of Sitting Bull surrender, 1, 4, 6; at US–Canada border, 383; of war, 409
prospectors, 60, 62, 78, 80, 83–87, 90, 94, 96, 127–128, 238–239, 331
Provost, Constant, 361
Pryor Creek, 38

R
railroads: construction of, 31–37, 43–44, 53–54, 381, 413–414; Indian opposition to, 36–37, 39, 43–44, 53; survey work for, 31–34, 40–42, 49, 52–53, 72, 210, 395
Rain in the Face, 51, 53, 80, 123, 132, 146, 174, 205, 206, 216, 238, 384, 396
rations, 56, 89, 272, 275, 276, 323–324, 327, 391, 392
Rattle Blanket Woman, 294
Rattling Hawk, 180
Rawhide Butte, 14
Raynolds, William, 71
Red Bear, 323, 370
Red Bird, 286
Red Canyon, 75
Red Cloud, 14, 275; Black Hills and, 79–80, 85, 92–93; buffalo hunt and, 338; at Camp Robinson, 335; Crazy Horse and, 328, 329, 341; Crook and, 128, 129, 341; embrace of agency life by, 26; Fort Laramie Treaty and, 21; leadership of, 37; notoriety of, 19; peace negotiations by, 325–326
Red Cloud, Jack (Above Man), 133, 150, 158, 188
Red Cloud Agency, 25, 57–58, 66, 72, 73, 79–80, 85, 88, 231, 234; arms trade at, 64–65; Articles of Agreement signed at, 259; confiscation of ponies and firearms

at, 275, 276; Crazy Horse at, 329, 332, 343; creation of, 46–47; flag pole affair at, 297; food shortages at, 56–57; Lakotas at, 337–340; peace-talkers from, 319; return to, by Northern Indians, 388–389
Red Cloud's War, 19–22, 41, 106, 417
Red Cloud Trail, 47
Red Coats, 352–356, 376, 393, 404
Red Dog, 92, 337, 341
Red Feather, 199, 206, 211
Red Fork, battle of, 282–294, 305, 308, 312–313
Red Hawk, 164–165, 206–208, 212, 228–229, 382
Red Horn Bull, 212
Red Horse, 120, 133, 218, 221, 228, 245, 254, 256, 300, 307, 322
Red Leaf, 275
Red Ripe, 286, 291
Red River War, 274
Red Sack, 300, 307, 319
Red Skirt, 270
Red Sun, 270
Red Tomahawk, 422
Red Water River, 45, 252
Reno, Marcus, 224
Republican River country, 20, 54, 90; buffalo hunting in, 56
Richard, Louis, 88, 89
Riel, Louis, 392–393
rifles, 16, 48, 64, 66, 227, 246, 256, 302. *See also* firearms
Robinson, Levi, 57, 58
Rodman Gun, 402
Roman Nose, 254, 294, 308, 320, 322
Rosebud Agency, 389
Rosebud Creek, 7, 43–45, 60–62, 235, 281; camp at, 127, 130–133, 138–139, 144, 313; Sun Dance on, 83–84
Rosebud Creek, battle of, 147–168, 300; aftermath of, 169–185; plunder from, 171–172
Rosebud Narrows, 151
Rotten Grass Creek, 232
Rowland, William, 290
Rule of 1876, 4
Runs Fearless, 243
Runs the Bear, 303
Runs the Enemy, 139, 149, 165, 171, 192, 193, 201, 203, 216
Rupert's Land, 17, 352

S

Sacred Hat Lodge, 131
Sage Creek, 327
Sand Buttes, 2
Sand Creek, 120
Sans Arcs, 26, 36–38, 52; aligned with Crazy Horse, 294; arrest of, 252–253; at Ash Creek, 173; Battle of Little Big Horn and, 191–192; in Canada, 376, 391; defections by, 308; departure of, from Sitting Bull's camp, 245, 252; Fort Laramie Treaty and, 21; homeland of, 11; in Sitting Bull's camp, 121, 179, 182; surrender by, 269–271, 320, 322–323, 396
Santee Sioux, 28, 29, 49; in Canada, 261, 304, 351, 357, 370; departure of, from Sitting Bull's camp, 251–252; Fort Laramie Treaty and, 21; joining of Indian coalition by, 122, 125; in Sitting Bull's camp, 179; skirmishes between soldiers and, 42
Saones, 11–12
Saville, John J., 58, 64, 73, 79, 85, 89–91, 94, 99
Scabby, 164, 286, 291
Scott's Bluff, 57
Seen by Her Nation, 8
Sentinel Butte, 14
Seventh Cavalry, 3, 289
Shane, Baptiste, 361
Sharpshooter Ridge, 185
Shave Elk, 106, 149, 171, 182, 205
Sheep Creek, 122
Sheridan, Philip, 96, 99, 241, 314, 340, 412, 419, 421; army forts and, 279–280; on end of war, 333–334, 408; Pony Campaign of, 274–276; summer campaign of, 250; surrender terms and, 315, 380; tactics of, 78
Sheridan's Army, 249–250, 333–334. *See also* US Army
Sherman, William T., 315, 358, 378
Short Bull, 102, 106, 107, 115–116, 119, 130, 133, 257, 294
Short Pine Hills, 14
Shorty, 333
Shoshone-Arapaho Reservation, 422
Shoshones: allied with US Army, 171, 279; at Rosebud Creek battle, 153, 156–157, 159, 164, 165
Shot in the Eye, 213
Shoulder Blade Creek, 229
Sibley Scout, 337
Sicangus, 10
Simmons, A. J., 48–49
Sioux Commission, 77
Sioux Country: Black Hills in, 71–99; confrontations in, 241–242; firearms trade in, 64–67; Ghost Dance movement in, 421–422; landmarks, 2, 14–15, 83, 90, 94, 211, 242, 258, 293, 308; soldiers in, 137–141; white incursions into, 95. *See also* buffalo country; Great Sioux Reservation

Sioux people: buffalo and, 9–10; in Canada, 353–359, 376, 378–379, 389–393, 407; clashes between Métis and, 17, 47–48; culture of, 10–13, 16; divisions of, 10–12, 18, 25; end of prairie life for, 408; farming, 381, 421; fighting between Crows and, 81–83, 126; fighting between Whites and, 18–20, 45–46; of Great Plains, 10–11; lodges of, 44–45; movement of, 12–13; surrender by, 394, 402–403; territory of, 10–15, 20–22, 26–27, 90. *See also* Lakotas; *specific groups*
Sits in the Night, 284
Sitting Bear, 281–282
Sitting Bull, 97, 169, 225; after Battle of Little Big Horn, 223; Allison and, 398–401; arrest of, 422; at Arrow Creek, 38–39, 58; attempt to capture, 340; at Battle of Little Big Horn, 194, 202–203, 220, 228; Black Hills Expedition and, 76–77; Bruguier and, 262–263; buffalo hunting by, 61; in Canada, 3, 339, 353–359, 361–367, 370–373, 377, 380–381, 389–390, 393–408; character of, 7, 8; communication of Grant's ultimatum to, 103–104; Crazy Horse and, 306; Crows and, 81; daughter of, 2, 406–407; early life of, 7; exile of, 419–420; Fort Buford and, 22; Fort Pease and, 82–83; Ghost Dance movement and, 421–422; government attitudes toward, 97–99; as holy man, 7; household of, 8, 179, 194; Indian coalition and, 120–141; interviews of, 365–367, 383–386; killing of, 422; leadership of, 26, 122–124, 131, 134–135, 175–176, 182–183, 243; messengers sent to, 143–144; Métis and, 29, 47–48; peace envoys to, 355–356; peace negotiations by, 264–267, 269, plan to flee to Canada of, 251, 260–261, 304, 306, 350–353; post-war life of, 419–422; at Prairie Dog Creek camp, 303–304, 306; prayer by, 134, 184–185, 188; Red Cloud's War and, 22; reputation of, 103; resistance to railroads by, 37; return to Standing Rock by, 420–421; return to US by, 379; at Rosebud Creek battle, 149, 154; sale of Black Hills and, 89, 93–94; at Sitting Bull Commission, 361–366; Spotted Tail and, 86; at Sun Dance, 83–84; surrender by, 1–7, 398–399, 401, 407–410; territory occupied by, 21–22, 26–27; as traditionalist, 23–25; visions of, 7, 131–132, 136, 142, 168, 188–189, 197, 223, 225–226; Walsh and, 355, 389–390, 393–394, 399, 404, 407; welcoming of refugees by, 116–117; Whites and, 15–16, 18, 22–23, 31, 37, 39, 44, 51, 117–118; wives of, 8
Sitting Bull Commission, 360–367
Sitting Bull of the South, 92, 259, 296–297, 310
Sitting Bull's camp, 69–70, 93–94, 112, 120–121, 136–137, 142–143; after Battle of Little Big Horn, 222–224; after Rosebud Creek battle, 173–185; Allison at, 398–399; at Ash Creek, 145–146; attacks on, 193–196, 201–202, 268–271, 273; in Canada, 367–372, 376, 379–381, 384–385, 405; at Cedar Creek, 265–271; councils at, 182–183, 230, 243–244; daily routines in, 180, 186–187; dances in, 183; defense of, 149, 182, 194–196, 201–202; growth of, 126–127, 133–134; hunger at, 377, 390, 391, 393, 399, 405–406; in Little Big Horn Valley, 174–189, 193–196; movement of, after Little Big Horn, 229–238, 243–245, 260–264; movement toward Fort Peck, 271–273; Nez Perce at, 367–368; at Prairie Dog Creek, 303–307; refugees in, 116–117; return to US by Indians in, 379–381, 387–389, 404; size of, 175, 179–181; splintering of, 230–232, 237–238, 244–245, 273–274, 404–405; at Willow Bunch, 405–408; winter camps, 80, 107–108
Sitting Bull's Sun Dance, 135–137
Sitting Bull-Sully clash, 245
Sitting Bull's War, 10, 24, 27, 147–148; attempts to avoid, 146, 176, 227–228; beginning of, 99; Belly Butte battle, 300–303; Cedar Creek attack, 268–271; debates over ending, 306–307; end of, 6–7, 394–395, 408; fall campaigns in, 278–299; holdouts in, 331–334; Indian coalition in, 120–141, lead-ups to, 131; legacy of, 411; Little Big Horn battle, 186–224, 225; Milk River fight, 382; Muddy Creek fight, 331–334; peace negotiations during, 20–21, 264–269, 295–299, 307–314, 319–321, 325–326; Powder River attack and, 109–119; press coverage of, 1, 4, 6, 336–337, 409–410; Red Fork battle, 282–294; Rosebud Creek battle, 147–168; Sheridan's Army failures in, 249–250; Skirmish at Warbonnet Creek, 240–241. *See also specific battles*
Sitting Eagle, 157
Skunk Horse, 369, 381–382, 388, 389
Slim Buttes, 14; attack at, 254–257, 260, 275, 301
Slotas, 17, 29, 47
Slow Bull, 73, 326

Smith, Edward P., 96, 97, 99, 101
Smith, Henry W., 242
Smith, John, 66
Smith, John Q., 25, 73, 105
soldiers: after Little Big Horn battle, 198–199, 202, 207–208, 226–229, 232; attack at Slim Buttes by, 254–257; attack on Sitting Bull's camp by, 193–196; in Battle of Little Big Horn, 189, 196–202, 204–221; in buffalo country, 19, 50, 141, 145, 150, 175, 177, 189–190, 249, 265, 312, 331; camps of, 233–234; pursuit of Indians by, 252, 253; retreat by, after Rosebud Creek battle, 170–171, 172; at Rosebud Creek battle, 152, 154–156, 159–167, 169; warrior attacks on, 263–264; in Yellowstone country, 260, 263. *See also* US Army
soldier scouts, 151–153, 191, 196, 249, 285, 300
Soldier Wolf, 202
southern agencies: bloodshed at, 56–59. *See also specific agencies*
Southern Cheyennes, 18, 24, 121–122, 150, 239
southern herd. *See* Buffalo South
Southern Lakotas, 10–11, 18; relocation of, 46–47; winter counts, 54–55. *See also* Brulés; Oglalas
Spider, 308
Spirit Lake Massacre, 122
Spotted Bear, 92, 263
Spotted Eagle, 26, 36–38, 245; in Canada, 362, 376–377, 384, 390, 391; joining of Indian coalition by, 121, 307; at Poplar River Agency, 400; post-war life of, 416–417; surrender by, 396
Spotted Elk, 107, 271, 296, 307, 320, 322
Spotted Horn Bull, 193
Spotted Tail, 20, 26, 40, 54, 88, 256, 275, 314; Black Hills and, 91–93; Boucher and, 124, 247; buffalo hunt and, 338, 339; Crazy Horse and, 343, 344; Indian surrenders and, 323; miners and, 85, 86–87; peace negotiations by, 307–308, 319–322, 324; relocation of people of, 46
Spotted Tail Agency, 57, 58, 80, 124, 259, 314, 344; creation of, 46–47; food shortages at, 323–324; Sioux Commission at, 77; surrender at, 322, 323, 368; treatment at, 143–144
Stabber (One Stab), 73, 86, 92
Standing Bear, 34, 70, 73–74, 76, 171, 172, 216, 221–223, 226–227, 240
Standing Bear, Emily, 187
Standing Elk, 309, 316, 317
Standing Rock Agency, 6, 175, 237, 238, 269; confiscation of ponies and firearms at, 275; Sitting Bull at, 420–421; transfer of Lakotas to, 407, 410
Stanley, David, 33, 54, 67; Gall and, 41–43, 48; Spotted Eagle and, 36–37
starvation, 3, 45, 313, 378, 391, 399, 405–406, 408. *See also* food shortages
Steam Boat, 38
steamboats, 50, 81–83, 243–244, 247, 251–252
Steps, 367–368, 420
Stillson, Jerome, 360, 362, 364–366, 409
Suicide Boys, 183, 187, 213–214
Sully, Alfred, 203
Sully campaign, 417
Sun Dances, 7, 12, 25, 37–38, 83–84, 131, 135–137, 338, 357, 421
surrender terms, 272, 294, 298–299, 307–311, 314, 319–320, 328, 355, 358, 362, 380, 392–393, 398; Rule of 1876, 4
surveyors, 31–34, 40–42, 49, 52–53, 60, 64, 67–69, 72, 80–81, 83, 210, 395
Sweet Medicine Chief, 109
Sweet Taste Woman, 309, 310
Swelled Face, 252, 253, 300, 301, 306
Sword, George, 319

T

Tackett, Charlie, 342
Tall Bull, 166, 200
taureaux, 29
Terry, Alfred, 315, 360–364, 382, 398, 400
Teton Sioux, 10–11, 29, 33. *See also specific oyates*
Thompson, James H., 393, 399
Thompson Creek, 109, 112
Thunder Hawk, 180
tiyospayes, 10
Tongue River, 81, 82, 88, 106, 131, 138, 233, 236
Tongue River Cantonment, 265, 274, 296–297, 299, 305, 315, 355
Touch the Clouds, 294, 308, 320, 322, 337, 340, 342–344, 348
trade: firearms, 16–17, 48–49, 64–67, 104–105, 124–125, 246–249; furs, 16–17, 48, 352–353, 375; illegal, 30, 48, 65–66, 105, 124–125, 246–249; with Métis, 16–17, 29–31, 47–49, 59, 69, 105, 124, 246, 261, 350, 370; with Whites, 11–12, 16–17; with Yanktonais, 271–272
trading posts, 12, 16, 22, 29, 31, 65–66. *See also specific posts*
traditionals, 25–27, 80, 97; agencies and, 25, 35–37, 80; aligned with Crazy Horse, 294–295; coalition of, 120–141; dispersal